In Praise of
Canadian Plays of Italian Heritage

As a Canadian and an immigrant, the question of identity, visibility and representation has been and continues to be, for me, a giant pea under the many mattresses of discomfort. In this collection of works for theatre, by Canadians of Italian Heritage, Professor Anna Migliarisi's clarity is truly revealing and intelligent and intensely accurate. The works cited in this anthology are those of a generation of artists/writers whom I followed and whose work was inspiring in my own quest to communicate my writing as a Canadian/Italian author. The first generation of artists from my community to bring to the stages of Canada their Canadian stories which reflected their Italian Heritage in all of its light and darkness, humour and tragedy. The assumption that they were Italian plays, or ethnic theatre, is wrong as Migliarisi makes clear. They are a uniquely authentic theatre of a generation that wrote the reality of their times and have never been given the respect or recognition they deserve. This is an invaluable anthology not only for its artistic substance but for the history it provides for generations to come.

—**Gianna Patriarca**, author of *Italian Women and Other Tragedies*,
This Way Home, and *All My Fallen Angelas*

With clarity and passion Migliarisi launches us on an exciting voyage of discovery. She generously provides us with what we need to start our journey: history, context and an introduction to a brilliant community of playwrights. This book is a guide to a culturally rich area that is too little known and yet full of rewards. Migliarisi is to be thanked and congratulated for bringing us this vibrant collection of plays that reveal the poignant and complex Italian Canadian experience.

—**Antoni Cimolino** C.M., Artistic Director of the Stratford Festival

ESSENTIAL DRAMA SERIES 39

Canada Council for the Arts — Conseil des arts du Canada

ONTARIO ARTS COUNCIL
CONSEIL DES ARTS DE L'ONTARIO
an Ontario government agency
un organisme du gouvernement de l'Ontario

Ontario

Canada

Guernica Editions Inc. acknowledges the support of the Canada Council
for the Arts and the Ontario Arts Council. The Ontario Arts Council
is an agency of the Government of Ontario.
We acknowledge the financial support of the Government of Canada.

CANADIAN PLAYS
of
ITALIAN HERITAGE

Selected and Edited by
Anna Migliarisi

Special thanks to
Rocco Galati, Co-Publisher

GUERNICA
EDITIONS
TORONTO · CHICAGO · BUFFALO · LANCASTER (U.K.)
2025

Thank you to the following for granting permission to reprint
the following materials in this collection:
Michael Macina. *Johnny Bananas.* © 1983. Martin Hunter Papers,
Thomas Fisher Rare Book Library, University of Toronto.
Used by permission of Sarah Hunter.
Diana Iuele-Colilli and Christine Sansalone.
Ma Che Brava Gente! (Oh, What Good People!). © 2009.
Reprinted by permission of Soleil Publishing.
Dalia Katz. Photographic stills. *Paolozzapedia.* © 2023.
Photographic stills reproduced by permission of Dalia Katz.

Guernica Founder: Antonio D'Alfonso

Rocco Galati, Co-Publisher
Michael Mirolla, General Editor
Anna Migliarisi, Editor
Interior and cover design: David Moratto

Guernica Editions Inc.
1241 Marble Rock Road, Gananoque, ON K7G 2V4
2250 Military Road, Tonawanda, N.Y. 14150-6000 U.S.A.
www.guernicaeditions.com

Distributors:
Independent Publishers Group (IPG)
600 North Pulaski Road, Chicago IL 60624
University of Toronto Press Distribution (UTP)
5201 Dufferin Street, Toronto (ON), Canada M3H 5T8

First edition.
Printed in Canada.

Legal Deposit—First Quarter
Library of Congress Catalog Card Number: 2024939681
Library and Archives Canada Cataloguing in Publication
Title: Canadian plays of Italian heritage / selected and edited by Anna Migliarisi.
Names: Migliarisi, Anna, editor.
Series: Essential drama series ; 39.
Description: Series statement: Essential drama series ; 39 | Co-published by
Rocco Galati. | Includes bibliographical references.
Identifiers: Canadiana 20240390725 | ISBN 9781771839952 (softcover)
Subjects: LCSH: Canadian drama—Italian authors. | CSH: Canadian drama
(English)—Italian Canadian authors. | LCGFT: Drama.
Classification: LCC PS8305 .C365 2025 | DDC C812/.0080851071—dc23

How can a nation, a community, a people exist without theatre?
It would be inconceivable. A people without theatre is a dead people,
with no cultural aspirations.
   —Bruno Mesaglio (1911–1977)

TABLE OF CONTENTS

FOREWORD

I AM THANKFUL to have this opportunity to explain why I support this project and publication of this anthology.

I am a constitutional lawyer by profession, as an "actor on the world stage." The crux of constitutional law is history. Without a reference to it, no challenges could ever be mounted. Without a respectful and deep knowledge of it, no success could ever be achieved.

For better or for worse, predominantly for worse, history is inevitably tribal.

We are forever confronted and negotiating two distinct forms of history: institutional and individual. Institutional history is often oppressive, distorted, controlling, and imposed without choice. Individual history is mostly liberating, an expression of the human spirit and choice.

Institutional history is the stuff of Kings, Queens, Sultans, and other despots and governments alike. Individual history is the stories of individuals: literature.

Individual history is largely unwritten. When unwritten, it is buried with the individual.

When you bury enough individual historians of a tribe, you've buried that tribe, no matter what your definition of that tribe is.

Ironically enough, it is the history written by individuals, literature, that is more permanent and relevant than institutional history. We have been discussing Homer and his journey since 750 BC. Virtually no one mentions King Italus, the founder of Calabria, 1,500 BC, or any of its leaders in between to the present. We still discuss that Homer was afraid to pass through the Strait of Messina, for fear he would fall off the edge of a flat world and descend into hell.

It is a cliché that literature, the stories told in it, reflect and try to make sense of us, as individuals, and our trajectory through time and space, and our place in the universe. This is why it is timeless. Institutional history is self-serving to its own interests, and when its interests end, it ceases to be relevant to us, if it ever was, except in its non voluntary imposition over us as free individuals. It is only timeless in its irrelevance to us as free individuals.

As a constitutional lawyer, I have lived and observed this reality, in the administration of justice and injustice, albeit under a professed constitutional right to equality and multiculturalism.

The ignoring, avoidance, diminishment, denial, and in fact the outright suppression of our rights, as Canadians of Italic heritage, has been historically pronounced in Canada. This includes our literature.

However, this *de facto* denial by "Canadian" society, and the governments of Canada, became the more repulsive starting in 1971 when the multiculturalism policy of Pierre Trudeau was publicly announced and endorsed, the *Multiculturalism Act* passed in 1988, and then the patriation of our constitution, where multiculturalism was constitutionally entrenched by virtue of section 15 of the *Charter*, which guarantees equality rights, and by the specific provisions of section 27 of the *Charter* which reads as follows:

Multicultural Heritage

> **27** This Charter shall be interpreted in a manner consistent with the preservation and enhancement of the multicultural heritage of Canadians.

At this juncture "multiculturalism" ceased to be an academic interest and became a constitutional imperative. Yet, even the Supreme Court of Canada has neglected the law, as witnessed by the fact that it has yet to grant permission to hear a case based on substantive racial discrimination under s.15 of the *Charter*.

Multiculturalism is ignored on the ground, in the institutional halls of government activities and programs, including the arts, and the arts councils of this country, who treat Canadians of non-English, non-French, heritage as something other than Canadians: something lesser than Canadians. There is a massive confusion and fraud perpetuated that because we are an officially bilingual country, we are also an officially bicultural country. This notion was explicitly rejected by Prime Minister Trudeau, in 1971, in announcing the multiculturalism policy in Parliament. It was further slammed by *The Multiculturalism Act* of 1988, and the *Canadian Charter of Rights and Freedoms* of 1982, also drives this point home.

Canadians of Italic heritage are not the only voices silenced. Consider all we are missing and being deprived of from voices and literature of the Indigenous peoples of Canada, the Japanese, the Chinese, South Asians, African, Latino, etc., the list goes on.

The Italo Canadian community, regardless of how you want to define it, has been, unfortunately, suppressed, ignored, and buried with respect to our stories. We need to take our fate and history into our own hands. The only way to do this is to tell and publish our individual stories. My hope is that all non- mainstream voices, and individual historians of other communities, do the same.

This anthology is but a small step towards that redress.

Rocco Galati, BA, LLB, LLM

PREFACE

THE FIRST QUESTION facing the editor of a collection such as the present one is whether to identify the plays as Canadian plays of Italian heritage or Italian Canadian plays. The choice is not a matter of indifference, since the label "Italian Canadian", whether or not it is hyphenated, could be easily interpreted as an invitation to read them as plays of the Italian diaspora in Canada, a new chapter in the historical development of Italian theatre informed by the experience of emigration and immigration. Anna Migliarisi makes her position very clear in the title itself: these are Canadian plays, to be read, produced and examined in the context of Canadian theatre practice and social history. The plays reflect the cultural self-understanding of the authors, who do not regard themselves as Italian playwrights living in Canada but as Canadian playwrights of Italian origin, playwrights who seek recognition for their contribution to the national theatre of Canada.

Given the cultural diversity of Canada, a fact that is currently being taken much more seriously than previously on many fronts, the idea of a national Canadian theatre that is not in a constant state of flux could not make much sense at the present time. It would mask the presence of a canon of sorts serving the ideology of individuals and institutions content with paying lip service to diversity. Still, we might usefully invoke the idea heuristically as the provisional heterogeneous background of themes, dramatic forms, production conventions and audiences against which the plays in this volume ought to be read, produced and studied, as authentic Canadian plays whose authors seek, among other things, to bring about a readjustment of the background itself. They all attempt to add their own to the plurality of voices that constitutes Canadian theatre. They pursue this goal by expressing the tensions that run through the cultural and ideological self-understanding of the communities from which they emerge, to which they refer and which they address. In different ways, each is concerned with the community's location in Canadian multiculturalism and with the experience of immigration into Canada. Only secondarily are the plays about emigration from Italy, usually described only as a source of tension in the here and now of life in Canada.

By placing the plays in this context, Anna Migliarisi rejects the notion that they can or that they should be studied in relation to the Italian literature of emigration, as works by playwrights of the Italian diaspora in Canada, with the stress on Italian rather than Canada. And yet with the odd exception, it is in courses in university departments of Italian studies that they are occasionally studied, departments with little or no contact with programmes in Canadian studies or the theatre department of the same institution. Though it represents an attempt to validate the plays and to record their existence, this practice in Canadian universities comes with the heavy risk of legitimizing the hegemonic undercurrent active in the view of multiculturalism espoused by mainstream culture. An excellent counterexample comes to us from Italy. In his history of Canadian theatre in the last three decades of the twentieth century, the distinguished scholar Giulio Marra discusses Canadian plays of Italian heritage by grouping them with plays from other immigrant communities (Italian, Greek, Korean,

Jamaican, Caribbean, etc.) in various cities of Canada.[1] He identifies the commonalities and explains the differences, careful throughout his analysis not to yield to the rhetoric of multicultural or politically correct theatre, at times used as a platform for alienating judgments by arbiters of plays.

The plays in this volume were selected from a large corpus and grouped in categories designed to foreground commonalities representative of the period and make them "reader-friendly", something to the aid of which the editor contributes an introduction to Canadian theatre of Italian heritage in general that offers the reader a panoramic view of its historical development. It is hoped that the anthology can generate critical and artistic reflection on the individual plays and help amend a common perception of Canadian theatre history.

Domenico Pietropaolo
Professor Emeritus
University of Toronto

---

1. Giulio Marra, *Teatro canadese degli ultimi trent'anni*. Fasano: Schena Editore, 2004.

INTRODUCTION

Italian Canadian Theatre: A Brief History

THIS ANTHOLOGY TOOK root in 2017 when I was invited to give a paper on Italian Canadian plays and playwrights at the Department of Italian Studies at the University of Toronto. I began by researching the history of Italian Canadian theatre and performance and compiling an inventory of original plays intended for a digital archive. Whenever I told people about my study, I was bombarded with the same questions: Are there *many* Italian playwrights out there? What do they write *about*? Are they any *good*? Why haven't I *heard* about them, apart from Tony Nardi and the "Letters" and Vittorio Rossi? I called my paper "Where Are the Italian Canadian Playwrights?" I began with two questions: How many Italian Canadian playwrights are out there? And why are the "famous" ones not better represented in standard critical sources?

The rabbit hole I fell into was deeper than I could have imagined, and my project became a voyage of discovery and recovery. I delved into plays and performance histories; poured through production programs, reviews, and old photographs; followed leads; cross-referenced; spoke with writers; recorded testimony; gathered data; ultimately letting the emerging volume of work speak for itself. By necessity my research encompassed a range of disciplinary frameworks and is in constant evolution—it is a historical archive in-the-making. What I did not expect along the way was my having to confront my own lack of knowledge. How is it that I did not know about this rich tradition?[1]

This anthology endeavors to set the historical record straight, but it is just a starting point. My focus is to provide information and avenues for further research rather than complete analysis within the limits of this piece. There is so much more work to be done, rendering it impossible to fill each historical absence in this introduction. My purpose, accordingly, is to present the collection of plays in this anthology, but first to situate these works in a broader historical context. The omission of influential

---

1. Anna Migliarisi, *"Where Are the Italian Canadian Playwrights"*, presented on 21 September 2017 in my capacity as Emilio Goggio Visiting Professor at the University of Toronto's Italian Department. The title of the paper was deliberately confrontational. I "stole" it from Italian American novelist Gay Talese, who in March 1993 wrote a controversial essay for the *New York Times Book Review* called "Where Are the Italian American Novelists?" in which he made disparaging comments on the reading and book-buying habits of Italian Americans. This essay prompted intense public debate and extensive discussion in the Italian American literary community and beyond. I wanted to play on this controversy in an Italian Canadian theatre context through a flippant reference to Talese's treatise. And in answer to the question of my paper's title, I replied: Italian Canadian playwrights are everywhere. This anthology is an amalgamation of influences but would not have proceeded without the commitment and support of actor-author Tony Nardi and Professor Domenico Pietropaolo, who honors it with his *Preface*. Professor Bancheri at the Department of Italian Studies also deserves recognition for inviting me to serve as Visiting Professor and to pilot the first dedicated course on Italian Canadian plays and playwrights. I am indebted to the pioneering work of the late author and icon Helen Barolini (1985) who shaped so much of my thinking and framing of ideas and questions in this introduction and throughout my research. Errors in referencing are wholly unintentional and mine.

innovators such as Signor Lenzi, Mario Duliani and Bruno Mesaglio speaks to the further challenges of piecing together the definitive story and history of Italian Canadian theatre.

Origins: Production and Practice

The chronicle begins with a Sugar Sculpture. *Trionfi di tavola*. The date is June 18, 1786, in Halifax, Nova Scotia. The occasion is an extravagant birthday celebration for British Queen Charlotte:

> A brilliant assembly was opened at the Pontac, where the splendid array of the Cytherean train, and the confectionary preparations of *Signor Lenzi* (my italics) exhibited a most celestial appearance. The ball began at half after eight … At the close of the fifth contradance, supper was announced in the most romantic manner, by the sudden elevation of a curtain that separated the two rooms, and displayed to the enraptured beholders a complete masterpiece of pastry work. In the middle … sprang up an artificial fountain, in defiance of the frost itself; and on each side, at proper distances, were erected pyramids, obelisks and monuments, with the temples of Health and Venus on top and bottom. During the course of the repast, the music attended to delight the ear, and pleased the more delicate senses, while the great variety of most exquisite dishes served to gratify the palate …[1]

This is the earliest extant reference to an *Italian*—known only as Signor Lenzi—in English Canadian theatre and performance practice. It is found in Murdock's *History of Nova Scotia* (1867), which I came across in A.V. Spada's *The Italians in Canada* (1969). The latter is contested often in Italian Canadian studies on account of its hagiographic slant and adulatory tone[2] notwithstanding the correspondingly worthwhile historical particulars it brings to light.

For clarification, when referring to the *sugar sculpture* of Signor Lenzi I mean *performance art* which stands as a distinct genre in theatre studies. It encompasses wide-ranging dramaturgical modes, from more scripted to less scripted, from solo performance, spoken or sung, to performative art experiences. Performance art is well represented in the catalogue of Italian Canadian dramatic literature and the present anthology features solo pieces that consciously play with notions of performativity and textual hybridity. In 1786 the theatrical *text* was sculpted out of sugar and artfully displayed on a table and afterwards consumed by the audience. Like *tableau vivant* and *masques, sugar sculptures* were firmly established aesthetic forms in Italian Renaissance

---

1. Beamish Murdock, Esq., Q.C. *A History of Nova-Scotia or Acadie Vol. III* (Halifax, N.S. James Barnes, Printer and Publisher, 1867), 47–48.
2. The account on Signor Lenzi may be found in Spada 221. *Hagiography* refers to the glorification of ancestors, in this case the early *Italian* explorers, artists and exiles in historical studies. Robert F. Harney discusses the issue in several works, including "The Uses of the Italian-Canadian Past" in Perin and Sturino 37–61. See Filippo Salvatore's response to Harney in "Discoverism in the Work of Italian-Canadian Historians" in Minni and Ciampolini 161–183.

and Baroque theatre throughout Western Europe. Signor Lenzi, along with the earliest Italian migrants effectively imported these art forms to Canada.

It should be noted that Canada, was not Canada, but the *Colony of Canada* in the year 1786—and *the Canadas* a few years after that—and English Canadian theatre was decidedly *English* not Canadian. What's more, Italy was not Italy in the sense of a unified nation-state, but an aggregate of city states with their own share of political antagonisms and class inconsistencies.[1] Naming Lenzi an Italian, then, is consciously expedient on my part and more orientational than historically accurate.

The community of Halifax was established as a trade and military colony of Great Britain in 1749. The colony was populated sparsely with gentlemen officers, political elites, garrison amateur actors, as well as merchants, sailors, and laborers. By all accounts, they valued theatrical culture as part of settlement life. This included popular entertainments, contemporaneous British plays held in makeshift flexible performance spaces, masquerades and other exclusive social affairs, naval, and regimental spectacles.[2] In 1786, to honor Queen Charlotte, Signor Lenzi created political allegory in the form of performative table art.

Murdock's original account—which I will analyze—is more detailed than Spada's. A second account in *History of Halifax City* (1895) by chronicler Thomas B. Atkins substantiates Murdock's description of the event and the confectionary masterpiece "all constructed of sugar." It provides a little more information on the organization of the evening and effusively celebrates the artistry of "one Signor Lenzi." Both accounts are based on a first-hand description in the *N. S. Gazette* published on January 20, 1786, two days after the celebration.[3] There appear to be no written accounts from the standpoint of Signor Lenzi or any information in his biographical particulars.

Who was Signor Lenzi? New World settler? Artiste voyager? Political exile? Was he strictly the architect of the *confectionary masterpiece* or the director-curator of the entire festivity? It is conceivable—though not verifiable—that he was both. The use of the deferential appellation *Signor* speaks volumes about Lenzi's standing in that unambiguously homogenous Anglo-Saxon social context. At the same time, the narrative is told from a privileged Colonialist viewpoint. Without doubt, Lenzi, an exoticized foreigner, was an individual with sophisticated knowledge of performance and the decorative arts.

---

1. The term *the Canadas* came into use in 1791 and appears in early records of North American travelling theatre companies through the 19th century. See Johnson 90–105. There is a considerable amount of interdisciplinary writing on Italian Unification (1861 to 1871) and its aftermath. Of note: OPERAZIONE TERRONICA!—The first Toronto CONFERENCE ON THE UNTOLD STORY OF ITALY'S 1861 "Unification" (The Invasion and Massacre of Southern Italy), held at the Columbus Centre on November 13, 2011. Produced by Canadian constitutional lawyer, Rocco Galati and actor-writers Nick Mancuso and Tony Nardi, the participants featured Pino Aprile, Antonio Ciano and Rocco Galati moderated by Antonio Nicaso. Facebook: http://goo.gl/FOT7O.

2. The Pontac Inn was built on the Halifax waterfront in 1754 and served as the central location of all major political ceremonies and social events. It contained assembly rooms large and flexible enough to accommodate theatrical entertainments. The first designated bricks-and-mortar theatre in Halifax, the New Grand Theatre, was built in 1798. See Fergusson 419–427 and Hall 278–309. See also Anthony J. Vickery, Glen F. Nichols and Allana C. Lindgren, eds. *Canadian Performance Documents and Debates: A Sourcebook*. University of Alberta Press, 2022.

3. Thomas B. Atkin *History of Halifax City* (1895), 89. The *N. S. Gazette* 20 January 1786.

The documented indeterminacy is the point. Fragmentary records pre-Confederation and inconsistent migration statistics post-Confederation, paint an incomplete picture of Italian persons like Signor Lenzi and their presence and influence in Canadian theatre histories. In addition to providing a pre-Confederation reference for non-literary performative practice, 1786 sits at an intersection of historical Italian Canadian and (mainly English) Canadian theatre studies. What's more, the indeterminacy speaks to the basic premise of this first anthology of original plays by Canadians of Italian heritage: *if it's not on the record it effectively does not exist.*

By my accounting, we have had upwards of 90 writers of Italian Canadian heritage working in professional, educational and community theatre contexts across the country[1] and over half are still actively working in theatre today. Notably, half of these writers identify as women. They have written over 300 original plays, many of which have been produced or workshopped. The first written plays appear in the 1930s and through the 1960s and 1970s several people were actively writing for the theatre mostly in Quebec and Ontario. Nonetheless, most of these plays are from the early 1980s onward. Italian theatrical practice before this time was so vibrant, especially in Toronto, that sources describe it as a Golden Age of Italian theatre.[2] Though earlier documentation is negligible, Italian theatre was active during the first wave of mass migration at the turn of the 20th century through World War II: an area that begs for critical attention.

Studies and criticism of Italian Canadian dramatists narrating in their own voices are practically non-existent in established anthologies on Canadian theatre. Some of the thirteen plays in this collection are being published for the first time. Most of the existing work on Italian Canadian performance views it through the lens of *multicultural* or *hyphenated* or *post-marginal* or some other contextual hinterland. In Italian Canadian studies, the focus is on poetry and novels instead of theater. There has been *some* critical and journalistic attention paid in recent years. I am thinking of the work of Vittorio Rossi and Tony Nardi—and Marco Micone, who is the writer most often cited. However, this treatment is incomplete. I can pretty much count on one hand the extant sources on Italian Canadian theatre.[3]

Very few university course reading lists include original Italian Canadian plays, with only one or two exceptions such as University of Toronto Mississauga and Laurentian University.[4] The University of Toronto is the largest university in the country, located in the country's largest city and touted as the world's most multicultural with the largest population of Canadians of Italian heritage in a nation that's presumably a world model of cultural diversity. Nevertheless, there is no dedicated course or

---

1. The inventory of plays is an ongoing archival project which I began in 2017.
2. Julius A. Molinaro and Maddalena Kuitunen. "Introduction." *The Luminous Mosaic: Italian Cultural Organizations in Ontario.* Soleil, 1993, p. 8.
3. These include 1) Bancheri and Pugliese 2) DiCenzo, 3) *Polyphony* 5, No. 2 (Fall/Winter 1983) and shorter pieces such as Di Giovanni's "*Italian Theatre in Toronto*" and Spezzano's "Tribute to Bruno Mesaglio" in *Italian Canadiana* Vol. 26–29 (2012–2015), 167–190, which includes stills and reproductions from various *Piccolo* shows.
4. For example, the *Maschere Due Mondi* at University of Toronto at Mississauga, initiated by Salvatore Bancheri and Guido Pugliese, and *Le Maschere laurenziane* at Laurentian University, established by Paul Colilli, Diana Iuele-Colilli and Christine Sansalone. These endeavors exist on a continuum that dates to 1853—which is the first reference to Italian language theatre at the University of Toronto (Kuitunen 6–8 and Molinaro).

stream of study at the University of Toronto's Centre of Drama, Theater and Performance or, amazingly, in the Italian Department.

If Italian Canadian plays and playwrights do not show up on course reading lists and in anthologies, and critical studies, and subject headings do not come up on basic research retrieval sites like Google Scholar and World Cat, how are we to know that they exist? If plays are underrepresented in publisher catalogues, then how are actors, directors and artistic directors supposed to know they exist? How can they be produced on publicly funded stages? The question becomes where do we address Italian Canadian performance and a catalogue of 300 texts in Canadian history? When a body of practice is denied a legitimate formal place in our recorded history, it becomes vulnerable to all sorts of simplistic misreading and ethnocentric polemics. Moreover, as critics like Helen Barolini propose, the conspicuous absence signals that the work is unworthy of critical reflection and recognition in the public domain. This leads to the mistaken notion that there is no tradition of dramatic literature and theatrical practice to build on.[1] Unfortunately, it must be acknowledged, however, that the silence, the invisibility, the historical *absence* on the record emanates as much from within Italian Canadian communities as from without.[2]

Sugar Performance Art

The *trionfi di tavola* or *table triumphs*[3] created by Signor Lenzi in 1786, emerged from the decorative arts in the wealthy courts of Renaissance Italy with the Republic of Venice as its world leader. Venice was a prosperous multicultural trading base with political and economic links across the eastern Mediterranean and access to rare and exotic foodstuffs and spices from across the cultural spectrum, notably, the Arab world. Sugar, an extravagant commodity, was controlled by the Venetian monopoly through to the 18th century. Fittingly, sugar art was the fashionable demonstration of the all-powerful dukedom.[4]

The process of creating sugar art involved heating vast amounts of raw sugar into manipulable paste or sugar frost and shaping it into three-dimensional sculptures. Not unlike the techniques behind alabaster or marble sculptural reproductions, sometimes the artist made use of pre-prepared specialized molds.

1. These matters are queried by Barolini in her seminal *"Introduction"* to *The Dream Book (1985)*, 28–29, 34, 43. Her insights have shaped my work as have those of Giunte 1–13, 15–33.
2. Through the course of my research, I have had the privilege of engaging with many Italian Canadian theater artists in person or by phone or by email. I have discovered that the remarkable history of Italian Canadian history is for the most part unknown to most of them too. Dina Morrone, represented in this anthology, noted: "I think that we too have to own the absence and the silence. I mean it is also our fault, isn't it? It took us along time to come to this place, this place of feeling pride in our being Italian Canadian. I see this writing as our legacy." (Telephone interview July 4, 2017). At the same time, I wish to hold up a critical mirror to the Italian Canadian community—or communities—and its relationship to investment in its theatre artists. There are exceptions, of course, but a common theme in my research is that theatre artists tend to feel unsupported and undervalued; the thwarted promise of building a permanent theatre—a *teatro stabile*—comes up time and again in the literature and in interviews.
3. These were a kind of non-literary performance art rooted in Italian theatre and European traditions such as allegorical processions, street pageantry and stunning spectacle; the social aspect of these forms was most important.
4. Courts were centers for creative research and development of decorative as well as theatre and visual arts. See Ewa Kociszewska and June di Schino.

One of the most famous and well documented immersive sugar art works was created in Venice in 1574 to commemorate the entry of French Monarch Henry III to the Republic of Venice. It was an exemplary affair with finely crafted pieces from swaying trees to delicate tableware and linens all created out of sugar and designed by all accounts to crumble at Henry's touch.[1]

Whether Signor Lenzi was acquainted with this production even anecdotally, cannot be confirmed. However, the aesthetic effects of pleasure and pageantry created in Venice are similar to what Signor Lenzi undertook to achieve for Queen Charlotte in Halifax, though at a much smaller scale. The extant account of the evening refers to sensual "pleasure, lively abandon, and enraptured beholders" in concert with the "political excitement" of the moment.[2]

In Halifax one of the featured sugar sculptures was of *Cytherean* or *Cythere*, the legendary birthplace of the Greek goddess Aphrodite, Venus to the Romans. She emerged from the frothy effervesce and cut across the shore on a magical seashell—as did Queen Charlotte, allegorically, on a majestic fleet of ships with British flags blowing over the Atlantic heading towards the Halifax harbor.

Declared a public holiday the celebration began with Queen Charlotte's ceremonious entry onto the waterfront followed by triumphant naval and military demonstrations from Citadel Hill and culminated in an exclusive dance ball and festive meal and confectionary display at "Willis' rooms in the Pontac. The two rooms were separated by a curtain" for the occasion (Atkins). The guests assembled and danced away on one side of the curtain and on the other side rested the sugar sculpture—dutifully concealed by the curtain until the moment of revelation.

The sequence went something like this: the ball began at "half after eight". Presumably at that late hour the space was lit with oil lamps and candles. The dance room was packed to capacity with excited guests zealously waiting for the scheduled contradances[3] to get underway. The unexpected overcrowding caused "a little bit of confusion" in the room, Murdock tells us. However, the crowd was marshalled without incident by a coterie of "gentlemen [who] officiated as managers." This "impartial regulation" created "additional" pleasure to every one present. Of course, we have no information on the officiants and their communication system, or on who may have served in a stage or house management capacity, but we can suppose someone was in charge—if only to guard the sugar sculptures.

At the end of the 5th contradance, supper was announced "in the most romantic manner": the dividing curtain was suddenly and dramatically elevated and the masterwork was displayed to the appreciative gasps of "enraptured beholders". The source of

---

1. See Mark Greengrass.

2. These and following quotations are taken from the account of Murdock (pages 47–48). I will integrate references to Atkin's (89) account into the text where necessary for ease of reading.

3. The contradance, composed typically of two lines of partnered dancers facing each other, had roots in 17th century Italian court masques and French inspiration. It migrated to New France by the mid-1800s and like ballet emerged as a popular form in British and French settlements. A Monsieur Renault reportedly introduced ballet lessons in 1737 Montreal and by the late 18th century (on account of the Canadian National Railway) the Canadas emerged as a primary circuit stop for touring American ballet and dance companies. The "perverse irony" to use Linda Hutcheon's term is that while privileged guests in Halifax danced elatedly into the night, Indigenous dance and culture was being unjustly censored and eradicated. There is no mention of the Mi'kmaq or any other First Nations people in the Halifax account, but we know they were present.

the cue and signal system to raise the curtain and the precise nature of the romantic announcement cannot be determined. Who gave the cue? Was it romantic by way of the speaker's voice? Gesture? The dialogue itself? In 1786 the primary meaning of the word "romantic" was *extravagant*. What we can say is that a systemization plan of some kind would have been in place. The revelation of the artwork and its calculated impact on the royal guest of honor would not be left to chance.

The sculpture was a magnificent fountain made of sugar frost with water seemingly flowing out into the air flanked upstage and downstage with temples of Apollo and Venus, representations of Health and Love, respectively. The sources mention pyramids, knowledge of which would have been scarce because the 17th century was only the start of exploration and studies of these Egyptian ancient structures.

The entire display was, literally, a sweet ode to British greatness. The sequence of the presentation from scene to scene—from preparation to revelation—is rooted in classical performative practice. Indeed, all the sugar models and imagery are typical of the *mise-en-scène* in 17th and 18th century Italianate opera which Signor Lenzi successfully metamorphosed into British colonial terms.

After the display an "exquisite" dinner of various dishes was served to "delicate and pleasing" music, but the organizational details cannot be determined. Who served the meal? Where was the kitchen located? How were the tables set up? Just how was the presentation of the meal paced and synchronized with the music? Was the music vocal or orchestral or both? Surely someone was in charge.

Forerunners in Italian courtly theatre, masques and banquets are helpful in visualizing the structure and sequencing of the event. I am thinking of the famous banquet at the Gonzaga court in Mantua documented by Leone De Sommi in his 1562 manual *Quattro Dialoghi*.[1] It illustrates, conceptually, the specialized knowledge of performance aesthetics, organization, and choreography required to realize these elaborate enactments. It is conceivable that a confectionary table artist like Signor Lenzi in 1786 Halifax would have had rudimentary knowledge of these long-standing old-world traditional celebrations and their artful implementation.

Were the confections consumed? It is difficult to verify. The descriptions by Murdock and Atkin mention the delirious effects of the festivities—and elaborate meal—on the dancing guests. In fact, the evening reached into the next day: "they did not go home till morning" (Atkin). Whether this documented elation was on account of guests devouring the sugary confections—in combination with the delirious effects of spirits and dancing—cannot be determined. Sugar sculptures were generally created for show, but miniature confections were edible, and their design and creation was considered a singularized art.

Historian John Zucchi, one of the several prominent sources on early Italian settlement in Canada,[2] tells us that in mid-1840s in Toronto—then known as the Town of York—a gentleman called Franco Rossi known universally as a "scientific confectioner" and "artist" established the first *pasticceria* and *gelateria* in the King and Bay streets area of the Town. Reputedly Mr. Rossi's shop was a popular gathering place for

1. "Theorizing Comic Performance: Leone De Sommi's Dialogues on the Art of Direction" in Anna Migliarisi *Renaissance and Baroque Directors*. Legas, 2003, pp. 49–53.
2. For pre-WWII see Zucchi 1988, Zucchi 1992, Principe *Italiani a Toronto*, Sturino 1990, and their extensive bibliographies.

elite British migrants who procured sweetcakes, liqueurs, and other confectionary delicacies for feasts like Christmas and other social events. Mr. Rossi was also known for establishing the first import business of alabaster reproductions of famous Florentine sculptures like Apollo and Perseus. These were widely admired in the New World and through the 1830s and 1840s in Toronto.[1] This curious alignment seems to corroborate overlaps between the techniques in sculpturing and those of confectionary and sugar arts.

Vagabondi

Like Signor Lenzi in 1786 Halifax the documentation on Mr. Rossi in the Town of York is ambiguous, but we know that several named but mostly unnamed artisans and performers were present in burgeoning Italian settlements in the Canadas through the late 19th century and beyond. Known at that time as *vagabondi*, in the etymological sense of the term,[2] or strolling players, street musicians, singers, and monologists, the list is long and shadowy.

Since travel between Pre-Confederation Canada and Pre-Civil War America was commonplace, artists and exiles were treated favorably, with tolerance.[3] Most of these migrants were from Northern Italy: Veneto, Piedmont, and Lombardy regions. Reputedly, Italian Street musicians were seen in 1825 around the time that wooden sidewalks were built to accommodate British colonial settlers. In various settlements in the 1830s and 1840s, in addition to highly regarded artisans and trades people including bakers, lace-makers, mosaic tile-makers, and language and music instructors, there are references to organ-grinders and street performers including children.[4]

In comparison, as documented by R.H. Harney and other historians, itinerant actors and street musicians arriving in Canada in the wave of migration prompted by the ravages of the 1861 Unification of Italy faced a barrage of hostility and racialized debasement.[5] Most of these migrants came from the Southern regions of Italy, from Calabria, Sicily, Abruzzi, Molise as well as from the northeastern region of Friuli. The first distinct records here are of an organist in 1860 and a street musician from Genoa in 1870 in the Town of York. Then in 1872 Ottawa, there is a record of an organ-grinder with his monkey and blind male accordion player singing operas led by a young girl who accompanied him on a violin.[6] By the turn of the century street musicians and itinerant actors were a common back drop in the major urban centers across the

---

1. Principe 98–120. Zucchi *Italians* 78.
2. The term literally means *wanderer or vagrant* in Italian and has negative connotations today. I use the term to name strolling players or itinerant actors. For street music and itinerant activity see Zucchi *Italians*: "Work and Enterprise," 68–140 and "The Way of the Notables," 141–165 as well as Principe 98–120.
3. See Harney, Robert F. "*Italophobia.*" On travel between USA and Canada, see Ramirez, Saddlemyer, and Johnson, and their bibliographies.
4. Zucchi *Little Slaves* 6, 122, 148, 164–7. See also Smith 6–22, and Cohen and Greenwood.
5. The pioneering work of R.F. Harney in the 1970s and 1980s inspired extensive scholarly work on Italian Canadian migration and its aftermath through WW II from various interdisciplinary perspectives. In addition to Harney see the many discussions and bibliographies of Perin, Sturino, Iacovetta, Fanella, Bagnell.
6. Zucchi (1998): 32, 36, 116. See also Smith.

country. Inevitably, restrictive non-vagrancy regulations against these non-mainstream foreigners followed.[1] Time and again, the striking juxtaposition between high-brow and low-brow Italian cultural expression—between privilege and poverty—played itself out in increasingly brutal fashion across the country.

The larger social, cultural, anthropological, and political reasons for this backlash in Canada and United States are well documented, including the shadow of *Nativism*. This gave way to a clash of perceptions over social and racial hierarchy and "whiteness."[2] Southern Italians were simply not welcome in the Canadas as were their Northern counterparts. The literature cites the tensions between masses of Italian unschooled workers toiling like animals in scattered coal mines, steel plants, train tracks and other labor sites and the fascination of Italian language and culture among Anglo-Saxon elites. Negative responses of the Canadian religious establishment to the *Italian problem* are also well documented. The showy religious celebrations—*feste*—featuring processions and religious iconography—were decried as pagan theatrics, not serious and dignified religious observation.[3] Sources have it that in 1901 Sault Ste. Marie a shopkeeper was startled to find a man presenting a paycheck made out simply to "Italian, No. 151."[4] Ironically, as early as 1840 the first Italian language course was introduced into the curriculum at the Upper Canada Academy in Cobourg, Ontario.[5] This tension between ancient custom, performative modes and literary expression is very much part of the history of Italian Canadian Theatre and indeed of the canon of plays—which range in form and style, from polished literary works to broad farces and burlesques of everyday life.

R.H. Harney—who essentially birthed Italian Canadian studies and the documentary systemization of immigrant theater—warned of two-tiered methodological approaches in interpreting the presence of Italians in Canada. He named it "hagiography" or, as mentioned in my introductory paragraph—the alleged critical fixation on the glorious past of Italians in Canada—like Signor Lenzi, arguably—at the expense of frank accounts of ordinary folk who abandoned their ancestral homes in late 19th century Italy to take up the not-so-easy path of emigration to North America. In the impressive body of Italian Canadian social histories, these complex issues have been duly recognized. But in the Italian Canadian theatre community—critics, audiences, publishers, and artists—this collision of ideologies and perceptions of what is artistically worthy has not been sufficiently addressed.

---

1. See R.F. Harney *Chiaroscuro* 143–67.
2. The multi-disciplinary literature on Nativism and racial hierarchy and the concept of "whiteness" is extensive and beyond the scope of this introduction. The question becomes to what extent does the dilemma of racial "in-betweenness" around Italians in Canada, which has a formal history that goes back to the Great Migration (1880–1920), play itself out in Italian Canadian theatre and drama, from the perspectives of representation, character typology, and performance?
3. See the many discussions and bibliographies in Bancheri and Pugliese, R. F. Harney, Iacovetta, Perin, Sturino, DeMaria, Harney, and Giuliano as well as Robert A. Orsi's iconic *The Madonna of 115th Street*. As well, *Orsi's* 1992 study in *American Quarterly* on the intersection of faith and racial in-betweenness speaks to many of the issues in this section.
4. Heron 84–85. This study provides extensive primary references to immigrant labor in steel plants in Sault St. Marie, Hamilton and Halifax and the clusters of workers and societies that formed: "Each ethnic group retained its own language, developed its own mutual benefit societies ... and patronized its own set of shops, cafés, community halls, bands, choirs, and theatres" (85).
5. Kuitunen p. 2.

In Western theatre the 1800s through the 1920s was the era of the great theatre tours and the great actors among them.[1] While itinerant performers were literally singing for their supper in the streets of the Town of York, the Great Italian Actors—Ernesto Rossi, Tommaso Salvini and Eleonora Duse—were touring through the Americas and served as archetypes for Constantin Stanislavsky's conception of virtuosic acting.[2] Notably, Ontario audiences were quite taken with Mr. Rossi for his portrayal of *Hamlet*, in Italian but supported by an English-speaking cast. Reviews indicate audiences were "properly impressed" but they wished he would speak English.[3] If there is a thread—a line of development in Italian Canadian theatre practice—it rests surely in this perversely ironical space.[4]

While Italian Canadian theatre does not emerge in any formal way until the Second World War period, we have passing references in local papers of the 1920s and 1930s of performative entertainments taking place in social clubs and church-related theatre groups.[5] In addition to attending to the practical needs of migrants, these gathering places, many of which exist to this day, provided a *context* for the emergence of an Italian theatre culture in Canada in the form of popular entertainments. In Montreal, Toronto, Winnipeg, Vancouver, and in smaller communities from Trail, British Columbia to Dominion, Nova Scotia, essentially a mining town, storytelling to vocal and instrumental musical production to vaudevillian performance[6]—not to

---

1. Angelo Principe (1991) is the foremost source on these early players. In the Town of York (Toronto), the professional husband-and-wife team of actors Mr. and Mrs. Cipriani associated with the Company of Comedians from Montreal made an appearance in 1810 in a play called *Douglas or the Noble Shepard!* Signorina Teresa Parodi who, fresh off tours in London, Paris, Milan, and New York, performed the great arias of Verdi and Rossini at St. Lawrence Hall in 1851 and in an unprecedented 1855 return engagement—to rival the great Swedish soprano, Judy Lind. Several Italian (and other European) singers and actors performed regularly in established venues during the summer months of the 1840s and 50s in the Town of York and Montreal as part of the Canadas-United States theatre tour circuit, but beyond names and dates, performance details cannot be firmly established. Naturally the insubstantial evidence makes it difficult to do anything but lay historical markers for this early practice, but it invites further critical work to be done (comparative work on early theatrical tours, for instance) and raises issues of what we permit to fall in the cracks.
2. Stanislavsky devotes an entire chapter of *My Life in Art* to Salvini ("*Tommaso Salvini the Elder*") and discusses Duse, Rossi, and Salvini as inspirations for his System in the now legendary chapter "*The Beginning of My System*" 265–276, 458–467.
3. Saddlemyer describes Rossi's appearance as the "most exotic event of the season" and cites two reviews: "They found him handsome—a broad, impressive forehead, dark eyes, curly hair, and a fine figure. His voice was clear and powerful and his manner and movements graceful. 'Perhaps the most remarkable characteristic of his temperament is intensity,' wrote one reviewer of *Hamlet*. [...] Said another: 'His conception of the Danish prince varies on many points from the conventional Hamlet as portrayed by Irving and McCullough and other noted actors and this variation rather increases than deteriorates from the effects of this rendition.' (London *Free Press*, 17 January 1882.)." The second review was on Rossi's portrayal of Romeo: 'The contrast was ... most marked. In the one [*Hamlet*] he gave full vent to the passions and emotions which stirred the Danish Prince and in the other he was all gentleness, full of poetry and sentiment. (ibid., 18 November 1881). 154.
4. I borrow this concept from Linda Hutcheon's *Splitting Images*.
5. This aspect of Italian Canadian culture has been covered from interdisciplinary critical perspectives and from political perspectives but there is more work to be done in the context of performance history: on the relationship between club activity and the development of plays and performance. Bancheri and Pugliese describe a formal *rehearsal protocol* for shows emerging around parish churches in "*Italian Theatre*," 80–81. This protocol challenges preconceptions of these endeavors as slipshod amateurism unworthy of critical analysis.
6. Based on oral testimony we know that in Cape Breton, Emilio Pace (1898–1955), originally from Abruzzi, played various instruments—violin, mandolin, trumpet, guitar, and piano—and composed original music in different genres. He played in an orchestra that accompanied silent movies at the Strand Theatre in

mention dances, festive meals[1] and picnics and religious processions and fireworks took place. An array of events happened in immigrants' homes as well, not unlike the antics of the Mummers of Newfoundland.[2]

These were not literary-based proscenium-arch theatre practices, but instead regionally based *divertimenti* that were visceral, grounded, and meaningful. Italian migrants carried this performative context with them from the homeland; however, there seems to be no distinct causative line of development from one point in time and place to the next. There were bursts of performative activity and seemingly random local and regional enactments. Folkloric some might say, strolling players in the safe embrace of parish or club or "on the road" was one thing, but performance presumes to draw attention to itself, and this is the last thing most foreigners were prepared to do. Like the Medieval theatre you had to be cautious, or you'd end up in Ecclesiastical Hell Mouth.

Despite the challenges of incomplete and sporadic records, my research indicates there is enough of an evidentiary trail to begin piecing together all this activity from a performance studies perspective and its transformation into what sources call the Golden Age of Italian Canadian theatre. We have potential research crossovers as well between Italian immigrant theatre performance[3] and the many other pre-World War II groups in Canada. For example, the active Ukrainian theatre or the Toronto- and

---

Sydney, Nova Scotia. Pace later played in the Montreal orchestra of the renowned Lucio Agostino (1913–1996). He was also a gifted monologist and singer as was Mrs. Pace. The couple toured between Quebec and Nova Scotia along with their children who played the piano and saxophone respectively. During World War Two Pace reportedly performed for the Canadian troops as did musical performer Mario Pina (1919–1997) from Glace Bay, Nova Scotia. Pina was reputedly also a part of the Canadian Army Service Car and played in various legions throughout the Maritimes. (Migliore and Di Pierro pp. 230–238) We can trace a line of development of vaudevillian performance from Emilio Pace in the 1920s to the routines of actor-comic Bob Vinci and his *Teatro Comico Italiano de Toronto* in the 1970s to solo spoken-word performance of the present day. All this output merits reclamation and critical examination.

1. Italian migrants, unschooled and degraded by a history of colonization, were nonetheless rich in ancient cultural traditions and performative rituals. Some of these involved food—the table—and the act of gathering around it. In Atlantic Canada the Italian Canadian community coalesced at the end of World War One. Migrants settled in mining towns like Dominion Nova Scotia where in 1936 the landmark Dominion Hall was built (and still stands today). Community meals and festive picnics were open to everyone in Dominion. Food as 'public art' in tandem with musical acts and dramatic performances—the social heart of the community—were being played out in much the same way in Dominion Halls across the country. For Dominion Hall see De Gasperi 142–153. There is a huge body of creative and scholarly literature on Italians and food, from personal memoir to anthropological studies. See Cioni for example. Less attention is paid to the subject (and iconicity) of food in Italian Canadian theatre literature and yet it is a source for critical investigation. Food, its creation, presentation, and consumption, features as a motif in many plays in the Italian Canadian theatre catalogue: Lucia Frangione names her critically acclaimed 2000 play *Espresso*. Adam Paolozza offered espresso to audience members at the top of his theatre fringe version of *Paolozzapedia*. ("*Yes, we offered coffee. It wasn't exactly espresso ... it was drip. But it was coffee.*" Email. August 21, 2023.) Raffaele, the patriarch in *A Modo Suo (A Fable)*, takes refuge in his basement cantina of preserved vegetables, wine, and a gallon of metaphorical callouses from a lifetime of labor and familial strife.

2. See Lynde 429–434 and Fanella 37–41.

3. Regarding the terms, *immigrant theatre* and *theatre of immigration*, we must bear in mind that Italians in pre-WWII Canada weren't automatically *immigrants* but *migrants* or *itinerants* or Americans travelling back-and-forth on different trajectories. These terms underscore that immigrant performance is a little studied historiographic tradition in Canadian theatre. Robert Harney's 1983 essay on immigrant theatre in *Polyphony* established the field but Italian immigrant theatre has not been adequately studied and remains subject to oversimplifications and mischaracterizations because the history is not known. Giuliana Muscio notes the absence of studies of immigrant stage performers in Western United States in her 2019 article cited in the bibliography.

Montreal-based Yiddish theatre communities. We have American associative histories and sources to work with, such as the Italian immigrant theatre of Washington Square Theatre in San Francisco and the Old Bowery Theatre on New York's Lower East Side.[4] No matter the locale the essential fabric of this popular—literary and non-literary—performance practice and its impact in reflecting the hardships of immigrant life and providing a foundational cultural mirror—is not altogether different. Every social club and church basement in the Italian Canadian community—and in other immigrant groups no doubt—was either built or furnished with *a stage* or a dais that could be converted into a performance space.[5] All these communities share this basic theatrical ideal.

Mario Duliani (1885–1964)

One of the individuals who emerged out of this shadowy context was the extraordinary Mario Duliani. While Dominion Hall was being built by hand by Italian immigrants in 1930s Cape Breton, journalist and author Mario Duliani was developing his craft as a playwright and theatre director first in Paris, France and then in Quebec at the Montreal Repertory Theatre (MRT). A figure of some controversy in Italian Canadian studies, Duliani arrived in Montreal in 1936 to work at *La Presse* as a journalist and involved himself soon after in the growing theatrical and cultural life of the city. The MRT, subsequently renamed the Mont-Royal Théâtre Français, was primarily an English-language theatre, but founder Martha Allan envisioned it as an all-inclusive space for theatrical experimentation and consequently created a school for theatre training and a French-language section. Duliani thrived as its duly appointed Director.

Between 1936 and 1940 Duliani trained actors, directed a range of classical and contemporaneous plays, introduced the plays of Pirandello in French to Quebec audiences. According to sources, he broke new ground in French-Canadian print journalism by promoting local writers and up-and-coming performers in Montreal's cultural scene.[6]

Duliani was a prolific writer. He authored twelve plays including comedies, satiric sketches and radio plays published in French in the 1920s and 1930s. He wrote and published a substantial body of prose including two books on humor, *Deux Heures de Fou Rire* (1944) and *Quatres Heures de Fou Rire* (n.d.) and a collection of essays on the visual arts called *Sculpture et Peinture* (1908).

His unpublished manuscripts include short stories, and a full-length novel called *The Return*. His controversial memoir called *La ville sans femmes* (1945) is considered to be the first Italian Canadian novel. *La ville sans femmes* documents his three-and-a-half-year detention in internment camps in Petawawa, Ontario and Fredericton, New

---

4. Obviously, migration patterns were different in the United States. Most Italians arrived at Ellis Island and other ports at the turn of the 20th century. In 1910 there were half a million Italians in East Harlem alone, in contrast to the 60, 000 or so in Canada. See Aleandri's *Italian-American Immigrant Theatre of New York City, 1746–1899.*

5. R.F. Harney makes this important observation (*Immigrant Theatre* 8)

6. Basic bibliographic details can be found in the works by Perin *Actor or Victim?* Other sources include Eisenbichler *Forgotten Italians,* Mazza's preface to *The City Without Women,* Salvatore *Ancient Memories* and Beraud *350 ans de théâtre au Canada francais.*

Brunswick during the Second World War. Duliani was arrested in June 1940 like hundreds of other Italian nationals living in Canada deemed enemy aliens following Mussolini's declaration of war against the Allies.[1]

The generic categorization of *La ville sans femmes* is at the heart of many interdisciplinary disputes. Is it a true account? A picaresque novel? Reportage? The critics do not seem to agree though Duliani himself calls it a novelesque account. Some critics argue that *La ville sans femmes* is full of historical misrepresentations. They claim Duliani was a Fascist sympathizer. There is an evidentiary trail that he ultimately whitewashed the internment in *La ville sans femme*, for personal gain, causing irreparable harm to the Italian Canadian community. Others position him as a misunderstood martyr and downplay the dark threads in *La ville sans femme* entirely or they foreground the artistry of the man, which was substantial.

How do we make sense of this? I find historian Roberto Perin's notion of the ambivalent narrative[2] helpful in reading Duliani and making sense of his place in Italian Canadian theatre. Duliani was a complex man, obviously, and his legacy is full of perverse ironies that are hard to ignore but they seem to reflect the larger uneven history of theatre in the Italian Canadian community that I am grappling with. I wonder if his problematic legacy is one of the reasons that Duliani has been glossed over in Italian Canadian theatre studies.

In 1948 Duliani authored a 146-page treatise on the art of the actor called *La Fortune Vient en Parlant* or *Fortune Comes by Speaking*.[3] The *Préface* is by Edith Piaf. Published in French in Montreal, the book represents the first dedicated manual for actors ever published in Canadian theatre history. It has never been published or translated into English—other than the critical edition I am preparing—or into Italian or any other language from its original French. Remarkably, it has never been studied. As a practitioner I find this historical omission perplexing considering the absence of works on the actor's art in Canada during this time.[4] Duliani's ideas reflect the cornerstones of the enormously influential acting System introduced by Russian actor-director-theorist Constantin Stanislavsky in the early 20th century. They were highly controversial in the 1940s and certainly in the context of established rhetorical styles

---

1. The WW II internment of Italians in Canada is featured in several plays in the Italian Canadian catalogue, including Lucia Frangione's finely crafted *Fresco*, published here for the first time, which looks at the internment from a nuanced, decidedly female perspective. Also, the trilogy of Vittorio Rossi (*Paradise by The River*, *Carmela's Table* and *The Carpenter*), written between 1998 and 2007, and the manuscript-in-progress of Tony Nardi, *Terminus: Things That Happen Only to the Living*—the totality of which cry out for dedicated comparative analysis.

2. Roberto Perin *Actor or Victim?*

3. Duliani, Mario. *La Fortune Vient En Parlant. Préface De Edith Piaf.* Montréal: Les Editions Fernand Pilon: 1948.

4. At any time, I should say. The dearth of Canadian acting texts is discussed in Mann's 1999 Doctoral dissertation. Mann noted that the subject of actors and acting as well as Stanislavsky's influence on Canadian actors, teachers and directors was a neglected area of research in English-language performance studies. The situation hasn't changed significantly since Mann completed her work. The Russian System of acting was introduced in Canada primarily through American teachers, among them David Pressman and Paul Mann in the 1930s. In the 1940s Yiddish performer and teacher Chayele Grober brought Stanislavsky's System to Montreal. As an original member of the Moscow Habima, Grober was personally trained by Stanislavsky and his protégé Vahktangov and she describes this work in "Stanislavsky and His Influence on World Theatre," a chapter of a 1952 memoir called *Mi-shene tside ha-masakh*, published in Yiddish in 1973. Other than a translation I commissioned for my own research (*Stanislavsky*); no study of this invaluable account exists.

of acting in English and French Canada. The reason I am highlighting this book is because it is another example of a unique and important document in the rich history of Italian Canadian theatre that has yet to be studied.[1]

Despite mentions in some of the French sources, the work of Duliani as a theatre director and teacher of acting have never been thoroughly studied. Yet he was actively contributing to the theatre culture and nurturing young artists at a time of transformative change in Quebec. In 1961 he was the first Italian Canadian to be appointed a member of the *Le Counsel des Arts de Quebec*. The late historian Filippo Salvatore points outs this glaring omission in a 1998 article, but nothing after that has been done.[2] Notably, Duiliani's plays do not readily appear on library shelves either. They have never been performed or translated into English, and yet their historical significance in the catalogue of Italian Canadian and Canadian dramatic literature cannot be underestimated.

The Golden Age

Italian Canadian theatre culture comes into its own with founding of the Toronto's[3] *Piccolo* theatre by Bruno Mesaglio (1911–1977)—actor, director, designer, and arguably one of the biggest impresarios in Canadian theatre history that nobody

---

1. Another example of notable historical neglect I discovered during my research for this anthology is a book by Ukrainian Canadian playwright and director, Myroslav Irchan (1897–1937), *The Stage: A Textbook for Worker Farmer Drama Circles*, published in Ukrainian in 1928. This work appears to be the first such instructional manual in Canadian theatre history. Ninety-five pages in length, it is divided into five major sections with illustrations covering the staging of drama from a directorial perspective: selecting plays, working with actors, conducting rehearsals, and finally putting it all together in performance. In the *Preface*, Irchan also discusses the aesthetic as well as ideological nature of drama. I am engaged in preliminary work on an English-language critical edition. However, along with Duliani's *La Fortune Vient En* Parlant (1948) and Grober's "Stanislavsky and His Influence on World Theatre," (1952), *The Stage: A Texbook for Worker Farmer Drama Circles* (1928) is a major significant addition to the literature, one that has hitherto escaped the notice of Canadian theatre scholars.

2. Salvatore p. 72. I discovered what appears to be Duliani's original director's copy of the play, *La Rolls Royce; comedie en 3 actes de Mario Duliani et Jean Refroigney [n.d.]* preserved at the Library for the Performing Arts at the Lincoln Center, New York Public Library. Typewritten in French on onionskin, the 49–page script is well-worn, with indentations and red inked underlines of stage directions, setting descriptions and secondary directions. For example, on page 4: "*Gaston, protestent*"; "*Nicole, un peau rêveuse*"; "Anna, *vexée … elle sort*". There are several corrections by hand of typographical errors as well. Curiously, the front matter of the manuscript shows two different New York City addresses, belonging most likely, according to the NYPL archivist, to Duliani's American literary agent, I. S. Richter This extremely rare document, indeed, the only one in existence, merits focused critical examination.

3. The sources use the term *Golden Age* to describe Italian Canadian theatre production in Toronto, but theatre activity was taking place in communities across the country though shaped by population and settlement patterns. There were only about 2,000 Italians living in Canada in 1880 and 60,000 in 1911. In the early days of WW II there were 150,000 Italians on record and that number reached to half a million between 1948 and 1970. Montreal was the community with the largest settlement of Italians until the post-WW II wave of immigration when Toronto became the largest center, followed by Montreal and Vancouver. Each settlement like each wave of migration and range of theatre activity is unique and reflected in the larger inventory of plays and theatre production. At the time of writing most of the playwrights in my catalogue are from Ontario (roughly 60%), Quebec (20%), and British Columbia and the rest of the country (20%) respectively. It is notable that while the Piccolo Teatro was established in Toronto, Mesaglio and founders conceived it as *teatro italiano nell'Ontario*—theatre serving the cultural needs of the broader Italian community of Ontario. Menasse, Joseph. "*Perchè si deve incoraggiar il teatro*" *A Ricordo Del Suo X Anno Di Attivita* (1950–1960). *Il Piccolo Teatro* Program 1960.

knows—apart from a handful of historians and members of the Italian Canadian community who still speak of him. Mesaglio was born in Udine and served as cultural attaché at the Italian Embassy at The Hague before immigrating to Toronto in 1948. Once there, he joined the well-established drama group at St. Agnes Church in the west end of the city. Soon after, Mesaglio assembled a group of actors and in 1949 established the *Piccolo*, a name and production model inspired by Giorgio Strehler's *Piccolo Teatro di Milano* (literally "Little Theatre of the City of Milan") founded in 1947.[1]

Housed administratively at Brandon Hall,[2] home of the Italo-Canadian Recreation Club at 33 Brandon Avenue in the west end of the city, the Toronto *Piccolo* flourished for over two decades.[3] The company played to well-attended audiences in various venues—from Hart House at the University of Toronto to movie theatres such as the Pylon and Lansdowne cinemas in the city center, to mainstream spaces like the St. Lawrence Centre and Crest Theatre. In the early years, the Piccolo's repertoire included mostly lighthearted plays and operettas,[4] but by the late 1950s, the company added plays by Pirandello and Goldoni. The Goldoni works were performed in full-on traditional *commedia dell'arte* masks. Productions of Goldoni's *La Locandiera* in 1957 and *Il Bugiardo* in 1960 are frequently cited as markers for the troupe's growing regard by both the Italian and English mainstream communities—as well as in Italy. The *Piccolo* was in fact honored in 1960 with the prestigious Lion of San Marco by the City of Venice.[5]

Reviewers in Canada and Italy frequently commented on the high degree of professionalism and skill of the *Piccolo* actors. A number of them, including Mesaglio, went on to make appearances in English-language mainstream television shows of the 1950s and 1960s, including the CBC *Playdate Series* (*The Aspern Papers* by Henry James featuring Bruno Mesaglio and Alberto De Rosa, directed by Fulvio Marchi) and the 1966 pilot ("*Tell them the streets are dancing*") of the famous *Wojeck* television series.[6]

---

1. The model made sense in post-WW II Toronto as a means of building a sense of community and overcoming prevailing antagonism against Italians in Canada at that time. See Grohovaz A. Gianni. "*A Quest for Heritage: Piccolo Teatro Italiano.*" In *Polyphony* 5, No. 2 (Fall/Winter 1983): 47–56.

2. The legendary Italian Canadian Recreation Centre, also known as Brandon Hall, was built in 1948 in the Dufferin and Davenport area of Toronto, one of the city's four major settlement areas. When the building was sold in 1980, furniture, archives, and all, it caused heated controversy in the Italian Canadian community. Brandon Hall was the administrative home to the Piccolo and so who knows what was lost in terms of primary sources material. See Grohovaz A. Gianni, "*See You at Brandon Hall. OH! ... I Mean the Italo-Canadian Recreation Club.*" In *Polyphony* Vol. 7, No. 2 (Fall/Winter 1985): 98–103.

3. Members included Luigi Speca, *il sarto di Toronto* (Toronto's tailor) who went on to fame at Malabar's for his costuming for the Canadian opera company and other production companies throughout the world, Vittorio Mesaglio, Bruno's brother, well-known *truccatore* (make-up master), Augusto Saccucci who served in the traditional role of the "prompter", and actor Alberto De Rosa and director Fulvio Marchi.

4. The production values in these musical comedies and operettas were impressive and typically involved musical accompaniment of well-known musicians, Amilcare Zanni (orchestra) and Luigi Rovazzi (piano). Grohovaz *Quest* 48.

5. Italy was quite taken with the Toronto Piccolo: The Milan newspaper *Il tempo* praised the 1957 production of *La Locandiera* and printed a production still in the *December 26, 1957*, issue. In the 1961–1962 season Mesaglio and company were awarded the prestigious award, *Leon d'oro* from the city of Venice. See Bancheri and Pugliese 86 and Grohovaz *Quest* 50–51.

6. Bancheri and Pugliese 86 and Spezzano 190. Whereas radio through the 1940s was the principal source for entertainment and day-to-day news and information, television broadcasting was just getting underway in 1950s Montreal and Toronto. Professionalization of acting in both English and Italian and French communities was closely tied to the field of radio acting. Italian Canadian actors as well as writers

Mesaglio transformed relatively inexperienced actors into a cohesive company with a deep commitment to craft and demonstrated ability to deliver fine-tuned performances in the context of an increasingly demanding repertoire of plays.

There was no mistaking Mesaglio's depth of knowledge of acting and stagecraft or his deeply rooted belief in theatre culture as a corrective to the realities of immigrant existence. The *Piccolo* was a model of community, a thriving extended family—not unlike the organizational structure of the classic *commedia dell arte* troupe—with Mesaglio as its *capocomico*—Arlecchino—keeping everyone deftly in line.

The front cover of the Fall/Winter 1983 issue of *Polyphony* magazine reproduces a picture of Mesaglio wearing the costume of that classic trickster—a role, it is said, he played with great skill. Notice the body language, the exuberance and poise (*sprezzatura*); a wide-open smile and an elegant lean into a stack of newspapers—which when we flip the image over are Italian language newspapers from across the country. This picture is a powerful symbol, not only of a growing demographic, but also of the status and influence of Mesaglio in the development of Italian Canadian theatre.[1]

That such a prominent figure should be so little known, so glossed over in Canadian theatre sources, is another sign of historical neglect and erasure of an important Italian Canadian cultural model. Mesaglio's approach to actor training, his use of *commedia dell'arte*, and his directorial methodology remain undocumented in any comprehensive way. We have only a couple of short pieces to draw on. Mesaglio articulated his theory of drama—on the utilitarian effects of theatre in tempering feelings of "otherness" and marginalization—in a number of sources.[2] But these are not included in any studies of Canadian theatre or in dramatic theory courses that I am aware of. It was a revelation to learn that Mesaglio trained students and directed productions in theatres across the University of Toronto campus, including the Robert Gill Theatre where I spent my formative years. I knew nothing of this history.

The Piccolo ceased production in 1971 but its influence was reflected in the emergence of several new companies, such as the *Compagnia dei Giovani* and Edu-Art (and others)[3] who advanced the foundational work of the Piccolo in innovative ways. The *Compagnia dei Giovani* (1971–1980) emerged from the University of Toronto as an experimental bilingual entity meant to thrive beyond the confines of an academic setting.[4] Whereas Mesaglio focused on Italian classic plays mainly for the Italian community with the concept expanding over time, the *Compagnia dei Giovani* envisaged linguistic accessibility and inter-cultural outreach to the English-speaking mainstream community as central to their practice.

A challenging repertoire appealed to the widest possible audience. It included classics like Goldoni's *La Locanderia*, socially charged material like Machiavelli's *Mandrag*ola and new contemporary writers, such as the very first Canadian production

and musicians were at the forefront of these developments in radio and television and merit added critical attention. See Miller 86–96 and Kirkley 75–95.

1. The image of Mesaglio on the cover of *Polyphony* (Fall/Winter 1983, Vol. 5 No. 2) may be found on the website of the Multicultural History Society of Ontario. "Immigrant theatre," 1983, (CU13056757) edited by Robert F. Harney. Courtesy of Local Histories Collection, Libraries and Cultural Resources Digital Collections, University of Calgary.

2. Bancheri and Pugliese 79–104 cite the various print sources on this.

3. Bancheri and Pugliese are the major sources here but see also Fracassa 45–47.

4. Damiano Pietropaolo recalls the company was "named after a well-known and much-admired Italian theatre troupe—*Compagnia dei giovani* founded in 1954." *Hyphenated Identities* 25.

in 1973 of Dario Fo's one-act farce called *L'uomo nudo a l'uomo in frak (One was nude and one wore tails).*[1]

The troupe included English-speaking actors and they performed in both English and Italian languages. Supported by federal arts grants and inspired by the newly established Multicultural Theatre Association (1971), they toured extensively in Ontario and Quebec winning critical recognition and awards for their increasingly sophisticated work. They made several appearances in Italy as well owing to the ingenuity of the troupe's resident producer, Alberto Di Giovanni.[2] They brought an English translation of Pirandello's one-act 1913 play *Cecè* to the 5th International Pirandello Congress in Agrigento, Italy (Pirandello's birthplace) on December 9, 1978. *Cecè* was performed along with a second short play, *The Man With a Flower in His Mouth* (1922), in its original Italian, with Damiano Pietropaolo playing the central role. These performances received positive reviews in the Italian weekly magazine *Gente* and instigated a program of "cultural exchanges" with Italy.[3]

During this period, three of the company members—Laura Springolo, Mariella Bertella and Celestino De Iuliis—started translating Canadian authors "*in an attempt to link the Canadian reality to the Italian community and vice versa.*"[4] They translated Michel Tremblay's *A toi pour toujours ta Marie-Lou* into Italian and presented it in early March 1979 at Hart House Theatre in Toronto followed by performances March 19–22 in Rome, Italy at the *Teatro Goldoni*. Staged by Damiano Pietropaolo, one of the troupe's resident directors, the production received favorable reviews by local Roman newspapers *Paese Sera* and *Daily American*.[5]

The *Compagnia dei Giovani* developed a methodology of production in answer to the larger social transformations that were taking place in this post-1968 student movement era. Damiano Pietropaolo introduced the company to an innovative collective directing theory known as *regia del collettivo* which he had studied in Italy in 1972. To the best of my knowledge, no critical work has been done on their directorial

1. The Dario Fo play was staged at Hart House in April 1973 along with another one-act *La patente* by Pirandello to positive reviews. The level of professionalism and potential significance of the Compagnia in mainstream theatre was noted by Renato Ciolfi in *The Corriere Canadese* (16 April 1973) 6. See Bancheri and Pugliese 91, 102.

2. Company *impresario* and sometime director, Alberto Di Giovanni remains a figure of standing not only in the Italian Canadian community but in the non-English and non-French theatre communities of Ontario and Italy. As principal animator of the Multicultural Theatre Festival established in 1971, Di Giovanni served as the Theatre Association's first director and remained active in the organization for many years. Di Giovanni has maintained a personal archive of primary resources on the Golden Age of Italian Canadian theatre that begs for documentation and critical analysis. Among his publications is *Italo-Canadians: Nationality and Citizenship* (Guernica, 2015).

3. Bancheri and Pugliese (1993): 95. According to primary sources in the Alberto Di Giovanni archive, the *Compagnia dei giovani* performed in Agrigento on two occasions: December 1978 (*Cecè* and *The Man With the Flower in His Mouth*) and December 1979 with Pirandello's *Ma non è una cosa seria*, in Italian. Damiano Pietropaolo. Telephone Interview. August 14, 2023.

4. Mariella Bertelli. Bancheri and Pugliese 95.

5. See Damiano Pietropaolo's discussion of the Roman production of Tremblay in *Hyphenated Identities* 15–29. Roman reviews of *A toi, pour toujours, ta Marie-Lou* appeared in *Paese Sera* (21 Marzo 1979) and *Daily American* (March 24, 1979). Pietropaolo performed in *Compagnia dei Giovani* productions but focused much of his attention on directing and producing before moving to an accomplished career at CBC radio. His writing, directing, producing at CBC Radio Drama and Features, and Radio Arts & Entertainment remain internationally recognized. The Damiano Pietropaolo Papers at the Thomas Fischer Rare Book Library archives contain numerous original draft and production radio scripts by countless Canadian authors including Nick Mancuso, Caterina Edwards, Paula Wing, and others.

experiments in any form or in the context of emergent contemporaneous developments in the Canadian alternate theatre movement.[1] Despite a significant history of production over nine seasons with an intercultural bilingual focus and a provocative repertoire the *Compagnia* has escaped notice of Canadian theater scholars.[2]

The Compagnia's commitment to inclusivity and accessibility inspired endeavors such as *Pinocchio on The Road*. Created in 1973 by Laura Springolo and Mariella Bertelli and funded by a Local Initiative Project grant, actors from the *Compagnia* performed folk tales in both English and Italian throughout the greater metropolitan of Toronto, in schools, libraries, parks and community centers.

Through the 1970s the bilingual troupe Edu-Arts Service created by Franco Spezzano and Cosmo Barranca brought a range of plays, many of them original, to countless adults and young people in schools and community settings. As the name Edu-Art Service implies there is a connection between theatre and instruction and community service—a recurring strand in the history of Italian Canadian theatre and its dramatic literature. As Mario Duliani said in *La Fortune Vient en Parlant*, theatre is for "life". Philosophically and practically the techniques involved in the actor's work are a foundation for a humanist education: whatever your profession or station in life the basic principles are precious and useful (*très precieux, et très utile*).[3]

---

1. The absence of the *Compagnia dei Giovani* in Canadian theatre studies is inexplicable. 1) It was a bilingual, experimental collective that flourished for a decade in 1970s Toronto amidst a thriving alternate theatre movement in which collectivity was a preoccupation by artists and critics alike. The *Compagnia*'s approach to directing known as *colettiva regia* (collective directing) was inspired directly by theatre practice in Italy. Notably, Europe had provided several models for Canadian theatre: Toronto Free Theatre (Germany's Free Theatre) and Toronto Workshop productions (Joan Littlewood) for instance. 2) The theatre mainstream was not "alien" to Italian Canadians at that time: Nick Mancuso, for example, was busily engaged at Toronto Free and Theatre Passe Muraille as was Louis Del Grande who was also presenting his early plays such as *So, who's Goldberg? A comedy in one act* (1972). Bruno Gerussi as well was a regular face on national television after a successful stage career. 3) Instead of finding pathways and intersections for collaboration *with* Italian Canadian theatre artists, it appears that Toronto's Italian Canadian community was fodder for the gaze of non-Italian theatre folk. An example of this approach is a cycle of plays at Theatre Passe Muraille created and directed by Paul Thompson known as "The Immigrants." These productions were devised for Italian, Greek, and Portuguese community clubs to enable TPS to "reach" new communities and audiences. I cannot speak to the Greek and Portuguese plays, but managed to track down archival reviews, pictures, and posters of the "Italian" show at the University of Guelph library. It was called *Adventures of an Immigrant* (1974); one of the reviewers described it a "docudrama" (*Globe and Mail* 25 February 1974). There is no script since the play was improvised, but Rick Salutin is named "writer" in the archival material and the actors included Eric Peterson, Anne Anglin and the late David Fox. Performances were presented in Italian community "clubs" and on the Queen Street streetcar—on the streetcar (!). The actors would break out and perform "scenes of Italian life" while the streetcar was moving from stop to stop. There were no artists from the Italian community involved in this production. The reviews indicate that Italian audiences did not show up. Critics such as Robert Wallace reported the experiment was "not always successful" in Wallace, Robert. "Growing Pains: Toronto Theatre in the 1970s." in *Theatre and Performance in Toronto*. (2009): 15. Without diminishing the honorable careers and contributions of Mr. Thompson and Mr. Salutin to Canadian theatre history, based on the extant archival materials, this endeavor was a minstrel show at best. I imagine the company would look back at that initiative through a different lens today. I thank Frank Canino who first mentioned "an Italian show on a streetcar in the early 1970s" over coffee (December 2019), a conversation which led to this discovery. Apparently, Italian immigrants and their stories were popular literary subjects in the 1970s especially in literature for young people. Examples include the award-winning play, *The Magic Carpets of Antonio Angelini* (1976) by Gwen Pharis Ringwood produced in Winnipeg at the National Multicultural Theatre Festival in July 1976 and the book *The Sandwich* by Ian Wallace and Angela Wood published by Kids Can Press in 1975.

2. First-hand accounts of the troupe's philosophy and *regia del collettivo* may be found in Bancheri and Pugliese 88–92, 102–103.

3. Duliani, Mario. "*En Guise De 'Lever De Rideau'*" Duliani 7–16.

In English Canada, the process of establishing a national theatre identity came about almost exclusively in the context of amateur and university theatre activity. When Mesaglio was training his company of actors in 1950s Toronto, acting was hardly recognized as a "real" profession.[1] You will notice that I have not used the words amateur or professional in my account thus far. A couple of the sources use them, describing the Piccolo as an amateur company and the *Compagnia dei Giovani* as semi-professional. One cannot deny that in the 1980s we saw a complex cultural shift, with more and more members of the Italian Canadian community entering the professional theatre world. Sometimes words like "amateur" disguise the true nature of the quality of the work—which is the measure that matters. The Habima had immigrant roots. The Group Theatre had amateur roots. Stanislavsky, perhaps the most famous amateur in performance history, changed history. Mesaglio never used the terms amateur or professional. Craft was the ultimate measure. *The work was good, or it was not.*[2]

Dora Mavor Moore's New Play Society (est. 1946) had an amateur non-profit basis, and the Crest theatre (est. 1951)[3] grew out of University of Toronto student theatre productions. Similarly, the *Piccolo* grew out of the Italian community and the *Compagnia dei Giovani* emerged from the University of Toronto expanding their reach from there. Valuing "amateur" theatre roots ought to include amateur non-English and bi-lingual Italian English theatre. Italian Canadian theatre progressed *alongside* the growth and professionalization of English Canadian theatre, and these histories and activities intersected at various points in time.[4] This parallel history is not claimed, and these cultural intersections are all but ignored by mainstream theatre as *legitimate* or *Canadian enough* in the hierarchy of significance that permeates our theatre history.[5]

Italian Canadian practice has always been a central part of the culture even though it is still difficult to penetrate in terms of representation, visibility, and access. Italian theatre did not seek *authorization* from the mainstream culture but rather recognition to do what they have always done: create, educate, and entertain. I believe there is a space of deep connection between "mainstream" theatre and Italian Canadian theatre, but the roots are not known. The influence of Italian culture on Canadian theatre from Signor Lenzi to the grand tradition of the *Vagabondi* to today's unsung playwrights has never been fully acknowledged.

---

1. Acting was "part-time, a secondary occupation," Nathan Cohen famously observed (*Theatre for Canada* 226). Actor David Gardiner recollects: "At the end of that year [1951] I submitted my expenses, my income tax expenses for touring for hotels, meals out, etc. as a touring actor. 'What category are you?' I was asked. 'Actor,' I replied. My income tax form was returned to me saying 'we have no category for actor in this country at this time, so we have taken your expenses and we have re-classified you as a travelling salesman,' which was not far off! Again, an indication of where we were in this country professionally speaking." (McNicoll 15).
2. This quotation of Mesaglio was gathered in an-person interview I conducted with Frank Spezzano (July 6, 2017).
3. See Sperdakos on the New Play Society and Goodwin on the Crest Theatre.
4. For example, Memorial Day co-productions in the 1960s and 1970s: Gianni Grohovaz's realistic play, *Il ragazzo del '99*, about a fallen soldier performed (and apparently) filmed in honor of 1962 Memorial Day; and a musical allegory called *From Flanders Field to the Italian Alps* presented November 4, 1975, to the accompaniment of the Saint Cecelia Choir. The latter is cited as one of the first formal multilingual plays produced in Canada; it combines Italian, Friulana, English and French (Baxa and Grohovaz *Quest for Heritage*).
5. Notably, Playwrights Canada published *The Enchanted Loom* by Suvendrini Lena in both English and Tamil in November 2022 and its first play in English and Farsi, *Winter of '88* by Mohammad Yaghoubi, in March 2023. Annie Gibson, Playwrights Canada Press. Email Exchange. July 31, 2023.

The first known play on record by an Italian Canadian in the post-WW II period dates to 1946. It was never published or staged and is preserved in original typescript at Library and Archives Canada. It is called *I Fled Him* and was written by Leo Armand Ciceri (1924–1970). You may recognize the name because Ciceri was an actor in the early years of the Stratford Festival. By all accounts he was a gifted actor—it is said that he played a fiery Paris opposite Bruno Gerussi's Romeo in the 1960s—but Ciceri died tragically in 1970 at the age of 46. An award in his name was established by the Stratford Festival to be given annually at the National Theatre School to a promising young talent. What is little known about Ciceri was his interest in playwriting and in theatre education—the latter a recurring stream in the development of Italian Canadian theatre practice. In addition to coaching young actors at the Stratford Festival, he wrote and presented talks on Shakespeare and theatre to secondary students and teachers. This original writing—which I am presently working through—is also preserved at Archives Canada.[1]

I mention Leo Ciceri because not only does he stand for the tentative beginnings of a tradition of writing for the theatre, but also because he embodies the multidimensional hybrid nature of many playwrights in the catalogue of plays by Canadians of Italian heritage and in this anthology. Ciceri was an actor, teacher, public speaker, and experimental playwright. His language of birth was Italian. He was raised in a province that was predominantly French. He received classical theatre training in the UK and performed in English in both Canada and the US. He gave public lectures on theatre. This amalgam of métier—of language—of cultural identification—indeed of cultural perspective—seems a proper jumping off place in talking about these Italian Canadian dramatists.

When I say Italian Canadian dramatists, I mean individuals that have connection with—or relationship to their Italian Canadian heritage. I recognize this term means different things to different people. Do we include the hyphen[2] or not? Do we mean theatre and plays by Italians born in Canada or by Canadians who are Italian by

---

1. In one talk Ciceri writes that theatre is intrinsically multicultural, multilingual, multidisciplinary, and multi-difference, and references a production of *Oedipus Rex* that had played at the Century Theatre in New York City. It "was written by a Greek, translated by an Irishman [William Butler Yeats], directed by a Frenchman [Michael Saint-Denis] and acted by Englishmen [Laurence Olivier and the Old Vic company]." The only thing America supplied was a space and that is not good enough, he says. "What we are practicing today in the name of theatre has almost nothing to do with the theater ... Drama is all around us, in the very air we breathe. But the odd thing is, it isn't in our theatre." As a gathering place theatre should reflect what is true, the community it represents. "Otherwise, it isn't theatre." (Ciceri *Speech About the Theatre*). These are rather prescient forward-thinking views. It is also true that during the late 1940s Ciceri had to leave Canada to study acting. The Massey Commission was released in 1951 in the same year as the founding of the Théâtre du Nouveau Monde in Montreal. The Stratford festival was established in 1953 and the Canadian branch of Canadian Actor's Equity was opened in only 1955. Acting was not recognized as a legitimate profession in Canada in those days and so it is not surprising that some of ideas that Ciceri is wrestling with are majoritarian and decidedly British since that is what was available to him.
2. There is a great deal of (Canadian and American) scholarly discussion and creative literature about hyphens and hyphenation. There are two prevailing spellings of the term 'Italian Canadian'—one *with* and the other *without* the hyphen. A unifying *slash* (*Italian/Canadian* and/or *Italian/American*) is often used as well. These markers imply different things: connection and belonging or displacement and marginalization. For the purposes of this introduction, I favor the *space* in between Italian and Canadian.

heritage? Do we mean theatre and stories about Italians in Canada or stories written by Italians in Canada, or do we mean both? Moreover, what do we mean by Italian Canadian community? What are the boundaries for a play to be classified as Italian Canadian? Is there *something in common* beyond culture and pedigree?[1] Some 2nd and 3rd generation writers do not address issues of cultural identity in their plays, which begs the question: *Where do we start and stop in the project of classification?*

These subjects are far too large to address properly in this introduction, but my view is that being Italian Canadian amalgamates diverse histories, languages, and modes of expression and crisscrosses geographies and generations. It is an ever-evolving heterogeneous entity and as such there is no one monument of Italian Canadian theater authors.

In the catalogue of 300 plays this referent is sometimes overt and explicit—I am thinking of the characters Frank and Rocco in Vittorio Rossi's *Little Blood Brother* (1986) or matriarch Concetta in Salvatore Antonio's *In Gabriel's Kitchen* (2006). Sometimes the referent to heritage is ambiguous such as in the work of Rose Napoli in *Lo (or Dear Mr. Wells)* (2020) in which 15-year schoolgirl Laura is not identifiably Italian Canadian. Sometimes characters and plot situations are not identifiably Italian Canadian except by intimation or association. Sometimes the playwrights draw on historical figures of Italian Canadian heritage—as Frank Canino does in his play about Italian immigrant Angelina Napolitana (1882–1932) in *The Angelina Project (2000)*—to give us insight into matters of universal value and resonance.

What matters most are the assorted ways in which heritage plays itself out in the respective written works of Italian Canadian dramatists and actor-artists. I acknowledge the problematic notion of presenting a body of presumably identifiable Italian Canadian plays. It raises all sorts of questions about power and privilege. What is included? What is left out? Who sanctions acceptance and by what standards? These are important questions. I am hyper-aware of the kind of language I use and inadvertently re-marginalizing the plays and playwrights.[2]

For the most part these playwrights write entirely in English or in a theatrical bilingualism, English with interjections of Italian that makes them perfectly understood. Several write their plays in French. Others write in Italian or in one of the regional Italian dialects or in *Italiese*—which is a fusion of Standard Italian or an Italian dialect with English. A number write in combinations of one or more of these languages.[3]

---

1. This phrase is from Jason Sherman's closing remarks in *Modern Jewish Plays*.
2. This is not a new dilemma as the far-reaching and inspiring body of Italian Canadian literature and criticism by pioneers such as Joseph Pivato, Linda Hutcheon, Giorgio Di Cicco, Caterina Edwards, Marco Micone, and many others in the field to the present day demonstrate.
3. The issue of language and theatre in Canada is perpetually complex and intersects theoretical as well as pedagogical and practical subjects which cannot be dealt with here. It is ironic that the 300 plays in the Italian Canadian catalogue are written mostly in English. Of note, Filippo Salvatore's essay "The Voiceless People Speak Out" 94–99, discussions and bibliographies of Paul Colilli and Diana Iule-Colilli "*Italiese* as a Literary Language," Caterina Edwards "Discovering Voice," and Pivato's well-known article on Marco Micone cited in the bibliography. On a historiographic note, I recall one of the most poignant responses to the 1990 production of *A Modo Suo (A Fable)* from Robert Crew of *The Toronto Star*. He described how he felt like "an outsider ... shut out of the work"—notwithstanding what was obviously a fine show and strong reaction from the audience. "*A Modo Suo* Needs Subtitles," he wrote on April 22, 1990. Of course, one wants to reach the widest audience, but that is not always possible. The question becomes: Can theatre of this sort with its inherent limitations co-exist in 'Canadian' theatre? See Migliarisi "Production History."

They write tragedies, comedies, farce to social satire, musicals, and plays for young people and plays for puppets. They write stories of emigration, history plays, plays based on poetry or inspired by folklore or short stories. They translate 20th century classics from French to Italian (Tremblay) or from Italian into English (Pirandello). They write a variety of solo works as well as site-specific plays and plays for social justice and everything in between. They write with their bodies as well, as memorialized in the movement plays of Winnipeg actor-mime Giuseppe Condello.[1]

From one-acts and solo pieces to sprawling collective creations, interdisciplinary spectacles and immersive experiences, the plays draw on many dramatic styles and conventions, from kitchen-sink realism to expressionism to post-modern strangeness. Most of the playwrights write in a distinguishable style—and on recognizable themes—but some experiment with different storytelling modes within their own *oeuvre*. Categorizing these plays and playwrights in any definitive way is an ongoing point of issue. What we can say for certain, however, is that the central attribute of this body of work is breadth and variety in subject matter, form, style and tone.

One of the writers said to me, *Anna, please don't include my early plays. They're not very good*. A focus of my larger project of retrieval, inventory, and cataloguing is to acknowledge how *much* is out there. The weird and wonderful are all a part of the official record and deserve to be recognized. The dramaturgically unsophisticated works are valuable if only as expressions of an honest impulse to create something meaningful.[2] I am not minimizing the authority of craft—on the contrary. Acknowledgment does not prevent critical evaluation and a lack of technical sophistication is hardly a measure of inherent worth. The multiplicity of styles and structures in the catalogue disrupts any monolithic labeling such as ethnic, minority, marginal or immigrant. Instead, in their totality, these rich works constitute a diverse body of difference. Put another way difference is the common.

The plays in this anthology are organized purposely into groupings that draw attention to their multifaceted dramaturgic, stylistic, thematic, and linguistic intersections. They include family dramas, comedies, plays based on historical figures or rooted in historical events, one-person narratives, and social dramas. Themes and conflicts play themselves out in different psychological, socio-cultural, intergenerational, narrative, and performative territories. The complexity is both the point and inherent contribution of this body of work.

Each play in this collection (other than *Che Brava Gente* which emerged out of an educational context)[3] has a professional production history and received reviews and in most cases honors and accolades. Even though they played and appealed to both Italian Canadian and non-Italian Canadian audiences and a broad swath of creative people involved in the productions, most of the plays represented here have never been

---

1. Mentored by Etienne Decroux in Paris, France, Giuseppe Condello is internationally recognized for his mime-movement plays and performances. His distinctive approach to actor training has been captured in a recent documentary: *Corporal Mime: The Actor's Art of Movement*.

2. Barolini underscores this idea in relation to "unknown" Italian American women writers. See also Fazio, Venera and De Santis and Di Giovanni, Caroline.

3. The play was presented in February 2009 by *Le maschere laurenziane*, a student theatre ensemble housed in the Italian studies program at Laurentian University, Sudbury, Ontario. *Le maschere laurenziane* has employed theatre practice as a pedagogical tool and meeting place for cultural enrichment for over two decades. See Iuele-Colilli.

published. Martin Hunter, for example, co-director of the production of *Johnny Bananas* at the Adelaide Court Theatre in 1984, was not Italian, but he recognized something of profound value in *Johnny Bananas* beyond the narrow confines of an "immigrant" story.[1] The point was inclusivity and a widening cultural reach, sentiments I reflexively set sights on for the plays in this anthology. The fact that *Johnny Bananas* and others in the collection have not been included in standard anthologies of Canadian drama is not a value judgment on the plays, but rather on the mainstream perception of the plays and catalogue.

The collection begins with *A Modo Suo (A Fable)* because it stands as a turning point in the history of Italian Canadian theatre in Toronto. In the Golden Age of the 1960s and 1970s Italian Canadian actors, directors, designers, producers, and a handful of writers, put down a foundation for a vibrant *performance* practice.[2] It is in the 1980s that we see the emergence of a body of *theatrical writing* that grows and intensifies into the 1990s and beyond. This change was a result of complex social, cultural, political, and economic factors. The availability of government theater arts funding, in both the Italian and Canadian theatre communities, inspired new voices entering the professional theatre mainstream.

Their plays depicted, for the very first time, Italian Canadian characters and situations set against an Italian-Quebec Canadian reality. These plays include *Gens du Silence* by Marco Micone (1982) staged in French in 1983 and a few years later in English translation as *Voiceless People* (1984). Vittorio Rossi's *Little Blood Brother* (1986) and *Backstreets* (1987) which were written and staged in English at the Centaur Theatre, and Tony Nardi's first play, co-authored with Vince Ierfino, *La Storia dell'emigrante* (1979–1982), was written and staged in Italian in Montreal and Toronto.

A number of women were also developing their craft and making their voices heard in a range of theatrical contexts from fringe festivals to mainstream theatres—such as Caterina Edwards in *Homeground* (1986); Eufemia Fantetti in *The Last Moon* (1987) and *Italian Tale* (1987); and Maristella Roca, who would go on to explore the lives of Italian Canadian women in original plays like *Clutching the Heat* (1990) and *Poveri Fiori* (1993), both written in English. Roca also co-authored with the late Luciano Iacobelli *La Storia Calvino (1985)*—the first collective creation of Italian Canadian actors for Acting Company.[3] *Johnny Bananas* (1983) was being workshopped

1. The production was co-directed by Damiano Pietropaolo.
2. Several writers were producing in the 1960s and 1970s. They include James de Felice (Edmonton), Louise Del Grande (Toronto), John Juliani (Vancouver), and Michael Mirolla (editor of this volume) and Dominique de Pasquale (Montreal). Nick Mancuso describes the agit-prop experimentation inspired by Artaud's Theatre of Cruelty that he created and performed with Damiano Pietropaolo: "*Teatru streetucarru* was the name of the theatre group of misfits and malcontents and it started at the Bar Diplomatico that wasted summer." (Nick Mancuso. Email. August 24, 2023). This period of multi-focused and multilingual theatrical experimentation—including the fine work of *Le Maschere* theatre troupe in Montreal—merits critical study, considering it established a terrain out of which further work emerged.
3. The text was a collage of stories devised from the actors' personal experiences interwoven with select fables of Italo Calvino. The collective included Mario Romano, Tony Nardi, Alvaro D'Antonio, Anna Starnino and me. It was directed by Alec Stockwell with dramaturgy by Mimi Meckler. The production played at the Tarragon Theatre to critical acclaim and earned Dora nominations (*La Storia II* was subsequently developed). One of its most interesting aspects in my view was the scenic design and conception of space. The centerpiece was a massive wooden table—painted in striking colors in quasi-Futurist style—carved out in interlocking sections that could be pulled apart and back together in various configurations, depending on the scene, much like a puzzle. By the end of the show all the actors gathered

in various Toronto theatre venues. While this production falls into an ill-defined category of semi-professional theatre, it featured up and coming and well-known professional actors such as Geza Kovacks, Anthony Rizacos and Rod Beattie in addition to individuals from the highly regarded *Compagnia dei giovani* in the Italian Canadian community.

A Modo Suo (A Fable) was a historical landmark in 1990 performed at Canadian Stage during a time of shifting values and accepted cultural norms. The play remains the first recorded depiction of the lives of post-World War Two Italian Calabrese speaking in their own language performed in an English-language mainstream theatre. The play is published here for the first time in its original Calabrese along with an English translation. The story of *A Modo Suo (A Fable)* is not only the play but also the controversially embattled production.[1] The piece provoked numerous questions about the reception and critical evaluation of plays written in a language other than English and French and First Nations that are as relevant today as they were in 1990.

Many of the new voices in 1990s were women. They included Toronto-based actor Toni Ellwand who was beginning to write and produce a series of personal plays on the Italian Canadian experience from a female perspective such as *Cause Unknown* (1994), published here for the first time. Actor Norma Dell'Agnese, who in addition to her film work began writing one of several solo pieces in English; and Montreal-based Mara Rantucci was writing plays in Italian in Montreal. Eleonor Albanese was writing in these years, and many of her plays were staged at Magnus Theatre in Thunder Bay. Among them was *The Two Rooms of Grace* (1999), a play that is told through the eyes of an 87-year-old woman—Grace—who is looking back at her life and her marriage to an Italian immigrant. Paula Wing was writing in this period as well. Her well-known translations include *Naomi's Road* (1992) recognized by both Dora Mavor Moore and Chalmers theatre awards. In that period, Vancouver-based playwright Lucia Frangione, author of the play *Fresco* published for the first time in this anthology, was also starting to write for the Fringe Festival circuit. Frangione is one of Canada's most prolific playwrights. At last count she has written 30 plays of striking range and depth, and dramaturgical sophistication. The major ones have been produced internationally, published, and recognized with honors.

One of the pleasures of working through this inventory is discovering how skilled Italian women playwrights are at writing comedy and creating multi-layered female characters. I am thinking of Mary Melfi who wrote her first comedy, *Sex Therapy*, in 1996, and went on to write her recent black comedies *My Italian Wife* and *Foreplay*

---

around it in a sort of *tableau vivant or table art*. There is no comprehensive production history of *La Storia Calvino* or studies of the collective experience itself which raised all sorts of questions from ethnocultural and intercultural perspectives. The innovative text is worthy of critical appraisal, considering the groundswell of experimental drama emerging in the 1980s. The impressive early history of collective creation in Italian Canadian practice, which includes Guillaume Bernardi's theatrical innovations in the 1990s, has escaped critical attention.

1. See Migliarisi *A Modo Suo*. Journalistic pieces in both Italian and English mainstream dailies on this controversial production are abundant. Of note, Leonard, Paul. "Of Plays Canadian" and Baldassare, Angela, "Fable Restricted by Language" cited in the bibliography. There has been no dedicated historiographical study on *A Modo Suo (A Fable)* but it invites dedicated analyses from multiple disciplinary perspectives in English Canadian history and Italian Canadian theatre studies. The unprecedented support *A Modo Suo (A Fable)* received from the Italian Canadian community, notably the famous Columbus Centre and then President Pal Di Iulio, was also a significant aspect of this storied production.

(2012). I am also thinking of Fantetti and her heartbreaking *13 Scenes (and a Few Jokes) From the Life of a Depressed Comic* (2012), as well as the many other women writing and performing solo works—from Debra Di Giovanni to Sandra Battaglini to Sonia Di Placido. All these writers portray characters and situations that defy ubiquitous one-dimensional depictions of Italian Canadian women.

Italian Canadian male writers are also deft at comedy. I am speaking not only of Frank Spadone, Guido Grasso, and other popular solo performers, but also of Montreal-based writer and actor Tony Calabretta who has developed a smart ear for dialogue and comical situations as seen in his play *Damn Those Wedding Bells!* (1996). This play was subsequently translated into French by none other than Michel Tremblay and staged in 2006 in Montreal—a recognition that speaks for itself.

The year 2000 is another point of change in the history of Italian Canadian drama. *Canadian Theatre Review* published an issue devoted to Italian Canadian Theatre in the fall (Number 104) of that year with a photo of Charly Chiarelli on the front cover. Chiarelli is recognized for his popular 1995 solo-play *Cu' Fu*. Edited by Maria DiCenzo this issue includes an English language translation of Nardi's *A Modo Suo (A Fable)* and a number of other short pieces focused mostly on contemporary practice. None are particularly comprehensive in scope; however, Di Cenzo's editorial is a strong concerted effort in historicizing Italian Canadian theatre and in marking it out as a rich reservoir for further critical study.[1]

In the 2009 summer issue, *Canadian Theatre Review* published a short play called *Professionally Ethnic* (2009) by Bobby Del Rio—reprised as part of the Summer Works Festival in Toronto in 2017. "*As an Italian Chinese Canadian I'm always on the outside,*" he told me in an interview.[2] His play deals with the problematic entity called multiculturalism as seen through the eyes of an ethnically ambiguous theatre artist. In some ways *Professionally Ethnic* and its author reflect the eclecticism that characterizes Italian Canadian theatrical practice in the new millennium.

This outsider theme is recurring in Italian Canadian drama. One of the most striking examples is *Two Letters ... and Counting!* (2006–2013) by Tony Nardi—arguably one of Canada's most famous or depending on your perspective infamous outsiders—who takes on the entire Canadian cultural establishment in addressing themes of art and power.[3]

In recent years newer and younger voices are making their presence felt. They include Montreal-based Michaela Di Cesare whose plays include a dramatic exploration of the mysterious woman behind the man in her *In Search of Mrs. Pirandello* (2015); Marco Soriano and the rest of the comic writers of Vancouver's Bella Luna Productions; Toronto-based Melissa D'Agostino, solo performer and writer of the award-winning digital series, *Tactical Girls*; Adam Paolozza and his Jacque Lecoq-inspired theatrical pieces and Daniele Bartolini and his provocative urban installations with *Dopo Lavoro Teatrale*; and the multidimensional Liana Cusmano, a poet, playwright, spoken-word performance artist, filmmaker, and culture critic working fluidly in English, French and Italian languages.

---

1. "Performing Ethnicity: Italian Canadian Theatre." in Maria DiCenzo (2000): 3–6.
2. In-person interview August 15, 2017.
3. Nardi, Tony, et al. *Two Letters—and Counting! Two Incidents Provoked—*. 1st ed., Guernica, 2013.

There are no signs that theatrical writing in the Italian Canadian community is slowing down. Plays of varying degrees of dramaturgical complexity and aesthetic gradation happily coexist in Italian Canadian theatre—extending a colorful history of live practice that goes back hundreds and hundreds of years in Mother Italy. We may well say that we are in a New Golden Age encompassing new forms that include social media and other technologies. Some of the struggles faced by the *Piccolo* and *Compagnia dei giovani* and the establishment of a theatre writing tradition—of getting produced and published and recognized—remain the same. The question is: Do today's Italian Canadian theatre makers and writers seek "acceptance" by the "mainstream" in the way their predecessors did?

I have organized the thirteen plays into "categories" to make them user-friendly for the reader. However, I do not intend to impose rigid literary boundaries, rather I want to highlight the connections between the plays and their inherent overlaps. We can look at these plays through the lens of theme but also in the context of history or histories. Where do they stand in the development of Italian Canadian theatre history and its literature?

The first two—*A Modo Suo (A Fable)* by Tony Nardi and *Cause Unknown* by Toni Ellwand—are family plays, but only at the most simplistic understanding of plot. There are no happy families here. The next category is comedy. *Ma Che Brava Gente!* by Iuele-Colilli and Sansalone is a comedy of language (Italiese). *Moose on the Loose* by Dina Morrone is a comedy of character and *Damn Those Wedding Bells!* by Tony Calabretta is a situation comedy. The third category is historical plays based on either historical figures or events. *Johnny Bananas* by Michael Macina, a portrait of an immigrant in Toronto based on the life of Macina's great grandfather, Giovanni Macina, is a cross between scripted *cinema verité* and vaudevillian show. In *In Search of Mrs. Pirandello* by Michaele Di Cesare the main character confronts history by conjuring up Mrs. Pirandello and effectively demarginalizing her in the present. Drawing on the kaleidoscope of theatricality to make sense of history, *Fresco* by Lucia Frangione is a deeply personal view on the Internment of Italians in Canada. The next category is modern-day social dramas. *God Is a Gangster* by Nick Mancuso being a solo character piece about a homeless man that rages on the page. Mancuso is unique among this group because he came to playwriting after an extraordinary career as an internationally recognized and respected performer in theatre, film, and television. In addition to authoring several plays, his recent pursuits include an important body of writing on the actor's work that merits compilation and analysis. *The Summoned* by Fabrizio Filippo is a futuristic meditation on the question of how far from our human nature will technology take us. The final category is biographical musings. In *Professionally Ethnic* Bobby Del Rio wins us over by personally challenging the constructs of representation through social satire. Encompassing many performative disciplines rooted in *commedia dell'arte, Paollozapedia* by Adam Paolloza is a moving personal exploration of identity, roots, culture, and mortality. *Boyfriend* is eloquent in its bare-naked simplicity. Liana Cusmano employs performance poetry, a form with roots in classical oratory that has come full circle to express their poignant soul. Through *spoken word* they reveal the theatricality of their heart.

While I was researching the three hundred plays for this anthology, I unearthed a veritable bounty of riches. The compilation is a treasure trove of truly unique writings that I believe to be of utmost importance to the development and recorded history of Italian Canadian Theatre. My challenge became not so much what to include in this book, but what not to reluctantly exclude. Limited by time and space, I chose the following thirteen plays, but there are many more that deserve your attention. So, dear reader, I leave it to you to discover these historic gems in your own time and possibly glimpse—as I did—fragments of yourself, your friends, your ancestors.

In summary, trusting in reader discernment, I have assembled these works with generic tractability. They are more than their classifications. At the risk of echoing what has already been said or worse, presenting one-dimensional understandings, let me emphasize the aim of this collection: Let the plays speak for themselves.

Blibliography

Atkin, Thomas Beamish, 1809–1891. *History of Halifax City.* s.n.,1895.

Aleandri, Emelise. *The Italian-American Immigrant Theatre of New York City, 1746–1899.* Edwin Mellen, 2006.

Bagnell, Kenneth. *Canadese: A Portrait of the Italian Canadians.* Macmillan, 1989.

Baldassare, Angela. "Fable Restricted by Language." *Metropolis* 26 April 1990: 25.

Bancheri, Salvatore and Guido Pugliese. "Italian Theatre." *The Luminous Mosaic: Italian Cultural Organizations in Ontario.* Soleil, 1993.

Barolini. Helen. *The Dream Book: An Anthology of Writings by Italian American Writings.* Syracuse University Press, 1985.

Baxa, Paul. "La Festa Della Fratellanza Italiana: Gianni Grohovaz and the Celebrations of Italian Memorial Day in Toronto, 1960–1975." *Quaderni d'italianistica*, Volume 31, No. 1, 2010, pp.197–225.

Beraud, Jean. 350 *ans de théâtre au Canada français*, Montreal, Le Cercle du livre de France, 1958, vol. I.

Ciceri, Leo Armand. *"Speech About the Theatre"* (n.d.) Library and Archives Canada.

Cioni, Maria. *Spaghetti Western: How My Father Brought Italian Food to the West.* Fifth House, 2006.

Cohen, David, and Ben Greenwood. *The Buskers: A History of Street Entertainment.* David and Charles 1981.

Cohen, Nathan. "Theatre for Canada" (1956). Rubin, Don. *Canadian Theatre History: Selected Readings.* 2nd ed., Playwrights Canada Press, 2004.

Crew, Robert. " *A Modo Suo* Needs Subtitles." *The Toronto Star* 22 April 1990, C9.

De Gasperi. Giulia. "'The Hall was us': Roles and Functions of the Italian Hall, La Sala Italiana in the Italian-Canadian Community of Dominion, Cape Breton Island, Canada." in *Folk Life*, 49:2 (2011), pp. 142–153.

Del Rio, Bobby. In-person Interview. Toronto. 2017.

DiCenzo, Maria. Editor. "Italian Canadian Theatre." *Canadian Theatre Review.* Number 104. Fall 2000. University of Toronto Press, 2000, pp. 3–6.

…, "Performing Ethnicity: Italian Canadian Theatre." *Canadian Theatre Review.* Number 104. Fall 2000. University of Toronto Press, 2000, pp. 3–6.

Di Giovanni, Alberto. *Italo-Canadians: Nationalism and Citizenship.* Guernica, 2015.

Di Giovanni, Caroline Morgan. *Italian Canadian Voices: an Anthology of Poetry and Prose (1946–1983).* Mosaic Press, 1984.

Di Schino, June. "The Significance and Symbolism of Sugar Sculpture at Italian Court Banquets." *Food and Material Culture: Proceedings of the Oxford Symposium on Food and Cookery 2013*, ed. McWilliams, Mark, 111–22. Totnes: Prospect Books, 2014.

Duliani, Mario. *La Fortune Vient En Parlant.* Préface De Edith Piaf. Les Éditions Fernand Pilon, 1948.

Edwards, Caterina. "Discovering Voice: The Second Generation Finds Its Place: A Polemic." *Italian Canadiana* Vol. 2 No. 1 (Spring 1986), pp. 63–68.

Eisenbichler, Konrad. Ed. *Forgotten Italians: Julian-Dalmatian Writers and Artists in Canada.* University of Toronto P, 2018.

Fanella, Antonella. *With Heart and Soul: Calgary's Italian Community.* University of Calgary Press, 1999.

Fazio, Venera and Delia De Santis, Eds. *Exploring Voice Italian Canadian Female Writers. Special Issue of Italian Canadiana.* Volume 30 (2016).

Fergusson, C. B. "The Rise of the Theatre in Halifax." *Dalhousie Review*, Vol. 29, 1949, pp. 419–427.

Filippo, Salvatore. "Discoverism in the Work of Italian-Canadian Historians." C. Dino Minni and Anna F. Ciampolini, Eds. *Writers in Transition.* Guernica, 1990, pp. 161–183.

Fracassa, Rosa. "A selected Chronology of Italian Canadian Theatre in Toronto from 1950 to the Present." *Canadian Theatre Review.* Number 104. Fall 2000. University of Toronto Press, 2000, pp. 45–47

Galati, Rocco, Nick Mancuso and Tony Nardi. OPERAZIONE TERRONICA! The first Toronto CONFERENCE ON THE UNTOLD STORY OF ITALY'S 1861 "UNIFICATION" (The Invasion and Massacre of Southern Italy). Columbus Center, Toronto, November 13, 2011. Facebook: http://goo.gl/FOT7O.

Gardiner, David. McNicoll, Susan. *The Opening Act: Canadian Theatre History, 1945–1953.* Ronsdale, 2012.

Annie Gibson, Playwrights Canada Press. Email Exchange. July 31, 2023.

Giuliano, Bruce B. *Sacro O Profano? A Consideration of Four Italian-Canadian Religious Festivals.* National Museums of Canada, 1976

Giunte, Edvige. *Writing with an Accent.* Palgrave, 2002.

Goodwin, Jill Tomasson. "A Career in Review: Donald Davis Canadian Actor, Producer, Director." *Theatre Research in Canada.* Vol. 10, no. 2, (1989), pp. 132–51.

Greengrass, Mark. "Henri III, Festival Culture and the Rhetoric of Royalty"' *Europa Triumphans* (2004).

Grober, Chayele. "Stanislavsky and His Influence on World Theatre," *Mi-shene tside ha-masakh*, 1952. Trans. Yosef Aha'i. *Pinat ha-sefer*, 1973.

Grohovaz A. Gianni. "A Quest for Heritage: Piccolo Teatro Italiano." *Polyphony* 5, No. 2. (Fall/Winter 1983). Multicultural History Society of Ontario, 1985. pp. 47–56.

Grohovaz A. Gianni, "See You at Brandon Hall. Oh! ... I Mean the Italo-Canadian Recreation Club." *Polyphony* Vol. 7, No. 2. (Fall/Winter 1985), pp. 98–103.

Hall, Frederick A. "Musical Life in Eighteenth-Century Halifax." *Canadian University Music Review.* No. 4, (1983), 278–309.

Harney, Nicholas De Maria. Editor. *From the Shores of Hardship: Italians in Canada. Essays by Robert F. Harney. Preface by Alberto Di Giovanni.* Soleil, 1993.

..., *Eh, Paesan: Being Italian in Toronto.* University of Toronto Press, 1998.

Harney, Robert F. "Chiaroscuro: Italians in Toronto 1885–1915." *Italian Americana*, Vol. 1, No. 2, (1975), pp. 143–67.

..., and J. V. Scarpaci. Editors. *Little Italies in North America*. Multicultural Society of Ontario, 1981.

..., "Immigrant Theatre" in *Polyphony*. Vol. 5. No 2. (Fall/Winter 1983), pp. 1–14.

..., "The Uses of the Italian-Canadian Past." *Arrangiarsi: The Italian Immigration Experience in Canada*. Eds. R. Perin and F. Sturino. Guernica, 1989, pp. 37–61.

..., "Italophobia: An English-speaking Malady?" *From the Shores of Hardship: Italians in Canada*. Soleil, 1993, pp. 29–73.

Heron, Craig. *Working in Steel: The Early Years in Canada, 1883–1935*. University of Toronto Press, 2008.

Hutcheon, Linda. *Splitting Images: Contemporary Canadian Ironies*. Oxford University Press, 1991.

Iacovetta, Franca. *Such Hardworking People: Italian Immigrants in Postwar Toronto*. McGill-Queen's University Press, 1992.

Iacovetta, Franca, Roberto Perin, and Angelo Principe. Editors. *Enemies Within: Italian and Other Internees in Canada and Abroad*. University of Toronto Press, 2000.

Iuele-Colilli, Diana. "Documenting *Italiese*." *Italian Canadiana*, 32 (2018), pp. 55–67.

Paul Colilli and Diana Iule-Colilli. "Italiese as Literary Language" *Italian Canadiana*, Special Issue, Vol. 31 (2017), 91–102.

Irchan, Myroslav. *The Stage: A Textbook for Worker Farmer Drama Circles*. 1928. Manuscript in Ukrainian. Slavic Collection Elizabeth Dafoe Library, University of Manitoba.

Johnson, Stephen. "Getting to Theatre History: On the Tension Between the New History and the Nation State." *Theatre History Critical Perspectives* Vol. 13 (2009), 90–105.

Kociszewska, Ewa. (2020). "Displays of Sugar Sculpture and the Collection of Antiquities in Late Renaissance Venice." *Renaissance Quarterly*, 73(2), 441–488. doi:10.1017/rqx.2020.2

Kirkley, Richard Bruce, "John Hirsch and the Critical Mass: Alternative Theatre on CBC Television in the 1970s." *Theatre Research in Canada* 15.1 (Spring 1994), 75–95.

Kuitunen, Maddalena. "Italian and Italians in the Academic Institutions of English-Speaking Canada 1840–1887." *Italian Canadiana* Volume 2, Number 1, Spring (1986), pp.1–13.

Leonard, Paul. "Of Plays Canadian." *TTA Reports*. April-May 1990.

Lynde, Denyse. "Christmas Mummering Plays in Newfoundland." Anthony J. Vickery, Glen F. Nichols and Allana C. Lindgren, eds. *Canadian Performance Documents and Debates: A Sourcebook*. University of Alberta Press, 2022, 429–434.

Mancuso, Nick. Email Exchange. August 24, 2023.

Mann, Laurin Marie. "Actor Training in Toronto: Theory in Practice." Diss. University of Toronto, 1999.

Mazza, Antonino. *The City Without Women: a Chronicle of Internment Life in Canada During the Second World War*. Mosaic Press, 1993.

Menasse, Joseph. "Perchè si deve incoraggiar il teatro" *A Ricordo Del Suo X Anno Di Attivita (1950–1960). Il Piccolo Teatro* Program 1960.

Migliarisi, Anna *"A Modo Suo (A Fable)*: A Production History." *Canadian Theatre Review* (2000), pp. 48–51.

..., "Theorizing Comic Performance: Leone De Sommi's Dialogues on the Art of Direction." Migliarisi, Anna. *Renaissance and Baroque Directors*. Legas, 2003.

..., "Stanislavsky in Canada: A Critical Chronology." *Stanislavsky and Directing*. Legas, 2008.

..., *"Where Are the Italian Canadian Playwrights?"* Public Lecture. 21 September 2017, University of Toronto.

Migliore, Sam, and A. Evo Di Pierrro. Eds. *Italian Lives, Cape Breton Memories*. Cape Breton University Press, 1999.

Miller, Mary Jane. "Television Drama in English Canada." Wagner, Anton. Ed., *Contemporary Canadian Theatre, New World Visions: A Collection of Essays*. Simon & Pierre, 1985, pp. 86–96.

Minni, Dino C. and Anna F. Ciampolini. Eds. *Writers in Transition* Guernica 1990.

Molinaro, Julius A., and Maddalena Kuitunen. "Introduction." *The Luminous Mosaic: Italian Cultural Organizations in Ontario*. Soleil Publishing, 1993.

Molinaro, Julius A. "Italian Outside the Classroom at the University of Toronto (1881–1940). *Italian Canadiana* Vol. 2. No 1. (Spring 1986), pp. 14–29.

Morrone, Dina. Telephone Interview. July 4, 2017

Murdock, Beamish. Esq., Q. C. *A History of Nova-Scotia* or Acadie Vol. III. Halifax, N.S. James Barnes, Printer and Publisher, 1867, pp. 47–48.

Muscio, Giuliana. "East Coast/West Coast: The Long Tradition of Italian Immigrant Performers." *California Italian Studies*. Vol. 9. 1 (2019): n. pag. Web.

Nardi, Tony, et al. *Two Letters—and Counting! Two Incidents Provoked —*. 1st ed., Guernica, 2013.

N. S. Gazette 20 January 1786.

Orsi, Robert A. *The Madonna of 115th Street Faith and Community in Italian Harlem, 1880–1950*. 3rd ed., Yale University Press, 2010.

..., "The Religious Boundaries of an Inbetween people: Street Feste and the problem of the Dark-Skinned Other in Italian Harlem, 1920–1990." *American Quarterly* Vol. 44, No. 3 (Sep., 1992), pp. 313–347.

Paolozza, Adam. Email. August 21, 2023.

Perin, Roberto., and Franc Sturino. *Arrangiarsi: The Italian Immigration Experience in Canada*. Guernica, 1989.

..., "Actor or Victim? Mario Duliani and His Internment Narrative." Franca Iacovetta, Roberto Perin, and Angelo Principe *Enemies Within: Italian and Other Internees in Canada and Abroad*. University of Toronto Press, 2000.

Pietropaolo, Damiano. "Hyphenated Identities in/and the Global Village." *Italian-Canadian Culture in the New Millennium. Special Issue of Italian Canadiana*. Volume 22 (2008): 25.

..., *Telephone Interview*. August 14, 2023

Pivato, Joseph. "Italian Canadian literature." Toye, William, and Eugene. Benson. *The Oxford Companion to Canadian Literature*. 2nd ed., Oxford University Press, 1997.

..., "Five-Fold Translation in the Theatre of Marco Micone." *Canadian Theatre Review* 104 (2000): 11–15.

Principe, Angelo. *Italiani a Toronto prima del 1861. Italian Canadiana* Volume 7 (1991), pp. 98–120

Ramirez, Bruno., and Yves. Otis. *Crossing the 49th Parallel: Migration from Canada to the United States, 1900–1930*. Cornell UP, 2001.

Saddlemyer, Ann. *Early Stages: Theatre in Ontario 1800–1914*. University of Toronto P, 1990.

Salvatore, Filippo. "Mario Duliani's La Ville sans femmes." *Ancient Memories, Modern Identities*. Guernica, 1999. pp. 64–73.

…, "The Voiceless People Speak Out" *Ancient Memories, Modern Identities*. Guernica, 1999. pp. 94–99.

Sherman, Jason. Ed. *"Outra." Modern Jewish Plays*. Playwrights Canada Press, 2006, n.p.

Smith, Murray. "Traditions, Stereotypes, and Tactics: A History of Musical Buskers in Toronto." *Canadian Journal for Traditional Music*, Vol. 24 (1996), pp. 6–22.

Spada, A. V. *The Italians in Canada*. Riviera Printers and Publishers, 1969.

Sperdakos, Paula. *Dora Mavor Moore: Pioneer of the Canadian Theatre*. ECW Press, 1995.

Spezzano, Frank. *Italian Canadiana*. Vol. 26–29 (2012–2015), pp.

Stanislavsky, Constantin. *My Life in Art*. Theatre Arts Books, 1948.

Sturino, Franc. *Forging the Chain: A Case Study of Italian Migration to North America, 1880–1930*. Multicultural History Society of Ontario, 1990.

Vickery, Anthony J., Glen F. Nichols and Allana C. Lindgren, Eds. *Canadian Performance Documents and Debates: A Sourcebook*. University of Alberta Press, 2022.

Zucchi, John. E. *Italians in Toronto: Development of a National Identity, 1875–1935*. McGill-Queen's University Press, 1988

…, *The Little Slaves of the Harp Italian Child Street Musicians in Nineteenth-Century Paris, London, and New York*. McGill-Queen's University Press, 1992.

FAMILY PLAYS

A MODO SUO (A FABLE)

A Play in Four Acts
English version
Tony Nardi

Copyright © August 1988
December 30, 1989
March 12, 1990
April 1990
May-July 1995
1998 (with Antonino Mazza)
September 2023

Playwright's note on the translation:

Soon after the production of *A Modo Suo (A Fable)* in 1990, I approached fellow Calabrian and late poet Antonino Mazza to execute an initial translation of the play in an effort to take the text (and me) outside the confines of its Calabrian linguistic context. Culturally and linguistically, and in the immediate aftermath of the performance run, the play's characters spoke (to me) and lived in Calabrian. Due to my lack of distance from the original, I was incapable of putting English words into the characters' mouths as if they were speaking Calabrian. My objective had always been to work from a translated version and then bring the text closer to the musicality and performance blueprint of the original. Although Antonino's translation had a marked literary strain, it nonetheless emphasized respect for the text's cultural and etymological roots, for which I am eternally grateful. In the late 1990s, thanks to Antonino's initial translation and my relative distance from the original Calabrian text, and as part of the original intent, I was able to incorporate some of the musical rhythm, textual bite, and performance architecture of the original into his English translation. Our different approaches and focuses were natural and made perfect sense since Antonino's background was poetry and mine theatre and performance. Our collaboration, and my reworking the original (Calabrian) text, resulted in the publication of the play in the Fall 2000 issue of *Canadian Theatre Review*. The present translation is a continuation of the work I began in the late 1990s. It draws upon the Calabrian original, the translation I collaborated on with Antonino, a version I worked on in 2005, and a recent mini reworking of the original. My aim was to bring some of the play's language closer to the original's textual musicality, psycholinguistic character, and performance blueprint and explore certain dramatic dynamics within the existing narrative and dramaturgy. In order to retain the spirit, thrust, rhythm, and intent of the original, as a performance text, it was sometimes necessary to use words that did not translate literally. Additionally, proverbs inherently possess a literary/poetic quality that cannot be removed through translation. Antonino's profound understanding of the play's characters and their Calabrian cultural and linguistic backgrounds ensured that even his literary translation respected and maintained the integrity and foundation of each character. It would not have been possible for me to get here without Antonino's important linguistic bridge.

Playwright's note on performance

The content in *A Modo Suo (A Fable)* represents a specific—at times personal—immigrant reality (one of many) steeped in and influenced by particular cultural, sociological, and historical contexts. It is also a tribute to a 'lost' generation of Italian immigrants and their children, whose lives, particularly the 'downs' of a toxic family environment and violence, aggravated by—but not exclusively because of—an old-world view in a 'new' Canadian setting, were largely undocumented in theatre before 1988.

The form, the theatrical game or 'le jeu,' draws from *commedia dell'arte* and Greek tragedy, and not as cosmetic components but as dramaturgical and acting templates. The text serves both as a performance blueprint and musical score for the actors for both the comic and dramatic moments. The actor is the center of the storytelling, inhabiting (while standing alongside) their character, having one foot in *commedia* and one in drama, and at times playing both at the same time. This duality, or quick change of gears, rooted in the actor's craft and improvisational knack, is the play's only 'style' and integral to the content. It is important to note that I am not referring to *commedia dell'arte* as the broad, physical, or pantomimic manifestation of 'style' commonly associated with its practice, but as a dramaturgical and performance template rooted in improvisation both in the writing and acting. Therefore, it is primarily the "commedia of the actors," an actor's technique or foundational acting method that relies on the actor's "bravura" in performance, since it is "on their shoulders that leans the entire theatrical game." [*Dario Fo's The Tricks of the Trade (Manuale minimo dell'attore), 1987.*]

As with jazz or *commedia dell'arte* performances, the play's structure and text remain the same throughout each performance, but the 'how' (the improvisational element) can vary. As in a fully scripted *commedia* play (in contrast to a *canovaccio*, the brief scenario that requires actors to improvise action and text), the actor in this case must work backwards, and, using the text, its architecture and music, must decipher 'the game' the writer played (as an actor) when writing the play. This writer-as-actor 'game' runs parallel to each character's intentions. Moreover, this writer-as-actor/character duality allows both the actor and their character to simultaneously inhabit both farce and drama and unleashes the play's inherent melody, comedy and drama. Where the dramaturgical 'game' (performance blueprint) and music are clear, the actor will experience no difficulty. Where they are unclear (due to my limitations), I nonetheless trust the actor to save the day—so long as their process, creativity, and imagination are supported and not hindered by the director.

A Modo Suo (A Fable) was first produced in Toronto, in Calabrian, at The Stage Upstairs (Canadian Stage), by Mimesis Theatre in April/May 1990, with the following cast:

Tony Nardi *Raffaele*
Mary Long *Carmela*
Lucy Filippone *Rosina*
Frank Crudele *Salvatore*
Anna Migliarisi *Linda*
Dom Fiore *Pasquale/Dottore*
Directed by Alberto Fortuzzi and Tony Nardi.
Set Design Teresa Przybylski
Costume Design Beata Marzynski-Groack
Lighting Design Teresa Przybylski, Alberto Fortuzzi, Tony Nardi, Roger West
Producers Mary Long, Anna Migliarisi, Tony Nardi
General Manager Brenda Bazinet
Production Manager Leslie Lester
Stage Manager Maria Bonanno

A Modo Suo (A Fable) was also produced, in Calabrian, at Laurentian University, in 1995.
Professors Cristina Zepedeo and Diana Iuile directed a cast of students of Italian Studies.

Cast of Characters
RAFFAELE, *father*
CARMELA, *mother*
ROSINA, *Carmela's sister*
SALVATORE, *son*
LINDA, *daughter*
PASQUALE, *relative from Italy*
DOCTOR PINO, *neighbours' son*
DELIVERY MAN, *offstage*

ACT ONE

Act 1, Scene 1: MOTHER, FATHER

> *Sunday, Summer, late seventies. It's Father's Day. We are in the basement
> of Raffaele's duplex in St. Leonard, the populous and 'upscale' Italian
> district of Montreal. The basement consists of a living- and dining-room
> area, a kitchen (Offstage), a washroom (Offstage), garage and wine
> cellar (Offstage). The stairway to the first floor is located downstage left.
> There is an unfinished spiral staircase located upstage center intended to
> eventually connect the basement to the main floor of the house as well
> as the apartment on the second floor. The family sleeps on the main
> floor— upstairs. The upstairs kitchen and living-room are seldom used.
> They're showrooms.*
> *MUSIC (diegetic, playing on the radio) "Il Cuore É Uno Zingaro" by
> Nicola Di Bari.*

Lights up on Father in the basement 'living room.' He is searching, calmly at first, for his personal pen on his 'scrivania' (a pen that he unconsciously holds in his hand). The 'scrivania' is where he keeps his documents, leases, birth certificates, medical files, in short, his office, headquarters, which he keeps tidy and spotless ... a symbol of order, organization, and readiness. Also, it is a safe with drawers that only he has the keys to, which he locks after each use, always double checking, unlocking and relocking them, to ensure that they have been locked properly. He walks over to the TV, places the pen on top of it, unaware, then begins channel surfing—as always— with the concentration and carefully measured motions of someone who is not familiar with the remote control. Finally, he locates the Italian program, turns up the volume, returns to his scrivania, and using one of the keys on the massive key chain in his pocket, he begins to unlock, search in, and lock drawer after drawer.

FATHER

Goddamn fucken devils! (*Calls out at the top of his lungs*) Carmè! Did you see my pen?! ... Carmè! (*To himself*) JESUS CHRIST! (*Becoming increasingly desperate in his search, he deliberately and methodically empties the contents of each drawer onto the floor—partly to 'punish' those 'responsible' for 'misplacing' his pen*) THE PEN, JUDAS FUCK!

MOTHER

(*Offstage, at the top of her lungs*) I don't know!

FATHER

(*To himself*) Ten years! It's always been here! And now, it's gone! And nobody knows! (*to Mother*) Ten years! You hear me?!

MOTHER

(*Offstage*) There must be a hundred in this house!

FATHER

I'm looking for mine, Mother of Christ! ... 'Cause it's already noon, and I have to miss the news, too! (*Fuming and fretting, he begins flinging things all over the place, swearing with each toss, in German, in Italian, in English, in French, in gibberish, inventing words, inventing saints' names, cursing the devil, God the father, God the son, the virgin Mary, her mother, and anyone else he can think of. The desk now stands in total disarray, a symbol of destruction, as if hit by a bomb. Pause*) Carmè! The fucken pen ... where is it?! Po, po, po, po, po ... (*Smouldering, he paces the room, passing his fingers through his hair, repeatedly and vigorously, massaging his brain, his memory, and rubbing out any curse along the way. He notices pen on T.V. set. Pause.*) Never mind, forget it. ... I found it!

MOTHER

(*Offstage, at the top of her lungs*) And why don't you look before you talk, you nightmare!

(*The pen is one of those 25-cent jobs from a super marché that he has had for many years, never leaks, and never runs out of ink. Father polishes the pen, pulls out a file from the messy pile on the floor, and mutters to himself* "Funerals ... weddings!" *Sits in his easychair, tries to write. Pen does not write*).

FATHER

Damn the fucken devils of the Virgin Mary! Ten years! … it's always worked! (*He tries pen again. It does not write. He puts it in his mouth, warming the ballpoint, shakes it. He tries writing again. Pen writes*) Okay! Let's see! Pasquale the Creek. (I brought him) 100 dollars for 4 people in n-i-n-e-t-e-e-n s-i-x-t-y three! Ok, let's put 200 dollars … for 4 … so, 4 people, at 50 dollars a plate—200, yeah! … ah … plus gift, makes two-hundred-and-f-i-f-t-y dollars. No, let's make it 300 dollars. More than ten years have passed! (*since '63*). (*Beat*) Rosie the Hunchback! Fuck! I brought them 100 dollars for two people in '68. That was money back then! (*Beat*) Let's see … (*Counting*) … there're Rosie, her husband, two children, with husband and wife, and two kids each! … that makes … (*Having problems with pen again*) … who the fuck's been using this pen! … makes … 10 people … at 50 dollars a plate … ok, even for the kids let's put 50 dollars, fuck it! … makes (*Calculating methodically*) … makes … five hundred! Let's add a gift of 200 … makes a total of s-e-v-e-n hundred dollars that they should bring me—at least! … Heh, what're you gonna do with seven hundred dollars these days?! We'll see! (*Beat*) Angie the Cripple and family … that fucken bow-legged, cadaverous, shit-faced idiot, who should have been dead by now and buried alive! … (I brought him) 200 dollars for 2 people … and this … in '74 … And my wife asks me where all the money goes! (*Beat*) Ok, Angeluzzo, wife, the daughter, if she comes, the son, with wife and son, Ah, and the aunt! Okay, let's invite the aunt too and make everybody happy! (*Mumbling, he's having problems with pen again*) … Jesus Christ!! … 8 people… 8 times 50 makes? … makes 400 … yeah, 400, that's what I said, plus 150 gift … and it comes to a grand beauty of 550 dollars! (*Beat*) That lame-footed prick doesn't even work, poor bastard! Ok, but, we always bring'em a Christmas gift. Every year! Fuck it! 500 dollars for the Cripple and family and if he doesn't like it, he can go fuck himself! (*Beat*) Alright. Rosina. Who the fuck put this name …? My wife, for sure! … Rosina the Viper and Joe the Asthmatic … that disgraceful motormouth bitch who doesn't have one bone of respect in her whole fucken body! … And that lazy vegetable, marshmallow of a fucken husband, who never once gave me a hand with my wine! But to drink it … (*A sudden, forceful rebuttal*) They never invited me to their kids' weddings!!! And I still sent them the envelope! Fuck you! 900 dollars for Rosina, Giuseppe and company! And if you don't come—even better! Send the envelope! 900 dollars! Then if you want to put more, 'up to you, 'your fucken business!

TV

THE DAILY NEWS! … (*Music intro*)

FATHER

Everybody quiet! The news!

> (*He rushes to the NuTone radio intercom wall unit by the kitchen and turns up the volume.*)

RADIO

Italian Newshour!

TV

Massacre in Bologna! …

RADIO

Eighty people dead, hundreds wounded …

TV

Fifteen wounded, seventy-seven dead …

RADIO

… in a terrorist attack at the Rome-Fiumicino Airport.

RADIO

… Devastating earthquake in Sicily …

TV

Here are some images …

FATHER

Look at that—look at that! Carmela! Look at that! … (*Talking to his 'family'*)
Ok, go ahead, do it your way … go, go … 'cause that's how you're gonna end up!

MOTHER

(*Enters from the kitchen*) I don't wanna see these things. Poor people! Time to
eat, Raffaè!

TV

In Naples, a new tragedy.

RADIO

A house engulfed in flames! …

TV

… five dead! …

RADIO

… all dead! …

TV

… desperate, they jumped out the window!

RADIO

… in Naples …

TV

… some post-tragedy images …

MOTHER

Dear God, protect us! Poor souls! Help them, dear Jesus!

FATHER

Oh yeah, Christ is sure gonna help you if you don't help yourself! You're talking
to Christ? Look at that, look at that! No arms! Look at that one, no legs! Just like
the war! Quiet! let's see …!

TV

Palermo has rationed its water …

FATHER

And here they let it run all day long! That's what I should do … make you wash
the dishes with pasta water, if you don't watch it! Just like the war! So you all
learn the meaning of life! … And from now on, I'm gonna do the shopping!

MOTHER

Go ahead! Do it! (*She exits to kitchen*)

TV

Italy's unemployment rate went up again! …

FATHER

What else is new?!

RADIO

... 11 percent of the Italian work force.

TV

Seventy-five percent ...

RADIO

... of the 11 percent ...

FATHER

... should starve!

RADIO

... is under the age of thirty.

FATHER

Your son's age! Lazy piece of shit! I'd line them up against the fucking wall, and, one by one, ta ta ta ta ta ta ta ta, I'd shoot'em all! Right there! Fuck it!

RADIO

Half of Italy headed for the ski slopes.

FATHER

And the other half doesn't work!

RADIO

The state is floundering.

TV

The new government defeated.

FATHER

No?!

RADIO

According to an opinion poll, Italians remain optimistic!

FATHER

Yeah, yeah—like a snowstorm with no snow.

RADIO AND TV

The Parti Québécois announced today that during this election campaign separation ...

FATHER

(*Turning off the TV*) Mangiè la mmerde! ... When are we gonna eat, Carmè?

MOTHER

(*From the kitchen*) Soon, soon!

FATHER

I don't see anything on the table. (*Beat*) Two women in this fucken house, and we always eat at midnight—with the vampires!

MOTHER

(*Enters from kitchen*) I have only two hands!

FATHER

What, and I have four?! looking after everybody and doing everything?

MOTHER

Listen, royal highness! I really need four fucken hands! I do this! Do that! Clean here! Iron there! Wash here! Wash there! Prepare here! Boil there! Put in there! ...

Serve here! … Turn of this, turn off there. Pee here! Shit there! That's my life! I'm going crazy!

FATHER

D'you finish?

MOTHER

Crazy!!

FATHER

And where is the little princess? … Always locked inside that cursed room?! But one way … those books, I'm gonna burn them … all of them … One by one! … Once, we used to go to mass on Sunday … all of sudden, today! …

MOTHER

When was the last time <u>you</u> went to mass?

FATHER

Carmè! … the virgin Mary!!! The children have to learn! I've prayed and confessed enough times!

MOTHER

You had sins to confess!

FATHER

And if you don't shut the fuck up, I'm gonna go confess again.

MOTHER

You *already* confessed! Now you can do whatever you want. (*Daring him to 'go ahead'*).

FATHER

Carmè! (*Warning her. Pause.*) Get my medicine, my back is killing me, fuck!

MOTHER

(*Finally notices the mess he has made*) What happened here?!

FATHER

What happened was that my pen was not where I left it. Her, for sure! Or you! … I said it a thousand times, Mother of Christ … when you take something from somewhere, you put it back where you found it—where it's supposed to be!

MOTHER

Ma[1], did you have bad dreams? Goat head! … So?! … (*Mother gets a bottle of Absorbine Junior from the cabinet*) Couldn't we try to talk nice to each other? "Get my medicine!" I'm your wife! (*Soliciting an answer*) Huh?

FATHER

What, you got an itch? You need something touched or … ? (*Aiming for her crotch*)

MOTHER

I don't want anything <u>touched</u>! That's not what I want!

FATHER

'Course not! God forbid!

MOTHER

That's all you're good for. But you don't know… a woman's legs are like a book. Always ready! Open and read. But you have to know how to open, and how to read! (*Pause*)

---

1. Here, the word "ma" refers to the words "but," "I mean," or "listen."

FATHER

Carmè, I am so fucken amazed by you! You talk like you have no idea what's going on! No sense of responsibility!

MOTHER

What's going on where?

FATHER

In here! (*Pointing to his head*) All the thoughts—*worries* I have!

MOTHER

That's it!

FATHER

That's it? That's it?!! You think it's nothing? My brain is pounding like a fucken …! … rub, just rub! (*Mother massages his shoulders*) You have to constantly think of the worst if you want to live, experience, enjoy the good! Can you imagine how much this head weighs?

MOTHER

Today is Sunday, Father's Day! Can't you let that head rest a little?

FATHER

Those who rest are lost!—That's enough, thanks! Fuck, you're rough! (*Pause. To himself, audibly*) Mother of Christ … sometimes I feel like setting fire to this fucken house, with everything in it! That's what I feel like doing sometimes!

MOTHER

(*Distracting him with an order*) Go wash your hands, it's almost ready! (*As she exits to the kitchen*) And bring a bottle of wine from the cantina!

FATHER

(*Beat*) Did the other one call?

MOTHER

Noooo!

FATHER

Leave him alone, leave him! … raise animals, not children! I don't give a fuck anymore! He got fired, for sure … and now, he's too ashamed to show his face! Piece of shit lawyer! He could have made a killing!! Instead, out on his ass and nothing to show for it! He should be shot! (*Pointing to throat*) Right here! Without wasting two bullets. Just one. Bang! That's what he deserves! His only salvation! May God strike me with lightning if I give him another hand! Not even a *finger*! … He comes around, and calls only when he needs *this*, see (*Making the money gesture by repeatedly rubbing his thumb over the tip of his index finger and middle finger*)? A fucking sponge! … 'Cause had he done it *my* way … things would be different now. … money, house, kids … like everybody else!

MOTHER

He always said he's not like everybody else.

FATHER

His loss! I'll show him the feast I'll throw for his sister—if she's good! You think I care?!

MOTHER

(*Over " You think I care?"*) **Feast**?! Do me a favour … get this *feast* idea out of your head!

FATHER

Shut up! I decide! What, is she a nun? Others are raising kids already! Only mine! ... I calculated ... roughly *thirty thousand dollars* for the little princess' wedding ... what goes out, what comes in ... *thirty thousand*!—If she's good!

MOTHER

Cause it won't cost us anything?!

FATHER

That doesn't count. *We're* throwing the feast ... *we're* paying for it ... it's our *gift*. Whatever comes in, she keeps. ... Do you know how much blood I had to sweat to earn 30,000 dollars?!

MOTHER

Ok, stop it, or she'll hear you! (*Short pause*) I see black ahead!

FATHER

If you see black, change your glasses! ... Did you mention anything?

MOTHER

Like you told me!

FATHER

And don't say anything! ... News from Italy?

MOTHER

Nothing.

FATHER

When's that parcel gonna get here?!!! Anyway ... let's wait for Italy first! To the little princess ... tomb! ("*lips sealed." Pause*)

MOTHER

At this point ... I'm already resigned to not having grandchildren.

FATHER

God forbid ("*you should look at the bright side*"!) ... How's the eye? ... Did she go looking for work today?!

MOTHER

You <u>know</u> ... If she doesn't find work she likes she won't go! (*Short pause*) She's talking about going back to school.

FATHER

Again *school*?! She's studied enough! Others didn't even allow their daughters to finish grade eleven! I let her finish!

MOTHER

Raffaè ...

FATHER

Tell her to bury the fucken thought! If she were a boy, okay ... more school the better! Now it's time to think about *other* things. ... Her brother went to school! Where did it get *him*?

MOTHER

She'll stop eating if you don't let her go!

FATHER

She won't—her loss! (*Beat*) ... Won't eat?! Because she always ate cut grass served on a fucken platter, never had to lift a finger! Won't eat? I'll show her "won't eat"! As for that other piece of shit, as far as I'm concerned, he's dead! I'm even gonna put a sign on the front door! MY SON IS DEAD!

MOTHER

Why don't we talk like human beings once in a while. Today is Sunday!

Doorbell rings.

FATHER

(*In a loud whisper*) Because I'm *ashamed*! I don't even know what to tell people anymore! From now on—the truth! *Shame*!

Doorbell rings, they freeze. Beat.

FATHER

(*In a loud whisper*) You answer! Maybe it's the tenant upstairs! ... Wait! Check the window! I wonder what the fuck she wants. (*Mother goes to window by stepping on the half-finished spiral staircase, that's half-way up against the upstage wall*) Close the light first! Close the fucken—or she'll see you! You make me so fucken! ...

MOTHER

But if I close the light, she'll notice!

FATHER

Okay, okay, forget it! And then if she tells you she wants to move out without paying the rent, *you* deal with it! Go, go, open it! (*Mother goes to the door*) Wait! If it's those Church people, those evangelists, I'll answer it! And this time, I'll take that magazine, whatever it's called, and shove it up their fucken ass! (*He goes to the door, mother goes to the window again*) Wait! (*in a loud whisper*) If it's your son, I'm not here!

MOTHER

Your son's upstairs!

FATHER

What do you mean upstairs? (*Doorbell rings*) Damn every son of (bitch) ... I asked you if he called, and you ... *nothing*! And me talking about that son-of-a-bitch for the last hour! ... That's how you wanna play?

MOTHER

He came late last night! You were sleeping! *He* told me not to tell you!

FATHER

Look at how mother and son get along ... *connive*. See.

MOTHER

He wanted to surprise you, *beast*! ... seeing that today is Father's Day! (*Doorbell rings. Mother goes to window*) It's Rosina!

FATHER

Rosina?! I don't want to see her here!

MOTHER

She's my sister!

FATHER

I don't give a fuck! I don't owe anybody anything! Just her name makes my blood boil! She's gotta spy around the house, see what you have, if yours is better than hers! A witch! Always talking about her Club!

MOTHER

Club my ass! It's a *centre*! They have courses in English or French!

FATHER

Never mind courses in English, French! You're fifty years old! Italian's enough!

MOTHER

... Listen, I told you! One of these days I'm gonna do something terrible! Real fucken terrible! ...

FATHER

Do it! (*Beat*) The less you see her the better ... for me, for you, and everyone else!
          Doorbell rings.

MOTHER

I'm answering!

FATHER

WAIT! (*Short pause*) I'll get it! (*He clears his throat. Unlocks door, removing the multiple security chains and bars*) Hide the crystal! (*He opens the door*).

Act 1, Scene 2: FATHER, MOTHER, ROSINA

> *Rosina is standing in the doorway. Everything about her suggests that she is very different from all the people inhabiting this "world," and yet, she could only be of that world. Her clothes are flashy, tacky and shrill. Her manners are raw, coarse, and earthy. She is forthright and loud.*

ROSINA

(*Pause*) Hey, Carmè! Hey, Raffaè! Bojoù! Bojoù!

FATHER

(*All smiles*) Great! Beautiful, just beautiful! ... nailed to the door, listening to other people business!

ROSINA

Up yours! I rang ten times! What the fuck is *that* about. Don't you answer the door anymore? ... Then I thought, maybe they're busy, in the garden ... or in some other place ...

MOTHER

Yeah, yeah ... Too much to do around here ... now the sausages, then the tomatoes ... if it's not one thing, it's another!

ROSINA

(*To Carmela*) It's time to find a lover ... What d'you say, Carme? ... Cause these husbands, once they get old ... (*to Raffaele*) Eat rice ... it makes it firm and nice— (*Pause*) Are you gonna invite me in?

FATHER

To be honest ...

MOTHER

Raffaè ...

FATHER

... The sooner you leave ... the better ...

MOTHER

(*Over "you leave"*) Raffaè! (*Laughs*) Always teasing!

FATHER

I don't *joke*. I *weigh* my words. And the mother of idiots is always pregnant.[1] (*Pause*) If you're gonna come in, come in! Shnell!, shnell!, like the Germans say! Arioppa! Arioppa![2] (*pointing to himself*) ... 'cause Ciccio pays the air conditioning! You know how much it eats up daily?

ROSINA

Raffaè, with all that fucken money you have in the bank ... under your bed, kitchen table, you're worried about the air conditioning?! ... See that ... they even bought "l'air conditioné"!

FATHER

There was a time when a husband's *word* was <u>enough</u> (sufficed). Today, *they* also have to have their say. (*Beat. To mother*) I'm in the garden.

ROSINA

You better offer me something or I'm gonna leave for real!

FATHER

What about an *enema* ... by mouth?

ROSINA

Fuck you! ... What—'cause I didn't bring you a gift?

FATHER

A gift ... from *you*?! You've given me enough gifts!

ROSINA

Good, 'cause I brought you nothing!

FATHER

Exactly what I asked for!

ROSINA

(*Referring to unfinished spiral staircase*) Hey! Nice! What's this?

FATHER

Nothing! It's what you see!

ROSINA

Compris Carmè?! ... "It's nothing!" ... I bet you it's for the upstairs apartment ... so, when Salvatore gets married you can go up and down, down and up, without going outside! Convenient! ... Why not start it on the first floor? Do you guys sleep in the basement, too? I've never seen the front entrance to this fucken house! Always through the garage.

MOTHER

We're always down here!

ROSINA

Enjoy your fucken house, live in it! (*Wiping off sweat from her cleavage with a kerchief*) Where is Salvatore?

FATHER

Out, minding his own business!

ROSINA

What the fuck! I never see him! Don't tell me he's not even coming today? I mean *today*! ...

---

1. The world is full of idiots.
2. Arioppa, from the English *hurry-up*.

MOTHER

He's always running here and there! That's busy people for you! Now here, now there ...

ROSINA

I heard he wasn't practicing law anymore! Is it true? I forget who ran into him in Toronto, I forget where. .... That's what Filomena said.

FATHER

Filomena the *windbag*?

ROSINA

She's got a sister in Toronto.

MOTHER

(*Over "windbag"*) Eeh! That clubfooted gasbag is deaf and blind from way back in Italy! She's a chatterbox ... got nothing better to do than gossip all day long!

FATHER

Gossiping, scheming, spreading, spitting lies!

ROSINA

But is it true?

FATHER

It's not my custom to discuss family matters at the door ... especially with strangers!

ROSINA

Up yours and all your ancestors! ... I'm a *stranger* now?! ... Carmé, you didn't give him a massage last night? ... *Stranger*?!

FATHER

No. Just someone who likes to stuff her nose wherever it fits ... and even if it doesn't fit, she still manages to stuff it in!

ROSINA

Raffaè, enough!

FATHER

She asked!

MOTHER

But you don't have to be rude! (*to Rosina*) No, Rosì, Salvatore is doing very well ... He works on his own, now ... opened a big office ...!

FATHER

(*Under his breath*) Big, yeah ... you can see it from here! ...

MOTHER

He's his own boss! He has five or six people working under him!

FATHER

(*Under his breath*) Yeah, in the basement!

MOTHER

The office is in Toronto, downtown, with all the big shots! No, thank God, we can't complain! Rosì, the kids are always fine, and those with no conscience do even better!

FATHER

What's that supposed to mean?

MOTHER

I'm talking to her! Go do what you have to do!

ROSINA

And the little princess, she find "u ciommo", yet?[1]

FATHER

Ciommo? Did you have "un chum" at her age?

ROSINA

I had kids at *half* her age! ... She found a *husband*, then!

FATHER

No one's getting married ...! If anything changes, I'll send you an invite!

ROSINA

So, there is still hope?

FATHER

"Hope," in what sense?

ROSINA

She who gets married, is happy for a day. ... He who slaughters a pig, is happy for a whole year! So, may she eat sausages and think of her health!

FATHER

Lamb should be eaten young, when it's tender! It tastes better.

ROSINA

I was talking about your daughter—not sheep! ... Maybe I misunderstood!

FATHER

(*Over "misunderstood!"*) Rosì! ... Nosy people have only one problem ... It's not the size of their nose! No! The problem is where they try and stick it! If they'd stick it more often in their own fucken business, the world would be a better place!

MOTHER

Rosì, did you eat? Want to join us?

ROSINA

My kitchen is waiting!

FATHER

Finally! The first sane and sacred words you said so far!

ROSINA

... Then I have to prepare some things for tonight's 'réunion.'

FATHER

I don't want to hear talk about fucking meetings, gatherings and assemblies in this house! The Church was made for *praying*!

ROSINA

Excuse me ... Plug your ears—I'm talking to her!

FATHER

Talk to Cheech, not to Carmela!

ROSINA

Why don't you come, too ... that way you'll see?

FATHER

Who, *me*?!

ROSINA

Yeah, *you*! We embroider! Read! Talk! Debate! ...

---

1. *Ciommo*, from the Québécois '*chum*' (boyfriend).

FATHER

Okay, okay, okay! ... You hear me?!

ROSINA

(*Beat*) I better leave! Just dropped by ... cause my husband ... if his food isn't ready at a certain time, I'll never hear the end of it!

FATHER

You blame him? The wife gets educated ... movies, dances, assemblies, with his money—his sweat and blood! And he stays home all alone, like an ignorant mule! Nice, isn't?

ROSINA

He's only interested in going to the bar to play cards with his buddies. All graduates of poker and billiards!

FATHER

For once we agree! I never liked people who go to bars! My brother always had a weakness for that!

ROSINA

He does what he wants, I do what I want!

FATHER

I'm warning you, stop giving examples!

ROSINA

Let him play cards, poor man ... he works very hard!

FATHER

At least you admit that he works hard! You recognize *that* at least!

ROSINA

Why not? ... I recognize anyone who deserves recognition, man or woman!

FATHER

I get it! I already know about your ... ! And you do me a big fucken favour if you'd stop preaching your way of seeing things in my house!

ROSINA

It's her house, too!

FATHER

Talk to Ciccio, not with her!

ROSINA

You're a *minor*! Too young for these discussions. (*Beat*) When you're hungry, she's a woman, but to talk she's a little girl? Do me a fucken favor ... reserve your mule logic for your wife .... she doesn't seem to mind.

FATHER

You wouldn't either, trust me.

ROSINA

Hey, I don't want to waste oxygen on my husband. He's a beast. He should be sliced in half—at the throat!

MOTHER

Rosì! ...

FATHER

(*Pause*) According to you, you and your husband are *equals*?

ROSINA

No! Equals no!

FATHER

Thank God! ... I thought ...

ROSINA

He's an embryo! Brain's too weak! He's yet to be born!

FATHER

One has to be in charge! One boss!

ROSINA

Who, *him*?

FATHER

Him, yes! *He* busted his fucken ass in the coal mine for ten years! He worked night and day to support his family! *Him*!

ROSINA

Him?

FATHER

The boss, yes! *He* resigned himself to ignorance for the sake—for the *good* of the family!

ROSINA

He never busted anything for no one! I've shat more blood and sweat in one day than he's likely to see in ten lifetimes ... I raised the kids! ... Our ceiling is dripping, full of holes! I can't do it ... he's too busy playing cards ... we have no money! ... let's wait for him to win a few fucking games!

FATHER

I bet you anything that you brought him to this state!

ROSINA

Me?

FATHER

What's the poor guy supposed to do? ... He sees how his wife behaves! ... what's he supposed to do?! Kill her and dishonour the family?!

MOTHER

Raffaè!

FATHER

No! ... Instead, he breaks up all inside, keeps it in there. ... swallows his tongue, his pride, and lives one day at a time ... and not to go completely mad, he goes out to play a few games of cards! ... What is he, an animal?! ... But I bet that if you'd spend more time at home, if you followed a more *normal* way, you know what I mean, according to our ways, instead of those short skirts!—Enough! You know what I mean! ... I bet you, he'd come back to life in a second! ... You give him a little massage here ... he's happy, everyone's happy! And he'd spend more time at home! There's a family! ... If there's no family what satisfaction can a man possibly have in plugging all the holes in a home, *if you know what I mean*!

ROSINA

I'm supposed to what encourage him, *cuddle* him, breast feed him and burp him?! Please! ... What we need is the wisdom—the *conscience* he doesn't have, and the money he loses every night at the bar! That's what we need! Fuck the cuddles!

FATHER

My mother, bless her soul, used to say that a wife has to put water on the fire, not hay! A proper woman knows how to *minister* the soup, not *spoil* it! (*He includes his wife in the conversation*) But she has to know *how*! (*to Rosina*) Because, even if everything you say is true ... is that the way to talk about your husband? ... Love your husband with his vices, because a husband is like the sea, if he doesn't deliver today, he'll deliver tomorrow!

ROSINA

When pigs fly! ... If you're born *square*, you can't be buried in a round hole!

FATHER

A wife has to put water!

ROSINA

This well has dried up!

FATHER

Jesus fucken Christ! ...

MOTHER

It's Sunday!

FATHER

... Ask yourself what people are <u>saying</u> about you!

ROSINA

My husband doesn't care about his reputation, why should I care about mine?

FATHER

He's forgiven! Ah! That you didn't know!

ROSINA

Whoever forgives *him* can forgive me, too!

FATHER

A *mother* brings honour to the family! ... Whatever a husband does, even if it's, I don't know, whatever ... doesn't matter ... understand? But one little mistake from his wife, it's all over! Honour! ... A husband, even if he *murders* his wife, betrayal or something ... he goes to prison ... but he's always forgiven! The *mother* ... Honour! That word mean anything to you?

ROSINA

No!

MOTHER

Honour, Rosì!

ROSINA

You calling me a whore?

MOTHER

Rosì!

ROSINA

What, it's just a word! ... *Whore*! ... You see, nothing happened! (*To Father*) I didn't hear you!

FATHER

Okay! Maybe you're not one, but there's one out there! ... for sure! (*Beat*) When you spend time with cripples, you end up limping too after a year!

ROSINA

Have you ever seen me limp?

FATHER

(*Pause*) It's not right, okay?!

ROSINA

According to whom?

FATHER

According to Jesus Christ nailed on the fucken Cross! People!

ROSINA

Who exactly are these people? Men, women? . . .

FATHER

Forget who they are! They're there!

ROSINA

Okay! But who in particular? Give me a name, a last name! Just one!

FATHER

Don't worry about first and last names! . . .

ROSINA

But who the fuck are these people!

FATHER

Everybody! People! If they don't say it to your face, they *think* it! When people's mouths start flying, try and catch'em, try! Try and stop it!

MOTHER

Come on, Rosì! I know what you're trying to say! . . .

FATHER

Ah, you agree with her?!

MOTHER

(*Explodes*) Let me talk! . . . that when you talk no one can get a word in! (*To Rosina*) I understand your problems, and even Raffaè told you, he doesn't like people who go to bars. But, *honour*! Rosì! I mean . . .! Rosì, let's be honest, all those women at the centre . . . according to you . . . those women are women? You know what I mean.

FATHER

Vipers!

MOTHER

I know two or three of them myself . . . no husband, divorced! . . .

FATHER

They preach the gospel of witches . . . the American way!

ROSINA

And what are *you*?

FATHER

Italian, for fuck's sake! Not a mixed salad! Did you know of any women's clubs like that in Italy? . . . in the village? You ever seen any? . . . And I've travelled around!

MOTHER

Come on, Raffaè, over there it's a different thing!

FATHER

Ah . . . over there what they're idiots?!

MOTHER

Over there . . . they always think old-fashioned!

FATHER

I get it, and here we're more modern! ... (*Beat*) All those hens in that church basement ... with no rooster in sight, can you imagine?! In your old age you wanna be young chicks again! Instead of going to church to confess their sins, they go there to commit them! And what's the purpose of this conference of chickens? I'll tell you! ... To undermine the husband! Saints in Church! Demons at home! If this gaggle of hens continues, you'll see where you'll all end up!— Where the world is gonna end up!

ROSINA

(*Beat*) Is that why you won't let your wife come tonight?

FATHER

Christ Almighty! ...

ROSINA

Of course, you never know ... she might become "one of those"!

MOTHER

Rosì! ...

FATHER

(*Beat, pointing to Carmela*) She studied English right after we got here ... Night classes, twice a week. No, I said, ... at home with the family. She'll tell you.

> *Pause.*

FATHER

In the world you need sacrifices of all kinds!

ROSINA

And a little pinch of trust!

FATHER

Your husband trusted you once.

ROSINA

(*Pause*) You're scared of losing her?

FATHER

Cunning! Not fear! This is how the world works—by nature, remember that, and two or three chickens in a church basement won't change the world in a day! Not even Mussolini succeeded! 'Cause whoever said, "A wife is like an egg, the more you beat it, the better it comes," was right! ... But ... who can't feel shame in their soul can't feel blows to their body.

> *Pause.*

MOTHER

(*To Rosina*) I don't even feel like going. *I* don't want to go, not that *he* won't let me.

FATHER

What, if I told you 'no,' you'd still go?

> *Pause. Phone rings. Father and mother freeze, terrified at the thought of who it might be. They let it ring a few times.*

FATHER

I'll get it! (*Clearing his voice, using a sober/suspicious tone*) Alò. ... (*All is clear*) Heh Philì! ... Your wife? ... Yeah, yeah, she's here! ... What's that? ... We were yakking! ... Yeah ... come by one of these days, so we can talk eye to eye! ... What? ... You haven't eaten yet? ... Neither have I! What are you gonna do?! ... Patience! ... Yeah, yeah ... here she is!

ROSINA

Poor man! ... Tell him I'll be there in ten minutes!

FATHER

Philì, she's leaving right right now! ... Ten minutes she'll be there. ... Yeah, yeah, I understand. (*to Rosina*) You better talk to him. It's between you two. ... Hasn't eaten since this morning!

ROSINA

(*Taking receiver from Raffaele*) What's the matter *my little sparrow*? ... Hungry? ... I didn't eat either! ... Why don't I come right now and *fix you* something?! ... *m'a t'arranger ca*1 ... Afraid you'd lost me? ... No, the centre is tonight. ... I'm coming, I said. ... And you poor thing didn't know where the pots were ... you're right! ... They *are* heavy ... And you'd have to bend down ... your back, of course! ... To heat up that pasta in the fridge is a terrible strain, I know ... Obviously, it takes practice, much too complicated for you *my little sparrow*. ... What about your card game? Oh, right, today is Sunday ... your day off? ... Oh! It's at 8:00?! ... Yeah, okay, okay I better hurry, yeah, I understand ... it's a disgrace if you're late. ... I can hear you just fine *my little sparrow*. ... Starving? ... yeah, yeah ... well, sitting on your ass like that can make you hungry! ... Oh, I'd love to give you a big smackeroo *my little scoundrel* ... I'm leaving *right now* ... I'll even give you a massage ... A <u>massage</u>, yeah! ... that's why! (*to Father and Mother*) He's so adorable. (*Into phone*) Yes, my *little bully sparrow* ... my little *bully bully bully bully bully dove*! ... Okay ... till I get there, eat this! (*She blows a raspberry into the phone and hangs up*) Kiss my ass! (*To herself*) Fuck you!
    Pause.

FATHER

Rosì, jokes aside, you'd better go before he buries you.

ROSINA

I'll eat the fucker raw. Right off the bone. And then I'll grind the bones!

FATHER

My mother used to say ... When a woman doesn't come running at the first call, it's because she doesn't like the song!

MOTHER

(*Angry*) Raffaè, don't start! My God! You two, always like cats and dogs! What the fuck! Calm down!!

FATHER

(*Calm*) I'm calm. I'm only saying, listen to what the Bible says ... 'cause Jesus Christ was a *man*! Instead, soon you'll try to convince me that he was a *woman*!

ROSINA

If he had been a woman, he'd have carried more than one cross!

FATHER

My mother used to say, "God protect us from men with no beards, and women with mustaches!"

ROSINA

I don't have a mustache!

---

1. "m'a t'arranger ca" (Literally *I will fix that for you*)

FATHER

And you don't have a beard either!

ROSINA

(*Short pause*) Better (to be) a woman with no beard than a man with no balls! (*She exits, slamming the door*)

FATHER

Who're you slamming the door at?! Always has to have the last word! I'll show you who you're slamming the door at! (*To Mother*) Someday I'll tame that one! . . . Poison! That's what she deserves! I'll be nice to a certain point, but then! . . .

MOTHER

Yeah, yeah, my dear . . . You <u>enjoy</u> being with her. When you talk with her, you talk like . . . as if you'd want to eat her with your eyes! Me, instead, you treat me like shit! You should have married *her*!

FATHER

And *why*, according to you?

MOTHER

<u>That</u> one definitely would make you dance!

FATHER

You're pushing! (*Brief pause*) You think I'm afraid of her?! . . . 'cause she really ended up with someone with no—y'know what I mean. You'd see how she'd walk straight if she were with me. Anyway, enough! Make lunch, if you're gonna make it! She's already spoiled my appetite! . . . I'm going in the garden. When it's ready, call me! (*Father exits*)

MOTHER

Death never comes to those who wish it! (*Mother exits*)

Act 1, Scene 3: MOTHER, SON

> *Enters Sal, thirty years old, but looking much older. Wearing a handsome bathrobe and combed back hair, he walks down the stairs with strained authority, while smoking a cigarette and observing the surroundings as if he were looking at paintings in a museum. Enters Mother.*

MOTHER

Salvatò! You know what time it is? Twelve noon! . . . Every time you come here, you sleep all day. That's what your father says!

SON

Mà . . . I need to catch up on all the sleep I lost. And then . . . I don't even sleep. (*Sigh*) Ah, dear mother . . . you wouldn't ask these questions if you knew the pounding in my head! (*Brief pause*) I don't know! . . .

MOTHER

You and your father, with your pounding brains! . . . 'cause you smoke first thing in the morning . . . okay, it's not even morning anymore! But, on an empty stomach! . . . Eat a banana! You want a banana?

SON

Mà! I'm trying to have a certain kind of discussion with you and you ask me if I want a banana? (*Beat*) ... Ok I'll take one.

MOTHER

(*Going to the kitchen*) An empty stomach can't reason. When you don't eat, you're fighting death.

SON

Where is he?

MOTHER

Where is he. In the garden! The only place he's happy! He whistles and plants. He's even doing the neighbours' gardens, now! ... At his age! As long as he leaves me alone he can do whatever he wants. He can even *die* there if he wants! He's not a kid anymore! ... He gets mad at me 'cause I don't know anything about gardens ... "You wanted the garden?! You look after it!" The kids were enough for me ... (*Beat*) Why don't you go help him. You never take an interest in his garden. And then ... he doesn't even want help. Just the gesture ... that's all he wants!

SON

I dreamt we were fighting ...

MOTHER

(*Banana in hand*) ... Here, eat this ... do you want it peeled?—Who?

SON

(*Trying to make sense of it*) In the dream, he was always stronger than me ... always had that extra energy more than me, or a longer arm ... I mean *really* long ... always fucked me up, had the edge ... We were fighting. I don't even know *why*, and all of a sudden ... he grabs my balls! ...

MOTHER

Eyyy!

SON

... right between the legs! Bang! ...

MOTHER

Stop being vulgar!

SON

It's true! ... Every time I'd try to fuck him up, bang! he grabs my balls! And wouldn't let go ... he squeezed and squeezed, I'm telling you, gave me such a stomach ache! ... Then he'd let go. ... I try to throw him down again, and, bang! ... he *grabs*! ...

MOTHER

I get it!

SON

And he would squeeze and squeeze! ... I don't know how he did it ... (*Beat*) My stomach still hurts!

MOTHER

You want me to make you a glass of water and sugar ... it's good for the stomach! ... (*Beat*) Heh? (*Beat*) Eat this then ...

SON

(*Absentmindedly*) No, forget it. (*Beat. Absorbed in thought*) Nothing's changed! Everything is the same! ... since the day you bought the house ... (*Without looking he points to a standing ashtray)* This ashtray has been here since '74, always in the same place! ... (*Beat*) If only it could talk ... with all it's seen ...

MOTHER

Put it someplace else if you don't like it there.

SON

... Even my room ... still has that same smell! ... that ... (*Beat*) the whole house ... (*Beat*) You know why I got up? I can spend entire days in bed, but you know why I got up? ... (*Beat*) The <u>sauce</u>! You can feel it's Sunday. It smells of Sunday! A Sunday without sauce is not a Sunday! Even the Italian radio you can hardly hear ... the same announcer, same *voice*! Year after year always the same ... the same songs! Sunday songs! ... And as long as I can smell that sauce, I feel good ... that everything's okay ... calm, in bed ... the only sounds, those from the kitchen! (*Brief pause*) Then I get up, come out of the room, and all that sediment starts coming up ... the dregs, that fucken *shit*! ... and my insides quiver!

MOTHER

Today is Father's Day, I'm warning you!

SON

What are we celebrating?

MOTHER

What a disgraceful son of a—don't make me swear! ... He's your *father*! He brought you into the world! He gave you *life*! Like it or not, he's your father ... for *life*!

SON

(*Beat*) How precious you are, mà! ... if you only knew! ... That sauce makes my head spin! ... it won't let me talk ... it's a sedative!

MOTHER

Don't talk! The best words are those unsaid! The more you talk, the more your head spins. We're gonna eat, now. ... The man who fasts has the devil up his ass! Don't you know that? ... Sit here! ... The tongue is rich, a thing of beauty, but it kills more than the sword!

> Son sits in Father's easy chair with some difficulty. Mother places a cushion behind his head, she removes his sandals from his feet, resting them on an ottoman. It's the treatment he gets from his mother every time he visits.

SON

Mà, no, it's okay ... (*Without resisting*)

MOTHER

You sleep with your socks on? Your feet won't breathe! What's wrong with you—are you mentally ill? (*Brief pause*) Did you bring anything to wash ... underwear, dirty shirts ... heh? (*Massaging son's head*) If he sees (this) ... (*Beat*) Listen, before you go to bed, you should do this, you see ... (*demonstrating on her own head*) three times ... on the head, like this, so you won't have bad dreams! Because when the devil pets you, he wants your soul. (*Goes back to massaging son's head*) Like this.

SON

Ah, dear, dear mother... all that flour and eggs has done wonders for your hands! ... What you're worth to me ... you'll never know! (*Suddenly, Mother yanks her son's hair violently back and forth*) Ahhhhh! Careful!—I'm losing my hair as it is!

MOTHER

Lord Jesus Christ! … Things were going so well! Now, you have no job, alone, no woman, no children … and I bet you have no money either! You tell me, can a mother be at peace if she does not even know what you eat? … or if you have money to pay the rent?! Eh?! … What do you eat?! … Eh?!!! You're bent on making me die!!! Find a woman, at least! … Then at least you'll have someone to cook for you, iron a shirt!

SON

They don't make those anymore, mà!

MOTHER

I mean, even for company! What are people going to think? A man like you, all alone! *Now* what're you gonna do? In Christ's name, what do you want to be?!! You have a diploma!

SON

(*Beat*) Mà … I'm trying to keep death at a distance. (*Beat*) People go looking for lawyers, mà, only when they're in trouble! You think you'd run into a smile once in a while? Never! They all come in, shoulders down to their knees, faces sweeping the floor. Then, you help them … and they tell you to go fuck yourself! … And if you die or get sick, not one of them gives a fuck! … In fact, they may benefit if you die … save a few dollars. Not one gift from a client! Not one! Not because I wanted one … It's the whole culture. It's corrupt. They resent you for defending their rights—successfully … and having to pay for it! They hate you, mà! It's a hate-infested relationship! A lawyer is a spittoon! There's no lawyer I know who enjoys being a lawyer!

MOTHER

But they pay you well!! No one gets rich if you're poor!

SON

I don't give a fuck! (*Pause*) Pay you well—Italian clients are the worst! They're doing <u>you</u> a favour by hiring you so you should do it for *free*. They want a *refund* when you *win*. Between discounts, favours, and complaints, I might as well work in a factory! I'd make more!

MOTHER

Ah, if your ass only had money!

SON

Money is a curse!

MOTHER

You're the curse! … Everything you touch you destroy! … Money can restore sight to the blind, in case you don't know! A man with no money is a walking corpse! (*To herself*) Imagine what people are gonna say …!

SON

People can go fuck themselves! (*Pause*) "I have a duplex, but Ciccio has a triplex! Yeah, but Nicola, he has a fiveplex! No, no, wait! Pasquale owns a three-story apartment block!" … And then there is Peppino, who sells everything and buys a bungalow! That's it, everyone sells and buys a bungalow! That's people! Sheep!

MOTHER

And you're a beggar!

SON

I have to look after my health, mà! ... Life is short! I'm suffering from a very serious illness ... in my *caput, cor,* and *rectum*! ... I haven't gone to the bathroom for over a month. ... Let's wait ... see what happens!

MOTHER

Let's-wait-and-see-what-happens my *ass*! ... that today is Sunday! We'll be old by then! ... People die *every day*! ... Didn't you hear that Pino the doctor's grandfather just died? (*Beat*) Mind you, God bless, they put on a *beautiful* funeral. So many wreaths, I tell you, ... big, beautiful, ... the flowers! ... from the children, nephews, even from Italy! ... And they rented that beautiful funeral home up there ... on Jarry Street. No, it was really beautiful. Everyone was really impressed! ... (*Beat*) *Now*'s the time to enjoy life! *Now*! Not tomorrow! *Now*!

SON

Now! ... (*Pause*) Way back, I used to be like *this* with Jesus Christ. Like *this* ... me and Jesus! He understood when I didn't have time to pray ... And even if he was busy in confession with someone else ... He'd wink at me, you know, like saying "Don't worry about, I'll see you later." ... Like *this*! We were really close. Buddies! ... (*Beat*) And serving mass ... every morning ... watching all those poor, pathetic fools kneeling in Church, old women with disgusting clown faces and parched lips painted in every color, extending their pitiful quivering *tongues*, waiting for that Host, waiting for death! ... I understood that I wasn't normal. ... I was certain that Christ had brought me into this world to leave something behind ... a *mark* or something. To make a *difference*!

MOTHER

You should have been a monk or a priest!

SON

(*Beat*) Everything seemed to exist for a reason ... Everything seemed like ... things were arranged ... seemed like they were there for a *reason* ... Everything! ... Even the fact that I was *there* ... seemed to be for a *reason*! ... (*Beat*) Here's the best part ... I'm not even angry at the wasted time. ... Even worse.

MOTHER

Leave-a-mark my ass! A lawyer means *nothing*? Just the word L A W Y E R ... says something! Makes an impression! To say Salvatore the shoemaker, or Salvatore the L A W Y E R—the A T T O R N E Y—it's a whole different thing! No?! What's bigger than that? The Lord Jesus, maybe! Heh! (*Brief pause*) Only you know what you're taking. ... You probably trusted someone ... took a cigarette ... and they drugged you without you even knowing it! It doesn't take much! ... I don't know you anymore! ... You're already thirty years old! ... (*Beat*) But ... if a donkey hasn't grown a tail after three years, he'll never grow one!

SON

Enough, mà! No more talking about donkeys and mules and thirty years old! You're right! Thirty years! Thirty fucken years devoted to duty! (*Pause*) I don't know ... I lost the will. ... It's as if I already knew the end! ... and I'm suspended from ... I don't know where ... waiting for death ... or something to amuse me ... to pass the time ... to avoid being bored ... I can't move. (*Pause*). The smallest effort becomes a burden when you're old! (*Brief pause*) Oh, how beautiful it would be to have a vacuum cleaner that could suck *everything* out of my head and leave a little *space* for a little *peace*!

MOTHER

You need a Doctor! ... A tree that doesn't bear fruit, should be cut down, the saying goes! The only mark you're ever gonna leave is that of your feet going round and round counting other people's footprints—*forever*! Enough! ... Even today you have to make me miss the third episode of the Italian soap! Stop it! I don't want to talk about it anymore! Every time you come here, you talk to me! You tell me everything! That's what he says. He's jealous! He's dying of jealousy! He says I treat you better than him! (*Brief pause*) You think your sister doesn't say the same thing?!

SON

(*Beat*) Where is she?

MOTHER

Where is she ... where she always is! In her room! Night and day! Always with her books! Your father is really gonna burn those books one day! He already burned half of them. ... He threw them out the window ... made a nice little stack ... and burned them in the garden.

SON

Mà, they're just books!

MOTHER

Just books?! ... You can't recognize her face anymore! Now you'll see how thin she is! She doesn't talk to anyone anymore! From her room to the bathroom, that's her life! People come to visit, she locks herself in her room, 'cause she doesn't wanna see anyone! ... She talks to herself! ... I find her in her room staring at the walls ... the window closed, the blinds closed, a book in her hands, and the music so loud you can hear it even from Jean-Talon! ... I call her ... she doesn't hear me. I call, "Linda!" ... nothing. ... staring at I don't know ... sitting on the bed! (*Loud music coming from Linda's room*)

> MUSIC: "School" by Supertramp. It begins at the 'scream' just before the lyrics "After school is over ..."

MOTHER

Signorina! Come down and set the table! Signorina! Come down! I'm telling you, your father is gonna kill you! (*MUSIC stops. Brief pause*) You see? Doesn't give a damn! Has to do things her way. She never lifts a finger in this house! ... But now ... You'll see how blows are gonna start flying around if she doesn't put on some sense ... *something*! ... She'll *have* to smarten up! ... Your father has decided to marry her off! Don't you say anything. (*Son looks at mother*) What're you looking at? At fifteen a female is either married or quartered! ... She's already old! ... No, she has put it in her *damn* head that she's in charge!

SON

And you haven't chopped her head off?

MOTHER

Yeah, yeah, watch your tongue! ... 'cause before you can fool me ...

SON

Mà, she's twenty-nine, almost thirty! Can't you give her a little freedom?

FATHER

(*Offstage*) When you're in your own house, you can do what you want! In my house, I do what I want!

SON

(*To Mother*) He's got ears!

MOTHER

Please ... it's Sunday. A Holy Day!

Act 1, Scene 4: FATHER, SON, MOTHER, LINDA

FATHER

(*Enters, carrying some garden vegetables*) Sunday? ... For your son it's always Sunday! It's already twelve-thirty ... the hour when aristocrats finally wake up! Isn't it true, Salvatò? (*To mother*) Did you at least bring his excellency coffee in bed?

SON

'Morning.

FATHER

Good evening, what good morning! (*To Mother*) I already put in a whole day's work ... with the help of no one! ... My mother used to say, bless her soul, "He who sleeps doesn't catch fish."

MOTHER

The hen lays the egg, and the rooster complains about an itchy ass.

FATHER

Yeah, yeah ... you want to compare your work with mine?! I still don't see *anything* on the table. I haven't eaten since six this morning! ... Where is the little princess?

MOTHER

Where is she ...!

FATHER

Still locked up in that goddam room? I'm telling you, I told you! ... Call her! The table needs to be set! ... that lazy, ungrateful parasite! ... If she doesn't behave and start doing something around here, I'm going to **fry her heart in a frying pan!** ... And I told you a thousand times! ... when she's in her room, she needs to leave the door open ... unless she wants me to rip it off the wall. (*Door slams upstairs. To Mother*) Look at this beautiful lettuce, God bless! Here, wash it and see what you want to do with it. (*Father exits*)

> Linda enters, coming down the stairs with a smile on her face,
> mumbling in pig Latin which only Sal understands.

LINDA

Iay atehay histay uckenfay ousehay. Iay atehay histay uckenfay ousehay. Iay opehay ehayiesday, uckenfay astardbay! Iay opehay ehay iesday! Iay opehay heytay ieday! Iay eallyray oday! Maybe a bird! That would be nice! (*She exits to the kitchen. Offstage*) Hi, Sal!

MOTHER

See that?

FATHER

(*Offstage*) I told you! In this house, we speak Italian! I told you a thousand times!

LINDA

(*Offstage*) La la la la la …

FATHER

(*Offstage*) Tell me something … what time did you close the light in your room last night?

LINDA

(*Offstage*) la la la la la …

FATHER

(*Offstage*) I am talking!

LINDA

(*Offstage*) la la la la la—I don't know!

FATHER

(*Offstage*) It was two in the morning! I warned you, Mother of Jesus! … If the light is not closed at exactly twelve midnight … I'll get rid of every lamp in your room! You understand me?

LINDA

(*Offstage*) I'll read as late as I want!

FATHER

(*Offstage*) And I say no, Jesus fucken Christ! … that today is Sunday! You get up early in the morning and read. Nights are for sleeping!

LINDA

(*Offstage*) As long as you sleep, why should you give a fuck about others? It's not like I'm disturbing you. … You snore like a pig!

> *Father slaps her. Pause.*

FATHER

(*Offstage*) Jesus Christ and the Virgin Mary! … I'm telling you so you'll learn.

> *Pause.*

MOTHER

Night and day, always like this! … Dear Jesus, what are we missing?! We have everything! … food, health … only peace! Never had any peace in my life! (*Pause*) I think all these nerves your father has is because of you!

SON

He was born a nerve, and he'll die a nerve!

MOTHER

You're never here! … He sees other sons … and suffers! He had so many plans for you … He still left that stairway half-finished! For who did he buy the house? All for you! You're the son! To him, these things are important! I don't know what to say to you, son. … How many days are you staying?

SON

I'm leaving tomorrow.

MOTHER

Ah, great! That way you'll make him nice and happy!

SON

Mà, I need money!

MOTHER

Ahhh!—Ask your father!

SON

You don't have any? ... I'll pay you back ... at the same interest as the bank!

MOTHER

Go to the bank—but are you crazy? How am I supposed to do that? Your father! Ask him! 'Cause your father ... and he warned the little princess ... that if she has the same ideas as you ...

FATHER

(*Offstage*) May Jesus Christ do me the grace of finding you dead in bed tomorrow morning.

        Pause.

MOTHER

Talk to him! He's you father! He's your blood!

SON

He's fuck all to me!

MOTHER

My God, what a disgraceful, shameless shit you are ... He'd give you the shirt off his back!

SON

Mà ... I come here for you!

MOTHER

Quiet, don't let him hear you! (*Loud sottovoce*) Zip it! ... (*Brief pause*) What's past is past! If we all looked at the past, we would all have to kill ourselves! ... Everything he did, he did it to teach you both. He's made that way, you know that. He can't change! But you, fuck! ...

SON

Every day, I say to myself—careful! ... he took this path ... turn ... find another way! He took a step to the right, you, take one to the left ... —Enough, ma! Don't make me think about it! ... because through these fucken veins runs ...

FATHER

(*Offstage*)—Carmè! The pot is boiling!

        Pause.

MOTHER

My dears, you have to learn how to swallow your tongue! If you wanna live in peace ... look, listen and be silent! And it takes a lot of patience! ... Shit, the more you stir it, the more it smells! ... I swallowed many tongues ... and I didn't die! ... Neither will you!

SON

Mà, he's not for you!

MOTHER

He's my husband!

FATHER

(*Offstage*) Carmè! Sacred Mother of Jesus! I'm dying of hunger!!!

MOTHER

(*Beat*) Don't tell him what you need. Just talk to him. Ask him if he needs help with anything ... And you'll see that he'll give you the money without you asking for any. (*Pause. Angry*) You know ... he hasn't forgotten the knife!! He always talks about it. He keeps it nice and safe in his desk! God help those who touch it! ... Till the day he dies, he said!

Father enters, stands by kitchen door where he can't be seen.

SON
He's a fucken child! **Worse!**

FATHER
If you came here to start a war in the house, you can leave! ... 'cause you don't do me any good here! ... and you never have! ... If you don't like the way things work around here, va sciènne, as the French say! ... A Frenchman in my place would have thrown you out of the house when you were ten, with only your underwear and no shoes! One of *those* is what you *deserve*! ... I already told your mother what to do when I die! I'll even write it down on a piece of paper! ... (*as if delivering an official decree*) **You are not to set foot in the funeral home**. And if anyone who respects me sees you come in, they have to throw you out immediately! I told your mother! ... And no one forces you to come here! **You piece of shit lawyer!** I always did the work alone around here ... even sick as a dog with a 40-degree fever, to feed all you animals, who sleep till twelve noon! 'Cause the food I fed you and your sister, did more harm than good! If I had fed you crumbs instead of bread, my circumstances would be different today. ... Modern life, is that it? Children who are ashamed to be Italian! Do like the *English*?! ... 'Cause when my father just *looked* at me, I'd tremble! Tremble, Jesus Christ! You piece of shit—rotten pus of a lawyer! Pino is not ashamed! ... and he's a doctor! ... You should have been the *pearl* of the family. The *pearl*, damn all the saints in heaven! ... (*Beat*) The world has to know! Do you *understand me*?! ... you shameless, disgraceful piece of shit waste of fucken life! So take your things and get out!

Pause.

SON
I'm not ashamed of being Italian, I'm ashamed of being your son! ...

FATHER
One doesn't respect their parents after they're dead!

Linda enters, smiling.

LINDA
The table is ready! Ladies and gentlemen, please!

MOTHER
C'mon, let's go, I even made a cake! Then, we'll open the gifts and take some pictures! Let's go!

FATHER
(*To SAL, throwing a five-dollar bill on the floor*) Here!

MOTHER
What's that?

FATHER
To buy a rope so he can hang himself!

Son exits house with robe on, slams the door. Linda goes upstairs, slams the door. Father exits to cantina, slams the door.

MOTHER

(*Beat*) The cake! may you all die!

Act 1, Scene 5: MOTHER, FATHER, LINDA, SAL

FATHER

(*Enters, with an empty garbage bag*) Child?! A CHILD?! 'Cause he heard *you* say that ... that's why he said it. Because you've always defended him!

MOTHER

I defend no one! I defend peace! I want peace! I don't understand how you reason.

FATHER

How I reason?!, or how *he* reasons? He better not ***dare*** show his face around here!

MOTHER

Quiet, or people will hear!

FATHER

I don't care even if the almighty *God the Father* hears me! I don't want to see even a handkerchief of his in this house!

MOTHER

Where're you bringing those bags?

FATHER

Not even a *handkerchief*! I'll bury them in the garden! First I'll burn them, then I'll bury them! All of them! ... I'll light a match and Gone! ... to hell! (*Going from wall to wall, removing everything that belongs to his Son or was a gift from him*) Who brought this? Gone! This, too. Gone! I don't want to see any pictures of him in this house! Gone!

MOTHER

Look at you! ... you're behaving exactly like a child! (*Father stops, stares at mother for a moment*) The plastic bags are going to make an awful smell, and the smoke is going to ruin all of the clothes on the line! ... Listen, those are memories! ... and I paid for half the stuff ... !

FATHER

Money thrown to the wind! A child?! ... You'll pay for that! 'Cause you've always encouraged way too many ***confidences*** between you! But a mother needs to set an *example*! ... He's worse than a *woman*!

MOTHER

He is my son! Lame, stupid, beautiful or ugly, he is my *son*! ... No ... you know what the problem is? You should *never* have had children! That's the problem! And if your son is a disgraceful shit, it's because he takes after your fucken family! He's just like you! Both of you, hard-headed!

FATHER

(*Over " Both of you"*) My family?—okay! Just try and let him enter this house again, and I'll show you who he takes after! I'll kill *him* and then *you*! ... And if you want, you can take your things and leave, too!

MOTHER

I should do it for real, to show you! ...

FATHER

Go ahead! DO IT! I'm better off alone! I don't need anyone!

MOTHER

I might live a day longer! ... (*Grabbing the garbage bag and trying to tear it from his hands*) Don't you *dare* throw that stuff! I'm warning you ... Give me those bags! ...

FATHER

... Careful, you're hurting me! ...

MOTHER

... 'Cause I *swear* you won't see me *ever* again!

FATHER

What are you waiting for? **DO IT!**

> *Father stops suddenly. Pause.*

FATHER

I hear a car! Close the lights! Go look from the window! (*Whispering loudly*) **GO SEE WHO IT IS, Jesus Christ!**

MOTHER

(*Looking out the window furtively*) The French people upstairs ... husband and wife. No. ... Oh my God ... oh my *God* ... it's not her husband!

FATHER

The slut! ... Of course! ... her husband is out of town, *working*, and now she *feasts* ... the good life! ... (*Beat*) Who is it? ... Her 'chum'! Today all these women like her have a ciommo!

MOTHER

Like what?

FATHER

(*Irritated*) Jesus! ... ! She's *French*! ... Always going out and leaving that poor kid at home alone with that young cousin of hers who always looks like she's on drugs ... Then you read in the papers that they find babies in ovens, in fridges, and people wonder why! ... Wait till I see her husband! ...

MOTHER

You mind your own $%$#@* business! Take care of your own house!

FATHER

Yeah? ... and if she leaves ... without paying the rent?! Ah! ... 'Cause if she's capable of doing this to her husband, what's it take for her to leave without saying a word? ... (*Looking out the window. Beat*) Look, look! ... see the dress? ... so you can see her legs, her thighs, her ... look, look ... her whole ass is exposed. ... Every time she goes up those stairs, she walks with those kinds of moves ... y'know what I mean? ... that scare even the dead. To show off her ass! ... The slut!

MOTHER

And why do you look?

FATHER

(*Beat*) I look, just like that ... I don't look to *look* ... you never know! ... sometimes someone might be trying to break in ... one can never be sure! And then ... you put a plate of pasta in front of my face, I'm not gonna look at it? ... 'specially if I'm hungry!

MOTHER

You're really a beautiful piece of something!

FATHER

(*Looking out the window*) You see ... look, look ... They went for a nice little pic-a-nic. Slut!

MOTHER

But how do you know she's a slut? He could be a relative, a cousin!

FATHER

Yeah, yeah, relative here! (*Pointing to his crotch*) Maybe she can fool you ... but to fool **me**? ... she's gotta <u>eat</u> a lot more <u>sausages</u> and <u>picnics</u> to fool me! ... (*Looking out the window*) Damn all the fucken devils in hell! I see a **<u>cat</u>**! See if I'm wrong!

MOTHER

Oh my God, look at that ... it's a cat!

FATHER

Holy Mother of Christ! I told her, No animals! We even wrote it in the lease! ... That's it! ... now I'll fix you both! ... (*Cleaning his throat in preparation for a confrontation*)

MOTHER

Wait! What are you doing? Let Salvatore speak to her when he comes back!

FATHER

Don't ...! (*Beat*) I told you!

MOTHER

Then, let Linda talk to them when her husband comes back! You don't know how to talk to them. (*Father stares at her*) Then you get mad, <u>**see**</u>, make her mad, and then she's gonna leave for sure!

FATHER

(*Broadcasting it to the world*) No cat, I said! Jesus Christ on the cross!

MOTHER

Why are you telling me?!

FATHER

We even wrote it in the fucken lease! (*Looks outside, with increased urgency*) See—the fucken!—they're bringing it upstairs! Call your daughter! ...

MOTHER

Signorì!

FATHER

... Since Réné Lavecchia ... They became arrogant *overnight* because of **him**! All these airs. What ... you think this one upstairs is not a separatist?

MOTHER

I didn't ask her! I don't go looking at how they vote or shit!

FATHER

That's why she's doing it!!! You don't see—you're not sharp! ... but I see everything! ... She *insisted* on having the lease in French!

MOTHER

They are French!

FATHER

And if I wanted to give it to them in English?! I'm the landlord!

MOTHER

You're a beast! ... 'Cause they're French doesn't mean they're separatists! ... There are good French people, too.

FATHER

Yeah, yeah ... okay, do me a favour ... let's not even talk about it anymore! 'Cause when it comes to politics you understand zero and nothing!. You're a parrot! ... This Lavecchia is doing what he's doing to *provoke*, if you don't understand! ... so you become weak, soften up, sell your house, business, move to Ontario, and then they're the only ones left! You understand now? (*Goes to window*) Bastards! Did you call your daughter?!

A door slams upstairs. Linda walks down the stairs.

LINDA

What do you want?

FATHER

(*At the window, waving to the tenant, embarrassed and totally under her spell*) Bojoù madame!

MOTHER

You see—she saw you!

FATHER

So what? I say hello and pretend like nothing! (*to Linda*) What were you doing?

LINDA

It's none of your business!

MOTHER

Oh my God, look at that!

Pause.

FATHER

Tell me something ... you ever see your mother rest? (*Pause*) Come closer. (*After a short pause, Linda takes one small step towards him*) A little closer! (*She takes a smaller step towards him*) **COME CLOSER**, I said! (*She takes a full step towards him.*) You see this piece of paper? (*She looks straight ahead in defiance. Father points to a piece of paper on the floor*) ... **THIS ONE HERE ON THE FLOOR!** ... It's been here since yesterday morning! ... Two days, and no one saw it!

LINDA

You saw it!

FATHER

'You doing it on purpose? I have other things to think about ... your mother's always cleaning, day and night!

LINDA

I've got other things to do, too! (*Referring to the piece of paper*) It's such a fucken little thing! Bullshit!

FATHER

(*Beat*) We all eat, we all work! Write those words down!

LINDA

More bullshit!

FATHER

That's the second time you said that word!

MOTHER

    Linda! ...

LINDA

    It's him!

FATHER

    Who, *him*? I don't want to hear *him* or *her*! Mother or father! You understand?

LINDA

    Yes, 'father.' And what's my name ... servant?

FATHER

    Don't make me swear ... Jesus Christ Almighty!! ... 'cause I'll feed you poison instead of food! ... it's in the cabinet.

LINDA

    You're the poison!

MOTHER

    Linda!

LINDA

    (*Crying*) You called me! What d'you want?!

FATHER

    A piece of paper ... what's it take? A *servant*? (*Pause. Throws a large ring of keys on the floo*r) Get me the lease for upstairs ... in my desk.

MOTHER

    And then re-heat the pasta.

LINDA

    (*Holding back the tears*) I'm not hungry!

MOTHER

    But **we** have to eat, signorì!

LINDA

    Yes, Madam!

MOTHER

    Another diet? You're so thin, soon you'll disappear before my eyes! ... you reek of famine!

LINDA

    When I was fat, it shamed you!

MOTHER

    And now you're still an embarrassment! ... Fat? You were a vat! Not fat! ... And now, you're a ghost!

FATHER

    Okay, let's do what we have to do *first*.

MOTHER

    Today I want to see you eat! ... like a human being! ... You have the face of a witch! ... If not, I'll feed you myself!

LINDA

    I said I'm not hungry!

FATHER

    No arguing or shenanigans! OK?! (*Beat*) There is no shortage of food in this house. And I don't want to see it go to waste!

LINDA

    (*Grabs the keys off the floor, then to Father*) If I were you, I'd watch what *you* eat …
'Cause one day … you'll find that poison in (on) your plate!

        *Linda exits. Mother chases after her. Lights fade leaving a spot on
        Father as he looks towards the upstairs apartment.
        MUSIC (diegetic, playing on the radio)
        "Il Pallone" by Rita Pavone.
        We are in the mid 1960s. Father hasn't moved, obsessively
        listening to the cat noise coming from the upstairs apartment.*

MOTHER

    (*Offstage*) Raffaè! Linda! Salvatore! It's ready! And bring the wine from the
cantina! (*Lights come up. Father re-enters the dining area*) How many fucken
times do I have to call you? Mother of Jesus, the pasta is gonna overcook, and
then it gets all pasty!

FATHER

    Half an hour to find that lease!

MOTHER

    Linda! Salvatore!

FATHER

    You hear the cat?

MOTHER

    But that's their kid!

FATHER

    What kid?! It's the cat! Don't you hear it running around? Tatatatum, tatatatum,
tatatatum! (*With the end of a broomstick, Father knocks on the ceiling*)

MOTHER

    But d'you have to make enemies with <u>everyone</u>?

FATHER

    He who has a hundred enemies never dies! (*Tenant responds by knocking same number
of times from above*)

        Enter Sal and Linda. He's eleven years old, she's ten.

MOTHER

    Ma, what are you, lame, or impaled on a cross?! (*Beat*) Gimme that wine!!! (*Takes
wine bottle from Sal*)

FATHER

    Did you wash your hands?

SAL and LINDA

    Yes! I did. Me, too! … Happy Father's Day. (*They kiss Father on both cheeks, who
accepts their greetings like a head of state, as a matter of duty. Linda and Sal then
give Father a Father's Day greeting card. Linda's card is in a heart-shaped (pink)
envelope, while Sal's is a rolled-up sheet of paper with a thin red ribbon carelessly
wrapped around it.*)

FATHER

    Thank you.

LINDA

    (*Giving father keys and lease*) Here!

FATHER

Let me see your hands? (*He inspects both their hands*) Go wash your hands, both of you! ... lying, disgraceful, miserable, little shits! (*They exit in a hurry*) ... All over these walls nothing but black handprints! ... And wash'em nice and clean ... or I'll come in and wash'em for you! ... and if the foam doesn't come out white like snow ... make the sign of the cross ... I'll give you both a swollen face and chop off your hands! ... (*Beat*) You hear me, Salvatò?! (*Beat. To himself*) Ma what ...

       Father studies lease. Mother serves the pasta singing under her breath.

FATHER

(*Calmly*) Get me the salt. (*Pause*) Where's the salt? (*Pause*) Is it possible to set the table nice nice when we eat?

MOTHER

What're you missing? (*Exits singing*) La la la la la ...

      Without moving from his chair, Father searches the room for salt.
      Can't find it.

FATHER

(*Exploding*) Jesus Christ! I am talking?!

MOTHER

Are you crazy?!

FATHER

Three times I asked for the salt, and no one nothing!

MOTHER

I didn't hear you! I'm sorry, Missiù ... (*Beat*) Did your hands fall off?

FATHER

(*Beat*) Carmè, d'you wanna see how I set the table? (*Beat*) I'll show you right away! ... This is order?! ... (*Beat*) It's ok, forget it, I'll get it myself! (*He exits, returns with napkins which he places on the table.*) No salt!

MOTHER

Eat without it!

FATHER

Carmè! First no napkins, then no salt!

MOTHER

Ask the little princess!

LINDA

(*Offstage. Top of her lungs*) I didn't touch it!

FATHER

(*Incredulous*) What does it take to put things back where they belong?

MOTHER

You! ... Don't interfere with the affairs of the kitchen. That's *my* business!

FATHER

What?! Only the kitchen you have to worry about in this house ... and you can't even do that! ... If it weren't for me, the kitchen would be upside down. Cups where they don't belong ...!—And it's not over! Find the salt!

      Mother exits and quickly re-enters.

MOTHER

(*Plunks down a box of salt in front of Father*) Here's the salt!

FATHER

I want the salt that goes on the table! The one in that little thing, the container, whatever the fuck it's called! The one that goes here, right here ... in its proper place! That's the one I want!

MOTHER

Jesus Christ Almighty! ... I'm gonna go jump off a mountain! (*Hysterical*) I didn't touch it!

FATHER

Ok ... where is it, then? ... Vanished ... like that ... all by itself? You didn't touch it, she didn't touch it ...

MOTHER

Linda a a a!

LINDA

(*Offstage*) I didn't touch it!

FATHER

Po, po, po, po, po, po, po, po ... I feel this fucken rage!!

        Enters Linda and sits at the table.

MOTHER

Ma, what are you guys doing in that toilet? Where did you put the salt?

FATHER

(*Studying the lease, to himself*) Bo! ... (*to Linda*) Linda ... read the lease, and see if it says, "no cat!"

MOTHER

(*Brusquely, as in "I'm eating"*) Bon'appetito! (*She eats*)

LINDA

(*To herself*) Auf!

FATHER

Without huffing and puffing 'cause I busted my ass to send you to school!

LINDA

(*Takes a quick look at the lease*) It's in French! (*Beat*) Don't you know if it's written in?

FATHER

(*Beat*) I asked Ciccio the neighbour to write it in! He specifically wrote, "No cat!" ... I can't see that well ...

LINDA

(*Takes another quick glance at the lease*) Nothing about a cat. It's not there.

FATHER

What do you mean, it's not there? "PAS DE SHIÀ"... it's not there? What's there?

LINDA

(*Reading*) "Le lo-ca-taar" ...

FATHER

Loca*terre*, not, locatarro.

LINDA

If you know, why d'you ask me? (*Father raises hand, as if to slap her with a backhand. Pause. Linda continues to read*) "Le locaterre et les per-sonnes a qui il per-mettes l'access a l'im-meubles ..."

FATHER

... What does that mean?

LINDA

It's in French! I don't understand this word.

FATHER

Ok, ok, go on. (*Beat*) Bo!

LINDA

... "do-i-vent se condu-ire"

FATHER

What?

LINDA

Bo!

FATHER

(*To himself*) Bo. I wonder what the fuck the word means? ... (*Reading*) "Dav se cond" ... Damn all the fucken misery in this world ... if I had *schooling*, **I'd make the world tremble, Jesus Christ**! ... "PAS DE SCIÀ"! ... Is it there or not? ... Or maybe it says, "no animal!"

LINDA

(*Mumbling, directed at Father*) Animal!

FATHER

What? (*Brief pause*) Is it there?! YES or NO?!

LINDA

I told you once already!

FATHER

And even if I ask you a hundred times!

LINDA

But I told you, it's not there! Why would I say it's not there, if it's there? 'Cause it's not there!

FATHER

(*Takes the lease from her violently*) Okay—never mind! (*To himself*) Not there!

LINDA

The writing is half-Italian, half-French.

FATHER

Because Ciccio wrote it for me ... because my children were not capable!

MOTHER

It means he forgot!

FATHER

You're siding with her, now?

MOTHER

Listen! ... if you're so smart, you find it!

FATHER

Why raise kids then?! ... I didn't do any fucken schooling! My father, God bless his soul, died when I was six and a half!

MOTHER

(*Over "I was six ..."*) Okay, I get it, the same old music!

FATHER

Carmè, I told them a thousand times! ... "Learn French" ... because if Lavecchia gets in with these separatists, bad times are right behind them!

MOTHER

What can we do? We'll adapt!

FATHER

Listen to her, listen to her! ... This guy is worse than Mussolini! Mussolini at least was Italian! ... With *this* guy, who doesn't speak French, _out_! ... (*Emphatically*) *He is dangerous*! And they can even take the house if they want! Like the Communists!

MOTHER

And what are we supposed to do now? Kill ourselves?! When that day comes, it comes!

FATHER

That day has come!

LINDA

What did the cat do to you? He's so cute! The lady upstairs even lets me play with him.

FATHER

You touched the cat?!

LINDA

So? ... He's always making a big deal about little things! Bullshit.

FATHER

(*Slaps her hard across the face*) That's the third time today! I warned you! Bullshit?! BULLSHIT?! Is that what you learn from your teachers? 'Cause I'll pull you out of school <u>tomorrow</u> and make you <u>sweat</u> for your food! Bullshit?! ... Cats are dirty ... they stink up the whole house with their shit and urine! And they bring bad luck! ... You didn't learn that in school? ... (*Beat*) Did you ever see anyone domesticate a cat? They do whatever they want! A modo suo![1] ... (*Beat*) Disease is all they bring!

MOTHER

But we have to eat! Now's the time to do these things?

FATHER

Who has time doesn't wait for time!

MOTHER

You're unbearable!

FATHER

(*Slaps Linda*) For every time you <u>talk</u>, or <u>defend</u> her ... she earns a back hand!
      Pause. Enters Sal, scratching his bum, vigorously.

MOTHER

(*To Sal*) And what are you doing in that toilet all that time?! Did you shit fire?! ... Half an hour!

FATHER

What? ... This one always has to shit when it's time to eat! (*to Sal*) You're not going to break that habit?

---

1. 'A modo suo' (Italian) do, act or behave in one's own way.

SAL

(*Sits at the table*) Ma, I like more that pasta in the cans.

MOTHER

I'm gonna put you in a can! Piece by piece!

> *Linda is still crying. Sal is oblivious to it all, he's used to it.*

SAL

(*Whispers in Linda's ear, then*) It's true, I couldn't hold it any more ... 'cause I knew like if I came home they wouldn't let me go out again ... then I wiped it with a leaf, you know ... but some of it still stuck ... I think I did it too hard, like, when I wiped. I'm itchy! There's blood!

FATHER

(*Slaps Sal across the back of the head*) Italian! ... or French! ... What did he say, Linda?

MOTHER

Are you crazy hitting him like that on the head?

FATHER

(*Hits Sal again*) I told you, don't defend the children in front of their father! (*Pause*) I hit him here! (*Hits Sal*) ... you see?

MOTHER

And is that not the head?

FATHER

Where do you hit him?

MOTHER

But if you hit like this, (*Hits Sal*) you'll kill him! You should never hit children on the head! They can become dumb! Ask whoever you want!

FATHER

'Cause you don't know how to hit! I on the other hand know where to hit! Here, (*Hits Sal*) ... you see ... where it's hard. You, instead, hit here, (*Hits Sal*) where it's soft! It's a whole different thing. There, for sure it's more delicate! So you have to do like this, (*Hits Sal*) not like this, (*Hits Sal*) or else of course they're gonna become retarded! ... I learned this from Olga the Tedesca when I was working in Germany. You gonna teach me how to hit the kids? (*Linda is about to exit*) You didn't touch the meat!

LINDA

Too much fat.

MOTHER

Eat your meat!

FATHER

When we were growing up, fatty meat was all we knew, once a year, at Christmas! Eat the meat! That's not bullshit. That's hard-earned money! Eat the meat!

MOTHER

(*To Linda*) Don't let me tell you again!

> *Linda takes a piece of meat and swallows it whole.*

MOTHER

Jesus Christ, she's swallowed it whole!

FATHER

(*Trying to retrieve the piece of meat from Linda's mouth*) Spit the meat on the plate! Spit the meat out, I said!

> *Linda smiles.*

MOTHER

No, she swallowed it! Little bitch!

LINDA

There's too much fat!

MOTHER

(*Grabs Linda's hair and pulls her head back and forth*) Are you crazy to swallow a whole piece of meat like that?! You'll die!

FATHER

Be careful, you're gonna hurt her like that! (*To Linda, calmly, staccato*) Eat the meat, like a human being! Chew it nice nice, like you're supposed to!

       Linda takes another piece of meat, swallows it whole.

MOTHER

My God! Again!

FATHER

Chew the! ... (*Grabs Linda by the jaw and forces her to open her mouth*) This is how you do it! Like this! (*He takes a new piece of meat from her plate, shoves it in her mouth, moving her jaw up and down*) Chew the fucken meat! (*Linda fights back. To Mother*) Carmè, hold her hands! Jesus Christ and all the saints, 'cause if you think you're hard-headed, I'm more hard-headed than you! (*Father shoves another piece of meat in Linda's mouth, though she has yet to swallow the last one*). Chew the fuc ... (*Linda spits the meat in his face*) Jesus Christ, stubborn fuc ...! Carmè! ... Salvatò, get me the belt in the cabinet ... disgraceful shit, chew! Chew the fucken ...! Salvatò! Get the ...

LINDA

I'll hate you!

FATHER

(*Threatening to slap her face*) No English, I said! I'll show you—"It you!"—Salvatò!

MOTHER

(*To Sal*) Go, or he's gonna hit you too!

LINDA

I swear on the Bible, Sal, I won't ... (*as in, "I'll never forgive you"*)

FATHER

Ah! (*Smacks her*) She bit my hand, the shameless shit! Salvatore! be a good boy, and get me the fucken belt! ... You go Carmè! (*Sal fetches belt from the kitchen cabinet. Linda breaks away. Still has a piece of meat in her mouth. Stops and stares back at them, one by one. She stares at Sal, who is still holding the belt, feeling guilty. Looking at father, she reveals the piece of meat, then swallows it whole. She smiles and exits. Pause.*) Is that what you think? Okay ... go to your room. You'll pay for this! Half an hour with gravel under your knees! ... May the Almighty Jesus Christ strike me dead if I'm lying! (*Door slams upstairs*) And I don't want to see any lights in that room! (*Door slams again. Then, to Sal*) And you, when I tell you get the belt, now, not tomorrow! (*Sal exits with the belt. Pause*) How is one supposed to raise a family and carry it forward? How? ... <u>How</u> (the fuck) do you carry, move a whole people forward ... when there is no order? ... We'd never move forward! ... But forward we must go, not backward! 'Cause if everyone does as they wish—***each in their own way***, the family, "caput," as the Romans used to say. ... (*Beat*) They're all doing it on purpose! ... (*Beat*)

We'll see who wins! (*Pause, touches his face*) That shameless little shit even scratched me!

> *Lights change. Back to the present. Father remains immobile down centre. Linda enters, with bruised face. She places the Father's Day cake on the table. Lights one candle. Exits to kitchen.*

FATHER
I was right there with him ... I saw him write, "NO SHIÀ!" ... Bo! ... "It's not there!" ... Ciccio's daughters ... God ... they read you letters, documents, government papers, just like that, tah, tah, tah, tah, tah, in French, English, <u>Italian</u>, everything! And even those pensions from Italy, tah, tah, tah, two minutes—amazing! (*Short pause. Glances at the ceiling*) ... Who knows what that cat is up to?

MOTHER
(*Beat*) Eat your pasta ... it's gonna get cold!

> *Radio news signal.*

FATHER
Quiet! The news! Nobody move! ... Let's see what they say.

> *End of Act One.*

ACT TWO

Act 2, Scene 1: MOTHER, FATHER, PASQUALE

> *Lights up on father in downstairs living-room. He's wearing construction gloves and appears to be fertilizing a chive plant. Enters mother.*

MOTHER
What's that?

FATHER
The slut! ... I took it from the balcony upstairs, without anyone seeing me! And now, I'll bring it back ... This is some kind of onion grass ... (*Beat*) Come closer ... look ... see here ... and even here! ... All of this side has been chewed up by the cat ... She's got four or five plants up there, but the cat always goes for this one ... I'll fix him!

MOTHER
And what are you gonna do with this plant?

FATHER
'Vitamins!' ... This one's super special! ... A friend at work gave it to me, 'cause he always reads books ... In just ten minutes, this 'vitamin' will level even a bull—cold stiff! No mercy! ... Now we put a little medicine here (*Applies the 'vitamin'*) ... and we'll straighten him out nice and stiff. ... They will remember my name for a long time!

MOTHER
But isn't it easier if you just talk to her? Or Ciccio next door can talk to her!

FATHER

What? "Portè alla courte", she told me! What're you gonna tell her! Go to court, go! ("*see what happens*") Ma, "mangiè la merda!"[1] ... This is all because her husband never let her taste a backhand from day one! ... Now, she changed pharmacies. She cures herself with vitamins from her ciommo!

MOTHER

This whole thing is crazy!

FATHER

What? ... 'cause if you had seen what I saw when I took the plant ... your hair would stand up! ... I looked in the kitchen window ... And don't I see her sitting on the sofa ... with nothing on? ... one leg here, the other leg there ... and her ciommo kneeling on the floor reciting his prayers (*With hand and mouth he mimes eating*).

MOTHER

Oh, my God, look at that! ...

FATHER

What? ... And him ammucca ammucca ammucca! ...

MOTHER

... Jesus on the Cross! ...

FATHER

That way he had antipasto, first, main course and dessert!

MOTHER

Listen, I don't want to hear those things!

FATHER

Of course, I know! ... everything scandalizes you! ...

MOTHER

In any case! ... go talk to her!

FATHER

Are you crazy or what? ... She offers me a coffee ... falls on the floor, breaks a leg, calls the police, and tells them I did it!

MOTHER

What, you're afraid she'll eat you?

FATHER

What? ... That slut is capable of eating ten at the same time! ... Her husband wasn't there ... she calls me to pay the rent. ... I find her with no underwear— only a shirt ... that she tucked between her legs ... shoved it right between you know—me firm, Jesus Christ! ... as if nothing. ... (*Beat*) To not pay the rent! ... She has to eat a lot of sausages ("*to fool me*")!

MOTHER

Instead, you like going up there first thing in the morning, 'cause you know you'll find her in her bikini underwear! ... maybe she'll invite you to eat ... some milk and cookies!—Why do you go?!

FATHER

Okay, enough! Watch your tongue ... 'Cause I didn't give you a fat lip like your brother does with his wife! ... That's why you have that tongue on you, now!

---

1. Mispronunciation of the Québécois *mange de la merde.*

MOTHER

Touch me and see! (*Pause*) You only see the bad in people! But not everyone is like you! ... One does not look behind a door unless they've stood behind a door.

FATHER

Enough, I said! ... Mother of God! ... All this arguing just to defend that whore upstairs! ... The cat has to scratch my walls?! ... I should give in—I have to be under the thumb of a separatist cat?! ... I'll show you! ... we'll see who wins! I'll put an ad in the paper ... and throw her and the cat *out on the street* ... NO CAT, I said!

> *Doorbell rings. Father and Mother freeze, look at each other. Father quickly hides the plant, and the poison, in the same closet where he keeps the belt. He answers the door, removing the many security bars and locks first. A huge trunk (baule) is standing in the doorway.*

FATHER

Carmè, give me a hand!

MOTHER

My God, look at that!

> *They both drag the trunk inside.*

FATHER

Finally! (*He locks the door again with the security bars*) Close the blinds, drapes, everything! Mother of God, if anybody finds out! ... They don't allow these into the country anymore. (*He smells the trunk*) You can *smell* it's from Italy! Smell, smell! ... This, my dear, is the purging we needed! Home-made ... prepared the old way! ... Now you'll see how its gonna loosen things up ... and revive the signorina's appetite!

> *Father opens the trunk, out pops a young man in his late twenties to early thirties wearing a white suit and pink fedora*

PASQUALE

Wuayy papà, wuayyy mamma! Malboro! Yu wanna lait? Yea, no, okay, latur, whatti? ... Pasquali the worm! ... you remember?! (*Affecting the voice of an American movie gangster and striking a pose*) Sticca mappa, Giacca! Se non la smettie ti rompoe il cooloe![1]

Blackout.

Act 2, Scene 2: MOTHER, FATHER, PASQUALE, LINDA

> *Lights up. Father, Mother and Pasquale stand by the entrance (gates) of the upstairs living room, wearing paper slippers, like those found in doctors' offices. It is a dark, ostentatious, mausoleum-like chamber with ornate, European Rococo drapes (dark red), a massive wooden 'sarcophagus' (a 1970s Zenith chromacolor television set in pristine condition), and a makeshift altar (credenza) made of wood and granite*

---

1. 'American' pronunciation of the Italian *Se non la smetti ti rompo il culo!* (*If you don't stop it I'll break your ass!*)

stacked with deceased relatives' photos and unlit votives. Small and tall
Dieffenbachia plants fill the room. The sofas are covered in plastic.

MOTHER
It's a living-room, Pasquale ... simple ... nothing special.

FATHER
(*To Mother*) I don't understand the difference between here and downstairs. A living
room is a living room! It's better downstairs.

MOTHER
(*To Father*) We're never in here! ... since '74, the year we bought the house.
Today's the perfect day! Sit down, please! (*They sit*) Oh my God! (*She stands up*)
Look at the dust on my clothes! I'd better change!

FATHER
Carmè! Sit down! (*She sits*)

PASQUALE
(*Referring to the framed memorial cards*) Dead?

FATHER
Why?! You think only the living live in this world? (*Beat*) Their suffering is over.
Not ours! ... (*Beat*) It all depends on you! ... (*Beat*) From the letters I got ...
from what your mother tells me ... your feelings for my daughter seem sincere.

PASQUALE
Of course! (*In a broad American accent*) "Shore!" ... Wuay papà, I was only this
high, and already for your daughter ... uh huh ... understand me? ... —Always
with respect, of course!

FATHER
She is as pure as the Virgin Mary!

PASQUALE
God forbid! ("*She should be otherwise*")

FATHER
Since day one, we've guided her in a strict manner!

PASQUALE
I have no doubts!

FATHER
Till recently, she used to go to Church every Sunday.

PASQUALE
Practically a Saint!

FATHER
She was always first of her class!

PASQUALE
Thank God! 'Cause me, school ... nada!

FATHER
Maybe one year she came second. A <u>beating</u>! The next year, <u>first</u> again!

PASQUALE
(*To Mother*) He's something, heh!

FATHER
A cookie and a blow, makes a boy grow!

PASQUALE

Daughter in this case ...

FATHER

(*Sudden anger*) He who spares the rod, Jesus Christ ...!

PASQUALE

(*Explodes*) Hates his *daughter*! ... "Punish them with the rod and save them from death!"

FATHER

Ahh, you know that one!

PASQUALE

And how! ... I've had my share of beatings! Thank God! I graduated with honours from the finest institution of Beatarorium! Beatings to the left, beatings to the right, beatings up and down!, teachers, priests, parents! Beatings from everybody!

FATHER

Men of every colour would like to marry her. ...

PASQUALE

So many races in America! God bless!

FATHER

Of every kind ... Idiot!

PASQUALE

Ah ... I thought ...

FATHER

... but I'm giving her to you! ...

PASQUALE

Thank you.

FATHER

Shut up! ... because I know your family ... I know your parents' sacrifices!

PASQUALE

(*Moved*) I'm touched. ... What does the future bride say?

FATHER

(*Dead serious, sticking to his 'sermon'*) Love is like wine ... the more you care for it—with patience, the stronger it gets! But it's a job and a half! ... And you need a pair of big ones! (*Gestures, holding thumbs and index fingers in a wide circle over his crotch. Pause*) Remember, your wife, my blood! I looked after her, and carried her, like this! (*Extends his right hand, keeping his palm open, to show that he raised her with the greatest of care*). And I want her treated like a queen!

PASQUALE

Wuay papà, I'm not complicated! As long as she can cook ... let's me find a minestrone, a penne or two with sauce every night, at exactly eight o'clock ... raises a couple of kids, the way it should be done ... that's all I want! Better than a queen! She won't even have to raise a finger! Nada! I'll do all the work! Heh! More than that ("*I rest my case*") ...

FATHER

(*To Mother, proud*) Amazing ... look at that! ...

PASQUALE

Better than that, you die!

FATHER

(*To Mother*) Just like his father!

PASQUALE

(*Beat*) My God, what a palace! Ah, America! It's a marvel! All the streets nice and straight! All these beautiful homes, in rows, lined up like twins. Can't tell one from the other! They do it right, here! Ah, America! (*Affecting an American accent*) "NAICE!" … Wuay papà! I bought some English books. (*In a thick Italian accent*) I, yu, he, she, her, we, yu, me! … I forget the rest, now. We'll practice together!

FATHER

Outside, yes! Inside, no!

PASQUALE

What'd you say papà?

FATHER

In this house we speak Italiano!

PASQUALE

That's all I can speak!

FATHER

Good! Outside speak whatever the fuck you want! More languages you know the better!

MOTHER

But you can also speak French.

PASQUALE

Ouì papà, like you wish! I adapt!

MOTHER

If this Lavecchia wins! …

PASQUALE

Which "vecchia?" …

FATHER

The one who wants to destroy Quebec! If he wins, he'll give five thousand dollars to the French for every child they make! Understand? So, once you're married, get going! Don't waste any time!

PASQUALE

Don't you worry, papà! When we joke we joke, but when we have to huh, huh! … I … (*"you know"*) …

FATHER

Are we clear?!

PASQUALE

Yes, my lord!

FATHER

Don't call me Lord! There is only one lord! And he's up there! (*Pointing upwards*) I don't have hair on my tongue!

PASQUALE

Thank God!

FATHER

(*Sudden anger*) Look me straight in the eyes when I talk to you, fuck! …

PASQUALE

Sorry, papà …

FATHER

She lost her tongue.

PASQUALE

That I didn't know!

FATHER

Speak to her in Italian—shemonite![1]

PASQUALE

Ah! … that tongue! We'll find it again, don't you worry!

FATHER

On certain things, I don't blame the French! They know how to play politics, sure, but, they're right! … You don't mix wine with beer … or dogs with cats, if you know what I mean. Cats with cats, dogs with dogs. … As for you … Fortify her with all you know, show her by example. Don't be shy! Seed new cabbages, but don't pull out the old ones!

PASQUALE

Who's pulling them out!—Let them try!

FATHER

Quiet! … All these Italian kids, who don't want to know anything about Italian … They stink of shame! I'm talking about our race! … those who have betrayed their roots and smoke drugs! You understand, now?! … I've seen them with my own eyes … 'cause I travel around downtown for work! … A pick and shovel is what they deserve! Because they sleep on their parents' sacrifices! … All my father had to do was just look at me … one look, and I trembled with fear. … I mean for real! I trembled Jesus Christ! Today, there's no respect anymore! … If I was chief of police … "Off with the shoes and socks, let's go!" … And then, with a pair of pliers, I'd pull out their fucken toenails, one by one. Zang, zang, zang, zang … that blood would flow through the streets like in Caserta during the war! Zang, zang zang, Jesus Christ! … Then, bread and water, for a year— minimum! … No pity! Then, you'd see!

> Pause.

MOTHER

(*Drained by the story's impact*) It really takes luck in this world! (*Suddenly coming back to life*) Take the neighbour next door. He's got two kids. The boy's name is Pino.

FATHER

Ah, Pino! (*To Pasquale*) A Doctor!

MOTHER

I tell you, that boy is like a piece of fresh-baked bread!

FATHER

He doesn't dare smoke a cigarette in front of his father!

MOTHER

Always helping his mother with this or that! …

---

1. Shemonite from the Italian *scemonito* and *scemo* (idiot, stupid)

FATHER

His father calls him, he's right there! Always ready. Stops whatever he's doing ... even if he's taking a shit!—don't let me get graphic! ... He's free to do whatever he wants. He even has his own room, all to himself ...

MOTHER

And he's so *clean*! ... His mother told me that when he has to cut his toenails, nice and calm ...

FATHER

Listen, listen! ...

MOTHER

... he lays a handkerchief on the bed, and then, lays his feet on the handkerchief ... and clips!

FATHER

(*To Pasquale*) See how delicate! ...

MOTHER

(*To Pasquale*) Can you believe it?!

FATHER

A *Doctor*! ... His father comes home tired from work, he goes to get him the slippers ... but, without his father even asking him! He does this on his own ... like ... from his own idea.

MOTHER

A boy like that is worth a lot more than bread!

FATHER

And the parents treat him like this (*Hand extended with open palm*). With a son like that, of course a father can go to his grave in peace!

MOTHER

Actually, he also had his eyes on Linda!

FATHER

Shut up!

MOTHER

Why 'shut up?!' It's nothing! (*To Pasquale*) But then, rumours started flying around that he wasn't ... normal! ... too delicate ... maybe he didn't really like women ...

FATHER

A faggot! Just say it!

MOTHER

I refuse to believe it. He's a Doctor!

FATHER

(*To Pasquale*) I can see that you have your head screwed on straight! (*To Mother*) Look at him, just like his father! Jesus, what a worker in Germany! (*To Pasquale*) Don't hold yourself back because you have no schooling! Forget about Doctor or not a Doctor! School is good for you, but you earn a living with these, you see! (*Demonstrating his calloused hands*) Without these ... ("*you're fucked!*") ... You only need a strong will, and good health! ... He who has health is rich and doesn't know it. *Everything* is possible! ... (*Beat*) Remember ... I'm not a fool, I *play* the fool, but playing the fool, I make a fool out of *you*!

PASQUALE

Wuay papà, that's a good one. I gotta write that down!

FATHER

(*Deadly serious, with urgency*) Life is a decaying fucken corpse, Jesus Christ! If it can, it'll fuck you! without mercy! ... You need a strong liver and balls the size of bricks! ... When you walk, look straight ahead ... eyes straight, ears open. Don't trust anyone! Look straight ahead! Don't look down! The more you bend over, the more you expose your ass! Better your mouth closed, than your ass open! *A fucken corpse, this life*! Today it's up your ass ... and tomorrow *again*! ... Bo ... A man, once warned, is half saved! ... What are your plans?

PASQUALE

Wuay, Papà, I am seriously considering one of those big professions!

FATHER

Good, good! You gotta have will!

PASQUALE

Exactly!

FATHER

Hard work!

PASQUALE

Precisely!

FATHER

And luck!

PASQUALE

That's what *I* say!

FATHER

So, then?

PASQUALE

Wuay, papà, I wanna be an artist! (*Imitating an American movie gangster*) "Ey, yu, wisey gai!" I spent two months in Rome doing T.V. commercials. I specialized in the department of medicine!

MOTHER

What medicine?

PASQUALE

·A cream.

FATHER

For what?

PASQUALE

To apply ...

FATHER

Where?

PASQUALE

In the ass!

FATHER

(*Slaps him*) You're disgusting!

PASQUALE

It was a cream commercial for haemorrhoids! On RAI TV! But you see only the face ... and the cream next to the face, like this, see? ... They told me I had the right face for that kind of thing! The right kind of expression!

FATHER

But your mother told me you were interested in becoming a carpenter, or a mechanic.

PASQUALE

I thought it over!

FATHER

Think again! If not, we'll close the book, and that's all!

MOTHER

(*Short pause*) Let's just say that that kind of thing is not a normal profession for our kind of people.

FATHER

Profession? ***Profession***?! Where men are women, and women are men—if you know what I mean? ***Profession***?! ... One day they'll shove it up your ass, too, and no cream or Jesus Christ is gonna save you then! ... <u>Then</u> it'll be too late to run home to your parents crying with a swollen ass! So, think it over, *carefully*!

MOTHER

He'll think about it, don't worry! He's too tired now! After such a long trip, and without eating!

FATHER

See the staircase? If you're good, I'll finish it. That way, you and Linda, instead of living down here with us, you'll be *alone* in your *own* apartment *upstairs*! ... If you're good, you can even give me a hand ... (*Beat*) There's the crucifix, there's my wife! Witnesses! (*Emphatically*) All that was destined for my son, I will give to you ... everything everything everything ... May Jesus Christ make me find myself stiff dead in bed tomorrow morning if I lie! If you <u>want</u>, I'll even sign a paper in front of my wife and the crucifix! *Dead in bed* if I'm lying, Jesus Christ! ... But you gotta earn it, or else I'll cancel *everything*, including <u>you</u>. ... I will ***erase*** you, Jesus Christ on the cross! ... (*Beat*) Understood? Do good, forget it. Do evil, look out!

MOTHER

Okay, okay! ... I'll call Linda now, and we'll have a little glass of something! (*Calls out*) Linda!

> Enters Linda, stoned out of her mind, mascara running down her face, walking in a catatonic state towards Pasquale.

PASQUALE

My God! Who's this horror?!

FATHER

WHAT?! (*About to slap him!*)

PASQUALE

No, I meant this creature! This apparition!

MOTHER

This is the little princess! See how beautifully dressed she is? (*Pulling Linda by the hair back and forth. To Linda*) You demented idiot! ... You don't say anything?!! This is your husband!

PASQUALE

(*Kneeling before her*) Joy of my life! (*With an Italian accent*) Yu ar oll mai laif! Oui, oui!

A red liquid substance pours out of both corners of Linda's mouth. She drops to the floor.

Blackout.

Act 2, Scene 3: FATHER, MOTHER, DOCTOR PINO, LINDA

Father is pacing in downstairs 'living room.' Enters Doctor (Pino) from upstairs, followed by Mother.

FATHER
So, Doctor, any news?
MOTHER
What'd she say, Pino?
DOCTOR
Eh, signora, everything's okay. . . . Nothing serious . . . let her rest.
FATHER
All she does is rest, Dottò! Always in her room!
DOCTOR
Yes, but . . . leave her alone for now. . . . Go easy . . . bit by bit.
MOTHER
But it's already two days! . . . Go easy!
DOCTOR
Yeah, but . . . a bottle of Acqua Velva . . . small bottle of iodine! . . . Un mélange dangereux!
MOTHER
I don't know what the hell got into her head, Lord Jesus!! . . . And the thing we found. Did you ask her?
DOCTOR
Eh, signora Carmela . . . I don't want to lie to you, but it's not necessary to get upset.! That's not going to help anybody.
MOTHER
Of course, Dottò!
FATHER
That's why we called you!
MOTHER
To help her!
FATHER
(*Beat*) Heh! . . . ummm—Pino!
DOCTOR
(*Beat*) It's marijuana.
FATHER
<u>Mariana</u>, Jesus Christ!
DOCTOR
It's a dried leaf, of the hemp plant, an aromatic herb of Asian origin. It grows once a year in India, but now it's cultivated everywhere. For centuries, it has

been used in traditional medicine and recreationally. They also use the plant for making cloth, rope, like the ones you see on ships!

MOTHER

But is it drugs! … *yes*, or *no*?

DOCTOR

It goes by different names … bhang, cannabis, marijuana. … Yes, signora, it's a drug.
> *Mother and Father instantly erupt, each in their own way,*
> *walking aimlessly in different directions.*

FATHER

Jesus Mary, Mother of Jesus Christ, I'll make sure she doesn't see tomorrow morning!

MOTHER

(*Over "Mother of Jesus Christ"*) Oh, my God! A disaster! A disgrace!

FATHER

I'll gouge her eyes out, Jesus Christ! … and bury her in the garden!

MOTHER

(*Over "bury her"*) Our Lady of Carmine, look what's become of us! Shame and disgrace!

FATHER

(*Over "disgrace"*) **MARIANA**! Jesus Christ! … just like the ones I see downtown when I work nights!! That disgraceful shit!

MOTHER

(*Over "shit"*) Holy Mother of God in Heaven, help me! That selfish, pigheaded bitch! …

FATHER

Enough! … (*Beat*) So, what do you think, Pino? What's your advice?

MOTHER

… Did you ask her where she got it?

DOCTOR

Signora, you can find it everywhere. … It's normal today!

FATHER

Normal? You think it is **normal** for a daughter that age to still have no sense of judgment? … to drug herself like that? **Normal**?!

MOTHER

And when you ask her, "*what's wrong?*" she says *nothing*! We thought maybe she's sick, that she's got *something* or, I don't know—that she's not happy! … she never wants to eat, 'cause she has to lose weight! Seven or eight years ago she got fat like a vat—a tub she was so big. Then, she went on one of those crazy diets … and now, she doesn't wanna touch anything!

FATHER

Because she was busy drugging herself behind our back! **Mariana**! That's *exactly* what they take, those guys downtown! She was dieting on MARIANA!—How could she be hungry?!

MOTHER

But who could have imagined!

DOCTOR

Calm down! … I didn't mean 'normal' like it's a good thing. But, it's not *serious*. She won't die!

FATHER

Too bad! … Pino, please, stop talking for Christ's sake! Don't say another word … or I'm gonna tear all my hair out, **like this! You see?** … **You see how I'm gonna tear my hair out!** … (*As he pulls at his hair, and rag dolls his head in an attempt to get rid of it*)

MOTHER

You're gonna get hurt!

FATHER

(*Over "get hurt"*) That disgraceful liar has been a curse and torment —from day one! … 'Cause the way we raised her … the way we *nurtured* her, *cultivated* her … is this what we deserve? You tell me, Pino! Is this what we *deserve*? That evil, dishonourable, shameless, lying piece of shit!

MOTHER

But just the thought of it … how—where did she get the money?!

FATHER

Okay, Carmè, just stop, please! "Where did she get it?" … in your **purse** that you always leave lying around! Let's not talk about it anymore, Carmè, for the love of Mary, Mother of Jesus Christ! Or I'll bury *both* of you in the garden … damn all the fucken Saints in heaven!

DOCTOR

Signor Raffaele, calm down! …

FATHER

(*Over "Signor"*) I beg you, Pino, stop with the "signore." 'Cause if there was a god, he would have **done** something about this by now!

DOCTOR

I understand how you feel … but that's the first thing you should do … try to calm down! … It's obvious she's angry about something.

FATHER

That *too*? She's *angry*?!

DOCTOR

She's fragile. … You have to go easy on her.

FATHER

But who's going *hard*?! She has everything she wants! Her friends have shoes that are like *this*, okay let's buy them like *this* for her too. She wears them *once*, throws them away … "They're out of *style*!" Okay, let's buy her the ones that are in *style*, 'cause my kids have to follow the *fashion*! You know how many pairs of shoes— and *dresses* she has? Not even the Queen has that many! I even sent her to school, all the way to *grade eleven*!

MOTHER

Look, Pino, there are other daughters, who have had *less*, and listen *more*! 'Cause, it's true, the more you give them, the worse they become!

Pause.

DOCTOR

That bruise over the eye … the blow …

FATHER

I told you! She fell like that—batababum, all of a sudden! Nobody touched her!

MOTHER

Yeah, all by herself.

FATHER

Heh! Drugged as she was! ...

DOCTOR

Here. These should be taken twice, or even three times a day ... you see what's best.

FATHER

'What's best!" You're the Doctor. I know what's best, I don't call you! (*Doctor hands him the prescription*) ... And what are these?

DOCTOR

It's a kind of tranquillizer. Helps one sleep.

FATHER

Okay, but I don't know anything about these things! Did you explain to her when she's supposed to take them! ... Before or after eating? ... Did you tell her?

DOCTOR

These are for *you*! ... For her—just rest. ... Okay, call me if there's anything else. If necessary, I could give you stronger pills. (*He begins to leave*)

FATHER

But, Pino, did you at least tell her, ... "**Why** these drugs?!" Why do you have to make your parents *suffer* like this ... especially her mother with the blood pressure. What does she need? Did you tell her?

MOTHER

Raffaè, he has to go now! You can ask her that yourself, later.

DOCTOR

Yes, please excuse me, but my mother puts the pasta on at exactly seven o'clock. Actually, by seven the pasta is already on the table. It's *ten* to seven ... and it takes seven / eight minutes for it to cook. ... Then, it depends which pasta ... if it's De Cecco, it takes a minute longer to cook, so if I leave now, I'll get there right on time, ready to eat at seven o'clock sharp! Then, if it's egg noodles I'm late already—'cause that one cooks in two minutes!

FATHER

Okay Pino, thank you. (*Pulling out some bills from his wallet*) How much do I owe you?

DOCTOR

No, don't worry. Nothing!

FATHER

What, 'nothing'? If I go to the shoemaker, he's gonna give me a pair of shoes for free? So, then?!

DOCTOR

Yes, but, no, it's my pleasure. Really!

FATHER

Don't make me angry—fuck! Here's the money! What do I owe you, and that's all! (*He throws a fifty-dollar bill on the floor*)

MOTHER

If he told you *no* it means *no*, *no*?

FATHER

I'm *talking*! ... Listen to me, Pino! Money is on everybody's lips, but in nobody's pockets! So, when you're owed, don't refuse it, 'cause money has wings.

DOCTOR

A friend in a piazza is worth more than a pocket full of money.

FATHER

No, no, listen to *me*! With friends and godfathers always speak your mind! A clear understanding makes for a better/longer friendship ... (*Trying not to fall apart*) Debts, you pay, sins, you cry—Holy Mary Mother of God!

DOCTOR

Good night!

FATHER

Okay, Pino, thank you! We'll settle the account later!

MOTHER

Good night, Pino, my best to your mother!

FATHER

And I'll call your father when it's time to make the wine, *okay*?

DOCTOR

Good night. (*About to exit*)

FATHER

Heh! Pino, please! ... About this, not a word ... to NO ONE! I beg you! ... pretend that ... understand? You're a tomb!

DOCTOR

A tomb.

FATHER

A ***tomb***, Jesus Christ! 'Cause if people find out ... they're gonna have to lock me up! Understand?

DOCTOR

No need to worry! Good night. (*He exits*)

FATHER

(*Follows Pino out the door*) Go, go! The pasta is already on the table! (*Short pause. Father comes back in, closes the door. To Mother*) That's a son! ... Only mine ...

MOTHER

My God!

FATHER

Did I not tell you?! ... she's sick in here! (*Pointing to his head*)

MOTHER

We can't go on like this! ... What are we gonna do?!

FATHER

You tell me! 'Cause I'll send her to the nut house! ... And I told you a thousand times ... "Pay attention to what your daughter does!" And you ... Leave her alone, she's in her room! READING! ... "Please Carmè, help her, advise her! ... I beg you, Carmè, guide her—every minute, because one day she's gonna have to be able to manage a home, a kitchen ... even better than her mother!"

MOTHER

Okay, I get it! It's always my fault!

FATHER

Why, it's <u>mine</u>?! Always after her, instructing her, to be careful!... My mother, bless her soul, raised <u>ten</u> children <u>without</u> a husband, and they walked a straight line! All of them!

MOTHER

Listen! Do me a *fucken* favor! Leave your mother in peace where she is! Stop throwing her name in my face all the time. ... Your mother <u>this</u>, your mother *that*! ...

FATHER

It's **<u>her</u>** loss!

MOTHER

We know, I **_know_**! Don't you see what she's become?! A ghost! We'll pretend she's dead, and that's it!

FATHER

Never mind! If she's hungry she'll eat! She won't die! No one had to beg us to eat.

MOTHER

Children are the <u>ruin</u>! We weren't made to have kids! They're the RUIN!

FATHER

Never **_mind_**! ... the worst is yet to come!

> *Doorbell rings.*

FATHER

(*Beat*) Look in the window <u>first</u>!

MOTHER

(*At the window, stunned*) It's a black woman. See for yourself!

FATHER

Black? ... I wonder what the fuck she wants. (*Goes towards the door, stops*) ... I get it!

MOTHER

Go talk to her!

FATHER

Call your daughter!

MOTHER

But she can hardly get up! ... <u>You</u> talk to her! If it's for the apartment, tell her no! And that's it!

FATHER

Carmè! ... Why don't <u>you</u> go talk to her, then?!

MOTHER

(*Short-tempered*) You don't have to get angry! (*Beat*) SIGNORINA!

> *Doorbell rings again.*

FATHER

Get away from the window, she'll see you!

MOTHER

LINDA! (*To Father*) Ma, can't you tell her it's rented, and that's all!

FATHER

Call your daughter, goddam it! ...

MOTHER

... LINDA!

> *Linda enters slowly, languidly, almost somnolent, but*
> *methodically, sporting a black eye. She is high.*

MOTHER
THREE TIMES I called you! DRUG ADDICT!

FATHER
(*To Linda, calmly*) There is a woman at the door. See what she wants. If it's for the apartment, tell her 'no messì, it was just rented today.'
> *Linda goes out the door, in her nightgown.*

MOTHER
In her *nightgown*?!

FATHER
Quiet!
> *Pause. Linda enters.*

LINDA
She's black!

FATHER
Okay, we know she's black!

LINDA
She wants to know how much for the apartment.

MOTHER
(*Loud whisper, baffled*) He told you to tell her it's already rented!

LINDA
(*Beat*) She wants to know how much!

FATHER
(*Beat*) Okay, tell her it's eight hundred dollars a month!

LINDA
Eight hundred dollars?!

FATHER
Eight hundred dollars, I said! ... If she wants it, that's the price!
> *Linda goes out again.*

MOTHER
Are you crazy or what? You just told her it's rented!

FATHER
Do me a favour, keep quiet—let me handle it! It's _my_ business! ... Who's gonna take it for eight hundred dollars?
> *Pause. Linda enters. Shuts the door.*

FATHER
What'd she say?

LINDA
(*Beat*) Nothing. She left.

FATHER
Good! ... 'cause these people ... I wouldn't rent it to them even for a thousand dollars in cash! In two days, they'll turn an apartment into a pigsty! (*Linda is about to go upstairs. To Linda*) Where you going?!

LINDA
Read!

MOTHER
Look at that face, look!

FATHER

Tell me ... In God's name ... what kind of idea did you get in that head of yours!

LINDA

Me, nothing.

FATHER

When I look at you ... I see the <u>devil</u>! (*Linda doesn't answer. Pause*) Nothing?! You want to play it that way? (*Pause*) **Do you not even have one ounce of shame at thirty fucken years of wasted life?!**

MOTHER

(*Beat*) Yes, or No! (*No answer*) Ma what ... she won't answer! ... now she's on drugs! ... Isn't it *true*?! Drug addict?! Because you have the face of a devil for real! Ugly witch!

FATHER

(*Reasoning*) Did someone turn your head around, or what? ... Always in your room talking to yourself? ...

MOTHER

Like an idiot—a lunatic!

FATHER

(*To Mother*) ... *I'm* talking! (*Pause. To Linda. Calmly*) Are you doing it on purpose, or what?

MOTHER

Yeah, yeah, she won't answer!

FATHER

I'm talking, I said! (*To Linda*) I want you to explain to me why you did what you did! ... **Why**? ... <u>Where did you get the</u> drugs? Look at me in the eyes! ... Look me straight in the eyes when I'm talking to you, 'cause I'm talking to you with blood in my eyes! (*Pause*) I'm gonna bury you in the garden! I told your mother!

LINDA

It's not my fault!

MOTHER

What? It's **our** fault? (*To Father*) Hear that?! The nerve! (*To Linda*) I'll pull your eyes out!

LINDA

My things are <u>mine</u>! No one told you to go through my personal things.

FATHER

You want me to smash the other eye?! ... *Personal*? ... There is no such thing as "personal" in this house! <u>Everyone</u> has to know <u>everything</u>! 'Cause I'll smash your other eye in a second! ... then I'll chop your head off and suck out all that poisonous blood of yours!

MOTHER

That's it! You will never set foot outside of this house ever again!! May they cut off my arms!

LINDA

Where did I get to go before?

FATHER

And where do you have to <u>go</u>? See what you did without going out! Imagine!

MOTHER
    ... and you get a <u>job</u>! ... Even in a factory! ... I don't give a shit! Others do it!

LINDA
    That's what you think.

FATHER
    You are finished with school! That's <u>final</u>! You've already had too much! Go bust your ass and sweat for your meals like everybody else!

LINDA
    I told you!

MOTHER
    No, she didn't understand! ... She pretends she can't hear! Drugs are nice, huh?

LINDA
    I already applied ... I was accepted. ... I said yes.

FATHER
    You shameless, selfish delinquent!—is that what you think?! Mother of Christ, she really wants to destroy me! I swear, I'll eat your <u>intestines</u>!

MOTHER
    (*To Linda*) You got some nerve!

LINDA
    You have the money.

FATHER
    The money's always been there ... for one who listens to her parents. Yesterday, you said goodbye to thirty thousand dollars ... and don't think it's over yet!

LINDA
    For me it is.

FATHER
    Thirty thousand dollars to the wind! According to you ... you made a great impression on Pasquale? Pray to God he doesn't go spreading the word all over Italy <u>and</u> Montreal! ... I gotta be laughed at, now?!

LINDA
    (*Beat*) I'm not ruining my life for a work permit!

FATHER
    That's not *ruining* life? It's <u>giving</u> life! Giving someone an opportunity! Why, didn't <u>we all</u> do it?! Your uncles?! ... That's life when times are hard!

LINDA
    Times are not hard!

FATHER
    Not for you! 'Cause you never saw war! ... All those years going to weddings ... why did I go? Tell me, **WHY**? ... To dance? ... To enjoy myself? No! I went for you!—and your brother! ... For your <u>future</u>!! That's why I went!
        Linda laughs.

MOTHER
    My God, she's laughing! ...

FATHER
    Your brother already lost his chance!—and share! ... and all the money I brought, wedding after—*year* after year! ... and now, <u>*you*</u>, you want to do the same thing?!

Before I throw away another thirty thousand dollars, I'll make sure to get myself locked up!—for life!

LINDA

No one told you to bring money. You had a choice!

MOTHER

It's our <u>duty</u>! Just like it's <u>their</u> duty now to bring it to you!

LINDA

When I'm dead, yeah.

FATHER

And <u>death</u> is exactly what you're gonna see!

LINDA

I know hell … death can't be worse! And if I have to choose <u>death</u> … I prefer the one without a husband! (*Pause*) No problem, I can earn my own money. … Besides … selling my ass to Pasquale or a stranger is the same. At least a stranger pays <u>better</u>. … and I don't have to spend the rest of my life with him!

> Pause.

FATHER

Starting today …

LINDA

(*Mimicking Father*) Starting today …

FATHER

(*Brief pause*) … like your mother said …

LINDA

(*Mimicking*) … like your mother said …

FATHER

(*Beat*) No more going out! …

LINDA

(*Mimicking*) … no more going out …

FATHER

(*Raising volume and tone*) You hand over your house keys to your mother right now!! … If you <u>have</u> to go out … you go with your <u>mother</u>, or with <u>me</u>! Choice? Did you learn that word in school? In <u>books</u>? **Choice**?

LINDA

I wish I had never <u>met</u> books! … They've been nothing but a curse, my great misfortune … <u>traitors</u>, every fucking one of them! … But, my <u>first</u> misfortune … the <u>really</u> <u>big</u> one … was being born a woman in this sick, cursed, piece of shit fucken family!

FATHER

(*Beat*) You haven't seen famine!

LINDA

And no life either! (*She's about to exit*)

FATHER

I haven't finished! … God help you if I catch you reading or playing music in your room. (*Turning to mother*) I'm saying this to you too! (*To Linda*) Actually, the record player, starting today, locked up in the storage! The books, you give them to your mother! Tomorrow, I'll burn them all! … I'll also put a lock on the door. If you have to go to the toilet ... call ... your mother will take you! From now on, you don't eat with us! In your room. Alone! In the dark! And if you push me you will eat and sleep in the closet ... standing up! If you eat, you eat, if you don't ... (*Beat*) Go stare at those four walls ... and rethink your plans! The date is fixed. The <u>choice</u> is yours. ... You can enter the Church two ways ... with a husband, or in a casket! You understand me?

> *Linda stares at him, and smiles.*

MOTHER

Look how stubborn she is! (*Mother pulls Linda by the hair*) Your father asked you if you understand! **Drug addict**! ... and take that smile off your face!

FATHER

Never on the head, I said!

MOTHER

Did you understand?

LINDA

Yes.

> *Linda stares for a moment at Father, smiles, then exits. Door slams. Pause.*

FATHER

(*To Mother*) Open the radio, the news is on!

> *Blackout.*

ACT THREE

Act 3, Scene 1: MOTHER, ROSINA, FATHER

MOTHER

Come in, come in ... don't let anybody see you!

ROSINA

What happened? Is the world coming to an end?

MOTHER

Dear Lord Jesus, I don't even wanna talk about it, you can't imagine! 'The devil has found his way to my house, and *misfortune* is now my godmother!' ... (*Giving her a small photo*) Here!

ROSINA

Who is it?

MOTHER

Filth, shit, trouble, ruin, and more ruin! A plague! You tell me!

ROSINA

I don't recognize him. A relative he's not, for sure! ... He's black!

MOTHER

(*Loud whisper*) Quite!, don't let anybody hear! (*takes photo back*) ... I found it in her purse! There were others ... I don't even want to think about it but I can't get them out of my head! A fucken disaster!

ROSINA
Raffaè?
MOTHER
Are you crazy?! ... We'd be in the papers already! I don't know what to do ...
That disgraceful, inconsiderate shit with no conscience! *__May she die__*! Rosì, my
little sister, you gotta help me! Put yourself in my place, and give me advice ...
'cause if her father finds out ... he'll cut her to pieces! ... My dear little sister!
<u>Guide</u> me!
ROSINA
What advice can I give you?! ... When there's a feast, there are no sisters and
godmothers. In a disaster, we are all sisters and godmothers.
MOTHER
Finished? That's it? That's all you have to say? Let's leave it to chance, and good
night?! (*She looks at photo*) Dear Jesus, look at that face! ... Like seeing *the devil*
himself!
ROSINA
(*Beat. Speak-singing*) Love poisons where it bites, and no one can spare you!
MOTHER
That's your advice? ... It's a <u>death</u> sentence! Please Rosì ... You shouldn't laugh
at the poor and the damned! ... What's <u>*love*</u> got to do with this? This is a *sickness*
in her head! ...
ROSINA
(*Speak-singing*) It's her fucken business, not yours! ... (*Back to her speaking voice*)
Carmè! Don't try to get any fat from a little chick, you'll starve!
MOTHER
You call this a little <u>chick</u>?! ... There is enough fat here to fry us all! (*To herself*)
My luck! ... Other daughters fall in love with doctors, accountants, ministers
and councillors! Mine falls in love with a fucken black! Of all the colours, she
had to pick this one! ... And if you saw the other pictures I found! I can't even
("*think about it ...*") ... I get a pain right here in my stomach! Dear Jesus, Mother
of God, how much more can I endure?! ... I feel the urge to curse all the Saints
in Heaven!
ROSINA
Wuay Carmè! She fell in love! Rejoice! Who experienced love in our days? Black
or white, what do you care?! Even in Cosenza now, Moroccans, Blacks, Asians.
... Those who fall in love with teeth and hair, fall in love with nothing!
MOTHER
If it was just a matter of teeth and hair it would be nothing! '*__Husbands and
cattle from your own town__*,' the saying goes!
ROSINA
When? Before Christ? ... And where did it get us?
MOTHER
(*Her mind is spinning out of control*) You imagine if someone saw her doing something
with that man?
ROSINA
What? Should she have done it with a <u>woman</u>?

MOTHER

You know what? … YES, it would have been better if she'd kissed a woman—or even a dog, or a monkey—or any other animal other than this one! YES!

ROSINA

Your daughter, whatever she does, she does it, and will go on doing it for herself! What?! She should pay attention to you? Ma, mind your own fucken business, 'cause sooner or later <u>that's</u> what's gonna nail you to your cross! 'Cause those who don't mind their own fucken business are just chasing after disaster with a lantern! And those who fight for their honour, only win shame!

MOTHER

You wanna see me dead? … She's gotta get married this winter with Pasqualino from Carolei!! I already made her a wedding dress. … White! And she's out there like a whore! …

ROSINA

(*Brief pause*) Ah … these men deserve to be killed. No matter which way you turn, they manage to stick it up your ass!

MOTHER

Don't start, Rosì! I'm begging you! Men, men! … On certain things I agree with you, but on this—for all the Saints in fucking heaven, don't make me curse, now, NO! … If you only knew what we found in her room, you wouldn't talk like that! DRUGS! Quiet! … In her dirty underwear, of all places! So don't say *men*! Never in my life! Never! I never heard anybody do such a thing, not even the French! and you know how they are! … Her father is right … the more you give them … the more they take advantage of you. … May God cut my hands off if that bitch ever leaves that room! My hands off!

ROSINA

You can turn and flip it any way you want, but the problem is always one! Your husband! Your husband is your husband, and there's 'nothing' you can do about it!

MOTHER

But how the fuck do you reason, Rosì? 'Cause now you're really making me fucken angry! What's my husband got to do with it?! I'm talking about that disgraceful shit!

ROSINA

You're afraid of <u>him</u>! You don't care about your <u>daughter</u>! And you care even less about <u>yourself</u>! … You don't know how to make him respect you!

MOTHER

Me? … I don't … no, no! You're not making any sense!—Ok, LOOK, I don't want to talk about this! 'Cause if it's a question of husbands, I'm sorry, but I'd choose mine over yours any day!

ROSINA

Keep him! I've already cured mine!

MOTHER

<u>What</u> did you cure? ***What***?!

ROSINA

Filippo was sick! Thirty years! Now he's cured! Thank God! I gave him a purgative! … (*Beat*) Heh dear sister, my problems are huge … and yours … a walk in the park.

MOTHER

(*Curious*) What did he have?

ROSINA

Stones. (*Beat*) In the head! And I shook them off! ... I took one of his belts, and I beat him black and blue! On the head, the spine, the ribs, the arms, but mostly on the legs!

MOTHER

Oh, my God, my heart just stopped! And he let you, without breaking your head?

ROSINA

My son was there, for protection! ... He called his father to the kitchen and told him, very politely, "Mother wants to talk to you! If you touch her, I will kill you." I went downstairs, and ventilated my anger! ... What a joy! I beat him until there was nothing left to beat! He even started to cry—in front of his son! "Cry, cry ... you know how many tears you have to shed to catch up to what I went through?!" ... His suitcase nicely packed and ready ... and out!

MOTHER

Oh, my God! Don't let Raffaele hear! ... Dear Mother of Heaven! No, no! You go too far, dear sister! ... *You* should have married my husband, that way you'd have killed each other! ... (*Beat*) Where is he now? ... Where did he go?

ROSINA

Who knows! Who gives a fuck! ... He couldn't have gotten too far! His legs were so swollen that ... (*she laughs*) When it comes to horses, cards, bars, friends, and girlfriends—he's great! ... With his wife! ...

MOTHER

You laugh? He who laughs on Friday, cries on Saturday, dear sister!

ROSINA

Thirty years! ... (*Beat*) And everybody knew! ... He even brought them home! When we first arrived ... in Sudbury, where did he take them? ... to the house ... almost every night ... and he'd tell them I was the cleaning woman. ... I didn't speak any English ... and, if I said anything, he'd beat me and punch me., I mean! ... (*Beat*) We were alone, no relatives, no friends, who are you gonna talk to?, always in the house ... you were still in Italy ... so I kept my mouth shut! ... Me in the kitchen, and them in the bedroom! ... It takes nerve! ... Thirty years! I endured it all! Not a day went by that I didn't have his dinner ready on time! You know how many dinners I cooked that he didn't come home for?! And when he did eat, I'd have to run after him, to wipe the sauce off his mouth! ... 'cause he had to hurry back to play cards with his friends! Play cards! ...

MOTHER

(*Stunned*) Dear God in heaven!

ROSINA

... (*Beat*) When my son was born, I said to myself, if there is a God, he'll pay for all of it one day! ... After thirty years, your ovaries explode! ... Understand? And then your little boy becomes a man of conscience ... (*Beat*) That's why, dear sister ... listen to me ... 'cause you don't find a sister on every street corner!

MOTHER

... (*Beat*) Ma what do you think? That all husbands are like yours?! I can't even get Raffaele to go out of the house! He's worse than a woman! Washes dishes, windows! He changed more diapers than I ever did! You know that?! Every year he hangs the Christmas lights outside! He's worse than a woman that way! He never let his children go without shoes! What the fuck do I have to complain about?

ROSINA

Great! Let Christmas lights and clean diapers enchant you to your grave! ... Not all red things are cherries! (*Beat. Concerned. Firm*) Where is Linda?! ... Where is your ***daughter***?!

MOTHER

(*Righteous*) Where she <u>should</u> be. And <u>that's</u> where she's staying! ...

ROSINA

(*With urgency, but measured*) Dear sister ... for the blind there's no daylight.

MOTHER

(*Trying to hold it together*) Listen, LISTEN TO ME! ... Quiet! There are women who can't even put on lipstick! ... or paint their nails! You understand? (*Reprovingly*) ... My husband never laid a hand on me ... and he doesn't go losing his money in bars—or touching other people's wives!

ROSINA

Calabrians and mules never piss alone! They're all cut from the same cloth, Carmè! Men—by *nature*—chase after tits and asses! Get over it!

MOTHER

(*Horrified*) What are you trying to tell me?!

ROSINA

That if *horns* were trees, the world would be a *forest*! And unfortunate are those who seek doctors and justice! ... The safest wound is to not cut yourself!

MOTHER

(*Fighting to keep from breaking down*) Listen, Rosì! You do what the fuck you want! But leave me alone! ... don't make things worse for me ... 'cause here, there's no shortage of troubles. ... I mean, ***what have we come to, GOD!!*** ... Please, Rosì, go, go! ... I want you to go! ... Thanks for the advice, but go! 'Cause if my husband finds you here, God help us! He has enough bugs in his head! And he always says that you put ideas in my head! So please, if you care about me, go now! Go! Go break your husband's head, go! Break even his horns! Whatever you want! Burn down the whole world if you want! But go! Jesus Christ will be the judge!

ROSINA

(*Beat*) Those who 'hope' die in shit, dear sister!

        Enters Father, doesn't notice Rosina.

FATHER

(*Slamming the door*) I'll show you, "MUUZIT 'TALIEN"[1] ... those bastards! ... She lost the fucken cat! ***What do I know?!*** I didn't <u>touch</u> the cat! Get out of my face! ... You don't want to pay two months?! I'll show you! ... Registered letter and RAUS! ... You like going to Florida every year? Then VA SCIENNE, CAVALISSE! ... PAY! ... I never take holidays! I've never been to a pic-que-ni-que! My balcony is good enough for me! ... But I own a <u>house</u>! "MUUZIT TALIEN" to me? Fuck you! I pay taxes! ... I'll fix them! They leave us the fridge and stove,

---

1. "Muuzit 'Talien" equals "maudit Italiens," which means "Damn Italians."

and MANGIÈ' LA MERDA! 'Cause I'm capable of renting it even to a Black, if I have to! Get out of my sight!

> *Father notices Rosina. Pause.*

FATHER
When the rooster is away, the chickens …

ROSINA
(*To no one in particular*) Okay, I'm gonna go now! (*Lingering*) Let that girl go out once in a while, I never see her! Fresh air is good for you!

FATHER
Cold air goes to the head!

ROSINA
(*Beat*) When the *end* is near, there is no point in saving!

> *She exits.*

FATHER
Always has to take a shot! (*Mother exits to kitchen*) What'd the gargoyle want?

MOTHER
(*Offstage*) Oh, do you always have to have your nose in everything?! … Women's stuff!

FATHER
Where's the little princess? (*Beat*) Where's your daughter!

> *Phone rings.*

MOTHER
Where you left her!

FATHER
(*Beat*) And keep her there!

> *Phone rings.*
> *Phone rings.*

FATHER
The phone! (*Phone rings. Pause*) Somebody get that phone! (*Phone rings*) Does anyone hear the phone?! (*Phone rings*) Okay, forget it, I'll answer it! (*Clears his throat, answers the phone*) Alò … Chi vulè vu? … Quà? … Ahh, Filomena! … Yeah … Uh-huh … Uh-huh …

> *Blackout.*

Act 3, Scene 2: MOTHER, FATHER, LINDA, SON

> *Mother and Father in the basement 'living room,' waiting. The room is dark except for a small amount of light cast by the television screen that illuminates their faces. The volume has been completely turned down. It's three in the morning.*

FATHER
(*Sottovoce*) She came back. … saw that her window was closed … all the lights closed …

MOTHER
Three o'clock! … not even criminals are out at this hour!

FATHER
    ... then she tried to open the door. But I put the lock on, two chains, and the broom ... (*Beat*) She's gotta ring for sure!

MOTHER
    You think she *cares*! She'll use the excuse that we locked the door! ... I mean, just *thinking* about it ... that Filomena the Chatterbox should have *seen her*, of all people! ... she's got such a mouth! ...

FATHER
    Filomena told me that he kept insisting, wanted a kiss ... and she ... just let herself go! And people stood there and watched ... shocked! ... "An Italian girl with one of those!" (*Beat*) I see malediction. (*Beat*) I see blood!

MOTHER
    He must have drugged her! ... You see how they are on TV. ... Gave her a cigarette ... and she ... without being aware of it ... then, she got hooked ... with *him* and with the *drugs*!

FATHER
    Quiet! Maybe it's her!

            In the distance, faint footsteps.

MOTHER
    (*Beat*) No ... it's the one next door over here. This is her normal hour ... she works at the club over there ... Langelier, where they have those naked women. ... No ... she by now ... for certain ... by *now* ...

FATHER
    Quiet! (*A cat meows in the distance*) The cat of *the slut*! See how they come back when they're hungry. Quie ...

MOTHER
    The door is locked!

FATHER
    (*Beat, sottovoce*) I removed the locks ... left only the broom. ... Look out the window. Don't open the curtain! ...

MOTHER
    Can't see anyone.

FATHER
    Then, it's her! Hurry! Go to the kitchen ... pretend you're crying! ... (*Loud sottovoce*) Let's go, *pretend*!

MOTHER
    I haven't cried enough?! ... I even have to *pretend*, now?

FATHER
    (*Loud sottovoce*) Go, I said!

            Doorbell rings. Mother exits to the kitchen. Father goes upstairs.
            Pause. The front door opens, slowly. The broom leaning against
            the door on the inside falls to the floor.

LINDA
    (*To herself, sottovoce*) Shit!

            Linda removes her shoes. Closes the door. Tiptoes towards the
            kitchen. Stops. Mother is heard crying. Her weeping gets

progressively louder as her fake whimper turns to real tears, then to a wail, as if she were at a funeral.

MOTHER
      (Offstage)

Oi Dio mio, I can't take it anymore!

Oi Gesù mio, what a nightmare! A disaster!

Oi Dio mio, I'm gonna kill myself, I'm gonna poison myself! That's what I'm gonna do!

Oi Dio mio, why didn't you make her die when she was born!

You cursed me with my own blood!

THE SHAME! I'm finished … My life is over!. **It's over dear God**!

      Lights up. Father is standing on the top landing.

FATHER
(With calculated restraint) Where were you?

LINDA
(Short pause) Out.

MOTHER
(Offstage) Is she *back*?!, My *nightmare*?! …

FATHER
(Same restrained tone) Where were you?

MOTHER
… *(Offstage)* 'Cause from the day the disgraceful bitch was *born*, I haven't seen *one* day of *peace*! I told him I didn't want any more children!

FATHER
(Same restrained tone) I am asking you calmly … where were you? … I'm not gonna hit you.

LINDA
(Short pause) Out.

MOTHER
(Enters, and darts towards Linda) Waste-of-life! Nightmare! Disease! … Do you know what time it is?!

FATHER
(Relatively calm and restrained, with a warning) I'm talking, Carmè! *(To Linda)* So this is the life you chose? … I say, NO … and you say YES! … *(Controlled explosion)* WHO GAVE YOU PERMISSION?!

LINDA
(Beat) I don't need permission!

MOTHER
… Phoning everywhere! … nobody knows anything! … Waiting and waiting! … Worrying, that maybe she's dead! … *(Suddenly spewing 'venom')* I wish you *had* been dead, that way I could live a day longer! … But HER?! … she already forgot about her mother!

FATHER
(Calm and restrained, with a warning) Carmè! *(To Linda)* You think it's great … what you're doing to your mother? … putting her through this hell?

MOTHER
If there's a God, he'll make you pay for *all of it!!* … *Everything*! … Yes, YOU!

FATHER

Mother of God, Carmè! How many people have to talk?! ONE or two? 'Cause If you had spoken from day one, I wouldn't be in this nightmare today! (*Father unbuckles his belt. To Linda*) What were you doing in the park at Viau and Jean Talon?

       Pause.

MOTHER

Look at that face! ... (*Beat*) We know **everything**! ... We got a call from Filomena the Gazette! She saw you!

LINDA

I told you, I was out. Alone.

MOTHER

... Liar!

FATHER

(*Beat*) Swear on the *crucifix*!

LINDA

(*Makes the sign of the cross, mechnically*) I swear!

MOTHER

Oh My God, look at the *liar*!

FATHER

Careful, it's a _sin_! (*Beat*) *Swear* on the *crucifix*, "That I should never see another tomorrow if I'm lying!!" Go on, swear!

LINDA

(*She kneels, making the sign of the cross, mechanically*) That I should never see another tomorrow if I'm lying!

MOTHER

My God, what a LIAR!

FATHER

I said, _careful_, 'cause Jesus-Christ-on-the-cross is gonna make you die for real!

LINDA

You believe in that?

FATHER

I believe in the almighty God the Father, creator of heaven and earth, and in Jesus Christ, his only Son, our Lord, who didn't make you die when you were born! Tell me the truth! I already know the truth, but I wanna hear it from you!

LINDA

(*She stands up*) It's none of your fucken business!

MOTHER

My God! ... What're you waiting for?! **_Hit her_**!

FATHER

Carmè! I'm gonna make the two of you disappear from the face of the earth tonight—and lock myself up! So stop talking! (*Pause. To Linda*) I want to know everything! Where you went? With who? And why?

MOTHER

Drug-addict whore!

FATHER

... Where <u>were</u> you till now, when even the clubs are closed? ... **EVERYTHING**! Now! ... Confess ... or make the sign of cross!

LINDA

If you touch me ...

FATHER

Touch you? ... Tonight I'll baptise you again! Tonight is your feast! Tonight we dance! We'll do the tarantella! ... Carmè, put the music on.

MOTHER

Now we're gonna play records?—at this hour?!

FATHER

Put the music on! ... or I'll make _both_ of you 'dance!' (_to Linda_) And don't make me waste time ... 'cause in three hours I have to go bust my ass in ditches and _sewers_ to feed you animals. ... D'you know where home is, YES, or NO? Do you know what _family_ means?

LINDA

I read the meaning in the dictionary, in books.

FATHER

Last time!

LINDA

Listen! I did nothing worse than what you did at my age ... and nothing better!

MOTHER

Oh my _God_, I'm going to have a paralysis! She even admits it, **even admits it**! ... You disgraceful!—_wait_! ... wait till you have children! Then, you'll see! Then, you'll learn!

LINDA

Me, _children_? ... (_"Sorry"_) Only by mistake! And I'd kill them!—instead of letting them see this world!

MOTHER

That was my wish, too! But I learned to live with my _mistakes_! And so will you!

LINDA

You're wrong! ... I _erase_ my mistakes! Trust me! I already did it once! ... (_Beat_) Yeah, I did it! And I did it willingly! ...(_Matter-of-factly, detached throughout, yet calculated_) I would have liked to have seen it being born ... if it was a boy or a girl ... just to _see_ it ... that way I could have killed it with my own hands ... slowly ... _suffocate_ it ... to see it dead with my own eyes! And to have another one and do the same thing ... squeeze every single _one_—empty out my _insides_ until there was nothing left and _no more_ could be born! ... But I couldn't wait! ... I couldn't risk seeing it! (_To Father_) I was afraid that it would look like you! ... And if that were true, it would have suffered a worse death! ... But it didn't deserve what I could do to it! (_Pause, smiling/crying_) I chose the least cruel way. It had to die! That's why I had it.

FATHER

(_Pause_) Who gave you permission?

LINDA

(_Beating her chest, then her head, repeatedly_) Me! Me! Me! Me! Me! Me! Me! Me! Me! Me!

MOTHER

Dear God! _look_ at her! ... what she's _become_!

LINDA

Why, you give a fuck?! ... what happens to me?! ... And I don't give a fuck either! It's my fucken business! ... And I'm so happy to know that this hurts you more than it hurts me! ... (*Pumps herself up to snap out of her emotions*) Cause I'm fucking *hard*! That's right! (*To Father*) Hit me! ... C'mon, Hit me! What? You don't have the courage? ... Pretend you're slaughtering a pig! It's the same thing for you ... It's the only thing you know how to do ...

MOTHER

(*To Father*) What are you waiting for? ... Pluck her eyes out!

LINDA

(*Laughing*) Oh, ma! ... (*Mimicking mom exaggeratedly*) "Pluck her eyes out!" ... (*Beat*) You're so ugly! ... cruelty suits you! (*To Father*) What, you need help? (*Intentionally provoking him*) ... Ignorant bastard! ... Go ahead, kill me! ... In here though ... you'll never touch me! ... In here, I'll always hate you! (*She smiles*)
> *Father strikes her with the belt.*

FATHER

Whose daughter are you? What devil conceived you?

MOTHER

Why did you come back! Why?!

LINDA

(*Controlling her emotions*) Where should I go? ... ('*Smiling*') The devil I know is better than the one I don't know!

FATHER

The devil **here?!** ...

LINDA

... Maybe I came to *talk*. Just <u>that</u>. ... ('*Smiling*')

FATHER

Don't get close, Carmè. 'Cause now she's nice and drugged, you never know ... maybe she could be hiding something somewhere!

MOTHER

(*Suddenly cautious, even scared*) You think so? How do you know?

FATHER

You can see it in her eyes! ... That's not your daughter!

MOTHER

Who is it, then? What is she?

FATHER

A beast! A wild cat! ... A demon! ... You see how the eyes shine with that light?!
> *Linda immediately embodies and acts out the cat/demon/beast image!*

LINDA

Musica!

> MUSIC: *Calabrian Tarantella. Fades in.*
> *As the cat/demon/beast, Linda dances the tarantella throughout*
> *the following action. She knocks over things (intentionally), and*
> *gradually, methodically, wrecks the place, all the while staring*
> *Father down, as she circles around him and he backs off. Then,*
> *with one motion of her arm she sweeps off the photos of dead*

ancestors that make up the shrine on the mantelpiece. Mother is horrified and quickly tries to salvage the pieces! Linda then takes down her parents' wedding portrait from the wall, smashes glass and frame. The Tarantella MUSIC STOPS suddenly. Linda removes the wedding photo from frame, and scratches it slowly, deliberately, "meowing" and "hissing" sottovoce.

MOTHER

My God, look! ... The only picture we have!

LINDA

(Genuinely concerned) Don't be angry, ma. ... It's only a picture! ... I never knew them! Did you? ... They were smiling! Photos are often like that! ... *(In sottovoce)* Not if you look closely. ... *(To Father and Mother)* What happened to those smiles? ... *(Suddenly vengeful)* My parents are dead! Bastards! ... See what I think of you?! *(She tears up their wedding picture to pieces. Father belts Linda on her back. Linda's body jolts)1* Bastard! *(Father belts her again)* Bastard! *(Father belts her again)* Bastard!

> *MUSIC "O' veni sonne di la muntagnella" (Calabrian lullaby, traditional version, author Anonymous). FADES IN after the third "Bastard."*

> 0 veni sonno di la muntanella
> *Oh, come now sleep from behind the mountain,*
> lu lupu si mangiau la pecurella, o mammà
> *The wolf has devoured the little lamb. Oh, mother,*
> 0 la ninna vo' fa'
> *Sing me a lullaby.*

> *As Father continues to belt Linda, she slowly walks away from him, downstage, drawn by the lullaby, but still reacting to Father's blows, physically and vocally with "Bastard."*

FATHER

Carmè! hold her legs! *(Mother remains immobile, stunned, and speechless)* Carmè, per la Madonna!2

> *Linda joins the lullaby (in sottovoce), her body still registering (reacting to) the sting of each blow, like a memory, like waves of aftershocks. Behind her, at a distance, Father's stationary rhythmic belting evokes images of a construction worker swinging a pick with tireless dedication.*

---

1. During the initial belting, the actor playing the Father stands two to three feet upstage of the actress playing Linda. When Linda walks away from Father to downstage center (and Father continues to belt her), the two actors will be roughly seven feet apart. From the audience's perspective, the distance between the two actors should not appear as great as it is, even when the actors are further apart.

2. The literal meaning of the phrase is *'by" or 'for' the Madonna*; however, it is commonly used to mean *'damn the Madonna'*.

Veni sonno di la landa mia
Oh, come, sweet sleep from our land
La mia figghiola muta mi vurria, o mammà
My baby child wants me silent. Oh, mother,
0 la ninna vo' fa'
Sing me a lullaby.

> *During the above stanza, Linda slowly drops to the floor and goes*
> *to sleep. The MUSIC ends.*

MOTHER

Raffaè, she's not moving! (*Father panics. Throws belt across the room. Gnaws his hand in despair*) Raffaè! Oh my God! Raffaè! Raffaè! Go look! Raffaè!
> *Father slaps Mother across the face. He leans over Linda.*

FATHER

(*In a gentle tone*) Linda! ... Linda! ... Come on ... get up ... Linda ... c'mon, be a good girl, okay? ... Carmè!, get me a glass of water, some lemon—*something*!

MOTHER

She looks paralysed! (*Taking Father's belt and wrapping it around her neck*) I'm gonna kill myself! See what I'm gonna do?!

FATHER

Get me that glass of water, idiot!

MOTHER

Leave me alone, I'm gonna kill myself! (*Tightening the belt around her neck*) I'm gonna kill myself!

FATHER

Call Pino the Doctor!

MOTHER

She's not moving at all, look!

FATHER

It's that son of a bitch's fault! ... She saw her brother slacking off, taking advantage of what he was given, wasting his life, and she did exactly the same thing! (*Kneeling, gentle tone*) Linda ... beautiful angel of papa! ... Linda ... my precious little pumpkin of papa! ... Linda!
> *Linda rises quickly, laughing hysterically.*

MOTHER

Mother of God! She's gone mad! ... She really has the eyes of the devil! Raffaè, call the police! I don't recognize her anymore!
> *Linda is still laughing. The laughter turns to a cry. She drops to*
> *the floor.*

LINDA

I hope you die! You fucken bastards! I wanna die! die! die!
> *Pause.*

FATHER

Raise children ... raise pigs. ... Raise a child ... so that one day ...

> *Lights fade. Spot on Father. He is still kneeling. He notices and*

pulls a rolled-up PINK SHEET of paper with a RED RIBBON wrapped around it from the debris surrounding him and examines it. It's the Father's Day card Linda gave him when she was 10 (Act 1, Scene 5). Father exhales and begins to read silently.

We hear Linda's voice for the first four lines.

LINDA
You've packed your first 20 years ...
With Gun on your shoulder, no shoes on your feet ...
You meet hell in Belgium ...
In a mine that's too deep ...

Father joins Linda for the next six lines

LINDA & FATHER
Many go in ... not as many come out ...
No further ahead ... and more bellies to feed ...
Hope comes in the mail ... (*Father only "It did"*)
A relative, a brother, a poor bastard like you.
You pack up your life, wife, kids and appetite ...
And push that trunk out to sea ...
(*Father only "We didn't come by ship, though"*)

From "Now the battle begins" till the end Father recites alone without reading from the card, not because he has memorized the text but because it is his story.

FATHER
Now the battle begins! ...
And with *fortune* leaning gently on your back
You're as good as any sailor ...
You're the boss, you're the captain,
So, you navigate and battle!
Just a little moment's rest ...
Troubles to the east ...
LOOK OUT! TO THE WEST! ... (*Father takes a look around*)
The devil pets you with a wave ...
A few wounded, zero dead! ...
With good health and a piece of bread,
Never look back, always forward ...
With each storm you endure ...
With each malignant wave you manage to evade ...
Make the sign of the cross ...
And if a smile should cross your face ...
Put it deep inside your pocket.
LOOK OUT! TO THE EAST! ...

All safe, once again! (*Father takes smile, stuffs it in his pocket*)
Now your courage spreads its muscle ...
The terrain still unknown ...
You fortify and fortify ...
Strength is in your liver not your 'sword' ...
Some lose hope ...
Some protest and revolt ...
Some sleep and don't care ...
You keep guiding! Look ahead! ...
If you're tired, do not doubt ...
Think what's in your pocket ...
Now it's calmer on the sea ...
You can also see the sun ...
Slowly in the distance,
you see nothing but land, mountains of treasures and endless (perpetual) toil
Raus, schnell and arioppa ...
The abundance overflows ...
You take those smiles from your pocket ...
Now's the time to *show* them all ...
Now you'll see what it means to laugh ...
A major laugh! ... A hearty LIFE laugh!
In your mouth one by one ...
> Beat.
Where are the soldiers?!

> *Father looks around and observes the destruction in the basement
> room. He sees Mother and Linda silently recovering, each absorbed
> in their own world and predicament.
> A strong wind sweeps across the stage. Lights start to change.*

FATHER
(*Pleading his case*) God of heaven and earth ... All custodian Angels ... All the
Jesus Christs of the Virgin Mary ... And all the Saints and higher Saints in
Paradise ... Open your ears—and suspend your purpose! I haven't finished yet!

> *Suddenly, we're in Raffaele's BACKYARD. A typical Montreal
> WINTER BLIZZARD, freezing cold. It's 3:00 a.m. Father is
> still kneeling center stage, greeting card in hand, lit by a SHAFT
> OF LIGHT from inside the cantina, door half open.*

FATHER
(*Upset at stubbornness of God & Company, shakes his head, to himself*) Ma what?!
... Muleheaded! ... every one! ... LET ME FINISH!
SON
(*At a distance, standing on the balcony landing, wearing pants and shirt only*) Pà ...
at this hour? The cold will kill you!
FATHER
(*Beat*) I don't feel the cold. (*Pause*) Too much to do before *winter*.
> *Father looking at the greeting card. The BLIZZARD rages on.*

SON

(*Referring to the 'greeting card'*) She wrote that on the bus one day. For school.

Pause

FATHER

(*Beat*) What for ... for who? (*Beat*) As the ancients used to say ... While the doctor studies, the sick die.

> *Father crumples card into a ball and throws it on a pile of garbage and waste. Father then fetches several gallons from the cantina and sets them centre stage. SON retrieves the "greeting card" without Father noticing.*

SON

And all these gallons?

FATHER

(*Starts digging*) In the garden you need fertilizer, in the world ... luck! (*Starts digging*) All of this is waste! I have to bury it! Everything in the soil! What we don't eat, or can't stomach, the earth eats! The earth is generous, it doesn't refuse anything! All waste is manure! Vitamins! ... Give me a hand.

SON

(*Pointing to a gallon*) And what's in here?

FATHER

(*Holding up the gallon to the night light*) Calluses. Thirty years of calluses! ... Thirty gallons! ... Let's see ...: this one's from '51. (*He pours the contents into the hole*)

SON

Charming! From the hands or the feet? ... Throw it out, throw it out! ... ... What are we gonna do now, an exhibition of calluses in the credenza?

FATHER

(*To himself*) Oh, yeah.

SON

And this one?

FATHER

Salt water.

SON

To preserve the calluses?

FATHER

Thirty years of sweat!

SON

Only one gallon? (*Sarcastic, more to himself*) Modest!

FATHER

Are you crazy?! I had saved five demijohns! *Distilled*. But the cantina is too warm in the Summer ... bit by bit, the water evaporated! That's all that's left! (*Opens the gallon and smells contents*) Eeeew! Mother of God, it stinks! (*Empties the gallon into the hole, methodically*) Times were good when times were bad!

SON

> Good, that's _good_! Throw it out, throw it out! ... Bury it and think about living! (_Beat_) WAIT! ... And this?

> _Cock crows._

FATHER

> (_Drops the gallon_) Nothing! ...

> _Cock crows._

SON

> Pollo vulgaris![1]

FATHER

> (_To everyone, pleading_) Don't close the light in the cantina!

> _Cock crows._

SON

> Pa', you turned it off yourself. Just now!

> _Father looks towards the Cantina. Now the LIGHT GOES OUT in the cantina._

FATHER

> God of heaven and earth!

> _Blackout._

Act 4

MOTHER, SON

MOTHER

> (_Giving son a glass of water and sugar_) Here, take this, it's good for the belly! ... With you, always those damn dreams?!

SON

> (_Beat_) It's the way it is, mà! Some people spend the night reflecting on what they did during the day ... I spend the whole day thinking about what I dreamt at night! (_Mother sings_) You're singing!?

MOTHER

> Singing? I don't sing ... I hum ... or _bark_! ... like that, when I'm doing some work! ... I take off with my voice without even being aware of it. ... God knows where it goes ... I wake up _even the dead_! ... He gets mad! (_She looks towards the_

---

1. Latin pullus vulgaris.

cantina. She sings) He's probably spying right now. ... He saw you come in ... without saying hi to him ... he's thinking ... "Look, look, right away chit-chatting with his mother ... making her waste time." That's what he's saying. (*Takes a fly swatter*) Fucken flies! ... where the fuck are they coming from? (*She chases a few flies. Pause*) Why did you come?

SON

(*Observing Mother*) I don't know ... maybe just for this glass of water and sugar.

MOTHER

You drank it?! Now you can go! ... You even forgot how to use the phone ... that's what he says!

SON

Mà, ...

MOTHER

(*Interrupting Son, in her singsong voice*) 'After they robbed Santa Chiara's they put up an iron door.'

SON

Where is he?

MOTHER

Where is he?—Always at the same place! ... He rented the apartment upstairs to a French couple. ... husband and wife. ... We'll see! ... Anyway, who you gonna rent it to?! Now that the separatists won ... everyone else is packing their bags! ... (*Beat*) He already brought them tomatoes from the garden ... two nice big ones ... and they, "Oh, messi bucù!," all happy! (*Wiping her hands on her apron*) We'll make a little plate of pasta, quick quick, with fresh tomatoes!

SON

Mà, ...

MOTHER

Don't you have to eat?! ... We'll make penne! ... I know you like them. ...

SON

Not even half a penne!

MOTHER

Tubbettini in broth? ... It's good for the belly! ...

SON

Say hi to them! ...

MOTHER

What, you wanna starve, now?! I already started making the sauce!

SON

Wine! I want wine! A nice glass of wine! ... it'll make everything just right!
(*Massaging his temples while going towards the cantina to get a bottle of wine*)

MOTHER

(*Mother gets in his way*) When you eat, you drink! ... (*Beat*) You see? To *drink* the wine, you're all good at that ... but when it's time to make it! ... That's what he says.

SON

(*Observing her*) Mà, please ...

MOTHER

These fucken flies! ... (*Beat*) What d'you think wine is, now?! ... water?! You'll get drunk, 'specially if you don't eat anything. ... It'll go straight to your head!

SON

If it goes to the head, mà, it's because that's where it does the most good! Wine is not stupid.

MOTHER

But on an empty stomach?! ... aronno![1] You have to eat something?!

SON

(*Explodes*) I DON'T WANT TO FUCKEN EAT, MÀ! ... JESUS CHRIST! ... Fuck!

Pause.

MOTHER

Your sister's gone. (*Loud, bitter whisper*) **Disappeared**! ... (*Pause*) You don't say anything? (*Beat*) Your father had already gone to work ... She was in her room ... still sleeping. ... (*Beat*) I leave the house to meet Ipatia at the corner. ... the bus came, we get in ... and looking towards the house ... don't I see her walking towards the bus stop ... with two nice big bags with all her stuff! ... Lord Jesus! ... my heart went in my throat! ... and to do it right in front of my face! ... In front of all my friends from work! ... (*Beat*) The bus was already moving. I saw her just like that ... for a second. ... I didn't even look back ... in case the others hadn't noticed ... but inside ... I could feel death! (*Pause*) She hasn't called. Nothing! ... See the kind of heart she has?! Malignant! ... *Three days* now! (*Looking towards the cantina*) That one ... (*Suddenly*) God what an idiot! I have to wrap the sandwiches for his lunch ... he's gotta work today! (*Son takes lunch box and throws it across the room. Mother clenches her left breast, and quietly picks up the lunch box. Pause*) Did the little princess tell you that we found drugs in her room? In her dirty underwear ... you understand?! ... Did she tell you?! ... We even called Filomena the Gazette ... 'cause she cures people of many awful maladies and things, and ... we thought ... who knows, somebody gave her the evil eye! Let's take it away! ... Filomena came, and while the little princess was sleeping, she put pig's feet and fresh uh rabbit's blood under her bed ... aronno ... in any case, a cure specifically for this kind of thing. ... for drug addicts. (*Beat*) Nothing! ... Where's my luck! ... The next morning your sister left. ... And Filomena cured lots of people! ... (*Beat*) No. ... I guess your sister was beyond saving ... already gone to another world! ... And if the devil should take her! ...

SON

(*Beat*) Only her bones lived here, mà! ... a skeleton!

MOTHER

A skeleton? ... The **DEVIL** was living here, not a skeleton! True, she got so ugly, thin. ... Your father gave her such a beating that ... What skeleton?! THE DEVIL! Enough! ENOUGH! Don't make my blood boil! ... I don't want to hear anymore! ... What was she missing? Stop it! ... 'cause if your father hears, he'll end it for all of us!

SON

Let him hear! He hears only what he wants to hear! LET HIM HEAR!

Mother turns on the radio.

---

1. Aronno from the English *I don't know*

RADIO
Giornale Radio!
MOTHER
Quiet, the news!
> Son yanks radio unit from the wall, throws it against another wall.

MOTHER
(*Trying not to give in to her pain*) **This house reeks of shame!** These walls weep and howl with scorn! And people are *laughing* at my misfortune! A few cry, but most of them <u>laugh</u>! ... And <u>talk</u>! They can't even look me in the eyes anymore! ... And no mercy, not even from God! ... (*Beat*) I'm telling you! ... once you start eating like *them*, *out there*, English or French, you'll never touch another plate of pasta! 'Cause *that's* where the damage started! Out there! *That's* where they ruined you! And don't say no! In Italy, the two of you were sweet as bread. Everybody said it! Here, you started seeing things differently! ... you turned everything upside down! (*Erupting*) This America was not the beginning! It was the end! It destroyed us! Can't you understand?!

SON
(*Referring to her outdated ideas*) Empty those trunks, ma! ... get rid of the old rags ... more ancient than the ancients! Throw them away!

MOTHER
Better to stick with the old things ... they're more secure!—Cut the roots, cut!

SON
I'm cutting nothing!

MOTHER
Get rid of them!—You gotta keep your people closer ... starting with the family!

SON
Family? The <u>appearance</u> of a family! ... And in the middle of this *fucking family <u>display</u> <u>window</u>*, there's <u>you</u> ready with a fucken plate of pasta!

MOTHER
(*Bewildered, then accusingly*) We were *born* this way! Old rags?! Those that kept you warm till now, instead of choking you?! Old Rags?! You're being a smart ass? ... 'cause you went to school? You <u>rotten pus</u> of a lawyer!—there, you made me say it! ... You're a smart ass with me, but not with your father!

SON
Forget fathers, Jesus Christs, and husbands, mà! ... Think of Carmela!

MOTHER
Exactly! *That's* the problem! ... *That* was my mistake! We always thought of the kids first! ... and you thought only of yourselves! ...

SON
(*Grabbing Mother by the shoulders*) Burn those rags, mà! And **bury** them!

MOTHER
(*Great difficulty suppressing her pain*) You never loved him! That's the truth!

SON
I loved him in silence, mà, like him! That's how he taught me!

MOTHER
You come here once a year, ONCE! ... just to fan the flames! ... That's what he says!

SON

And what do you say, mà? Right in here, what does Carmela say?

MOTHER

(*Blowing up*) I'm **thinking** about Carmela! That's **exactly** who I'm thinking about!

SON

And you can say to me that you're happy here?

MOTHER

Yeah, yeah, let's go with happiness! ... Who's happy? ... WHO?! You? ... Only those who have more powerful saints in heaven, *maybe*! ... I should go live alone now like a gipsy for the rest of my life?! (*Looks towards the cantina*) To think ... (*Desperately tries to contain her pain, but can't, and wails*) Oh God! ... all the sacrifices! ... (*Shuts down her emotions and snaps into focus*) ENOUGH! Let's end it ... 'cause he! ...

SON

Why this fear, mà? Why?!

MOTHER

Because I want blessed peace in this house! ... House or no house ... this is it?

SON

Houses are built every day, mà!

MOTHER

Quiet, he'll hear you! (*Intensely aware that Father might be listening*)

SON

And let him hear! LET HIM HEAR!

MOTHER

What a bastard you are! How the fuck dare you?! *Who the fuck are you?!* ... that you know better than anybody else what I should do! **I** have to live the rest of my life with him! **Me! NOT YOU**! How dare you?! ... Everyone's found the cure?! Everyone with the purgative! ... But there are no cures! You understand?! Is that why you came back? To give me a cure?! (*Throwing plates at him, and anything else in sight*) Get out of my house! Ugly beast! Get out! Don't think I forgot about what your father said! He still has that knife upstairs! Get out! I don't want to see your face again! GET OUT! (*Son is about to slap mother across the face, stops himself in mid action, shaking. Beat*) You're worse than your father! ... Worse! Worse! Worse!

Pause.

SON

... That day in the cantina, mà, with the knife ... when you found him on the floor, crying ... that day, mà, I came so close to killing him! ... and I was capable ... I was almost there, mà —almost there! ... But I didn't do it ... he looked me in the face, and for the first time he saw fire in my eyes ... And me, mà, I only wanted to see fear in his eyes ... In that moment, mà, I only wanted to see what he had seen in my eyes till that day ... And I saw it, mà! ... real fear ... bestial ... like a trapped rabbit with huge round eyes ... and his destiny in my hands! ... And I thought, "What satisfaction can one get to see that kind of fear in someone's eyes! Why?" ... And you know, mà, while I was letting him have a little taste of his own medicine, even if only for a moment ... you know, mà, I was actually enjoying seeing him with that fear! And the more I was enjoying it, the more I pitied him, and the more I wanted to kill him, to stick that fucken knife in his throat, to smash his head against the wall, also because I was ashamed of myself for having reduced him to the state of an animal ... I wanted to erase that moment ... But I couldn't! ... The fear was already there, mà ... I was too attracted to it ... And right in his eyes, mà ... he was no longer my father! ... he was this pathetic animal, with no connection to anything that's human ... And I thought of that day when I was still in school, when on the road, me and a friend found a bird that couldn't fly ... We took him and brought him in the Metrò ... in our hands ... like that ... and people were looking at us and thinking, "What nice little boys to save a poor bird!" ... You could see that's what they were thinking. That bird, mà ... we brought it to school ... but it was dying ... We didn't know how to save it. ... we decided to bury it ... because it was time to go to class. ... It was still alive ... so, we laid him on the train tracks ... and, me first ... then Sam ... with a stone we broke it in two! ... He wouldn't break at first, but with the stone again, Zang! We found him to save him ... and now ... without pity ... <u>nothing</u> ... in cold blood ... we enjoyed seeing how many pieces we could cut him into. ... again, with the stone, Zang! ... to see who would be the first to break off the head ... We buried him ... and when we came out of school, we dug him up again, and again with the stone, Zang!, until there was nothing left! ... it was all fucken (pieces) ... Zang! Zang! Zang! Zang! Zang! Zang! Zang! Zang! Zang! Zang! Zang! Zang! Zang!! ... We were so fucken thrilled! It was a rush! ... Like that day in the cantina, mà ... I was looking at an animal. Papa was the bird. ... Without knowing it the poor fucken idiot was looking in a mirror. ... maybe he had seen something even uglier than his rage ... my rage! ... And he deserved worse than the bird. ... As a person, mà, he deserved a lot fucken WORSE! ... but he's my father. ... so I didn't ... (*Pause*) Mà ... if you don't kill a rabid dog ... sooner or later ... it bites! Nothing left!

> *Pause.*

MOTHER

Bark, don't bite ... bark, 'cause the worst never dies. ... When you see a rabid dog, you need a heart. ... don't shoot it ... he's not crazy ... he's only mad ... and only he and Jesus Christ know what he's been through! (*Pause*) Okay. It's time to eat! Sit down if you want! ... Sit down! ... (*Calls out*) Raffaè, it's ready! And bring a bottle of wine from the cantina, we don't have any in the fridge! (*Turns on TV. Low volume*) Open that radio, the news are gonna be on soon ... and you know your father ... has to listen to the weather! (*Pause*) Okay, I'll open it! ... Sit down, I said. (*She notices the damaged state of the NuTone radio intercom wall unit. Says nothing. Pause. She gives SON a folded piece of paper.*) Here! Your father wrote it a couple of months ago. You never came!

SON

(*Looks at the cheque*) It's too much!

MOTHER

If you don't need it, *you* tell me. ... With that, do whatever you want! Use it to develop the horns on your head if you want! (*Serves Son a plate of pasta*) Eat it, now … I already made it! It has to go to waste?! … From now on I won't give you anymore! … (*She sits down to eat, shakes her head*) He's always like that! Never comes when it's ready! Never! … 'Has to finish his work! Finishes one thing, starts another! … Always has to make the pasta get cold … 'cause then, you know how it gets … it grows … and becomes all dry and mushy. … I'm eating … bon'appetito!

SON
I'll go call him.

MOTHER
Leave him alone! … Don't feel strange now that he gave you that … And half is from me. … It's yours now, and that's all. He doesn't want anything. … Tell him merci and that's all … If it gets cold, his problem. Leave him alone!

       Pause.

SON
I'm gonna call him … And I'll get the wine. too.

       Son exits.

       Long Pause.

SON
(*Offstage*) Mà.

       Son enters with a bottle of wine

SON
Mà, papà is in the cantina … hanging.

MOTHER
Heh! He's been there since the day before yesterday! Three days!

SON
Mà, he's dead.

MOTHER
Okay, sit down and eat, or else … yours is gonna get cold, too!

       Son sits down to eat.

       MUSIC: "Swordfisherman's Cry" (Grida Per Il Pesce Spada) by Bova G. Di Michelangelo1

       Son devours the pasta. Mother pours him a glass of wine.

       Lights fade to black.

       The End

---

1. "Southern Italy and the Islands," *The Columbia World Library of Folk and Primitive Music*, Compiled and Edited by Alan Lomax, 1957.

A MODO SUO (A FABLE)

A Play in Four Acts
Calabrian version

Two 'dialects,' one play:
The use of Calabrian in *A Modo Suo* (*A Fable*).

"La Calabria, geograficamente ben definita, mostra, dal punto di vista dialettale, scarsa unità." (*Calabria, geographically well defined, shows, from a dialectal point of view, little unity*). Devoni, G., & Giacomelli, G. (1972). *I dialetti delle regioni d'italia*. Sansoni.

My Calabrian 'dialect' originates from Carolei in the province of Cosenza, where I lived for the first (almost) 7 years of my life. The dialects of Cosenza and Carolei are virtually identical. My parents, however, were from Dipignano, which borders Carolei but is separated by a valley through which flows the Busento. Despite Carolei and Dipignano being equidistant from Cosenza, the Dipignanise dialect differs slightly. Since my father was born and raised on the Carolei valley side of Dipignano, his dialect was almost indistinguishable from that of Carolei. My mother moved from Dipignano to Carolei when she married, thus her dialect eventually also reflected a strong "Carolitano" influence.

According to the municipality of Carolei website, the correct denonym for the inhabitants is "Caroleani." Yet, all the years I have interacted with people from Carolei, including those living in Montreal, Toronto, Vancouver, Sudbury, Sault St. Marie, Edmonton, New York, and Carolei, they have always referred to themselves as "Carolitani" and their dialect as "Carolitano." Dipignano residents have always been referred to as Dipignanisi, and their dialect as Dipignanise—even within my extended family. The Italian equivalents are Dipignanesi for the residents and Dipignanese for the dialect. In many aspects, the Carolitano and Dipignanise dialects are very similar. To illustrate two differences between the two Cosentino dialects, Carolitano uses a double "d" sound whereas Dipignanise uses a double "l" (for example, for the word "there," 'dda vs 'llà, or 'dduacu vs 'llocu/'lluacu). Likewise, where Carolitani use "r" Dipignanisi use "l", e.g., ara casa (Carolei) vs. alla casa (Dipignano). The *A Modo Suo* text incorporates both dialects. Since the text is primarily a performance blueprint, phonetic concerns were often prioritized over grammatical considerations.

In *A Modo Suo*, the Calabrian dialect is further interspersed with 'Italian' (an Italianized Calabrian). Although I did so partly to ensure that actors from different Italian regions were able to read and perform the play (and that audiences from different Italian regions could understand it), there is another, more important reason for Italianizing the dialect. As a child, and even after moving to Canada, the dialect was spoken mainly at home and among close relatives. It was considered impolite, however, to use dialect when conducting official business with authorities and institutions, or dealing with teachers and professionals, or even when conversing with strangers from the same town. In public, "standard" (proper) Italian was encouraged and enforced, even with a backhand to the head if necessary. Italian was often spoken at home, too, but particularly when one (usually a parent) wished to emphasize a point, reprimand, or threaten, or when receiving guests outside the extended family. In fact, the dialect and Italian often coexisted in the same sentence, making it easy to distinguish what was being stressed and why. Thus, in the home, standard (colonial) Italian became the official (and sometimes feared) language of authority and reproach. As with a decree, a warning or reproach in Italian raised the stakes and placed significant weight on the potential consequences. *A Modo Suo's* Calabrian text attempts to preserve this linguistic duality, since it pertains to character traits, attitudes, and intentions. By understanding the hierarchy of language in the play, how it operates, and why, actors can utilize it effectively in a performance by switching between Calabrese and Italian as necessary.

The cast of the1990 production of *A Modo Suo (A Fable)* at the Stage Upstairs (Canadian Stage) performed the following Calabrian text, albeit in an earlier version.

Personaggi / Characters
(in order of appearance)
Tony Nardi *Raffaele*
Mary Long *Carmela*
Lucy Filippone *Rosina*
Frank Crudele *Salvatore*
Anna Migliarisi *Linda*
Dom Fiore *Pasquale/Dottore*
Directed by Alberto Fortuzzi and Tony Nardi.
Set Design Teresa Przybylski
Costume Design Beata Marzynski-Groack
Lighting Design Teresa Przybylski, Alberto Fortuzzi, Tony Nardi, Roger West
Producers Mary Long, Anna Migliarisi, Tony Nardi
General Manager Brenda Bazinet
Production Manager Leslie Lester
Stage Manager Maria Bonanno

Personaggi / Characters
(in order of appearance)
RAFFAELE, *father*
CARMELA, *mother*
ROSINA, *Carmela's sister*
SALVATORE, *son*
LINDA, *daughter*
PASQUALE, *relative from Italy*
DOTTORE PINO, *neighbour's son*

ACT ONE

~~

Act 1, Scene 1: MOTHER, FATHER

Sunday, Summer, late 1970s. It's Father's Day. We are in the basement of Raffaele's duplex in St. Leonard, the populous and 'upscale' Italian district of Montreal. The basement consists of a living- and dining-room area, a kitchen (Offstage), a washroom (Offstage), garage and wine cellar (Offstage). The stairway to the first floor is located downstage left. There is an unfinished spiral staircase located upstage center intended to eventually connect the basement to the main floor of the house as well as the apartment on the second floor. The family sleeps on the main floor—upstairs. The upstairs kitchen and living-room are seldom used. They're showrooms.
MUSIC (diegetic, playing on the radio): "Il Cuore É Uno Zingaro" by Nicola Di Bari.
Lights up on Father in the basement 'living room.' He is searching, calmly at first, for his personal pen on his 'scrivania' (a pen that he unconsciously holds in his hand). The 'scrivania' is where he keeps his documents, leases, birth certificates, medical files, in short, his office, headquarters, which he keeps tidy and spotless . . . a symbol of order, organization, and readiness. Also, it is a safe with drawers that only he has the keys to, which he locks after each use, always double checking, unlocking and relocking them, to ensure that they have been locked properly. He walks over to the TV, places the pen on top of it, unaware, then begins channel surfing—as always—with the concentration and carefully measured motions of someone who is not familiar with the remote control. Finally, he locates the Italian program, turns up the volume, returns to his scrivania, and using one of the keys on the massive key chain in his pocket, he begins to unlock, search in, and lock drawer after drawer.

FATHER
    Mannaie tutti i diavoli! . . . (*Calls out at the top of his lungs*) Carme'! . . . avissi vistu a pinna?! . . . Carmè! . . . (*To himself*) GESÙ CHRISTO! (*Becoming increasingly desperate in his search, he deliberately and methodically empties the contents of each drawer onto the floor—partly to 'punish' those 'responsible' for 'misplacing' his PEN*) . . . A PINNA! PORCO JUDA!
MOTHER
    (*Offstage, at the top of her lungs*) Nun sacciu nende!
FATHER
    (*To himself*) Diec'anni! Sembre cca' è stata! . . . e mo nun se trove. Bo . . . (*To Mother*) Diec'anni! Ai capito?!
MOTHER
    (*Offstage*) Ci ne sunnu cientu 'ndra sa casa!

FATHER

Io vado cercando a mia, madonna e Gesu Christo! ... ch'è già mezzogiorno, e devo mancare puru u giornale radio! (*Fuming and fretting, he begins flinging things all over the place, swearing with each toss, in German, in Italian, in English, in French, in gibberish, inventing words, inventing saints' names, cursing the devil, God the father, God the son, the virgin Mary, her mother, and anyone else he can think of. The desk now stands in total disarray, a symbol of destruction, as if hit by a bomb. Pause*) Carmè! ... a cazz'e pinna dov'è andata a finire! ... Po po po po po po po po po (*Smouldering, he paces the room, passing his fingers through his hair, repeatedly and vigorously, massaging his brain, his memory, and rubbing out any curse along the way. He notices pen on TV set. Pause.*) Lassa stare, lassa. L'ho trovata!

MOTHER

(*Offstage, at the top of her lungs*) E pecchì nun cerchi prima di parlare, guerra mia?!!!

The PEN is one of those 25-cent jobs from a super marché that he has had for years, never leaks, and never runs out of ink. Father polishes the pen, pulls out a file from the messy pile on the floor, and mutters to himself "Funerali ... sposalizi!" Sits in his easychair, tries to write. PEN does not write.

FATHER

Tutt'i diavoli da madonna! Diec'anni! ... ha scritto sembre. (*He tries pen again. It does not write. He puts it in his mouth, heating the ballpoint, shakes it. He tries writing again. PEN writes*) Allora! ... Pasquale du fiume, 100 dollari per 4 persone, il m-i-l-l-e n-o-v-e-c-e-n-t-o s-e-s-s-a-n-t-a—tre! Mettiamo 200 dollari ... sono 4, per 4 persone, a 50 dollari u piatto—200 sì! ... ah ... più regalo, fà due cento cinquanta dollari. No. Mettiamo 300 dollari. Sono passati più di diec'anni! (*Beat*) Rosanna a Sgobbata! Azzo! Ci ho portato 100 dollari per due persone il '68. Eranu soldi chissi! (*Beat*) Va bene, allora, Rosanna, il marito, piu' due figli, cu marito e moglie, e due figli l'uno ... fanno (*having problems with pen again*) Chi cazzo a use sta pinna?! ... fanno ... 10 persone, per 50 dollari u piatto, ... e si pure per i bambini mettiamo 50 dollari ... fanno (*methodically*) ci vi ci vi ci vi ci vi ci ... fanno c-i-n-q-u-e c-e-n-t-o dollari! Piu' mettiamo 200 dollari di regalo, fanno ... 700 dollari che mi dovrebbe portare. Eh!, ca oggi che ci fai co' 700 dollari?! Vidimo. (*Beat*) Angeluzzo u Zuappu e famiglia ... Chillu scondricato e merda, ch'ancora un n'è muartu, e ch'avissinu e dorbicare vivo ... 200 dollari per due persone ... questi ce l'ho portati il '74. E muglierma me domande dove vanno a finire i soldi! Allura. Angeluzzo, mogliera, figlia, se ci vene, e figlio, con mugliera e figlio, e fiqlia ... ah, e la zia ... va bene, invitamo puru a zia, e facimu contenti a tutti! Fanno (*mumbling, having problems with pen again*) Gesu Christo!! ... 8 persone ... 8 per 50 fanno? ... fanno 400 ... si, così ho detto, 400 dollari, piu' 150 di regalo e siamo arrivati a na bellezza di? ... 550 dollari! (*Beat*) U Zoppo nemmeno lavure povaraccio! Va bene, pero' u regalo a Natale c'e l'abbiamo portato sembre! 550 dollari per u Zoppo e famiglia e u jissi pigliare 'ngulo! ... Ah, Rosina ... e chine cazzu cià misu stu nume? Muglierma sicuru! Rosina e Calacala e Giuseppe u scondricatu ... quella disagraziata che non ha mai portato rispetto ... e chillu scondricatu vacabbunnu e merda che non m'h'aiutato una volta a fare u vino. Ma, per su vive? (*Arguing with himself*)

A mia unn'è che m'ann'invitatu aru sposalizio di fligli. I sordi ce le mannati u stessu! Fa 'ngulo! 500 dollari per Rosina, Giuseppe e famiglia ... e si nun ce veniti me faciti puru nu piacire! 500 dollari! Poi, se c'è ne vuliti mettere di più ... sono cazzi vostri!

TV

Il telegiornale!

FATHER

Citto tutti! E notizie!

He rushes to the NuTone radio intercom wall unit by the kitchen and turns up the volume.

RADIO

Giornale radio!

TV

Massacro a Bologna! ...

RADIO

Ottanta morti, e centinaia di feriti ...

TV

Quindici feriti, settantasette morti! ...

RADIO

... in un attacco all'aeroporto di Fiumicino a Roma ...

RADIO

Terremoto in Sicilia ...

TV

Ecco le immagini! ...

FATHER

Guarda ccà guarda. Carmela! ... guarda ccà nu pocu ... Va bene, belli mii ... fate come vuliti voi ... che lì andate a finire.

MOTHER

(*Enters from the kitchen*) Iu un voglio vide se cose ... povera gente ... sa de mangiare ... Raffaè!

TV

A Napoli, nuova tragedia! ...

RADIO

... in fiamma una casa ...

TV

... cinque morti! ...

RADIO

... tutti morti! ...

TV

—disperati si sono lanciati nel vuoto ...

RADIO

... Questo a Napoli! ...

TV

... Ecco le immagini!

MOTHER

Oh Dio mio, penzacce tu! Povera gente ... aiutali tu Gesù Christo mio!

FATHER

Mo t'aiute Gesù Christo si non t'aiuti sula. Parli con Gesù Christo? … Guarda ccà guarda … senza braccie … guarda chillu guarda … senza gamme … propio cumu i tempi e guerra … Citto vidimo!

TV

A Palermo acqua razzionata.

FATHER

E invece ccà, a fanno scorrere sembre. Così avissi de fare io. Ve fazzu lavare i piatti cu l'acqua da pasta se non stati attenti! Come i tempi e guerra! Così v'imbarati il significato della vita … Ca de muni avanti a spisa a fazzu io.

MOTHER

E falla tù! (*She exits to kitchen*)

TV

In Italia sale il numero dei dissoccupati!

FATHER

Loggico!

RADIO

… l'undici per cento della forza del …

TV

… il settantacinque per cento …

RADIO

… del l'undici per cento …

FATHER

… Avissin' e murire e fame! …

RADIO

… ha meno di trent'anni! …

FATHER

… L'anni di tuo figlio! Vagabondi! … Che io li mettessi tutti in fila … e ad uno a uno … ta ta ta ta ta ta ta ta … I sparassi TUTTI! VIA!

MOTHER

É figliu pur'a tia!

FATHER

Citto vidimo!

RADIO

… Mezza Italia sullo ski lift …

FATHER

E l'altra meta' nun lavure!

RADIO

La nave affonda.

TV

Il governo battuto!

FATHER

Quann'è mai!

RADIO

Un sondaggio d'opinioni subito dopo la vicenda mostra che gl'Italiani sono ottimisti …

FATHER

Allegria, festa! Ma iati pigliatu ndru cu …

TV

La nave Italia va alla grande!

RADIO

… torna l'inflazione.

TV

… la sua navigazione puo' essere fortemente disturbata …

FATHER

'Ndra meduddha!

RADIO

Inflazione.

TV

Prezzi si calmano ma spesa cala.

FATHER

Euh, com'i nervi!

RADIO

Nonostante la crisi, L'Italia a tutto gas.

FATHER

Si, aria di culo!

TV

Oggi la Repubblica regala "la Salute."

FATHER

Si, si … quannu iazze e nun fa niva.

RADIO and TV

Notizie del Quebec … Il partito Quebecois ad annunciato oggi che durante questa campagna elettorale il separatismo …

FATHER

(*Turning off the TV*) Mangiè la merde! … Quando se mangie Carmè?!

MOTHER

Mo mo.

FATHER

Iu un vidu nende supr'u tavulu. (*Beat*) Due fimmine dra sa cazz'e casa, e se mangie sembre all'ora di cani.

MOTHER

Due manu tiegnu!

FATHER

Ed io ne ho quattro?, che riesco a fare tutti i lavuri?!

MOTHER

Senta, signorino mio! Per me ce vonnu veramente quattru manu! Fai ccà, fai 'llà! … Pulisco ccà, stiro 'llà … Lava ccà, lava là! … Prepara ccà, bolle llà, mindi là! … Minestro ccà, stuta ccà, stuta llà! … Caca ccà, piscia 'llà! Questa è la vita mia! Alla fine esco pazza!

FATHER

(*Beat*) Ai finito?

MOTHER

PAZZA!—

FATHER

E la signorina dov'è?! ... Sembre chiusa dra quella Maledetta stanza?! ... Però 'ngu giorno ... chilli libri ci brucio tutti! ... ad uno ad uno! ... Na volta e Domeniche si andava ara missa. Oggi ormai ...

MOTHER

E tu de quando tiempu ca nun canusci a chiesa?!

FATHER

Carmè! Per la madonna! ... I figli si devono imbarare. Ho pregato volte io ... mi sono confessato volte.

MOTHER

Si vede ch'avie peccati di confessare!

FATHER

E se non te stai zitta, me vaio confesso di nuovo.

MOTHER

Ormai ti sei confessato. Mo po fare chillu chi vue, no.

FATHER

Carmè! (*warning her. Pause.*) Pigliame a medicina di spaddhi, ca me fannu male per la madosca ...

MOTHER

Ma ccà ch'èsuccesso?!

FATHER

È successo che la pinna mia non ere dove l'ho lasciata io. *Issa* sicuro! O forse tu! ... E ve l'ho detto mille volte, per a madonna, ca le cose dopo usate, si mettono aru posto suo!

MOTHER

Ma t'ha sunnato 'nguà cosa brutta?! ... **Mundune!** ... E allura? (*Mother gets a bottle of Absorbine Junior from the cabinet*) Un se putissi parlare bellu bellu! "Pigliame a medicina!" Te signu mugliera! ... (*Soliciting an answer*) Eh.

FATHER

Chi tieni? Vo tuccato 'nguà cosa, forse?

MOTHER

Io non voglio toccato nente! Un n'è chillu ca vuagliu.

FATHER

Eh, Dio ce ne libera! ...

MOTHER

Ca tuni sulu per chiddu si buano. Ma un nu sai, ch'e fimmine sunnu cume nu libro. Sembre pronte. Apri e leggi. Ma le sapir'aprire. E leggere. (*Pause*)

FATHER

Carmè, mi meraviglio di te. Parli cumu si nun sapissi nente de chillu chi succede! Senza responsabilita'!

MOTHER

Chi succede duve?

FATHER

'Ndra ccà! (*Pointing to his head*) Tutt'i pensieri che ho!

MOTHER

Sulu chissu?

FATHER

Sulu chissu? **Solo questo?!** È nende secondo te?! Ca su cervello mio palpite che ... Fai si massaggi fai! ... (*Mother rubs his shoulders*) Si deve pensare sembre aru peggio per ne trovare nel bene! T'ammaggini quando pese sa capu?

MOTHER

Oggi è Domenica. U giorno di patri ... a puo' fare riposare nu pocu sa capo?

FATHER

Chi si ferma è perduto!—Basta grazie! ... Cazzo come sei roffa! ... (*Pause. To himself, audibly*) Per a madonna, ca de vote me vene la voglia de ce minde fuoco a sa casa, cu tutt'e cose e dintra! Cussi vulissi fare de vote! ...

MOTHER

Va te lava e manu ca fra poco è quasi pronte! (*As she exits to the kitchen*) E porta na buttiglia e vino d'a cantina!¹

FATHER

(*Beat*) A chiamato l'altro?

MOTHER

Noni!

FATHER

Lasciu stare, lascia ... cresci animali, no figli! Me ne frego io! Questo sicuro che l'hanno slaccatu! E mo tene puru vergogna de se fa vide a faccia! Avvocato e cazzo! Ca putie fare soldi a palate! Mo', cu lu culu ruttu, e senza cerase! Che quello se meritassi sulu sparato! Sutta cca'! Senza consumare due pallotte ... una abbaste! **Bang**! Chissu se meritassi! L'unica salvazione sua! Che Dio me fulminassi si ce dugnu cchiu' na mano ... Manco nu dito! Che viene e chiame sulu quannu a bisogno chissi, i vidi ... (*He makes the money gesture, repeatedly rubbing his thumb over the tip of his index finger and middle finger*) Na spugna! ... Ca se lui faceva a modo mio ... oggi se trovava differente ... soldi ... casa ... figli ... come tutti gl'altri!

MOTHER

T'ha detto sembre che non è come tutti gl'altri

FATHER

Peggio per lui! ... E mò ce fazzu vedere io chi bella festa ce fazzu ara sorella—se fà la brava! Minne frico io!

MOTHER

(*Over "Minne frico io"*) **Festa?** ... Per piacire levate s'idea de festa da testa!

FATHER

Zitto! Comando io! E' fatta na monaca?! L'atri gia' criscianu figli ... sulu i mii! ... Trenta mila dollari ho calcolato per u sposalizio da signorina! Si fa la brava.

MOTHER

Ch'a nui un nne custe nende?!

FATHER

Quello non conta! A festa c'ia facciamo noi ... paghiamo noi ... è lu regalo nostro ... quello che entra si tene issa. Che io c'iò perduto sangue per 30, 000 dollari!

MOTHER

Va bene, smettila, si no te sende! (*Short pause*) Io ci vedo brutto!

---

1. Cantina is the wine cellar/cold room.

FATHER

E cambiate l'occhiali se ci vedi brutto! Cià ditto 'nguà cosa?

MOTHER

Cumu m'ha ditto tu!

FATHER

E nun ce dire nente! … Notizie d'Italia?

MOTHER

Ancora nente!

FATHER

Chi sa quannu arrive? … Comunque … aspettamu primo ch'arrive lu pacco dell'Italia. A la signorina … muta! (*Pause*)

MOTHER

Ormai ce signu rassegnata ad un n'avire niputi.

FATHER

Eh … ca tuni … (*Beat*) L'occhio cchi nova? … eh? … È andata a cercare lavoro oggi?

MOTHER

Chilla tu a sai … s'un trove lavuru che piace ad issa, ha detto che non ci và. (*Short pause*) Sta parlando ancora d'andare ara scola.

FATHER

Ancora sa scola?!! … A studiato abbastanza! Vedi che l'altri, are figlie, non ce l'hannu fatta finire a undici!

MOTHER

Raff …

FATHER

Su levassi da testa su pensiero! … S'ere maschio ochè. Mò s'ha de pensare ad atre cose … C'è jiutu u frate, a vistu chi fin'ha fattu?!

MOTHER

A ditto ca si nun cia mandi … un mangie cchiù!

FATHER

(*Beat*) Peggio per issa!—Nun mangie? … Chissu è pecchi ha mangiato ad erba tagliata fino a mo'! … Ce fazzu vedere io s'un mangie! … Per quando riguarde lu pellizzune, per me è morto. Ci metto pure na tabbella fore a porta! "MIO FIGLIO El MORTO!"

MOTHER

Ma pecchi un parlamu cumu i christiani, na vota ogni tanto. Oggi è Domenica!

Doorbell rings.

FATHER

(*In a loud whisper*) Pecchi tegnu **vergogna**! … Ara gente un sacciu più cumu ce dire! … ma de mò avanti, a verita' … **Vergogna!**

Doorbell rings.
Father and mother freeze. Beat.

FATHER

Rispunna tu! … ca forse è l'inguilina … **Aspetta!** … Va guarda da finestra …

sapimu chi cazzu vue ... (*Mother goes to window by stepping on the half-finished spiral staircase, that's half-way up against the upstage wall*) **Chiud'a luce prima**, si no ti vede!

MOTHER

Ma si chiudo a luce issa se ne accorge ...

FATHER

Va bene **lascia stare!** ... ca se poi dice ca se ne vuole andare senza pagare l'affitto, te la vedi tu! ... Vai, vai, apra ... (*Mother goes to the door*) **Aspetta!** Si sono quelli da chiesa ... quelli vangelisti, rispondo io. Che sta volta li mando a 'fangulo per d'avvero! (*He goes to the door, mother goes to the window again*) **Aspetta!** (*in a loud whisper*) ... S'è tuo figlio, io non ci sono!

MOTHER

Tuo figlio è sopra!

FATHER

Come sopra? (*Doorbell rings*) Mannai tutti i cornuti! ... ti ho domandato se ha chiamato, e tu <u>nente</u>! E io per mezz'ora a parlare du pellizzune[1] scialerato![2] ... Cussi dici tu?!

MOTHER

È arrivato tardi ieri sera! Tu dormivi! M'ha ditto issu per nun tu dire.

FATHER

Vedi come si mettono d'accordo mamma e figlio.

MOTHER

T'ha voluto fare na sorpresa, bestia! ... visto che oggi è festa! (*Doorbell rings. Mother goes to window*) É Rusina.

FATHER

Rusina?! Un na voglio vide ccà!

MOTHER

M'è suaro!

FATHER

Non me ne frego! Io un tegnu debiti cu nessuno! Solo il nome me fà venire u sangue a la testa! ... A de fare a spìa dintra a casa! ... per vide quello che tieni ... su tuo è meglio du suo! Na strega! ... sembre a parlare du clubbu!

MOTHER

U clubbu e mammata! Nu centro! Fannu corsi d'inglese o francese! ...

FATHER

Lassa stare corsi e no corsi! Tieni 50 anni! L'Italiano t'abbaste!

MOTHER

... Vedi che te l'ho detto! 'Ngu jiorno fazzu 'nguà cosa brutta io! <u>Bruttissima!</u>

FATHER

E fallo! ... meno a vidi a chilla, e meglio è ... per mia, per tia, e per tutti quandi!

        Doorbell rings.

MOTHER

Io rispondo!

---

1. *Pellizzune* from Italian *pezzo di stoffa (rag, worthless person)*
2. *Scialerato* from Italian *scellerato (criminal, cruel, evil)*

FATHER

>Aspètta! (*Brief pause*) ... rispondo io. (*He clears his throat. Unlocks door, removing the multiple security chains and bars*) Ammuccia i cristalli! (*He opens the door*)

Act 1, Scene 2: FATHER, MOTHER, ROSINA

>*Rosina is standing in the doorway. Everything about her suggests that she is very different from all the people inhabiting this "world," and yet, she could only be of that "world." Her clothes are flashy, tacky and shrill. Her manners are raw, course, and earthy. She is forthright and loud.*

ROSINA

>(*Pause*) Wey Carmè! ... Wey Raffaè!!! Bojoù, bojoù!

FATHER

>(*All smiles*) Bella cosa questa! Bella robba! Nghiovata alla porta ad ascoltare l'affari degl'altri!

ROSINA

>(*Over "ad ascoltare"*) Chi te vonnu rumb'e corne!! Che ho sonato dieci volte! E chi cazzo?! Non risponditi mai!!Penzavo che forse eravati bisì 'ndru giardino ... o 'ndra 'ngu natra parte ...

MOTHER

>Si si ... Troppo cose de fare ... mo e sazizze, poi i pummaduari ... s'un n'è na cosa è natra.

ROSINA

>Ne tocche de ne truvare u ciommo! Un n'è ru vero Carmè! Ca si mariti, arrivati alla vecchiaia ... Mangiative risu ca vu fà tene bellu tisu! (*Pause*) Ma me fa entra', si o no?

FATHER

>A te dire a verità ...?!

MOTHER

>Raffaè ...

FATHER

>... Cchiù priestu ti nne vai, e megliu è!

MOTHER

>(*Over "ti nne vai"*) Raffaè'! (*Laughs*) Sembre scherzannu!

FATHER

>Iu nun scherzo. Io e pisu e parole! E la mamma dei imbeccili è sempre incinta.[1] (*Pause*) Si devi entrare, entra! ... Facimula svelta! ... schnell schnell, come dicono i tedeschi! ... Arioppa! Arioppa![2] ... che l'aria condizzionata a paghe Ciccio! ... e si ne mangie litama!

ROSINA

>E tuni Raffaè! ... Cu tutt'i cazz'e sordi che tien ara banca, sutta u liettu e ru tavulu ... ti n'e frichi de l'aria condizzionata?! ... Ai visto, puru l'air condizzioné s'hannu fattu!! ...

---

1. The world is full of idiots.
2. Arioppa, from the English *hurry-up*.

FATHER

Ca na vota abbastave a parola du marito. Oi invece hannu e dire puru a sua. (*To Mother*) Iu signu dru giardino.

ROSINA

Ed offrame 'nguà cosa si no mi nne vaiu pe d'avvero!

FATHER

Veleno ... ne vue?

ROSINA

Ma va pigliala 'ngulo! ... Ch'un te purtato 'nguà cosa, nu regalo?

FATHER

Regalo?! Tu a mia? Mi nn'a fattu già troppo!

ROSINA

Ch'un te purtatu nente! ...

FATHER

Ca io chi t'e chiesto?! ... chissu ... Sai quando m'arricchiscainu i ragali tui?!

ROSINA

Cum'è bella! ... E chissa?!

FATHER

Va bene dai ... è nente ... e' quello che vedi.

ROSINA

Compris Carmè?! Annestenne?![1] È nente! ... Scommetto ... che chissa è per l'appartamento e sopra. Così quando se sposa Salvatore, potiti andare sopra e sotto, sotto e sopra senza uscire fuori. Visto che commodita'?! ... Ma pecchi un na cominci e supra. Chi te serve dru bassamento. Sempre dru bassamento. L'entrata e supra mancu a canuscio, ca trasu sembre du garaggiu!

MOTHER

Ca sembre cca simu!

ROSINA

Goditivilla sa cazz'e' casa! (*Wiping off sweat from her cleavage with a kerchief*) E Salvatore?

FATHER

Fore! ... a fare e cose sue!

ROSINA

E chi cazzo! ... non lo vedo mai! È possibile che non si fa vide oggi? Che oggi ...

MOTHER

Chillu va sembre curriannu curriannu! Cosi sono e gente bisì! Mò ccà, mò 'llà ...

ROSINA

... ma io e sentito dire ca non fà più l'avvocato ... e ru vero? ... un sacciu chine ha visto a Toronto ... un sacciu duve ... cussi a dittu Filumena da Cicala.

FATHER

Filomena Gazzetta?!

ROSINA

Ca ce tene la suaru a Toronto.

MOTHER

(*Over 'Ca ce tene'*) Iiiiiiiii ... ca chilla papara è cieca e surda de quannu eramu nui in Italia. Porta staffette!

---

1. Understand?!

FATHER

… pettegolannu, mbattocchianno e spatocchiannu, cose ch'un sù vere! …

ROSINA

Ma è vero?

FATHER

Non è l'abitudine mio de discutere affari e famiglia ara porta … specie cu forestieri.

ROSINA

'Ngul'a tutt'a razza tua! … E che sono na forestiera io?! … Carmé, un ci ai fattu i massagi ieri sira? … *Forestiera*?!!

FATHER

No. Una chi le piace a ficcare u naso d'ovunque trase. E puru s'un ce trase, cciù 'ngufizze lu stessu!

MOTHER

Raffaè, smettila!

FATHER

M'ha domandatu!

MOTHER

Un n'è necessario de fare u mal' aducato[1] … (*Beat*) No, Rusì, Salvatore sta buanu! Mo s'ha messo n'ufficio grande per conto suo! …

FATHER

(*Sottovoce*) Grande chi …

MOTHER

Issu è lu bossu. Ci'à cinque o sei operai che lavorano sotto di lui! …

FATHER

(*Sottovoce*) Eh! … All'abbassamento!

MOTHER

L'ufficio è a Toronto 'llà … bascio città, duve sunnu tutt'i bigghi sciotti! … No grazie a Dio, nun ce putimo lamentare! … I figli stannu sembre buani … e chilli senza cuscienza stannu <u>megliu</u>!

FATHER

E chi vo dire mo'?

MOTHER

Staiu parlannu cu issa! Fai chillu ch'e fare?

ROSINA

E la signorina s'ha truvato u ciommo?

FATHER

Ciommo?! Tu ne conoscevi ciommo quando eri giovane?

ROSINA

Allora s'ha trovato u marito?

FATHER

Non si sposa nessuno! … Caso mai … te mannu l'invito.

ROSINA

Allura, c'è speranza!

FATHER

Speranza in che senzo?

---

1. Mal' aducato = maleducato (rude)

ROSINA

Chine se spuse, sta cuntenta per na giornata ... chine ammazze nu maiale sta cuntentu per n'annu! Allura mangiassi sazizze e penzassi alla salute!

FATHER

I capretti se mangiano quando sò giovani. Sono più saporiti!

ROSINA

(*Over "Sono più saporiti"*) Scusa, io sto parlando de figliatta! ... no di capretti. Forse e malecapitu.

FATHER

(*Over "no di capretti"*) Rosì ... i ficcanasi hanno solo un problema ... non è la grandezza del naso. No. Ma il problema è dove lu ficcanu ... Se lo ficcassino più spesso 'ndri cazzi loro ... il mondo fossi più ricco!

MOTHER

Rusì ... te puazzu soffrire[1] 'nguà cosa?

ROSINA

Noni ... A cucina m'aspette.

FATHER

Ecco! A prima parola sana e santa ch'ai detto!

ROSINA

E poi devo preparare certe cose per u mittingu stasira.

FATHER

Per piacire nun me faciti sentire parlare de mittingu 'ndra sa casa!
A chiesa è fatta per pregare!

ROSINA

Ma scusa 'ndippate e ricchie! ... Stò parlando con Carmela!

FATHER

Parla con Ciccio, no cu Carmela!

ROSINA

Pecchi un ce veni puru tù? ... Cussì vidi!

FATHER

Chi *io*?

ROSINA

Hah! ... ricamamo, leggiamo, facimo discorsi ...

FATHER

Hey, ho capito, **va bene!**

ROSINA

É meglio ca me ne vado ... signu passata così ... ca maritumma, ... si nun vide lu mangiare pronte a na cert'ura ... nun la finisce mai!

FATHER

Ci dai torto?! A mugliera a s'educare, a jire aru cinema, balli, mittinghi, cu li sordi e li sudori du marito ed issu rimane sulu sulu 'gnorante, cumu nu lambasciune. Bello questo eh?

ROSINA

Issu è interessato ad andare aru barru, a giocare are carte con l'amici ... tutti laureati in scopa e briscula!

---

1. To *suffer*, a play on words on *offer (offrire)*.

FATHER

Bo, per n'avota siamo d'accordo … ca a mè … gente de barro … nun m'hannu mai piaciuto! Maritutta l'ha sembre avuto su brutto vizio!

ROSINA

Eh! Issu fa quello che vuole … Iu facciu chillu chi vogliu io!

FATHER

Ti prego, non dare esempi!

ROSINA

Fallu giocare are carte … povaraccio, che ha lavorato troppo forte.

FATHER

Almeno l'ammetti che ha lavorato. Questo lo riconosci!

ROSINA

E come no?! Io riconosco tutto quello che si merita riconoscimento. Sia de fimmine ca de uomini!

FATHER

Si si, e capito! Sono già al corrente di tutto! … E me facissi nu grande piacere si stu modo tuo di vedere le cose, lo praticassi il più meno possibile 'ndra casa mia!

ROSINA

E pure casa sua no?

FATHER

Parla con Ciccio, no cu Carmela!

ROSINA

Ma tu si minorenne per discutere se cose. (*Beat*) Ch'è fatta na ragazzina mò muglierta? Quannu teni fame, è <u>fimmina</u> … ma per parlare è na <u>quatrareddha</u>! … Ma mu fai nu cazz'e piacire Raffaè! Su modo tuo e parlare adoperalu cu muglierta … ca iddha c'è stà!

FATHER

Ce stassi puru tu, un te preoccupare.

ROSINA

Guarda un parlamu e maritumma … ca maritumma è na bestia e se meritassi cchiu' tosto scannato!

MOTHER

Rusi'!

FATHER

(*Pause*) Secondo te … tu e maritutta sieti pari.

ROSINA

No. Pari no! …

FATHER

… pensavo …

ROSINA

Lui povaraccio è debbole di cervello … da capozza! 'Ndra meduddha ce tene materia! Ancora a de nasce!

FATHER

—UNO a de comandare 'ndra casa! U bossu è uno!

ROSINA

Allora lui?

FATHER

Si LUI! LUI a sgobbato u culo in miniera! LUI a lavorato notte e giorno per supportare a famiglia, LUI!

ROSINA

Lui?

FATHER

U bossu SI! LUI s'è rassegnato all'ignoranza per il bene e l'interesso da famiglia!

ROSINA

Lui per a famiglia non si ce rumbe ne a testa nemmeno u culo …
Ne cule lu tetto … tutti buchi buchi … Iu nun signu capace … Maritomma è troppo bisì co le carte … sordi nun n'avimo … aspettamu fina ca vince 'nguà partita …

FATHER

Io scommetto che ciai portatu tu a se condizzione!

ROSINA

Io?

FATHER

Ca de fà chillu povaraccio?! Vede come si comporte la moglie. Ca de fare? Ammazzàre a mugliera e dissonoràre a famiglia?!!

MOTHER

Raffaè!

FATHER

NO! Invece lui … crepa dentro … se codde ra lingua, l'orgoglio, e penz'a campà … e per non escere pazzu completamente, se fa na partitella! Ch'è fatto? Na bestia?! Ma io scommetto che se tu passassi più tempo a la casa, a seguire na strada più normale, m'ha capito … com'è l'usanza nostra, inceve de se veste corte—basta, ho parlato! … isso scommetto che subito subito se riprende! … C'e fai nu massaggiciaddhu! … contento lui, contenti tutti! E passe più tempo ara casa puru isso! Ecco famiglia! Si famiglia non esiste che sodisfazzione può avere uno a tappare i buchi da casa, se mi capisci! …

ROSINA

Adesso lo devo incoraggiare?! Ci devo fare e coccole? Ma vai vai! Ci vuole u giudizio che non tene, e li sordi che perde ogni sera allu barru! Quello ci vuole! No e coccole!

FATHER

A bon'anima da mamma mia diceva sembre che na moglie a de minde acqua nel fuoco … no paglia! A fimmina destra conze la minestra! Ci dovete sapere fare però! … Che puru se fossi vero tutto chillo che dici … Così si parla del marito?! … Ama u marito tue cu li vizi sui! … ca nu marito e cumu u mari … s'un porte oggi, porte dumani! … Na mugliera a de minde acqua!

ROSINA

A voglia aspettare! Chi nasce quadrato nun pò murire tondo!

FATHER

Na mugliera a de minde acqua!

ROSINA

U pozzu mio s'è seccato!

FATHER

Ma per ra madonna!

MOTHER

È Domenica!

FATHER

Tu ti devi domandare chillu che dicono e gente!

ROSINA

Maritumma un ce fa casu a la reputazione sua ... e nemmeno io a la mia.

FATHER

Ma lui è perdonato! ... Ah questo non lo sapevi?!

ROSINA

E chine perdona a lui può perdonare pur'a mia!

FATHER

Na <u>mamma</u> porte onore a una famiglia! ... Quello che fa fà nu marito, puru si fossi nun sacciu chi—m'ha capito, non conta ... Ma na <u>piccolezza</u> che fà la moglie ... finito tutto! ONORE! ... Nu marito ... puru s'ammazze ra mugliera per 'ngu tradimento, per esempio ... va in prigione ... però è sembre perdonato! Na mamma ... ONORE! Nun vo dire nende sa parola per tia?

ROSINA

No.

MOTHER

Onore!

ROSINA

Secondo te, signu na puttana?

MOTHER

Rosina!

ROSINA

E ditto giusto na parola! PUTTANA! ... Ai visto, nun n'è successo nente! (*To Father*) Non mi rispunni?

FATHER

Va bene ... se non ci sei tu ... 'nguna c'è! ... **sicuro!** ... (*Beat*) Chine pratica cu li zoppi, dopo n'annu zoppichìe!

ROSINA

E tu m'avisto mai zoppichiare?!

FATHER

(*Pause*) Non è giusto va bene!

ROSINA

Secondo chi?

FATHER

Secondo Gesù Christo morto! **E gente!**

ROSINA

Chine sunnu se gente? Uomini, fimmine ...?

FATHER

Lassa stare chine sunnu! Ce sunnu!

ROSINA

Va bene! Ma chi in particolare? Damme nu nume, nu cugnume! Uno m'abbaste!

FATHER

Non ti preoccupare de nomi e cognomi.

ROSINA

Ma chi cazzo su se gente!!

FATHER

Tutti! Gente! Se non tu dicono 'ndra faccia, u penzanu! Quando vule la vucca de gente, valla 'ndippa va!

MOTHER

Dai Rosì ... Io capisco quello che vuoi dire tu ...

FATHER

—Ah, tu sei d'accordo?

MOTHER

(*Explodes*) Famme parlare! Ca quando parli tu, l'atri un ponnu dire mangu na parola! ... (*To Rosina*) I problemi tui i capisco ... e t'ha ditto puru Raffaele ch'un ce piacianu gente de barru. Però, **però!** ... voglio dire ... ONORE ... Dicimulu all'apierto Rosì ... tutte quelle fimmine aru centro, secondo te, sunnu fimmine? ... M'ha capito.

FATHER

Streghe!

MOTHER

... che due o tre le conosco io ... senza marito, divorziate.

FATHER

Predicano il vangelo d'e Streghe! All'Americana!

ROSINA

Ca tu chi sini?

FATHER

Italiano per la madonna! No na insalata mista! (*Beat*) Tu ne conoscevi centri de fimmine così in Italia? ... 'ndru paise? ... na visto mai? E vedi che ho viaggiato io!

MOTHER

Dai Raffaè, 'llà è natra cosa!

FATHER

Ah, 'llà sono più fessi?!

MOTHER

'Llà pensano sembre all'antica!

FATHER

E ccà siamo più moderni, e capito! Tutte se galline ara chiesa ... senza gallo ... te lo puoi immaginare?! ... che a la vecchiaia vuliti fare e pollastre! Invece de si confessare i peccati ... i combinano! E qual'è lu scopu? Pecchi sa conferenza de gaddhine? Te lo dico, io! ... di mettere sotto il marito! Sante 'ndra chiesa ... diavole 'ndra casa! (*Beat*) Vedrai! ... si continue su pollaio, dove andate a finire! Dove andrà a finire il mondo!

ROSINA

Apposto un cia fai venire a muglierta stasira.

FATHER

(*To himself*) Mannaie! ...

ROSINA

Eh si, pecchi un se sa mai, arrassu sia pò diventare "una di quelle."

FATHER

(*Beat, pointing to Carmela*) Issa studiave l'inglese appena simu arrivati. A sira! Due vote a settimana! E io ho detto NO! … ara casa, cu ri figli! In *famiglia*! … Fattu dire!

(*Pause*)

'Ndru munnu ce vonnu sacrifici de tutt'i culuri!

ROSINA

E nu spicciuliddhu e ficucia.

FATHER

Puru maritutta t'avie dato fiducia n'avota.

ROSINA

(*Pause*) Tieni paura ch'a pierdi?

FATHER

Furberia!, no paura! U munnu è nato così … ricordatillo! … E due o tre galline non cambierannu u munnu 'ndra na giornata! … Mancu Mussolini c'è riuscìto! … Che aveva raggione chi diceva che na moglie è come l'uovo … "più o sbatti e meglio vene!" … "Ma chi nun sente scorno, nun sente bastonate"

Pause.

MOTHER

E poi, iu un ce tiengnu mancu e ce jire … Un ce voglio jire io … no ca un mi ce manne issu …

FATHER

E ca si iu dico no, tu ce jissi u stessu?

Pause. Phone rings. Father and mother freeze, terrified at the thought of who it might be. They let it ring a few times.

FATHER

Vado io! (*Clearing his voice, using a serious/suspicious tone*) Alò … (*All is clear*) Eh Filil … muglierta? … sini si, è ccà … Cumu? Eh, stiamo chiacchierannu! … E fattila na camminata 'ngu giorno … cosi' parlamu a quattr'occhi!!! Come? Non ai mangiato ancora? … e nemmeono io … chi vo fà? … pacienza! … si si, ca ta fazzu parlà!

ROSINA

Povaraccio! … Diciaccie che fra dieci minuti arrivo!

FATHER

Filì … sta partiennu mò mò … Dieci minuti ed è arrivata … Si si t'e capito. (*to Rosina*) È meglio ca ce parli tu. Sunnu i cazzi vuastri! … (*into phone*) Ochè Filì (*to Rosina*) Non ha mangiato di sta mattina!

ROSINA

(*Taking receiver from Raffaele*) Chi c'è *passerotto mio*?! …. fame? … nemmeno io e mangiato … mo vengo preparo … *m'a t'arranger ca*1 … Avevi paura che m'avevi perso? … Noni. … u centro è stasera. … e mò vegnu ti ho detto! … E tu povaraccio non sapevi dov'eranu e cassarole … ai raggione … e poi pesano … ti devi piegare troppo … a schiena … eh si! … È na fatiga a te riscaldare chilla pasta 'ndru friggidero … è loggico, ci vuole pratica, … è troppo complicato per tia *passerotto mio*! … E la partita? … ah già oggi è Domenica … giorno di riposo

---

1. "m'a t'arranger ca" (Literally *I will fix that for you*)

... Ah, a le otto e mezza? ... Si si me sbrigo ... ca è vergogna si fai ritardo ... Vedi che ti sento benissimo passerotto mio! ... fame, si si. ... e chi vò ca te dico ... chi si vergogna de lavurare avessi d'avire vergogna de mangiare! ... Cumu e ditto?! ... Ch'a meglia parola è china ca 'un se dice ... Te vulissi dare nu vasune malandrino mio! ... si si parto mò! ... Ca mo viegnu e te fazzu puru i massaggi! ... I <u>massaggi</u> si! ... <u>Apposto</u>! (*to Father and Mother*) Com'è simbatico! ... (*to the phone*) Sini belluccio mio! Belluccio uccio uccio mio! ... Va bene, fina ch'arrivo mangiate chissu (*She blows a raspberry into the phone and hangs up*) Mavaffangulo!
> *Pause.*

FATHER
Rosì, a part'i scherzi ... è meglio che te ne vai prima ca chillo te fa vedere l'altro mondo.

ROSINA
A chillo mu mangio sano sano. Me spruppulu puru l'osse!

FATHER
Mamma mia diceva ... si a fimmina un corre ara prima chiamata ... vo dire ca canzune un ce piace.

MOTHER
(*Angry*) Raffaè! Non cominciare!! ... Eh Dio mio! Vui due sembre cumu cani e gatti! Calmatevi! **E chi cazzo!**

FATHER
(*Calm*) Calmo sono io ... Io dico solo—sentite a quello che dice la bibbia. Ca Gesù Christo era <u>uomo</u>! ... Invece fra poco me vuliti fà crèdere ch'ere <u>fimmina</u>!

ROSINA
S'ere fimmina avissi portatu cchiù de 'na crucie!

FATHER
Mamma mia dicie 'Dio ne scanza de uomini senza barba e fimmine mustazzuali'!

ROSINA
Io mustazzi un ne tiegnu!

FATHER
E nemmeno barba tieni!

ROSINA
(*Brief pause*) Meglio essere fimmina senza barba che uomo senza palle!
> (*She exits, slamming the door*)

FATHER
(*To Rosina, who is offstage*) A chine a sbatti a porta?! (*to Mother*) A de sembre dire l'ultima parola! (*to 'Rosina'*) Te dico io a chine sbatti a porta! (*to Mother*) Ca a chilla a domestico io 'ngu jiorno! Se meritassi veleno! Chissu se meritassi!! U bravo u faccio fino a nu certo punto ... ma poi ...

MOTHER
Si si, beddhu mio! Tu te sciali cu issa! Quannu parli cu issa, parli cumu si ta vulissi mangiare cu l'occhi! A mia invece me tratti cumu na merda! ... A quella ti dovevi sposare tu!

FATHER
E pecchi, dici tu?

MOTHER
Chiddha si' che te facissi abballlare ...

FATHER

Vida ch'ai già misu pede. (Beat) Tiegnu paura e iddha?! ... ca ha ngappato davvero uno senza ... mla capito Cu mia vidi cumu filassi! ... Basta ... Prepara e mangiare s'e preparare!—ca gia' m'ha guastato l'appetito chissa! Iu signu dru giardino! Quannu e' pronte chiama! (*Father exits*)

MOTHER

A morte desiderata un vene mai! (*Mother exists*)

Act 1, Scene 3: MOTHER, SON

> *Enters Sal, thirty years old, but looking much older. Wearing a handsome bathrobe and combed back hair, he walks down the stairs with strained authority, while smoking a cigarette and observing the surroundings as if he were looking at paintings in a museum. Enters Mother.*

MOTHER

Salvato' ... ma chiss'è ura? Sono le dodici! ... Ogni vota ca veni ccà, dormi sembre ... Così dice patritta!

SON

Ma. Devo raggiungere tutto u sonno che ho perduto. E poi, non è che dormo ... Eh mammarella mia ... si tu sapissi cumu palpite u cervello mio ... un facissi queste domande ... (*Brief pause*) Nun sacciu ...

MOTHER

Tu e patritta cu su cervello chi palpita ... ca fumi a prima matina!! ... Eh!? Già che non è più matina ... ma di giuno! ... mangiate na banana ... a vò na banana?

SON

Ma, io sto provando à fare certi raggionamenti, e tu mi domandi se voglio na banana? (*Beat*) ... va bene ma pigliu.

MOTHER

(*Going to the kitchen*) A panza di giuno non raggiune! ... Quannu nun mangi, combatti cu la morte!

SON

Duv'è issu?

MOTHER

Dru giardino, duv'è. Sulu là è cuntientu! ... fischie e piante. Sta faciennu u giardino puru ari vicini! ... Ara vecchiaia! Abbasta ca me lassassi in pace pò fare chillu chi vue ... C'e po puru crepare ... ormai è grande. ... Issu se ngazze ca un signu pratica de giardino, cumu l'atre fimmine! "A vulutu u giardino? E mu crisciatillo" ... A mia m'hannu abbastato i figli! (*Beat*) ... Pecchi un nu vai aiuti ... un t'interessi mai du giardino ... de nente ... E poi un n'è ca vò aiuto. Sul'u gesto ... sulu chillu vue.

SON

Me sunnatu ca ne luttavàmu ...

MOTHER

(*Banana in hand*) ... Te mangiate chissa ... a vo munnata?—Chine?

SON

'Ndra su suannu, issu ere sembre cchiù forte e mia … avie sembre quella poco d'energia più di me … o na mano più lunga … me fricave sembre … Bo … stavamu luttannu … un me ricordo nemmeno pecchi … e tutt'a n'avota m'acchiappe le palle—

MOTHER

Eyy!

SON

Propio ndre gamme, bum!

MOTHER

Emmè chi scostumato!

SON

(*Over "Chi scostumato"*) Ogni vota ca u volevo fregare—bum—m'acchiappe le palle! … E poi non lassave … stringeva e stringeva, te dicu, ca me venuto nu dolore e panza … Poi lassave … Io di nuovo provu a lu buttare per terra … ed issu, bum! … ancora m'acchiappe …

MOTHER

E capito! …

SON

E stringeva! … Non sò come faceva! … Ancora me fà mal' a panza.

MOTHER

Vo fattu nu bicchiere d'acqua e zuccheru … ca è buanu per la panza … (*Beat*) Eh? (*Beat*) Allura mangiate chissa mangiate …

SON

(*Absentmindedly*) No, lassa stare … (*Beat. Absorbed in thought*) Nente è cambiato! … Tutto è lu stesso! … pulito … du primu juarnu ch'a v'aviti cumbratu sa casa. … Su portacenere c'è du '74. E sembre ccà è statu! … (*Beat*) Si putissi parlare … visto tutto chillu ch'a visto! …

MOTHER

E mindalu a 'ngu natru postu s'un te piace duacu!

SON

Puru a stanza mia. Ci'à sembre chillu stesso odore … profumo … (*Beat*) cussi tutt'a casa! … (*Beat*) Tu lo sai pecchi mi sono alzato … Iu puazzu passare jiornate sane 'ndru liettu! Ma lo sai pecchi mi sono alzato? **U sugo!** Si sente ch'è Domenica! Addure de Domenica! … Pur'a radio 'taliana ch'appena se sente … stessu annunciatore … stessa *vuce* … pe' anni ed anni sembre a stessa! … cu chille stesse canzune. Canzune de Domenica! … E fina ca pozzu addurare su sugo, mi sento bene … tranquillo, 'ndru letto, i soli murmuri, chilli da cucina … (*Beat*) Poi mi alzo, esco fore da stanza … e saglie tutt'a fezza! U sedimento! … é tremu e dintra!

MOTHER

Oggi è lu jiornu e patri. Ti averto.

SON

Chi celebramo?

MOTHER

EMMÈ CHI DISGRAZIATO! … T'È PATRE! T'HA PURTATU ARU MUNNU! T'HA DATU A VITA! TE PIACE O no, t'è padre … per vita!

SON

(*Beat*) Quandu vali tu mammarella mia! Su sugo me fà girare a capo ... un me fà parlare!! ... è nu calmante!

MOTHER

Un parlare! ... E meglie parole sunnu chille ch'un se dicianu! ... Cchiù parli e cchiù te gire la testa! Ca mu mangiamu. ... L'uominu dgiuno tene lu diavulu 'ngulu! Un nu sai chissu? Sedate cca! Ch'a lingua é na richezza, ma ammazze cchiù da spada!

> *Son sits in Father's easy chair with some difficulty. Mother places a cushion behind his head, she removes his sandals from his feet, resting them on an ottoman. It's the treatment he gets from his mother every time he visits.*

SON

Ma, no, lassa stare ... (*Without resisting*)

MOTHER

Ma tu duarmi cu li quaziatti?!—chi piedi nun rispiranu! Ma guarda chi cosa e pazzi! Na purtato robba e lavare? ... mutanne, cammise lorde, eh? (*Massaging son's head.*) Vidissi chiddu ... Tu, prima di andare a' letto, e fare cussì, u vidi (*Demonstrating on her own head*). Tri vote cussì, supr'a capu ... cussi un te suanni brutti suanni! Ca quannu t'allisce lu diavolo vuole l'anima. (*Goes back to massaging son's head*) Cussi! ...

SON

(*Enjoying the treatment*) Ah, mammareddha mia! ... Quando vali tu! ... A farin'e ove ciannu fattu bene a se manu. (*Suddenly, Mother yanks her son's hair violently back and forth*) Ahhhh! Vida ca capiaddhi ne tiegnu pocu!

MOTHER

Ma Gesù mio! ... E cose stavano andando così bene! Mò, si senza lavuru ... solo ... senza fimmina ... senza figli ... e scommetto che sei pure senza soldi! Ma dimmilo tu ... può stare tranquilla na mamma si nun sacciu nemmeno chillu chi te mangi, o si teni soldi per pagare l'affitto! Eh? Chi te mangi?! Eh?! Tu m'e fare murire afforza! ... Almeno trovate na fimmina ... cussì almeno c'è quella chi te pò preparare 'nguà robba ... stirare 'nguà cammisa ...

SON

Un ne fannu cchiù.

MOTHER

Ma puru per compagnia! Ch'annu e dire e gente? N'uominu cussi, sulu! Mo che devi fare? Chi Gesù Christo te vo fare? Te si laureato!

SON

(*Beat*) Vai cercannu a vita, mà ... per evitare a morte. (*Beat*) E gente vannu truvannu l'avvocatu sulu quannu tenanu problemi. Ca vidissi na faccia sorridente na vota u jiarnu? Mai! Entrano tutti, con la faccia nterra, e spalle gobbate fin'e ginocchie ... Poi l'aiuti, e te mannanu a fangulo! E si muari or cadi malatu si nne fricanu nente! ... Anzi, si muari, ponnu guadagnare 'nguà cosa! ... risparmiare 'ngu dollaro! ... Mangu nu regalo! Uno. No che m'aspiettu! È propio a cultura. È corrotta! S'e ngazzanu ch'annu e pagare per ce difendere i deritti, puru si vinci! Te odìanu, mà! È na cultura de odio! E l'avvocato è nu pisciature!

MOTHER

Ma si pagato bene! Cu li poveri un si ce fà ricco nessuno!

SON

Minne frico! … (*Beat*) Pagato bene patate!—i clienti 'taliani sunnu i peggi! Tra sconti, favori, e lamenti … chi guadagni?! Quando *vinci* vonnu u rimborso! Te *vonnu* … ma nun vonnu pagare! TÙ 'e ringraziere a loro! Guadagnu miegliu 'ndra na fattoria!

MOTHER

Eh, su culu avissi sordi!

SON

I sordi sunnu a ruvina!

MOTHER

Tu sini a ruvina! … chillu chi tocchi tochhi, *ruvini*! I sordi fannu venire a vista a li cecati, su vo capire! E n'uominu senza sordi è nu muartu chi cammine! … U sai cumu dicono e gente …!

SON

E gente andassino affangulo! (*Pause*) "Io tegnu nu duplex, Ma Ciccio tene lu triplex … Si, ma Nicola tene lu cinqueplex! **Però**, **Però**, Pasquale tene lu bloccu apartamentu! … e poi c'è Peppino, ch'ha venduto tutto, e se cumbre nu bungalò! **Subito!** Tutti vendono! Tutti se cumbrano u bungalò! Chisse sunnu e gente! Pecore!

MOTHER

E tu si nu pecuraro!

SON

Iu me guardare a salute, ma! A vita é curta! Tegnu na malatia gravissima ara *capum*, *corum*, e *culum*! … nu mise ch'un vaiu buanu e cuarpu! … Aspettamu … vidimo chillu chi succede.

MOTHER

Aspettamu a fiss'e mammata! … Tè ca ma fatta dire, ca oji è Duminica! Cussì ne facimu tutti viecchi! Ca ne mòranu tutt'i jiuarni! Ch'avisto ch'è muartu u nonno de Pinu u dottore. (*Beat*) Però benediche hannu fattu nu bellu funerale … si vidi quandu curune c'eranu mamma mia … grande belle … tutt'i fiori … di figii … nipoti … pure de l'Italia … Poi s'hannu affitatu chilla bella sala grande, llà … a Jarry. No, ere bellu d'avvero. Hannu fattu na bella figura! A vita te le gode *mò*. *Mò*! No domani! *MÒ*!

SON

Mò! … (*Pause*) N'avota ero *cussì* cu Jesù Christo. *Cussì*! … Io e Jesù Christo! Mi capiva quando non avevo tempo per pregare! … Issu, puru s'ere occupato con qualch'uno che si stava confessando … me zinnave cu l'occhio "Va bene ce vidimo dopo." Eramo proprio vicino. Amici! E serviannu a missa … tutt'e matine … guardannu tutti chilli poveri fessi nginocchiati 'ndra chiesa, che facienu schifo e pietà a li vide cu la lingua e fore, che ci tremava, e fimmine cu labbre pittate de tutt'i culuri … ed è capito ch'un ero normale … Ero sicuro ca Christo m'avie portato 'ndra su munnu per lassare 'nguà cosa, 'nguà traccia!

MOTHER

T'avie fare o monaco o prete!

SON

Tutto sembrave come si fosi per 'nguà raggiune … tutto sembrave cumu … e cose eranu arrangiate … sembravano cumu si fossino 'llà per 'nguà raggiune … tutto, <u>tutto</u> … e lu fatto ca c'ere io … sembrave ca ere per 'nguà raggiune … A bella è … nun signu mangu ngazzatu per sa perduta e tiempu … ancora peggio!

MOTHER

… A traccia e mammata! Ca avvocato è nente?! Sulu a parola A V V 0 C A T 0, vo dire na cosa … fà n'impressione … A dire Salvatore u scarparu o Salvatore L'A V V 0 C A T 0, è tutta natra cosa! … Cchiù granne e chissu chi c'è? Gesù Christo forse! EH! (*Beat*) Tu sai quello che ti prendi! Accapace che hai dato fida a qualch'uno … 'nguà sigaretta … e chillo t'ha drogato! … Un ce vo nente! … Non ti conosco più … Ca tieni già trent'anni! … (*Beat*) Ma si u ciuccio un na fatto a cuda dopo tri anni, un na fà cchiù!

SON

Basta ma! … nun parlamu de ciucci e no ciucci e si trentlanni! A raggiune! Su passati trentlanni! TRENT'anni dedicati al dovere! … (*Pause*) Un sacciu … e perso a voglia. E cumu si già sapissi u resultato … ed io sospeso … un sacciu duve … aspiettu a morte … o 'nguà cosa per me divertere … per un me noiare … per me fare passare u tiempu! … Un me pozzu move … A la vecchiaia ogni fatiga è piso. … (*Beat*) Ehhh cumu fossi bellu ad avire na spirapolvere ca me sucassi tutto da capo, e lassassi nu pocu e spazio per nu pocu e pace.

MOTHER

(*Beat*) Beddhu mio, trovate 'ngu dottore! … N'albero senza frutto va tagliato, se dicie n'avota … Ca a sula traccia chi lassi tu, e chilla di piedi chi vannu ingiro ingiro cuntannu e pedate de l'atri! … e ch'un se feramnu mai! … Basta! Ca tu oggi me fare mancare puru a terza puntata du filmu taliano. Un ne parlamu cchiù!!! … Ogni vota ca veni ccà, parli cu mia … a mia me raccunti tutto! … Cussi dice issu! È geloso, bello mio! Crepe da gelosia! … Dice ca trattu megliu a tia ch'a d'issu! (*Beat*) Ca tua sorella un dice la stessa cosa.

SON

(*Beat*) Adduvie?

MOTHER

Adduvie? … dove solito! Dintr'a stanza! Notte e giorno! Sembre cu **libri!** Patritta 'ngu jiornu ci brucie tutti si libri! Metà ci'à già bruciati … L'ha buttati fore a finestra … ha fatto nu bello mazzo … e l'ha bruciati ndru giardino!

SON

Ma, sunnu sulu libri!

MOTHER

Solo libri? … Nun se canusce cchiù d'a facia! Mo vidi cumu s'è fatta magra! … Un parle più cu nessuno! Da stanza ara toletta! … chilla è la vita sua. Venanu visite—e se va chiude! … ch'un vò vide nessuno! Parle sula. … A truavu 'ndra stanza ngantata. Cu le finestre chiuse. E blainde chiuse, nu libro ndre manu, e la musica chi sone, chi se sente puru de Jean Talon. … A chiamo, e mancu me sente. Chiamo "Linda," e nente. Ingantata, seduta supra u liettu! … Bo. (*Loud music coming from Linda's room*)

>   MUSIC: "School" by Supertramp. It begins at the 'scream' just
>   before the lyrics "After school is over …"

MOTHER ·

SIGNORINA! Veni prepara a tavola! Signorina! Dai! … Vedi che patritta t'ammazze! (*MUSIC stops. Brief pause*) … Hai visto? … Non se ne frega! Fa a modo suo! Non fa nente 'ndra sa casa! … Però mu vidi cumu vulanu e palate s'un minde giudizio. S'a de minde a forza u giudizio! … Patritta a vo fa spusare. Tu però un dire nente. (*Son looks at mother*) Chi me guardi? Quannu na fimmina è arrivata a quindici anni, o a spusi o a scanni! … È fatta vecchia! … No … s'ha misu 'ndra capo, ca deve comandare issa!

SON

E non ci aviti tagliato a capo ancora?

MOTHER

Si si … guardate a lingua … ca per me pigliare fissa à mia …

SON

Ma, tene 29 anni, quasi **trenta!** … na poco de liberta' cia potiti dare.

FATHER

(*Offstage*) Quannu sini ara casa tua, fai come vuoi tu … ara casa mia, fazzu come voglio io!

SON

E tene le ricchie!

MOTHER

Per piacire … è Domenica! Giorno santo!

Act 1, Scene 4: FATHER, SON, MOTHER, LINDA

FATHER

(*Enters, carrying some garden vegetables*) Domenica? … Eh, per tuo figlio è sembre Domenica. Già mezzoggiorno e mezza … l'ura dell'aristocratici! … Non è lu veru Salvatò? … (*To mother*) C'è l'ha purtatu almeno u caffè 'ndru liettu a l'eccellenza?! Eh?

SON

Bongiorno.

FATHER

Buonasera, quale buongiorno. Ho fatto na giornata sana gia' … senza aiuto di nessuno … Diceva la bon'anima de mamma mia, "chi dorme nun piglie pisci".

MOTHER

A gallina fà l'uavu e aru gallu le bruce lu culu …

FATHER

Sini sini … vo mettere i lavuri tui cu li mii? … Ancora nun vidu nente supr'a tavola. Un ne mangiato de sei sta matina … Adduv'è la signorina?!

MOTHER

Duv'è!

FATHER

Ancora chiusa 'ndra quella stanza maledetta?! Vedi che te l'ho detto! … Chiamala! U tavolo è da preparare! … sciagurata che non è altra! … Se non si da de fare 'ndra sa casa, me frijo u core 'ndra na padella! … e quannu è 'ndra stanza lassassi la porta aperta … Ve l'ho detto mille volte! … si no cia cacciu completamente!

(*Door slams upstairs. To mother*) Guarda benediche chi lattuche! Te, lavali e vedi che ci devi fare. (*Father exits.*

Linda enters, coming down the stairs with a smile on her face, mumbling in pig Latin which only Sal understands.

LINDA

Iay atehay histay uckenfay ousehay. Iay atehay histay uckenfay ousehay. Iay opehay ehayiesday, uckenfay astardbay! Iay opehay ehay iesday! Iay opehay heytay ieday! Iay eallyray oday! Maybe a bird! That would be nice! (*She exits to the kitchen. Offstage*) Hi, Sal!

MOTHER

Hai visto?

FATHER

(*Offstage*) Ve l'ho detto! ... 'ndra casa se parle Italiano! ... Te l'ho detto mille vote!

LINDA

(*Offstage*) La la la la la.

FATHER

(*Offstage*) Dimme na cosa ... a che ora a chius'a luce 'ndra stanza ieri sera?

LINDA

(*Offstage*) La la la la la ...

FATHER

(*Offstage*) Ho parlato io!

LINDA

(*Offstage*) La la la la la ... non lo so'

FATHER

(*Offstage*) Erano le due da matina. Ti ho avertito, per la madonna! ... Se la luce non è smossa a mezzanotte preciso ... ti levo tutt'e lampe da stanza ... hai capito?

LINDA

(*Offstage*) Io leggio fin'a l'ora che voglio!

FATHER

(*Offstage*) Ed io dico NO!, per Gesù Christo! ... ca oggi è Domenica! ... Te alzi a matina presto, e leggi. A notte è per dormire ...

LINDA

(*Offstage*) Abbasta che dormi tu, chi ti nne frichi degl'altri?! ... Non è che ti disturbo ... russi cumu nu puarcu!

      Father slaps her. Pause.

FATHER

(*Offstage*) Mannaie tutt'i cornut ... lo fazzu per v'imbarare.

      Pause.

MOTHER

Nott'e giorno ... sembre così! Gesù mio!, chi ne manghe? ... C'è pane, salute ... sulu a pace ... pace non ce ne stata mai 'ndra vita mia! ... (*Pause*) Io penzo ca tutti si nervi chi tene patritta ... è pecchi a tene con tè!

SON

È nato nu niervu, e more nu niervu.

MOTHER

Non ci sei mai! ... Issu guarde a l'atri figli, e soffre ... Aveva tante idee per tia! ... Ancora sa scala a lassata a mezza! A casa per chine a cumbrata! ... Tutto per

tia! Si u figliu! Issu ce tene a se cose … (*Brief pause*) Nun sacciu cumu te dire,
bellu mio … Quando jiorni rimani?

SON

Parto domani.

MOTHER

Ah!, cussì a patritta lo fai bello contento! …

SON

Ma, tiegnu bisognu e sordi.

MOTHER

Ahhhh … —domand'a patritta!

SON

Tu un ne tien? … Te li ridò … allu stesso interesso da banca.

MOTHER

Vat'a ra banca—ma tu si pazzu?! Cumu fazzu iu?! A patritta! Ca patritta! … E ci
ha detto a la signorina, che si tene le stesse idee tue …

FATHER

(*Offstage*) … Che Gesù Christo me facissi na grazia e te facissi truvare stisa
morta 'ndru letto domani mattina!

        Pause.

MOTHER

Parlacce! T'è padre. T'è sangue!

SON

M'è cazzo!

MOTHER

Dio mio, chi disgraziato, svergognato e merda! Te dassi la cammicia de spalle!

SON

Ma … iu viegnu ccà per tia! …

MOTHER

Cittu un te fa sente! (*Loud sottovoce*) Muto! … (*Brief pause*) Si guardassimo tutti
u passato, n'avissimo e ammazzare tutti! … Tutto quello ch'ha fatto ha fatto per
v'imbarare! È fatto cussì. U sapiti! D'a natura fino la sepultura. Issu non può
cambiare! … ma vui cazzo!

SON

Ogni giorno che cammino, me dico … Attento! De ccà c'è passato issu! Gira …
trova atri modi … issu ha fattu nu passa ara destra … tu, piglialu ara sinistra—
basta ma! … nun mi ce fa pensare … ca 'ndra se vene mie corre na cosa …

FATHER

(*Offstage*)—**Carmè!** … a cassarola bolle!

        Pause.

MOTHER

Beddhi mii, v'aviti e mbarare a va cuddhare a lingua! Si vo vive in pace … senta,
vivi e taci! … e ci ne vò pacienza! Ch'a merda più a manipoli e cchiù puzze! …
Mi ne cuddhatu lingue iu … e nun signu morta … E nun muriti nemmenu vui!

SON

Ma … non è per te.

MOTHER

È mio marito!

FATHER

(*Offstage*) … **Carme'**! Santa madonna!, che sto crepando da fame!

MOTHER

(*Beat*) Tu senza ce dire nente. Parlacce. Domanda si vo aiuto a fà 'nguà cosa … e tu vidi ca chillu ti dune li sordi senza chi ci domandi … (*Pause*) Vida ca u cortello un s'ha dimenticato! Ne parle sembre! U tene conservato bellu bellu 'ndra scrivania! … e guai a chi lo tocca! … Fin'a morte, a dittu!

> Father enters, stands by kitchen door where he can't be seen.

SON

È nu bambino ecco! **Peggio!**

FATHER

Si sei venuto per minde guerra 'ndra casa, te ne puoi andare! Ca à me ccà, bene non me ne fai! … e non me ne hai fatto mai! … Se non ti piace come funzionanu e cose ccà! … **Va scienne** come dicono i francesi! Ca se fossi statu nu francese aru posto mio t'avissi cacciato da casa a diec'anni—sulu cu le mutanne! e senza scarpe! Uno di quelli ti meritavi! … A mammata c'e'l'ho detto come deve fare quando moro io! … Lu lasso scritto puru supra na carta! **Tu, 'ndra sala mortuaria non ci devi mettere piedi.** E si te vide entrare 'nguno che me rispette ti deve cacciare fuori! … C'e l'ho detto a mammata! E nessuno te forze de ce venire ccà! **Avvocato e cazzo!** I lavori l'ho fatti sembre solo pure con la febre a 40, per dare a mangiare a voi animali, che dormite fino a mezzogiorno! … ca il mangiare ccà vi ha fatto male, no bene! Ca si v'avissi datu muddhiche invece de pane, oji me truvassi in differente condizzione! A vita moderna?! Figli che hanno avuto sembre vergogna d'essere 'taliani! Faciti all'inglese?! Ca quando patrimma me sulu guardave —**tremavo! Tremavo,** per a madonna! Avvocato e cazzo! Pino vergogna non ne ha! … ed è **dottore!** … Avissi e esse *la perla* della famiglia. La perla, maledetti tutti i santi del paradiso! … Il mondo lo deve sapere! Hai **capito** sciagurato, sventurato, svergognato, disgraziato e merda?! Allora pigliat'e cose e vatinne!

> Pause.

SON

Iu un tiegnu vergogna d'essere 'taliano … tegnu vergogna d'essere tuo figlio …

FATHER

I genitori non si rispettano na vota morti!

> Linda enters, smiling.

LINDA

A tavola è preparata! Signori prego!

MOTHER

Iamu ja … ch'e fatto puru a checca! E dopo rapimu i regali, e pigliamu e fotografie! Iiamu!

FATHER

(*To SAL , throwing a five dollar bill on the floor*) Te!

MOTHER

E chissi?

FATHER

Per se cumbrare a corda per se mbicare!

> Son exits house with robe on, slams the door. Linda goes upstairs, slams the door. Father exits to cantina, slams the door.

MOTHER

(*Beat*) A checca, chi vuliti murire!

Act 1, Scene 5: MOTHER, FATHER, LINDA, SAL

FATHER

(*Enters, with an empty garbage bag*) **Bambino! Bambino!** Ca ti ci'à sentito dire a tia! Apposto a ditto! Pecchi tu hai sembre difenduto ad issu!

MOTHER

Io difendo nessuno! Io difendo a pace! Voglio pace! Ma guarda cume raggiuni!

FATHER

Come raggiono **io o issu?!** . . . Nun se facissi vedere a faccia!

MOTHER

Zitto ca te sendanu e gente!

FATHER

E me sentissi puru u patr'eterno! Non voglio vedere mancu nu falzoletto suo 'ndra casa!

MOTHER

Dov'e porti se beghe?!

FATHER

Mancu nu falzoletto! . . . E dorbico ndru giardino! Prima e brucio . . . e poi e dorbico! Tutte! . . . fiammifero e Via! (*Going from wall to wall, removing everything that belongs to his Son or was a gift from him.*) Questo chi l'ha portato? . . . Via! . . . questo pure—Via! . . . fotografie sue 'ndra sa casa non ne voglio vedere! . . . Via!

MOTHER

Ma guarda ccà! . . . *propio* come i bambini stai faciennu! (*Father stops, stares at mother for a moment*) Ca se beghe de plastica fannu na puzza da morire . . . e u fumo me ruvine tutt'i panni e fore. . . . Vida bellu mio ca chissi sunnu ricordi! . . . e mezze robbe ce le combrate iu!

FATHER

Soldi buttati aru vientu! . . . **Bambino?!** . . . va bene, chissa la pagherai! Che tu ce dai troppo confidenza! Na mamma avissi de dare esempi!

MOTHER

M'è figlio! Zoppo, stupido, bello o brutto, m'è figlio! . . . U sai qual'è lu problema? . . . che tu, figli non ne dovevi avere! Ecco il problema! I . . . E si figliutta è nu disgraziato, è pecchi ha pigliato tutto da razza tua maleditta! Tutt'e tia ha pigliato! Tutti due testardi!

FATHER

(*OVER "Tutt'e tia ha pigliato"*) Da razza—va bene . . . permettate du fare entrare 'ndra casa . . . e poi te lo dico io de quale razza ha pigliato! Ammazzo ad isso ed a tia! . . . E se vuoi, te po pigliare puru tutt'e cose tue, e ti ne puoi andare puru tu!

MOTHER

Io avissi de fare davvero, per te fa vide!

FATHER

E fallo! Che da solo sto bene io! Non ho bisogno di nessuno!

MOTHER

Ca forse vivu nu jiornu e cchiù! … (*Grabbing the garbage bag and trying to tear it from his hands*) Vida un jiettà sa robba! T'aviertu! …

FATHER

Ahi ca me fa male!

MOTHER

Ca tu giuro dumani un me vidi cchiu'!

FATHER

… ch'aspìatti!—**Fallo!**

> *Father stops suddenly. Pause.*

FATHER

Sento na macchina! Stut'a luce! Va guarda da finestra! **VA GUARDA CHI È, Gesù Christo!**

MOTHER

(*Looking out the window furtively*) I francesi e supra … marit'e moglie … No … emme, **emme'** … non è lu marito!

FATHER

Quella troia! … Eh si! … u marito lavure fore città … e mo issa fa festa!—a bella vita! … Chin'è? u ciommo! … Oggi tutte queste così tenanu u ciommo!

MOTHER

Cumu così?

FATHER

Oi … e francese! Sembre ad uscire fuori, e a lasciare quello povero figlio solo … cu chilla cugina giovane … ca pare sembre drogata! Poi leggi 'ndri giornali che trovanu bambini 'ndri stufe—'ndri friggideri … e la gente se meraviglie … Quando vedo u marito …

MOTHER

Tu fatt'i cazzi tui! Vedat'i fatti da casa tua!

FATHER

Eh si! … e se si ne và? … senza pagare l'affitto? Ahhhh! … Che questa s'è capace de fare questo a lu marito, che ci vuole a se ne andare senza dire na parola a nessuno! … (*Beat*) Gua gua … vedi chi vesta? … Così si vedono e gamme, e cosce, a—**vedi vè** … tutt'u culo e fore! … Ogni vota chi saglie le scale … cammine cu certe mosse—hai capito … ca fa spaventare puru i muarti! … per se fa vide u culu! **Troia!**

MOTHER

E tu pecchi guardi?

FATHER

Io guardo così … no ca guardo per guardà … non si sa mai … de vote qualch'uno va trovannu d'arrubbare … Uno un po stare maì sicuro! … E poi … me metti nu piatto e pasta davanti a faccia, non lo guardo? … specie si me fa fame …

MOTHER

Chi bella robba ca sini …

FATHER

Hai visto … guà guà … sono andati aru picchinniccu. (*Beat*) Troia!

MOTHER

Ma tu chi ne sai s'è na troia? Ce può essere parente, cugino …

FATHER

Si si, parente ccà! (*Pointing to his crotch*) . . . A te forse, ti ce piglie per fissa . . . ma per pigliare fissa a mia . . . na de mangiare sazizza e picchinnicchi! . . . (*Looks out the window*) **MANNAIE TUTTII CORNUTI DU DIAVOLO!** Vedo nu gatto! Vedi si me sbaglio.

MOTHER

Iiiii emmè . . . è nu gatto!

FATHER

Per la madonna! C'è l'ho detto! . . . **no animali!** C'è l'abbiamo scritto puru ndru baio! . . . Mo v'arrangio io. (*Cleaning his throat in preparation for a confrontation*)

MOTHER

Aspetta!!! Chi fai?! Facce parlare de Salvature quannu ritorne!

FATHER

Te l'ho detto!

MOTHER

Allura faccie parlare de Linda quannu vene lu marito! Ca tu non ci sai parlare . . . (*Father stares at her*) U vidi! . . . **Poi t'engazzi subito** . . . e a capace ca fai ngazzare puru ad issa, e poi sinne và veramente!

FATHER

GATTO NO!, ho detto! . . . porca miseria!

MOTHER

Pecchi mu dici a mia?!

FATHER

Ci'abbiamo scritto ndru cazz'e baio! . . . (*Looks outside*) Vidi disgraziata, u portanu sopra!—Chiam'a figliatta!

MOTHER

Signorì!

FATHER

. . . Ca cu sa Levecchia s'hannu misu tutti sa prepotenza! . . . Ca questa e sopra non è separatista?!

MOTHER

Non ci ho domandato! . . . Iu un vaiu guardannu ne cumu votanu e ne cumu cacanu!

FATHER

Apposto lo fà! . . . Tu non sei furba . . . ma io vedo tutto! . . . A voluto u baio a forza in francese!

MOTHER

Sunnu francese!

FATHER

E se io ce lo volevo dare in Inglese?! Sono il padrone!

MOTHER

Sei na bestia! . . . ca sono francesi, un ne ca vò dire ca sunnu separatisti! . . . Ci sono puru i francesi buani!

FATHER

Si si . . . va bene per piacire, un ne parlamu de nente! ca tu de politica capisci poco e nente! Si na pappagalla! **Questo** lo fa' per provocare . . . se non capisci! . . . cussi' indebolisci, vinni casa e bottega, e rimangono solo loro! Hai capito mò?!

(*Goes to window*) Disgrazziati! A chiamat'a figliatta?!

A door slams upstairs. Linda walks down the stairs.

LINDA

Chi vuliti?

FATHER

(*At the window, waving to the tenant, embarrassed and totally under her spell*) Bojoù madamme.

MOTHER

Hai visto ca t'ha visto!

FATHER

Chi fà? Saluto, e faccio finta ca nente! (*to Linda*) Cosa stavi facendo?

LINDA

Un sunnu affari tui

MOTHER

Emmè!

Pause.

FATHER

Dimme na cosa … a mammata la vedi mai riposare? (*Pause*) Avvicinate cca (*After a short pause, Linda takes one small step towards him*) … più vicino ancora (*She takes a smaller step towards him*) … **AVVICINATE ti ho detto!** (*She takes a full step towards him*) U vedi su pezzo e carta? (*She looks straight ahead in defiance. Father points to a piece of paper on the floo*r) **QUESTO QUÀ PER TERRA!** … C'è de ieri matina! … Due giorni, e nessuno l'ha visto!

LINDA

L'ai visto tu!

FATHER

Mu fai apposto? … Io tiegnu atri affari e penzare! … mammata è sembre a pulire da matina ara sera!

LINDA

Puru io tiegnu atre cose de fare … Su fissarie!

FATHER

Tutti mangiamo, tutti lavoriamo! Scrivatille se parole!

LINDA

Atre fissarie!

FATHER

Vedi ch'è la seconda volta ch'ai ditto sa parola …

MOTHER

Linda! …

LINDA

È **dissu!**

FATHER

Chine ISSU?! … Non voglio sentire **ISSU o ISSA!** Mamma o papà. Hai capito?

LINDA

Si **papà**. … Ed io come mi chiamo … SERVA?

FATHER

Non mi fare bestemiare per la mbiculita! Ca invece de te dare mangiare, ti do veleno io. Ca ndru stipo è!

LINDA

Tu si u veleno!

MOTHER

LINDA!

LINDA

(*Crying*) M'aviti chiamato!—Chi vuliti?!

FATHER

Nu pezz'e carta. Che ci vuole. SERVA? (*Pause. Throws a bundle of keys on the floor*) Pigliame u baio de chilla e sopra dra scrivania.

MOTHER

E dopo riscald'a pasta.

LINDA

(*Holding back the tears*) Non ho fame.

MOTHER

Ma noi dobbiamo mangiare, signorì!

LINDA

Si signora!

MOTHER

N'atra dieta? Che fra poco sparisci davanti gl'occhi! ...

LINDA

Quando ero grossa ti facevo vergogna!

MOTHER

E mò fai puru vergogna! ... grossa? Na vutta! ... no grossa ... e invece mu si nu spirdu!

FATHER

Va bene, facimu i lavuri prima.

MOTHER

Io oggi ti voglio vedere mangiare!—come na **cristiana!** ... Ca fattu a faccia de na strega! Si no te civo io!

LINDA

Non ho fame ti ho detto!

FATHER

Senza mutetti! Un mangiare 'ndra casa un ce manche! ... E unnu voglio vedere perde!

LINDA

(*Picks up the keys from the floor, then to Father*) Si fossi a lu posto tuo, facissi attenzione a chillo chi te mangi tu ... 'Ngu juarnu u veleno te lo fazzu trovare ndru piatto!

> Linda exits. Mother chases after her. Lights fade leaving a spot on
> Father as he looks towards the upstairs apartment.
> MUSIC (diegetic, playing on the radio):
> "Il Pallone" by Rita Pavone.
> We are in the mid 1960s. Father hasn't moved, obsessively
> listening to the cat noise coming from the upstairs apartment.

MOTHER

(*Offstage*) U **mangiar'è pronte!** Raffaè, Linda, ... **SALVATORE!** ... E portati u vino d'a cantina! **È pronte!** (*Lights up. Father renters the dining area*) Quandu cazz'e vote ve chiamare?! Gesù mio!, ch'a pasta se scoce, e dopo se fa tutta brutta brutta!

FATHER

Mezz'ora quella, per trovare su baio!

MOTHER

Linda! **Salvatore!**

FATHER

(*Beat*) U sienti come corre lu gatto!

MOTHER

Ma quello è lu figlio!

FATHER

Che figlio! È lu gatto! Un senti come corre … tatatatum, tatatatum, tatatatum. (*With the end of a broomstick, Father knocks on the ceiling*)

MOTHER

Ma tu te fare nemici con tutti?!

FATHER

Chi ci'à cento nimici nun more mai! (*Tenant responds by knocking same number of times from above*)

        Enter Sal and Linda. He's eleven years old, she's ten.

MOTHER

Siti ciunghi? Sit'impalegrati?! Damme su vino! (*Takes wine bottle from Sal*)

FATHER

Vaviti lavat'e manu?

SAL AND LINDA

Si … Io ye … Auguri … buona festa. *(They kiss Father on both cheeks, who accepts their greetings like a head of state, as a matter of duty. Linda and Sal then give Father a Father's Day greeting card. Sal's card is in a white rectangular-shaped envelope, while Linda's is a rolled-up PINK SHEET of paper with a RED RIBBON wrapped around it.)*

FATHER

Grazie!

LINDA

(*Giving father keys and lease*) Te!

FATHER

Facitime vidire e manu. (*He inspects both their hands*) Cammina iative lavat'e manu! Buggiardi, sciagurati, svergognati e merda! (*They exit in a hurry*) Ca tutte se mure mure manate nere! … E lavativille belle belle! … Si no, vengo 'ndra toletta, e ve lavo io! … E si a schiuma non esce bianca bianca come a neve … facitive a croce, ca ve gonfio u musso, e ve tagliu e manu! … (*Beat*) Hai capito Salvato'?! … (*Beat. to himself*) Ma chi! …

        Father studies lease. Mother serves the pasta 'canticchiannu,'
        singing under her breath.

FATHER

(*Calmly*) Pigliame u sale … (*Pause*) Adduv'è lu sale? (*Pause*) È possibile d'avere u tavolo preparato bello bello quando se mangie?!

MOTHER

Chi te manghe? (*Exists singing*) La la la la la.

        Without moving from his chair, Father's eyes search the room for
        salt. Can't find it.

FATHER

    (*Exploding*) **GESÙ CHRISTO! STO PARLANDO!**

MOTHER

    Ma sei pazzo?!

FATHER

    Tre volte ho domandato per u sale! E nessuno nente!

MOTHER

    Non ti ho sentito! **Scusa Missiù!**[1] ... a tia te su cadut'e manu?

FATHER

    Carmè! Voi vedere come ti preparo u tavolo io?! Ca t'u fazzu vedere subito subito!
    ... (*Beat*) Questa è sistemazzione?!! (*Beat*) ... Lassa stare, ... me lo prendo solo.
    (*He exits, returns with napkins which he places on the table. No salt*) Non c'è!

MOTHER

    (*Beat*) Mangia senza sale!

FATHER

    Carmè! ... Prima no serevietti, poi no sale ...

MOTHER

    Domanda alla signorina!

LINDA

    (*Offstage. Top of her lungs*) Io non l'ho toccato!

FATHER

    Che ci vuole a mettere e cose a lu posto suo.

MOTHER

    Tu, un te mischiare ndre cose da cucina! ... sunnu affari mii!

FATHER

    Chi? ... Che solo da cucina ti devi preoccupare ... e non sei nemmeno capace!
    ... Se non fossi per mia, a cucina fossi capo sotto. Tazze dove non appartengono!
    —E ancora non è finita! ... Trovati u sale!

        Mother exits and quickly re-enters.

MOTHER

    (*Plunks down a box of salt in front of Father*) Ecco il sale!

FATHER

    Io voglio u sale che va sopra a tavola ... quello ndru piccolo cosu ... u recipiente,
    cumu cazzo se chiame ... quello che si mette ccà ... propio ccà ... a lu postu suo!
    Quello voglio!

MOTHER

    Gesù mio ca me vaiu jiettu de na muntagna! (*Hysterical*) **NON L'HO TOCCATO!**

FATHER

    Va bene ... Allora dov'è? ... Sparito? Così! Solo solo. (*Pause*) Tu un n'ha tuccatu!
    ... Chiddha un n'ha tuccatu! ...

MOTHER

    Liiindaaa! ...

LINDA

    (*Offstage*)—**NON L'HO TOCCATO!**

---

1. Missiù from the French *Monsieur*.

FATHER

(*To himself*) Po po Po po po po po po po po po po po po popopopopopo ... ca me vene na raggia!!

Enters Linda and sits at the table.

MOTHER

Ma chi stati faciennu 'ndra sa toletta?!! U sale adduve a misu?!

FATHER

(*Studying the lease, to himself*) Bo ... (*to Linda*) Linda! ... leggi tu su baio, e vedi se c'è scritto "no gatto."

MOTHER

(*Brusquely, as in "I'm eating"*) Bon'appetito! (*She eats*)

LINDA

(*To herself*) Ouff!

FATHER

Senza sbruffare, bella mia! ... Ca per ve mannare ara scola ho sgobbato u culo!

LINDA

(*Takes a quick look at the lease*) È in francese. (*Beat*) Tu non lo sai si c'è scritto?!

FATHER

(*Beat*) C'è l'ho fatto scrivere de Ciccio affianco! ... ci'à scritto specialmente ... "no gatto." ... Io non ci vedo bene.

LINDA

(*Takes another quick glance at the lease*) Non c'è nente de gatto.

FATHER

Come non c'è? "PAS DE SCIÀ"... non c'è? ... Come c'e' scritto?

LINDA

(*Reading*) Le lo ca taar ...

FATHER

Loca*terre*, no locatarro.

LINDA

E se lo sai, pecchi me domandi? ... (*Father raises hand, as if to slap her with a backhand. Pause. Linda continues to read*) "Le loca*terre* et les per-sonnes a qui il per-mettes l'access a l'im-meubles" ...

FATHER

E chi vo dire chissu?

LINDA

(*Beat*) Bo. È in francese. Non la capisco sa parola.

FATHER

(*Beat*) Va bene va bene, continua. (*Beat*) Bo.

LINDA

... "doivent se conduire" ...

FATHER

Come?

LINDA

Bo.

FATHER

Bo. Chi sà che cazzo vo dire sa parola! ... Vidimo ccà ... (*Reading*) "Dav se cond ..." Per a miseria! Che s'avissi scola io, facessi tremare il **mondo, Gesù Christo!!** ... "PAS DE SCIÀ"! C'è o non c'è?! ... 0 forse c'è 'no animal'

LINDA

    (*Mumbling, directed at Father*) Animal.

FATHER

    Come? … (*Beat*) C'È, SÌ o NO?!

LINDA

    Te l'ho detto na volta già!

FATHER

    E pure se te lo domando cento volte!

LINDA

    Ma t'ho detto, NON C'È! Pecchi dicissi ca non c'è se c'è?! Perche' non c'è!!

FATHER

    (*Takes the lease from her violently*) Va bene, lascia stare! (*To himself*) Non c'è.

LINDA

    Sa scrittura è mezza 'taliana, mezza francese.

FATHER

    Pecchi me l'ha scritta Ciccio … chi figli mii non erano capace!

MOTHER

    Vo dire ca s'è dimenticato.

FATHER

    Puru tu sei d'accordo?

MOTHER

    Senti! … tu ca si tanto sperto … trovalo tu!

FATHER

    E pecchi crisci figli?! Io non ho fatto scola e cazzo! A bon'anima e patrimma è morto quannu avie sei anni e miezzu! …

MOTHER

    (*Over "quannu avie sei …"*) Ahah. … Va bene, chilla stessa musica.

FATHER

    Carme'! C'è l'ho detto mille volte! "Mbarative u francese!" … ca si trase sa Vecchia cu si separatisti trasanu i tempi brutti!

MOTHER

    Ch'a me fare? Ci adattiamo!

FATHER

    Sentila sentila … Ca questo è peggio di Mussolini! Mussolini almeno ere 'taliano! … Cu chissu, chi nun parle francese, **fuori!** È tremende! … E se possono prendere puru a casa, se vogliono! *Cumu i comunisti*!

MOTHER

    E che dobbiamo fare mo'?! Ci'ammazziamo?!! Quando arrive lu giorno arrive!

FATHER

    È **arrivato!!**

LINDA

    Chi te fa lu gatto? … È cosi bello. A madama e supra mi ce fa giocare.

FATHER

    Tu hai toccato u gatto?

LINDA

    So? … S'appriche sembre a se fissarie.

164

FATHER

(*Slaps her hard across the face*) La terza volta oggi! E ti ho avertito! Fissarie? ... FISSARIE?! Quello che t'mbarano e maestre? ... ca io ti faccio lassare a scola domani, e te mindo subito subito a sudare u pane! **Fissarie?!** I gatti sono sporchi! ... te profumano tutt'a casa cu la merda e la pisciazza! E portanu sfortuna! Chissu nun te l'hannu mbarato alla scola?! Hai visto mai domesticare nu gatto? Anne fare a modo suo! ... portanu sulu malatie!

MOTHER

Ma s'a de mangiare! Mo è tempo de fare se cose?

FATHER

Chi ha tempo, non aspete tempo!

MOTHER

Sei **insupportabile!**

FATHER

(*Slaps Linda*) Per ogni volta che parli, o che la difendi ... abbusche nu schiaffo! *Pause. Enters Sal, scratching his bum, vigorously.*

MOTHER

Ma che stai facendo 'ndra sa toletta tutto su tiempu tu natru?! A cacare fuoco?! ... Mezz'ora!

FATHER

Chi? Ca chissu ha de sembre cacare quannu se mangie! Un tu cacci su vizio?

SAL

Ma, a mia me piace cchiù chilla pasta ndre buatte.[1]

MOTHER

Vida ca ti ce mindu a tia ndre buatte. A piezzi piezzi!

     Linda is still crying. Sal is oblivious to it all, he's used to it.

SAL

(*Whispers in Linda's ear, then*) It's true, I couldn't hold it any more 'cause I knew like if I came home they wouldn't let me go out again ... then I wiped it with a leaf, you know ... but some of it still stuck ... I think I did it too hard, like, when I wiped. I'm itchy! There's blood!

FATHER

(*Slaps Sal across the back of the head*) **Italiano!** o francese ... Cos'ha detto Linda?

MOTHER

Ma tu si pazzu a lu minare ara capo?!

FATHER

(*Hits Sal again*) E te l'ho detto ... Non difendere i figli davanti al padre. (*Pause*) Io l'ho minato ccà (*Hits Sal again*) u vidi.

MOTHER

E unn'è la testa?

FATHER

E tu dove i mini?

---

1. 'Buatte' from the French *boîtes*, (*cans*).

MOTHER

Ma si tu mini così ... (*Hits Sal*) ... L'ammazzi! I figli non se minanu alla testa!—che ponnu diventare cioti. Domanda a chi vuoi!

FATHER

Ca non sai minare! ... Io però saccio dove mino ... a ccà (*Hits Sal*)—dov'è duro, u vidi. Tu invece mini ccà (*Hits Sal*) dov'è mollo ... è tutta natra cosa. 'Llà sicuro ch'è più delicato, e se ponnu rimbambire!. Invece si fa così (*Hits Sal*), no così (Hits Sal) si no sì che diventanu matti! Questo m'a 'mbarato Olga a tedesca, quannu lavoravo in Germania ... Mi vuoi mbarare tu come minare i figli? (*Linda is about to exit*) A carne non l'hai toccata.

LINDA

Troppo grassa.

MOTHER

Mangiat'a carne!

FATHER

Quannu cresciamu nui, solo a grassa si conosceva. Una volta a l'anno—NATALE! ... Mangiat'a carne! Questa non è fissaria! Chissa su soldi! Mangiat'a carne!

MOTHER

Non te lo fa dire natra vota!

     Linda takes a piece of meat and swallows it whole.

MOTHER

Emmè, se l'ha ngoiata sana sana!

FATHER

(*Trying to retrieve the piece of meat from Linda's mouth*) Butt'a carne ndru piatto! **Butt'a carne, ti ho detto!**

     Linda smiles.

MOTHER

No, s'a cuddhata! Che cornuta!

LINDA

È grassa!

MOTHER

(*Grabs Linda's hair and pulls her head back and forth*) Ma sei scema de te cuddhare nu piezzu e carne sano sano, ca muari!

FATHER

Vedi che 'a fai male così. (*To Linda, calmly, staccato*) Mangiat'a carne come i cristiani. Masticala belle bella!

     Linda takes another piece of meat,
     swallows it whole.

MOTHER

Emmè! 'Natra vota!

FATHER

Mastica! (*Grabs Linda by the jaw and forces her to open her mouth*) **Così s'à de fare! Così!** (*He takes a new piece of meat from her plate, shoves it in her mouth, moving her jaw up and down*) **Mastica sa cazz'e carne!!** (*Linda fights back. To mother*) Carmè!, tenacc'e mano! Ca per la madonna, si tu si testarda, io sono più testardo e tia! (*Father shoves another piece of meat in Linda's mouth, though she has yet to swallow the last one*) **Mastica sa ...** (*Linda spits the meat in his face*) Per a madonna, cum'è dura e capu! … **Carmè!** … Salvatò, va piglia a cinta ndru stipo—**disgraziata—mastica—SALVATÒ!, vai a prendere** …

LINDA

(*To Sal*) I'll hate you.

FATHER

Non parlare inglese!!! (*Threatening to slap her face*) Te lo dico io "IT YU!" **Salvatò!**

MOTHER

(*To Sal*) Vai!, se nò te mine puru a tia!

LINDA

I swear on the Bible, Sal, I won't …

FATHER

Ai! (*Smacks her*) M'ha muzzicato a manu sa disgraziata! … **Salvatore!**, fai u bravo 'e papà, e pigliame sa cazz'e cinta! … Vai tu Carmè! (*Sal fetches belt from the kitchen cabinet. Linda breaks away. Still has a piece of meat in her mouth. Stops and stares back at them, one by one. She stares at Sal, who is still holding the belt, feeling guilty. Looking at father, she reveals the piece of meat, then swallows it whole. She smiles and exits. Pause*) Così dici tu?! Va bene … vate 'ndra stanza. Questa la pagherai! Mezz'ora cu petre sott'e ginocchie!, m'avissi de fulminare Gesù Christo!!! (*Door slams upstairs*) … **E non voglio vedere luce!** (*Upstairs door slams again. Then, to Sal*) E a tè, quando te dico pigliame a cinta, mò, no domani! (*Sal exits with the belt. Pause*) Come fà uno a tirare e crescere na famiglia? … Come … **come** fà uno a tirare nu popolo? … se non c'è sistemazione? … Mò s'andassi avanti!! … Ma avanti si deve andare!, no indietro! Ca si tutti comincianio a fare a modo suo, a famiglia "afallesce" diceva nu barese! … (*Beat*) Me la faciti tutt'apposto! … (*Beat*) Vediamo chi la vince! (*Pause*) Chilla disgraziata m'ha puru graffiato!

> Lights change. Back to the present. Father remains immobile down centre. Linda enters, with bruised face. She places the Father's Day cake on the table. Lights one candle. Exits to kitchen.

FATHER

C'ero io presente … l'ho visto scrive, "NO SHIÀ." … Bo … "non c'è." … Chille figlie e Ciccio … te leggiano lettere, documenti, carte de governo, così ta ta ta ta ta … Francese, Inglese, 'Taliano. Tutto! … Pure quelle pensione de l'Italia … ta ta ta due minuti, ch'è na meraviglia! (*Short pause. Glances at the ceiling*) … Chisà che combine chillu gatto?

MOTHER

Mangiat'a pasta, ca se rifridde!

> Radio news signal.

FATHER

Zitto! E notizie! Fermi tutti! … Vediamo che dicono loro!

End of Act One.

ACT TWO

Act 2, Scene 1: MOTHER, FATHER, PASQUALE

Lights up on Father in downstairs 'living-room.' He is wearing construction gloves and appears to be fertilizing a chive plant. Enters Mother.

MOTHER
E questa?

FATHER
È d'a **troia!** Signu andato sopra u balcone, senza mi vedere nessuno, e me l'ho presa. E mo ce la riporto. ... (*Beat*) Questa è na spece d'erba cipollina ... (*Beat*) Avvicinate ... Vedi quà ... e pure quà ... tutto quì se l'ha mangiato u gatto. ... Tene quattru o cinque piante, ma u gatto và toccando sembre questa. Adesso la sistemo io!

MOTHER
Teee, e mu chi ce fare cu sa pianta?

FATHER
A vitamina! ... Questa è speciale! ... m'a data n'amico du lavuru ... ca lui legge sembre libri ... In termine di dieciminuti, sta vitamina, stenne puru nu toro ... Mo ce mettiamo na poco e medicina, e lo sistemiamo bello tiso tiso. (*Beat*) Il nome mio se lo devono ricordare!

MOTHER
Ma non è più facile se ci parli?! ... O facci parlare de Ciccio affianco.

FATHER
Chi? ... "Portè alla courte" mi ha detto! ... Chi ce va dici? ... Vate alla curta vate! Ma mangiassi la merda! ... ca questo è pecchi u marito un ci'à fatto provare e manu du primo giorno! ... Ormai iddha ha cambiato farmacia! ... Mu se cure cu la vitamina du ciommo!

MOTHER
Ma guarda chi cosa e pazzi!

FATHER
... Ca si vidisssi chillu ch'e vistu io ... quannu e pigliatu a pianta ... te azassino i capiaddhi! ... (*Beat*) E guardato da finestra da cucina ... un ta vidi seduta supra u divano senza nente ... na gamma ccà ... na gamma 'llà ... e lu ciommo nginocchiato per terra ca dicie le preghiere. (*He mimes 'eating' with one hand and mouth*)

MOTHER
Iiii, ma guarda ...

FATHER
Chi? ... e chiddhu ammucca ammucca ammucca.

MOTHER
Gesù mio da crucie ...

FATHER
Cussì ha fatto primo, secondo e contorno.

MOTHER
Senda!, un voglio sentì de se cose ...

FATHER

Iii ca tuni ... tutto te scandalizze ...

MOTHER

Insomma **ce va parli!**

FATHER

Ma sei scema? ... me offre nu caffè ... cade per terra ... si rombe na gamma ... chiame la pulizia, e ce dice ca ce l'ho rotta io!

MOTHER

Ma tieni paura ca te mangie?

FATHER

Come? ... Ca chissa troia se ne mangiassi dieci! ... Non c'ere il marito ... me chiame per pagare l'affitto ... e la trovu senza mutandine, solo cu na maglietta ... che si tirava mezz'e gamme ... s'a ngufizzave propio mezz'—Io **fermo!**, Gesù Christo! ... finta che niente! ... (*Beat*) Per no pagare l'affitto!!! ... Na de mangiare sazizze ...

MOTHER

Invece a tia ti ce piace a ce jire a prima matina ... che lo sai che la trovi sulu cu le brachissine! ... forse t'invite per mangiare ... nu pocu e latte e biscotti!—pecchi ce vai?!!

FATHER

Va bene, basta! Guardat'a lingua! Ca n'un t'e rotto u musso come fa tuo fratello cu la mugliera! Apposto hai messo sa lingua!

MOTHER

E toccame per vide! (*Pause*) TU, vidi sulu u male de gente, ecco! Ma e gente non sono tutte com'e te! ... A gatta da dispensa, com'è se penza!

FATHER

Smettila per la madonna! ... Tutta questa storia per difendere sa puttana e supra! M'ha de grattare i muri su gatto?! Mi devo far mettere sotto de nu gatto separatista?! ... E mo ve fazzu vide ... vediamo chi la vince! ... Metto n'annuncio ndru giornale ... e cacciu ad issa e ru gattu! ... No gatto ho detto!

> *Doorbell rings. Father and mother freeze, and look at each other. Father quickly hides the plant, and the poison, in the same closet where he keeps the belt. He answers the door, removing the many security bars and locks first. A huge trunk (baule) is standing in the doorway.*

FATHER

Carmè, damme na mano!

MOTHER

Ma guarda chi cosa!

> *They both drag the trunk inside.*

FATHER

Finalmente! (*He locks the door again with the security bars*) Chiuda blainde, tente tutto!! Per a madonna ... ca s'u vene a sapire 'nguno! ... Chissi un ni fannu entrare più! (*He smells the trunk*) Si sente ch'è de l'Italia! Addura addù ... Questa bella mia, è la purga! ... Robba de casa ... fatta a l'uso nostro ... Mu vidi cumu scioglie sa purga! ... e cumu ce fa venire l'appetito alla signorina!

> *Father opens the trunk, out pops a young man in his late twenties to early thirties wearing a white suit and pink fedora.*

PASQUALE

Wuayy papà, wuayyy mamma! Malboro! Yu wanna lait? Yea, no, okay, latur, whatti? ... Pasqualino u Vermiciellu ... ti ricordi?! (*Affecting the voice of an American movie gangster and striking a pose*) ... Sticca mappa, Giacca! Se non la smettie ti rompoe il culo![1]

Blackout.

Act 2, Scene 2: MOTHER, FATHER, PASQUALE, LINDA

Lights up. Father, Mother and Pasquale stand by the entrance (gates) of the upstairs living room, wearing paper slippers, like those found in doctors' offices. It is a dark, ostentatious, mausoleum-like chamber with ornate, European Rococo drapes (dark red), a massive wooden 'sarcophagus' (a 1970s Zenith chromacolor television set in pristine condition), and a makeshift altar (credenza) made of wood and granite stacked with deceased relatives' photos and unlit votives. Small and tall Dieffenbachia plants fill the room. The sofas are covered in plastic.

MOTHER

È nu salotto Pasquà ... Semplice ... nent'e speciale.

FATHER

(*To Mother*) Io non capisco che differenza c'è di qua e sotto ... Salotto è salotto! Sotto si stà meglio.

MOTHER

'Ndra ccà non ci siamo mai! ... du '74, forse e più ... l'annu chavimu cumbratu a casa ... Oggi c'è l'occasione! **Seditive!** (*They sit*) ... Emmè, Dio mio!, è megliu ca me vaiu cambio! ... tutti si panni pieni di polvere!

FATHER

CARMÈ! Sedate! (*She sits*)

PASQUALE

(*Referring to the framed memorial cards*) Tutti morti?

FATHER

E pecchi u munnu è fattu solo dei vivi secondo te? (*Beat*) Loro hanno finito di soffrire. Noi ancora no. (*Beat*) Tutto dipende da te. (*Beat*) De lettere che ho ricevuto ... di quello che mi dice tua mamma ... i sentimenti tuoi verso mia figlia sembrano sinceri.

PASQUALE

Sicuro! **Sciore!** Wuay papà, ero tanto, io, e già per tua figlia, mi capisci.—Sembre cò' rispetto però!

FATHER

È pura come la vergine Maria!

PASQUALE[2]

—Ci mancherebbe?!

---

1. 'American' pronunciation of the Italian *Se non la smetti ti rompo il culo!* (*If you don't stop it I'll break your ass!*)
2. In this case, dashes before the dialogue do not necessarily indicate an overlap per se but the rhythmic

FATHER

—Ci abbiamo fatto sembre avertimenti!

PASQUALE

—Non ho dubbi!

FATHER

—Fin'a poco fà, andav'a chiesa ogni Domenica—

PASQUALE

—Na santa praticamente!

FATHER

—È stata sembre la prima da classe!

PASQUALE

Meno male! . . . che io scuola, poco e nente!

FATHER

—Solo n'anno forse, ch'è stata seconda. **Palate!** L'anno dopo **prima** da classe!

PASQUALE

(*To Mother*) È forte però!

FATHER

—Mazze e panelli fanno i figli belli . . .

PASQUALE

—Figlie in questo caso . . .

FATHER

(*Over "caso"*) **Panelli** senza maze . . .

PASQUALE

—Fannu i figli pazzi!

FATHER

—Ahh!, a conosci questa?!

PASQUALE

—Come no! . . . Grazie a Dio, ne ho avuto palate io! Io sono grandissimo studioso de palatorium! Palatum a destram. sinistram, sotto e soprum!

FATHER

—Uomini de tutt'i culuri sa vulissino sposare.

PASQUALE

—Benediche, ce ne sono razze a s'America!

FATHER

—Ma io la dò a te!

PASQUALE

—Grazie

FATHER

—Citto! . . . Perchè conosco a famiglia . . . Conosco i sacrifici dei genitori tuoi.

PASQUALE

(*Beat, moved*) Sono commosso . . . Come dice la futura sposa?

FATHER

(*Dead serious, he sticks to his 'sermon'*) L'amore è come u vino . . . più u curi, cu la pacienza, e più vene potente! Ma è n'impegno! . . . e ce vonnu chille quadrate!

---

call-and-response between characters, that is, the *fast-paced dialogue entry* by a character following the dialogue of the previous character, which is why they start with Pasquale's first response.

(*Pause*) Ricordate, moglie tua, sangue mio! Così l'ho tenuta! (*He extends his right hand, keeping his palm open, to show that he raised her with the greatest of care*) E come na regina a voglio trattata!

PASQUALE

Wuay papà, io non sono complicato! Abbasta ca sà cucinare! ... me fà trovare na minestra calda o due penne asciutte ogni sera, alle otto precise ... e me crisce nu paru de figli come si debe ... Solo quello voglio io! ... Altro che regina! Non deve alzare nemmeno na mano! I lavori i faccio io! Eh! Più di quello ... ("*I rest my case*") ...

FATHER

(*To Mother*) Guarda come raggione!

PASQUALE

Meglio di così si muore!

FATHER

(*To Mother*) Tutt'u patre!

PASQUALE

Madonna che palazzo! ... Eh, s'America! Na meraviglia! ... E poi tutte le strate belle diritte! Tutte se case belle! Tutte gemelle! Ci sanno fare ccà! Ah, America! "NAICE!" ... Wuay papà! ... mi sono combrato libri inglese I, yu he, she, her, we., yu, me ... poi non mi ricordo preciso. Poi pratichiamo insieme!

FATHER

Fuori sì, dentro no!

PASQUALE

Come dici papà?

FATHER

In questa casa si parla i t a l i a n o!

PASQUALE

E solo quello sò parlare!

FATHER

Bene così! ... Fuori parla quello che cavolo vuoi! Più lingue conosci, e meglio è!

MOTHER

Ma però, puoi parlare francese ...

PASQUALE

Ouì papà, come vuliti voi! Io m'adatto!

MOTHER

Ca mò si entra Lavecchia!

PASQUALE

—Quale vecchia?

FATHER'

Quello che vuò rovinare il Quebec! E si vince, regale cinque mila dollari a li francesi, per ogni figlio che fannu! ... Capito? ... Allora, n'avolta sposato, dunat'e fare! Non perdere tempo!

PASQUALE

No dubitare papà! Quando si scherze si scherze, ma quando si uh huh! ... io ... !

FATHER

Simu capiti?

PASQUALE

Si signore!

FATHER

Non mi chiamare signore! Ce n'è solo uno! La! (*Pointing upwards*) Peli alla bocca non ne ho io!

PASQUALE

Meno male!

FATHER

(*Sudden anger*) Guardami 'ndra l'occhi quando ti parlo!

PASQUALE

Scusa papà …

FATHER

Issa ha perso a lingua.

PASQUALE

Questo non lo sapevo!

FATHER

Parlacci in ITALIANO scemo!

PASQUALE

Ahhh, quella lingua!! E la ritroviamo, state tranquillo!

FATHER

Iu per certe cose, a li francesi non ci dò torto! A politica a sannu fare! … Però hannu raggiune! … U vino un se mischie cu la birra. I cani un se mischianu cu li gatti, se mi capisci … Cani per cani, gatti pel gatti! … Tu rinforzala con quello che conosci. Non avere vergogna! Pianta cavoli nuovi, ma i vecchi non i scippare!

PASQUALE

Ma chi le scippe?!

FATHER

Tutti si giovani 'taliani ccà che non vogliono sapere niente del italiano! … <u>puzzano</u> di vergogna! Io parlo da razza nostra! … che hanno tradito e radici … e fumano <u>droga</u>! Hai capito mò?! … Io l'ho visti con gl'occhi mii … ca io giro per bascio città, cu lu lavuru! … Se meritassinu pico e pala! … perchè ci dormono sopra i sacrifici di genitori! … Quandu me sulu guardave patrimma, io **tremavo** … ma nel senso vero … **TREMAVO!**, Gesù Christo! … Oggi tutti hanno perdutu rispetto! Se fossi capo de polizia, "Levativ'e scarpe e le calzette, **subito!**" e con na tinaglia, ce tirassi tutte l'ugne di piedi, ad uno ad uno. Zang, zang, zang, zang, che il sangue deve scorrere per le vie come scorreva à Caserta durant'a guerra! Zang, zang, zang, per la madonna! … Poi, pane ed acqua per n'anno! Minimo! Senza pietà! Poi vedi!

> *Beat.*

MOTHER

(*Drained by the story's impact*) Ci vò veramente fortuna! (*Suddenly coming back to life*) Prendi u vicino e ccà. … Ci'à due figli. U maschio se chiame Pino.

FATHER

—Ah Pino … (*To Pasquale*) Dottore!

MOTHER

—Ma te dico … nu pezzo e pane quello figlio!

FATHER

—Non si permette de fumare sigarette davanti al padre!

MOTHER

—Sembre ad aiutare a mamma! ...

FATHER

—U chiame lu padre ... sembre pronto! Lasse puru de cacare! È libero di fare quello che vuole. Ci'à la stanza sua, per conto suo!

MOTHER

—Ed è così polito! ... A mamma mi ha detto che quando si deve taglaire l'ugna di piedi, bello bello,

FATHER

—Senta senta ...

MOTHER

... mette nu falzoletto sopra il letto, e li piedi sopra il falzoletto ... e taglie!

FATHER

Vedi che delicatezza!

MOTHER

Ma guarda tu!

FATHER

—Dottore! ... Viene il padre stanco del lavoro, ci và a prendere e sandola ... ma senza ciù domandare il padre. Questo lo fà propio lui de l'idea sua! ... Peggio de na fimmina!

MOTHER

Uno di questi vale più del pane!

FATHER

E li genitori lo tengono <u>così</u>!! (*Hand extended with open palm*) Sicuro ca nu padre more tranquillo!

MOTHER

Anzi, issu vulìe puru a Linda

FATHER

E citto!

MOTHER

Chi citto?! Un n'è nente! (*To Pasquale*) Ma poi è uscita a parola ca un ere ... insomma ... normale ... ca forse, un sacciu, un ce piacianu veramente e fimmine ...

FATHER

—Ricchione e basta!

MOTHER

Ma io non ci credo. ... È dottore!

FATHER

(*To Pasquale*) Si vede che tu 'a testa ce l'hai avvitata abbastanza bene! A pigliato tutt'e patritta! Cazzu chi lavurature in Germania! ... Non ti frenare pecchi un tieni scola ... Lassa stare dottore o no dottore!! ... A scola fa bene, ma u pane se guadagne cu chisse, e vi'! (*Demonstrating his calloused hands*) ... senza chisse ... Ci vuole solo la buona volontà, e la buone salute! ... Chi ha salute è ricco e non lo sà! Tutto è possibile! ... (*Beat*) Ricordate, io non sono fesso ... faccio u fesso ... ma faciennu u fesso, prendo pe' fesso a tè!

PASQUALE

Wuay papà ... questa sì ch'è forte. Mo me la scrivo!

FATHER

A vita è na carogna! Se può ti frega! Senza pieta'! Ci vuole <u>fegato</u>! … Quando cammini, guarda avanti! Gl'occhi diritti! Ricchie aperte. Non dare fida a nessuno! Guarda avanti! Più t'abbassi e più mostri u culo! Meglio bocca chiusa ca culo aperto! **Na carogna a vita!** Oggi va 'ngulo a te … e domani puru!! … Bo! … L'uomo avvisato è mezzo salvato! … (*Beat*) Che teni intenzione de fare?

PASQUALE

Eh, io sto pensando ad una professione di quelle grande!

FATHER

Buono buono! Ci vuole volontà!

PASQUALE

Ecco!

FATHER

Fatiga!

PASQUALE

Preciso!

FATHER

E fortuna.

PASQUALE

Appunto!

FATHER

Allora?!

PASQUALE

Wuay papa, mi voglio fare n'artista! (*Imitating an American movie gangster*) "Ey yu, wisey gai!" Ho passato due mesi a Roma a fare annunci di publicità! Io specializavo nel dipartamento di medicina!

MOTHER

Chi medicina?

PASQUALE

Na pumata.

FATHER

Per fare chi?

PASQUALE

Per applicare.

MOTHER

Dove?

PASQUALE

Nel culo!

FATHER

Scostumato! (*Slaps him*)

PASQUALE

Ere uno annuncio publicitario per le murroidde! Sulla RAI! Ma però si vede solo la faccia … e la pumata vicino a faccia così! Ecco! … Mi hanno detto che ho la faccia adatta per se cose! L'espressione giusta!

FATHER

Ma tua mamma m'aveva detto ch'eri interessato a fare falegnama, o meccanico …

PASQUALE

Ci ho ripensato!

FATHER

E ripensacci di nuovo! Se no chiudimo libro, e dazzol![1]

MOTHER

(*Short pause*) Diciàmo ca questo non è nu mistiere normale per gente nostre.

FATHER

Mistiere?! **Mistiere?!**—Dove l'uomini sono fimmine, e le fimmine uomini … se mi capisci! **Mistiere?!** Ca poi te lo mettono 'ngulo pur'a te' … e non te salve no pumata, e no Gesù Christo! E dopo è troppo tardi d'andare piangento a mamma e papà con il culo rotto! Pensacci bene!

MOTHER

E si ca ce penze! Ca mò è troppo stanco! Nu viaggiu così lungo! È digiuno!

FATHER

Vedi se scale?! Se fai u bravo, le finisco. Così tu e Linda invece d'abbitare con noi ccà, stati per conto vostro sopra nell'appartamento! … Si fai u bravo … mi puoi pure aiutare … (*Beat*) Tu dico davanti a mia moglie … e davanti u crucifisso … Ca Gesù Christo m'avissi de fare truvare stisu muartu ndru liettu dumani matina si dicu bugie … Tutto quello ch'era destinato a mio figlio lo do a te … tutto tutto tutto … Stisu muartu, per Gesù Christo! … Quello che non si ha meritato lui lo do a te … E firmu puru na carta si vue … davanti a mia moglie e ru crucifisso … come testimonia … Ma lo devi meritare … si no cancellu *tutto* … pur'a *tia*. … Ti **cancello**, sopra il crucifisso! (*Beat*) Capito? … Fai bene, scordati … fai male, guardate!

MOTHER

Si si … ca mò chiamo a Linda e ne facimo nu biccherino! LINDA!

> *Enters Linda, stoned out of her mind, mascara running down her face, walking in a catatonic state towards Pasquale.*

PASQUALE

E sa bestia chi è?!

MOTHER

Questa è la signorina! Hai visto com'è vestita bella bella! (*Pulling Linda by the hair back and forth. To Linda*) Rimbambita scemonita!!! Un dici nente?! Questo è tuo sposo!

PASQUALE

(*Kneeling before her*) Gioia da vita mia! (*With an Italian accent*) Yu ar oll mai laif! … Oui oui!

> *A red liquid substance pours out of both corners of Linda's mouth. She drops to the floor.*
> *Blackout.*
> *MUSIC: "Vedrai, Vedrai" by Luigi Tenco. It starts with the first chorus, "Vedrai, Vedrai."*
>
> *Intermission.*

---

1. Dazzol from the English *that's all*.

Act 2, Scene 3: FATHER, MOTHER, DOTTORE, LINDA

Father is pacing in downstairs 'living room.' Enters Doctor (Pino) from upstairs, followed by Mother.

FATHER
Allora dottore, che novità?
MOTHER
Cos'ha detto Pino?
DOTTORE
Eh signora, tutt'okay ... non è niente di grave ... facitila riposare.
FATHER
Ca issa è sembre riposata dottò! Sembre 'ndra stanza!
DOTTORE
Si, ma voi lasciatela stare ... piano piano.
MOTHER
Ma sono passati due giorni! ... piano piano!
DOTTORE
Eh, si ma ... na bottiglia sana sana d'Acqua Velva ... e una piccola bottiglia di iodio! Un mélange dangereux!
MOTHER
Ma chi le venuto 'ndra capu a chissa Gesù Christo mio! ... (*Beat*) E chillo ch'abbiamo trovato? ... ce l'hai chiesto?
DOTTORE
Eh signora Carmela ... non vi voglio dire bugie, ma non è necessario de v'ingazzare ... perchè quello non aiut'à nessuno.
MOTHER
Ma sicuro dotto'!
FATHER
Apposto v'amo chiamato ...!
MOTHER
—Per l'aiutare!
FATHER
—Eh! Cosu, cumu te chiami—Pino!
DOTTORE
È marijuana.
FATHER
Mariana, GESÙ CHRISTO!
DOTTORE
Sono foglie disseccate di una canapa Indiana ... n'erba aromatica. Cresce una volta a l'anno, d'origine indiana, ma coltivata praticamente d'appertuto. Per secoli è stata utilizzata nella medicina tradizionale e a scopo ricreativo. Cu sa piante ce fannu puru stoffa ... corde ... come quelle che usano sulle nave!
MOTHER
Ma è droga si o no?

DOTTORE

Ha parecchi nomi ... bhang, cannabis, marijuana ... Sì signora, è droga.

Mother and Father instantly erupt, each in their own way,
walking aimlessly in different directions.

FATHER

Pe' ra madonna che non ci fazzu vedere domani io!

MOTHER

(*Over "Per a madonna"*) Oh Gesù mio! Che rovina! Chi vergogna!!—

FATHER

—Ca ce scippo l'occhi, per a madonna, e la dorbico 'ndru giardino! ...

MOTHER

(*Over "e la dorbico"*) Vida tu, Madonna mia del Carmine dove siamo arrivati!
Che vergogna! Vergogna da vita mia!!

FATHER

(*Over "che vergogna"*) **MARIANA!**, Gesù Christo! Sì sì, come quelli che vedo
bascio città quando lavoro di notte! Disgraziata!

MOTHER

(*Over "disgraziata!"*) Madonna mia du cielo, aiutame tu! **Farabbutt'e merda!!**

FATHER

—**Basta!** ... (*Beat*) Allora come dici tu Pino? Come consigli?

MOTHER

Ce l'hai domandata dove l'ha pigliata?

DOTTORE

Signora, si trove d'appertutto chissa ... oggi è normale.

FATHER

Normale?! Normale che na figlia di quest'età ancora non ha messo giudizio?! ...
A se drogare così! **Normale**?!

MOTHER

E quando ce domandi "che tieni?" ... un dice nente! ... Noi a penzare che forse è
malata, ca tene 'nguà cosa o aronno ch'un n'è contenta ... non vuole mai mangiare,
ch'a de dimagrire! Sette o otto anni fà s'ere fatta grossa cumu na vutta. A fatto
na dieta de chille bone ... e mò non vuole toccare niente!

FATHER

Perchè dietro le spalle nostre se pigliave la droga ... **MARIANA!** ... propio questa
se pigliano quelli de bascio città! Facie la dieta d'a MARIANA, può avere fame?!

MOTHER

Chi s'a 'mmaginava!

DOTTORE

Calmatevi! ... No voglio dire ch'è normale come si fossi na cosa buona ... Però,
non è grave ... non muore!

FATHER

Peccato!—Pino zitto pe' piacere!—che io me tirassi tutt'i capelli da capo, **cussi i**
vidi?!—U vidi cumu mi scippu tutti io?! ... (*As he pulls at his hair, and rag dolls*
his head in an attempt to get rid of it)

MOTHER

—Ca te fa' male!

FATHER

(*Over "ca te fa' male"*) Ca questa disgraziata ci ha dato solo fil'e torce! Che come l'abbiamo cresciuta noi, come l'abbiamo coltivata, questo ne meritiamo?! Diciammillo tu Pino! … questo ne meritiamo?! Sciagurata, disgraziata, dissonorata di merda!

MOTHER

Ma io solo a ci penzare … dove ha pigliato i soldi?!

FATHER

Va bene Camè! … non ne parliamo più per piacere! … 'dda pigliati … 'ndra borsa tua che lasci sembre ingiro! … NON NE PARLIAMO PIÙ PER LA MADONNA! … Che io vi sotterro ndru giardino a tutt'e due! … per u santissim accioma!

DOTTORE

Signore Raffele, calmatevi! Questa è la prima cosa che dovete fare!

FATHER

(*Over "Signore"*) Ti prego Pino, basta cu su 'signure'! … ca si ce *fossi* lu signore, avissi già fattu 'ngua cosa! …

DOTTORE

Vi capisco come vi sentite … ma provate a vi calmare! … È ovvio che è ingazzata per qualche cosa.

FATHER

Pure questo? È ingazzata?!

DOTTORE

È fragile … Ci dovete andare piano piano.

FATHER

E chi ci và forte?! Tene quello che vuole! … L'amiche cianno e scarpe così, combriamoccelle così pur'a issa! Se le mette na volta e le jette! "Non è la moda!" Va bene, combriano quelle che sono de moda … chi figli mii sunnu e moda! Sai quando par'e scarpe e veste che tene? … Che non ce l'ha nemmeno la regina! … A la scuola ce lo pure mandata … fino a undici!

MOTHER

Vedi Pino, che ci sono altre figlie, che hanno avuto <u>meno</u>, e ascoltano di più! Ca è vero, più ci dai, e peggio se fannu!

DOTTORE

(*Pause*) Chill'ammaccatura sopra l'occhio … quella botta …

FATHER

E te l'hò detto! È caduta così—batababum, di un colpo! Non l'ha toccata nessuno!

MOTHER

Si, sola sola

FATHER

Eh! … drogata cum'ere!

DOTTORE

Ecco. Questi si prendono due volte a giorno, o pure tre … vedete voi.

FATHER

'Vedete voi,' non chiamo a tia … tu sì dottore. E cos'è questo?

DOTTORE

Questo è na specie de rilassante. Fa dormire.

FATHER

Va bene ... ma io non ne capisco di queste cose. Ce l'hai spiegato quando se li deve prendere ... prima o dopo mangiato ... ce l'hai detto?

DOTTORE

Questi sono per voi! ... Pe' issa, riposo ... Okay chiamatemi se c'è qualche cosa. In caso mai, ve posso dare pinnoli più forte. (*He begins to leave*)

FATHER

Ma Pino, tu ce l'hai detto ... Perchè sa droga? ... Perchè deve fare soffrire i genitori così ... specialmente a mamma ca tene la pressione. Che ci manca? Ce l'hai detto?

MOTHER

Raffaè, se ne deve andare mò! Questo poi, ce lo puoi domandare tu dopo.

DOTTORE

Si, scusate, che mamma alle sette precise mette la pasta. Anzi a le sette è già sopra il tavolo. Sono le sette meno dieci e ci vuole sette, otto minuti per si cuocere. Poi, dipende quale pasta usa. S'è De Cecco, ci vuole un minuto di più per si cuocere, così arrivo preciso preciso e pronte per mangiare alle sette! Poi s'è pasta all'uovo, sono già in ritardo che quella se coce subito subito!

FATHER

Va bene. (*Pulling out some bills from his wallet*) Quando ti devo dare?

DOTTORE

No no lasciate perdere ... niente!

FATHER

Come niente?! Se vado allu scarparo me li dà gratis nu par'e scarpe?! ... E allora!

DOTTORE

Sì ma ... no ... mi fa piacere ... veramente!

FATHER

Non mi fare sumare i cazzi! Ecco i sordi! Quanto ti devo dare e basta! (*He throws a fifty-dollar bill on the floor*)

MOTHER

Si t'ha detto no, vuò dire no, no?

FATHER

Muta tu!—Sent'a mia, Pino! I denari sono sulla bocca di tutti e nella tasca di nessuno! Allura quannu t'aspettanu, un ni rifiutare. Chi sordi tenanu l'ale.

PINO

Vale più an amico in piazza, che cento ducati in tasca.

FATHER

No no, sent'a mia! ... Con l'amico e il compare parla chiaro! Che i patti chiari conservanu a lungo l'amicizia. (*Trying not to fall apart*) I debiti si pagano ... ed i peccati si piangono!, per a madonna!

DOTTORE

Buonasera!

FATHER

Va bene Pino, grazie! ... Ne facimu i conti n'altra volta.

MOTHER

Buonasera Pino ... salutam'à mammata! ...

FATHER

Si, che poi a patritta lo chiamo io quando a me fare u vino, ochè? ...

DOTTORE

Buonasera. (*About to exit*)

FATHER

Ehi! Ti prego Pino … di questo … A NESSUNO. Ti prego. Tu finta ca … m'a capito? Sei una tomba!

DOTTORE

Tomba.

FATHER

Tomba pe' Gesù Christo! … Che se lo sapissin'e gente … mi vado chiudo! … capito?

DOTTORE

Statte tranquillo. Buonasera. (*He exits*)

FATHER

Si vai vai, che la pasta è già sopra il tavolo. (*Short pause. Father comes back in, closes the door. To mother*) Vedi che figli'e di pane!! solo i mii.

MOTHER

Gesù mio!

FATHER

Te l'avevo detto io … ndra <u>ccà</u> è malata!

MOTHER

Così non si può continuare! Come dobbiamo fare!

FATHER

Diciammillo tu! … Che io la mando al manicomio! E te l'ho detto mille volte! Vedi quello che fà tua figlia! E tu, lasci'a stare, ch'è dentro a stanza! A LEGGERE! "Un chiuditi a porta da stanza! Vi prego! Facci i avertimienti, ti prego Carmè, che un giorno deve essere capace d'agire na casa, cucina, meglio da mamma!"

MOTHER

Ho capito basta! … a colpa è sembre da mamma!

FATHER

E ci colpo io?! … a ci fare sembre avertimienti! … Che la mamma mia a cresciuto dieci figli … senza marito … e filavano tutti!

MOTHER

Senta! Famme nu cazz'e piacire! … A mammata a lasci stare 'mbace duve se trove! Non mi nominare sembre a mammata … ca mammmata chisso, mammata chillo! …

FATHER

Issa ce perde!

MOTHER

Eh! Un na vidi com'è ridotta! Nu spirdu! … Facimu nu cuntu ch'è morta, e dazzol!

FATHER

Lassa stare! Si tene fame mangie! Nun more! A noi non ci doveva pregare nessuno per mangiare.

MOTHER

I figli sono a rovina! Non eramu cosa d'avire figli noi! A ROVINA!

FATHER

Lassa stare! … che il peggio deve arrivare ancora

> *Doorbell rings.*

FATHER

Vedi prima da finestra!

MOTHER

(*At the window*) Teee, emmèèèè ... è na nera!

FATHER

Na nera?! Sapimo chi cazzu vue?! (*Goes towards the door, stops*) ... Ho capito!

MOTHER

Va ce parla tu!

FATHER

Chiam'a figliatta!

MOTHER

Ma quella a pena si può alzare! ... parlacci tu! ... S'è' pe' l'appartamento ce dici "NO" ed è finita lì!

FATHER

Carmè! Pecchi non ci parli *tu* allora?!

MOTHER

(*Short-tempered*) Non ce bisogno de t'arrabbiare! (*Beat*) SIGNORINA!

> Doorbell rings again.

FATHER

Esci davanti a finestra se no ti vede!

MOTHER

LINDA! (*To Father*) Ma non ci puoi dire ch'è già stat'affittata e dazzol!

FATHER

Chiam'a figliatta per la 'mbicolita!!

MOTHER

LINDA!

> Linda enters slowly, languidly, almost somnolent, but
> methodically, sporting a black eye. She is high.

MOTHER

Tre volte ti ho chiamato, DROGATA!

FATHER

(*To Linda, measured and calmly*) Vedi che c'è una femmina ara porta. Vedi che vuole. S'è per l'appartamento, diciacce "non messì ... ch'è stato affittato giust'oggi"!

> Linda goes out the door, in her nightgown.

MOTHER

Cu la vestaglia!

FATHER

Cittu!

> Pause. Linda enters.

LINDA

È nivura.

FATHER

Va bene, lo sò ch'è nivura!

LINDA

Vo sapire quand'è l'appartamento?

MOTHER
(*Loud whisper, baffled*) Ti ha detto de ce dire ch'è già stat'affitato!
LINDA
(*Beat*) Vo sapere quand'è!
FATHER
(*Beat*) Va bene, diciacce ch'è otto cento dollari u mese!
LINDA
Otto cento dollari?!
FATHER
Otto cento dollari ti ho detto! Se lo vuole, questo è il prezzo!

> *Linda goes out again.*

MOTHER
Ma guarda chi scemo … ci hai detto mò ch'è stato affittato!
FATHER
Zitto per piacire. Sono affair mii! … Chi se lo prende per otto cento dollari?!

> *Pause. Linda enters. Shuts the door.*

FATHER
Cos'ha detto?
LINDA
(*Beat*) Niente. Se n'è andata.
FATHER
Meglio così … Ca a questi neache per mille dollari ciu dassi. Dentro due giorni … n'appartamento te lo riducono a na stalla di porci! (*Linda is about to go upstairs. To Linda*) Dove vai?!
LINDA
A legge!
MOTHER
Guarda chi faccia, guarda!
FATHER
Ma dimmi, che ti ai messo dentro a capo?
LINDA
Io nente.
FATHER
Vedi che quando vede tè … vedo il diavolo! (*Linda says nothing. Pause*) Cosi' dici tu? (*Pause*) CE N'AI VERGOGNA CA TIENI TRENTIANNI BRUCIATI!, SI O NO?!

> *No answer.*

MOTHER
Chi … un te rispunne! … ormai è drogata. Non è lu vero DROGATA! Brutt'e faccia! Che hai fatto na faccia de diavolo per davvero!

FATHER

Qualch'uno t'ha girato a testa o chidi? ... Parli sembre sola 'ndra stanza ...

MOTHER

Come na ciota!

FATHER

Sto parlando io! (*Pause*) Lo fai apposto o chidi?

MOTHER

Si sì, non ti rispunne!

FATHER

Sto parlando io t'ho detto! ... (*To Linda*) Tu mi devi spiegare perchè hai fatto quello ch'ai fatto ... perchè? <u>Dove</u> hai <u>pigliato</u> <u>sa</u> <u>droga</u>?! Guardami negl'occhi! **Guardami negl'occhi quando ti parlo io!**, che io ti parlo co' il sangue negl'occhi!! (*Pause*) Vedi che io ti sotterro ndru giardino! Ce l'ho detto a mammata!

LINDA

A colpa non è mia!

MOTHER

A colpa è la nostra? ... Emmè, **ca io ti scippo l'uacchi!** ...

LINDA

E robbe mie sono mie! Non v'ha detto nessuno d'andare girando ndre cose mie personale.

FATHER

Voi ammaccato l'altr'occhio?!! ... <u>Personale</u>?! ... Non esiste personale 'ndra sa casa. Tutti devono sapere tutto! Che io te l'ammacco subito subito l'occhio! ... E poi te taglio a capo e me succhio tutt'u sangue tuo velenoso!

MOTHER

Basta! Tu di questa casa non esci più! M'avissin'e tagliare e mano!

LINDA

Che prima dov'andavo?

FATHER

E dove devi andare? Hai visto quello ch'ai combinato senza uscire! Immagina!

MOTHER

E vai lavori! ... Puru 'ndra na fattoria! ... non me ne frego! L'altri u fanno!

LINDA

Lo dicete voi.

FATHER

A scola è finita per te! Ne hai fatto già troppo! Vai a sgobbare u culo e a te guadagnare u pane come tutti gl'altri!

LINDA

Ve l'ho detto! ...

MOTHER

No, no ha capito! ... Fa finta che non sente ... È bella a droga, eh?

LINDA

Ho già fatto l'applicazzione ... M'hanno accettato ... ci ho detto sì.

FATHER

Disgraziata, farabbutta ... così dici tu? Per la madonna che mi vuò mettere propio sotto! Vedi che mi mangio e budelle!

MOTHER

Ma tieni coraggio!

LINDA

I soldi aviti.

FATHER

I soldi ci sono stati sembre ... per una chi ascolta li genitori. Tu ieri hai buttato via trenta mila dollari, e non è finita!

LINDA

Per me sì.

FATHER

Trenta mila dollari jettati aru vientu! ... Secondo te hai fatto na bella figura davant'a Pasquale?! Speriamo a Dio che non dice niente a l'Italia! Che la gente devono ridere di mè?!

LINDA

Io non sono interessata a me rovinare a vita per nu permesso di lavoro!

FATHER

Non è rovinare! È <u>dare</u> vita, questo! Dare opportunità! Perchè, non l'hanno fatto tutti ... i zii tuoi ...? Quando i tempi sono brutti, così è la vita.

LINDA

I tempi non sono brutti!

FATHER

Per te no!! Che non hai visto guerra! ... Che io tutti st'anni ad andare a sposalizi ... perchè ci sono andato? PERCHÈ?! Per abballare?! Per me divertire?! ... Per voi ci sono andato!!

Linda laughs.

MOTHER

Emmè ride.

FATHER

Tuo fratello l'ha già fatti perdere i suoi ... e tutti quelli che ho portato io! ... E mò TU, vo fare a stessa cosa?! ... Prima che butto via trenta mila dollari io, mi vado chiudo!

LINDA

Non te l'ha detto nessuno de ci portare. Avie a scelta!

MOTHER

È dovere! Com'è dovere che adesso li portano à tè!

LINDA

Morta sì!

FATHER

E quella vedrai! A morte!

LINDA

Conosco già l'inferno ... a morte non può essere peggio! Si devo scegliere a morte ... preferisco quella senza marito! E cchiu naturale. (*Pause*) Non c'è problema, i soldi me li pozzu guadagnare sula ... Tanto, a dare u culo a Pasquale o a nu forestiere, è la, stessa cosa. Almeno u forestiere me paga bene ... e non ci devo passare u restu da vita!

Pause.

FATHER

Di oggi in poi …

LINDA

(*Mimicking Father*) … Di oggi in poi …

FATHER

(*Brief pause*) … Come ha detto mammata …

LINDA

(*Mimicking*) … Come ha detto mammata …

FATHER

(*Beat*) **Non esci più!** …

LINDA

(*Mimicking*) … non esci più …

FATHER

(*Raising volume and tone*) Le chiave da casa le consegni adesso a' mammata. Se devi uscire … o cu mammata, o cu mia! <u>Scelta</u>? T'hannu 'mbarata-ara scola sa parola?! Ndri libri?! **Scelta?!**

LINDA

Quella è stat'a maledizzione … Ere meglio si nun avissi mai conosciuto libri! … Per mia è stat'a sfortuna! … tradituri, tutti! … Però … a prima sfortuna mia … chilla grande … è d'essere nata fimmina 'ndra sa maleditta casa, famiglia e merda!!!

FATHER

(*Beat*) Non hai visto fame!

LINDA

Nemmeno a vita! (*She's about to exit*)

FATHER

Non ho finito! … Guai se ti trovu 'ndra stanza a leggere o a giocare dischi … (*To Mother*) E chissu u dico pur'a tia! Guai! (*To Linda*) Anzi, u sistema de musica, di oggi in poi, chiuso ndru sgabozzino!, con le chiave! **I libri** li consegni tutt'a mmammata! Domani li brucio tutti! … Ara porta du stanza, ce mindu na sicura! Devi andare ara toletta? … chiama! T'accumpagne mammata! De mò avanti, non mangi più con noi! 'Ndra stanza! Sula! Ndru buio! … E se insisti, te chiudo ndru stipo! E 'llà mangi e duarmi! … all'impiedi! Si mangi mangi. S'un mangi, criapi! … Va guarda chille quattru mure … e ripenza quale intenzione tieni! A data è fissata. A scelta e ra tua! … Dra chiesa ce po' trase in due modi … o cu marito … o cu tavuto! Hai capito?

Linda stares at him, and smiles.

MOTHER

Emmè. Ma guarda chi testarda! (*Mother pulls Linda by the hair*) Patritta ti ha domandato se hai capito?! **Drogata e merda!** … **e** levate su risu da vucca!

FATHER

Mai a la testa ho detto!

MOTHER

Ai capito?

LINDA
Si.

> *Linda stares for a moment at father, smiles, then exits. Door*
> *slams. Pause.*

FATHER
(*To Mother*) Apri a radio che ci sono e notizie!

> *Blackout.*

ACT THREE

⤳

Act 3, Scene 1: MOTHER, ROSINA, FATHER

MOTHER
Trasa tra … un te fa vide de nessuno!
ROSINA
Ma ch'è successo? S'è sciusu u munnu?!
MOTHER
Gesù mio, un ne parlamu e nente!! 'U diavolo s'ha 'mbarato a strada d'a casa …
e la sfortuna è diventata cummare! (*Giving her a small photo*) Te.
ROSINA
Chin'ie?
MOTHER
Guai, merda, catuaio, ruvina e stra ruvina! Na pesta! Diciammillo tu!
ROSINA
Chi nne sacciu! Parente un n'è sicuro! … È nu vivuru!
MOTHER
(*Loud whisper*) **Cittu** un te fa sente! (*takes photo back*) Le truvata 'ndra borsa da
signorina! … Ne truvatu atre … si sapissi … Un ce voglio mancu penza, ma un
me pozzu cacciare da capu! <u>Svendura</u>!
ROSINA
Raffè?
MOTHER
Ma si pazza?! … Su sapissi fossimo gia 'ndri giornali! … Iu un sacciu ch'e fare …
chilla disgraziata, senza cuscienza e merda!! **Chi vo crepare!!** … Rusi', Rusinella
mia!, me aiutare! Mittate tu aru posto mio e consigliame! … ca su su vene a sapire u
patre … a fà a piezzi piezzi! … Soricella mia!, <u>consigliame</u>!
ROSINA
Chi te consiglio?! … Però, 'Quannu c'e' festa, ne cummare e ne sorelle! Quannu
c'e su' guai, tutte cummare, tutte sorelle!'
MOTHER
Finito? Sulu chisso? Lassamu tutto a la speranza e bonasira?! (*She looks at photo*)
Gesù mio guarda chi faccia! Cumu si vidissi lu diavolo in persona!

ROSINA

(*Beat. Speak-signing*) Carmè, l'amuri duve morde, avvelene! E nessuno te pò scanzà!

MOTHER

Chissu è consiglio?! Chiss'è sentenza'e morte! Citto Rosì! ... Un scherzamu cu li poveri e li dannati! ... Ma chi c'intre l'amuri?! Chissa è na malatia sua da capo!

ROSINA

(*Speak-signing*) Sunnu cazzi da signorina! (*Back to her speaking voice*) Carmè, Chi va' cercamu grassu ndru puricino rimane ngamato!

MOTHER

Puricino! ... S'è puricino chisso?! ... Ca u grasso che c'è ccà ne frigge a tutti! ... (To herself) Ma guarda chi fortuna! ... L'atre figlie se 'nnammuranu de dottori, contabili, ministri e consiglieri ... a mia se innamure de nu cazz'e nivuru! De tutt'i culuri, propio chissu ce vulìe! ... E si vidissi l'atre fotographie ch'e truvatu —un ne parlamu e nente madonna mia!, ca me vene nu male propio a lu stomaco! Gesù mio, quandu n'e passare! ... Ca me vene na voglia de bestemiare tutt'i santi du cielo!

ROSINA

Wuay Carmè! S'è 'nnammurata!! Allegria! Chine u canuscie l'amuri a li tempi nostri?! 'Bianco nero, che te ne freghi?! Chi se 'nnammure de denti e capelli, se 'nnammure de nente!

MOTHER

Ca si fossino sulu i dienti e li capiaddhi fossi nente! MARITO E BUE DU PAISE TUE!

RUSINA

Si, quannu? ... avanti Christo?! ... quannu criscìamu nui? E chi bene n'ha fattu?!

MOTHER

(*Her mind is spinning out of control*) T'a 'mmagini si 'nguno ha vista cu chissu faciennu 'nguà cosa?!

ROSINA

E cu chine avie de fare ... cu na <u>fimmina</u>?

MOTHER

Quasi quasi, avissi fatto meglio s'avissi baciato na fimmina si! ... o 'ngu cane, 'nguà scimia! ... na bestia, qualsiasi cosa, oltre chissu! SI!

RUSINA

Figliatta ... chillu chi fà fà, lo fà, e lo farà pe issa ... Chi? ... a de dare retta a vui forse? ... ... Guardat'i cazzi tui!, ca prima o poi, *chilli* te nghiodanu ara crucie! Ca chine un se fa' i cazzi sui va truvannu i guai cu la lanterna! E se litighi per l'onore, acquisti vergogna!

MOTHER

Tu me vo vide morta beddha mia?! S'a de spusare st'inverno cu Pasqualino de 'mPed'a Terra! ... Ce fatto già a vesta! Bianca! ... Ed iddha a far'a puttana!

ROSINA

(*Brief pause*) **Eh** si uomini se meritassino tutti ammazzati! ... de duve te giri giri, tu mittanu 'ngulo!

MOTHER

Un conicia' Rusì! Ti prego!! L'uomini l'uomini! Su certe cose signu d'accordo, ma su chissu—pel tutt'i santi, ca bestemio puru io mù, NO! ... Ca si u sapissi

chillu ch'avimu truvatu 'ndra stanza, un parlassi a cussì! A DROGA!—**Cittu!** …
Dre mutanne lorde, nente meno! Là sa tenie!. Allura nun parlamu de uomini!
… Mai nella mia vita!' MAI! Nemmeno a li francesi e sentito fare se cose …
ca sai cumu sunnu! Ca tene raggiune u patre! … cchiù ci ne duni e cchiù
s'approfittano! M'avissino de tagliare e manu si chilla cornuta esce d'a stanza!
E manu m'avissino de tagliare!

ROSINA

Però, gira e vota cumu vue, u problema e sembre chillu! … maritotta! … Maritotta
el maritotta, e un ce nente da fare!

MOTHER

Ma cumu cazzu raggiuni Rosì?! Ca mu me fai sumare propio i cazzi!!! Chi centre
maritomma?! Io sto parlando da disgraziata!!

ROSINA

Invece si! Tieni paura e maritotta! De figliatta ti nne frichi pocu e nente! … De tia
un ti nne frichi propio e nente! Un te sa fa rispettare!

MOTHER

Iu … un te … no, no … un te segue propio … Va bene un ne parlamu propio! Ca
si se trattassi de mariti, scusa ca tu dico … ma sceglissi cento vote u mio e no u tuo!

ROSINA

Tenatillo! U mio le già curato!

MOTHER

Ch'a curato? Chi?!

ROSINA

Filippo è stato malato! Trent'anni sa malatia! … Mo grazie a Dio è curato! Ce datu
a purga! … Eh, soricella mia, i problem mii su' gruassi e li tui me peranu nu spassu!

MOTHER

Ch'avie?

ROSINA

Petre. (*Beat*) Ara capu! … E ce le scotulate! E pigliatu na cinta de sue … e le fatto
nero di palate! A la testa, a le spalle … alle coste … ma più tosto a le gambe! … i
dottori un ce putianu fa' nente!

MOTHER

Gesù mio ca mi se ferme lu core! E s'è fatto minaret da' mugliera senza te rumbe
a capo?

ROSINA

C'ere figlioma pe' sicurezza! … Ha chiamato u patre 'ndra cucina, e ci'à detto
bello bello, "mamma te vo parlà! Se la tocchi, t'ammazzo!" Sono scesa sotto, e mi
sono sfogata! … Chi scialata! Ce ne ho dato—de tutt'i culuri! Si è messo purla
piangere … avanti u figlio! … Piangia piangia … ca ce ne vogliono pianti per
arrivare a chilli che ho passato io! A valigia bella preparata … e fuori!

MOTHER

Iiii! Un te fa sente de Raffaele! Mammarella mia du cielu! No, NO! Tu esaggeri
bella mia! Tu t'avie spusare veramente a maritomma … cussi v'ammazzatevi
l'uno e l'atru! … E de se trove mò? … d'e jutu a finire?

ROSINA

Chine sacciu! CHI SE NE FREGA! … Lontano un n'è potuto andare sicuro! E gamme ce le gonfiate chi! … (*She laughs*) Cu ri cavalli, carte, barri, amici, ed *amiche* ce sa fare! … ma cu la mugliera! …

MOTHER

Ridi? Chi ride de venneri piange de sabato soricella mia!

ROSINA

Trent'anni!!! Ho sopportato tutto! … E lo sapevano tutti! … Che non le portava a casa? …… Quannu simi appena arrivati de l'Italia … quannu eramu a Subberi' … a duv'e purtave … ara casa … quasi ogni sira … e ce dicie ca iu ere la serva … Iu l'inglese un nu parlave. Si dicie 'nguà cosa, issu me riempie de palate, cazzotti! … c'eramu sulu nui 'llà … parenti un ci n'eranu, amiche nemmeno … cu chine parli … sembre 'ndra casa … vui ancora eravati in Italia … e cussì me signu stata cittu. Chi sente e tace vive in pace. E cussi e fattu! Iu 'ndra cucina, ed iddhi 'ndra camera e liettu! Vida ca c'e' vue coraggio. Trent'anni! … Non è passato nu giorno che non ci ho fatto trovare u mangiare pronte! Ne ho fatto pranzi che non si ha mangiato! E quando se li mangiava … a ci correre appresso appresso per ci strofinare u musso pieno di sugo! … ch'aveva pressa che si doveva fare a partita!!! *Partita*!

MOTHER

Dio mio du cielu!

ROSINA

… (*Beat*) Quannu é natu figlioma, e dittu, si c'è Gesù Christo, 'ngu giorno le pagherà tutte! … Vedi che dopo trent'anni lovarie scoppiano! … Ai capito?! … e poi, u figlio ragazzino è diventato n'uominu cu la cuscienza. … (*Beat*) Apposta soricella mia! Sentame! … ca sorelle poche se ne trovanu per le strade! …

MOTHER

… (*Beat*) Ma chi pienzi? Ca tutti i mariti sunnu cumu i tui? Ca a Raffaele un nu puazzu nemmeno cacciare d'a casa! È peggio e na fimmina! Lave piatti, finestre! Ha cambiato cchiù pannizzi issu ca io! U sai! … Ogni anno minde le luc'e natale fore! Ce tene a se cose! Peggio de na fimmina! I figli un n'a fatti andare mai scalzi! De chi cazzo me lamendare!

ROSINA

'Ngantate de luce de natale e pannizzi puliti, ngantate! Non tutte le cose rosse sono ciliegie!

(*Beat. Concerned. Firm*) Adduv'e Linda?! … Adduv'e **figliatta**?!

MOTHER

(*Righteous*) Duve se mèrita! … E 'llà ha de stare!

ROSINA

(*With urgency, but measured*) E soricella mia … per u cieco, un se fa mai juarnu!

MOTHER

(*Trying to hold it together*) Senta beddha mia!, ce sunnu fimmine ch'un se ponnu minde nemmeno rossetto ara vucca … o a se pittare l'ugne! Ai capito?! … (*Reprovingly*) In somma, u marito mio, un m'ha mai toccatu e un se và jocannu i sordi aru barru, e tuccanu e mugliere e l'atri!!

ROSINA

Calabresi e muli non pisciano mai suli! … Sunnu tutti da stessa stoffa, Carmè! L'uomini de natura guardanu minne e culu! Svegliate!

MOTHER

(*Horrified*) E chi vo dire mo?!

ROSINA

Se corne fossino alberi, tutt'u munnu fossi nu bosco! E amaro chine cerche medico e giustizia! ... A meglia ferita è de nun te tagliare!

MOTHER

(*Fighting to keep from breaking down*) Senta Rosi'! Fai come cazzo vuoi! Ma à mia lasciami stare! ... Un me minda ndri guai! ... ca ccà pane e guai un ne mancanu mai! ... Ma dico io DOVE SIAMO ARRIVATI?!! ... Per piacire Rusì, vatinne và! ... grazie du consiglio, ma vatinne! Ca si maritumma te trove ccà, Dio ce ne libera, ca già i tene li cazzi a la capo! ... e dice sembre ca tu me mindi idee 'ndra testa! Allura pe' piacire, si me vo' bene, Vai! Va rum'a capo a maritotta va'! ... Rumbacce puru e corne! ... Quello che vuoi! BRUCIA PURE IL MONDO! ma **vatinne!** ... ca c'è provvide Gesù Christo!

ROSINA

(*Beat*) Chi vive sperannu, more cacannu, soricella mia!

Enters Father, doesn't notice Rosina.

FATHER

(*Slamming the door*) Ve lo dico io "MUUZIT 'TALIEN"[1]—si bastardi! ... A perduto u cazz'e gatto! CHE NE SÒ IO?! Non l'ho toccato il gatto! ... Jativinne d'avanti a faccia mia!—Un vò pagare i due misi?! Ve lo dico io ... lettera raccomandata e RAUS![2] ... Ve piace ad andare alla Florida ogni anno?! Allora VA SCIENNE, CAVALISSE![3] ... PAGA! ... Io vacanze non ne prendo mai! Picchinnicchi non ho mai conosciuto! ... u balcone m'abbaste! ... Pero' ciò a casa!!! MUUZIT TALIEN a mia? Fa 'ngulo! E tasse e pago io! ... Li frego io! Ne lasse stufa e friggidero e MANGIÈ' LA MERDA! ... Che io sono capace d'affittare puru a nu nero! ... **Jativinne!** (*Father notices Rosina. Pause.*) Quando il gallo non c'e' ... e galline ...

ROSINA

(*To no one in particular*) Io vi saluto. (*Lingering*) Fati a esce fore ogni tanto a figliatta ... un na vido mai ... L'aria frisca fà bene! ...

FATHER

L'aria friddha dune ara capu!

ROSINA

(*Beat*) Alla *rovina*, un ce vò risparmio!

    She exits.

FATHER

A de sembre jettar'a botta! (*Mother exits to the kitchen*) Che voleva sa zingara?!

MOTHER

(*Offstage*) Oi, quannu cose va guardannu ... cos'e fimmine!

---

1. From the Québec French "*maudit Italien*" ('*damn Italian*').
2. From the German "raus" ("*out of here*")
3. From the Québec French "*Va chier*" ("*go shit*").

FATHER

A signorina duv'ie? (*Beat*) Adduv'è figliatta?!

Phone rings.

MOTHER

(*Offstage*) D'a lassata!

FATHER

(*Beat*) E 'llà a de sta'!

Phone rings. Phone rings.

FATHER

Il telefono. (*Phone rings*) Pigliati u telefono qualch'uno! (*Phone rings*) *Ma su telfono u sientu sulu io?!* (*Phone rings*) Va bene, lassati stare ... rispondo io! (*Clears his throat, answers the phone*) Alo' ... chi vule' vu? ... Come? ... Ahh, Filomena da Cicala. Si ... si.

Blackout.

Act 3, Scene 2: MOTHER, FATHER, LINDA, SON

Mother and Father in the basement 'living room,' waiting. The room is dark except for a small amount of light cast by the television screen that illuminates their faces. The volume has been turned down completely. It's three in the morning.

FATHER

(*Sottovoce*) Quella è ritornata. Ha visto ch'a finestra sua ere chiusa, e luce tutte chiuse ...

MOTHER

E tre! ... che neanche i malavita sono fuori a chiss'ura!

FATHER

... poi ha provato ad aprire a porta ... ma io ce messo u loccu, e due sicure, più a scopa ... così si prove la porta ... (*Beat*) A de sunare pe' forza!

MOTHER

Tu penzi ca se ne frega issa?! Trove la scusa che ci abbiamo chiuso a porta ... (*Beat*) Ma penzacce tu ... alla vedere nente meno FILOMENA DA CICALA ... ca quella tene na vucca! ...

FATHER

Filomena m'ha detto ca lui insisteva ... vulìe baciato ... ed issa, si lasciav'andare ... e le gente guardavano, meravigliate! ... "na 'taliana cu uno e chissi!" ... (*Beat*) che io vedo maledizzione! (*Beat*) Vidu sangue!

MOTHER

Si vede che questo l'ha drogata! Un ni vidi sembre ara televisione ... Ci'à dato 'nguà sigaretta ... ed issa senza se ne accorge ... e poi ci ha pigliato vizio ... cu issu e cu la droga!

FATHER
Zitto! … che forse è issa.

In the distance, faint footsteps.

MOTHER
(*Beat*) No … è quella d'affianco quà. Quest'è l'orario sue normale … lavure a lu clubbu 'llà … a Langelier, de ce sunnu e fimmine nude … No issa ormai … sicuramente … ormai …

FATHER
Zitto! (*A cat meows in the distance*) U gatto da troia! Vedi come ritornanu quannu tenanu fame! Ci …

MOTHER
A port'e chiusa.

FATHER
Ce levat tutt'e sicure … sol'a scopa ci ho lasciato … Vedi da finestra, senz'aprir'a tenda!

MOTHER
Non si vede nessuno …

FATHER
Allora ed issa! Priesto! Vai 'ndra cucina … fai finta che piangi! (*Loud sotto voce*) Dai fai finta!

MOTHER
Ca un n'e piangiut'abbastanza … mo devo fare puru finta?

FATHER
(*Loud sottovoce*) **Vai ti ho detto!**

Doorbell rings. Mother exits to the kitchen. Father goes upstairs.
Pause. The front door opens, slowly. The broom leaning against
the door on the inside falls to the floor.

LINDA
(*To herself, sottovoce*) Shit!

Linda removes her shoes. Closes the door. Tiptoes towards
the kitchen. Stops. Mother is heard crying. Her weeping gets
progressively louder as her fake whimper turns to real tears, then
to a wail, as if she were at a funeral.

MOTHER
(*Offstage*)
Oi Dio mio non ce la fazzo più!
Oi Gesù mio chi ruvina!
Oi Dio mio che io m'ammazzu, m'avveleno!
Oi Dio mio che non l'ai fatta murire quand'è nata!
Ch'i figli sunnu a maledizione!
Chi figura! Signu ruvinata! Oi Dio mio!

Lights up. Father is standing on the top landing.

FATHER

(*With calculated restraint*) Dove si stata?

LINDA

(*Short pause*) Fore.

MOTHER

(*Offstage*) È arrivata a <u>ruvina mia</u>!

FATHER

(*Same restrained tone*) Duve si stata?

MOTHER

... (*Offstage*) Che di quando è nata questa disgraziata non ho visto nu giorno de pace! C'avìe ditt'à lui che non volevo più figli!

FATHER

(*Same restrained tone*) Vedi che t'ho domandato con il calmo ... dove si stata? Nun te minu.

LINDA

(*Short pause*) Fore.

MOTHER

(*Enters, and darts towards Linda*) ROVINA! ROVINA da vita mia! ... ti pare ora?!!

FATHER

(*Relatively calm and restrained*) Sto-parlando io Carmè! (*To Linda*) Allora questa è la vita ch'ai scelto?! ... Io a dire NO ... e tu a dire SÌ! ... (*Controlled explosion*) CHI TI HA DATO PERMESSO?!

LINDA

(*Beat*) Non ho bisogno di permesso.

MOTHER

... A telefonare a tutt'e parte ... nessuno sa nente! ... Ad aspettare ed aspettare! ... cu pensieru, che fors'è morta ... (*Suddenly spewing 'venom'*) Ca fossi morta d'avvero!, cussi cambo 'ngu giorno di più'! ... Ma issa, a mamma, s'a già dimenticata!

FATHER

(*Calm and restrained, with a warning*) Carmè! ... (*To Linda*) È bello quello che stai facendo passare a tua mamma?

MOTHER

Si c'è Dio, te fa pagare tutto quello che stai facendo, bella mia! Sini ... propio TU!

FATHER

Santa Madonna Carme'! Deve parlare UNO o due?! Che s'avissi parlato tu del primo giorno ... nun me truvassi 'ndra se condizzione! (*Father unbuckles his belt. To Linda*) Cosa sei andat'a fare aru parco de Viau e Jean Talon?

    Pause.

MOTHER

Chi faccia! ... N'ha telefonato Filomena Da Cicala! Che t'ha visto! Sapiamo TUTTO!

LINDA

Te l'ho detto. Ero fore. Sola.

MOTHER

... Buggiarda!

FATHER

(*Beat*) Giura sopra il *crocifisso*!

LINDA

(*Makes the sign of the cross*) Lo giuro!

MOTHER

Emmè chi buggiarda!

FATHER

Vedi ch'è peccato! Giura sopra il crocifisso … 'Ch'un n'avissi d'arrivare a dumani matina,' *dai!*

LINDA

Ch'un n'avissi d'arrivare a dumani matina

MOTHER

Dio mio, che buggiarda!

FATHER

Vedi che Gesù Christo ti fa morire veramente!

LINDA

Tu ci credi?

FATHER

Io credo in Dio Padre onnipotente, creatore del cielo e della terra, e in Gesù Christo, suo unico figlio, nostro Signore, che non ti ha fatto murire quando si nata!! **Dici'a** VERITÀ! … Che io la sò già! Ma dimmi TU la *verità!*

LINDA

(*She stands up*) Un sunnu cazzi tui!

MOTHER

Dio mio! … Ch'aspietti?! *Minala!*

FATHER

Carmè! Ca ve caccio du munnu a tutt'e due stasira, e dopo me vado chiudo in galera! (*Pause. To Linda*) Io voglio sapere tutto! Dove sei andata? Con chi? E perchè'!

MOTHER

Puttana drogata!

FATHER

… Dove sei stata fin'a quest'ora, che pure i clubbi sono chiusi. **TUTTO!** Mo! Confessate o fatt'a cruce!

LINDA

Se mi tocchi? …

FATHER

Tocchi? … Stasera ti battezzo di nuovo! Stasera è la festa tua! Stasera s'abballe! Se fà la tarantella! … Carmè mind'a musica.

MOTHER

E mò mindimu dischi?

FATHER

Mind'a musica! … si no ve fazzu 'abbalare' a tutt'e due! (*To Linda*) E non mi fare perdere tempo! Che fra tre ore devo andare a zappare per dare mangiare a voi animali! … A casa 'a conosci?! … SI o NO?! A famiglia la conosci?

LINDA

E letto u significato 'ndru vocabbulario, 'ndri libri.

FATHER

L'ultima vota!

LINDA

Senta! Ho fatto nente de peggiu de chillu chi facìe tu a l'età mia! … e nente e megliu!

MOTHER

Dio mio ca me vene na paralisi! Pur'u dice! **Pur'u dice!** … Dissonorata! Aspetta!— Aspetta fino che teni figli tù! … poi vidi! Poi te'mbari!

LINDA

IO, <u>figli</u>? … S'avissi, solo pe' sbaglio! E l'ammazzassi! … invece de ce fa vide su munnu!

MOTHER

Puru io avevo sperato questo! Ma io ce signu imbarata a vivere cu li sbagli?! … e ti ce 'mbari pure <u>tu</u>!

LINDA

Te sbagli!! Io i sbagli i cancello! Cridame! L'e già fattu na vota! … Sì, l'ho fatto! E l'ho fatto volentieri! … M'avissi piaciuto du videre nasce … s'ere masculu o fimmina … sulu pe' lu vide … cussi dopo 'avissi potuto ammazzare cu le manu mie … piano piano … a lu fare soffocare … a lu vide morto cu l'occhi mii! E a n'avire natru e 'a fare a stessa cosa … a me svuotare tutta fina ch'un ce rimanìe nente … fina ch'un ne escìanu cchiù! … (*Beat*) Ma non potevo aspettare. Nun putìe rischiare d'u vide … (*To Father*) Avevo paura ch'assomigliav'a te! … E s'ere vero … avissi passato na morta più brutta! … Ma nun se meritàve chillu che ce putìe fare (*Pause. Smiling*) E scelto u modo ch'ere meno crudele. Doveva morire! L'ho avuto apposto!

FATHER

(*Pause*) Chi ti ha dato permesso?!

LINDA

(*Beating her chest, then her head, repeatedly*) IO! IO! IO! IO! IO! IO! IO! IO! IO! IO! IO!

MOTHER

Guarda com'è combinata?

LINDA

Ca vui vi'nne fricati?! … chillu chi succede a mia?! … E non me frego manch'io! Sunnu i cazzi mii! … E che piacere a sapire che fà cchiù mal'a vui! … Io signu tosta! (*To Father*) Miname … miname … Che? Te manche coraggio? … Fai finta che stai squartannu nu puarcu! È la stessa cosa per tia! È la sula cosa chi sa' fare …

MOTHER

Ch'aspetti tu natru?! … Scippaccce l'uocchi!

LINDA

(*Laughing*) Oh ma! … (*Mimicking mother*) "Scippaccce l'uocchi!" … Cumn si bruta! … A vigliaccheria te sta bene! (*To Father*) Vo aiuto? (*Intentionally provoking him*) … *ignorante*! … ammazzame! … 'ndra ccà pero' un ce trasi mai! … 'ndra cca', te odio sembre. (*She smiles*).

Father strikes her with the belt.

FATHER

A chi sei figlia? A quale diavolo?!

MOTHER

Pecchi sì ritornata? Pecchi?!

LINDA

Dove devo andare? ... U diavolo chi canusciu è megliu de chillu ch'un canusciu!

FATHER

Diavolo ccà?! ...

LINDA

... Forse signu venuta giusto per *parlare* ... sulu *chissu*. ... (*'Smiling'*)

FATHER

Un t'avvicinare Carmè! Ca mu chissa è bella drogata, e nun se sa mai ... a capace ca tene 'nguà cosa nascosta.

MOTHER

Tu pienzi? E tu cum'u sai?!

FATHER

Se vidre 'ndra l'uocchi! ... Chissa un'nnè figliatta!

MOTHER

E chin'ìe?

FATHER

Na bestia! ... Na gatta! ... nu demonio! ... I vi cumu lùciano l'uocchi!?

Linda immediately embodies the cat/demon/beast image!

LINDA

Musica!

> *MUSIC: Calabrian Tarantella. Fades in.*
> *As the cat/demon/beast, Linda dances the tarantella throughout*
> *the following action. She knocks over things (intentionally), and*
> *gradually, methodically, wrecks the place, all the while staring*
> *Father down, as she circles around him and he backs off. Then,*
> *with one motion of her arm she sweeps off the photos of dead*
> *ancestors that make up the shrine on the mantlepiece. Mother is*
> *horrified and quickly tries to salvage the pieces! Linda then takes*
> *down her parents' wedding portrait from the wall, smashes glass*
> *and frame. The Tarantella MUSIC STOPS suddenly. Linda*
> *removes the wedding photo from frame, and scratches it slowly,*
> *deliberately, "meowing" and "hissing" sotto voce.*

MOTHER

Emmè'! A sula fotografia ch'avimu!

LINDA

(*Genuinely concerned*) Un te 'ngazzare, ma! ... È sulu na fotografia! ... Chilli nun le mai conosciuti! Vui i canusciti? ... Sorridevono ... E fotografie sunnu spesso d'accussi! (*Sotto voce*) No si ce guardi cchiù vicino! ... D'aviti lassati i sorrisi? ... (*Suddenly vengeful*) I genitori mii sunnu muarti! Bastardi! U viditi chi pienzu e vui! (*She tears up their wedding picture to pieces. Father belts Linda on her back. Linda's body jolts)*[1] Bastard! (*Father belts her again*) Bastard! (*Father belts her again*) Bastard!

MUSIC—FADES IN after the third "Bastard."

O veni sonno di la muntanella
lu lupu si mangiau la pecurella, o mamma
O la ninna vo' fa'

*"O veni sonne di la muntagnella" (Calabrian lullaby) author
Anonymous. Traditional version.*

*As Father continues to belt Linda, she slowly walks away from
him, downstage centre, drawn by the lullaby, but still reacting to
Father's blows, physically and vocally with "Bastard."*

FATHER
Carmè! Tenacc'e gamme! (*Mother remains immobile, stunned, and speechless*) Carmè,
per la Madonna![2]

*Linda joins the lullaby (in sottovoce), but her body still registers
(reacts to) the sting of each blow, like a memory, like waves of
aftershocks. Behind her, Father's stationary rhythmic belting
evokes images of a construction worker swinging a pick with
tireless dedication.*

Veni sonno di la landa mia
La mia figghiola muta mi vurria, o mammà
0 la ninna vo' fa'

*During the above stanza, Linda slowly drops to the floor and goes
to sleep. The MUSIC ends.*

MOTHER
Raffaè!, nun se move! (*Father panics. Throws belt across the room. Gnaws his hand
in despair*) Raffaè! Gesù mio! Raffaè! Raffaè! Vedi tu! Raffaè!

Father slaps Mother across the face. He leans over Linda.

---

1. During the initial belting, the actor playing the Father stands two to three feet upstage of the actress
playing Linda. When Linda walks away from Father to downstage center (and Father continues to belt
her), the two will be approximately seven feet apart. From the audience's perspective, the distance between
the two actors should not appear as great as it is, even when the actors are further apart.
2. The literal meaning of the phrase is *'by'* or *'for'* *the Madonna*; however, it is commonly used to mean
'damn the Madonna'.

FATHER

(*In a gentle tone*) Linda ... Linda ... dai ... alzate ... Linda ... dai fai a brava, ochè? ... Carmè, vamme piglia nu bicchiere d'acqua, nu puco e limune, 'nguà cosa!

MOTHER

Pare paralizzata! (*Taking Father's belt and wrapping it around her own neck*) Che io m'ammazzo! U vidi cumu fazzu!

FATHER

Piglia stu bicchieri d'acqua, scemonita!

MOTHER

Lassa stare ca m'ammazzo! (*Tightening the belt around her neck*) Io m'a m m a z z o!

FATHER

Chiama Pino u dottore!

MOTHER

Non se move de nente! guarda!

FATHER

Che la colpa è di quello disgraziato! Issa ha visto minde corda a lu frate, e ha fatto u stesso pur'issa! ... (*Kneeling, gentle tone*) Linda, bella e papà ... Linda, coccò de papa. Fanciulla e papa ... Linda!

> *Linda rises quickly, laughing hysterically.*

MOTHER

Madonna mia du cielo! Ed uscita pazza! ... tene propio l'uocchi du diavolo!!! Raffaè!, chiam'a pulizia! Che non si conosce piu'!

> *Linda is still laughing. The laughter turns to a cry. She drops to the floor.*

LINDA

I hope you die! You fucken bastards! I wanna die! die! die!
Pause.

FATHER

Crisci figli ... crisci porci ... crisci figli ... che un giorno ...

> *Lights fade. Spot on Father. He is still kneeling. He notices and pulls a rolled-up PINK SHEET of paper with a RED RIBBON wrapped around it from the debris surrounding him and examines it. It's the Father's Day card Linda gave him when she was 10 (Act 1, Scene 5). Father exhales and begins to read silently.*

> *We hear Linda's voice for the first four lines.*

Parti tu, cu li vent'anni
Cu fucile e senza scarpe
Quindic'anni di miniera
Perdi guaddhera e c'è miseria!

Father joins Linda for the next four lines.

Poi arrive la speranza
Una littera de qualch'uno!
Cu moglie e figli e l'appetito
Si preparano i bauli!

*From "Mò comincie la battaglia" till the end Father recites alone
without reading from the card, not because he has memorized it
but because it is his story.*

Mò comincie la battaglia!
Cu fortuna mezz'u mare
Simu tutti marinari!
Tu si bossu e capitano
Allura navighi e combatti!
Nu minuto di riposo
Guai a destra e a sinistra!
U diavolo chi t'alisce! ATTENZIONE TUTTI 'A LONDA!
'Ngu ferito, zero morti
Cu salute e nu panino
Sembre avanti, mai indietro!
Cu ogni temporale che riesci a superare
Cu ogni onda mortale che riesci ad evitare
Fatt'a cruce, ca si vivo!
E si te vene 'ngu sorriso
Stipatillo dra sacchetta!
ATTENZIONE TUTTI A LONDA!
Tutti salvi, natra vota (*Father takes smile, stuffs it in his pocket*)
Cunt'e stelle, e cunt'i santi
Ca nel mondo, un sunnu tanti!
Mu aumente lu coraggio!
U terreno sconosciuto
Tu rinforzi e rinforzi
Ce vò fegato no cucuzze!
C'e' chi perde la speranza!
C'e' che mormora e ribelle
C'e' chi dorme e non se ne fregha
Tu dirigi! Guard'avanti
Si si stanco, un dubitare
Penz'a chilli ndr'a tasca!
Mo u mare s'è calmato
E se vide puru u sule
Piano piano, piano piano
Vedi terra, teraa, e terra,
Cu tesori e factica
Rauss schnell e arioppa

Abbondanza èsuverchia
Caccia fuori i sorrisi
Mo vi frego a tutti quandi!
Mo viditi che risata!
Na scialata number one!
Dintr'a bocca ad uno ad uno!
     (*Beat*)
À 'dde sunnu i suldati?!

Father looks around and observes the destruction in the basement
'living room.' He sees Mother and Linda silently recovering, each
absorbed in their own world and predicament.

A strong wind sweeps across the stage. Lights start to change.

FATHER

(*Pleading his case*) Dio del cielo e de la terra! Tutti l'angeli custodi! Tutt'i Gesu
Christi da madonna! E tutt'i santi e stra santi in paradiso. Aprit'e richhie ... e
suspenniti u scopo! Ca un n'e finito!!

Suddenly, we're in Raffaele's BACKYARD. A typical Montreal
WINTER BLIZZARD, freezing cold. It's 3:00 a.m. Father
is still kneeling center stage, 'greeting card' in hand, lit by a
SHAFT OF LIGHT from inside the cantina, door half ajar.

FATHER

(*Upset that God and company did not listen to him, shakes his head, then to himself*)
Ma che?! ... Testardi! Tutti! ... Famme finire!

SON

(*At a distance, standing on the balcony landing, wearing pants and shirt only*) Pà
achiss'ura?! Ca mùari e friddhu!

FATHER

(*Beat*) Iu un ne sientu friddhu. (*Pause*) Troppe cose de sbarazzare prima ch'arrive
l'inverno!
     Father looking at the 'greeting card.'
     The BLIZZARD rages on.

SON

(*Referring to the 'greeting card'*) L'ha scritta supra l'autobusso nu jiorno. Per ra scola. ...

Pause

FATHER

(*Beat*) A chi serve? Pe' chine? ... (*Beat*) Dicìanu l'antichi ... Mentre il medico
studia il malato muore.

Father crumples card into a ball and throws it on a pile of
garbage and waste. Father then fetches several gallons from the
cantina and sets them centre stage. SON retrieves the "greeting
card" without Father noticing.

SON

E tutti si galluni?

FATHER

(*Starts digging*) 'Ndra l'orto ce vo concime, 'ndru munnu—fortuna ... (*Referring to the gallons*) Chiss'è rifiuto! ... li devo sotterare tutti! Tutti sutta terra! Tutto chillu chi nun ne mangiamu nui ... o ch'un putimo stomacare ... su mangie la terra. A terra è benigna, un rifiute nente! ... Ogni rifiuto è litama! Vitamina! Damme 'na mano dà.

SON

(*Pointing to a gallon*) E dentro ccà chi c'è?

FATHER

(*Holding up the gallon to the night light*) Calli. Trent'anni di calli! ... trenta galloni ... vidimo ... quest'e du '51. (*He pours the contents into the hole*)

SON

Affascinante! De mano o di piedi? ... Butta butta ... che facciamo, mò, 'na mostra de calli dintr'a cridenza? ...

FATHER

(*To himself*) Sì, sì propio cussi.

SON

E chissu?

FAHER

Acqua salata!

SON

Per preservare i calli?

FATHER

Trent'anni di sudori!

SON

(*Sarcastic, more to himself*) Modesto. Solo nu gallone?

FATHER

Si matto?! N'avevo conservato cinque damigiane. *Filtrate*! Ma 'sa cantina è troppo calda l'estate ... piano piano, l'acqua s'è evaporizata! È rimasto solo questo! (*Opens the gallon and smells contents*) Ie la madonnna cumu puzze! (*Empties the gallon into the hole, methodically*) Eh, sì ... Si stava bene, quando si stava male!

SON

Fai bene, fai bene ... butta butta ... sutterra beddhu mio e penz'a campà! FERMO! E questo?

Cock crows.

FATHER

(*Drops the gallon*) Nente ...

Cock crows.

SON

Pollo vulgaris!

FATHER

Un stutati a luce 'ndra cantina!

> *Cock crows.*

SON

Pà, ha stutata propio tu! Propio mù!

> *Father looks towards the Cantina. Now the LIGHT GOES OUT in the cantina.*

FATHER

Dio del cielo e de la terra!

> *Blackout.*

Act 4

MOTHER, SON

MOTHER

(*Giving son a glass of water and sugar*) Te, prenditi questo, che fà bene a la panza! ... Ma sembre si cazz'e suanni?!

SON

(*Beat*) Cussì è! Certi passano a notte a riflettere chillo che hanno fatto u giorno ... invece io passo a giornata a pensare a chillo che mi ho sognato a notte! (*Mother sings*) Canti?

MOTHER

Cantu? ... Iu un cantu ... canticchio ... o abbaio! ... cussì quannu fazzu i lavuri! Parto cu la voce senza me ne accorge ... fazzu svegliare pur'i morti! Issu s'ingazze! (*She looks towards the cantina. She sings*) Chillu a capace che fà la spia ... T'ha visto entrare ... senza u salutare ... e sta penzando ... "Vedi ve' ... subito subito a parlare cu ra mamma ... ara fa' perd'u tiempu" ... cussì dice. (*Grabs the fly swatter*) Se cazz'e musche ... de dove cazzu venanu?! (*She chases a few flies. Pause*) Pecchi si venuto?

SON

(*Observing Mother*) Non lo sò ... forse sulu pe'su bicchiere d'acqua e zucchero.

MOTHER

T'ha vìppitu? Mù ti nne po' jire! ... Che t'ha dimenticatu puru u telefono ... così dice lui!

SON

Mà ...

MOTHER

(*Interrupting him, in her singsong voice*) "Dopo arrubbato Santa Chiara, ci hanno fatto a port'e fierru!"

SON

(*Beat*) A duv'è issu?

MOTHER

Sembre allu stesso posto … duv'ie?! … L'appartamento e supra l'ha affittato a due francesi! … marito e moglie … Vidimo … Eh!, a chine lo vai affitti?! Mò ch'hannu vinto si separatisti … l'atri se fannu e valice! … (*Beat*) Issu ci ha già portato pommodori du giardino … due belli grande … ed iddhi, tutti belli contenti, "Oh messì bucù'!"[1] … (*Wiping her hands on her apron*) Che mò facimo nu pocu e pasta asciutta subito subito cu li pummaduari frischi!

SON

Mà, …

MOTHER

E non devi mangiare?! Facimu e penne! ca te piacianu! …

SON

Mancu 'na mezza penna! …

MOTHER

Tubbetti in brodo? … Ca chilli sunnu buoni per la panza!

SON

Salutammilli! …

MOTHER

E devi morire di fame?! U sugo l'ho già messo à fare!

SON

Vino! Vino voglio! Nu bello bicchiere e vino! … mette tutto apposto! (*Massaging his temples while going towards the cantina to get a bottle of wine*)

MOTHER

(*Mother gets in his way*) Quannu se mangie se vive! (*Beat*) Ai visto? … Per lu bere u vino, siete tutti buani … ma pe' lu fare … Cussì dice lui.

SON

(*Observing her*) Mà, ti prego …

MOTHER

Se cazz'e musche! … (*Beat*) Ma u vino ch'è fatto?! … <u>acqua</u>?! … Ca poi te 'mbrìachi! … spece s'un te mangi nente! … te và dirittu ara capu!

SON

Si và ara capo, ma … è pecchi là fà bene … U vino un n'é fissa!

MOTHER

Ma cu ru stomaco vacante … <u>aronno</u>! … 'Nguà cosa un te le mangiare?!

SON

(*Explodes*) NON VOGLIO MANGIARE PE' GESÙ CHRISTO!! … Bo! … Fuck!

Pause.

MOTHER

Tua sorella se n'è andata. (*Loud, bitter whisper*) **Sparita**! … (*Pause*) Un dici nente? (*Pause*) Patritta ere già partito aru lavuru … Issa ere 'ndra stanza ch'ancora dormiva … (*Beat*) Io parto da casa per incontrare Ipatia aru cornu … Arrive lu bussu … saglimu … e guardannu verso a casa … un na vidu camminare verso u

---

1. "Oh messì bucù!" from the French *Oh, merçi beaucoup*.

stoppu du busso! … cu due beghe de carta belle grosse cu tutt'a robba sua! … Gesù' mio! … u core m'è jutu 'ndra gola! … a mu fare propio davant'a faccia! … avanti tutte e amiche mie du lavuru! … (*Beat*) U bussu già camminava. L'ho vista solo così … n'attimo! … Non ho mancu guardato indietro … in caso l'atre un n'avìenu vista … ma dintra … e passato a morte! (*Pause*) Non ha chiamato. Nente! … Vedi che core maligno! <u>Maligno</u>! … Sunnu tre giorni mò. (*Looking towards the cantina*) Quello … (*Suddenly*) Emmè chi ciota! C'e 'ngartare i sanguicci du lònciu! … ca issu oggi ha dde lavurare! (*Son takes the lunch box from her and throws it across the room. Mother clenches her left breast, and quietly picks up the lunch box. Pause*). … Te l'ha detto a signorina ca ci avimo trovato a droga 'ndra stanza?! 'Ndre <u>mutanne lorde</u>! … Ai capito? Te l'ha detto?! … Avimu chiamatu puru a Filumena da Cicala … ca chiddha cure gente de tante malatie brutte! … nui penzannu … chi sà, qualch'uno l'ha affascinata! Sfascinamula! … È venuta Filumena … e mentre ch'a signorina durmìe … ci ha messo … aspetta … piedi e puarci, e sangue frisco de coniglio sotto u liettu! … Aronno … insomma 'na cura adatta per se cose … pe' **drogati**! … Ma chi?! Dov'è 'sa fortuna! … A matina dopo tua sorella se n'è andata! … E vedi che Filumena n'ha guarito persone! … No! … si vede che tua sorella non ere più cosa de salvare! … ere già partita a 'ngu natru munnu! … E si s'a 'mbesata 'ngu diavolo! …

SON

(*Beat*) Mà, ccà ci abbitavano sulu l'osse … nu skeletro!

MOTHER

<u>Skeletro</u>?! … **U DIAVOLO** abbitave ccà! … no nu skeletro! … Sì, ch'ere ridotta così brutta, magra! … Patritta cià dat'e palate chi! … Chi skeletro?! U DIAVOLO! —BASTA!, un me fa' avvelenare! … un ne voglio sentire cchiù! … Chi ce mancave? <u>BASTA</u>! … ca si sentissi patritta! … la fà finita pe' tutti!

SON

E fallu sente! Chillu sente sulu chillu chi vo sentire! FALLU SENTE!

Mother turns on the radio.

RADIO

Giornale Radio!

MOTHER

Cittu e notizie!

Son yanks radio unit from the wall, throws it against another wall.

MOTHER

(*Trying not to give in to her pain*) **Sa casa puzze de vergogna!** E mure làcrimano de scorno! E gente **rìdono** da sfortuna mia! Qualch'uno piange! … ma la maggior parte <u>ridono</u>! … e parlanu! Un me puonnu guardare nemmeno cchiù 'ndra l'uacchi! … E un c'e misericordia! … Viditi belli mii, che n'avota che vi mettiti a fare a dieta "all'inglese" o ara francese, a past'as'ciutta un n'a toccati cchiù! Pecchi LÀ è stat'u danno! LÀ fore! LÀ fore v'hanno rovinato! E nun me dire no! … Quannu eramu a l'Italia, èrati figli e pane … Lo dicevono tutti! …

Ccà, aviti cominciato a vide e cose un pò diverse! E aviti misu u munnu tutto capu sutta! (*Erupting*)—S'America è stata a <u>ruvina</u>!

SON

Svota i bauli ma! … e butta via si stracci vecchi! … più antichi de' l'antichi!

MOTHER

È meglio a stare cu' le cose vecchie … sunnu più sicure! (*Cutting*) Taglia radici taglia!

SON

Taglia nente!

MOTHER

Butta, butta! … E gente tue t'e le tene più care … e se comincie in <u>famiglia</u>!

SON

<u>Famiglia</u>? Sulu l'<u>apparenza</u> … e mìenzu s'apparenza, sa *famiglia di vetrina* … ce sì tù pronte cu su piattu e pasta asciutta!

MOTHER

(*Bewildered, then accusingly*) Simu nati così!—Stracci vecchi?!! Chilli chi t'hannu mandenuto bello caldo fino a mò?!!!, invece de t'affucare!!! … STRACCI VECCHI?!!! Fai u spiritusu?, ch'ai fatt'a scola?! Avvocato e <u>cazzo</u>!!! Tu fai u spiritoso cu mia … ma nò cu patritta!

SON

Lassa stare patrimma, Gesù Christi e mariti, mà! … Penz'a Carmela!!

MOTHER

LÀ sono i guai! … LÀ ho sbagliato! … Che abbiamo penzato sembre primo ari <u>figli</u>! E vui aviti penzatu sulu a vui stessi! …

SON

(*Grabbing mother by the shoulders*) Brucia si stracci mà! E dorbicali!

MOTHER

(*Great difficulty suppressing her pain*) Un cià mai voluto bene ad issu! Ecco la verità!

SON

L'ho amato in silenzio, mà, come fà lui … così m'ha 'mbarato!

MOTHER

Veni ccà, 'na volt'a l'anno, solo per minde fuoco! Così dice lui!

SON

E <u>tu</u> chi dici?! Propio dintra, Carmela chi dice?!

MOTHER

(*Blowing up*) E propio a Carmela sto pensando! **PROPIO A CARMELA!**

SON

E tu me po dire che tu <u>ccà</u> sì cuntenta?

MOTHER

Sì, sì … jamu cu' la cuntentizza! Chine sta cuntientu?! CHINE? TÙ?! … Sulu chilli chi tenanu 'ngu santu più potente in paradiso forse! … Devo vivere sula come 'na zingara?! (*Looks towards the cantina*) A ce penzare … (*Desperately tries to contain her pain, but can't, and wails*) Oh Dio! … tutt'i sacrifici!!! … (*Shuts down her emotions and snaps into focus*) BASTA! <u>Finimula</u>! … ca chillo! …

SON

Pecchi sa paura, mà? Pecchi?

MOTHER

Pecchi io voglio santa pace 'ndra 'sa casa! Casa o no casa, chissa é!

SON

Case si ne costruiscono sembre mà!

MOTHER

Cittu ca te sente! (*Intensely aware that Father might be listening*)

SON

E fallu sente, ma! FALLU SENTE! . . .

MOTHER

Ma che cornuto che sei! . . . Come cazzo ti permetti!?! Chi cazzo sei tu?! . . . Ca tu sai meglio di tutti quello ch'avissi de fare io?! . . . IO ci devo fare a vita! IO! NO TU! . . . Come ti permetti?! Tutti quandi aviti truvatu a cura! Tutti cu la purga! Ma cure, un ci nne sunnu! . . . u vò' capire! . . . Apposto sei venuto?! Per me dare a cura?! (*Throwing plates at him, and anything else in sight*) Escia da casa mia! Brutta bestia! ESCIA! Ca un te penzare ca m'e dimenticato chillo ch'ha dittu patritta! U curtiaddhu u tene ancora supra! ESCIA! E nun te fa vide cchiù! ESCIA! (*Son is about to slap mother across the face, stops himself in mid action, shaking. Beat*) Tu si peggio e patritta! . . . Peggio! Peggio! Peggio!

> *Pause.*

SON

. . . Chillu juarnu 'ndra cantina, mà . . . cu ru curtiaddhu . . . ca tu dopo l'hai truvatu 'nderra ca ciangìe . . . chillu juarnu mà, signu arrivatu cussì vicinu all'ammazzare . . . ed ero capace! . . . c'ero quasi arrivatu mà—quasi arrivatu! . . . Ma nun le fattu! . . . m'ha guardatu 'ndra faccia, e pe' ra prima vota, ha vistu fuocu 'ndra l'uacchi mii . . . Ed iu mà, vulìe vide sulu a paura 'ndra l'uacchi sui . . . 'Ndra chillu momento mà, iu e vulutu vide chillu chi vidìe issu 'ndra l'uacchi mii fin'a chillu juarnu! . . . E l'ho vista mà . . . Paura vera . . . bestiale . . . cumu nu cunigliu 'ntrappulatu . . . cu l'uacchi rutunni . . . e lu destinu sue 'ndre manu mie . . . Ed e penzatu . . . "Chi sodisfazzione può avire uno a vide sa paura 'ndra l'uacchi de natru? Perchè?" . . . E tu sai mà, mentre ca c'e fattu assaggiare nu pocu da medicina sua . . . sulu pe' chill'attimu . . . sai mà, ca ce pigliavu gustu a lu vide cu chilla paura. E cchiù ce pigliavu gustu, cchiù me facie pena . . . e cchiù u vulìe ammazzare, a ce ficcare u curtieddhu 'ndra gola, e a ce ammaccare a capu aru muro! . . . puru pecchì avìe puru vergogna ca le potutu riducere a n'animale . . . vulìe cancellare chillu momentu, mà . . . ma nun putìe . . . a paura già c'ere . . . eru troppu attiratu a sa paura . . . E 'ndra l'uocchi . . . iddhu un n'ere cchiù patrimma . . . ere n'animale pateticu . . . senza nessuna traccia de nu essere umanu . . . Ed e penzatu a nu juarnu quannu jìe ara scola . . . ca pe'ra via, iu e n'amicu, avimu truvatu n'uccellu ch'un vulave cchiù. L'avimo pigliatu, e l'amu purtatu 'ndru metrù,[1] cussì, 'ndre manu . . . e re gente ne guardavanu, e penzavanu, "Chi belli guagliuni, a salvare nu pover'uccello". Chissu penzavanu! L'uccello mà, avimu purtatu ara scola . . . pianu pianu stave murìannu . . . Un sapìamu cum'u salvare . . . avimu decisu du dorbicare . . . pecchi ere tiempu d'entrare 'ndra classe. Ere vivu . . . allura, avimu misu supr'e tracche du treno . . . e primo iu . . . dopo Sam . . . cu na petra l'amu spaccatu in due . . . Un se spaccave in due . . . però nui cu la petra, di nuovo Zang! Avimu truvatu pe' ru salvare . . . e mù . . . senza pietà . . . nente! . . . sangue freddo . . . avìamu piacire de vide a quandu piezzi u putìamu

---

1. Metrù from the French *métro* (*subway*).

fare ... ancora cu ra petra, Zang! ... pe'vide chine arrivava primo a ce staccare a
capu! ... Avimu dorbicatu ... e quannu simu usciti d'a scola, avimu cacciatu fore
ancora, e ancora cu ra petra, Zang!, fina ch'un c'ere rimastu nente, Zang! Zang!
Zang! Zang! Zang! Zang! Zang! Zang! Zang! Zang! Zang! Zang! Zang!! ... che
sodisfazzione!! Eravamu cussi cuntienti! ... cume chillu juarnu 'ndra cantina mà.
Papà ere diventatu l'uccello. ... Senz'u sapire, u poveru fissa, se stave guardannu
'ndru specchiu! ... forse avìe vistu na cosa pure cchiù brutta da raggia sua ... a
raggia mia! ... E se meritave peggiu dell'uccello! Come persona si meritave
PEGGIO! ... ma m'è patre, e non l'ho fatto! ... (*Pause*) Nu cane arragiatu mà,
s'un n'ammazzi ... prima o poi muzziche!

> *Pause.*

MOTHER
... Abbaia, nun muzzicare! ... Abbaia, ch'u peggio nun more mai! ... Quannu
vidi nu cane arraggiato, ce vo' core ... un nu sparare ... un n'é matto ... e
sulu'arraggiato ... e solo isso e Gesù Christo s'annu chillu ch'ha patuto! (*Pause*)
Va bene. Ed ora de mangiare mù. Sedate si vùe ... Sedate! ... (*Calls out*) Raffaè!,
vedi ch'è pronte! E porta na buttiglia e vino d'a cantina., che non ce n'è 'ndru
friggideru! (*Turns on TV. Low volume*) Appiccia sa radio che frà poco ci sono e
notizie ... ch'a patritta lo conosci ... a de sente a temperatura (*Pause*) Va bene,
l'accendo io! ... Sedate ti ho detto! (*She notices the damaged state of the NuTone
radio intercom wall unit. Says nothing. Pause. She gives SON a folded piece of
paper.*) Te. Patritta te l'aveva scritta nu par'e misi fa ... Tu nun si venutu mai! ...
SON
(*Looks at the cheque*) Sono troppo!
MOTHER
Se non ti fanno bisogno, vedi tu. ... Cu chissi, facce chillu chi vue! Usali pe' te
sviluppare pur'e corne! (*Serves Son a plate of pasta*) Mangiate questa mò ... ormai
l'ho fatta! Si deve perdere? ... Di oggi in poi nun ti ne fazzu più! (*She sits down to
eat, shakes her head*) Sembre così lui ... non viene mai quand'è pronte. Mai! Che
deve finire i lavori. Finisce nu lavoro e ne comincie n'altro ... Deve fare sembre
rifriddare sa pasta ... che poi ai visto come cresce ... e si fà troppo asciutta! ... Io
mangio! ... bon'appetito!
SON
Lo vado chiamo io.
MOTHER
Lascialo stare!! ... Non te sentire stranu mò che t'ha dato questi. ... E metà te li
ho dati io! ... Fai cuntu ca sunnu i tui. Nun vuole niente. ... Diciacce merci, e
dazzol! ... si se rifredde, si frega! Lascialo stare.

> *Pause.*

SON
Lo vado chiamo ... E pigliu pur'u vino.

> *Son exits. Long Pause.*

SON
  (Offstage) Mà.

  Enters with a bottle of wine

SON
  Mà, papà è 'ndra cantina … 'mbicato.
MOTHER
  Eh! C'è d'avantieri sira! Tre giorni!
SON
  Mà, è morto.
MOTHER
  Va bene, sedate e mangia, che si nnò … se rifredde pur'a tua!

  Son sits down to eat.

  MUSIC: "Swordfisherman's Cry" (Grida Per Il Pesce Spada) by Bova G. Di Michelangelo[1]
  Son devours the pasta. Mother pours him a glass of wine.

  Lights fade to black.

  The End

---

1. "Southern Italy and the Islands," *The Columbia World Library of Folk and Primitive Music*, Compiled and Edited by Alan Lomax, 1957.

CAUSE UNKNOWN

1994
Toni Ellwand

To die,—to sleep;—
To sleep. Perchance to dream:—ay, there's the rub;
For in that sleep of death what dreams may come.
    —Hamlet

In every eye there is a spot that is incapable of sight. The optic disc exists as a black hole right next to the central point of clearest vision. Yet anyone who has not learned the trick of finding it would swear there is no such void.
    —Dr. Roland Summit,
        Lasting Effects of Child Sexual Abuse

List Of Characters
Felice Benvenuta
Mama Benvenuta
Papa Benvenuta
Dina Benvenuta
Sarah Riley
Fr. William
Doctor

SCENE 1

As the lights slowly rise up on stage, we hear angelic music. if possible, it should be similar to the theme music from the movie, I've Heard The Mermaids Singing. The music starts softly and rises to a crescendo when the lights are at their fullest. on stage we see the interior of a garage. in the center of the garage is a massive freshly-slaughtered pig, hanging from the ceiling. MAMA BENVENUTA enters. As the music and lights swell to a climactic peak, MAMA opens the legs of the pig and pulls out a length of Italian sausage. She exits. Lights out.

SCENE 2

Two conversations are taking place simultaneously, in different areas of the playing space. the Benvenuta kitchen and dining room is one area.

the neighbourhood leading up to the Benvenuta home is the second area.
MAMA and DINA are busily preparing the enormous easter meal. if
possible, this should be a real meal. FELICE BENVENUTA and her
student, SARAH RILEY, are approaching the house.

SARAH

Holy God, how do you people afford houses like these? They're intense!

DINA

And don't ask about the house. We don't want to get into another fight.

FELICE

You mean immense?

DINA

It's finished, it's done, okay?

MAMA

Tengo la bocca chiusa.

DINA

Good.

SARAH

No, I means intense!

MAMA

Arrimina lu sugo Di'!

DINA

I'm stirring, I'm stirring!

FELICE

Yeah, they are a bit much aren't they?

DINA

And don't say stupid things to her friend!

MAMA

A chi chiami stupida?

FELICE

Hard work and too many sacrifices paid for them.

DINA

It's because you're always putting your foot in your mouth.

SARAH

Felice? Am I dressed okay?

FELICE

You're fine. My sister may say something, but she's crazy so ...
           DINA puts some food in her mouth and MAMA slaps her.

MAMA

E you always putting troppo pancetta in your mouth!

DINA

Ouh!

MAMA

Help me wid de table invece di parlare sempre come un'imbecile!

SARAH

How long's it been since you were back here anyway?

FELICE
    Not that long but for my mother—
                FELICE starts rushing to the door of her parents' home.
MAMA
    Allestiti! You so slow!
DINA
    Don't start or I'm gonna go watch TV!
MAMA
    Okay, okay, ma help me!
SARAH
    What's wrong girl?
FELICE
    We're late! And wops, they love to make you pay, you know?
                FELICE rings the doorbell. DINA goes to answer it.
MAMA
    Dina, Dina, turn off de stove!
DINA
    What! Are you helpless all of a sudden. Jesus!
                DINA returns to turn off stove. doorbell rings again.
MAMA
    Ma why you so slow, va apri la porta!
DINA
    God, I could wring your neck!
                DINA exits. MAMA rushes around getting everything ready.
                she is breathing heavily. DINA, FELICE and SARAH enter.
MAMA
    Ma what happen? Why you so late! Tutto è pronto!
FELICE
    Sorry Ma, c'era troppo traffico—
MAMA
    (*In tears*) Oh Madonna Mia! I no see mia Felice for so many months!
                MAMA starts hugging and kissing FELICE violently.
DINA
    The prodigal child returns to the fold.
FELICE
    It hasn't been that long Ma!—
DINA
    Happy Easter!
MAMA
    Buona Pasqua!
SARAH
    Bona Pancia!
DINA
    (*Laughing*) Bona Pancia?!
                MAMA suddenly notices SARAH and her huge belly.
MAMA
    Madonna, che pancia!

FELICE

E incinta!

SARAH

I'm pregnant!

> *MAMA makes the sign of the cross over SARAH's tummy.*

DINA

So what, she's pregnant. What's in the box.

SARAH

A Easter sheep.

MAMA

Oh, la pecora di Pasqua, dat mean good luck!

DINA

Right!

FELICE

And cannoli siciliani.

DINA

Oh boy, oh boy!

> *DINA starts tearing into box. MAMA slaps her hand and takes the box away.*

DINA

Ouh!

MAMA

Dina, per carità!

DINA

I was just gonna take a look!

MAMA

I got to hide dem. (MAMA points ominously to SARAH's stomach). Se vede tutti questi dolci, si rovina l'appetito!

SARAH

Did I do something wrong?

FELICE

No, no. My mother's just worried that you'll crave the desserts.

DINA

And that'll ruin your appetite.

SARAH

I don't think so. I'm eating like the royal pig right now.

DINA

So, is my sister going to introduce you or are we going to play guessing games all night?

FELICE

Well, if you'd give me a chance—

DINA

Okay, here's your opportunity, Felice, here it is, 'Who is she?'

FELICE

Sarah Riley, my student.

DINA

Very good, Felice. Hi Sarah, I'm Dina, the sister who stayed.

SARAH

Hi. Felice's been telling me all about you.

DINA

Did she tell you I was crazy? Well, I'm not.

MAMA

Chi'è Di?

DINA

La sua studente.

SARAH

Felice's student, Sarah.

MAMA

Ah, Serafina, piacere.

DINA

Sarah!

SARAH

Serafina pacere to you too.

DINA

No, no, no.

SARAH

No?

DINA

No. It's just piacere which means, pleasure to meet you.

SARAH

I'd be pretty piacere to get a seat right about now. My back's killing me.

> *Everyone rushes to get SARAH a chair. MAMA is the big*
> *winner—after shoving everyone aside of course.*

MAMA

Per l'amore di Dio Di! You always in my way!

SARAH

Thanks.

> *Pause.*

MAMA

E quella casa, come va?

DINA

Ma!

FELICE

(*Laughing*) It's alright, Di. The house is great.

MAMA

See, she no get upset, 'cause I asking.

FELICE

Everything's been taken care of so—

DINA

So what's $5,000 for a few unexpected disasters.

MAMA

Cinque mila! O Dio Mio, Felice! Not on dat house. Ma te l'ho detto io.

FELICE

I thought you were supposed to be on my side!

DINA
 It just slipped out.
FELICE
 Thanks!
MAMA
 I tol you dat house is garbage. Ti hanno tirato gl'occhi!
DINA
 Ma she can afford it, she's a teacher.
FELICE
 Mmmm!
MAMA
 Dats right. Al meno she have a job!
FELICE
 Something smells really good!
SARAH
 I'm starving! What's for supper?
MAMA
 Now dat you lose alla you money on dat barraca—
DINA
 Ma, she asked you what you were cooking.
MAMA
 Be, is lasagne.
FELICE
 That's great Ma!
DINA
 And fried sausages!
SARAH
 Yum! I loves Italian sausages.
MAMA
 Fatti di casa!
DINA
 Hey, when my sister comes back, it's a special day. Look Felice, Ma's even got the
 good dishes out.
FELICE
 Dina—
MAMA
 Ma stai zitta adesso—
FELICE
 I'm starving too!
DINA
 Me three, let's eat.
    MAMA points toward the upstairs.
MAMA
 (*Loud whisper*) SHH! Scema, lascia stare. Is no time yet.
DINA
 Oh Christ. How much time?

MAMA

Dieci minuti.

DINA

He's already slept for 20!

MAMA

Se si sveglia troppo presto diventa un'orso. You know dat.

DINA

Ten minutes is too long! I'll die!

FELICE

But first you gotta give me a massage. Come on. Right here. She's a natural at this Sarah.

DINA

Awh ... okay. 'Ms. Dina Benvenuta, massage therapist to the rescue'!

FELICE

Yes, ouh! Oh yes, ouh! Oh that hurts! You should get a massage table and work out of the house.

DINA

Yeah! As if Italians in Maple are gonna come see me for a massage.

FELICE

It would be a job.

DINA presses hard on FELICE'S back.

FELICE

Ouh!

MAMA

Sempre le stesse. You two always get busy when you gotta help me!

SARAH

I'll give you a hand—

MAMA

No, no, no—

PAPA enters. everyone is aware of his presence.

PAPA

Levati Dina. I gonna do it.

MAMA

(*To SARAH*) Grazie, I mean, thank you. Dina, aiutami!

DINA

It's okay, I'm almost finished.

PAPA

My hands are stronge dan yours, go.

FELICE

You don't have to do it Papa.

PAPA

Sh sh sh. Is gonna make you feel better.

PAPA starts massaging FELICE. He notices SARAH.

PAPA

Hello. nice to meet you. Buona Pasqua.

SARAH

Uh, Buena Peshqua. I'm Sarah.

FELICE
Mia studente.
PAPA
Relax!
DINA
Coming through. Get your arms off the table Felice They're gonna get burned.
MAMA
Si, and I need room for the salad too.
FELICE
That's enough Papa. Thanks.
PAPA
It's okay. Buona Pasqua mia Felice.
FELICE
Buona Pasqua Papa.
PAPA
Okay, okay. Let's eat.
    Everyone sits.
PAPA
Il nome di Padre, Figlio, Spirito, Santo e cose sia.
    Lights shift.

SCENE 3

  After dinner. everyone is seated in the living room. SARAH, DINA,
  FELICE, and PAPA are watching t.v. it is italian programming. DINA
  and SARAH are also going through a photo album of the Benvenuta family.

DINA
This is me when I had my first communion.
SARAH
Is the other one of Felice?
DINA
Mhm, that's Felice.
SARAH
Felice, you looks some cute.
DINA
Yeah! What happened?
FELICE
Di, give it a rest.
SARAH
How come you had to dress up like miniature brides?
DINA
Because that's what we were.
SARAH
Oh I get it. It's like them East Indian cultures where they set you up when you're
a kid.

DINA

Better still, a good Catholic girl is supposed to marry Jesus when she's in grade two and stay a virgin for the rest of her life.

FELICE

It's not that extreme.

DINA

They'd like it to be.

SARAH

You're not still a virgin?

DINA

Well—

FELICE

Dina, shut up.

> *DINA flips through pictures.*

DINA

Look at this one. Who do you think that is?

SARAH

(Laughing) Oh no! That's the stundest outfit I've ever seen Felice!

DINA

Felice wasn't what you'd call the hippest person in her class but she was the smartest.

SARAH

The students voted her teacher of the year.

DINA

Oh yeah, well, big surprise. Felice got scholarships to all the universities she applied to. They sent my mother and father letters, begging for her, eh Felice?

> *(Beat)*

DINA

Not like yours truly, eh Felice?

> *(Beat)*

DINA

I had to beg them to let me in, didn't I Felice?

> *Silence.*

SARAH

Yeah?

DINA

But I'm perfectly normal.

> *DINA makes a face and they both laugh. MAMA enters with cookies and coffee.*

DINA

Right here Ma.

MAMA

Uno biscotto Di e basta.

SARAH

What was that?

DINA

I can have as many cookies as I want.

> *DINA and SARAH help themselves to cookies.*

SARAH
Mm! These are excellent!
MAMA
I make dem myself.
SARAH
I gotta tell you, Mrs. Benvenuta, this is the best meal I've had in ages. Them sausages were amazing.
PAPA
Fatti in casa. Homemade. When Felice little, we make alla de time, eh Felice?
DINA
(To SARAH) The first time we slaughtered a pig in the garage, the blood squirted out all over the walls. It was really gross.
MAMA
It start like baby pig and grow like de baby in your tummy.
SARAH laughs.
DINA
Felice fed the pig. She even gave it a name.
FELICE
Can we talk about something else, please?
DINA
Why? This is fun.
PAPA
Madonna, to catch dat stupid pig was so hard!
MAMA
Come gridava! It give me a head-ache after.
DINA
I had to get the two by four for Papa. Then I had to hold it by the back leg. Mama had one leg, I had the other.
MAMA
Felice no can do. She cry just like de pig.
DINA
It was a strong pig too. Papa wacked it on the nose and you could hear the skull cracking and the pig squealing and shaking and then its front legs gave in.
PAPA
And de pig face hit de floor of de garage e crack!
DINA
But it was still alive and drowning in its own blood. So I got the knife for Papa.
PAPA
E I cut de troat (Makes knife slashing sounds) very fast. Perchè se non si fa fast, de meat go bad.
DINA
And the blood! Jesus! It shot out of that pig!
MAMA
(To SARAH) Hai mai visto, you see how much blood a pig have?
DINA
It spattered the floors, the walls—

FELICE

Finiscila adesso!

DINA

Aw poor Felice. That pig was her baby.

PAPA

Errato troppo bella Felice; so cute.

DINA

Felice was so upset, papa had to go and make her feel better.

FELICE

Shut up, shut up, shut up!

DINA

What's your problem?

PAPA

Eh, you like to eat de sausages, no?

FELICE

No.

PAPA

(*Dismissing this*) Ma che dici!

DINA

We don't kill our own pigs anymore. We get it slaughtered first and then we hang it over the drain to drip. It's not as messy.

FELICE

Let's start going Sarah.

PAPA

Where you from?

SARAH

Wha?

PAPA

Where you from?

SARAH

Downtown.

PAPA

No, no, no. You talk different—where you from?

SARAH

You still heres it do ya? Hmm.

PAPA

WHERE YOU FROM?

FELICE

Pa lasciala stare.

PAPA

Oh dat's it. You do de bad ting eh?

SARAH

The bad thing? I'm from Newfoundland. Is that supposed to be a bad thing?

FELICE

Fa troppo caldo ma, open the window.

MAMA & DINA

No!

PAPA

Newfoundland? Che cos'e stu Newfoundland?

FELICE

I'm sweating.

DINA

It's a place.

FELICE

I'm sweating!

DINA

Are you nuts? The heat's still on.

MAMA

Caramia, bisogna mangiare. You too skinny bedrame.

MAMA gives FELICE cookies and coffee.

FELICE

We'd better start going.

MAMA

Ma, non hai preso il caffe.

FELICE stands.

FELICE

I don't want any coffee.

PAPA

Assettati.

FELICE sits.

PAPA

Ma questa ragazza, sta con te?

Silence.

PAPA

Felice, she live with you?

Silence.

SARAH

I'm only staying with Felice until my new place comes through. I'm at the top of the waiting list so it shouldn't be too long now.

PAPA

Ma, non è sposata?

Silence.

PAPA

Felice, she no marry?

SARAH

I sort of got a boyfriend. But he's not around right now so ...

PAPA

Where is he?

SARAH

Well, he kind of got messed up—

MAMA

Che cosa ha detto Di?

DINA

I'll tell you later.

MAMA

Che cosa ha detto?

PAPA

E drogato?

SARAH

Wha?

DINA

He's a crackhead?

SARAH

No!

FELICE

It's getting late Sarah.

PAPA

E allora he gonna be wid you, tomorrow?

SARAH

No.

PAPA

Ma, de baby gotta have a fader.

SARAH

My baby's got me.

PAPA

Ma dats not enough! Only de fader can take care of de family.

SARAH

Are you kidding?

PAPA

A baby need a fader.

SARAH

I can take care of it myself!

PAPA

No. no no little ghella. A baby's a big job. You gotta dress him, you gotta feed him, you gotta put him in nice bed.

DINA

Ma had to do all of that.

PAPA

Yeah, scema. Who bring home de money eh? Eh? Io! Il papa!

SARAH

Mr. Benvenuta, thanks for all your concern but—

PAPA

(Shouting) La responsabilità è con il papa! De sacrifice is wid de fader! You canna watch dis ghella, you canna watch yourself! You gotta come home adesso. Devi essere a casa con la famiglia. Non è giusto quello che fai tu!

FELICE

But Papa I own my own house now.

PAPA

What you want people to say? Dat you Papa canna take care of you eh? Dat he got no money per la sua famiglia?

FELICE
No Papa—
PAPA
E allora vieni a casa Felice because de people dey talk. Dey tell me to my face. Whats da matter, dey say? Why Felice no home? You lose you job? You got no money?
FELICE
But that's not true Papa everything's fine.
PAPA
No everting no fine, because you no home, e people say I no doing my job. E if I no do my job, che cosa va capitare? What happen to my family? My house? My life? Eh? Eh? Eh finita!
DINA
Pa relax!
MAMA
Calmati, calmati Antonino!
                    FELICE collapses.
SARAH
Are you alright?
DINA
What's wrong?
MAMA
Figlia mia, che c'è, che c'è?
                    Everyone surrounds FELICE.
PAPA
Felice, scusami ah, everyting gonna be good now. Stai qui. I canna make you your favourite soup. Chicken. Is gonna make you feel better.
FELICE
I don't want chicken soup. I've been trying to tell you that it's too hot but nobody wants to listen.
PAPA
Okay, okay, we turn de heat down.
DINA
But it's freezing outside.
MAMA
Dina, per carità.
PAPA
Dina, shut up.
MAMA
No, non poi andare in questa condizione. Sleep here tonight.
FELICE
SARAH! I need some air, let's go!
SARAH
Uh, yeah, okay!
DINA
Felice, come on.
PAPA
Felice!

MAMA

Is too early!

FELICE

It's time to go!

MAMA

Okay, okay!

Everyone tries to speak at the same time in the following dialogue.

MAMA

You gonna come back next week!

FELICE

No, I—

MAMA

Ma, si, you gotta help me wid de tomatoes—

FELICE .

Dina can—

DINA

Ma, I can—

MAMA

No, Dina too lazy—

FELICE

I've got—

PAPA

Felice, I need you per il computer—

MAMA

Devi venire Sabato—

PAPA

No, Friday, per tutto il weekend—

DINA

No, Felice, come Monday and stay for the damn week!

PAPA

Ma che dici scema!

MAMA

Scimunita, shut up!

FELICE

Okay, okay, okay! I'll see you next week—Sarah, let's go.

MAMA

Aspetta! I give you some food.

FELICE

No!

SARAH

Yes!

FELICE

Okay.

DINA

Ma, hurry up, get it and I'll put it in her car!

Everyone exits. PAPA is left alone. Lights out.

SCENE 4

Lights up on FELICE and SARAH. they are in FELICE's home. FELICE has a big plastic bag from which she is trying to lift out nugs (log bits), whore's eggs (a Nfld shellfish), a newfoundland calendar, seaweed, kelp, seashells, dried beached caplin (Nfld fish), etc. both women are laughing sarah. is smoking. FELICE takes a big piece of rope from the bag.

SARAH
Where'd you get that?

FELICE
Off the docks.

SARAH
You actually picked something up off those docks? go on!

FELICE
What?

SARAH
Awh, it's such a touristy thing to do.

FELICE
The old fisherman wanted me to take it. Isn't it wonderful? He was going to have to throw it away!

SARAH
Sure, well look at it!

FELICE
He came up to me! His face was all cracked and broken by the wind. He showed me his hands and I swear to you, they were just like leather. "It's from pullin' them ropes", he said, "Them ropes is a part of me. Go on, smell it!" It was that sea.

SARAH
When did you go?

FELICE
Last summer. Oh Sarah, it's so amazing! The beach is all rock.

SARAH
Yes, there's a few rocks maid.

They laugh. FELICE pulls out a bag full of dried fish. they are caplin fish.

FELICE
Beached Caplin.

SARAH
Dried smelt.

FELICE pulls out two whore's eggs.

FELICE
Whore's eggs!

SARAH
Sea urchins.

FELICE
I love Newfoundland! They give everything a name that's different from everyone

else's. They never follow the rules. Look at these. Whore's eggs! Don't you just love them?

>SARAH *laughs.*

FELICE

This one was floating right near the shore. I went in with my shoes and everything. I got completely soaked. But it was so much fun. Look at these beautiful treasures. My mother would have heart failure. She'd want to throw them all out. If you're talking to my family, don't mention that I went to Newfoundland. They'll never let it go. They'll say, I wasted my money. I should have spent it on the roof.

>*FELICE starts putting things away.*

SARAH

You looks so straight, but you're always doing all this wild stuff. Like that time you rented them costumes for class, dressing up in them outfits and walkin' around, reading Romeo and Juliet, looking up all them words in that fancy dictionary. I mean we all got the story, hey.

FELICE

It's my job.

SARAH

Yes girl, but you don't just sit there. You takes us on a ride.

FELICE

A package came for you. It's from Newfoundland.

>*SARAH grabs package and starts to tear it open.*

SARAH

My mother sent me something?! Shit, maybe she's getting it together!

>*FELICE takes a package of pills out of her pocket and pops a couple into her mouth.*

SARAH

When'd you start pill-popping?

FELICE

They're only caffeine pills. Here, read the label.

SARAH

Hey, you don't have to explain yourself to me.

FELICE

I just got some stupid bug and I'm still really tired so . . .

SARAH

So maybe you should see a doctor.

FELICE

I've been working too hard. I need a little rest, that's all.

>*SARAH pulls out a very skimpy outfit from the package. It can be anything as long as it is obvious that the outfit was meant for someone very slim and certainly not pregnant. SARAH stares at it for a moment.*

FELICE

It's, it's, wow. You're going to look like something in that.

SARAH

Yes girl, like in three years.

>*(Beat)*

SARAH

I sent her pictures.

FELICE

Maybe she sent this for after the baby.

SARAH

She's a fucking drunk, Felice.

FELICE

Oh.

SARAH

And I almost thought she cared. (Beat) I don't know how many times I picked her up off the goddamned floor. Too drunk and too beaten up to move. All she can see is her friggin' bottle. (Beat) And she never did a goddamn thing when her boyfriend beat the crap out of me. Didn't lift a finger. I thought, that's it. I've had it. I'm not takin' this shit anymore. And I left. (Beat) Felice, look, I haven't called Jessie's yet, but I will. As soon as an apartment's up for me, I'm outta here, I promise.

FELICE

Sarah, the important thing is you and the baby. We want the baby to be healthy and happy right?

SARAH

Yeah?

SARAH gets another cigarette. FELICE takes it away.

FELICE

So we have to take care of you. That makes sense, doesn't it?

SARAH

Yeah.

FELICE

You don't have to rely on an institution. This is your home. For as long as you want, okay?

SARAH

Okay?!

FELICE

You fainting in my classroom's turned out to be a boon for me. The first time I made a real meal in this house was when you moved in. I never wanted to eat again after getting away from my mother's house.

SARAH

I loves your mother's cooking.

FELICE

Oh great. Well, I said I'd go back there for the weekend. Any orders?

SARAH

Can you bring me back some sausages?

FELICE

They're my father's specialty.

They laugh. Lights out.

SCENE 5

Benvenuta home. MAMA is putting tablecloth on the dining room table.
FELICE enters

MAMA
Madonna mia!
>*MAMA starts breathing hard.*

FELICE
Ma, ma, I gotta talk to you.

MAMA
Oh mio cuore!
>*DINA enters.*

DINA
Mmm, something smells really good.

MAMA
MY HEART!

DINA
Oh my God, where are your pills?
>*DINA exits to get MAMA's pills.*

MAMA
No scema, I'ma happy! Sono troppo contenta vederti cosi, Felice.

FELICE
I know Ma.

MAMA
Oh cara mia, you well now.

FELICE
Ma, Ma, listen, there's nothing wrong with me. I've just been a little rundown.
Sono stanca, that's all.

MAMA
No no caramia io lo so. Io lo so qui. (MAMA points to her heart) Ma now,
everyting bad finish.

FELICE
Ma—
>*DINA enters. she has ma's pills and bread and Nutella. MAMA*
>*is breathing heavily.*

DINA
Ma what are you doing? Take your pills!

MAMA
Si, si.
>*MAMA takes her pills. DINA gives her water.*

MAMA
Mi devi scusare ah, I got too much emotion.

FELICE
Ma.

MAMA
Caramia, che c'è?

FELICE

Have you been up to some funny things this weekend?

MAMA

(Looks at FELICE innocently) Me? I don't know.

FELICE

I think you do know.

> *DINA makes herself a huge Nutella sandwich. FELICE picks up*
> *bulky soggy handkerchief sitting on the table and shows it to DINA.*

FELICE

Di, look what I found between my pillows.

> *DINA looks at the handkerchief and starts coughing.*

DINA

Woh, it stinks! What the hell is that?

> *MAMA grabs the handkerchief.*

MAMA

Ma che stai facendo?

FELICE

Ma?

MAMA

Eh che c'è?'

FELICE

I'm waiting.

MAMA

Eh! Why you tink you better, ah? I go to Signora Nancy dats why ... È vero, she
tell true, Signora Nancy.

FELICE

What'd she tell you ma.

DINA

Yeah, what'd she say ma, I'm all ears.

MAMA

(To DINA) Dispettosa, you no believe but it work. Signora Nancy tell me,
Somebody put a curse on mia Felice! Is true! Bad people do dat alla de time.

FELICE

Ma please.

DINA

I could think of a few people, I'd like to do it to.

FELICE

Yeah!

> (They laugh)

MAMA

Non ci credi? You no tink is true? Ma guarda questo fazzoletto! Ti hanno messo
il mal'occhio!

DINA

Mal' occhio, schmallocchio, why did Signora Nancy tell you to put this thing in
her bed?

MAMA

Scimunita, se stai-zitta per un momento I gonna tell you.

DINA

    This is gonna be good.

MAMA

    Signora Nancy tell me, I gotta wrap a ripe tomato in a pure white handkerchief and put it in bed where Felice sleep. E per venti quattr'ore, Signora Nancy light a hundred candles e pray for you in her special gypsy church. De next day, I suppose to take de tomato out of de bed and if it's covered wid black hairs den de curse is finish.

> *DINA and FELICE open up the handkerchief completely and reveal a ripe tomato covered in black hair. They look at each other and . . .*

FELICE

    No it can't be!

DINA

    No way!

MAMA

    Ma guardala!

> *MAMA grabs FELICE's face and hugs and kisses her violently.*

FELICE

    Ma, finiscila, basta, that's enough ma, please.

MAMA

    You better no?

DINA

    The proof's in the tomato, Felice!

> *They laugh.*

MAMA

    I gonna kiss Signora Nancy when I see her.

DINA

    And pay her the fat fee you owe her.

MAMA

    You, shut up!

> *MAMA slaps DINA.*

FELICE

    What are you doing, stop it.

> *DINA pushes MAMA.*

DINA

    Lay off me you old cow!

MAMA

    I no care how much it cost, I got my Felice back. I gave her life.

FELICE

    (TRYING TO INTERJECT) Can we discuss this like civilized human beings, for a change?!

MAMA

    Che cosa hai fatto tu per la tua sorella, ha?

DINA

    Ma va fa Napoli!

MAMA

Va fa Napoli a te! Felice ha fatto il successo, no tu. You, you canna even keep a job, no finish universita, noting!

DINA

And Fuck you too!

MAMA

You say dat to me, butana!

DINA and MAMA start slapping each other.

FELICE

ENOUGH PLEASE!

DINA

You again! You come back here and shit happens!

DINA picks up jar of Nutella and bread and starts to exit.

FELICE

What are you doing? What are you doing? We're gonna have dinner in a minute.

DINA

You eat the dinner. You need it to build up your strength, oh perfect one!

She exits. FELICE is suddenly drained of energy.

MAMA

(*Shouting*) Dina, I no like you eating all over de house. You get crumbs all over de carpet! Felice never do dat! She so good mia Felice. No like dat lazy, pezzo di merda sister.

MAMA goes about her work. She talks continuously. She is unaware of FELICE.

FELICE

Ma, basta. That's enough.

MAMA

Is no good. Trovo nutella sandwich sott'il letto. Chips sotto tutti i cuscini di lu couch! Oh Felice, you gotta come home. You gotta teach her de right way.

FELICE

Ma, I can't ... I have my own home ma.

MAMA

What you say?

FELICE

Questa non e casa mia.

MAMA

Ma che sei pazza? You tink dat piece of shit house is you home eh? No way.

FELICE sits. she is trying to fight off her fatigue. MAMA continues talking unaware.

MAMA

Affitala quella garbage house, come home e you fix quella butana di figlia. She's a pig. I tell her dat alla de time. Ma she no listen to me. Felice, muoviti, I-gotta put de dishes down. Felice, we gotta eat! Felice! Felice! Oh Dio, Oh Dio.

As MAMA exits, she is shouting to DINA off-stage.

MAMA

Dina! Dina! Va chiama Fader Fiori! Sta morendo! Dina!

FELICE is asleep. Lights out.

SCENE 6

DINA and PAPA are sitting in front of a computer. DINA is stuffing herself with chips. she eats throughout the scene. papa is trying to figure something out on the computer, but his attempts are unsuccessful. Finally...

PAPA
    (*In frustration*) AAHHH! STU CAZZU!
DINA
    NO! Press Enter, press Enter!.
            But PAPA wants no more to do with it.
PAPA
    Porca miseria!
DINA
    It's IBM compatible.
PAPA
    You tell me dat a million time ma no make no difference.
DINA
    Sure it makes a difference. It means that you learn on this one and then you'll be able to pick up on the one you're going to have to use at work.
PAPA
    Ma ci devi avere la testa per questi cosi, Di. Is too late for me.
DINA
    Pa, anybody can learn this. Even that kid Sarah, knows how to figure this stuff out. I saw her reading the books!
            PAPA grabs one of the computer books.
PAPA
    Ma sto libro, scimunita. Dis book, dese instructions ... Is de same book for both computer, eh?
DINA
    No but ...
PAPA
    No eh allora, what you trying to tell me? I just waste my time learning dis shit. E di più, non lo capisco.
            FELICE enters with her arms outstretched in front of her. she is in great pain because of the swollen lymph glands in her armpits.
DINA
    Why are you walking around like that?
FELICE
    My armpits are swollen!
PAPA
    Sei allergica a qualcosa.
DINA
    Yeah, this family.
FELICE
    Who knows. I can't put my arms down.

DINA
Maybe you're getting that virus that's going around.
PAPA
Fammi vedere.
DINA
No, let me see.
FELICE
Please be gentle.
DINA
You should go to the doctor.
FELICE
I hate doctors. I'm just run down, that's all.
DINA gently feels FELICE's armpits.
DINA
Woh, they're huge!
FELICE
It's like having golf balls inside my armpits.
DINA
You'd better see a doctor right away.
FELICE
Forget it. By the time I get an appointment, I'll be fine.
DINA roles her eyes and eats more chips.
PAPA
Let me see!
PAPA tries to check FELICE's armpits. She moves away.
FELICE
No. You're too rough.
PAPA
Ma che dici? Fammi vedere.
PAPA grabs FELICE.
FELICE
Ouh!
DINA
(*To Papa*) Lasciala stare Pa. (*To Felice*) You okay?
FELICE
Yeah.
DINA goes for more chips. PAPA grabs the chip bag and crumples it.
DINA
Why'd you do that for?
PAPA
You a pig. E pigs can't teach.
FELICE
Don't talk like that.
PAPA
Felice, please, Dina non capisce un cavollo come si deve insegnare.

DINA

I don't know how to teach huh? I've spent a month trying to get this into your thick head. But the minute she comes back, I can't teach. Here.

DINA gives FELICE the instruction book.

DINA

The peasant wants you St. Felice. This pig's had it. She's going to the trough. (SNORT, SNORT)

FELICE

Dina please, I can't help him. I can't put my arms down.

DINA

Tough! He's all yours honey.

FELICE

(*Yelling after DINA*) Dina! Come on! I can't help him! Dina!

PAPA

Ah finitela tuttedue. Ma che me ne frega di questo pezzo di merda di computer. Eh tu, whatsa matter wid you? (*He grabs FELICE and shakes her.*) Finiscela cu sti porcherie.

FELICE

Ahhh! Papa, don't, don't touch me, mi fa male.

DINA

Let go of her, you idiot.

> *DINA throws the remaining chips all over PAPA and starts pounding him. he is oblivious. PAPA hugs FELICE.*

PAPA

Felice, I love you so much!

DINA

Don't!

PAPA

My baby, I gonna make you some chicken soup. Felice mia Felice.

> *DINA is pounding her father. PAPA is hugging and rocking FELICE and she hugs him back. MAMA enters and takes DINA away.*

DINA

Let go!

> *MAMA pushes DINA out of the room.*

MAMA

Dina! Va mangia un sandwicho di Nutella, e shut up!

> *DINA exits. PAPA continues to hug FELICE. MAMA watches. Lights out.*

SCENE 7

> *Lights up. The Benvenuta home. DINA, FELICE and PAPA are seated, watching t.v. They are all dressed in their Sunday best.*

PAPA

Is a good program today.

FELICE

Yeah, a cliff-hanger

DINA

More like a boob-hanger if you ask me.

PAPA

Eh?

FELICE

Ci piace il show.

DINA

Yeah.

PAPA

Ma sure is a good show.

> *MAMA, also dressed up, enters. She places an enormous tray of*
> *Italian cookies on the coffee table right in front of DINA.*

DINA

Ma, please take these back into the kitchen until he shows up. I don't want to look at them. I'm trying to watch what I eat.

MAMA

No make me laugh Dina, per carità.

> *DINA pushes plate to the other end of the coffee table. silence.*
> *Everyone continues to watch t.v. it is Italian programming.*
> *MAMA does not watch. she is pacing. This goes on for a while*
> *until PAPA can't take it anymore.*

PAPA

O ti assetti, o you go upstairs, to your room.

> *Everyone watches t.v. MAMA tries to clean surreptitiously.*

PAPA

Oh, Arè stai cominciando?

MAMA

Ma, everyting so dirty.

DINA

I wonder why it's taking him so long. The last mass was at noon.

> *MAMA goes in front of the t.v. and gives it a thorough wiping.*
> *We hear laughter and wild applause.*

PAPA

Eh levati di mezzo!

> *PAPA pushes MAMA away from the t.v. DINA and FELICE laugh.*

PAPA

Cu sti cazzu di femmini, I no hear my show. Shut up adesso.

> *Everyone watches t.v. MAMA stands. Doorbell rings.*

MAMA

Finalmente.

> *MAMA runs to open the door. FR. WILLIAM rushes in.*
> *MAMA follows. FR. WILLIAM is dressed in full priest*
> *regalia with the purple sash around his neck. He has all the*
> *paraphernalia for the purposes of extreme unction.*

FR. WILLIAM

I came as soon as I could, Signora. I'm so sorry it took so long but there was a
drunk I had to ... oh never mind. Where is she? Is she upstairs? Which room is
she in? I hope I'm not, uhm, too ...

MAMA

Fader, Dov'è, where is Fader Fiori?

FR. WILLIAM

Oh, uh, he couldn't make it. He's extremely sorry but after the last mass today,
he drained, he was dr ... dr ... very drained. Worn out. So he asked me to come.
I mean to go. To va?

MAMA

Hah?

FR. WILLIAM

I'm sorry I'm not Italian—

MAMA

Is okay, is better!

FR. WILLIAM

Oh good. Oh, I hope I'm not too ... which is her room?

DINA

She's right here, Father.

FR. WILLIAM

Pardon?

DINA

She's right here. You see that woman there, Father, that's her, that's Felice. She's
the sick one.

> FR. WILLIAM *stares at* FELICE *for a second.*

FR. WILLIAM

Excuse me Signora, but Father Fiori told me that your daughter was, ahem, dying.

DINA

(Laughing) Holy shit! Uh, sorry!

MAMA

Ma si, Fader, non la vedi com'è? She so sick, Fader.

FR. WILLIAM

She looks, uh, she looks perfectly uhm, fine to me. But then again, I'm not a doctor.

MAMA

Ma no padre, she sick, she sick inside.

DINA

Ma ...

PAPA

Father, maybe you like a cookie o some espresso?

FR. WILLIAM

That would be ...

MAMA

No, you lissen to me, please. She got il Diavolo inside e you gotta take it out, pull
it out Padre!

FR. WILLIAM

She's got what inside her?

DINA

The Devil.

PAPA

Dina, I think you Mama heart acting up, please go get de pills.

MAMA

I no need no pills! Scusatemi ah, but, mi sento sana io. Is Felice, Fader, she have il vileno qui.

She places her hands on her lower abdomen.

DINA

(To Fr. WILLIAM.) A poison here.

DINA makes the same gesture as MAMA.

PAPA

Dina!

DINA

Ma!

MAMA

Is a poison snake fader e lo devi tirare fuori.

DINA

(To Fr. WILLIAM) You've got to pull a snake out of her.

PAPA

Dina!

MAMA

Felice, tell de priest, bedrame, please. Now is de time.

PAPA

Dina, please, de pills. Dey're in de kitchen.

MAMA

No, no le pillole, per piacere!

DINA

(*TO FR. W.*) She's refusing the pills.

PAPA

(*Boxing DINA's ears*) Allestiti, stonata.

DINA

Ouh!

PAPA goes to give DINA another wack but she's gone before he can hit her again. DINA exits.

MAMA

Felice, caramia, talk to him, tell him, è inglese. He gonna understand.

PAPA

Mama, dats enough.

MAMA

Talk to him! .

PAPA

Mama.

MAMA

No, è la mia figlia, la mia anima!

FR. WILLIAM

Signora, signora, please—

MAMA
    Padre, padre, per piacere—
FR. WILLIAM
    Signora, please—
MAMA
    Padre, please—
FR. WILLIAM
    (*Trying to top MAMA*) I DON'T DO EXORCISMS!
                    There is an embarrassed silence.
FR. WILLIAM
    Signora, in the morning, after you've had a chance to rest, perhaps you could call
    Fr. Fiori, explain it all to him and—
PAPA
    Ma, is no necessary, Fader. She got heart condition is all.
MAMA
    E chi mi l'ha dato questa 'condition' eh?
PAPA
    CALMATI!
MAMA
    Sorry. (MAMA is breathing heavily).
FR. WILLIAM
    Perhaps we could say a little prayer.
                    DINA enters with water and pills.
DINA
    That's a good one.
PAPA
    Dina, shut up!
                    *MAMA is still trying to persuade FELICE to talk to FR. WILLIAM
                    but she is having a hard time because her heart is in fact acting up.*
MAMA
    Felice, please—
PAPA
    Mama—
MAMA
    I canna help you no more—
PAPA
    Mama—
MAMA
    Non so più cosa devo fare—
PAPA
    BASTA ADESSO.
                    MAMA is sobbing wildly. PAPA picks her up.
PAPA
    (*As if talking to a small child*) Mama, is time you take de pill. Is gonna be better.
    You take you pill e you go to bed.
MAMA
    Si Papa.

PAPA

Dina take you moder upstairs e give her de pills.

MAMA and DINA exit.

PAPA

Sorry Padre. Fader?

FR. WILLIAM

William.

PAPA

Ah.

FR. WILLIAM

Your wife does seem to be very disturbed about something.

PAPA

E si, Padre. She suffer bad heart attack last year e sometime she get mix up, who sick, who no sick.

FR. WILLIAM

But your wife seems to have this idea that . . .

PAPA

When somebody a little bit sick, my wife tink somebody give dem il malocchio. You know what dat means?

FR. WILLIAM

I'm afraid not.

PAPA

De evil eye!

FR. WILLIAM

(*Pondering the meaning of this*) The evil eye?

PAPA makes a horn gesture with his hands.

PAPA

De evil eye!

FR. WILLIAM

(*Chuckling*) Oh dear!

PAPA

Be, my wife, since she got dis heart trouble, we have to watch out eh. She canna get too excite.

FR. WILLIAM

Yes, yes, . . . well . . .

PAPA

Tank you for you trouble.

FR. WILLIAM

Oh no trouble at all. HE RISES TOO. If there's anything I can do—

DINA enters with her *mouth full of food.*

DINA

Oh, oh Father, my mother asked that before you leave we all have a little praying session.

FR. WILLIAM

That would be—

PAPA

Ma, it's okay—

FELICE

Yes, Papa—

PAPA

I no think we need.

FELICE

If Mama wants it, we should have it.

FR. WILLIAM

Well uh, it would be my pleasure.

PAPA & FELICE

Fine.

FR. WILLIAM

Alright then, let's get down on our knees right here.

> *Everyone kneels.*

FR. WILLIAM

This is certainly a nice change from the wooden floors at the rectory.

PAPA

It's a new carpet.

FR. WILLIAM

(*Clears his throat*) In the name of the Father and the Son and the Holy Spirit ... who are we dedicating these prayers to?

FELICE

Mama.

PAPA

Felice.

DINA

No, me! Just kidding.

FELICE

We're all worried about Mama.

FR. WILLIAM

Fine then. Let's keep her in our thoughts.

PAPA

Okay.

FR. WILLIAM

Here goes: Our Father, who art in heaven ...

PAPA & DINA & FR. WILLIAM

Hallowed be thy name, thy kingdom come, thy will be done on earth as it is in heaven. Give us this day our daily Bread and forgive us our trespasses as we forgive those who trespass against us ...

> *As lights dim to darkness, we hear MAMA's voice.*

MAMA

Padre nostro, che sei nei cieli, sia santificato il tuo nome, venga il tuo regno, sia fatta la tua volonta ...

> *Black Out.*

SCENE 8

FELICE's home. SARAH and FELICE are talking. A box of food is on the floor.

FELICE

Hairy tomatoes, mangiachecca priests. Oh God.

SARAH

What about a doctor?

FELICE

My mother's on to that too. She's pushing me to see some guy our neighbour, Mrs. Pilari, told her about.

SARAH

I think you should see him, Felice.

FELICE

What for? All he's going to do is give me some drugs and tell me I'm depressed because I'm single.

SARAH

They're not all bad.

FELICE

I don't need a doctor, Sarah. Your massages are better than any drugs a doctor could give me.

SARAH

But, Felice, I'm not a nurse—

FELICE

Would you do my hands, please. They feel kind of stiff.

SARAH

Felice, I—

FELICE

Sarah, I—(*They laugh*).

FELICE

I've been thinking about the back room for the baby. It's a little small but it gets a lot of heat. Not like the rest of this house.

SARAH

I don't know—

FELICE

We could paint it pink and put up some cute border—

SARAH

What if it's a boy?

FELICE

Okay, yellow then. And, well, I might as well tell you now, I went ahead and ordered the crib. It's white. And we should do something about that thing you've been sleeping on. It's pathetic.

SARAH

But Felice—

FELICE

I didn't get any sheets or blankets—

SARAH

    Felice, it's not—

FELICE

    But I thought, maybe next week, we could take—

SARAH

    What, are you my baby's papa now? Felice! Mother of God, listen, Jessie's called. They got an apartment for me . . .

FELICE

    Oh.

SARAH

    You've been so good to me, Felice, with everything but, I'm not your kid and you're not my mother. Don't get me wrong, Felice. I'm really grateful for all you done, but I gotta take care of myself.

FELICE

    Uhuh.

        FELICE grabs the box of food and starts to exit. Suddenly she drops everything.

SARAH

    What the hell—

        SARAH starts collecting the stuff but she notices FELICE who is just standing there.

SARAH

    Felice, Felice are you okay?

        SARAH grabs FELICE.

SARAH

    Holy shit girl, are you ever cold.

        SARAH gets FELICE'S coat, wraps her up in it and sits her down.

SARAH

    Should I get you something?

FELICE

    No.

SARAH

    Are you sure you don't want nothing?

        FELICE starts to get up.

FELICE

    No. I'm fine, I'm—

        FELICE starts to get up.

SARAH

    Will you stop that. Sit down.

        SARAH forcibly sits her down.

SARAH

    You looks like chalk. I'm gonna call your mother.

FELICE

    No!

SARAH

    You gotta see that doctor, Felice.

FELICE
No.

> *FELICE starts falling asleep.*

SARAH
Don't you get it, you're sick!

FELICE
No.

SARAH
Oh shit. Look, I'm sorry. But …

FELICE
Mmm

SARAH
Felice? Felice?

> *FELICE sleeps. SARAH sits. Lights out.*

SCENE 9

> *Lights up. MAMA, DOCTOR, FELICE. FELICE is on examination table.*

FELICE
Vedi ma. Why did you drag me here. Ti lu disse iu. Chistu ca è scemo comu tutti latri.

MAMA
Ma stai zitta un minuto, Felice. Ci ha dare la chanza, no.

DOCTOR
Ladies, ladies, please, let's be fair. There are other patients—

FELICE
That's not our fault.

MAMA
Finiscila! Doctor please, un minuto.

> *MAMA stares at doctor for a second.*

MAMA
Ma dottor, you gotta a brother dats a priest right?

DOCTOR
No.

MAMA
You sure?

DOCTOR
Yes.

MAMA
Be, you look just like dis nice priest I know.

DOCTOR
I don't have any brothers.

MAMA
No?

DOCTOR
    No.
MAMA
    E perche no?
DOCTOR
    What?
MAMA
    Why no?
DOCTOR
    What do you mean, why no, I don't have any brothers!
MAMA
    Eh, maybe it's a part-time jobe!
DOCTOR
    Mrs.—please! Can we get on with this. I'm not a priest. I'm a doctor.
FELICE
    Ma, go wait outside with Dina, please.
MAMA
    Dottor, ascoltami, mia Felice, she no look sick outside eh, ma inside, doctor è
    smidollata. Non ha più forza per niente doctor.
FELICE
    Ma.
MAMA
    Non si puo guardare. Su Felice, spiegacilu.
FELICE
    I'm not going to tell him that.
DOCTOR
    Tell me what?
MAMA
    She canna take care of herself. E di più, she got a young ghella wid her e de ghella
    got a baby in her stomach. È grande così!
FELICE
    She's gone, Ma!
MAMA
    Oh che sfortuna! Who gonna call de hospital when you fall down like you dead ha?
FELICE
    What?
DOCTOR
    Pardon?
MAMA
    Yeah. Non ti riccordi? De last time she come home, she fall down, boom, right
    on my new carpet.
FELICE
    I fainted.
MAMA
    Vedi. If she fall down like dat in her house, hit her head and it bleed, who gonna
    see dat? Abita sola dottor. She no marry.

FELICE

Ma—be quiet!

DOCTOR

Ladies, ladies, I'm going to have to leave in a minute.

MAMA & FELICE

Okay.

The DOCTOR opens a file and starts writing.

DOCTOR

Have you had any flus or bad colds recently?

FELICE

Yes.

DOCTOR

Fever?

FELICE

Yes. But it didn't last long.

DOCTOR

And then?

FELICE

Then, the cold went away, but I still felt tired.

DOCTOR

How long have you been like this?

FELICE

I don't know, a few months.

DOCTOR

And then you noticed the swollen glands?

FELICE

Yes.

DOCTOR

Any arthritic pain?

FELICE

Yes.

DOCTOR

Depression?

FELICE

Yes. So you know what it is?

MAMA

Finalmente. I tol you dis doctor gonna know what it is.

DOCTOR

No, I don't know anything yet. Have you had unprotected sex recently?

MAMA

Eh, Madonna mia. Mia Felice, she still a—

FELICE

MA STAI ZITA! (To DOCTOR) No.

DOCTOR

Any blood transfusions?

FELICE

No.

DOCTOR
Any intravenous drug use?
MAMA
Ma che disse, Felice?
FELICE
Oh God!
DOCTOR
I'm sorry, but I have to ask.
FELICE
No.
DOCTOR
Any sores that have trouble healing?
FELICE
No.

The DOCTOR does a quick physical examination of FELICE.

FELICE
What is it?
DOCTOR
Let's do some blood tests first.
MAMA
What you tink doctor? Maybe she should eat more meat, huh? I gonna give her
una bella bistecca, full of blood when she come home. E she got to come home,
e doctor, whatta you tink? E la migliore cosa di fare no? E I give her salsiccia,
lasagne, eggplant—
DOCTOR
Mrs.—please!
FELICE
Ma, please!

DOCTOR writes prescription.

DOCTOR
Now I want you to get lots of sleep—
MAMA
You know doctor, is so hard for me. I got de heart condition e I live in Maple
dottor e she in de downtown. I canna go back e forth everyday to make sure she
no fall e kill herself. Please, tell her she gotta come home.
FELICE
WILL YOU SHUT UP!
DOCTOR
You have to try to relax.
FELICE
Can I go please?
DOCTOR
No, just a minute.

DOCTOR finishes writing his prescription.

DOCTOR
It could just be stress. These should help you relax.

MAMA

    E she gotta come home right?

DOCTOR

    Maybe you should go back to your mother's—

FELICE

    But—

DOCTOR

    It won't kill you to let your mother look after you, for a while.

FELICE

    How long is a while?

MAMA

    Che disse, Felice?

DOCTOR

    Don't fool around Miss. You need rest.

MAMA

    Che disse, Felice?

FELICE

    Disse, che devo ritornare a casa.

MAMA

    Oh grazie a Dio, grazie a Dio!

DOCTOR

    A little T.L.C. and a couple of links of homemade sausage could do wonders. I should be so lucky!

MAMA

    I bring you some next week. Grazie, grazie—

DOCTOR

    Get those tests done and book an appointment for two weeks. E Signora, Dio vi benedica!

        He exits. MAMA makes the sign of the cross.

MAMA

    È un miracolo!

        Lights Out.

SCENE 10

    Lights up. DINA is near FELICE's bed. FELICE is asleep. DINA and MAMA sit.

FELICE

    Mi fa male—

DINA

    What hurts?

        Door bell rings. MAMA exits and re-enters with SARAH.

MAMA

    Oh, caramia, is so wonderful dat you gonna be a mamma.

SARAH

Yeah. How are you Signora?

MAMA

Chiamami Mama.

SARAH

Mama. Hi Dina!

DINA

Hi ... Felice, wake up, you're student's here.

FELICE

(*In her sleep*) Is it over? Oh, thank you.

> *PAUSE*

SARAH

How is she?

MAMA

Oh mia Felice is very happy at home. I do everything for her, wash, clean, cook.
I make you a sandwich, eh, wid salsiccia.

SARAH

Thanks Mama, but I really came by to see how Felice was doing.

DINA

Well, she's sleeping. The doctor gave her these pills—

> *SARAH takes the pills and reads the label.*

SARAH

Anti-depressants.

DINA

Anti-depressants?

MAMA

Mia Felice tell you what she got?

SARAH

Uh, no. I was kind of hoping you'd be able to tell me.

DINA

We don't know anything, yet.

> *(Beat) Everyone looks at FELICE.*

MAMA

Io ho paura ch'e il mallocchio.

SARAH

Wha?

MAMA

Il mallocchio! De evil eye!

> *MAMA makes the evil eye gesture at SARAH.*

DINA

MA! Va metti l'espresso!

MAMA

Aspetta Di—

DINA

Ma—

SARAH

Is Felice gonna wake up soon?

DINA

Who knows.

SARAH

I wanted to ask her something. (*Beat*) Oh God, she's really sick!

DINA

Awh, she's just got some little thing. She'll get over it.

SARAH

It's not a little thing. If it was a little thing, Felice would be up right now. I mean, she goes overboard, helping people.

DINA

Yeah, well, my sister always did wanna be Florence Nightingale.

SARAH

If Felice hadn't come along, I probably would've lost my kid. (Beat) I was living in this place, and a lot of the kids were on drugs and stuff. I didn't sleep, I didn't eat. Felice came along and helped me out and—

DINA

And you moved into her house.

SARAH

I got my own place now.

MAMA

So you no lived wid your mama ha?

SARAH

No way. Are you kidding?

DINA

I still live at home.

SARAH

I know.

DINA

What did you wanna tell my sister?

SARAH

(*Beat*) I should go.

DINA

Tell me what you wanna tell Felice and I'll relay the message when she wakes up.

SARAH

I just wanted to talk to her about her will.

DINA

Her what?

SARAH

Her will.

DINA

A will? She made a will?

MAMA

Che cos'e? A will?

DINA

It's a thing you make before you die.

MAMA

Chi va morire?

SARAH

Sorry.

DINA

GET THE ESPRESSO!

SARAH

I'd better be going home.

MAMA

No, no, no, you gotta drink my espresso first.

SARAH

It's okay, Signora.

DINA

I don't get it! I'm her sister. She didn't tell me anything about a will! Anti-depressants!?
Oh my God—Why would she tell you that she wrote a will?

SARAH

She sent this note telling me that she left me her money.

DINA

Who the hell are you?

MAMA

Che cosa ha detto Di?

SARAH

I don't want it, okay.

DINA

I don't believe this. That fucking cow.

MAMA

Dina!

SARAH

I'm outta here.

DINA

(*Shaking FELICE*) Wake up, wake up, asshole! Wake up and say good bye to
your heiress!

> SARAH exits

FELICE

Don't, don't, don't, don't touch me, don't touch me, don't touch me—

> DINA is shaking FELICE.

MAMA

No, Dina—

FELICE

Please, mi fa male, mi fa male—

MAMA

Fermati—

DINA

Felice, Felice, it's me—

> FELICE wakes up, DINA and FELICE hug. MAMA makes
> the sign of the cross. Lights change. FELICE falls asleep again.
> MAMA and DINA exit.

SCENE 11

> *FELICE is asleep. lights change. music changes. This is FELICE's dream/nightmare. FELICE rises slowly from the bed and floats upstage. FR. WILLIAM APPEARS and ceremoniously places a pure white wedding veil over FELICE's entire body. FELICE slowly returns centre stage. She is a bride making her way down the aisle. As she reaches the front of her imaginary church, she stands waiting for her groom. No one comes. The music begins to slide closer to a nightmare. like a frightened child, FELICE calls for her PAPA.*

FELICE
    Papa, Papa, Papa, Papa, PAPA, PAPA—
> *PAPA enters. He comes up behind her and gently touches her shoulder. FELICE, now comforted, is lead back to bed by her PAPA. She removes the veil as PAPA pulls back the bedcovers. FELICE climbs in. Papa pulls the covers lovingly over FELICE, covering her completely like a corpse. The music soars to a cacophony. FELICE jolts awake and frantically pulls off her covers. Lights change.*

SCENE 12

> *PAPA looks at FELICE for a moment. FELICE is aware of PAPA. she pretends to sleep. PAPA has a bowl of soup.*

PAPA
    (*Quietly*) Felice, Felice. Felice, I make you some soup. I'm sick for you bellezza. Svegliati un pocchetino, Felice. Wake up. I gotta tell you someting. He gently nudges her.
FELICE
    (*In her sleep*) Don't, I have to sleep.
PAPA
    You gonna lose you jobe if you no go back to work.
FELICE
    I'm sick.
PAPA
    Nobody gonna pay you to sleep caramia.
FELICE
    Fammi dormire, please.
> *Beat.*
PAPA
    Why you so sick huh? Is like you wanna die. (BEAT) Errato troppo bella when you was small, ti riccordi? I almost want to eat you. You sit on my knee, you help me make de sausage, in de garage. Era bello no? Ti riccordi?
> *Silence.*

PAPA

Felice, ascoltami bedrame. Ti devo dire una cosa. Oggi, I lose my jobe.

> *FELICE turns towards PAPA.*

PAPA

I pretend I know everyting, for twelve years. Ho fatto finta per dodic' anni. M'adesso, il gioco è finito. Everything go good until dat computer come. Ci dicevo yes, yes, I know e quiet, quiet, I go home e you show me what I suppose to do. All you uncles, dey gonna laugh at me Felice. Everybody gonna know. Tu sei la furba nella famiglia eh Felice. You de smart one. Oh bellezza, I canna play no more. Quello computer mi ha fregato la vita.

> *He takes out an envelope from his pocket, looks at it for*
> *a moment.*

PAPA

See, nessuno mi vuole, bedrame, neanche tu. I noting no more.

> *PAPA crumples envelope and throws it.*

PAPA

Help me a little bit Felice. Come princessa. I canna tell you Mama. Tu ce lo devi dire. Please, you gotta tell her. For your Papa. Dai, su.

> *He pulls back her covers.*

FELICE

No, no—

PAPA

Adesso mi guardi con gl'occhi so full of hate.

FELICE

What are you talking about. I love you papa.

PAPA

Una sola volta, dis de last time—

> *PAPA tries to pull her up.*

FELICE

Go away—

PAPA

I promise—

FELICE

Go away—

PAPA

Aiutami Felice—

FELICE

I can't—

PAPA

I canna do it senza di te—

FELICE

Stop—

PAPA

I need you so much—

FELICE

No! I don't want to! Mi fa male, mi fa male, mi fa male . . .

PAPA

Sh, sh, sleep! Go sleep now. It's okay, it's okay. Sh! Stai zitta adesso, basta baby. Is finish now. Me ne vado, vedi, me ne vado. I love you bellezza. O come ti amo.

He tries to touch her and she pulls away.

FELICE

Mi fa male, mi fa male ...

PAPA

Don't worry. Non ti disturberò piu. Dats de lass time.

FELICE

Cumogliami Papa.

PAPA

Si si bellezza I gonna tuck you in.

He takes off his jacket and tucks her in with it.

PAPA

Vedi, is finish. Bye bye baby, bye, bye.

He exits. Pause.

FELICE

(*Softly*) Papa, Papa?

> *FELICE slowly exits upstage. Lights change. We see papa hanging. The pig is on the floor. Sausages are spilling from its guts. Lights out.*

SCENE 13

> *Lights up. The Benvenuta home. MAMA enters after a moment, DINA enters.*

DINA

Ma, what are you doing, go to bed.

MAMA

Sono troppo agitata per dormire.

DINA

È tardo.

MAMA

Lasciami stare, Di.

> (*BEAT*)

DINA

You wanna watch some T.V.?

MAMA

Sure, okay.

> *DINA turns on the t.v. A violent wrestling match is in progress.*

DINA

Do we have any chips?

MAMA

Ma chi ha fatto la spesa, Di.

DINA

It was a good turn out tonight.

MAMA

Be, dey all respect your fader.

MAMA starts to cry.

DINA

Ma, sh, sh, that's enough now. (*Beat*) Woh, did you see that?

MAMA

He's good dat guy.

DINA

I'll say.

MAMA

Dats it! Mezzo le coshe!

DINA

Right in the balls?

MAMA

Bravo!

FELICE enters.

DINA

Hey Ma, sleeping Beauty finally woke up.

MAMA

Felice, ti sei svegliata! You feel better!?

FELICE

I thought you just left.

DINA

We've been gone for hours.

MAMA

C'erano tanti genti, Felice.

DINA

They were crammed into that funeral parlor like sardines. You were missed.

MAMA

Oh come mi manchi Antonino.

FELICE

It's a really good match tonight.

MAMA

I'm all alone. Mi hai lasciato sola!

FELICE

Ugh, is that guy ever Fat. Oh Madonna, he's got breasts.

MAMA

Guanto fiori, eh Di?

FELICE

And a big zuchini between his legs.

DINA

Wall to wall flowers.

FELICE

He must eat a ton of Nutella sandwiches.

DINA

Era come una profumeria, eh Ma?

MAMA

Era troppo bello. You make a good job, Di.

FELICE

Oh God, that hamburger looks good.

MAMA

Oh Antonino, you no get to see you wrestling no more. Papa stay up ogni Sabato e watch de wrestling. He love it so much. Io mi sono sempre adormentata. Some night he come to bed so late, I don't know what he doing.

FELICE

Ooh, that must hurt.

MAMA

Hai visto lu bossu, Di?

DINA

Oh yeah, his boss was there. He came up to me and told me how sorry he was that they'd given Pa such an early retirement. He didn't think it would affect him so adversely. Dingbat.

MAMA

Be, he's a nice guy, Di.

FELICE

Ma guarda quello bestia!

DINA

Nice my ass!

FELICE

Oh my God!

DINA

If Mr. Boss had been nice, he would have given Pa some computer training. Or put him somewhere, where he would've been more comfortable, not fired him.

FELICE

I can't look.

MAMA

Ma che dici, fired?

FELICE

Holy shit!

DINA

What a lousy send-off. No watch, no nothing. Just a cheapo letter, saying, thank you for a job well done. (*BEAT*)

MAMA

Oh my heart!

FELICE

Ooh, that was bad. Where's the ref? Jesus! Oh my God, he's gonna do it again! Look at him go! He's gonna make that baby pay. I don't believe this, I don't believe this! Ring the bell. Holy shit! Porca miseria! Aiutaci Dio. No, not him. Why'd he ring that bell? Why'd he ring that bell? You're wrong asshole! Here we go! Hold on tight! Beat the shit out of him! Go on! Come on, come on ... That's it, that's it ... Mezo le coshe, mezzo le coshe ... Go for it, go for it, come on, KILL HIM, KILL HIM ... YAAAAY!! That was great.

MAMA

Oh Felice, I so happy you feel good. You can go shopping tomorrow.

FELICE

What for?

DINA

A black dress. You're going to need one for the funeral.

MAMA

Adesso le ghelle gonna fight in de mud.

DINA

They're gonna drown in all that mud.

MAMA

No, dey no gonna drown, but maybe dey gonna lose dere bikini!

DINA

You're cattiva tonight, Ma.

FELICE

I'm not going to get a black dress.

MAMA

Why, you got one already?

FELICE

No.

DINA

You gotta wear black Felice. We have to look perfect and be proud for Papa.

SILENCE.

DINA

So what about it Felice?

FELICE

Sorry but I'm leaving tomorrow night.

DINA

What?

MAMA

Eh?

FELICE

I have a ticket to Newfoundland.

DINA

I think I'm gonna have a heart attack.

MAMA

Is you Fader Felice. Almeno devi andare al suo funerale.

FELICE

I don't like funerals.

DINA

Are you out of your mind?

MAMA

Ma non è uno sconosciuto, è tuo Padre.

DINA

Everybody's going to laugh at us if you don't show up!

MAMA

Che devono dire la gente?

FELICE

Just tell them, I'm too sick to get out of bed.

DINA

Who did you book that ticket with?

MAMA

Felice, you just do this one thing e den you never have to do noting again okay.

FELICE

But it's never really like that, is it?

MAMA

Era meglio se avessi morto tu, instead of your fader!

DINA

Ma—

FELICE

Don't you think I know that?

DINA

Go to bed Ma—

MAMA

Sto impazzendo io! I going crazy!

> MAMA *is breathing heavily.*

DINA

Ma, vai a letto adesso—please.

> *MAMA IS CRYING.*

MAMA

If you no go to you papa funerale, he gonna go to hell! Non sara perdonato!

FELICE

He should have thought of that earlier!

MAMA

Butana!

DINA

MA SHUT UP!

MAMA

Okay, Dina. I'm sorry, I'm sorry. Non so quello che dico. Spiegacilu per piacere, tell her. La vergogna, de shame.

DINA

Okay, okay, okay, go!

> *MAMA Exits.*

DINA

You're going to that funeral.

FELICE

Leave me alone.

DINA

Do you know how this is gonna look?

> *NO RESPONSE.*

DINA

Do you know what it's been like sitting in that funeral parlor? Do you? And being given condolences by people who won't look you in the eye, because they know your father hanged himself? Do you have any idea what that's like?

FELICE
 I can't be there. You don't understand.

DINA
 I understand alright. I understand that I'm supposed to let you off the fucking hook! NO WAY!

FELICE
 OUH!!!

DINA
 WHO DID YOU BOOK WITH?
> *Lights Out.*

SCENE 14

> *In darkness, we hear MAMA's loud keening followed by a chorus of people keening. Even though this scene is not a dream, it should have a surreal quality. Lights up. An open casket is upstage centre on a raised platform. the side facing the audience is exposed showing the face of FELICE's father. There are two rows of chairs facing each other. One row is stage left the other is stage right. Seated on the chairs are people dressed in black with black veils over their heads. They are keening and rocking intermittently back and forth. FR. WILLIAM is standing in front of the coffin. MAMA, DINA, and FELICE are sitting on the chairs closest to the coffin. The audience could be viewed as other mourners or we could have stuffed bodies dressed in black, sitting in the other chairs.*

MAMA
 (*Wailing*) Voglio morire, voglio morire! Antonino, Antonino! Antonino! La vita è finita per me! ANTONINO! ANTONINO! ANTONINO!
> *FR. WILLIAM approaches mama with the cross. DINA and FELICE help MAMA rise. It is time to give PAPA a final kiss good-bye.*

MAMA
 (*Screaming*) ANTONINO! ANTONINO! ANTONINO! ...
> *FR. WILLIAM who is clearly over his head, is trying to console mama.*

FR. WILLIAM
 Signora, you should be happy—

DINA
 Father—

MAMA
 (*Screaming*) Antonino! Why you go away? Perchè mi hai lasciato?

FR. WILLIAM
 Oh Signora, it's not this life we're living in that's important—

DINA
 Father—

MAMA
> ANTONINO!

FR. WILLIAM
> It's … it's the after life!

MAMA
> ANTONINO! ANTONINO!

DINA
> Ma per carità—

MAMA
> ANTONINO!!!

DINA
> That's enough now. È troppo gia.

MAMA
> I gonna show you troppo!
> > *MAMA rushes to the coffin and tries to get in with PAPA.*

MAMA
> ANTONINO! I want to go too! Sono niente senza te. Portami con te—
> ANTONINO! ANTONINO!
> > *FR. WILLIAM and DINA try to pry mama away from the coffin.*

MAMA
> Let me kiss my husband—

DINA
> Ma please—

FELICE
> I'm sick for you bello.
> > *FELICE starts approaching the coffin.*

FR. WILLIAM
> Signora, please—

DINA
> She just needs a little air-

MAMA
> Voglio morire con te—

FR. WILLIAM
> I'm a bit concerned about opening the door—

MAMA
> ANTONINO!

FR. WILLIAM
> She's very loud.

DINA
> Well, you would be too, if your God damned husband just died!

FELICE
> Oh you're so beautiful. I gonna love you baby. Si ti amo. Errato troppo bello. Ti riccordi? No, non ti fa male. It doesn't hurt. I love you so much baby, I want to eat you.

FR. WILLIAM
> Priests don't have husbands—

DINA
Awh Christ—Where the hell is Father Fiori. She needs somebody Italian, somebody who can understand her—

MAMA
Un bacio—

DINA
Cut it out, this is embarrassing!

FR. WILLIAM
Well, I'm sorry I—Fr. Fiori's uh—

DINA
God damned vino—
> *MAMA makes another effort to get to papa and they grab her and pull her back.*

MAMA
Fammi abbracciare mio marito.

DINA
Ma chi si pazza? Basta adesso, everybody knows you're upset!
> *MAMA is breathing heavily.*

MAMA
I canna breathe!
> *The lights dim on mama and become stronger on Felice.*

MAMA
(Breathing heavily.) I gonna die too now, Antonino, si anch'io!

FELICE
Oh no baby you no gonna die from dat, no.

DINA
Ma where are your pills?

FELICE
Sh, nobody gotta know okay?

DINA
Le pillole, Ma? Dov'e sono?

FELICE
Sh. If you wake up somebody, I'm gonna kill you.
> *FR. WILLIAM and DINA are supporting mama.*

FR. WILLIAM
God's love is absolute Signora—

DINA
Quit the dog shit and get me a chair! Now!
> *FR. WILLIAM drops MAMA and rushes out.*

MAMA
VOGLIO MORIRE CON TE!

FELICE
Ah, dats so good.

MAMA
(Barely audible.) FAMMI ABBRACCIARE MIO MARITO!

FELICE
Vedi, gelato game nice.

DINA

Ma, think about your heart.

FELICE

Si, adesso—

DINA

Please.

FELICE

Justa one minute, no hurt.

DINA

Devi calmarti!

MAMA

Perchè? Perchè?

FELICE

Su, open up.

MAMA

Nessuno c'è più per me Antonino!

FELICE

Si, dat's it, dat's it.

MAMA

I WANT TO HUG MY HUSBAND!

FELICE

Ma shud up eh put you fist in you mouth!

MAMA

TI VOGLIO DARE UN BACIO, UN BACIO!

FELICE

Basta adesso. Bite you fist. You let me finish, I make you chicken soup after. Si!

MAMA

A KISS! A KISS!

       MAMA tries to crawl back to coffin. Lights up D.S. SARAH enters.

DINA

Come on Ma get up now. Stop that!

MAMA

SONO SOLA ADESSO! I gonna go wid my husband.

FELICE

This is what you want Papa, isn't it? Isn't it?

       FELICE climbs on top of PAPA'S dead body.

MAMA

ALL ALONE! VENGO, VENGO!

       MAMA suddenly sees FELICE.

MAMA

Felice?

FELICE

You gonna like it.

MAMA

FELICE!

FELICE

You gonna like it.

MAMA

Oh Dio Mio, Oh, Oh!

DINA

Felice! What are you doing?

MAMA

DINA—

> *MAMA collapses grabbing on to DINA. DINA can't loosen her grasp.*

FELICE

I'm here Papa, your princessa's here. Don't you feel it?

DINA

Ma, ma get up! Somebody help! Call an ambulance, quick!

FELICE

Come on Papa, wake up! Svegliati! I'm doing what you want, aren't I? So wake up!

DINA

It feels like she's dead. Ma, get up! Please! Father!

FELICE

Wake up! It's okay Mama, don't worry. I'm helping Papa get better!

DINA

WHAT'RE YOU ALL GAWKING AT, GET ME SOME HELP!

FELICE

Ti piace bellezza? Mi fa male papa. Ti piace bellezza? Mi fa male papa.

DINA

Somebody help me!

FELICE

He needs me to make the woosh happen Mama!

DINA

FELICE! FELICE!

FELICE

He tells me that's what he needs to get better. The whoosh!

DINA

FELICE!

FELICE

Ti piace bellezza? Si mi piace papa. I like it, I like it! I SAID I LIKE IT!

DINA

FELICE!

FELICE

SO WAKE UP! WAKE UP AND GET OFF ME. GET OFF ME, GET THE FUCK OFF ME NOW!

DINA

FELICE!

FELICE

PAPA!

> *LIGHTS OUT.*

SCENE 15

> *SARAH'S apartment. SARAH is smoking a cigarette and dancing to Nirvana. The place is a mess. she has not really moved in. there is a knock at the door but she doesn't hear it at first. then*

DINA

(*Shouting Off—Stage*) SARAH, SARAH, OPEN THE DOOR.

SARAH

Shit!

> *She puts out the cigarette, turns off the music and runs to answer the door.*

SARAH

Sorry uh, come on in.

> *DINA and FELICE enter. DINA has a huge, clear plastic bag which is filled with raw Italian sausages.*

SARAH

Uh, hi!

> *DINA hands SARAH the bag of sausages.*

DINA

Hi. Here. My mother told me to give them to you. She says they'll be good for your milk.

SARAH

Thanks. How's mama?

DINA

She's pretty weak. But the doctor says she's gonna be okay.

SARAH

And Felice?

DINA

How the hell should I know! She spent the night fondling, uh touching—I mean looking at this junk she brought home in a garbage bag. Then she tells me she went to Newfoundland for a holiday. I don't know what to believe anymore.

FELICE

You better think about getting that job.

> *DINA gives FELICE a dirty look and returns to SARAH.*

DINA

Listen, if something happens—

SARAH

Uhuh—

DINA

If you need me for whatever reason, if she does anything stupid, I'll be at this number. But don't call me unless it's urgent. (*Turning to FELICE*) This is an important interview, Felice. I'm responsible for this family now. So you better not screw it up for me.

FELICE

Good luck.

DINA

Yeah. It's 11 o'clock Felice, I'll pick you up in two hours. Got that, two hours! (*To SARAH*) Don't take your eyes off her.

> *She Exits.*

SARAH

Bye!? (*Beat*) What's with her?

FELICE

They think I'm crazy.

SARAH

… They always think that.

> (*Beat*)

SARAH

Hey, you want some lunch? I could fry up these sausages. And I got some cake too. It's Italian. There's a bakery down the road—

FELICE

I'm so happy to see you Sarah.

SARAH

Yeah, me too. Hey, I came over to visit you once, but you were asleep.

> *FELICE smiles. Pause.*

SARAH

Let me get the lunch—

FELICE

I'm not hungry.

> (*Beat*)

SARAH

What did the doctor say to you?

FELICE

They don't know anything.

SARAH

Yeah, but what did he say?

FELICE

They can't find anything wrong.

> *Silence*

SARAH

Felice … What about the funeral?

> *Silence*

FELICE

They did say, I should get a lot of rest.

SARAH

Yeah, but what about—

FELICE

And I have been. All I do is sleep.

SARAH

What happened—

FELICE

And eat of course.

SARAH

What happened—

FELICE

I'm tired all the time.

SARAH

Felice, I think you need—

FELICE

Nothing seems to work.

(Beat)

SARAH

You can't keep running away, Felice.

FELICE

Look who's talking.

Silence

FELICE

You hate me don't you.

SARAH

No, no—it's just that—you're my teacher. You're not supposed to be like this.
You're supposed to be okay!

Silence

FELICE

Papa was the last child in a family of girls. So when he was born, my grandmother
thought he came directly from God. Un regalo di Dio. (BEAT) Mi fa male.

SARAH

I don't speak Italian, Felice.

FELICE takes out a whore's egg.

FELICE

I brought you un regalo. A gift. This is the one I went into the water for.

(Beat)

SARAH

Felice, I wish—

FELICE

How about that cake?

SARAH

Okay.?

SARAH exits and talks off—stage. At some point, FELICE exits.

SARAH

Felice … I'm gonna make some coffee. (Beat) Hey, there's this great place I know
that has a ton of whore's eggs. Next time you get to Newfoundland, I'll draw
you a map. (BEAT) Felice, I don't know what went on between you and your
dad but … When I was little my mom, she'd take me to this place. It was by the
sea, and it was real rocky. And I'd boot it up to the top of them rocks and I'd
yell at that sea, real loud and then I'd sit there, and I'd wait and I'd listen. And
that sea, my dear, that sea—Felice—(Alone) that sea would always yell back.

Lights Out.

SCENE 16

Lights up. Upstage, FELICE is looking through her Newfoundland treasures. Lights dim. Lights up downstage on SARAH. At some point FELICE exits. Lights up on SARAH. SARAH is talking on the telephone. It is very late at night. She is smoking. She is holding FELICE's whore's egg.

SARAH

(Starting in a whisper.) Hi, Mum? It's Sare. Hi. No, no, I'm fine. Because ... because, it's late. There're other people in the building you know. No I'm not livin' there anymore, I got my own place now. Yeah, I got it. No I haven't worn it. I'm pregnant that's why. How old were you? Well, I beat you mom. I'm startin' a family one year younger. Hah! Yeah, the dad's around. Sure, sure, he loves me. Is he happy about it? How the—What does my teacher think? Uh, I don't know. Anyway, what does it matter what anybody thinks, it's my kid. Awh, mom, I never phoned to yak about my teacher. Listen mum ... I don't know. I'll name it after some musician, I guess. A musician! No, I'm gonna call it Grateful Dead, will you shut up a minute—(Beat) Oh. Is he there now? Good. Put some ice on it. So, nothing's changed eh. Too bad. I said too bad. I was callin' to tell you—will you straighten yourself out for a second. Awh mom, let's not start alright. No! Because! You know why. Yes, you do. I don't wanna talk about it long distance okay. I'm fine, I'm fine—you're such a fucking drunk! Aw shit! I'm sorry, I'm sorry, okay? My friend's father just died and I'm a little weirded out by it. He just died, he just died—will you stop crying! Listen, I gotta go.

> *She takes a deep breath.*

SARAH

Yeah, I'm calm now. (BEAT) Mom, I'm calling because ... I'm thinking of coming home for a visit but just for a visit, okay? I'm thinkin' about it. Yeah, start it off with some Newfie roots. Are you? Good. What? Uh, yeah, I guess a few bucks wouldn't hurt. I'll phone you again, okay? Take care of yourself. And, thanks. I gotta go now. Me too. Bye. Yes, I means it. Bye.

> *She hangs up. She exits. Lights out. Lights up upstage. We see a silhouette of FELICE. She is hanging. On a screen we see a picture of FELICE and her father, his arm around her. They are smiling. Around the picture see flowers and candles as if in front of a shrine. At the same time, we hear Pavarotti singing an Italian aria.*
>
> *Lights out.*

COMEDIES

MA CHE BRAVA GENTE! (OH, WHAT GOOD PEOPLE)

2009
Diana Iuele-Colilli and Christine Sansalone

"Moreover, we are dealing with a linguistic hybridism that seeks to capture the socio-linguistic and historical realities of the Italian immigrants of the 1950s-60s-70s in Canada. At times, the plays might appear as quasi-documentary in nature, and that is so because one of our key goals is to record and document the words, expressions, grammatical constructs that were the communicative lifeline for these Italian immigrants."
  —**Paul Colilli** and **Diana Iuele-Colilli**, "*Italiese* as a Literary Language (The Example of *Le maschere laurenziane*)" *Italian Canadiana*, Special Issue, Vol. 31, (2017), 91–102.

PERSONAGGI
(in ordine di apparizione)
FRANCESCA DELFINO ROSA BATTAGLIA
OTTAVIO DELFINO, marito di Francesca
SANTINA DELFINO, figlia
FILOMENA DELFINO, figlia CONTROLLORE
SPAZZINO
GIUSEPPE BATTAGLIA , marito di Rosa
TERESA, vicina di casa dei Battaglia
MARCO FERRi, barista
ASSUNTA, sorella di Ottavio
VITTORIO, fratello di Ottavio
LAURA BATTAGLIA, figlia di Rosa
MRS. CLARKSON, la maestra di Laura
GINO BATTAGLIA, figlio di Rosa
BETH, amica di Gino Battaglia

Introduzione

Ma che brava gente! è composta da una serie di sei vignette che delineano vari momenti della vita di due famiglie italo- canadesi che abitano nella West End di Sudbury dagli anni cinquanta ad oggi. I sei momenti includono l'arrivo a Sudbury con il treno e la confusione creata quando la famiglia Delfino è costretta a scendere alla stazione ferroviaria di Capreol invece di Sudbury. La seconda vignetta mette in evidenza l'emozione sentita dalla famiglia Battaglia quando si fa la prima telefonata ai parenti in Italia. La terza vignetta del primo atto è dedicata alla prima giornata di lavoro a Inco e i problemi nell'adeguarsi alla maniera di lavorare in Canada. Il secondo atto si apre con il primo colloquio con l'insegnate e i malintesi tra i coniugi Battaglia e la maestra d'inglese della loro figlia Laura. La seconda vignetta tratta i preparativi per un matrimonio italo- canadese e le discussioni che nascono dai desideri dei genitori che pretendono di avere un matrimonio in cui fanno bella figura e la sposa che non ne vuole sapere. L'ultima scena ha come movente le difficoltà che hanno gli emigranti italo-canadesi con la tecnologia. Ma la madre, Rosa Battaglia, è stupita dal fatto che si può registrare la musica dal computer ma poi non riesce a capire il valore del cellulare e il forno a microonde.

Essendo dei nuovi immigranti, i membri di queste due famiglie devono cimentarsi nell'ardua impresa di imparare una nuova lingua. Il problema si risolve con l'invenzione di un nuovo linguaggio coniato dalla comunità italiana non solo a Sudbury ma in tutto il Canada anglofono, cioè dell'italiese, una combinazione di italiano e inglese. È tramite l'amalgamazione non solo delle due lingue ma anche delle due culture e tradizioni che il processo di integrazione nel nuovo paese può avere luogo.

Il filo conduttore, quindi, della commedia è la lingua parlata dalle varie generazioni di emigranti. Si noterà l'uso classico dell'italiese, cioè la creazione di vocaboli inglesi con una fonologia italiana, dagli emigranti stessi. Di solito sono nomi per oggetti che non esistevano oppure non conoscevano al momento dell'emigrazione. Nel caso dei figli nati in Canada oppure arrivatici in età molto giovane, l'italiese prende una veste molto diversa. Si noterà nei personaggi più giovani un linguaggio che mescola l'italiese dei genitori con l'inglese e l'italiano standard imparato a scuola. Per tale ragione si è creduto opportuno includere un piccolo glossario alla fine della commedia stessa.

Questa commedia, infine, è una testimonianza della vita che gli immigranti italiani si sono creati nella loro terra adottiva e delle fatiche e degli ostacoli che hanno dovuto superare per sopravvivere e prosperare in questo nuovo mondo. La dedichiamo a loro.

Diana Iule-Colilli
Christine Sansalone
Laurentian University
Sudbury, Ontario (Canada)

ATTO I

> *La scena si apre nel corridoio di un centro commerciale a Sudbury.*
> *Due vecchie amiche, Rosa e Francesca, che non si vedono da tanto*
> *tempo, aspettano le loro rispettive figlie che stanno facendo delle compere*
> *in un negozio.*

FRANCESCA
Ma guarda chi si vede! Rosa, sei tu?
ROSA
Santa Maria, Francesca, sì, sono io. Mamma mia, da quanto tempo non ci vediamo?
> *(le due donne si abbracciano, si baciano e si siedono su una*
> *panchina a un lato della scena)*
FRANCESCA
Non lo so, da troppo tempo. E che ci fai qui?

ROSA

Eh, sai com'è. Mia figlia mi ha accompagnato dal medico ma aveva altre cose da fare e quindi sono qui ad aspettare mentre lei fa lo sciopping.

FRANCESCA

E che ci puoi fare. Mia figlia ha detto che ci sta uno speciale sullo zucchero al Wallimárti. Mi ha chiesto se ci volevo venire per farle un po' di compagnia, ma ora mi ha detto che vuole guardare in un paio di altri stori. Questi stori devono essere molto lontani perché aspetto qui da più di un ora. Non ce la facevo più a camminare. I piedi mi fanno un male da morire.

ROSA

A chi lo dici. Non siamo più buone a fare niente. I miei piedi si gonfiano subito adesso. Ti ricordi quando in una giornata facevamo tante cose e non ci stancavamo mai.

FRANCESCA

Sì, ma eravamo giovani e stupide. Siamo venute qui per farci una vita migliore ed eravamo disposte a fare tutto!

ROSA

Sì, hai ragione. Bisognava fare fortuna a tutti i costi per far vedere a tutti i parenti ed i paesani in Italia che emigrare era la cosa giusta da fare.

FRANCESCA

Certamente, Ottavio diceva sempre che saremmo restati solo cinque anni e poi saremmo tornati al paese con una montagna di soldi!

ROSA

(*sarcastica*) Sì, sì, proprio una montagna alta così (*indicando con le mani*). Per piacere, è meglio non parlarne (*pausa—pulendosi il naso*) Ti ricordi quando nemmeno sapevamo pronunciare Subburì?

FRANCESCA

Pronunciare! Non me ne parlare, che noi abbiamo avuto un sacco di problemi ad arrivarci!

ROSA

Veramente! E perché?

FRANCESCA

Perché ci avevano detto che dovevamo scendere dal treno alla stazione chiamata Subburì, invece non siamo scesi là!

ROSA

Ma come!?! E che è successo? Dove siete scesi?

> *La scena diventa buia. La luce si accende sul lato opposto della scena dove è ricreata la stazione ferroviaria di Capreol negli anni 50. Vi è una grand'insegna su cui è scritto CAPREOL.*

Scena I

> *L'arrivo a Sudbury*
> Francesca Delfino, moglie
> Ottavio Delfino, marito
> Santina Delfino, figlia

Filomena Delfino, figlia
CONTROLLORE
Spazzino
*La famiglia Delfino arriva a Sudbury dopo il lungo viaggio ferroviario
da Halifax.*

FRANCESCA

Mamma mia, che freddo! Mica fa 'sto freddo in Italia a maggio!

OTTAVIO

E cara mia, qui siamo vicini al Polo Nord! Però si guadagnano soldi a palate ...
anzi ... mio cugino Tonino mi diceva che i dollari crescono sugli alberi qui.

FILOMENA

(guardando fuori dal finestrino) Ma io non ne vedo di alberi con dollari attaccati!

SANTINA

No, ma che dici, abbiamo visto un sacco di alberi. Ma ha ragione Filomena.
(Guardando fuori) Gli alberi hanno solo foglie. Mamma, ma quando arriviamo!?

FILOMENA

Sono giorni che siamo su questo treno. Ma quant'è grande questo Canadà? Mi fa
male il culo seduta sempre su questa panchina (si alza per sgranchirsi le gambe).

SANTINA

E io ho fame. Abbiamo finito tutto il mangiare che hai portato dall'Italia? C'è
una frutta o un pezzo di pane?

FRANCESCA

(guardando nella borsa) Cara mia, abbiamo finito tutto. Ma voi due siete
sfondate!! Non fate altro che mangiare! Papà ha comprato un po' di cose al porto
di Alifáchisi per il viaggio sul treno. *(apre la borsa e prende della roba)*. Non c'è
molto. Scegliete qualcosa. Sono sicura che dovremmo arrivare fra poco. Non
avete bisogno di mangiare molto.
          (Le bambine scelgono qualcosa ciascuna)

SANTINA

(apre il panino coperto di carta velina) Mamma mia, che cosa schifosa. Che
panino piccolino. E poi, non ho mai visto un pane bianco così! *(annusando)* E
che cos'è 'sta roba che c'è dentro?
          (Francesca controlla i tramezzini)

FRANCESCA

Questo qui pare che è formaggio con una foglia di lattuga. Ma io non ho mai
visto questo tipo di formaggio così arancione! E quest'altro *(apre il tramezzino)*
mi pare marmellata e ... e ... questa roba marrone non lo so cos'è. Provate e vedete
se vi piace. Se lo vendono, si vede che la gente lo mangia!

SANTINA

No, io voglio un panino italiano.

FILOMENA

Sì, uno come quelli che fai sempre con la sopressata che ha fatto la nonna con il
caciocavallo e le melanzane sott'aceto. *(guardando il panino)*.

SANTINA E FILOMENA

Provalo tu!

FRANCESCA

Ma che cretine che siete! Volete mangiare sì o no! Non abbiamo altro (*ricoprendo di nuovo i tramezzini con la carta velina*). Abbiamo consumato tutto il pane, il salame, il formaggio e le sardelle che avevo impaccato per il viaggio. O questo, o niente! Scegliete voi.

OTTAVIO

Mannaggia all'abbondanza! Ci vorrebbe una guerra per sistemarvi a voi! Vorrei sapere che fareste se la scelta fosse tra il panino che hai in mano oppure una pietra. (*arrabbiato*) Dammi a me 'sti panini. Li mangio io (*li strappa dalle mani della moglie*)! Alla faccia vostra (*apre la carta velina*) e poi voi v'arrangiate! (*Comincia a mangiare voracemente un panino ma non riesce a masticare perché la bocca rimane bloccata. Parla con la bocca piena*) Santo Dio, che m'avete dato! Mo m'affogo! È tutto attaccato nella bocca!

FRANCESCA

Come attaccato? Ma che dici?

OTTAVIO

È tutto attaccato qua (*fa il gesto con le dita*). Mi hai dato il panino con la marmellata e (*apre il panino e annusa*) io sento il gusto di noccioline. Che schifo. Ci vogliono avvelenare qua! C'è un po' d'acqua ... non riesco ad ingoiare. Mo sputo tutto!

        (*Le figlie ridono a crepapelle*)

FRANCESCA

Ma basta, falla finita. Ecco un po' d'acqua! (*gli porge l'altro panino*) Tié, assaggia questo e vedi cosa ne pensi.

OTTAVIO

NOOOO! Assaggialo tu! Meglio morire di fame che mangiare quella porcheria. Quanto vale un bel panino fatto in casa!

FRANCESCA

E va be'. Quante storie (*assaggia l'altro panino e sta per affogare*). Madonna mia!!!! Avevi ragione. Il pane ti si attacca sulla bocca. Ma come lo fanno 'sto pane. Non sembra nemmeno cotto.

FILOMENA

(si avvicina e studia il tramezzino) Mi sembra tutto mollica.

SANTINA

Ma io ho fame! Come facciamo. (*pausa*) Mamma, è proprio schifoso il panino?

FRANCESCA

No, solo che s'attacca tutto nella bocca. Il sapore è buono.

SANTINA

Allora, dammelo, che ho una fame che non ci vedo. In questo momento mi mangerei pure una pietra! (*prende il panino e gli dà un morso*)

OTTAVIO

Ma guarda un po'! Santina sta diventando già canadese!

SANTINA

Non è male per niente. Ce n'è ancora?

FRANCESCA

No, era tutto quello che avevamo. (*Si sente una voce dalle quinte*)

CONTROLLORE

Next stop Capreol! End of the line! Everybody off! Next stop Capreol!

FRANCESCA

Che ha detto?

OTTAVIO

Boh, non ci ho capito niente! Forse ci stiamo avvicinando. È meglio che incominciamo a mettere tutto a posto.

CONTROLLORE

Next stop, Capreol! Everyone off the train!

Capreol! Capreol is the next stop! End of the line!

(Il treno si ferma e si vede l'insegna con su scritto CAPREOL)

SANTINA

(guarda fuori dalla finestra) Mamma, siamo arrivati a un posto chiamato CA … PRE … OL. Chissà quando arriviamo a Suddibúri.

OTTAVIO

Come, capriola. Che razza di nome è questo? *(Arriva il controllore che fa il gesto a tutti di scendere)*

CONTROLLORE

Everybody off! End of the line! Capreol is the end of the line!

(I Delfino non si muovono)

CONTROLLORE

(a Ottavio) Helloooooo! Everybody off! End of the line.

OTTAVIO

(alla moglie) Ma che sta dicendo questo? Perché grida? Che vuole?

FRANCESCA

E che ne so io! Chi lo capisce!

CONTROLLORE

You need to get off the train now! *(si rende conto che i Delfino non hanno capito).* These imigrants don't understand a thing. Now what do I do? *(parla lentamente con gesti)* YOU *(indicando ognuno dei Delfino)* YOU, YOU, and YOU, OFF THE TRAIN, NOW!!!! This is the end of the line. We need to clear the train. Understand?!?!?

OTTAVIO

Non ci ho capito niente. Non spostatevi che sicuramente sta gridando alle persone nel prossimo vagone.

CONTROLLORE

(irritato) I'm speaking to you! Are you deaf!?!?! You need to get off the train because this is the end of the line. *(molto lentamente con gesti esagerati)* You have to get off the train! This is the end! *(va a prendere le loro valige).* You need to get off or I'll get fired!

FILOMENA

Papà, questo vuole che noi scendiamo.

SANTINA

Ma non siamo arrivati a Suddibúri. *(al controllore lentamente con gesti)* Ma noi non possiamo scendere qui. Non siamo arrivati a Suddibúri. *(si rivolge al padre)* Papà, spiegaglielo tu!!

CONTROLLORE

Yes, Sudbury! Yes this is the Sudbury stop. *(gesticolando)* Off! You need to get off now! *(I Delfino non capiscono)* Damn! They don't get it.

(Ottavio prende i biglietti dalla tasca per mostrarli al controllore. Filomena glieli strappa e si fa avanti).

FRANCESCA

No Capriola. (*lentamente con gesti*) Noi … scendere … a Suddibúri … no Capriola.

CONTROLLORE

Yes, you're in Sudbury. You need to get off now! (*prende le valige e le butta dalla finestra*)

OTTAVIO

(*arrabbiato alla moglie*) Mannaggia alla miseria. Hai visto che hai fatto, Francé. Questo qui s'è incazzato e mo butta tutte le nostre cose dal treno. (*al controllore gesticolando*) Va bene, va bene, piano, piano, scendiamo! Ma non buttare le valige dalla finestra che ci sono tante cose delicate.

FRANCESCA

(quasi piangendo) Il vino, i sottaceti! 'Sto scemo mi rompe tutto. Santo Dio, (*al controllore gesticolando*) Fermati! Che scendiamo. Ma non buttate giù niente!

(Le figlie cominciano a piangere)

SANTINA

Ora che facciamo? Non solo non sappiamo dove siamo, non abbiamo più niente da mangiare. Mamma mia che fame che ho!!

FILOMENA

Ma cretina, tu pensi solo e sempre a mangiare! Come ci arriviamo a Suddibúri adesso?

(Prendono tutte le loro cose e scendono dal treno e si siedono sulle valige.)

FRANCESCA

Mannaggia all'America e il marito che mi ha convinto di venire. (arrabbiata al marito) Te l'avevo detto che era meglio morire di fame al paese che venire in una terra straniera dove non riesci né a capire né a farti capire.

FILOMENA

(*piangendo*) Io voglio tornare in Italia. Il figlio di Genuzzo il barbiere aveva promesso di sposarmi e ora mi trovo perduta chissà dove!!!!

SANTINA

Io voglio tornare alla pasta asciutta, alla ricotta secca e al mio bel pane calabrese. Anche se era duro come una pietra, almeno aveva un bel gusto!!!!

OTTAVIO

Dai, non perdetevi d'animo. (*camminando avanti e indietro e agitandosi*) Non fatemi incazzare!! Lo sapete che quando m'arrabbio non capisco più niente e non posso ragionare (*pausa*) Lasciatemi pensare!

(Sentono una voce nella distanza che canta qualcosa che conoscono.)

FRANCESCA

Io sento una voce zitti (la voce è più distinta adesso)

OTTAVIO

Ma questa è una canzone italiana! Magari parla italiano! Uei, là.

SANTINA

Magari ci potrà dire dove possiamo comprare un po' di pane e formaggio (*tutti la guardano arrabbiati*).

(Entra lo spazzino)

SPAZZINO

Yes!!! Chenna áia élpi iú?

FILOMENA

(*Quasi piangendo*) Ma no, questo parla inglese! Mo come facciamo?

SPAZZINO

Ma voi siete italiani?

SANTINA

(*sollevata*) Oh, sì. Siamo italiani. Potete aiutarci?

FRANCESCA

Quello scemo di controllore ci ha cacciati dal treno qui a Caprioli, ma noi dovevamo scendere a (*dimentica il nome del posto*).

OTTAVIO

A Suddibúri.

SPAZZINO

Ah, a Subburì. Ma questo è Subburì.

OTTAVIO

Ma il cartellone lì dice Caprioli!!

SPAZZINO

Sì, sì, la fermata si chiama Caprioli, ma Caprioli è la stazione di Subburì.

OTTAVIO

E caspita! Come sono complicate le cose in America. Se la fermata si chiama Suddibúri, chiamatela Suddibúri.

SPAZZINO

Eh, sì, lo so. Ei, paisà, qui si dice Subburì, no Suddibúri. Niente è semplice qua. Esiste la stazione di Subburì, ma quasi tutti i treni che arrivano da Alifáchisi si fermano solo qui. Non siete i primi a pensare di essere persi.

FRANCESCA

Meno male. Eravamo proprio disperati quando il controllore ha cominciato a buttare tutte le nostre cose dal treno.

SPAZZINO

Sì, ma quello là è uno stronzo. Non fateci caso!

SANTINA

Signor, spazzino. Scusate, ma ci sono negozi qua che vendono pane e formaggio? Io sto morendo dalla fame!

FRANCESCA, FIOLOMENA E OTTAVIO

Ma basta Santina!

FRANCESCA

Abbiamo problemi molto più grossi. (*guardandosi attorno*) Io non vedo nessuno. Come facciamo a trovare i nostri parenti?

SPAZZINO

Ma forse arrivano con il busso delle tre. (*guarda l'orologio*) Mancano un paio di minuti. Dovrebbe arrivare presto. Aspettate qui.

SANTINA

Il busso?

FILOMENA

Che è il busso?

SPAZZINO

Come, non avete mai visto un busso. Ma da dove venite? È un grande trocco e eccolo che sta arrivando!!

SANTINA E FILOMENA

(si guardano) Un trocco? Ma che cos'è un trocco.

OTTAVIO

(indicando) Ah, guardate ragazze, un trocco dev'essere una corriera in inglese perché sta arrivando una corriera. (Si avvicina alle quinte per vedere meglio e poi ritorna verso le figlie. Prende una valigia in mano) Ragazze mie, un busso è una corriera. Facile, no?!?! Dai prendete qualcosa.

FRANCESCA

Guarda che sta arrivando mio cugino, Nanduzzo! Andiamo, andiamo.

  (Prendono le valige ed escono)
  Si ritorna al presente. La scena è buia e si riaccende nell'angolo
  con Francesca e Rosa sedute sulla panchina dell'inizio della
  commedia.

ROSA

Mamma mia! Noi, invece, siamo stati fortunati a scendere alla stazione in città!

FRANCESCA

E che ci vuoi fare! All'inizio è stata dura veramente! Abbiamo avuto un sacco di problemi con la lingua, con la spesa, con la scuola, con il lavoro. Sono passati mesi prima che Ottavio ha trovato un lavoro decente.

ROSA

A chi lo dici. Se non era per la mia vicina di casa, chissà quando trovava una giobba buona Giuseppe mio.

FRANCESCA

Ma Giuseppe ha sempre lavorato a Inco?

ROSA

Quasi! Prima gli avevano offerto una giobba a Cecutti come panettiere, ma lui non voleva fare la stessa giobba dell'Italia. Diceva che voleva guadagnare tanto e subito. Voleva tornare subito in Italia. Quindi la vicina nostra gli ha dato una pusciata con il bosso suo che faceva il maneggére a Inco. A 'sto bosso, lei gli puliva la casa.

FRANCESCA

E gli è andata bene dall'inizio?

ROSA

Macché, mo ti racconto …

  La scena si rabbuia, escono Francesca e Rosa e le luci si accendono
  sull'altra parte del palcoscenico. Si ritorna al passato in una casa
  modesta di Gatchell.

Scena II

  Il primo giorno di lavoro
  Rosa Battaglia, moglie di Giuseppe Giuseppe Battaglia
  TERESA, vicina di casa

*La scena si apre nella sala da pranzo della famiglia Battaglia. In scena
vi è un tavolo da cucina con quattro sedie. Un attaccapanni e un
mobiletto. Rosa sta parlando con una vicina di casa.*

TERESA

Buona sera Rosa, è permesso, si può entrare?

ROSA

Ma certo, accomodati, tu sei la padrona qua. Dopo tutto quello che hai fatto per noi.

TERESA

A proposito, chissà come è andato il primo giorno di lavoro di tuo marito.
Speriamo che se lo tengono a INCO, che quella è una buona giobba, c'è la
sciuranza e ti danno pure la compestésciona se ti fai male!

ROSA

Che ti danno? Scusami comare Teresa, ma noi siamo appena arrivati da poco qui
in Canada e non sappiamo ancora parlare inglese.

TERESA

Non ti preoccupare, s'impara subito. È molto facile, ecco che ti insegno un paio
di parole utili (*indicando*) questo per esempio è "un garbiccio". Ripeti dopo di
me. GARBICCIO.

ROSA

GARBICCIO? Ma non si dice monnezza?

TERESA

Ma che monnezza! Questo è dialetto. Se vuoi fare fortuna, impara l'inglese.
Ripeti, garbiccio.

ROSA

Garbiccio.

TERESA

Brava, hai una buona pronuncia. Questo è un SANGUICCIO.

ROSA

SANGUICCIO? Ma è un bel panino alla mortadella!

TERESA

NOOO. Sanguiccio è la parola canadese. Il pranzo che hai preparato per tuo
marito da portarsi alla giobba si chiama "LONCIO.

ROSA

LONCIO!

TERESA

(indica dei biscotti sul tavolo) CUCCHÍSSI, no biscotti.

ROSA

CUCHÍSSI.

> *Si sente arrivare qualcuno. Entra Giuseppe vestito da lavoro
> (scarponi, casco, giacca, "lunch bag"), è stanco morto e trascina
> le gambe.*

GIUSEPPE

Mamma mia come sono stanco! Non mi sono fermato un attimo. (si siede e inizia
a togliersi le scarpe, il cappello e la giacca).

ROSA

Giuseppe, non vedi che c'è la comare Teresa?! Salutala, non fare lo scostumato! Dopo tutto quello che ha fatto per te, ti ha trovato questo bel lavoro!

GIUSEPPE

(*sarcastico*) E sì, grazie tanto di questa bella giobba!

TERESA

Compare Giò, buonasera. Allora, com'è andato il primo giorno a INCO?

GIUSEPPE

Che è questo Giò? Io mi chiamo **Giuseppe!**

TERESA

Ei, compà, ora siamo in America!

ROSA

(*tirando fuori una pagnotta e un pezzo di salame dalla borsa del marito*) Ma guarda un po', non hai finito il loncio, perché? Non ti è piaciuto questo bel salame con le rape?

GIUSEPPE

Ma che caspita è 'sto loncio? Ma parla come ti ha fatto mámmata. Non sono riuscito a mangiarlo tutto perché ci hanno dato solo 15 minuti di tempo per mangiare e poi tutti che mi guardavano! E che! questi canadesi non hanno mai visto pane e salame? Avevano tutti questo pane fino fino con una schifezza dentro. Compare Pino, che era con me, dice che si chiama pinebbára. Bo, ma che ne so.

TERESA

Ah sì compà, qui i canadesi mangiano marmellata e pinebbara per loncio.

GIUSEPPE

Ma che schifo. Ora però Rosa mia, tengo una fame che non ci vedo. Che hai preparato per cena?

ROSA

Ora ci pensa Rosa tua. Ho preparato una bella pastasciutta con la costolina.

GIUSEPPE

Ah, meno male. (*si mette le mani sulla schiena*) ahhhh che mal di schiena, ho dovuto spalare tutto il giorno. Mannaggia all'America e chi mi ci ha fatto venire! Tutto il giorno in quella miniera a spezzarmi la schiena! Era meglio rimanere al paese.

TERESA

Ei, non ti lamentare compà! Che questo lavoro ti dà da mangiare!

ROSA

Sai Giusè che la comare Teresa ha trovato un lavoro anche a (*calmandosi*) Mah, questa lingua inglese è strana! Io non la capisco.

TERESA

E non ti preoccupare che te la insegno io. Le parole più importanti che devi sapere qui in Canada sono taimenaéffa, céca e morghéggio.

GIUSEPPE

(perplesso) Come?

TERESA

Senti ora non ho tempo di spiegartele perché fra poco mio marito torna da lavoro e se non c'è la cena pronta, chi lo sente? Te lo spiego domani. (*si avvia verso la porta*)

GIUSEPPE

E va be, a domani.

ROSA

Ciao Terè, ci vediamo domani.

TERESA

Sì, a domani, gubbai (*Teresa esce*).

GIUSEPPE

(*di nuovo perplesso*) Cos'ha detto? GUBBAI???? Gli è venuta la gobba?

ROSA

Bo.

GIUSEPPE

Ma ora mangiamo che dopo cena passa compare Pino e ha detto che mi porta in un posto che si chiama Caruso Clobbi a giocare a carte.

ROSA

Ah sì ci sono stata oggi con Teresa a cucire insieme alle altre donne. Sai chi c'era?

GIUSEPPE

Chi?

ROSA

La sorella di Carminuzzo, il brigadiere del paese.

GIUSEPPE

Veramente! Ah sì, è vero! Me la ricordo. Anche lei era partita per l'America per sposarsi con un paesano che era già qua.

ROSA

E sai cosa mi ha detto la comare Teresa?

GIUSEPPE

Cosa?

ROSA

Che quando è arrivata, che si era sposata per procura, dopo solo sei mesi ha partorito un bel bambino, sano sano di 5 chili!

GIUSEPPE

E questa è bella! È il marito cosa ha fatto? Se l'è tenuta?

ROSA

Il marito ha fatto finta di niente e se l'è tenuta in casa come se niente fosse.

GIUSEPPE

Che bella roba! O è fesso, o non sa contare! Queste cose al paese non sarebbero mai successe! Si vede che si è fatto rimbambire dall'America.

> Si sente bussare alla porta.

GIUSEPPE

Ma chi può essere? È ancora troppo presto per Pino.

ROSA

Vado a vedere.

> Rosa esce e ritorna subito dopo seguita da Teresa.

ROSA

Vieni, vieni, entra. Che è, ti sei dimenticata qualcosa?

TERESA

No, scusate. Ma si è rotta una pippa nel bassamento e allicca dappertutto! Giò, non è che potresti andare ad aiutare marítoma? So che tu te ne intendi di pippe!

GIUSEPPE

(*allarmato*) Come! Di che m'intendo io? Ma come ti permetti? Ma l'America ti ha fatto diventare anche scostumata, Teré?

TERESA

Ma che dici, Giò, la pippa nel bassamento. Come si dice, il tubo allicca, perde acqua!

GIUSEPPE

Ahhh. Perde il tubo. Ma dove si trova questo bassamento? È lontano?

TERESA

Ma che lontano. È qui accanto. In casa mia. Il bassamento di casa mia.

ROSA

Giusé, il bassamento dev'essere lo scantinato. Perde un tubo nello scantinato della casa di Teresa.

GIUSEPPE

Ahh, ora ho capito. Vado subito.

(*Si mette la giacca e il cappello e corre fuori*)

ROSA

Scusa, Teré, ma noi ancora non lo capiamo bene l'inglese.

TERESA

Eh, pazienza. Anche noi ci abbiamo messo un po' a impararlo. Speriamo che l'acqua non mi rovina tutto lu floru. È già la seconda volta che succede quest'anno. E cara Rosa, le case qui non sono fatte bene come in Italia con i bricchi forti. Qui sono tutte di legno e marciscono subito.

ROSA

Come sono fatte di bricchi? Che strano. Non sapevo che si possono fare le case di bricchi. Ma bricchi d'acqua o di vino?

TERESA

(*frustrata*) Ma che dici? I bricchi! Quelli della costruzione!!! Quelli con cui si fanno i muri!!!

ROSA

Ah, i mattoni! Si chiamano bricchi in inglese?

TERESA

Sì, bricchi. Rientra Giuseppe

TERESA

Già fatto? Così presto? Hai già ficsato tutto?

GIUSEPPE

Veramente non ho fissato niente. La pippa era già fissata al muro, io l'ho solo aggiustata.

TERESA

Sì, allora l'hai ficsata. Ma ora vado a pulire quella messa che c'è.

ROSA

Come? Vai a messa a quest'ora? Ma non è domani la messa?

TERESA

(*frustrata*) La messa! Il casino! Vado a pulire il casino che ha fatto la pippa rotta.

ROSA

Ah, scusa.

TERESA

Gubbái e tencsalótto.

ROSA E GIUSEPPE

 Gubbái.

GIUSEPPE

 Cosa ha detto Teresa? Che tiene un salotto? Ma lo sappiamo che tiene un salotto (ripete lentamente) "tengo un salotto?" Ma, ci siamo stati ieri per un caffè. Bo.

ROSA

 Ma che ne so.

GIUSEPPE

 (*Si siede*) Senti Rosa, ma mi potresti stirare i vestiti meglio domani?

ROSA

 Perché? Non ti sei mai lamentato di come stiro. Ch'è successo?

GIUSEPPE

 Oggi a lavoro il maneggére non ha fatto altro che dirmi ARIAPPA, ARIAPPA e poi anche ora il marito di Teresa mi ha detto ARIAPPA, ARIAPPA. Si vede che ho tutti i vestiti arrappati.

ROSA

 Ma che dici? A me non sembrano arrappati, li ho stirati con tanta cura. Ci saranno loro arrappati quegli scostumati! E maleducati pure!

GIUSEPPE

 Ma ora Rosa mangiamo che non ne posso più dalla fame. E sai che ti dico? Al Caruso Clobbi non ci vado perché domani ho lo sciffiti delle 5:00 e mi passa a prendere Pino col trocco.

ROSA

 Lo vedi Giusè che anche tu adesso sai parlare inglese?

GIUSEPPE

 Ma che inglese e inglese! Non ho avuto altro che problemi oggi al lavoro.

ROSA

 E ch'è successo?

GIUSEPPE

 Prima di tutto non sapevo dove dovevo andare. L'Inco è così grande! Io pensavo di dover lavorare con i lavoratori di Compare Ciccio. E invece mi hanno mandato sotto terra. Immagina il mio terrore quando il mio capo mi dice di prendere la cheggia per andare al draie per prepararmi alla giornata. E chi l'ha capito?

ROSA

 Cheggia e draie!? Ma che caspita fai. Dove ti hanno mandato?

GIUSEPPE

 Prima di tutto il mio capo si chiama bosso.

ROSA

 Bosso? Che nome è? È italiano? È un cognome nuovo! Da che parte dell'Italia viene?

GIUSEPPE

 Ma che cognome! Qui, tutti i capi si chiamano "bosso".

ROSA

 Caspita! Hanno tanti parenti. Saranno immigrati da un sacco di tempo!

GIUSEPPE

 Rosa, ti prego. Già al lavoro ero muto perché non capivo l'inglese. Fammi almeno parlare qua!

ROSA

E parla, continua.

GIUSEPPE

Allora, dicevo che tutti i capi si chiamano bosso. È un titolo. Il mio bosso si
chiamo Smit. Ma si scrive con l'acca. Non è italiano. Compare Ciccio lo chiama
un povero mangiachecca!

ROSA

Che mangia?

GIUSEPPE

E che ne so che mangia. Compare Ciccio lo chiama così. Io non ho fatto domande.
Ho passato la giornata cercando solo di capire che cavolo mi stavano dicendo.

ROSA

E 'sto bosso Mangiachecca che t'ha fatto fare?

GIUSEPPE

Mi dice di prendere la cheggia e di andare al draie per stardare lo scíffiti!

ROSA

(*facendosi la croce*) Madonna mia, marito mio, io non ti capisco!

GIUSEPPE

E figurati io, che mi ci sono trovato. Quello mi parla, mi dice cosa devo fare e io
non capisco un cavolo. Volevo piangere, ma non potevo mica fargli vedere che io
non capivo. Sennò mi cacciava.

ROSA

E cosa hai fatto?

GIUSEPPE

Meno male che in quel momento è passato Lorenzo, il figlio di Arnaldo il postino,
che mi ha tirato da parte e mi ha spiegato tutto e mi ha fatto vedere dove dovevo
andare.

ROSA

Ringraziamo a Dio ... meno male. Allora, com'è andata poi la giornata?

GIUSEPPE

Aspetta, aspetta! Lo sai che cos'è la cheggia?

ROSA

Cosa?

GIUSEPPE

È 'na scatola grande, grande. Ci vai dentro e ci entrano tante persone, e ti porta
giù, giù, giù nella miniera dove lavorano.

ROSA

E non ci sono le scale?

GIUSEPPE

No, io non l'ho viste.

ROSA

Ma che cose curiose che ci sono qui in America!

GIUSEPPE

Ma poi, quando sono arrivato alla cheggia, ho trovato una stanza che si chiama
il draie. Qui tutti i lavoratori ci vanno se ci sono problemi, e ci vanno anche a
mangiare. Qui mi sono pure cambiato.

ROSA

E hai passato tutto il giorno a lavorare sotto terra?

GIUSEPPE

Dovevo, ma quando il bosso ha visto che stavo quasi per svenire, perché mi mancava l'aria, senza nemmeno una finestra e un caldo peggio dell'Italia a Ferr'agosto, mi ha mandato su a lavorare alla costrósciona.

ROSA

Alla dove? È un'altra parte della miniera?

GIUSEPPE

No, ero sempre a Inco, però lavoravo dove costruivano le cose. Qui si chiama costrósciona.

ROSA

E là che hai fatto?

GIUSEPPE

Qui mi sono trovato molto meglio, perché c'erano un sacco d'italiani che mi hanno spiegato tutte le parole nuove. Sono salito su uno scáfalo dove un altro uomo mi passava i tubbaifori per costruire le mura e il ruffo di un ufficio.

ROSA

Tubbaifori, scáfalo, ruffo. Basta. La lezione deve finire per oggi perché non ci capisco più niente e mi sta scoppiando il cervello.

(Giuseppe comincia a ridere)

GIUSEPPE

C'è voluto un po', ma dopo ho cominciato a capire e usare anch'io le stesse parole. Posso essere un contadino, ma stupido non ci sono.

ROSA

Basta che capisci tu, io sono contenta.

(Rosa prepara per la cena e Giuseppe legge un po' il giornale)

GIUSEPPE

Ma dimmi Rosa, ti piacerebbe un bel carro? Qui a Subburì i carri sono lunghi lunghi e così grandi.

ROSA

Ma che dici Giusé, dobbiamo ancora pagare questi quattro muri di legno che chiamiamo casa, e tu pensi al carro, ma cammina!

GIUSEPPE

Ma tu sei sempre così pessimista! Ora siamo nella terra dell'abbondanza. Facciamo un sacco di soldi e poi torniamo al paese con nu carro lungo da qui a lì (*fa il gesto con le mani*).

ROSA

(*mettendogli un piatto davanti*) Eh, mangia mangia, pensa a fare tanti dollari e alla macchina ci pensiamo dopo.

Si abbassano le luci e si riaccendono sul lato opposto della scena
dove sono sedute di nuovo Francesca e Rosa.

FRANCESCA

Santa Maria! Allora ve lo siete comprato poi il carro lungo, lungo.

ROSA

Sì, ma non subito come pensava Giuseppe. Si guadagnava bene ma non abbastanza per pagare subito la casa, comprare la fornitura e comprare il carro. Ci sono voluti anni e anni. Giuseppe diceva sempre che saremmo tornati al paese ricchi, ma non è mai successo.

FRANCESCA

Certamente, e non si poteva comprare niente. Ottavio mi diceva sempre che dovevamo risparmiare ogni penì che guadagnava.

ROSA

A chi lo dici!?!

FRANCESCA

L'unica volta che Ottavio spendeva soldi era quando telefonava in Italia.

ROSA

Gli piaceva parlare al telefono? Ottavio non mi sembra il tipo.

FRANCESCA

Macché! Prima ci faceva impazzire per prendere la laina per l'Italia e poi si metteva a piangere che nessuno lo capiva! La prima volta che abbiamo telefonato al paese era così nervoso.

ROSA

Ma perché?

> *Le luci si abbassano su Rosa e Francesca e si accendono sul lato opposto della scena dove ci troviamo in un salotto negli anni '50.*

Scena III

> *La telefonata in Italia*
> *Francesca Delfino, moglie di Ottavio*
> *Ottavio Delfino, marito di Francesca*
> *Marco, barista*
> *Assunta, sorella di Ottavio*
> *Vittorio, fratello di Ottavio*

OTTAVIO

(*gridando*) Francé, hai preso il bucco con tutti i numeri di telefòno? Se non telefoniamo adesso si fa tardi e poi mamma va a dormire.

FRANCESCA

(*entrando*) Va bé, va bé, arrivo. Non gridare. (*apre il libro e cerca il numero*) Allora, vediamo! Zia Rosetta, Compare Nico, ecco qua. Allora chiami tu o vuoi che lo faccio io?

OTTAVIO

(*un po' offeso*) Perché vuoi chiamare tu? Non ti fidi del mio inglese? Non ti preoccupare che non m'arrabbio e non mi metto a gridare. Se non capisco l'operéta, ti faccio parlare a te. Ok? E poi, è mamma a me e non a te!

FRANCESCA

Ok!! Ma mi raccomando, non metterti a gridare e plissi, non piangere quando senti la voce dei tuoi parenti. Fai sempre la figura del beibì.

OTTAVIO

(va al telefono e cerca di fare il numero ma non ci vede) Mannaggia alla miseria! Francé, portami gli occhiali (riattacca il telefono)

FRANCESCA
(prende gli occhiali e glieli porta) Ecco.

OTTAVIO
(*fa lo zero per il centralino*) Alò! Alò! Iesse! I uánna fare 'na telefonata to Italy.
(*ascolta*) Iesse. Isa … isa … (*cerca il libretto telefonico. Lo vede sul tavolo*) Mannaggia!
(copre il telefono) Francé, portami il bucco, che l'operéta sta aspettando. (*Francesca
gli porta il libretto*) Iesse. Cosenza, Italy. Iesse. Ok. (riattacca il telefono)

FRANCESCA
Allora?

OTTAVIO
Allora niente. Dobbiamo aspettare. L'operéta ci chiama indietro quando ci ha la láina.

FRANCESCA
T'ha detto quanto tempo ci vorrà?

OTTAVIO
No, m'ha detto solo "Ai colla you becca." (*squilla il telefono*) Ecco, magari è lei.
(corre al telefono) Alò! Iesse, sì, ah finalmente, *(alla moglie)* è l'operéta italiana.
Finalmente ci capisco. (*ritorna al telefono*) Sì, sì, Cosenza, nella provincia di
Cosenza (pausa) Serra Pedace, sì. Il prefisso? Sì, ma voi non lo sapete? Sì, io ce
l'ho. Ecco … zero, nove, otto, quattro. (*pausa*) Il numero? Sì, quarantatrè,
cinque, ottantasette.

FRANCESCA
(che sta ascoltando all'orecchio del marito). Allora?

OTTAVIO
Allora niente! (*contento*) Sta suonando il telefono.
Si accendono le luci sulla parte opposta della scena. Appare il
barista che sta pulendo un tavolo. Squilla il telefono.

BARISTA
Pronto!

OTTAVIO
(*gridando*) Alò! Alò?! Con chi parlo?

BARISTA
Qui il Bar del Corso. Chi parla?

OTTAVIO
Chiamo dal Canadà. Sono Ottavio Delfino.

BARISTA
Chi?

OTTAVIO
Ottavio Delfino (*pausa*) Ottavio 'e Spaventa!

BARISTA
Alla miseria! (*gridando*). Ottavio 'e Spaventa. Quello che è andato all'America?!!
(*Ottavio scuota la testa indicando sì*). Io sono Marco Ferri. Il figlio di Donato u
Cravunaru!

OTTAVIO
(*Si mette a piangere e la moglie scuote la testa*) Madonna mia! Donato ha un figlio
così grande!?!?!

BARISTA
Eh, sì. Ho anche una sorella più vecchia di me. Allora, che mi dici? Come va la
vita in America?

OTTAVIO

(*piangendo*) Tutto bene. Non ci possiamo lamentare (Francesca segnala il passaggio del tempo toccando l'orologio e facendo il gesto dei soldi) Senti Marco, io ho telefonato a te perché il vostro bar ha l'unico telefono al paese e io devo assolutamente parlare con la mia famiglia. Fammi un piacere. Io telefono di nuovo fra mezz'ora. Fammi il piacere di andare a chiamare i miei parenti e falli venire al bar così possiamo parlare.

BARISTA

Benissimo. Ora chiamo a papà, lo faccio scendere così io posso andare a chiamare a Vittorio, tuo fratello e ci pensa lui a portare gli altri. Va bene?

OTTAVIO

Veri guddi!

BARISTA

Come?

OTTAVIO

Niente, niente. Richiamo tra mezzo'ora. Bai, bai.

(*riattacca il telefono*)

BARISTA

(guarda la cornetta del telefono) Abbaia? Ma io non ho sentito nessun cane abbaiare. (*Alza le spalle*) Boh. (*riattacca il telefono e corre alla porta*) Papà! Papà! Scendi per piacere un momento. Ha telefonato Ottavio 'e Spaventa dall'America e m'ha detto di andare a chiamare il fratello Vittorio perché richiama fra una mezz'ora. Per piacere scendi che scappo e torno subito. (*si toglie il grembiule e corre via*)

Si abbassano le luci della scena in Italia.

OTTAVIO

Uau! Non ci posso credere che Donato u Cravunaru ha un figlio così grande. Come passa il tempo! Francé, portami il foglio con tutte le cose che devono fare alla casa. È meglio spiegare tutto, per filo e per segno a mio fratello perché non sempre ci arriva a capire le cose.

FRANCESCA

(*porgendogli un foglio di carta*) Magari verrà al telefono anche tua sorella Assunta. Lei è molto più vispa! Vieni a mangiare qualcosa adesso perché se ti fa arrabbiare tuo fratello poi ti passa l'appetito.

OTTAVIO

(*sedendosi*) Sai che è una buona pensata. (*si siede, mangia e legge il giornale*). Io non posso più aspettare. Chiamo l'operéta adesso. Chissà quando la prendiamo la láina. (*va al telefono e fa il numero*) Iesse, I uánna to telefóne to Italia. (*pausa*) Iesse, (*pausa*) Serra Pedace, (*pausa*) Iesse, Calabria. (*Pausa*). Ok. Tencaiù!

Ottavio va a sedersi al tavolo ma deve subito alzarsi perché squilla il telefono.

OTTAVIO

(*correndo verso il telefono*) Mamma mia! Come sono stati fésti questa volta! Alò! Sì, sì, la provincia di Cosenza (*pausa*) Serra Pedace, (*pausa*) il prefisso? zero, nove, otto, quattro, il numero? (*guarda il libretto*) quarantatrè, cinque, ottantasette.

Si riaccendono le luci nel bar in Italia. Sulla scena c'è il barista, Vittorio e Assunta che aspettano ansiosamente attorno al telefono.

BARISTA

Pronto! (*gridando*) Ottà, sei tu?

OTTAVIO

(*gridando*) Sì, sì! È arrivato mio fratello?

BARISTA

Sì, è qua. C'è anche tua sorella Assunta. Te li passo.

OTTAVIO

Veri guddi. Alò?

ASSUNTA

(*gridando*) Ottà, sei tu?

OTTAVIO

(*Piangendo*) Uei, soré. Come te la passi?

ASSUNTA

Mamma mia, come si sente bene, Ottà. Sembra che sei nella stanza qua vicino. Come state, tutti? Francesca, Filomena e Santina? Ma perché piangi? È successo qualcosa? Dimmi la verità!

OTTAVIO

Ma no, non è successo niente. Piango perché sono emozionato, basta. Noi stiamo tutti benissimo. Stiamo tutti bene, te lo giuro. Io lavoro ancora nella costròsciona a Inco, Francesca lavora a un grande storo dove cucina.

ASSUNTA

Una grande storia? Che cos'è? Forse non ti ho sentito bene.

OTTAVIO

Nu storo! Ma la láina non è chiara? Nu storo … un negozio. Poi Santina va ancora all'aiscula e Filomena si sposa fra un mese. Avete ricevuto l'invitésciona?

ASSUNTA

La cosa?

OTTAVIO

L'invitésciona (*pausa a se stesso—coprendo la cornetta del telefono*) Cavolo, come si dice?! L'invito! L'invito!

ASSUNTA

Ah, sì, sì. L'abbiamo ricevuto. E lo sposo, chi è? Un paesano?

OTTAVIO

No, no. Non è un paesano, ma almeno è italiano. La paura mia era che si sposava nu mangiachecca.

ASSUNTA

Che si mangia? La cacca! Che schifo! Povera Filomena! E tu non hai fatto niente?!?!

OTTAVIO

E che ne so che si mangiava?! (*capendo il malinteso*) No, sorella mia! Noi chiamiamo mangiachecca le persone che non sono italiane. (*cambiando il discorso*) Ma lascia stare. Carmine come sta? Lavora? E i figli, come stanno?

ASSUNTA

Stanno tutti bene. Carmine lavora qua e là dove c'è lavoro.
Gregorio e Ferruccio vanno tutti e due all'università.

OTTAVIO

Bravi, che smarti che sono 'sti nipoti miei! Hanno pigliato dallo zio! E mamma (*piangendo*) come sta? C'è là? Posso parlare con lei?

ASSUNTA

E come vuoi che sta, Ottà? È fatta vecchiarella. Piange tutti i giorni da quando è morto papà. Non l'abbiamo portata perché fa fatica a camminare. La malattia peggiora. (*pausa, piangendo e pulendosi il naso*) Ottà, non sta bene. Hai capito? Cerca di venire a trovarla, ora che ti può ancora riconoscere.

OTTAVIO

(*piangere ancora di più*) Mammarella mia! Provo, magari dopo il matrimonio di Filomena. Ma Vittorio è la? Gli voglio parlare della casa.

ASSUNTA

Sì, è qua. Te lo passo sennò spendi un sacco di soldi per questa telefonata. Statti bene e salutami a tutti quanti a casa.

OTTAVIO

Bai, bai, Assù. Statti bene! (Vittorio prende il telefono) Alò, fraté! (pausa, si mette ancora a piangere) Come stai?

VITTORIO

Uei, Ottà. Come si va? Tutti bene a casa?

OTTAVIO

Sì, sì, stanno tutti bene e ti mandano tanti saluti. Senti, Filomena quando si sposa viene in Italia per l'annimúnni.

VITTORIO

Un anno! E perché aspetta un anno per venire a trovarci?

OTTAVIO

Ma che hai capito? Viene appena si sposa, per l'annimúnni!

VITTORIO

Cosa? No, no Battista 'e Limune, non c'è più al paese. È emigrato in Argentina! Non lo sapevi?

OTTAVIO

Ma che me ne frega di Battista 'e Limune!? Senti, Filomena viene in Italia subito dopo il matrimonio. Io mando i soldi per aggiustare la casa con lei. Non mi fido di mandare tanti soldi per posta. Non si sa mai.

VITTORIO

Hai ragione. Fai bene. Io ho cominciato un po' di lavoro alla casa, ma io devo pensare alla mia casa, e sai com'è?

OTTAVIO

Non ti preoccupare che ci penso io a aggiustare la casa di mamma. Io sto lavorando a due giobbe per guadagnare di più per la casa di mamma e per il matrimonio di Filomena. Ci vuole una montagna di soldi per 'sti matrimoni. Tra bomboniere, fiori, braidismédi, e tutto il resto, io e Francesca stiamo impazzendo.

VITTORIO

I braidi cosa?

OTTAVIO

Sono come la commare, ma non esattamente la stessa cosa. (*sarcastico*) Filomena ne deve avere sei, una in più della cugina Anna, e a me tocca cacciare i soldi per i regali!

VITTORIO

Povero te, ci vuole un portafoglio grande così (*gesticola con le mani*).

OTTAVIO

Non mi ci fare pensare che mi viene un ardatacco!

VITTORIO

Fratello mio, non t'attacare a 'ste cose che non ne vale la pena.

OTTAVIO

(*confuso*) Senti a me, per la casa. Ti mando cinquemila dollari con Filomena. Lo so che ci sono tante cose da ficsare. Mamma ha scritto dicendo che il floro è tutto rovinato e che si deve cambiare.

VITTORIO

(*confuso*) Ma, mamma non ne ha fiori! Di quali fiori parla?

OTTAVIO

Ma quali fiori! Che hai capito!?! (*Toccandosi la testa con la mano*) Il pavimento, il pavimento!

VITTORIO

Ah, sì. È vero.

OTTAVIO

Poi ha detto che tutti quanti al paese hanno il battirúmmi dentro la casa. Ma è vero?

VITTORIO

Che vuole battere, mamma?

OTTAVIO

(*copre la cornetta del telefono alla moglie*) Ma 'sto fratello mio non capisce proprio niente. (*ritorna a parlare con il fratello*) Poi con i soldi che rimangono, ci potete mettere un ruffo nuovo per il battirúmmi e sicuramente potete pure comprare una tenca per l'acqua calda. Hai capito?

VITTORIO

No, non ci ho capito proprio niente. La casa ha bisogno di tanto lavoro, ma il lavoro sicuramento non lo farà un ruffiano, come dici tu! E poi, (*arrabbiato*) perché dobbiamo comprare una tenda quando Assunta le può cucire così facilmente.

OTTAVIO

Ma che caspita hai capito?! Il ruffo (*pausa*), il tetto della casa, non si deve aggiustare?

VITTORIO

Sì, e mbé, che c'entra?

OTTAVIO

E come caspita si chiama quella cosa che si mette nel bagno dove si riscalda l'acqua per farti un bagno?!?

VITTORIO

Ah, la caldaia. Madonna mia, fratello mio. Non ti capisco più quando parli!

Francesca indica il passaggio del tempo toccandosi l'orologio.

OTTAVIO

Allora, Vittò, ci siamo capiti. Dobbiamo finire di parlare perché io pagherò sicuramente làzza moni.

VITTORIO

(*perplesso*) Lazza chi? Iazzolino, quello 'e Tolla? Se n'è andato a Milano a lavorare. Ma come ti è venuto in mente adesso? (*copre la cornetta del telefono a parla alla sorella*) Ma Ottavio, non sta bene. Dice delle cose molto strane. (*a Ottavio*) Senti, fratello mio, tu manda i soldi con Filomena che ci penso io a fare aggiustare la casa di mamma. Salutami a tutti quanti in famiglia. Ciao, ciao.

OTTAVIO

Ok, salutami pure tu a tutti nella tua famiglia. Un abbraccio e un bacio forte forte a mamma. Bai, bai.

VITTORIO

Abbaia (*pausa*)! Boh, si vede che Ottavio ha un cane che stava abbaiando. (*a Marco*) O Marco, abbiamo finito. Che devo fare?

BARISTA

Niente, riattacca e basta.

> *Assunta e Vittorio lasciano il bar e le luci si abbassano in quella parte del palco. Ottavio riattacca anche lui il telefono.*

OTTAVIO

Ma quanto è cretino mio fratello. Non ha capito niente di quello che ho detto. Io ho parlato così chiaramente. Speriamo che aggiusta bene la casa. Io lavoro come un matto per aiutare.

FRANCESCA

Non ti preoccupare che farà una buona giobba tuo fratello.

OTTAVIO

Mi sa che mi toccherà andare in Italia dopo il matrimonio per assicurare che fanno una buona giobba con la casa.

FRANCESCA

(*seccata*) Ma è possibile che solo tu sai fare le cose. Non ti fidi di nessuno! Nemmeno di tuo fratello!

OTTAVIO

Guarda che io butto il sangue a due giobbe per fare sposare TUA figlia con un matrimonio con i fiocchi. Io voglio solo assicurarmi che fanno tutte le cose che vuole mamma. Perché, in fin dei conti pago io, no!?!

FRANCESCA

Va bé, fai quello che devi fare. Ma prima dobbiamo pensare al matrimonio di Filomena. Dobbiamo andare al clobbi a scegliere il mangiare e poi ci aspettano al flauer scioppi per decidere quali fiori vogliamo.

OTTAVIO

Madonna mia, aiutami! Io dovrò trovare una terza giobba per pagare per tutte 'ste cose che dobbiamo avere per sposare 'sta figlia. Andiamo, andià, non mi voglio perdere la partita di achi. Stasera gioca Toronto contro Montreálli. Siamo quasi ai pleiòffisi. Sarà una bella partita!

FRANCESCA

Va bé, andiamo.

> *Partono e si abbassano le luci. Si riaccendono le luci sulla panchina dove sono ancora sedute Francesca e Rosa.*

ROSA

Mi ricordo bene il matrimonio di Filomena. Che bello! L'invidia di tutti i paesani. Ma quanta gente avete invitato? Trecento?

FRANCESCA

No, ce n'erano quattrocentocinquanta. Era uno dei primi matrimoni nella òlla nuova di sopra al Caruso Clobbi.

ROSA

E poi Ottavio è tornato in Italia a vedere la giobba che ha fatto il fratello?

FRANCESCA

Ma certo. Ottavio si è sempre fatto a pezzi per la mamma. Risparmiava ogni penì per mandarlo alla mamma. Se mia suocera ha avuto tutta la casa ficsata, può ringraziare mio marito.

ROSA

(*guardando attorno*) Francé, io non so che fine ha fatto mia figlia, ma io devo andare al bagno. (*si alza*) Ti saluto.

FRANCESCA

Che saluto! Vengo anch'io. (*si guarda attorno*) Nemmeno io vedo mia figlia. Dai, andiamo, ti faccio compagnia.

> Le due donne escono e si abbassano le luci.

ATTO II

> Francesca e Rosa rientrano a braccetto sulla scena cercando le figlie.

FRANCESCA

Ma porca misera! Chissà dov'è andata Santina? Mannaggia allo sciopping! Quando viene qui alla mola, si scorda di tutto!!

ROSA

A chi lo dici. Mia figlia Laura, ci abiterebbe qui, se potesse. Conosce tutti gli stori!

FRANCESCA

Ma tua figlia, non ci lavora qua dentro?

ROSA

Una volta sì! È per questo che dico che conosce tutti i buchi.

FRANCESCA

Ma dove ha lavorato?

ROSA

A uno storo dove vendono le scarpe. Non mi ricordo il nome.

FRANCESCA

E ci ha lavorato per tanto tempo?

ROSA

Da quando aveva quindici anni. Ha fatto pure l'assistente maneggéra finché non si è fatta tíccera. Solo che a causa di questo lavoro, quasi quasi non finiva l'aiscula!

FRANCESCA

E perché?

ROSA

Sai com'è? Questi ragazzi, (*fa il segno dei soldi con le mani*) quando cominciano a vedere il dollaro. Vogliono solo lavorare e non pensano a niente altro. Una volta, mio marito la voleva strozzare perché quasi quasi non passava una materia.

FRANCESCA

E com'è andata a finire?

ROSA

Mo ti racconto. Un giorno torna a casa Laura …

> Si abbassano le luci su Francesca e Rosa e si alzano sul lato opposto della scena.

Scena I

Il colloquio con la maestra
Giuseppe Battaglia, marito di Rosa
Rosa Battaglia, moglie di Giuseppe
Laura Battaglia, figlia
Mrs. Clarkson, la maestra di Laura
La scena è la cucina della famiglia Battaglia, una casa modesta di
Gatchell. Vi è un tavolo con sedie ed altri mobili.
Laura entra con libri in mano.

LAURA

Hi, ma! I'm home.

ROSA

Ei, Lauretta, sei già tornata? Che ora è? (*guarda l'orologio*) Mamma mia, dove vanno le ore?

LAURA

What are you doing?

ROSA

Uátta iú minna, uátta áima dúinga? Cucino! Preparo la cena. Tu lo sai com'è tuo padre! Se la cena non è sul tavolo quando arriva, diventa una belva!

LAURA

Ma, ti devo fare vedere una cosa.

ROSA

(*preoccupata*) Che significa! Cosa hai fatto? Dove sei stata e con chi?

LAURA

Take it easy, ma! Non ho fatto niente. (*esitando*) It's my report card.

ROSA

Reporti carti (*sollevata*), meno male. (agitandosi) Ma, Laura, che succede? Non sei andata bene alla scuola? Tu hai sempre i màrchisi sempre più alti di tutti quei ciucci mangiachecchi nella tua classe!

LAURA

Sì, ma. (*sarcastic*) I know you think I'm a regular Einstein, but this is advanced English. We're studying Shakepeare. E non mi piace.

ROSA

(*dandole uno schiaffo alla nuca*) Aronché, se non ti piace. Tu devi studiare e basta. Fa' finta che ti piace! Fammi vedere 'sta pagella.

LAURA

Okay, but please don't be mad!

ROSA

(*legge all'italiana*) Matematica 80, benissimo; Fémili Studia 85, meglio ancora; (*fa fatica*) gi, gi, gi (*scocciata, mostra alla figlia*) come caspita si legge questo?

LAURA

Gym, ma, gym.

ROSA

E che è?

LAURA

Ginnastica.

ROSA

Ah, va bé, gimmi, 80, veri guddi. (*legge ancora all'italiana*) Inglisci (*rimane sbalordita dal voto*) mamma mia, figlia, un 51! Che cos'è successo? Non hai mai ricevuto un voto così basso! Forse non ti piace la tíccera? Forse non ti tratta bene?

LAURA

No, ma, non mi piace l'inglese. Leggiamo 'sti libri noiosi di secoli fa. Non m'interessa.

ROSA

(*arrabbiata*) Lo so io perché non t'interessa. Perché pensi sempre a lavorare. (*fa il gesto dei soldi con la mano*) Per te, i dollari sono diventati più importanti di studiare. (*apre un'altro pezzo di carta che legge difficilmente*). "Tu olla parenti, (pausa) opena áusa uílla tecca plesi atta da scuola atta ... (*pausa, arrabbiata*) stasera alle sette! Da quanto tempo avevi 'sta lettera?

LAURA

(*imbarazzata*) Dalla settimana scorsa.

ROSA

(*arrabbiata*) Lo so benissimo che non me l'hai fatto sapere perché non vuoi che io e tuo padre veniamo a parlare con la tíccera. Vero? Ma perché fai sempre così. (*si mette a piangere*) Perché ti vergogni di noi?

LAURA

(*cercando di calmarla*) Non è vero ma, solo che ho paura che tu e papà andate alla scuola e vi mettete a gridare.

Entra Giuseppe dal lavoro.

GIUSEPPE

Buona sera, che succede?

LAURA

(*imbarazzata*) Nothing, nothing, papà! Did you have a nice day at work?

ROSA

(*cercando di sdrammatizzare*) Náting. Laura giusta ghetta omma, e ...

GIUSEPPE

Ma perché mi parlate in inglese. Lo sapete che non mi piace quando fate così. (*arrabbiandosi*) Che cosa mi state nascondendo?

ROSA

Niente. Laura ha portato la pagella dalla scuola oggi e stasera c'è l'ópena áusa se vogliamo andare a parlare con la tíccera.

GIUSEPPE

Perché dobbiamo andare a parlare con la tíccera? Laura è la più smarta della classe. Non siamo mai andati a parlare con nessuna tíccera! (*alla figlia, sospettosa*) Che caspita hai combinato?

LAURA

Niente, papà! Sto avendo un po' di problemi con Shakespeare.

GIUSEPPE

E che caspita è? (*scandalizzato*) Ti sei messa a bere la birra scuola?!?!

LAURA

Ma no, papà che hai capito. Shakespeare è uno scrittore inglese e stiamo leggendo le sue commedie. Il corso non mi piace tanto e il mio voto non è molto buono.

GIUSEPPE

Che significa "non è molto buono"?

ROSA

Ha preso un cinquantuno.

GIUSEPPE

(*sorpresissimo e mettendosi la mano al petto*) Mamma mia. Ma hai fatto qualcosa alla tíccera?

LAURA

No, papà. Non mi piace il corso e basta.

GIUSEPPE

Dai Rosa, togliti 'sto grembiule e andiamo alla scuola a parlare colla tíccera.

ROSA

Ma, io ho cucinato. Mangiamo prima e poi andiamo. La lettera dice che la scuola è aperta fino alle nove.

GIUSEPPE

Ma che mangiare. Io non voglio mangiare. Ho perso l'appetito. Dai, preparati.

> *Giuseppe si cambia velocemente. Rosa si toglie il grembiule e si mette a posto i capelli.*

ROSA

Ok! Ok! (*voltandosi alla figlia*) Tu, resta qua e non ti preoccupare. Ci penso io a tuo padre.

LAURA

Please ma, keep him calm. All my friends' parents are going to be at the school. If papà blows up everybody will be laughing at me tomorrow at school. I swear, ma, if that happens, I'm dropping out!

ROSA

Statti zitta, plissi. Ci penso io a tuo padre!

> *Rosa e Giuseppe escono dalla stanza e emergono davanti al palco che funge da esteriore. Rientrano dalle quinte opposte e riappaiono sul lato opposto della scena dove si trova una maestra seduta alla sua scrivania. Rosa bussa alla porta.*

ROSA

Alò, Missi Clarchisonni? (*la maestra dice di sì con la testa—si volta al marito*) Ecco ci siamo. Per piacere fa parlare a me, ok?

GIUSEPPE

(*scocciato*) Ok, ok! Che lagna che sei! (*mettendosi avanti*) Alò, (*dando la mano alla maestra*) Aimma Laura Battaglia dora. Signora tíccera, my Laura, iffa she no do a gudda giobba for iú, iú canni itta er. Capisci? (*facendo i gesti con le mani*) Le puoi dare un sacco di palate con la mia benedizione! Ochidochi!?!

ROSA

(*dandogli una gomitata e parlando sottovoce al marito*) Ma cretino, sciarappa che fai fare brutta figura a tua figlia. Mannaggia alla misera, le hai appena detto che sei la figlia di Laura Battaglia! Lascia parlare a me. (*cambiando il tono alla maestra*) Echiscúsimi, signora Clarchisonni, Laura Battaglia issa áura dora.

MRS. CLARKSON

Your daughter?

ROSA E GIUSEPPE

Iesse, Iesse.

ROSA

Oua arri iú?

MRS. CLARKSON

Very well thank you. I imagine you are here to discuss your daughter's evaluation as of late.

GIUSEPPE

(nell'orecchio della moglie) Che cosa?

ROSA

(sottovoce al marito) Non lo so. (Si volta verso la maestra) Echiscúsimi?

MRS. CLARKSON

(*parlando lentamente*) You're here because Laura is having trouble with Shakespeare. Right?

ROSA

Iesse! Uatta Laura canni do to studiare (*correggendosi*) to stodi more e ghetti guddi márchisi?

MRS. CLARKSON

First Laura needs to do the readings, then she needs to do the homework and lastly she needs to come to class. She skips class regularly.

GIUSEPPE

Che ha detto?

ROSA

(*al marito*) Zitto, che poi ti spiego. (*si volta alla maestra*) Uaiti nu minuto. Laura, she ridda olla da táimi. She lova to ridda.

MRS. CLARKSON

She is obviously NOT reading for my class.

ROSA

E poi, Laura olauéis do da omiuórchi. Everi náiti!

MRS. CLARKSON

She's not doing the work for my class. She didn't hand in any assignments and did very poorly on the last test.

GIUSEPPE

(*alla moglie sottovoce*) Che ha detto? Mi sembrano tutte cose brutte!

ROSA

(*sottovoce al marito*) Infatti, è tutto brutto. (*si volge alla maestra*) Signora Clarchisonni, uatti sciuddi ui du?

MRS. CLARKSON

I don't know. Laura has to come to class.

GIUSEPPE

Uatta iu mina? Laura non coma to scula?

MRS. CLARKSON

(*facendo gesta*) She missed two classes this week and three days last week. If she continues like this she'll fail!

GIUSEPPE

(*alla moglie*) Madonna mia, quella disgraziata di figlia non viene alla scuola. Dove caspita va?

ROSA

(*al marito*) Mi faccio tagliare la testa che va alla mola a lavorare. Ha sempre soldi nel portafoglio.

GIUSEPPE

(*contento*) Brava figlia. Almeno se non viene a scuola, va a guadagnarsi il pane.

ROSA

(*mortificata*) Aima sorri, signora Clarchisonni. I tocca to my dora uenni we go omi. Ok?

MRS. CLARKSON

Thank you. I'd appreciate it. She doesn't seem to be interested in school at all. Maybe she would be better off going to a vocational school. I doubt that she would do very well at university.

> *Rosa si mette a piangere*

GIUSEPPE

(*alla moglie sottovoce*) Che succede. Che t'ha detto questa?

ROSA

(*al marito*) Pensa che a Laura non le interessa la scuola. Che forse è meglio che Laura va a quella scuola dove vanno tutti i ragazzi che sono ciucci. Dice che sicuramente Laura non può andare all'università (*continua a piangere*).

GIUSEPPE

(*alla moglie sottovoce*) 'Sta vipera! Ma chi si crede di essere! (*alla maestra in tono arrabbiato*) Cara signora Clarchisonni, io no spicchi inglisci (*pausa*) enti io no onisténdi inglisci veri guddi, (*pausa*) però, (*pausa*) batta, (*pausa*) mai figlia, mai Laura, she veri smarta. No stupida come dici tu. Iffa she no comma to da classe, isa, for sciuri bicósi, iú classe isa veri noioso! (*alla moglie sottovoce*) Andiamocene, Rosa. Questa cretina pensa di essere meglio di noi. Se non ce ne andiamo adesso m'arrabbio veramente.

ROSA

(*al marito*) Zitto, per piacere. Non farti capire sennò questa befana tratta peggio a Laura. (*alla maestra*) Tencaiù, signora Clarchisonni. We go omi nao enti tocca to Laura. Tencaiù veri maccia.

MRS. CLARKSON

Tell her to come to class and I'm sure her marks will get better.

ROSA

Tencaiù e guddi naiti.

GIUSEPPE

(gentilmente alla maestra) Guddi naiti (sottovoce alla moglie) Scema che non sei altro!

> *Escono e ritornano a casa facendo la stessa strada dell'andata.*
> *Si fermano a parlare per la strada.*

GIUSEPPE

Ma guarda un po'! (*alzando il tono della voce—incredulo*) Ma guarda un po'!

ROSA

Ma come facciamo?

GIUSEPPE

Che facciamo?! Troviamo 'na tíccera privata così Laura impara più di quella rimbambita che si fa chiamare tíccera. Ti faccio vedere io se mia figlia non sarà la più smarta della classe.

ROSA

Ma la figlia di Vera Valletta è una maestra, vero?

GIUSEPPE

La figlia che abita in quella casa bianca a Lógani Stritti?

ROSA

Bravo, proprio quella. M'ha detto Teresa, la nostra vicina di casa, che fa classi private. Perché non parliamo con lei.

GIUSEPPE

Benissimo! Ma adesso andiamo a casa che (*toccandosi la pancia*) mi sta venendo la fame.

Escono.
Le luci si riaccendono sulla panchina dove sono sedute
Francesca e Rosa

FRANCESCA

Mamma mia, e poi ch'è successo?

ROSA

Laura ha fatto classi private per un mese e alla fine dell'anno ha preso il voto più alto di quella maledetta classe.

FRANCESCA

Bella!

ROSA

Poi è andata all'università e si è fatta tíccera pure lei e la soddisfazione più grande l'ha avuta quando la signora Clarchisonni è ritáira e Laura ha preso il suo lavoro. (*guardandosi attorno*) Ma 'ste figlie nostre si sono proprio perse!!

FRANCESCA

Io non ci capisco niente. Santina lo sa che abbiamo un sacco di cose da fare con il matrimonio che sta arrivando.

ROSA

Hai ragione, il matrimonio quando è?

FRANCESCA

Fra un mese e Santina mi sta facendo impazzire perché vuole fare tutto a modo suo. Dice sempre che non vuole un matrimonio tradizionale italiano. Questa qua mi fa impazzire.

ROSA

Ma non ti preoccupare. Andrà tutto bene.

FRANCESCA

Ma scherzi! Se ti raccontassi le cose che ci sta facendo passare.

ROSA

E dai dimmi.

Si abbassano le luci. Rosa e Francesca lasciano la scena e
Francesca entra dalla parte opposta nella sua propria casa.

Scena II

> *La preparazione di un matrimonio italo-canadese*
> *Francesca Delfino, moglie*
> *Ottavio Delfino, marito*
> *Santina, figlia Filomena, figlia*
> *Siamo a casa della famiglia Delfino al giorno d'oggi. La scena si apre in*
> *un salotto con divano, tavolinetto e tavolo con 4 sedie. In scena c'è Santina*
> *vestita da sposa con la madre, Francesca che le aggiusta il vestito e le*
> *prende le misure per fare le alterazioni necessarie. Sul tavolino ci sono*
> *un sacco di bomboniere diverse.*

FRANCESCA

(*entrando*) Ecco le spille (*cerca di mettere una spilla sul vestito*) Santì, sta' ferma che sennò ti faccio male.

SANTINA

Ma, hurry up!!!

FRANCESCA

Eh, ariappa ariappa, ma vuoi che ti faccio una schifezza! Voglio fare una buona giobba con questo vestito, altrimenti tutti che diranno?

SANTINA

But Ma, Marco is coming to pick me up in a half an hour and I still have to shower and get dressed.

FRANCESCA

Ancora con 'sta sciàuera! Ma non te la sei fatta questa mattina? Ma quante volte ti devi lavare? Non sei stata mica a zappare nella iarda che ti sei sporcata! Ai tempi miei ci facevamo il bagno una volta alla settimana.

SANTINA

Ma, we are not (*fa una smorfia*) ai tempi tuoi anymore and we are not in a little village in Italy!

FRANCESCA

(*andando verso il tavolino e prendendo le bomboniere*) Senti Santì, prima di uscire devi scegliere le bomboniere per il matrimonio. Guarda come sono belle queste. Guarda che dobbiamo ordinarle subito, sennò non fanno in tempo ad arrivare. Ti piace questa?

SANTINA

Ma, I told you I don't want any of this bomboniere, shit! Marco and I decided not to have any.

FRANCESCA

(*scandalizzata*) Che???? Ma tu sei pazza!!! No bomboniere? Ma senti questa! E che siamo dei pezzenti che non abbiamo bomboniere al matrimonio di nostra figlia? Ma mi vuoi fare morire? E che diranno i parenti e i paesani? No, assolutamente no! Tu avrai le bomboniere, sennò no more eredità per te, hai capito?

SANTINA

Ok, do what you want. (*entra Filomena incinta*)

FILOMENA

Ciao ma, hi sis, come state?

FRANCESCA

Ciao Filomè. C'è tua sorella qui che mi sta facendo morire. Ora dice che non vuole le bomboniere.

FILOMENA

Santina, you shouldn't even try to argue, you know that no matter what the wedding is not going to be how you want it but how mom and dad want it, per non fare brutta figura. Vero ma?

FRANCESCA

Che hai da dire tu? Tu, grazie a me e a tuo padre, ti sei sposata come una regina!

FILOMENA

Ya, come una regina (*sarcastica*). I have to sit down. My feet are so swollen and my back is killing me.

SANTINA

I hope you don't have this kid during my wedding.

FRANCESCA

Filomè, hai portato la lista?

FILOMENA

Sì, ma, but this list is 10 years old and half of these people are dead now.

SANTINA

Oh good, that means that there will be half as many people that I barely know at my wedding. And mom, don't you think you are going to invite the entire Sudbury to my wedding. Capito?

FRANCESCA

Non ti preoccupare, invitiamo solo tutti gli italiani che i mangiachecche nella busta non ci mettono niente. Neanche una lira! Si presentano al matrimonio con un tóstero!

SANTINA

Oh my God!

FILOMENA

(*sarcastica*) Don't worry sis, we'll fill up that Caruso Club nice and tight. You'll see. How many people does it fit?

FRANCESCA

Cinquecento.

FILOMENA

(*sarcastic*) That's it? Oh, don't worry, we'll cram a couple of extra tables in there!

SANTINA

Shut up!

FRANCESCA

Uei, che è stu sciarappa. Guarda come parli a tua sorella.

(*si sente arrivare qualcuno*)

FRANCESCA

Ecco vostro padre. (*entra Ottavio*)

SANTINA E FILOMENA

Ciao papà.

OTTAVIO

Ciao Filomé, come stai? (*toccando la pancia di Filomena*) E questo bel bambino qua dentro come sta?

FILOMENA
Bene, bene, papà. Un po' stanca.

OTTAVIO
Filomé, questa volta me lo devi fare un bel boio, se no io in questa famiglia ci muoio circondato da tutte queste femmine.

FRANCESCA
Ma stai zitto vai, che ti manca? È proprio perché sei circondato da queste femmine che vivi come un rè, servito e riverito.

OTTAVIO
Sì, sì! (*alla figlia*) Filomè, l'hai portata la lista?

SANTINA
Sis, please, don't give him that list! I don't want those people at my wedding!

FILOMENA
Even if I don't give him the list, he will just make another one. He'll go through all his old address books and make mom write them out.

OTTAVIO
EI!!!!! Ma parlate come va fatto mammata! Che è questo inglese? Parlate inglese per non farmi capire, vi conosco io a voi!

FILOMENA
Papà, ma che dici, ecco la lista.

OTTAVIO
Ah, fammi vedere.
(*Guarda la lista, ma non riesce a leggere niente senza gli occhiali*)

OTTAVIO
Francé, pigliami gli occhiali che non ci vedo!
Mannaggia la vecchiaia!
(*Francesca prende gli occhiali che sono in un cassetto e li dà al marito*)

FRANCESCA
Eccoli.

SANTINA
Ma, I have to go. Marco is going to be here any minute now.

FRANCESCA
E la lista?

SANTINA
You and dad take care of that. It's not like you're going to listen to anything I have to say anyway, so what's the point of me being here?!?

OTTAVIO
Ancora con questo inglese! Mannaggia alla miseria! Ma non ti ricordi come parlavi bene l'italiano quando eri bambina e siamo venuti dall'Italia? Ma che ti è successo?

SANTINA
Papà, siamo in Canada now and we have to speak English. Capito? I can't believe you have been here for twenty years and you don't speak English!

OTTAVIO
Vedi come mi risponde TUA figlia Francé!

FRANCESCA
Santì, dazzinóffa! Vatti a preparare!
(*Santina esce*)

FILOMENA

Non ti preoccupare papà che ti aiuto io con la lista. (*si va a sedere vicino al padre*)

OTTAVIO

(*Prendendo carta e penna*) Allora, vediamo un po'. Compare Pippo e comare Franca. Al matrimonio di Filomena hanno messo una busta di cinquanta dollari. Per due persone cinquanta dollari. Ma non si vergognano! Francé, questi li eliminiamo dalla lista!

FRANCESCA

E fai bene. 'Sti svergognati. Non li invitiamo!

FILOMENA

Ma papà, io mi sono sposata 10 anni fa! Dieci anni fa cinquanta dollari erano tanti! Ci devi mettere il cost of living.

OTTAVIO

Ma che dici Filomè, cinquanta dollari sono cinquanta dollari. Me ne frego dell'inflazione. Basta, eliminati! Andiamo avanti. Comare Gisella e compare Francuzzo. Loro si sono comportati bene al tuo matrimonio. Hanno messo 100 dollari nella busta. Ok, a loro li invitiamo.

FRANCESCA

Sì, però bisogna stare attenti a non metterli allo stesso tavolo di comare Pina e compare Berto perché non si parlano da 15 anni per quel fatto della terra al paese e se li mettiamo allo stesso tavolo va a finire che si scannano.

FILOMENA

E state attenti a zio Michele, che al mio matrimonio ha bevuto così tanto che ...

FRANCESCA

Ah, mamma mia, mi ricordo, ha vomitato su tutto lo suitti tébelo a mezzanotte. Su tutti quei bei dolci! Mamma mia! Che rovina!

OTTAVIO

A proposito, hai parlato con il Caruso Clobbi? Gli hai detto che vogliamo un suitti tébelo grandissimo? Il più grande che hanno mai fatto! Con fontane di cioccolata. Così tutti i parenti moriranno dall'invidia! Sarà il matrimonio del secolo. Francé, ripetimi un po' il menù.

FRANCESCA

Ma te l'ho già detto.

OTTAVIO

E ripetimelo, dai!

FRANCESCA

Allora, prima c'è l'antipasto con prosciutto, melone, bocconcini, olive e melanzane, poi la minestra, poi ci sono le penne all'arrabbiata e poi i cannelloni e poi il pollo con le patate, e poi le fettine alla parmigiana e poi l'insalata, e poi ...

OTTAVIO

Come e poi l'insalata. E il pesce? Non c'è il pesce?

FRANCESCA

Ma che pesce. La mamma di Marco ha detto che è troppo.

OTTAVIO

Come?! È troppo? Ma che dici Francé. Niente è troppo! Ma che razza di matrimonio è senza pesce? Ma vuoi che facciamo la figuraccia dei morti di fame? Certo che la mamma di Marco ha detto così, perché LORO sono morti di fame, ma non

NOI! Ci sarà il pesce. Punto e basta! Andiamo avanti. (*pausa*) Lorenzo e Emilia, non hanno ancora il figlio di quarant'anni che devono ancora maritare?

FRANCESCA

Sì, e mbé, che c'entra?

OTTAVIO

Se li mettiamo allo stesso tavolo di Tommaso e Chiarina Struzzo, che hanno quella figlia racchia, magari si trovano quella sera e ci prepariamo per un altro matrimonio.

FILOMENA

Ma, papà, mind your own buisness.

OTTAVIO

Ma io i bisinissi miei me li so guardare molto bene. Non ti preoccupare. Se si accoppiano, facciamo un piacere a tutti e due. E poi che male fa? Ai tempi nostri così si faceva. Mica si facevano i "detti" che fate voi, che non fate altro che spendere soldi!

FILOMENA

O papà, you're so old fashioned.

OTTAVIO

Ma che dici, io m'affascino!

FRANCESCA

(*interrompendo*) Ma vedi che ha ragione Santina, stai qui da un secolo e ancora non capisci l'inglese. Filomena t'ha detto che sei all'antica.

OTTAVIO

Io, all'antica!?! (*Allargando il petto*) Se qua dentro c'è un giovanotto di vent'anni!!!

FRANCESCA

Ma per piacere, non mi fare ridere. Andiamo avanti.

Chi altro c'è sulla lista?

OTTAVIO

C'è Filippo e Carolina Rizzo. (*A Filomena*) Loro sono venuti al tuo matrimonio e hanno avuto il coraggio di non invitarci per il matrimonio della figlia che si è sposata due anni fa. Sonamabiccia! Non mi hanno rispettato dopo tutto il lavoro che ho fatto a quella scecca di casa che hanno! Disgraziato! Non li invitiamo!

FRANCESCA

Fai bene! Non mi è mai piaciuta quella pettegola di Carolina. Teresa mi ha detto che dopo il matrimonio di Filomena, Carolina andava in giro dicendo che noi avevamo fatto un matrimonio molto accippi.

OTTAVIO

Noi! Accippi! Disgraziati! Se abbiamo fatto venire Rocco del Sud e la sua banda da Toronto a cantare al matrimonio!

FILOMENA

Please! Don't tell me that Roccuzzo is singing at Santina's wedding too! She's gonna have a fit!!

FRANCESCA

No, hanno trovato una banda che si chiama (*pausa*) "Digei". Li cononsci? Sono bravi?

FILOMENA

Ma che hai capito, ma? Un DJ è un uomo che viene e suona dischi. Non c'è nessuna banda!

OTTAVIO

Madonna mia! Non c'è la banda!?! E che dice la gente?

FRANCESCA

Ci pigliano per accippi veramente!

OTTAVIO

No, no, no! Io chiamo subito a Antonio Sansalone a Toronto e lui ci fa certamente venire Roccuzzo che sono vecchi amici.

FILOMENA

Antonio Sansalone? E chi è?

OTTAVIO

È quell'amico mio che viene spesso e andiamo a caccia a Manitúli insieme. Non te lo ricordi?

FRANCESCA

Sì, sì, invitiamoli che quelli sono di Toronto e ci mettono una bella busta!

FILOMENA

I don't believe what I'm hearing. I gotta get out of here. Io me ne vado. Voi non avete bisogno di me. Vi lascio la lista.

FRANCESCA

Aspetta che ti accompagno io, che quasi quasi non ci passi più per la porta. (*al marito*) Ottà, torno subito.

FILOMENA

Ciao, pà. (*Si salutano*) (*al padre*) Papà, non studiare troppo la lista or you'll go blind.
              Le due donne escono.

OTTAVIO

Non ti preoccupare che io ci vedo benissimo. (*Si risiede*) Allora, ritorniamo alla lista …
              Si abbassano le luci e si riaccendono su
              Rosa e Francesca sulla panchina.

ROSA

Vedi! Ti stai preoccupando per niente! Sarà un matrimonio bellissimo. L'invidia di tutti i paesani che verranno. Ma dimmi una cosa. Quella bella fontana di cioccolata … l'avete trovata?

FRANCESCA

Sì, ce l'ha trovata Gianni, il maneggére del Caruso Clobbi. L'ha arrenditata da qualche posto.

ROSA

Proprio bella! Farete una bellissima figura.

FRANCESCA

Sì, ma mia figlia mi sta facendo sudare. 'Sti giovani di oggi vogliono fare sempre le cose a modo loro. Pensano di essere così smarti e di sapere tutto.

ROSA

Ma non lo raccontare a me, che ho due figli che mi stanno facendo impazzire.

FRANCESCA

E perché?

ROSA

Ma Francesca mia, dimmi un po' se alla mia età, io mi posso imparare a usare tutte 'ste mascine moderne che usano loro! Non è possibile!

FRANCESCA

Ma che cosa vogliono farti imparare?

ROSA

Senti che ora ti racconto!

Si abbassano le luci su Rosa e Francesca e si accendono dalla parte opposta del palco.

Scena III

> *La tecnologia*
> *Rosa Battaglia*
> *Gino Battaglia, figlio*
> *Laura Battaglia, figlia*
> *Beth, amica di Laura*
> *Siamo nel salotto di casa Battaglia. Ci sono un divano, un tavolinetto,*
> *una scrivania con sopra un computer e un paio di sedie.*

ROSA

(sta spolverando la stanza con un paio di mutande vecchie, ma quando arriva al computer non sa come fare) Mannaggia, devo pulire sotto 'sto maledetto compútero, ma come faccio. 'Sta televísiona, la posso muovere? (Cerca di spostare lo schermo ma lo trova pesante). Mamma mia, quanto pesa. È meglio che non lo tocco che se lo rompo, m'ammazzano i figli. Anzi, m'ammazza Giuseppe, che l'ha pagato lui. (Spolvera attorno ma guarda sotto lo schermo). Ma guarda quanta polvere! Devo pulirci. (Comincia a pulire e il computer emette un suono). (spaventatissima) Oh, Gesù, Giuseppe e Maria, che caspita ho fatto?!

> *Entra Laura*

LAURA

Ma, what are you doing?

ROSA

(*spaventata*) Uatta iú minna, uatta áima duinga? Sto facendo quello che dovresti fare tu! Sto pulendo 'sta maledetta mascína. Ma mi sa che ci ho fatto qualcosa, che sta facendo una noisa che fa pi pi, pi pi, pi pi.

LAURA

Oh, it's probably nothing mom. Let's see. (*Accende il computer*) So, when are you going to learn how to use this thing?

ROSA

(*scioccata*) IO, ma che dici?

LAURA

But, ma. It's not hard. If you learn how to use the computer, you could talk to your sisters and the rest of your relatives in Italy for free.

ROSA

Per fri! Ma tu scherzi! Non è possibile!

LAURA

È possibile sì. E poi, we can even find all the music you and papà like and I can make a CD for you.

ROSA

Ma va', va'. Tu mi fai i CD che abbiamo comprato a Musica Worldi a Wooddibríggi l'ultima volta che siamo andati a Toronto?

LAURA

Ya, those. Just that what I make you, doesn't have the fancy cover. You wanna try? Come and sit here beside me.

ROSA

Va be'. Ti faccio contenta. Attraiamo. Vediamo cosa puoi fare.

LAURA

Ok, what singer do you want me to find? Or is there a song you want?

ROSA

Ok, smarta che sei. Trovami le canzoni di Claudio Villa.

LAURA

Ok, just a second. How do you spell Claudio Villa.

ROSA

Come! Come si spella!?! (*pronunciando lentamente*) C-L-A-U-D-I-O VILLA

LAURA

Is that with due elle?

ROSA

Ma certo, cretina. Parli sempre in inglese che ti sei dimenticata tutto l'italiano che t'abbiamo imparato. Che tempo sprecato tutti quei sabato mattina che sei andata alla scuola italiana.

LAURA

(scocciata) Ok, ma! Don't worry about my Italian. Look Claudio Villa's waiting for you! Look at all these songs. Which one do you want? (Elenca) Buon giorno tristezza, Mamma, Tic Ti Tic Ta.

ROSA

(*si mette gli occhiali e guarda lo schermo*) Ma io non sento niente. Vedo solo le parole.

LAURA

Wait, I have to download them. That's why you have to tell me which ones you want.

ROSA

Che gli devi fare? Le devi dauna cosa?

LAURA

Download. Le devo daunlodáre. I'll show you, just tell me which songs you want.

ROSA

Le voglio tutte!

LAURA

Ok, let's start with Buon giorno tristezza.

ROSA

(*indicando*) E che è quella cosa che si sta muovendo?

LAURA

When that's full, the song is ready. (*pausa*) Look, 5 seconds left. (pausa) There. You wanna hear it?

ROSA

Già?

LAURA

Yes, ma, già. Here we go. (Si sente Buon giorno tristezza)

ROSA

(*canticchiando felicemente*) Ma come hai fatto? Da dove è venuta 'sta canzone? Dai, fammi vedere il CD. Dove l'hai nascosto?

LAURA

Ma, there is no CD. Listen, here's Tic Ti, Tic Ta and Arrivederci Roma. You believe me now?

ROSA

Ma santo Dio, come hai fatto? Noi stiamo qua a Subburì, la mascína è ploggata al muro. Da dov'è venuta la musica (*guarda la figlia*)?

LAURA

From cyberspace (*Rosa non capisce*). Dallo spazio.

ROSA

Ma chi ce l'ha messa la musica nella nostra mascína?

LAURA

Somebody in Italy put it on their computer and when I clicked on the song, I took it from there.

ROSA

(*scandalizzata*) Ma allora l'hai rubata, la musica!

LAURA

No, ma. It's shared music. It's too hard to explain. Do you want a CD, sì o no?

ROSA

Sì, sì, certo. Fammelo, fammelo. Entrano Gino e un'amica, Beth.

GINO

Hi, ma. I'm home. What's for dinner?

ROSA

(*al figlio sottovoce*) Te pozze strozzà! N'altra volta mi hai portato 'sta befana di mangiachecca in casa a mangiare. Mica sono una cuoca in un ristorante io!

BETH

(*pronuncia all'inglese*) Hi, Mrs. Battaglia! How are you? Thank you for inviting me to dinner again. What ever you're making smells wonderful.

ROSA

(*sottovoce*) Ma certo che smella guddi! A casa tua mangiate solo ottidoghi e framburger con quel pane schifoso. Lazza checiáppa e mostarda. Mmmm, mangia e muori!

BETH

Excuse me, are you making hamburgers and hotdogs for dinner? I love them. We had them for dinner last night at my place. (*A Gino*) Do you guys have relish and mayonnaise?

Gino fa cenno di no

ROSA

'Ste porcherie a casa mia non ci sono. No, ai mecca, ziti uita salsa rossa con costolette di maiale. Denni uí itta, fettine impanate con una bella peperonata e un'insalata.

BETH

(*a Gino*) I didn't understand a word she said.

ROSA

Come, iú no onistendi mai inglisci?

GINO

L'hai parlato troppo festa, ma. (*A Beth*) We're having pasta with a red sauce and a bunch of other stuff. You'll love it.

BETH

Oooh. Is it going to be as good as the Prego stuff my mom buys at the store.

ROSA

(*sottovoce*) Prego! Salsa comprata allo storo! Ma dove si crede di essere questa scema? Quelle sono cose che si comprano solo i mangiachecca. A casa mia neanche il cane si mangia quella porcheria.

LAURA

(*sdramatizzando*) Hey, bro, Beth. You wanna see this great video I found on You-tube.

Rosa ritorna a spolverare

ROSA

Va' a finire che ci sono pure i tubi in quella mascína.

I tre ragazzi vanno al computer. Si sente squillare un cellulare che si trova sul tavolino.

ROSA

Il telefono, Gi, rispondi.

GINO

No, ma, that's not mine. That's the phone we bought for you for your birthday. You answer!

ROSA

Oh, Dio! Ma quel telefono è solo per emergenzíe. Io non l'ho mai usato. Perché sta suonando? Rispondi tu!

GINO

No way. If you don't answer it, you'll never learn how to use it.

ROSA

Mannaggia! Voi mi volete fare morire di paura. Se lo rompo che facciamo?!

GINO

Ma, you're not gonna break it. Just answer the damn phone.

ROSA

Ok, ok! (prende il telefono e non sa come fare. Mette il telefono all'orecchio ma continua a suonare). Ma perché continua a suonare?

GINO

Ma, flip it!

ROSA

Che è 'sto flippa?

GINO

Open it!

ROSA

(lo apre, lo mette all'orecchio ma il telefono continua a suonare) Ma, suona ancora. (Lo scuote) Sci no uórca!!

GINO

Yes, ma (*imitandola*) She uórca! You have to press the button.

ROSA

E quale bottone devo pusciare? Qui ce ne sono tanti!

GINO

(*impaziente*) The one that says "talk".

ROSA

(prende gli occhiali e se li mette) Ma qui io non vedo T O C C A.

GINO

(frustrato si avvicina alla mamma e le prende il telefono dalla mano e le preme il pulsante) It's this one. It's says talk on it. (Glielo passa) Here!

ROSA

Alò? Alò? Alò!!!!! Ma qui non c'è nessuno. (*porta il telefono al figlio*) Te l'ho detto che questo telefono sci no uórca!!

LAURA

They probably hung up because it rang so many times

BETH

(*a Laura*) I stopped counting at 40!!!

ROSA

(*va dal figlio*) Bringa becca to da storo! Soldi bruciati.

GINO

All technology is soldi bruciati for you, ma. (*Alla sorella e a Beth*) Look, guarda! You see that box over there? I bought her a microwave last Christmas and it's still in the box!

BETH

In the box? How does she cook without a microwave?

LAURA

(*dà una gomitata a Beth*) Shhhh! This is a touchy subject.

ROSA

Uára iú mínna come cucino io? Che ci devo fare con 'sto microué? C'ho il forno e la stufa che mi funzionano così bene. Non mi serve. E te l'ho detto che alla televísiona hanno detto che fa venire il cánsero!

LAURA

Please ma, everybody uses it!

ROSA

E mica siamo evribódi noi. 'Sti microué servono per le persone lezi che non sono organizzate come me che mi ricordo di sfrizare la carne e non mangiamo niente dalle bóchise preparate. Quando voi vi sposate, ve lo potete portare che sicuramente tu (*a Laura*) non cucinerai, e tu (*a Gino*) che stai sempre con le donne mangiachecche userai il microué tutte le sere per preparare la cena. Poi non venite a casa mia a mangiare!!!

GINO

Ok, ma! We know you're the best cook in the world. Don't be insulted. I'll take it back to Canadian Tire.

ROSA

Bravo, bravo! La prima cosa buona che hai detto. Ripórtala alla Canada Táire. E i soldi che ti danno valli a mettere alla banca. Risparmiati i soldi e non mi comprare più 'ste porcherie! Ora basta. Andiamo a mangiare che alle sette c'è il mio sció al Telelatino e non me lo voglio perdere.

> *Tutti s'incamminano verso la cucina.*
> *Esce prima Rosa.*

LAURA

(*a Beth*) You should see her watch her soap.

BETH

What do you mean?

GINO

She yells and screams at the actors on the screen. She thinks they're real people!

BETH

It's the same thing at my house, only my mother watches the Young and the Restless.

LAURA

Oh, we watch (*facendo le virgolette con le mani*) the "Restiling" here too!

GINO

But we have to explain what's going on to her.

> *Tutti ridono e escono. Si abbassano le luci e si riaccendono su*
> *Rosa e Francesca sedute sulla panchina.*

FRANCESCA

Ma pure tu, ti guardi il "Restling"? Ma quel Vittorio! hai visto cosa gli è successo?

ROSA

Chissà se fanno la pace lui e Nichi? (*Si guarda attorno*) Guarda che 'sta figlia mia è proprio scostumata. Mi sta facendo passare ore qui seduta. Non sento più il mio culo! E se non fossi arrivata tu, come facevo io qua sola. Mica siamo in Italia dove al paese conosci tutti quanti!

FRANCESCA

(*rassegnata*) E lo so. Ma che ci puoi fare? Non siamo più in Italia.

ROSA

E lo so, ma certe volte mi ci vorrei proprio trovare. (*avvicinandosi all'orecchio dell'amica*) Ma dimmi la verità, non ti manca l'Italia?

FRANCESCA

Certo che mi manca. Ci sono nata! L'Italia avrà sempre un posto molto speciale nel mio cuore, ma ho passato la maggior parte della mia vita qui in Canada.

ROSA

Sì, anch'io. Ma certe volte ... (*pausa*) ... non lo so.

FRANCESCA

Ti ho capito benissimo amica mia! Però, se ci pensi, non ce la siamo passata poi così male qui. Va bene, che l'inverno è bruttissimo qua.

ROSA

Hai ragione. Abbiamo lavorato sodo qui però, il Canada e Subburì ci hanno dato tante possibilità.

FRANCESCA

Eccome se abbiamo lavorato! Notte e giorno ... facendo doppio scìffiti per guadagnare più soldi.

ROSA

Abbiamo lavorato tanto e ci siamo fatti rispettare da tutti.

FRANCESCA

(*scherzando*) Ci siamo fatti rispettare perché siamo brava gente.

> *Le due amiche ridono.*
> *Entra Santina con tante buste in mano.*

SANTINA

Hi ma! Hi signora Battaglia. How are you? *Si baciano sulla guancia*

ROSA

Santina, bella! Sto benissmo. Come ti sei fatta grande e bella! Sarai una bellissima sposa.

FRANCESCA

Ma santo Dio, figlia dove sei andate a finire?

SANTINA

(*togliendo qualcosa da un sacchetto di plastica*) Look, ma, I found the bomboniera you really liked!

FRANCESCA E ROSA

Che bella!

ROSA

Hai visto che tua figlia t'ascolta.

FRANCESCA

Meno male. Almeno questa soddisfazione me l'ha data. (*Guarda l'orologio*) Ma che ora abbiamo fatto?

ROSA

Sono le quattro!

FRANCESCA

Madonna! Dobbiamo partire subito sennò ci perdiamo a "Restiling" oggi!

ROSA

Cominciate ad andare. Vedi (*indicando*) sta arrivando mia figlia.

FRANCESCA

Rosa, non aspettiamo mesi e mesi per vederci. Mi sono così divertita oggi chiacchierando delle nostre famiglie con te.

ROSA

Hai ragione. Perché non andiamo a farci una camminata al bordiuocchi a Lecca Rémisi qualche volta.

FRANCESCA

Perfetto! E poi possiamo anche andare a farci un caffé a Timmi Ortins (*si salutano*).

ROSA

Ciao!

FRANCESCA

Ciao! Ci vediamo al matrimonio!

> *Rosa esce da una parte della scena e Francesca e Santina dalla parte opposta.*

FINE

Glossario

áchi hockey su ghiaccio, *hockey*
aiscúla high school, *liceo*
Alifáchisi Halifax
alliccáre colare, *to leak*
aló pronto, *hello*

annimúnni viaggio di nozze, *honeymoon*

ardatácco *a heart attack*

arrenditáta affittata, *to rent*

attraiáre provare, *to try*

áura la nostra, *our*

bái ciao, *bye*

bassamento scantinato, *the basement*

bátta ma, *but*

battirúmmi bagno, *bathroom*

becca indietro,*take back*

beibí neonato, *the baby*

bicósi perché, *because*

bisiníssi affari, *business*

bóchise scatola, *box*

bói maschietto, *boy*

bordiuócchi lungo mare, *boardwalk*

bosso capo, *the boss*

bottóne pulsante, *button*

braidismédi damigella, *bridesmaid*

bricchi mattoni, *bricks*

bucco libro, *the book* **bússo** corriera, *the bus*

Canada Táire *Canadian Tire*

cánsero cancro, *cancer*

Caprioli *Capreol*

carro macchina, *car*

Caruso Clobbi *Caruso Club*

ceca assegno "paga", *cheque*

checciáppa salsetta, *ketchup*

cheggia *the mining cage*

clobbi associazione, *club*

compestésciona *compensation*

compútero computer, *computer*

costrósciona edilizia, *construction*

cucchíssi biscotti, *the cookies*

dáuna sotto, *down*

daunalodáre scaricare, *to download*

dénni poi, *then*

détti appuntamenti, *dates*

digéi disk jockey, *DJ*

dóra figlia, *daughter*

il dráie *the mining dry*

emergenzíe emergenze, *emergencies*

evribódi tutti quanti, *everybody*

festi/a fare subito, *fast*

ficsare aggiustare, *to fix*

fláuera scioppi fioraio, *flower shop*

flíppa aprire di sopra, *to flip*

fornitura mobilia, *furniture*
floro pavimento, *the floor*
frambúrgher hamburger, *hamburger*
frí gratis, *free*
garbiccio immondizia, *the garbage*
gímmi ginnastica, *gym*
Gió Giuseppe, *Joe*
giobba lavoro, *the job*
gúddi buono, *good*
iárda giardino, *yard*
ítta picchiare, *hit*
iésse sì, *yes*
íffa se, *if*
inglísci inglese, *English*
invitésciona invito, *invitation*
láina linea telefonica, *the telephone line*
lázza tanto, *lots*
Lécchi Rémesi Lago Ramsey, *Lake Ramsey*
lézi pigro, *lazy*
loncio colazione, *the lunch*
maneggére direttore, *the manager*
mangiachecca *a non-Italian person*
manitúli Isola di, *Manitoulin Island*
márchisi voti, *marks*
mascína macchina, *machine*
mécca fare, *to make*
messa disordine, *the mess*
microué forno a micro onde, *microwave*
móla centro commerciale, *mall*
Montreálli città di Montreal, *Montreal*
morgheggio mutuo, *the mortgage*
mostárda senape, *mustard*
Música Uórldi *Music World*
natíing niente, *nothing*
níchi Nicoletta, *Nicky*
nóisa chiasso, *noise*
olauéis sempre, *always*
ólla sala, *hall*
omiuórchi compiti, *homework*
onesténdi capire, *understand*
operéta centralino, *the operator*
ottidóghi wierstel, *hot dogs*
penì centesimo, *penny*
pinebbára burro d'arachide, *peanut butter*
pippa tubo, *the water pipe*
pleióffisi campionato, *playoffs*
plissi per piaceres, *please*

plogáre attaccato al muro, *to plug*

pusciáre spingere, *to push*

pusciata bussata, *a push (helping push)*

repórti cárdi pagella, *report card*

Restiling nome di telenovella, *Young and the Restless*

rídda legge, *read*

ritáira andare in pensione, *retired*

ruffo tetto, *the roof*

sanguiccio panino, *the sandwich*

scáfalo impalcatura, *the scaffold*

scécca casupola, *shack*

sciáuera doccia, *shower*

scíffiti turno, *the shift*

sció programma, *show*

sciopping compere, *shopping*

sciuranza assicurazione, *insurance*

sfizáre sgelare, *defrost*

smarta/i intelligente, *smart*

smella profumare, *to smell*

Smit cognome, *Smith (surname)*

speciale saldi, *a special sale*

spelláre scrivere, *to spell*

spícchi parlare, *speak*

stardare mettere in moto, *to start*

stódi studiare, *to study*

storo negozio, *a store*

Subburí/Suddibúri *Sudbu-ry*

televísiona televisione, *television*

ténca caldaia, *tank*

tíccera maestra/insegnante, *teacher*

Tímmi Órtons *Tim Hortons*

tócca parlerò, *I'll speak*

tóstero tostapane, *toaster*

trocco camion, *the truck*

tubbaifóri misura di legname, *two-by-four*

Uallimarti grande magazzino, *WalMart*

uanna volere *want*

uátta cosa, *what*

uíta con, *with*

uuddibríggi *Woodbridge*

óua árri iú come stai, *How are you?*

sciaráppa sta' zitta, *shut up*

sci no uórca non funziona, *it doesn't work*

sonamabíccia figlio di buona mamma, *son of a bitch*

suítti tébele tavolo dei dolci, *sweet table*

taimenaéffi straordinario)- time and a half

tencaiú grazie, *thank you*

tencsalótto tante grazie, *thanks a lot*
uátta áima dúinga cosa faccio?, *what I'm doing?*
uátta iú mínna che significa)? *what do you mean?*
uátta sciúddi uí du cosa dobbiamo fare? *what should we do?*
uénni uí go ómmi quando andiamo a casa, *when we go home*

Frasi

ai cólla iú bec ti richiamo, *I'll call you back*
áima sóri mi scusi, *I'm sorry*
ariáppa sbrigati, *Hurry up*
aronché non me ne importa, *I don't care*
dazzinóffa basta, *that's enough*
echiscúsimi i scusi, *excuse me*
éveri náiti ogni sera, *every night*
fémili studia *Family Studies*
for sciúri di certo, *for sure*
chénna áia élpi iú? posso aiutare?, *Can I help you?*
gubbai arrivederci/ciao, *good-bye*
gúddi náiti buona sera, *good night*
ísa è, *it's*
lázza móni tanti soldi, *lot's of money*
Míssi Clarchisónni Signorina Clarkson, *Miss Clarkson*
ópena áusa porte aperte, *open house*
uétti nu minuto aspetta un minuto, *wait a minute*
véri gúddi molto bene, *very good*
véri máccia molto, *very much*

MOOSE ON THE LOOSE

**A comedy about an Italian family
and a Canadian moose
2011
Dina Morrone**

"The play falls into the category of idiosyncratic (character driven) humanist comedy. Think George S. Kaufman (*You Can't Take it With You*) and the films of Sicilian born Frank Capra where behavior is the story and every character is given time to be seen, heard and remembered. Whether they stand at the center or the edge of the narrative action, each is important. What they say and how they say it affects all of us."
>   —**Playwright's Production Notes**

Cast of Characters

Moose: A big tall guy, 40's, the eyes and ears of Way Up Bay. (double cast as Chief).

Giuseppe Tappino: Married to Maria; late 50's, father of four, thinks he's the boss, opinionated, frustrated, longs to see his mother in Italy.

Maria Tappino: Married to Giuseppe, late 50's, mother of four, she's the boss and runs the household.

Gina: Daughter, 35, single, big city girl, fashionable, bossy, high-strung, and preferably blonde.

Carmela: Daughter, 34, never left Way Up Bay, simple minded, sweet, and with a sharp contrast in demeanor to her older sister Gina; married to Darryl, her high school sweetheart.

Bruno: Son, 33, couch potato, lives at home, heavy-set, loves to wear plaid printed fleece hunting shirts.

Joseph: Son, 24, studies nursing, clean-cut, wears pressed dress shirts, lives at home.

Rodolfo Pupi: Maria's father, late 70's, slender, a man of few words.

Pina Pupi: Maria's mother, late 70's, slender, bossy and opinionated.

Darryl: Married to Carmela, 35, blonde, soft spoken, quietist guy in the room, lean, probably never picked up a weight at the gym.

Timothy: Darryl and Carmela's 9 year old son.

Honabigi: Bruno's Aboriginal girlfriend, 30's.

Chief: A big tall guy, 40's, a local cop, (double cast as Moose)

*The characters of MOOSE and CHIEF are to be played by the same actor.

Place

Way Up Bay, Ontario, Canada.

Time

Mid morning. Cold and snowy Sunday. November, 1999.

Setting

Inside a small suburban bungalow.

Note: Some characters speak with a very thick Italian accent. Therefore, some dialogue is intentionally written with poor grammar and the misuse of words to reflect the social class of these characters. Some words are written in pure Italian and some in the Calabrese dialect. *Calabria is a region in Southern Italy, near the tip of the boot.

Note: The play falls into the category of idiosyncratic (character- driven) humanist comedy. Think George S. Kaufman ('You Can't Take it With You') and the films of Sicilian born Frank Capra where behavior is the story and every character is given time to be seen, heard and remembered. Whether they stand at the center or the edge of the narrative action, each is important. What they say and how they say it affects all of us.

Note: Although *Moose On The Loose* is a comedy, it is not a farce and should not be performed as such. The characters are not caricatures or gross stereotypes, and should not be interpreted as such. All the characters are based on real Italian/Canadian families living the Italian/Canadian immigrant experience in Canada.

ACT ONE

The Canadian National Anthem begins to play.
At stage right there is a small bush area with snow, shrubs and trees. A very big guy, who goes by the name of MOOSE, walks out of the bush area. He is wearing a tattered brown fur vest, matching fur hat with large moose antlers, sorrel boots, and holding a Molson Canadian beer. The main playing area is comprised of the kitchen and family area. In the kitchen, a large pot of sauce simmers on the stove top while homemade bread bakes in the oven. A dining table and chairs are in the center of this busy kitchen. The window above the sink and the window on the back door are covered with frost. The porch area(raised, with steps and railing)is filled with a collection of winter boots, coats, scarves, old newspapers and junk mail. Next to the kitchen is the family room area with a television set and a small couch. (*note: please do not put plastic on the furniture).
At stage left there is a tiny jail with a desk and chair.
Once the Canadian Anthem has finished playing, MOOSE begins to speak.

MOOSE

Hey. How's it goin' eh? Cold enough for you? *(beat)* Oh, yeah. You can say that again. It's fricken freezin' up here in *Way Up Bay*. But not for me. I got my fur on. Locals nicknamed this desolate blue collar town of about twenty thousand, the *Frozen Tundra* because temps dip as low as minus fifty Celsius and wind chill off the lake ... well, that's just icing on the cake. Now, if you're looking at a map, that's *way up,* because it's *way up,* north-east of Duluth, Minnesota, near

Lake Nipigon … in Canada … on land once mainly populated by the Ojibway. And why was this land once mainly populated by the Ojibway? Because it was *their* land … it still is … kind of. Now you might have heard of their Spirit Nannabush or their Great Spirit Manitou, you know, Lord of everything. *(beat)* Well, if you haven't it's okay. They're both from around these parts and they're always up to something. *(beat)* It's November. That's moose season. And that's why I'm in town. I'm not into hunting. It's not my thing. I come around for a cup of coffee up at the Tim Horton's, a couple a Molson's down at the Lodge … the Moose Lodge … and mingle with the locals, you know, that kinda stuff. *(beat)* Now you may be asking yourself, who the hell lives all the way up here? And, you may also be asking yourself, if *you* had to immigrate, if *you* had to go somewhere else for a better life, why the hell would *you* come here? But instead you name em' we got em' all on the same block: Eye-talians, Poles, Finns, Ukrainians, Slavs, Portuguese, four Jewish people, one black family … the list goes on and on. You get the picture. Oh, and a lot of Scots and Brits. You know what they came here looking for … *beaver. (beat)* Oh come on people, this is a family show. The Ojibway trapped *beaver* and traded it for things the Ojibway needed like sugar, tobacco, blankets, whiskey. Brits shipped *beaver* back to England and turned it into beaver felt for top hats that were all the rage at the time. But fashions change. *Beaver* goes out of style. And that was good news for the *beaver* because there were only a couple of them left anyway. But it was bad news for the Ojibway. By then there were all these other things movin' in, Shipyards, Paper Mills, Grain Elevators. Lot's of work. But not for the Ojibway. For people like the Tappino family for instance who came over in the early 60's, the last real wave of immigration around these parts.

> Lights up as GIUSEPPE enters, followed by MARIA. They make
> their way to the kitchen. JOSEPH enters reading a textbook and
> makes his way to the kitchen table. BRUNO enters holding the
> remote control in one hand and food in the other as he makes his
> way to the couch.

MOOSE (CONT'D)

GIUSEPPE TAPPINO is married to MARIA. They're from Calabria, in Southern Italy. They got four grown kids all born here.

GINA. They wanted a boy, they got Gina. She moved to the big city.

CARMELA. They wanted a boy, they got another girl. She never left Way Up Bay.

BRUNO. Did I say they wanted a boy?

Well, be careful what you wish for. They really wanted a boy, they finally got a boy, and he's the gift that keeps on giving because he never leaves the couch and he's glued to the weather channel. And then there's JOSEPH, oops … let's just say … they weren't expecting him. *(GIUSEPPE exits)* CARMELA'S married to DARRYL, *not* Italian. They got a kid named TIMOTHY. MARIA'S parents, they live here too. There's PINA PUPI, the kids call her Nonna, and RODOLFO PUPI, they call him Nonno, together they are Nonni, and guess what?

The whole family will be here, in this house, for dinner, tonight. Now if you don't mind, I'm gonna go next door and *mingle* with the neighbors.

THE KITCHEN

> *MARIA puts on an apron. She is brewing espresso. GIUSEPPE re-enters buttoning up his shirt. He grabs his winter boots, walks to the table, sits down and begins to put them on. BRUNO sits on the couch holding a remote control in his hand. His eyes are glued to the Weather Channel. His mouth is busy eating. JOSEPH sits at the kitchen table reading a medical textbook.*

V/O WEATHER CHANNEL

Live from the Weather Channel. This is First Outlook. We can expect light flurries in the morning, giving way to blizzard conditions by evening for Way Up Bay and other parts of Northern Ontario including, Dryden, Nipigon, Kapuskasing, Marathon and Pickle Lake. We'll have updates every half hour so keep it here on the Weather Channel.

BRUNO

(*Shouting*) Hey ma. Blizzard.

MARIA

No. Please no today. Gina coming home today.

GIUSEPPE

Maria. Hurry up with my espresso. I gotta go *shovel* snow.

JOSEPH

Shovel? More like sweep.

BRUNO

The storm hasn't even moved in yet. There's barely a centimeter on the ground.

GIUSEPPE

I don't care if is only one millimeter. I like *my* driveway clean ... for *my* truck.

JOSEPH

You drive a four by four.

GIUSEPPE

Never mind what I drive. If I no shovel, who gonna do? No you. No your mother. And no your brother that's for sure.

MARIA

Giuseppe. Just go. And stop talk about it.

GIUSEPPE

What else I'm gonna do? I have to do something.

JOSEPH

You say the same thing every year when you get laid off.

GIUSEPPE

I no want Gina to slip.

MARIA

She gonna have a lot of things.

GIUSEPPE

Why?

MARIA

She no come for just one week.

GIUSEPPE

Why no?

MARIA
I no know.
GIUSEPPE
How long she stay?
MARIA
Maybe one year. I no know.
GIUSEPPE
One year? Where she gonna stay?
MARIA
Her room.
GIUSEPPE
Her room? Is full a junk.
MARIA
No. I clean yesterday.
GIUSEPPE
(Suspicious) Where you put all the junk?
MARIA
In the basement.
GIUSEPPE
Inna the basement? We gotta no more room inna the basement! Pretty soon we gonna have to move out just to make room for all *your* junk.
MARIA
Is no just *my* junk! You got alotta junk too!
GIUSEPPE
No like you. *(beat)* Why you no tell me before about Gina? Why I'm always the last one to know?
JOSEPH
Because you always make a big deal about everything.
MARIA
Bruno girlfriend, she come for dinner tonight too.
GIUSEPPE
Who?
BRUNO
Honabigi. (pronounced Ho-nah-bee-gee)
GIUSEPPE
Hona who who?
BRUNO
Honabigi. My girlfriend.
GIUSEPPE
Bruno got a girlfriend?
MARIA
Giuseppe, he gotta girlfriend.
GIUSEPPE
But why she come tonight?
MARIA
Because I say is okay.

BRUNO

I've been dating her for ten months.

GIUSEPPE

Ten months? Where you hide this girl? In the couch?

BRUNO

Forget it. I'll tell her not to come.

MARIA

No. She come. No listen to you father.

GIUSEPPE

One year? Why so long?

JOSEPH

You should have never told him Gina was staying.

GIUSEPPE

What she gonna do for one year?

MARIA

She gonna do what she gonna do. I don't know.

GIUSEPPE

Someone please explain to me because I still no understand, what kind of work Gina do?

MARIA

How many time I tell you? Mar-ke-ting!

GIUSEPPE

I know Maria, but what's a Mar-ke-ting?

JOSEPH

It's ... well, she *markets* things ...

GIUSEPPE

Forget it. I don't want to know.

MARIA

Then drink you coffee and shut up.

BRUNO

I'm trying to watch TV.

GIUSEPPE

Where did we go wrong? Carmela marry a baccala'. He got nothing to say. Gina, she getting old and she no marry. No children. One day she in Toronto, one day Italy, one day Istanbul. I no even know where she live. Joseph wanna be a nurse and I never see him with a girlfriend. And that one over there, Mr. stuck to the couch, he gotta the girlfriend and I think maybe she's an Indian.

BRUNO

She's not an *Indian*.

GIUSEPPE

She's *no* Italiano!

BRUNO

She's *Aboriginal*.

GIUSEPPE

I don't care if she's *original!* She's no Italiano.

BRUNO

That's it. I'm calling her.

MARIA

No. Giuseppe per favore. One son you no want to meet his girlfriend, the other you push to *find* a girlfriend. Leave the kids alone.

GIUSEPPE

When I was Joseph's age I have twenty, thirty girls all over Italy.

MARIA

When you was Joseph's age *you* was already married. To *me*!

GIUSEPPE

Oh yeah. *(beat) Get* me the Grappa.

MARIA

No. It's too strong.

GIUSEPPE

Maria. One shot.

MARIA

Okay. Just one shot.

GIUSEPPE

One shot in my coffee before I go outside.

> *MARIA places a bottle of homemade Grappa down on the table.*

MARIA

Here. But no let it go straight to you head. We got a lot to do.

BRUNO

Can you guys please keep it down. I'm trying to watch The Weather Channel.

MARIA

> *(yelling to Bruno)*

Why we all the time have to watch this boring show? Put on a funny show.

BRUNO

The Weather Channel's *not* a *show*. It's news.

MARIA

News? What news? I no need to know all the time every five minutes weather is going to be bad. I already *know* it's bad. It's *always* bad.

> *RODOLFO, dressed in slacks, pressed shirt, and a nice cardigan,*
> *and PINA, wearing a dress (hem below her knees), and a sweater,*
> *shuffle in. GIUSEPPE pours a shot of Grappa into his espresso.*

PINA

> *(Italian accent)*

Buon giorno. Hmmm. Coffee smell so good.

GIUSEPPE

Boys, make room for your Nonni.

MARIA

Giuseppe? You no go outside?

GIUSEPPE

A little more coffee first.

RODOLFO

> *(Italian accent)*

Gonna be cold today.

GIUSEPPE

No too cold.

RODOLFO

No. It's gonna be *cold*.

BRUNO

Minus fifteen.

GIUSEPPE

That's no cold.

JOSEPH

For November it is.

GIUSEPPE

When I work on the lake—

MARIA

No remind me when you work on the lake. I never sleep all night.

GIUSEPPE

You worry for nothing.

MARIA

I no worry about *you*. I worry if you drown you leave me a widow.

GIUSEPPE

Maria. Water was frozen.

RODOLFO

Six feet of ice.

GIUSEPPE

I could break my neck. But no drown.

> *GIUSEPPE pours another shot of Grappa.*

GIUSEPPE (CONT'D)

For one week on that boat was minus sixty-two.

JOSEPH

You mean minus sixty-two with wind chill?

GIUSEPPE

Just like Siberia.

JOSEPH

Christmas Eve, the year you were in the hospital Nonna …

PINA

I no remember.

JOSEPH

… that was brutal …

BRUNO

Yeah. It was minus fifty-six.

PINA

I no remember.

GIUSEPPE

But no like minus sixty-two.

BRUNO

If skins exposed for more than twenty seconds at that temperature, it's gonna freeze.

GIUSEPPE

Of course it gonna freeze. But, was *only* minus forty-six with wind when your nonna was in the hospital. I remember.

BRUNO
No. It was minus fifty-six.
GIUSEPPE
Forty-six.
BRUNO
Fifty-six. It was on the *news*.
JOSEPH
Who cares. It was freezing. The car tires felt like blocks of ice. When we got to the hospital two guys hooked up to IV's with hospital gowns open in back were standing outside smoking and coughing like it was the middle of summer . . .
BRUNO
Oh yeah, and remember Gina was trying to reason with them about getting a pneumonia and I told her not to waste her time.
GIUSEPPE
I say nothing important to Canadian people. They just smile and say, I'mma sorry, I'mma sorry. *(beat)* Sorry for what? Because we live here? In this cold. Crazy Canadian.
JOSEPH
Uh . . . Dad? Where do *we* live?
GIUSEPPE
I know where *we* live.
JOSEPH
And so what does that make us?
GIUSEPPE
No. You was born here. You Canadian. Me, I'm Italiano.
JOSEPH
But you became a Canadian—
GIUSEPPE
I became nothing! *(realizes what he said)* I know what I am.
RODOLFO
How a guy can smoke outside in this cold? *(beat)* When I first arrive in this country I go outside train to smoke. It was so cold my lungs hurt. I throw my cigarette on the snow and I never smoke no more. Then something very strange happen to me, in just a few minutes, I begin to grow ghiaccioli—
PINA
Here he go again with the same story. Mamma mia.
BRUNO
What did you grow?
PINA
He grow nothing!
RODOLFO
Ghiaccioli. Maria? How you say in English?
MARIA
Ice-ee-close.
RODOLFO
Yes. Ice-ee-close.

JOSEPH
    You mean *icicles*.
RODOLFO
    That's what I say. Ice-ee-close.
PINA
    He tell this story one hundred time.
JOSEPH
    What story?
PINA
    Nobody wanna hear this story now. Maria got a lot to do.
        MARIA places homemade bread and a bottle of Brandy on the table.
MARIA
    Papa' here's your coffee and a little Brandy.
PINA
            (referring to bottle)
    Put it back!
GIUSEPPE
    Try my Grappa. I make it last week.
            *The phone rings. RODOLFO reaches for Brandy bottle and
            pours himself a shot.*
RODOLFO
    No. Today I drink Brandy.
PINA
    Grappa, Brandy, it's all bad for you.
MARIA
            (answers phone)
    Allo ...? Eva ...?
GIUSEPPE
    Eva? Whadda she want now?
MARIA
    A moose?
            GIUSEPPE is all eyes and ears when he hears the word "moose."
GIUSEPPE
    A moose? Where?
MARIA
    In her back yard.
GIUSEPPE
    Back yard!? Ask if it got the corna?
MARIA
    Giuseppe want to know if the moose gotta the corna?
JOSEPH/BRUNO
    Antlers!
MARIA
    An-te-ler. *(to Giuseppe)* She say yes.
GIUSEPPE
    He's a man. *(beat)* How big?

MARIA

How big what?

GIUSEPPE

How big the corna?

MARIA

How big the an-te-ler? Oh! (to Giuseppe) She say big. (back to phone—listens for a few seconds and then a small gasp) Really?—(*Back to Giuseppe*) She say she go throw garbage outside—

GIUSEPPE

Outside? What she was wearing?

MARIA

(to Giuseppe)

Why you wanna know?

GIUSEPPE

It's important. Ask. Ask.

MARIA

(to Eva)

No. I talk to Giuseppe. He wanna know what you wear when the moose see you? *(to Giuseppe)* She wear a slip.

GIUSEPPE

A slip? To throw away garbage in the minus fifteen. *(beat)* Ask if she wear the perfume?

MARIA

Perfume? Giuseppe, you crazy. She say she turn around, she see the moose, and then she scream.

GIUSEPPE

(mounting excitement)

How she scream?

MARIA

Basta! Giuseppe! You ask too many stupid question! *(to Eva)* I close the phone. I have to cook. Eva, I no know what you should do. Call the Polizia. Okay. Ciao. *(hangs up the phone)*

GIUSEPPE

Shoot it!

MARIA

Her husband is no home to shoot.

GIUSEPPE

Maria, what she say?

MARIA

She say she see the moose and the moose see her and he get really scared and he try to run, but he too big so he *trip* and fall *inside* the camper trailer belong to her husband and now he stuck in there and he look really confuse and really stupid. *(beat)* Next time he no gonna go where he no suppose to go. Now you know everyting she say to me. Okay?

GIUSEPPE

Moose no trip and fall.

MARIA

Maybe he getta dizzy when he see her.

GIUSEPPE

But why you tell her to call the Polizia? What the hell the Polizia gonna do? *Arrest* a moose?

MARIA

I no know what they gonna do. Is no my problem.

> *RODOLFO and PINA look confused. MARIA busies about in the kitchen.*

PINA

What happen?

RODOLFO

I no know. *(beat)* Maria? Cosa? What happen?

MARIA

Bruno. Please explain to your Nonni.

BRUNO

It's nothing. Mamma just told Eva, you know, the nice looking Polish lady that lives down the road by the Pine trees ...

RODOLFO

Oh. Si. The Polacca.

BRUNO

Yeah. The blonde lady.

RODOLFO

With the big ... *(hand gestures large breasts)*

BRUNO

Yeah with the big ...

PINA

> *(smacks Rodolfo)*

What about her?

BRUNO

Well, it's not a big deal. It's just that she saw a moose and mamma told her to call the Polizia so they can come here and arrest all of us and the moose too.

PINA

No!

RODOLFO

What he say?

GIUSEPPE

Bruno! Why you say that?

MARIA

Bruno! That's no what I say! *(beat)* No listen to him.

BRUNO

> *(chuckles)*

I was just joking with you guys.

PINA

You no funny guy, that's a for sure.

GIUSEPPE

I go get my gun.

MARIA
You gun? For what?
GIUSEPPE
The moose.
GIUSEPPE stands up.
MARIA
Giuseppe!
JOSEPH
You can't just make your own rules. You're gonna get arrested.
GIUSEPPE
I break no rules.
MARIA
Giuseppe! Sit down!
GIUSEPPE sits down.
GIUSEPPE
I can catch this moose with one shot.
JOSEPH
As in *kill* it?
GIUSEPPE
No. I invite the moose for a *shot* of Grappa. Of course to kill it.
BRUNO
He's not gonna shoot anything.
GIUSEPPE
He's no suppose to be here. He's in the wrong place.
JOSEPH
You can't shoot a moose inside city limits. That's the law.
GIUSEPPE
What law?
JOSEPH
Dad ... hold on. *(beat)* How would you like it if one night you got lost while driving home?
GIUSEPPE
I don't get lost in Way Up Bay.
JOSEPH
Okay dad, you don't get lost but hear me out ...
GIUSEPPE
I know this place like the bottom of my hand.
JOSEPH
It's the *back* of your hand.
GIUSEPPE
It's *my* hand!
JOSEPH
Okay dad, it's your hand. But lets just say that ...
BRUNO
... say a tree falls on the road ...
JOSEPH
... yeah a tree, and you have to take another route. It happens ... right ...

BRUNO

... and say you get a flat tire ...

JOSEPH

... yeah, you get a flat tire in front of some guys house you don't know and say the guy who lives in the house doesn't know the law and he comes running out and shoots you because you were parked in front of his house. How would you feel?

GIUSEPPE

I feel like this is a stupido story.

JOSEPH

Okay dad. But really, how would you feel?

GIUSEPPE

I feel nothing. I be dead.

JOSEPH

That's my point. You'd be dead.

GIUSEPPE

My papa' was right ... "Is better to raise pigs then to raise children because when a pig getta big and fat you canna kill him, make a sausage and eat it." Whatta you gonna do when you kids getta big and fat and stupido? *(moment, thinks...)* I go getta my gun.

> *RODOLFO reaches for more Brandy and in doing so accidentally knocks over the bottle spilling Brandy onto the crotch area of GIUSEPPE'S pants. (Ad lib reaction)*

MARIA

Giuseppe! Sit down!

RODOLFO

Ahiah la puttana!

PINA

Look at what you do now.

GIUSEPPE

It's nothing. Just a little wet.

PINA

Here Giuseppe. I help you.

> *PINA grabs a tea towel and rubs down GIUSEPPE'S pants. His crotch area is drenched with Brandy.*

PINA

Rodolfo put the bottle away.

> *GIUSEPPE tries to turn away and escape while Pina continues to pat down his went pants. Awkward.*

GIUSEPPE

I'm okay. Okay. I'm okay.

MARIA

Go change you pants.

BRUNO

They're giving an update on that storm.

MARIA

Nobody care about a storm at a time like a this. Gina coming home.

GIUSEPPE

I go clean the driveway.

> *GIUSEPPE sees this as an opportunity to go outside. He scurries to the back door.*

MARIA

Your pants are wet. Cut the salami. Bruno stop watching TV and go clean your room. Joseph stop reading. *(beat)* I gotta do everything around here.

> *GIUSEPPE quickly puts on a cap and jacket.*
> *He opens the door and exits.*

MARIA(CONT'D)

No! Giuseppe! I say No!

PINA

Maria. You gotta *make* your husband listen to you!

> *Police siren. MARIA runs to the window.*

MARIA

Oh Dio mio! What happen now?

PINA

Alla bonura! (dialect—re siren: may it be nothing serious)

BRUNO

I guess Eva took your advice and called the cops.

> *MARIA grabs the Grappa bottle.*

MARIA

What we do now?

JOSEPH

What do you mean what do we do now?

BRUNO

They're not coming *here*.

MARIA

What if they *do*?

BRUNO

Well, we're *not* running a brothel.

JOSEPH

Or killing anybody.

MARIA

Turn off the television and do something.

> *MARIA pours the Grappa down the drain.*

JOSEPH

Papa's gonna go nuts when he finds out you poured his moonshine Grappa down the drain.

MARIA

Is illegal. I no gonna take a chance with the Polizia.

BRUNO

> *(at the thermostat)*

Did someone crank up the heat again?

MARIA

No talk to me about the heat when the Polizia is outside. Every day with this heat. I was cold. I turn it up. Okay.

BRUNO

But now it's like an oven in here.

BRUNO reaches for the knob on the thermostat.

PINA

Bruno! No touch the furnace!

BRUNO

(fanning himself)

But I'm dying.

MARIA

Then go outside to die. I no want to freeze in my own house.

PINA

Maria, all day he sit and he do nothing. That's why he getta too hot and he getta too big. He need to do something!

MARIA

(runs to BRUNO and gently kisses his cheek—mamma's boy)

Mamma . . . leave him alone.

RODOLFO

This morning I wake up so nice. A little coffee. Some Brandy. We talk. A little joke. So nice. Then I no know what the hell happen.

PINA

It's the Brandy.

RODOLFO

No. It's telefono. All the time it ring, is bad news.

JOSEPH

I still can't get over the fact that dad said he wanted to shoot it.

MARIA

He no serious.

JOSEPH

But the fact that he would even think it.

BRUNO

That's the Grappa talking. *(beat)* In all the times I've gone hunting with him he's never fired his rifle. Not once. The thought of killing an animal freaks him out. But he's not gonna admit it to his hunting buddies because . . . you know, he wants to fit in.

MARIA

Bruno right. He never kill a moose. No even a rabbit.

JOSEPH

I don't want to hear about rabbits.

PINA

You eat so many when you was little.

JOSEPH

Only because you tricked me into eating it by calling it the "special meat."

PINA

It taste much better than chicken.

JOSEPH

I'm a vegetarian.

PINA
Gina *was* a *vegetable* too. Then she get an enema and almost loose all her blood.
JOSEPH
Anemia. She had *gynecological* problems.
MARIA/PINA
What kind of problem?
JOSEPH
You know, down there.
MARIA
Down where? *(beat)* Oh. I no wanna know. I'm too busy now.
PINA
Is because she no eat the meat.
JOSEPH
No it's not.
BRUNO
Why do we always end up talking about Gina?
MARIA
Because to talk about you papa' is a waste a time. I don't know why he say the things he say.
JOSEPH
Well, ask him. He *is* your husband.
BRUNO
Yeah. You married him.

> BRUNO and JOSEPH laugh.

MARIA
They make me marry him.
BRUNO
What? *They* tied you to a chair and said *marry him or else?*
MARIA
No.
PINA
What did we do?
JOSEPH
Did you guys force mamma to marry papa'?
PINA
No!
RODOLFO
No!
MARIA
How many time I tell you, before I marry Giuseppe, I want to leave him because I was no sure he was the one for me? And you say no because would be a vergogna if I leave. A disgrace. Me? A disgrace. I was so young. Only eighteen. How I could be a disgrace? *(beat)* When I grow up, *parent* tell *you* what to do an *you* have to listen. Now kids tell parent what to do and parent have to shut up and listen or social worker come, put *you* in jail, and no more kids.
PINA
Was much better in Italy.

JOSEPH

Times change. It's not what it was when you guys left.

PINA

Is the same. Children over there listen.

RODOLFO

Pina. You make no sense. Stuttee cheetu.*(dialect: keep quiet)*

PINA

In my time women was serious. They was women. They act like women. Nobody do ... you know ... da *ting,* before they getta marry. Nobody. Remember Rodolfo? *(da "ting" disgusts her)*

RODOLFO

How I canna forget.

JOSEPH

I find that hard to believe.

RODOLFO

Credemi. Is true. *(believe me)*

PINA

No. Is no *hard.* You find someone. You make a plan. When you say yes, he gonna be the one for the rest of you life. But first you getta marry and *then* you learn *every-ting* you need to know about *every-ting.* No the other way around.

BRUNO

You're trying to tell us no one *did it* before they got married?

PINA

No one!

JOSEPH

Well, maybe *you* didn't but—

PINA

No one!

RODOLFO

No listen to her. First time I try to kiss her she no wanna kiss me because she think she was gonna make-a the baby.

PINA

Rodolfo! From a kiss. Rodolfo!

RODOLFO PINA RODOLFO

You no know what I put up with just to marry her.

PINA

Rodolfo!

MARIA

(blushing)

Mamma? Is this true? About the kiss? I never hear this before.

RODOLFO

My cousin Emilio house ... but I no gonna say no more. Finito.

PINA

Good! Is better for everyone. Non ti vergogni? *(Aren't you ashamed of yourself?)* *(beat)* No one do *da ... **da ting** before they getta marry! They wait. Why? Because if you play with *fire* you gonna getta burn. But now, everyone wanna *burn* because they love the *fire.* Every-*ting* is a schiffo.*(disgusting)*

JOSEPH

No it's not. It's just different.

RODOLFO

I'm a justta say one more thing. You old fashion when I meet you and you old fashion today. You never change.

PINA

Shut-uppa!

RODOLFO

Okay. Okay. I go watch my Italian Soap Opera. *(walks away)*.

PINA

Shave. And put on a clean shirt.

BRUNO

I don't think it's such a bad thing if couples wanna get to know each other *first*.

PINA

You no need to know *nothing first!(beat)* I go. Ciao. Mannaggia l'America. Che schiffo. Stupido.*(continues mumbling)*

　　　　　PINA exits.

MARIA

Boys, all my life I have justa one man … you father. Now I know, one man … *(reflecting) is no enough.* But look at you sister Gina, she change one man every time I talk to her. One in this country, one in that country. One she take, one she leave. Thanks to God you father he no know. Is no right.

JOSEPH

Says who?

MARIA

Me. I can no look Father Riccardo in the face when I take the communion.

BRUNO

Then stop telling him everything.

MARIA

What I'm suppose to talk to him about?

BRUNO

I don't know. Does anyone really need to go to confession? I mean, does the guy really need to know you cursed dad's dead relatives or that your daughter's easy?

MARIA

I never say this!

BRUNO

Why are we even having *this* conversation?

JOSEPH

Yeah. How'd we end up in another *Oprah* moment with mom? *(beat)* I'm going to my room.

　　　　　JOSEPH exits.

MARIA

Make your bed and no read, it make your eyes hurt. That's why you wear the glasses. Bruno, turn off the television and go getta the dish and wine glass downstair.

BRUNO

Gina's better with all that crystal stuff.

MARIA

Oh Dio mio. Gina gonna be home. I go fix my hair.

> *MARIA exits. BRUNO runs to the thermostat. Just as he's about*
> *to turn down the temperature, MARIA peaks her head back*
> *around the corner and smacks his hand. BRUNO goes back to*
> *the couch and turns up the volume on the TV.*

TELEVISION NEWS *(V.O.)*

We interrupt this program for a Way Up Bay news alert. A large moose has wandered out of the bush and made it's way into the back yard near the intersection of Chippewa and Wawa. All residents are being urged to remain indoors. Please, *don't go see the moose eh*. This is all the information we have for now. We'll be sure to pass along any updates as they become available.

> *Sirens. Chihuahua barking.*

GINA (O.S.)

(*yelling at barking chihuahua*)

Go! Shew! Go away! Go! Go home! This is a Prada bag. Go!

> *Front door swings open. GINA enters dragging a designer carry-on*
> *suitcase. Wind and snow blow into the house. She is visibly cold.*
> *Rambles on and on.*

GINA

Thank God the heat's on. It's freezing out there. What is it like minus a hundred?

BRUNO

Minus fifteen.

> *BRUNO doesn't move from the sofa. GINA begins to take off*
> *layers of winter attire while walking around the kitchen/living*
> *room area. She is rambling. It's been a long flight.*

GINA

> *Whatever. I left Rome thirty-two hours ago because of some stupid*
> *pointless strike at Fiumicino. Eight hours we sat in the terminal*
> *only so we could board and sit on the runway for two more hours*
> *while they fixed something. I don't even wanna know what . . .*

BRUNO

Hey sis. How's it goin?

GINA

. . . and there was this couple sitting next to me who reminded me so much of mom and dad because all they did was argue the whole way over, that is when they weren't asking me every twenty minutes how much longer before we landed. Like I was supposed to know. Do I look like an air traffic controller? And when we did land, finally, I missed my both of my connections by about a day, and of course my bags never even made it because fourteen extra hours wasn't enough time for them to get their *shit* together at Fiumicino, and then I got squeezed onto the very last seat of that puddle jumper—and thank God for that or who knows when I would be getting here—and so then of course they had to de-ice the wings, twice, and then it was up and down, and up and down, and up and down all the way to Sault Ste. Marie and then on to Thunder Bay and then onto here. And do you know how many times I threw up? Three! I threw up three times!

BRUNO

>Are you done?

>>*GINA notices the floor around her is wet from the snow on her boots. She walks to door and removes her boots.*

GINA

>Oh my God I forgot to take off my boots. *(beat)* And what the hell's going on out there?

BRUNO

>A moose.

GINA

>Because something's not right. That Ukrainian lady's Chihuahua was barking at me like I was trying to kill it.

BRUNO

>It's a Chihuahua. That's what they do.

GINA

>It's an unhappy dog.

BRUNO

>More rat than dog.

GINA

>Rat. Dog. It's going to be dead if it doesn't get out of the cold. Someone should call the Humane Society and report the owner.

BRUNO

>He likes the cold.

>>*GINA grabs a rag and some paper towels and begins wiping up the wet floor.*

GINA

>Nobody likes the cold. And the taxi had to drop me off at the top of the road at the corner, you know, by that Polish lady's house, because the area's completely blocked off. Did you know the entire area's blocked off? And I had to drag my carry-on, in the snow, all the way here and then no one even bothered to clean off the driveway. And what's with all the cop cars? Did somebody get shot?

BRUNO

>I said, it's a moose.

GINA

>A moose?

BRUNO

>Yeah. A wayward moose.

GINA

>Of course it's a wayward moose. What else could it be all the way up here?

BRUNO

>Get over it Gina. Some of us like it here.

GINA

>I never said I didn't like it here.

BRUNO

>Then what are you bitching about?

GINA

>I'm not bitching about anything. You think I'm bitching? If you wanna see bitching I can show you bitching ...

MARIA (O.S.)
Is that Gina?

BRUNO
Yep.

GINA
(yelling but restrained)
Yes mamma. It's me. I'm home. *(beat)* I'm sorry, Bruno. I'm exhausted. And you're right. I am being a bitch. But I'm happy to be home so let's start over again.
GINA walks over to BRUNO and as he reaches out to give her a hug she half pats his back and keeps on moving.

BRUNO
Yeah. Welcome home, sis. *(beat)* How's that shrink of yours doin'? Seen him lately?

GINA
Bruno. I haven't seen a shrink in years. *(beat)* You never said anything to mom and dad about him? Have you?

BRUNO
No. Why would I do that? Are you *crazy*?

GINA
Well ... good. And don't ever because they would never understand that whole going to the therapist thing.

BRUNO
Okay.

GINA
But do you remember when I first went away to University?

BRUNO
Yeah. I remember.

GINA
Remember the separation anxiety? Well, I went to see *him* and *he* listened to me. Bruno, *he* listened to *me*! *He* actually listened. And then he gave me Adivan ... but I haven't taken that in years and especially not now that I'm ...

BRUNO
That you're what?

GINA
Bruno. I'm pregnant. But please don't say anything. I want to be the first one to tell them—

MARIA
Gina!
GINA runs to her mother. They embrace. GINA nearly collapses in her arms.

GINA
Mamma. I'm so happy to be home. You smell so good.

MARIA
You say hi to you brother?

GINA
Yeah.

MARIA
Bruno? You say hi to you sister?

BRUNO
Uh. Huh.
MARIA
Where you put all your suitcase?
GINA
Long story. They'll be here.
MARIA
There is a moose in Eva yard.
GINA
Yeah, I heard about the wayward moose.
MARIA
You eat?
GINA
No. I'm fine.
MARIA
You want espresso? You so white. You have anemia again?
GINA
I'll have an espresso.
MARIA
You sure you want espresso? Too much coffee make you agitator and you already too agitator.
GINA
Forget it. I shouldn't be drinking espresso. I'll have water.
MARIA
No. I make it for you. I drink some too. Sit down. You like my hair? You sister cut it.
GINA
Yeah. It looks good.
MARIA
No. It look so good. *(beat)* Bruno? Go downstair and get the glass.
BRUNO
It's way too hot in here. *(exits)*
MARIA
I have to do everything.
GINA
So, where's papa'? Outside.
MARIA GINA
I didn't see him outside.
MARIA
Maybe he go inside garage.
GINA
Oh. Well, I didn't see him.
MARIA
Gina? You all right?
GINA
Yes.

MARIA
>   You quit you job?

GINA
>   No.

>   *MARIA picks up a little booklet.*

MARIA
>   Gina look.

GINA
>   What?

>   *MARIA hands GINA the booklet.*

MARIA
>   Look what I find. Tah-less A Da Tome-Tome.

GINA
>   *Tales Of The Tom-Tom.* Oh my God. Where did you find this?

MARIA
>   When I clean inside the closet. *(beat)* Fourteen year old you was when you make me buy you this little book when we go to K-mart. You drive me crazy to buy you this little book. And when you bring it home, you read to everyone and you papa' tell you to shut up but you no listen to him and you keep read. You never listen to no one. *(beat)* Gina, before I forget, you call *Sears* tomorrow.

GINA
>   Sears? What for?

MARIA
>   Dryer she no work again. I tell you papa' so many time to fix it but he no do.

GINA
>   You waited for me to come home so I can call Sears?

MARIA
>   I feel better when you do. I know it gonna get done right.

>   *RODOLFO and PINA shuffle back in.*

RODOLFO
>   Joyah. Bel e' nannoozzu. Joyah. You home. *(dialect: Honey, Nonno's sweet girl)*

GINA
>   Hey Nonna. Nonno ...

>   *GINA kisses her grandparents.*

RODOLFO
>   You looka so nice.

PINA
>   You looka so tired. What's a matter? You no sleep?

GINA
>   I never sleep on airplanes. I have a hard enough time sleeping in my own bed.

RODOLFO
>   Stuttee cheetu. *(dialect: keep quiet)* No listen to her. You looka so nice bel e' nannoozzu. *(beat)* Every time you come home you looka more and more like my mamma and my sister. Your hair. Your blue eyes ...

PINA
>   Your mother. Che brutta. Come un pippistrello. *(ugly like a bat)*

RODOLFO

Blonde. Beautiful. Tall. Just like you Gina.

PINA

Blonde, but not so beautiful.

RODOLFO

No talk about my mamma like that. She dead. Ask Maria?

MARIA

Yes. She dead.

RODOLFO

No! What's a matter for you? *How she look?*

MARIA

She look ... you right. Gina look like your mamma. When I was little I always wish I look like her.

PINA

You look like *my* father.

MARIA

Thank you mamma.

GINA

Nonno have a seat. You want an espresso?

MARIA

Gina gonna stay one year.

PINA

One year?

RODOLFO

One year? You go crazy here.

PINA

You quit your job? No.

GINA MARIA

No. She no quit her job.

PINA

Then why she stay?

RODOLFO

> *(infuriated)*

Ma che vuoi sapere? *(Why do you need to know?)* She stay because she wanna stay!

PINA

Ma va fan ... go put on a clean shirt!

RODOLFO

This a clean shirt. *(examines his shirt)*

PINA

Then put on another one.

> *RODOLFO ignores PINA.*

RODOLFO

Leave me alone. *(beat)* Gina, how you trip? Plane is good?

GINA

No. Thirty two hours.

RODOLFO

When I come it take thirteen days.

GINA

Thirteen days? I would have thrown up all the way here. I can't believe that of all the places in the world ... you guys picked the furthest place to settle.

PINA

We no pick nothing.

RODOLFO

When I first come to this country for work ...

PINA smacks him in the arm.

PINA

You tell this story one million time.

RODOLFO

(Mumbles to PINA) (beat) Gina? Tell me ... your life is good?

GINA

Yes nonno. It's all good.

RODOLFO

You like your job?

GINA

I love my job.

RODOLFO

Good. This is what I like to hear.*(beat)* Gina, listen to me. Enjoy your life now, you young. After you marry, it's like *Inferno di Dante.*

PINA

Don't encourage her. (*smacks RODOLFO again*)

Phone rings. MARIA makes her way to the phone.

RODOLFO

Okay. Okay. I go watcha my show. Ciao Gina.

RODOLFO exits.

MARIA

(into phone)

Carmela? Where you are? Yes. Gina here. No. Street is closed.

GINA

Tell her she's going to have to park at the corner and walk.

MARIA

Park at corner. And hurry up. *(phone rings again)* Allo.

THE YARD

Sirens, chatter and Police radio.

MOOSE

The thing about this place is, whereever you come from, whatever you're speakin' when you get off that train is what you're speakin' when you die.

MOOSE looks over his shoulder and notices GIUSEPPE holding a hunting rifle and poking his head around the corner of a large tree. MOOSE ignores GIUSEPPE and keeps on speaking.

MOOSE (CONT'D)

It's like you're tongue get's *frozen* in time. It's the isolation. The weather. All that being indoors. Keepin' with your own kind. You know, life takes over and the next thing you know thirty years go by just like that and you're still not speakin' English too good.

> *MOOSE looks back at GIUSEPPE, who has now moved even closer.*

MOOSE (CONT'D)

And for the kids born here, to these people, they sure got their work cut out for them because it's a whole lotta communication breakdown goin' on.

> *MOOSE turns to GIUSEPPE who is now standing mere inches away*
> *from him. GIUSEPPE'S gun is pointed at the MOOSE'S chest.*

MOOSE

What do you think you're gonna do with that thing?

GIUSEPPE

Whadda you *tink?*

MOOSE

I don't *tink* that's such a good idea.

GIUSEPPE

No. Is good.

MOOSE

No. *Is* not.

GIUSEPPE

Why no?

MOOSE

Because if you shoot, you're gonna go to jail.

GIUSEPPE

You lucky Eva husband no home, first he shoot then he talk.

MOOSE

I think you should put that thing away.

GIUSEPPE

I want to show my famiglia I can kill one.

MOOSE

Moose Technicians are on their way.

GIUSEPPE

They know nothing.

MOOSE

It's their job.

GIUSEPPE

Gonna die anyway.

MOOSE

No. They use a tranquilizer gun.

GIUSEPPE

Even with a tranquileezer.

MOOSE

No.

> *GIUSEPPE continues to hold up rifle.*

GIUSEPPE
Yes. One time a small baby bear, no so big, was in my friend Lino back yard.
Technician people shoot him with too much drug and he die.

MOOSE
No.

GIUSEPPE
Yes! I explain. After they shoot with the drug they take you back to the bush
where you suppose to be. But when you wake up you say "What the hell happen
to me?" And you go look for some food. But is hunting season now. So, when
you go look for food, me and some guy, we go look to catch *you* and bring you
back here where *you* are right now. Capisce? We cut *you* up nice, split *you* meat
mezza mezza, and we save a lot a money.

MOOSE
Money? Oh come on. This is about money?

GIUSEPPE
For sure. *(beat)* All these people. Fireman. Police. Moose Technician. For one
moose. Cost a lot of taxpayer money. And who gonna pay? Me. People like me.
And what do *we* get? *We* don't even get the meat.

> GIUSEPPE *walks away.* MOOSE *watches him as he goes on his*
> *rant.*

GIUSEPPE (CONT'D)
I have to eat. I have to feed my famiglia. I have to buy the boot and the shoes
and pay my house and the heat and light and water and the truck, gasoline, new
window, new roof, new floor, and now I no even work. No construction work in
the winter. When I do work Government say to me, "Hey you! You gotta pay
this tax bill too." Vafanculo! In this country I pay so many tax I have no money
left for me. *(beat) (his anger turns to reflection and longing)* I leave my mamma in
Italy to come here to make money. I no wanna leave my mamma but I have to
make money. But when you get money you get the bills and now I gotta no
money so who gonna pay the bills?

> GIUSEPPE *finds a stump. Sits. Defeated.* MOOSE *turns*
> *around and quietly exits.*

GIUSEPPE (CONT'D)
I dream to work hard, make some money and move back to Italy to be with my
mamma. But no, what do I get? Bills! What kind of man I am if I cannot take
care of my famiglia?

THE KITCHEN

> MARIA *is on the phone.* GINA *is seated at the table.* PINA *is cooking.*

MARIA
… A moose! No. No fire. They close my street for a moose! Maybe he got no
place to go so he come here. I don't know. He gonna do what he gonna do. He's
a moose! No. No. You no bother me. *(looks at phone receiver)* Oh. She hang up.
> MARIA *hangs up.*

GINA

Ma. You really should take it off the hook.

PINA

Maria, listen to Gina. Leave this moose alone.

GINA

Yeah leave it alone. All this moose talk. It's like the twentieth phone call. Pretty soon even our relatives from Italy are going to be calling to see how the moose is doing. Ma, just take it off.

MARIA

No. I never take it off! What if it's an emergency? *(phone rings again)* Allo.

THE BACKYARD

GIUSEPPE

I no need to kill this moose. What he do to me? He just in the wrong place. Just like me. Tomorrow I wake up and I go look for a job.

> GIUSEPPE *stands up and begins to walk away. MOOSE is now dressed as CHIEF OF POLICE; referred to as CHIEF.*

CHIEF

Sir?

> GIUSEPPE *doesn't hear him.*

CHIEF (CONT'D)

Sir? Can I have a *word* with you?

GIUSEPPE

> *(looks up, startled)*

Oh. Hello.

CHIEF

We need to talk.

GIUSEPPE

My English no too good.

CHIEF

It's not so bad.

GIUSEPPE

No so good.

CHIEF

W h a t—is—your—name?

GIUSEPPE

Tappino.

CHIEF

How about we try this, Mr. Tappino. *(slower)* Hand—me—the—rifle.

> GIUSEPPE *looks at the rifle, then quickly hands it over to CHIEF.*

GIUSEPPE

Here. Take. I was no gonna use.

CHIEF

You know it's against the law to carry a hunting rifle within *city* limits?

GIUSEPPE

    City?! This is no *city*. Rome! Now that's a *city*!

CHIEF

    Were you intending to *kill* the moose?

GIUSEPPE

    No. No! You crazy. I just look. I ... protect my property.

CHIEF

    It's not your property, sir. It's a back lane. And it's city property.

GIUSEPPE

    I pay my tax.

CHIEF

    It's still against the law.

GIUSEPPE

    (nervous ramble)

    I no understand what you try to say to me. You let me call my children. If my children come, they explain to me what you try to explain to me. I call Joseph. He want to be a nurse. A man who want to be a nurse. That's a job for a woman. I call Gina, my daughter, she work in a market. I don't know what this market is but I think is a job for a man, I call—

CHIEF

    Here. Make the call. *(hands him a large old model cell phone)*

GIUSEPPE

    Bruno ... he go to University to study History and then he quit. *(he tries figure out how to use the phone)*

CHIEF

    Make the call.

GIUSEPPE

    I say to him, why you wanna waste my money to study History? Why study something that happen one thousand year ago? Study something that *never* happen. Like you. Everyday you study things that never happen. Be a Police. *(beat)* It's busy. That's what I say to him. If you want to study things that never happen, be a police. *(beat)* Busy. *(hands CHIEF the phone)*

CHIEF

    (sniffing, then) Have you been drinking?

GIUSEPPE

    No.

    The CHIEF continues to sniff.

CHIEF

    You sure you haven't been drinking?

GIUSEPPE

    No. Just some ... espresso.

CHIEF

    That's not what I'm smelling.

GIUSEPPE

    Oh? *(then he remembers the Brandy bottle spill)* Oh. Oh yes. I wet my pants. Right here. Feel.

    GIUSEPPE touches the wet crotch area.

CHIEF
Pardon me?

GIUSEPPE
Right here. Feel. *(beat)* My father-in-law, he spill Brandy.

CHIEF
Mr. Tappino! Let's talk about *this* down at the station.
The CHIEF leads GIUSEPPE to the jail at stage left.

GIUSEPPE
Okay. *(beat)* My wife, she gonna kill me!

THE KITCHEN

MARIA is on the phone.

MARIA
Carmela? Yes was busy. I talk. Okay. *(beat)* Where you are..? *(to Gina)* Good thing I no take it off. *(into phone)* No. I talk with you sister. She always tell me what to do. *(beat)* What? What do you mean Darryl don't know where to park?

PINA
Her husband is no good for nothing.

MARIA
Tell Darryl to park and no be scared. Hurry up. Ciao.
MARIA hangs up the phone.

PINA
Maria. We have to cook.

GINA
I'm buying you guys an answering machine.

PINA
No throw you money away.
Phone rings again.

MARIA
Joseph already try to buy one but you father say was garbage and bring it back to Sears. *(beat)* Maybe is Carmela again. *(MARIA answers)* Hello. Oh. Luisa? You hear about the moose …? No. Then why you call …? A what …? A divorce! No. No too busy. So, she get a divorce? But why? She have a nice house. They should stay together for the kids …

THE JAIL

CHIEF examines GIUSEPPE'S ID. GIUSEPPE holds receiver to ear.

GIUSEPPE
Busy! Still busy! At my house all the time it's busy.

CHIEF

    Maybe it's off the hook.

GIUSEPPE

    No. My wife she never *take it off.* She's a talky talk, She talk so much my head hurt. My mother-in-law she's a talky talk. My daughter ... a talky talk. My Polacca neighbor, she's a talky talk. *(beat)* You married?

CHIEF

    Oh no.

GIUSEPPE

    Then you don't know my misery. If I do it all over again, I only marry a woman who don't talk.

THE KITCHEN

MARIA

    Luisa we talka tomorrow ... Luisa. Luisa! Luisa!! I gotta cook or we no eat tonight. Okay. *(hangs up phone)* Ciao.

PINA

    Maria. Adesso basta or no one gonna eat tonight.

MARIA

    Okay. Okay. Mamma. I listen to Gina. I take it off.
        MARIA takes the phone OFF the cradle.

THE JAIL

CHIEF

    Mr. Tappino, when was the last time you drove your truck?

GIUSEPPE

    Every day. I'm laid off. I go out.

CHIEF

    Your driver's license expired.

GIUSEPPE

    Expire?

CHIEF

    Six months ago.

GIUSEPPE

    Six month ago? Can not be. Let me see.
        CHIEF flashes the license to GIUSEPPE. GIUSEPPE sees the expired date.

GIUSEPPE (CONT'D)

    Son a ma gun. You right.

CHIEF

    Wait here. Now I'm gonna have to run you through the system.
        CHIEF exits.

THE KITCHEN

MARIA
Ivana daughter, she get a divorce.

GINA
I'm not surprised. The guy she married, I knew him back in highschool, and he was such a jerk.

MARIA
Maybe he no a good guy but at least she *got* someone.

PINA
You too picky. How you can find someone? You travel too much.

GINA
I'm not too picky. I just don't want to end up with something that I don't really want. That's all.

PINA
Then you gonna end up with nothing. *(beat)* You no getting no younger. Look at you face. You look so tired.

> *GINA can't listen to this. She exits.*

PINA (CONT'D)
How long you think you can look young? Look at me. One time I look justa like you.

> *Back door swings open. CARMELA, sweet and cheery,*
> *TIMOTHY bright and energetic, DARRYL, soft spoken and*
> *calm no matter what level of Italian family dysfunction and*
> *hysteria surrounds him, enter bundled up in winter gear.*

TIMOTHY
Nanna! Nanna! We're here.

MARIA
Teem-o-tee. Bello. Come kiss Nanna. Oh you so cute.

CARMELA
Sorry we're late. We finally made it, eh. Only after Darryl drove around and around all over the city. I told him to park where you said but he insisted on waiting it out.

DARRYL
I'm sorry. Your street was blocked off.

> *GINA enters.*

GINA
Carmela!

CARMELA
Gina. You're home.

> *GINA and CARMELA embrace.*

GINA
Carmela. You look so good with your hair up like this.

CARMELA
You look good too. *(beat)* Timothy? You see your Auntie Gina? Aren't you excited?

TIMOTHY
Hey Auntie Gina.

> *GINA squeezes TIMOTHY tightly.*

GINA

Timothy. You've grown so much since the last time I was home. Carm, he's really gotten big.

CARMELA

I know. He's gonna take after his dad. Darryl? You see my sister?

GINA gives DARRYL a half embrace.

DARRYL

Oh hi Gina.

GINA

Hey Darryl.

CARMELA

Tim, give dad your jacket.

DARRYL

I got it.

GINA

Carmela. Your boots.

TIMOTHY

I saw ...

CARMELA

Oh, let me show you what I baked. Here. *(handing over baking)* The marshmallow squares didn't get hard. I don't know what I did wrong. Maybe too much butter. And the Nanaimo Squares fell on the floor. It was a mess. Mamma, your bread smells so good. Everything you cook is so delicious. Right Darryl? My family hates my cooking.*(beat) Gina,* I'm so glad you're here.

GINA grabs a rag and begins to wipe up the wet floor from Carmela's boots.

GINA

I'm so happy to be here. Carmela, take off your boots.

TIMOTHY

I saw Nonno.

MARIA

You see Nonno? Oh you so cute. Eat some bread.

CARMELA

It wasn't him.

TIMOTHY

He was waving to me. From a police car.

CARMELA

I told you it wasn't him. Now say hi to your Nonni.

TIMOTHY

Hi Nonni. *(beat)* But it was. He was waving to me. From a police car.

PINA

Ciao. Piccolo.

RODOLFO enters. Walks past DARRYL.

RODOLFO

Ciao. Piccolo.

CARMELA
Darryl? You say hi to my grandparents?
DARRYL
Ciao.
PINA
Ciao.
RODOLFO
Ciao.
CARMELA
Hi Nonni. *(beat)* Gina I brought some pictures from our trip to Duluth. We had a great time. Right Darryl?
GINA
You brought pictures?
BRUNO and JOSEPH enter.
CARMELA
Timothy. Your uncles.
JOSEPH
Hey Tim. How's it going?
TIMOTHY
Hi uncle Joe.
BRUNO
Hey buddy, give me five. Good game last night.
TIMOTHY
Yeah. My first hat trick. That was pretty awesome.
BRUNO
Yeah. You were awesome.
CARMELA
Hi guys.*(beat)* Darryl? You say hi to my brothers?
GINA
The pictures.
DARRYL
Hey.
JOSEPH/BRUNO
Hey.
MARIA
Teem-o-tee eat some bread.
CARMELA
Darryl, you say hi to my brothers?
JOSEPH
Yeah Carm, we already said hi.
GINA'S exhausted and sits.
GINA
Carmela … the pictures.
CARMELA
Oh yeah, the pictures.
EVERYONE grabs a chair and sits, DARRYL is left standing looking for a place to sit. No chair. No place to sit.

CARMELA (CONT'D)
Darryl, you've already seen these. Why don't you straighten up the boots in the porch. You know how much my dad likes it when you straighten up the boots. He's always going on about what a good job you do. Right ma?

THE JAIL

> CHIEF has returned and is seated across from GIUSEPPE.
> With the passing of time, CHEIF and GIUSEPPE have opened up to each other.

GIUSEPPE
That baccala! Darryl! My son-in-law. His fault. Son-a-ma- beech! He say he gonna do and mail it. I say no to him. I don't want his help but Carmela start with me and she ask why I never let him help me. So, I ask him one time to help me. The only *ting* I ask him to do and he screw it up.
CHIEF
It could've gotten lost in the mail.
GIUSEPPE
No. *(beat)* How many time I tell my children to marry Italian people. No because I like Italian people or because I am Italian, but because it's easier to understand someone from my your own culture. *(slowly as if speaking to a child)*
M-o-g-l-i-e e b-u-o-i d-a-i p-a-e-s-i t-u-o-i.
CHIEF
Pardon me?
GIUSEPPE
Wives and bulls from you own town.
CHIEF
I don't know what that means.
GIUSEPPE
Hard to translate. *(beat)* I try to explain. *(beat)* If you want to marry a good woman, or you want to find a good bull to make the sexy with you cow, to make a good baby cow, then you must find one from *you* own village, because then you can trust that he is a good bull with the good meat and that his sperm is good so *you* cow canna make a good, strong, healthy, baby cow with good meat. *(beat)* Same thing goes for a wife.
CHIEF
Oh.
GIUSEPPE
She must be from *your* village. Your culture. Then you know the meat is good.
CHIEF
                    (really confused)
Okay …
GIUSEPPE
My daughter Carmela, she marry Darryl. He Canadian. We Italian. He no speak Italian. We no speak English too good. He eat a lot a cake. We eat alotta pasta.

We different. But Carmela, she try so hard to be more like him, like a Canadian. And you know what she do? She give to my only grandson an English name I can no even say.

CHIEF

What's his name?

GIUSEPPE

I can no say.

CHIEF

Then what do you call him?

GIUSEPPE

I don't know. *(beat)* Teem. Teemah. Teematee. Some *teeng* like that.

CHIEF

Timothy?

GIUSEPPE

Yes. That's the name.

CHIEF

It's the T-H sound. I know. It's a little difficult for some foreigners. I can help you with that.

GIUSEPPE

No.

CHIEF

Ah, come on.

GIUSEPPE

No.

CHIEF

You can do it. Just slide your tongue under your teeth. Like this. *(demonstrates)* It's like you're trying to clean your tongue with your teeth. Come on try ... TH—

　　　　　Overlapping while he tries to do it.

GIUSEPPE

TTT ... No. I can no do.

CHIEF

Try TH ...

GIUSEPPE

TTTTT

CHIEF

You can do it. TH ...

　　　　　GIUSEPPE is frustrated. He can't do it.

GIUSEPPE

TTT

CHIEF

THHHHHHH

GIUSEPPE

　　　　　(gives up)

How I can enjoy my grandchildren if I can no say his name? I go watch his hockey game and when he make-a the goal I say "Go Teem." Everyone tink I scream for the whole *team* but I just scream for Teem. You understand?

THE KITCHEN

DARRYL has come upon a stack of junk mail by the front door. In the middle of all the junk mail he has found one envelope that is addressed to GIUSEPPE and it looks important. He brings it to CARMELA.

MARIA
Carmela, tell your husband to stop clean the porch.
CARMELA
Darryl. Leave it.
DARRYL
I found this in that pile of papers.
MARIA
Is nothing. Just junk mail. We throw away tomorrow.
DARRYL
Uh. No. I don't think it's junk. It's addressed to Giuseppe from the Ministry of Transportation and it's dated June 18.
CARMELA
Darryl, just put it up on the fridge. Okay.
DARRYL
But, I think it's his renewed licence.
PINA
Tell him to sit down. He making me nervous.
        DARRYL places the envelope on top of the refrigerator.
CARMELA
Darryl. *(beat)* So, there's a moose out there?
BRUNO/GINA/RODOLFO
Eva's yard. / The Polish Lady. / Polacca house.
TIMOTHY
Can I go see the moose?
DARRYL
Sure.
CARMELA
No.
DARRYL
I think it would be all right.
TIMOTHY
Please?
CARMELA
No. You don't want to get your clothes dirty. Darryl? You feel like doing something about the kids?
DARRYL
        (almost flat, without emotion)
Settle down.
TIMOTHY
I'm settled. *(beat)* Hey auntie Gina will you come watch my game on Tuesday night?

BRUNO

I don't think so …

GINA

Bruno …

CARMELA

What's that supposed to mean?

BRUNO

Nothing. I just I think she's gonna freeze in there.

JOSEPH

He's right Gina. It's brutal.

TIMOTHY

It's a hockey arena. It's supposed to be cold.

JOSEPH

I can see my breath coming out of my mouth.

GINA

Yeah. Darryl shakes like a small dog. Right, Darryl? Why don't you guys mind your own business. I'll do what I want to do. Don't listen to them. Honey, I'll be there and I'll video tape it too.

TIMOTHY

You can come with Nonno.

CARMELA

Oh yeah, dad doesn't miss a game.

TIMOTHY

He really get's into it and yells at every kid on *both* teams.

BRUNO

I'm surprised he's never been kicked out.

CARMELA

Yeah. Tim's team will be losing and … Darryl, you tell them. Dad will be like … Darryl you should do it?

DARRYL

No.

CARMELA

Oh come on Darryl. Do the impression.

DARRYL

No.

TIMOTHY

Come on dad. Do the impression of Nonno.

DARRYL

(*flat, without emotion*)

No. Not now.

CARMELA

Oh come on Darryl.

TIMOTHY

Dad? Do it.

JOSEPH

Yeah Darryl. Do it.

TIMOTHY

Dad. Please.

DARRYL

I don't want Giuseppe to get mad at me.

GINA

He's outside. Just do it.

DARRYL

But what if he walks in while I'm doing it?

MARIA

No. He no gonna come inside. He busy someplace.

BRUNO

Do it.

CARMELA

Darryl. Just do it. He's hilarious when he does it.

TIMOTHY

Dad. Come on do it.

> *EVERYONE encourages him to do it.*

CARMELA

Darryl! Just do it.

DARRYL

Okay. Okay …

> *DARRYL stands up and sheepishly, then he begins to imitate GIUSEPPE. He doesn't sound anything like GIUSEPPE, but he thinks he does. He really gets into and enjoys being the center of attention.*

DARRYL (CONT'D)

"Number 8! Number 8! Take number 8 off! He can no skate. Trow him away. He so bad. He so bad, he no even good for the garbage can. Trow him away!"

> *CARMELA and TIMOTHY think he's funny. EVERYONE else is not impressed. Some politely smile. Look away. DARRYL sits down.*

DARRYL (CONT'D)

I'm sorry.

CARMELA

Darryl. You're so funny.

PINA

Funny for nothing.

JOSEPH

The kids' parents will be sitting two rows behind dad …

BRUNO

That's why I always sit as far away from him as possible.

JOSEPH

Thirty times a game I have to tell him to put a muzzle on it. And I have to keep reminding him that he's not at home watching hockey on TV.

TIMOTHY

Yeah. I can hear him on the ice and it's like so embarrassing. Some of the kids will be like, *what's he saying?* Unless they're Italian and then they'll just start laughing.

GINA

That is funny. *(beat)* Tim? You want something to drink?

TIMOTHY

No thanks.

GINA

Carm? You guys want an espresso?

CARMELA

Sure. I'll have one. *(beat)* So, you were in Rome, eh?

GINA

Don't remind me. Thirty-two hours. Darryl, you should take my sister to Rome one of these days. Go on a romantic vacation. *(beat)* I'm sorry, Darryl did you say you wanted an espresso?

DARRYL

No. A cup of hot tea please.

PINA

>   *(under her breath)*

What kind a man drink tea?

CARMELA

I heard that.

PINA

I just say he is *no* a man if he drink tea.

CARMELA

Nonna! Darryl is every bit a man. *(beat)* Darryl. Tell her yourself.

>   *DARRYL tries to speak but he can't get a word in.*

PINA

You can no bring him to Rome if he gonna ask for tea. He make you make a brutta figura. Better to leave him here.

>   *TIMOTHY sees that the receiver of the phone is off the hook.*

TIMOTHY

Nanna, your phone's off the hook.

>   *MARIA is too busy to really hear what TIMOTHY is saying.*

MARIA

That's okay.

TIMOTHY

I'll put it back.

MARIA

Oh you so cute. Here. Eat some bread.

>   *TIMOTHY puts the receiver back on the cradle. The phone immediately rings.*

CARMELA

Ma. Don't give him anymore bread. Darryl.

MARIA

Leave him alone.

>   *TIMOTHY answers.*

TIMOTHY

Hello?

THE JAIL

> *GIUSEPPE has made a connection.*

GIUSEPPE
> *(hysterical into phone)*

Teem!

TIMOTHY

Nonno? Is that you?

GIUSEPPE
> *(to CHIEF)*

Somebody answer my phone.

MARIA

Nonno?!

GIUSEPPE

Teeeem

> *TIMOTHY is now the center of attention.*
> **The following scene plays across the space between the kitchen*
> *and the jail.*

TIMOTHY
> *(shouting into phone)*

Nonno? What's wrong with you?

MARIA

Why is Nonno calling?

GIUSEPPE
> *(shouting into phone)*

Teeeeeeem!

TIMOTHY
> *(shouting into phone)*

I can't understand you.

CARMELA

Give your Nanna the phone.

CHIEF

Tell—them—you're—in—jail.

GIUSEPPE
> *(shouting into phone)*

I'm inna da jail.

TIMOTHY
> *(shouting and imitating his Nonno's accent)*

He's inna da jail.

GIUSEPPE
> *(louder, more emphasis)*

Inna da jail!

TIMOTHY
> *(louder, more emphasis)*

Inna da jail!

MARIA
 What is he doing inna da jail!?
TIMOTHY
            (shouting into phone)
 Whaddu you doing inna da jail?
            MARIA yanks the phone from TIMOTHY.
MARIA
 Giuseppe!!?
GIUSEPPE
 Maria! *(then to CHEIF)* It's my wife. Now she gonna kill me.
            CARMELA smacks TIMOTHY on his behind.
TIMOTHY
 Ouch! Why did you hit me?
MARIA
            (frantic)
 Giuseppe!
GIUSEPPE
 Maria. I'm inna da jail!
MARIA
            (turning to everyone)
 He's inna da jail.
TIMOTHY
            (shouting)
 I told you he was *inna da jail.*
            CARMELA smacks TIMOTHY again.
TIMOTHY
 Ouch!
GIUSEPPE
 Maria, you come here now!
MARIA
 Giuseppe! You no talk to me like-a that or you gonna walk home!
            MARIA slams down the phone. Everyone
            is stunned.
GINA
 Wait!
TIMOTHY
 I told you I saw him in the Police car.
CARMELA
 See Darryl, he was right. Why didn't you believe him?
DARRYL
 I believed him.
            MARIA is frozen in shock.
MARIA
 Everybody get in the car now!
            DARRYL takes orders and moves for his and TIMOTHY'S
            coats.

DARRYL

In the car.

CARMELA

I'm not going to a smelly jail.

MARIA

Giuseppe need us now!

BRUNO

All of us?

MARIA

All of us! We need to go now!

BRUNO

Okay. Okay. Then go get ready if we have to go.

GINA

(hysterical)

I just got home!

> *GINA turns off the stove. PINA scrambles to tidy up. MARIA
> barks out orders from the porch landing while BRUNO helps her
> to get dressed.*
> *EVERYONE begins to put on winter gear. JOSEPH helps his
> grandparents. Mayhem.*

MARIA

Cutlets, insalata, rapini need to be wash …

BRUNO

Ma. You wanna go or no go?

MARIA

I got so much to do.

GINA

Then don't go.

MARIA

Okay. I go. *(beat)* Joseph, go downstair and getta the deer sauseege in the freezer.

JOSEPH

No. I'm not touching deer sausage.

TIMOTHY

Bambi. I'm not eating bambi.

CARMELA

Timothy. Darryl!

DARRYL

No ones going to force you to eat a baby deer.

MARIA

I promise Giuseppe I make-a the deer for him and now he's inna da jail. Assunta gonna deliver flowers and new table cloth …

BRUNO

She'll leave them at the door. Get your coat.

PINA

Flowers freeze.

BRUNO
Then I'll stay home.

MARIA
No. You the only one who know how to drive you father truck.

GINA
Don't look at me. I don't know how to drive a stick.

CARMELA
Darryl? Do you?

DARRYL
(calmly)
Yeah. I know how to drive a stick.

PINA
Of course he don't know. He don't know nothing!

MARIA
Darryl. Put the milk in the fridge. Let's go.

CARMELA
Darryl. Put the milk in the fridge. Where are Tim's mittens?
Door bell rings. MARIA and PINA panic.
As everyone scrambles to finish getting ready.

MARIA
The door!

PINA
Dio mio. The door.

MARIA
Bruno. Open the door. (fearing for her life)
BRUNO walks to the door. EVERYONE watches him as he
opens the door.

BRUNO
It's Honabigi!
HONABIGI, BRUNO'S girlfriend enters. Everyone except
JOSEPH and MARIA don't even know that BRUNO has a
girlfriend. It's the first time any of them see her.

HONABIGI
Ciao.
No one knows who she is or what to say.

PINA
Who's that?

BRUNO
Honabigi. (beat) My girlfriend.

PINA
Bruno got a girlfriend?

HONABIGI
I heard about the moose.

PINA
(really confused)
When he find a girlfriend?

HONABIGI

I got a little worried so I came early.

MARIA looks her over.

MARIA

Nice to meet you. We gotta go.

BRUNO

Yeah. We gotta go. You're gonna have to come with us to jail.

HONABIGI

Jail? What for?

Mayhem stops when EVERYONE realizes they don't [know] why they're going to jail.

EVERYONE

Yeah. What for?

TIMOTHY

Nanna? Why **is** Nonno inna the jail?

MARIA pauses. Looks at phone. Then back at EVERYONE. She doesn't know the answer.

MARIA

I don't know. He no tell me! We gotta go!

Back to mayhem as EVERYONE scrambles to get ready to leave.

GINA

Why didn't you just ask him?

MARIA

Hurry up. He tell us when we get there.

JOSEPH

I'm taking my own car.

MARIA

I go with Bruno. (begins to exit)

EVERYONE including MARIA frantically begins filing out. The wind is blowing the snow in. It's a cold draft.

JOSEPH

Nonna, Nonno, you guys come with me.

MARIA comes back to the door. Meanwhile, off stage, EVERYONE ad libs: "I'm freezing, watch your step. It's slippery. You come with me, etc." JOSEPH is frantically trying to help RODOLFO and pushing him along because he is moving slowly. RODOLFO exits.

MARIA

Joseph make sure all the light is turn *off* or you papa gonna get really mad.

JOSEPH

He's in jail. I don't think he cares about the lights.

MARIA

Oh yes he do. He like the lights *off*! All the time he complain about the light bill …

JOSEPH

Okay. Ma. I'll turn them off! Just go!

> *As JOSEPH goes to turn off the lights and close the door,*
> *RODOLFO returns to retrieve his hat, which is hanging on the*
> *hook by the door. He grabs it and puts it on his head.*

RODOLFO

This morning, I wake uppa so nice. Then I don't know what the hell happen!

> *They exit. Black door closes.*

BLACKOUT

END OF ACT ONE

ACT TWO

∽

A POLICE STATION WAITING AREA

> *Lights up to reveal that EVERYONE is crammed into this tiny space.*
> *Some are seated on the two small benches (formed in an L-shape) and*
> *some are standing.*
> *All are bored, exhausted, over heated, and still wearing their outdoor*
> *winter attire. They've been there for some time.*

MARIA

Gina. Go ask how long?

GINA

Ma. We already asked three times.

PINA

> *(very concerned)*

They no gonna let him out.

MARIA

No. Mamma. Don't say that. Dio mio. Santo Cielo. My heart can no take too much. Gina. I feel funny. Gina. Feel my heart.

GINA

Ma. You're fine.

JOSEPH

Yeah ma. Your hearts fine.

MARIA

Gina. We been waiting too long. Go ask.

GINA

Ma. You gotta stop it.

JOSEPH

Yeah ma. Don't think about it.

BRUNO

Yeah. Think about something else. They'll call us when they call us.

363

CANADIAN PLAYS OF ITALIAN HERITAGE

GINA

Yeah. Think about … Look ma *(pulling out book from her purse)* the book you found … I'll read you a little story from Tales Of The Tom Tom. That'll take your mind off of it.

JOSEPH, BRUNO and CARMELA roll their eyes.

MARIA

Like when you was fourteen year old.

GINA

Yeah, like when I was fourteen. "As White Man became numerous, Nannabush spent more time away from home and Wife became lonely. To pass time, she spent many hours hunting until Nannabush returned home one day tired and hungry.

Angered by her absence he raged at Wife, and when she scolded him for leaving, he raised his great hand and struck her down?" What the …?

MARIA

Gina!

GINA

That was a bad idea.

MARIA

Gina. That's no help. This story make me more nervous.

JOSEPH

Gina. Put that thing away.

BRUNO

Yeah. Put that stupid book away.

GINA

I'm sorry. It was a bad idea. Okay. At least I tried. *(beat)* So. Honabigi? Was that the right pronunciation, Nannabush.

HONABIGI

Close. It's Na-Na-boosh. Ooosh. *(beat)* But we also call him Nanabijou and Nanna-Bo-zho.

TIMOTHY

(chuckles)

Nanna-bozo. Dad, that's funny.

DARRYL

Settle down.

HONABIGI

Well, you think it's funny because he's a trickster spirit. He's always doing something silly and stupid. He appears in the form of a big rabbit we call Mishaawooz.

Moment. PINA turns to HONABIGI.

PINA

Excuse me. Whaddu you say you name is?

HONABIGI

My name? It's Honabigi.

BRUNO

Honabigi.

PINA
Oh.
> *Moment.*

MARIA
Is no so easy to say you name.

PINA
Is no so hard. Ohn-a-beach.

BRUNO
No.

HONABIGI
Bruno, it is different than maybe what they're used to. It's okay.

BRUNO
I'll break it down for you. Just say *HO*.

PINA/MARIA/RODOLFO
OH.

BRUNO
Then NA

PINA/MARIA/RODOLFO
NA.

BRUNO
Then BEE GEE.

PINA/MARIA/RODOLFO
BEEGEE. BEEG.

BRUNO
Okay. Now put it all together ... Ho-na-bi-gi.
> *PINA tries to say it.*

PINA
Ohn-a-beach.
> *MARIA doesn't even bother.*

MARIA
How about I just call you Ho?
> *GINA is mortified. BRUNO is furious. EVERYONE is*
> *uncomfortable except MARIA, PINA, and RODOLFO. They*
> *have no idea what Ho means.*

BRUNO
No! That's not her name ...
> *BRUNO is upset and embarrassed. MARIA doesn't have a clue*
> *as to why.*

HONABIGI
Bruno. Don't worry about it. *(beat)* You can call me whatever's easiest.

BRUNO
No.

HONABIGI
Bruno ...

BRUNO
Oh man. This is so embarrassing.

MARIA
Gina? What's the problem?

GINA
I'll explain it to you when we get home.

BRUNO
Yeah. When she tells you *her own* problem.

GINA
Bruno.

CARMELA
What problem?

GINA
No problem. It's just Bruno. He's always being Bruno.

CARMELA
Well, I gotta tell you, I'm so happy you're here. Right Darryl?

DARRYL
Right.

CARMELA
You're gonna take a lot of pressure off me doing everything for mom and nonna.

MARIA
What do you do for me? You cut my hair. One time.

CARMELA
Oh come on. I take you to the Doctor, I take you to the grocery store, I take you …

PINA
You always so busy with you family.

CARMELA
I work. Darryl works. I have kids.

GINA
Carmela. Don't get upset. Leave her alone. I'm home. I can take you. Ma. I said I would.

CARMELA
Timothy! Get off the floor. It's full of germs. See what I have to deal with everyday. Darryl? *(TIMOTHY wanders off)* Timothy, get back here. Darryl!

DARRYL
I got it. *(goes off to find TIMOTHY)*

PINA
It's a sign. That's what it is.

CARMELA
What's a sign?

PINA
That we here. *(beat)* What's gonna happen next?

MARIA
I should never talk to Luisa. She all the time bring my famiglia malocchio.

JOSEPH
Ma. Please don't start with your evil eye stuff in here.

PINA
It's no stuff. It's true.

MARIA PINA
    Some people in Italy *die* because of *malocchio*. *(beat)* Ciccio, his sister Brunella, was a very bad story. You know her. She live by the yard with the big chestnut tree . . .

RODOLFO
    Olive tree.
PINA
    Chestnut tree. I know difference between olive and chestnut.
RODOLFO
    Olive.
MARIA
    You talk about the property next to the farm of Zio Francesco where they gotta the black goats?
RODOLFO
    No. She talk about the big field with big olive tree.
MARIA
    When you pass stone bridge beside old fruit store?
PINA
    Yes. The stone bridge that bring up the mountain by Concetta, who work for my cousin Luigi. That's the place where this guy Ciccio sister *live* . . . and *die* . . . from *malocchio*!
TIMOTHY
    (*as DARRYL and TIMOTHY return*) When is nonno coming out?
MARIA
                    (*very concerned*)
    Something is no right.
PINA
    Cristofero Colombo! Everything is his fault! That's what is a no right!
JOSEPH
    Christopher Columbus?
PINA
    Yes. Cristofero Colombo.
BRUNO
    What does Christopher Columbus have to do with anything?
PINA
    Everything. If he never discover America, we never come here. And we no be here now.
MARIA
    And you father no be in jail.
JOSEPH
    Okay. That's just ridiculous blaming Christopher Columbus.
RODOLFO
    He a great man. Italian hero.
PINA
    A facista!
RODOLFO
    Facista? No. You think of Mussolini.

PINA

Him too. That other idiot.

RODOLFO

What do you know? You Communista.

PINA

I'm no a Communista. Io sono per i diritti of the people. *(to TIMOTHY)* Your nonno is pazzo.

BRUNO

There's lot's of people who feel no love for Christopher Columbus.

RODOLFO

Like who?

BRUNO

Like people who were here before any of us arrived.

RODOLFO

It's no his fault. It's people who come after him. Spagnioli. Inglesi. No. Irish! Those people. Italian people hurt no one.

TIMOTHY

Is Nonno coming out or not?

> *CHIEF enters. No one sees him.*

MARIA

I'm going to kill him when I see him.

CARMELA

Ma. Don't talk like that in front of the kids.

MARIA

He ruin everybody day.

CHIEF

Is there a Mrs. Tappino?

GINA

Oh. Yes. Right here. *(beat)* Ma. He's talking to you.

> *MARIA stands up. Slowly.*

MARIA

Joseph. Come with me.

JOSEPH

Gina's here.

MARIA

She tired.

CARMELA

I can go.

MARIA

No. You watch you kids.

GINA

I'll come.

JOSEPH

No. I'll go.

CHIEF

Somebody decide.

GINA

    I said I'll come.

JOSEPH

    I'll come with you.

               JOSEPH and GINA stand next to MARIA.

MARIA

    I'm Mrs. Tappino.

JOSEPH

    Joseph. *(beat)* This is my sister Gina.

               GIUSEPPE calls from wings.

GIUSEPPE

    Psssst.

CHIEF

    Uhm. Excuse me.

               CHIEF steps away to wings.

MARIA

    What happen?

JOSEPH

    I don't know.

GIUSEPPE

               (to CHIEF—loud whisper)

    Why everyone come? Why Maria bring Teem? I no want Teem to see me in this place. And who that lady over there? I never see her before. Why she come? Tell everyone to go home. Just talk to Gina.

               CHIEF returns to address family.

CHIEF

    Gina? Can I have a word with you?

               GINA walks to CHIEF. CHIEF whispers in her ear.

               EVERYONE leans in towards GINA to try and listen in to what

               CHIEF is saying.

GINA

               (to CHIEF)

    I got it. I'll take care of it. *(then turning to family)* Okay, so here's the deal. Joseph, you and I are going to stay here and deal with this. You can stay ma, but it's better if everyone else goes home. We don't know much longer we're going to be here and there are too many of us in this small waiting area.

DARRYL

    Okay. Tim, let's go.

CARMELA

    Wait. Why are we going?

BRUNO

    We should have stayed home.

TIMOTHY

    Where is Nonno?

CARMELA

    Why can't we just stay?

GINA

Because Carmela it's the way dad wants it to be. Just go home and finish cooking and we'll get there when we get there.

CARMELA

And how long do you think that will be?

GINA

(losing her cool)

Carmela. Just go! And stop making a scene!

EVERYONE begins to exit. Slowly.

RODOLFO

Gina, tell me what happen.

GINA

I'll tell you at home. Nonno, just go.

JOSEPH, GINA, MARIA stay behind.

CHIEF

Mr. Tappino, you can come out.

GIUSEPPE enters. MARIA and GIUSEPPE'S eyes meet and it's love at first sight.

GIUSEPPE

Maria!

MARIA

Giuseppe!

They embrace tightly. They are overcome with emotion and love for each other.

GIUSEPPE

Carissima! (embracing)

MARIA

Giuseppe. You alive.

GIUSEPPE

Amore. Maria. Maria. Maria. Amore mio.

MARIA

Giuseppe. Amore mio.

GIUSEPPE

I miss you so much

MARIA

I miss you too.

They break their embrace but remain close.

GIUSEPPE

Maria, when the Polizia take me away I see Teem and Teem see me, and I sit inside the police car and I think to myself, what I am doing?

GIUSEPPE turns to GINA.

GIUSEPPE (CONT'D)

Gina. You home.

GINA

Yes papa'. I'm home.

GIUSEPPE
That's good. *(beat)* Maria, then I think about the first time you come with me to see the movie in Cosenza, in the big round piazza, in the new cinema. We take the train with your mother, my mother, your sister, my sister, my cousin, your uncle ...

MARIA
(she's in love)
I remember ...

GIUSEPPE
If I want to see *you*, I have to bring the whole famiglia. Amore. Grazie. Thank you for coming. I was so scared. I promise I never do it again. *(kisses her)*

MARIA
But Giuseppe, what did you do?

GIUSEPPE
(pause) Nothing. Let's go home.

CHIEF
Well, he ... we did a breath test because there was some suspicion he might have been intoxicated and you know, guns and alcohol don't mix no matter what city you're living in.

MARIA
Alcohol?

GINA
Guns?

JOSEPH
You were drunk?

CHIEF
He's a very lucky man. The tests came back negative so he's free to go.

MARIA
Negative? Oh no.

GINA
Negative. That's a good thing.

JOSEPH
Yeah. Negative is good.

CHIEF
Oh, and even though his weapon wasn't loaded we're gonna hold onto it until he pays the fine that we'll mail out in a day or two. Pay the fine get your weapon back.

JOSEPH
Okay. So we're good to go then.

CHIEF
Oh, and one more thing, his drivers licence is expired. Make sure he gets that renewed. Okay.

GIUSEPPE
Yes. Gina home now. She gonna do it for me.

GINA
I'll make sure it gets paid. Thank you.

CHIEF

Your welcome. Well, we're all done here. Gina, I hope you enjoy your stay. I'm sure everyone's thrilled to have you home. *(beat)* Joseph, your dad tells me you want to be a nurse?

> JOSEPH nods YES. (long pause) Chief looks at Mr. Tappino, then Joseph.

CHIEF

> *(to Joseph)*

That's okay. *(turns to Mr. Tappino)* Mr. Tappino, it's O-KAY. *(beat)* Mr. Tappino, I hope I never see you around here again. Now go home and have a nice supper. Arrivederci and ciao.

> CHIEF watches for a moment then exits.

JOSEPH

You're really lucky to be walking away from this one Rambo.

MARIA

Good thing I throw all you Grappa down the sink.

GIUSEPPE

You what? You throw my Grappa down the sink?

JOSEPH

Don't look at me. I told her not to do it.

GIUSEPPE

Maria, Grappa is the *only* ting that keep me *warm* when it's cold.

MARIA

Buy a heater! It's *illegal* to make Grappa in *my* house!

THE KITCHEN

> MARIA, GIUSEPPE, GINA and JOSEPH enter and begin to remove their winter attire. Lot's of commotion. Some FAMILY members are seated around the kitchen table, some are helping to prepare the meal. MARIA puts on an apron.

CARMELA

You're home.

JOSEPH

Yeah. We're home.

BRUNO

It's about time you guys got here.

TIMOTHY

Yeah. I'm starving. Me too.

JOSEPH GINA

I'm exhausted. This is the longest day of my life.

> GINA collapses onto the sofa, throws a blanket over herself and falls asleep.

PINA

Giuseppe, they let you out.

MARIA
Yes mamma. They let him out.
TIMOTHY
Nonno. I saw you in the Police car. You were waving to me.
GIUSEPPE
Oh. Yes. I see you.
TIMOTHY
What was it like *inna da jail*? Were you scared?
GIUSEPPE
No. I no scare. *(beat)* You play hockey today?
TIMOTHY
No. Just practice. *(beat)* So, did you make any friends?
GIUSEPPE
No. No one make *friends* inna da jail.
BRUNO
So dad, you gonna tell us what you were doing in the big house?
MARIA
Bruno. Quiet. We gotta company.
BRUNO
Company? She's my girlfriend. She's not company.*(beat)* Dad. This is Honabigi.
                    GIUSEPPE is embarrassed.
GIUSEPPE
Oh. Hello.
HONABIGI
It's so nice to meet you.
GIUSEPPE
Giuseppe. *(beat)* Tappino.
HONABIGI
I came to the jail too. So, what happened?
BRUNO
You gonna tell us what you were doing there?
MARIA
Bruno. Quiet!
JOSEPH
I'll tell you later.
TIMOTHY
I'm starving. Where's the meatballs?
PINA
Leave room for supper.
MARIA
Grazie mamma. You cook.
CARMELA
What about me? I helped too. Right Darryl?
DARRYL
Yes. You did. *(beat)* Could someone please pass the meatballs?
CARMELA
So what did the Chief say?

MARIA

Carmela. We have the company. He do nothing.

DARRYL

(sheepish)

The meatballs please.

MARIA

What do you want?

DARRYL

The meatballs please. For Tim.

PINA

If he talk a little louder maybe someone can hear him and pass him the balls.

CARMELA

Nonna. You're always picking on him.

PINA

He can no speak. He have no tongue.

CARMELA

No. He speaks when he has something important to say.

DARRYL

Thank you, Carmela.

PINA

Nobody eat meatballs now. Wait for supper. I make lots of food.

CARMELA

(to Bruno and Honabigi)

So, how'd you guys meet? I always like to hear how couples first met. Right Darryl?

BRUNO

Well, we met ...

HONABIGI

I was driving to work, and I saw this guy, all covered in snow, trying to get it started. So, I stopped the car, and that's when I first met Bruno. I gave him a hand with his ski-doo. We started talking about the trail he was on, and yeah, turns out we have a lot in common. We both like history ... anyway, it went something like that.

GIUSEPPE

So, your skoo-be-doo break? When?

BRUNO

Ten months ago.

GIUSEPPE

Ten months ago?

BRUNO

Yeah. Ten months ago.

GIUSEPPE

So you like the skoo-be-doo?

BRUNO

She likes all that outdoor stuff. She works at the Ministry.

GIUSEPPE

The Ministry? Oh. What do you do?

HONABIGI
Game and Wildlife.

GIUSEPPE
You? No. Really? *(beat)* You come for the moose?

HONABIGI
No. I'm not a moose technician. I enforce fishing and wildlife codes.

GIUSEPPE
Oh. That's a good job.

HONABIGI
Mr. Tappino, if you ever wanna go fishing or hunting in some really great places, off the grid, I can hook you up.
> *The phone rings.*

GIUSEPPE
Really? (pleased)

BRUNO
Yeah. Really..
> *MARIA answers the phone.*

MARIA
Allo? Eva.

GIUSEPPE
Again with the Polacca!

PINA
She's trouble. Hang up.

GIUSEPPE
What she want now?

MARIA
Everything is okay. We happy they take *him* away.

GIUSEPPE
Shhh. Maria. Don't tell her about *me*.
> *MARIA covers receiver with her hand.*

MARIA
I talk about the moose! *(to Eva)* No. I talk to Giuseppe. What …? Your husband shoot a moose?

GIUSEPPE
A moose? Son a ma gun. Where?

MARIA
Inna da bush.

GIUSEPPE
Inna da bush? I suppose to go with him inna da bush today.

MARIA
You was suppose to sit down an shut-up. *(beat) (to Eva)* No. I talk to Giuseppe. Eva, I gotta go. We talk tomorrow. Ciao.
> *MARIA hangs up the phone.*

GIUSEPPE
He always go inna da bush. She let him go inna da bush whenever he wanna go inna da bush. She never say no to da bush. No like you. You never let me go inna da bush.

MARIA

Giuseppe. Basta with da bush. You go inna da bush so many time and you never shoot *nothing!*

RODOLFO

(looking at his watch)

Pina! The show!

PINA

The show! Madonna mia. The show!

They drop everything and run to the sofa/TV.

RODOLFO

I almost forget the show.

PINA

It start in five minutes. I no wanna miss.

RODOLFO

Tonight gonna be good show.

PINA

Bruno. Open the TV.

GIUSEPPE

Bruno. The show.

MARIA

Hurry up.

JOSEPH

Bruno, please don't turn on that Italian Soap Opera.

TIMOTHY

I'm starving.

CARMELA

Yeah. Let's eat.

The music from the Italian Soap Opera opening credits fills the room. MARIA, GIUSEPPE, PINA and RODOLFO stand directly behind the sofa where GINA is sound asleep. They stare intently at the TV screen. This is an Italian Soap Opera they watch every Sunday night.

PINA

Tonight Mariella gonna marry Lorenzo.

RODOLFO

No. She no gonna marry him.

PINA

Why no?

RODOLFO

Because she in love with *Vittorio.*

MARIA

No. She no love him.

PINA

She too beautiful for that brutto.

GIUSEPPE

She a witch. A strega.

RODOLFO

    No. She nice.

PINA

    She no nice. You no see what she do to Filippo.

RODOLFO

    I know what she do. I no miss one show.

GIUSEPPE

    She gonna have his baby.

RODOLFO

    No. Is *Vittorio* baby.

MARIA

    No. Is Filippo baby.

RODOLFO

    No. I say is Vittorio baby.

        GINA is waking up from her sleep.

GINA

        (groggy)

    I'm going to have a baby.

PINA

    No. Mariella gonna have da baby.

        GINA stands up and faces them.

GINA

    No. I'm going to have a baby.

        GINA begins to walk away. She stops.

GINA

    I'm pregnant.

BRUNO

    It's about time you told them.

        They finally realize what she has said.

MARIA

    Cosa?

CARMELA

    Pregnant?

PINA

    Who pregnant?

BRUNO

    Gina.

GINA

    Me.

JOSEPH

    Pregnant

CARMELA

    Gina's going to have a baby? Oh my God, isn't that exciting?

PINA

    I told you, you play with fire, you gonna getta burn.

MARIA

    Good thing the priest no come for dinner tonight.

        CARMELA hugs GINA.

CARMELA
  Oh my God Gina that is so exciting. Darryl!
MARIA
  Carmela. Shut-uppa.
GIUSEPPE
  Maria? You know?
MARIA
  No! You crazy? You think I could hide something like this?
PINA
  She no even have a husband. How this thing can happen?
RODOLFO
  Pina. These *ting* happen.
PINA
  No they don't. She's no the Virgin Mary!
MARIA
  She no the Virgin no more that's for sure.
GIUSEPPE
  Why you no wait?
GINA
  Wait for what? I'm thirty-five years old.
GIUSEPPE
  I don't care if you one hundred. You should know better.
PINA
  Che brutta figura we make. Maria is all you fault.
MARIA
  My fault? *(beat)* Gina? See what you do now?
GINA
  Yeah. I see.
GIUSEPPE
  She too old to make this kinda mistake. Why you no say something?
MARIA
  Giuseppe, I no tell Gina what to do. *(beat)* This is number three. First the
  moose, then you Giuseppe, now Gina. One more thing happen and we gonna be
  in real trouble. *(beat)* Luisa.
PINA
  Luisa. All the time she bring the malocchia.
JOSEPH
  You guys are way over reacting.
BRUNO
  Yeah. What are you stressing about? It's awesome news.
GIUSEPPE
  She no marry.
BRUNO
  Who cares.
            GINA tries to say something.
PINA
  A woman make a baby by herself is no good.

BRUNO

Times change. So what if she's not married.

PINA

Times no change.

JOSEPH

It's not a sin to have a baby out of wedlock.

BRUNO

Yeah. Everyone's doin' it.

GIUSEPPE

No talk like that in front of Teem.

CARMELA

But he's right. Look at all those actresses on TV.

PINA

We no actress in dis house.

GIUSEPPE

And dis place is no Hollywood!

MARIA

This is Way-Uppa-Bay.

PINA

Cristoforo Colombo. Is all his fault.

GINA

I've become the moose.

BRUNO

Are you okay?

MARIA

Gina eat something.

GINA

I've become the moose.

GIUSEPPE

Now you talk stupido. You no the moose.

MARIA

Gina, go lie down.

GINA

No. I *am* the moose. Someone please shoot *me* and take me away on the hood of a truck.

MARIA

That's no nice. Why you say this?

GINA

I know it's not nice, but every time I come home it feels like what the hell did I just wander into? Like the moose.

> *Moment.*

GIUSEPPE

Maria? What the hell she say?

MARIA

She say ... I don't know what she say she speak English.

DARRYL

> *(sheepish)*

We're all the moose. (*silence as everyone looks at DARRYL*)

PINA

Did he say something?

TIMOTHY

Shhh. Everyone. My dad's gonna say something.

DARRYL

No. That's it Tim.

TIMOTHY

Go ahead dad. Say something.

DARRYL

Oh that's OK Tim. Never mind.

CARMELA

Darryl, if you have something to say then say it.

DARRYL

(measured and sheepish)

What I was saying was we're all displaced ... like the moose.

EVERYONE waits for DARRYL'S next word.

GIUSEPPE

Maria? We gonna eat or no eat?

DARRYL stands up.

DARRYL

I'm not from here either. My grandparents immigrated from England to Saskatoon, and I married Carmela and she's Italian and I'm English and we love each other very much. And sometimes I feel like I'm standing outside that window, in the snow, looking in at everyone.

Moment.

PINA

Is he still talking?

DARRYL

No. I'm done.

DARRYL sits.

HONABIGI

Then may I say something?

DARRYL stands.

DARRYL

Not yet. What I'm saying is I'm not outside. I'm in here. With you. Where I belong. This is my family too.

CARMELA

That's right Darryl.

DARRYL feels empowered.

DARRYL

I'm Darryl and I'm here.

DARRYL slams his hand down on the table. All eyes are on him. He walks to the fridge and gets the white envelope he found at the front door containing GIUSEPPE'S Drivers License.

PINA

Did he finish?

CARMELA

Yes Nonna. He finished.

DARRYL hands GIUSEPPE the envelope.

DARRYL

Giuseppe, this is for you.

GIUSEPPE looks inside and sees that it's his renewed Drivers Licence.

DARRYL (CONT'D)

Honabigi, you were going to say something.

BRUNO

Yeah. You were gonna say something.

HONABIGI

I was just going to ask Gina if *she's* happy?

GIUSEPPE

What kind of question is this?

BRUNO

She's talking to Gina?

HONABIGI

I just want to know, Gina are *you* happy?

GIUSEPPE

Who's happy?

BRUNO

She's talking to Gina.

RODOLFO

Gina? You happy?

PINA

Nobody is happy!

RODOLFO

Nobody ask-a you. Everyone quiet. *(beat)* Gina, you happy?

GINA

Yes Nonno. I'm happy. *(beat)* I'm going to be sick.

GINA runs out of the kitchen and heads to the bathroom.

MARIA

She so smart. I no understand why she do something so stupido.

GIUSEPPE

Too much education. That's the problem today.

PINA

Kids today know too much.

TIMOTHY

I'm going to have a baby cousin.

CARMELA

That's right, and I'm going to be an Auntie. Right Darryl?

GINA returns.

CARMELA (CONT'D)

Are you okay?

GINA

It was a false alarm. I'm okay. I just need to sit down.

CARMELA

Here Gina, have a seat.

> *GINA walks to the table. Sits.*

MARIA

Drink some water.

GINA

No. I'm fine. I just need to breathe.

GIUSEPPE

So, now we know why you come home.

GINA

Yes, now you know. I want my baby to be born here.

BRUNO

Here!? You sure you wanna do it *here*?

JOSEPH

Here? In the frozen tundra?

GINA

Yes. With work I never know where I'm going to be and I don't want to be alone. I know none of you would be able to leave your lives here and come take care of me or my baby.

PINA

No look at me. I'm scare to fly.

BRUNO

I'm just asking because you know what you're like when you come home.

JOSEPH

Yeah. You know what you're like.

GINA

Yes. I know what I'm like. But it's not about the place and it's not about all of you. It's the effort. The effort to get here. After a couple of days, I settle in, I feel better, I'm fine, but I go through the same torment every time I have to come here because coming home means leaving again.

MARIA

Gina, no one ask you to leave.

GINA

I know ma. But there's no work for me here. *(beat)* And from the time I'm packing my bags to come here, I'm already thinking about the day I have to leave and say good-bye again. When that tiny little plane takes off and we're climbing up, I look down on all of *this* covered in snow, like a big white sheet of snow, the frozen rivers, the smoke billowing out of chimneys, and I watch as we get further and further away and everything gets smaller and smaller, the trees, the homes, the white sheet, and then I tell myself that if I just keep staring at the white sheet that somehow I'll be able to hold onto everything that's here just a little bit longer, and then just like that, we fly into a big cloud and puff, its all gone. Then I wipe my tears away and I try to get it together and then this shift happens inside of me where I see myself enter into another reality, the reality of where I'm headed. Another place. Another city. Am I from there? From here? Or not? And then suddenly it all becomes a great big blur that I was even here. And it's like that every time I come home.

GIUSEPPE

So, who is the father? Please no tell me he come from a *plastic cup*. I just need to know he is *somebody*.

GINA

Did you just say plastic cup?

MARIA

Like Miranda.

GINA

Who's Miranda?

MARIA

Portuguese lady daughter.

GIUSEPPE

Forty year old and just like you, she no marry.

MARIA

She have a baby by herself.

GIUSEPPE

Please no tell me you do that?

GINA

Who are you talking about?

JOSEPH

Fernanda, this lesbian lab technician who works at the hospital.

GINA

And what's the problem?

JOSEPH

There is no problem. She had twins.

MARIA

Poor kids. They gonna be so confuse.

PINA

How they gonna know who is the mamma and who is the papà when they gotta two mamma and no papà? You tell me?Maybe

JOSEPH

They won't be confused. And and as far as I'm concerned, if she's not going to get married or have sex with a man in this lifetime, it doesn't mean she won't be a good mother. Okay. Besides, it shouldn't be any of our business.

MARIA

People talk. They gonna talk about *you* too.

JOSEPH

Who cares what other people think. She's *happy*. I'm *happy*. *Gina's happy.*

GIUSEPPE

Happy! Happy! Happy! Everybody talk about happy. What does happy mean? *(beat)* Let's say you wanna take drugs. Okay. You steal the money. You buy the drugs. You take the drugs. Okay, now you happy? Is this *happy?*

GINA

No. That's not happy. *(beat)* And look, in answer to your question about the plastic cup, I did not go to a sperm bank.

MARIA

Thanks to God.

GIUSEPPE
    Thanks God.
PINA
    Now they gotta *bank* for everything.
GINA
    He's from Italy.
MARIA
    Italy?
GIUSEPPE
    Who from Italy?
GINA
    The father. The father of my baby is Italian.
GIUSEPPE
    Father is from Italy?
GINA
    Yes. He's Italian.
GIUSEPPE
    Italiano?
RODOLFO
    Italiano?
PINA
    She say he's Italiano.
MARIA
    Which part?
GINA
    Which part what?
MARIA
    Which part?
GINA
    All of him. He's all Italian.
JOSEPH
    I think she means is he from the South?
GINA
    His name is Michele and he's— *(pronounced Mee-kay-lay)*
GIUSEPPE
    Michele?
PINA
    My brother name is Michele.
GIUSEPPE/MARIA
    Michele! That's a nice name.
GINA
    He's from Rome.
GIUSEPPE
    Rome! Now that's a city!
CARMELA
    Darryl, he's from Rome. Did you hear that?

DARRYL
Rome.

MARIA
What he do?

GINA
He's a pilot for Alitalia.

PINA/MARIA/RODOLFO
A Pilot.

GIUSEPPE
He's a Pilot?

GINA
Yes. A pilot.

PINA
Oh no. It's no good. You can no trust a Pilot when he all the time go up there ...

RODOLFO
Pina. Stuttee cheetu. Gina. You do good.

BRUNO
And just in case you guys didn't hear it, he's Italian.

MARIA
And he got a good job.

CARMELA
Isn't that exciting Darryl?

DARRYL
Yeah. I'm happy for you Gina.

RODOLFO
When he come to meet *us?*

GINA
I don't know. When he get's some time off work.

MARIA
He coming here? When?

GINA
I don't know. At some point.

GIUSEPPE
Where he gonna sleep?

GINA
With ah ... I don't know. The couch.

BRUNO
I don't think so.

GINA
Look, I don't know where he's going to sleep. I haven't really thought about it.

MARIA
We figure it out when he come.

GIUSEPPE
Maria, maybe if you no put all you junk inna da basement we can make a some room and put Michele inna da basement.

MARIA
Giuseppe, maybe I put you inna da basement with all you junk.

GIUSEPPE

It's no just my junk, you got alotta junk too.

BRUNO

Honabigi must think we're completely nuts. *(beat)* I'm so sorry. It's not always like this.

DARRYL

Oh yes it is. Everyone's always loud and emotional here.

PINA

That's because we alive!!!

MARIA

Ho? *(beat)* No one talk loud at you house? They no argue?

PINA

Maria, maybe at *Ho* house she never sit at kitchen table with her family. Many family in this country *never* eat together.

BRUNO

Nonna! Please.

HONABIGI

My parents are divorced since I was five.

GIUSEPPE

Divorce?

MARIA

Oh. Divorce.

PINA

Divorce? That's no good.

HONABIGI

No. Maybe it's not good in some cases, but sometimes it can be better. You see, now my parents are both happily remarried. My mom has a new husband, and my dad has a new wife. And sometimes we all eat together. And sometimes, we argue—just like every family does. You know. But it's all good. We're still a family. And we all love each other, too.

BRUNO

Sixty percent of married couples end in divorce.

GIUSEPPE

No.

BRUNO

Ask Father Riccardo. He knows.

GIUSEPPE

No us. We stay marry no matter what. We never get a divorce. No like people in this country, one fight and right away it's "*let's get a divorce.*"

PINA

Fifty-five year we marry. We fight everyday. Sometime we wanna kill each other. But we don't. And what I'm gonna do? Leave him? Now? For what? And who gonna want *him?* Nobody.

GIUSEPPE

Maybe we no *love* each other like you think *love* is supposed to be. Like *love* is in the movie. But we ... we *do love* ... me and you mamma.

MARIA

"L'amore non e' bello, se non e' stuzzicarello."

HONABIGI

What does that mean?

MARIA

It mean love is no beautiful unless is prodded and poke.

GIUSEPPE

It mean you have to fight for something or you risk to fight for nothing. That's why the marriage they break up. No one fight for what is important.

MARIA

> *(shaking her head)*

That's no what it mean.

GIUSEPPE

> *(slams fist on the table)*

That's what it mean!

MARIA

Ok. Giuseppe, that's what it mean.

GINA

I know you "love" each other but we've made different choices, me, Carmela, Bruno, Joseph, and it doesn't make us disrespectful because our choices are different than yours.

JOSEPH

Yeah. We make different choices because that's who *we* are.

MARIA

Let me say something. *(beat)* We know we think different from our children. And this is no just for me, but for many people from all over the world. When you are Immigrant, you go to make a better life, and you bring everything you know, who you are, you tradition, because you want to teach this to future generation ...

PINA

But when you come here everything is different and everything change and every day you feel more and more of who you are to slip away ...

MARIA

Gina, I know you is no more a little girl. I know you old enough. And I know is you choice, but is no tradition for us. And is still hard for us to understand. Okay. But we ...

GIUSEPPE

We try. Okay. We try.

> GIUSEPPE picks up the white envelope containing the renewed
> Drivers License and holds it up for DARRYL to see.

GIUSEPPE

Darryl. Grazie.

> *Moment.*

PINA

Darryl, you no so bad.

RODOLFO

When I first come to this country ... Pina, please shut-uppa and letta me talk!

PINA

Okay. Okay. I shut-uppa. Talk.

RODOLFO

All day I try to tell this story. If we no tell are stories to our grandchildren, what we leave to them? Money? Money can buy shoe and food, but our story is worth something more.

PINA

Okay. Okay. Rodolfo finish the story.

RODOLFO

When I come to this country, I no even know how to say one word in English. No "yes"—no "hello." Nothing. And I no even know where I go. I just know I go to America. I got no school. I can no read, no write. Before I leave, someone write for me *Way-Uppa Bay* and number to my sister Gianna house on a small piece of paper just in case I getta lost. Nine days on ship to Halifax, four days on train to here. Thirteen day it take me. When train stop in big city like Toronto, lots of people get out, but no me. When train stop here, I so tired, just-a me, I go out by myself . . .

JOSEPH

But why Way Up Bay?

GIUSEPPE

Was a different time Joseph. Now if you gotta the money, or if you no gotta no money, you go where you wanna go. Do what you wanna do.

RODOLFO

We no have choice where we go. Someone ask you to come, send letter, and say there is work for you, or was no immigration. My sister husband, he come many year before, 1952. He send letter and he invite me.

JOSEPH

And no one bothered to look at a map?

PINA

You tink we have a map?

RODOLFO

A map? We so poor sometime we no eat.

PINA

Who could afford a map?

GIUSEPPE

So poor I sleep in one bed with all my brothers until I marry your mother.

RODOLFO

Everyone want America.

BRUNO

It's Canada Nonno. We live in Canada.

PINA

Canada. America. It's all the same. Bruno, it's America.

BRUNO

No it's not.

GINA

Bruno! *(beat)* Nonno. Please finish your story. So, you were saying that you were the only one who got off the train.

RODOLFO

Si Gina. I finish. *(beat)* I go outside train. I put my suitcase on the snow and I sit on my suitcase and wait for my sister to come pick me up. I begin to pray. I trust God I make right decision to come here. Wind blow. Snow come down. I wait maybe ten minutes an then you know what happen to me? Something never I see in my life, ice-ee-close. Was so cold that big ice-ee-close grow under my nose. I never see ice-ee- close hang from someone nose before.

> *TIMOTHY doesn't know what ice-ee-close are. He looks over at JOSEPH and BRUNO.*

JOSEPH/BRUNO

Icicles.

TIMOTHY

Oh.

RODOLFO (CONT'D)

(pulls out his wallet) I think to myself, I sacrifice a lot to come here. I leave my country to come all this way, ship and train, *(pulls out a small crumpled piece of paper out of his wallet)* and for what? To die? Frozen to death without my wife and my famiglia? With ice-ee-close hang from my nose, holding this piece a paper.

> *RODOLFO looks at the paper. GINA grabs it out of his hands and looks at it.*

GINA

Nonno. Can I see that?

RODOLFO

Here.

JOSEPH

He still has it in his wallet after all these years?

BRUNO

That's crazy.

> *GINA hands the paper back.*

CARMELA

Darryl? Did you see that little piece of paper? He still has it in his wallet. Timothy did you see? It's very special.

DARRYL

Yeah. That's a very special piece of paper.

> *PINA jumps in.*

PINA

After two years when I come with your mamma and Giuseppe, everybody tell me we was so lucky to leave Italy. But I no feel too lucky when we arrive. I look around and I think to myself, this … this place is no my beautiful sunshine Calabria. This place will never be my Calabria. And then I remember why we come, and I remember Rodolfo wait for us in the new house he buy with money he make here. First house we buy with our own money. And then I tell to myself, is better to be cold and free, where I can own my own house, then to be in Italy where we sweat for the *padrone* and own nothing. This is why we come. *(padrone: landowner, boss)*

RODOLFO

This is why we come.

TIMOTHY

Hey. Everyone. Wow. Look outside. The snows really coming down.

Commotion and mumbling about the snow.

BRUNO

I told you we were gonna get dumped on.

HONABIGI

Yeah. It's really coming down now.

GIUSEPPE

I go clean the driveway.

TIMOTHY

I'm coming with you.

GIUSEPPE

You go ask you father first.

MARIA

No one go outside!

CARMELA

So Gina, how many months are you?

GINA

Four.

MARIA

Four month? Giuseppe, you got a lot to do.

GIUSEPPE

How long you know this guy?

CARMELA

Four months? It doesn't even show.

GINA

Yes it does. Look.

CARMELA

Oh please. I looked like a cow when I was pregnant.

PINA

I weigh just one hundred and twenty pounds when I have Maria.

GINA

At nine months?

PINA

Yes. You gonna take after me.

MARIA

No Mamma. That's no good. When I was born I look like a mouse. A sick mouse.

PINA

How you know how you look?

MARIA

Everybody tell me, "You look like a sick mouse."

PINA

Yeah, maybe you right. You don't eat too much when you was inside but when you come out, you start to drink-a the milk from my breast and you never stop.

TIMOTHY

Oh. That's so gross.

CARMELA

My breasts were humongous.

TIMOTHY

Mom! Stop.

CARMELA

Remember Darryl?

DARRYL

I remember.

TIMOTHY

Dad!

GINA

I'll start packing on the pounds now that I'm home.

MARIA

Never mind how much you weigh. You have to eat for two.

TIMOTHY

Nonno's on TV!

EVERYONE

What? Nonno? TV? Where? What do you mean?

TIMOTHY

He's on the TV!

GIUSEPPE

Maria. Gina. Shhh! The news.

> *GIUSEPPE'S face is plastered on the TV. EVERYONE runs to
> the TV.*

CARMELA

Oh my God Darryl. Dad's on TV!

PINA

Darryl, move your head.

> *PINA pushes DARRYL out of the way.*

GIUSEPPE

Turn it up. Look. I'm in da TV.

> *The news camera has panned over to the exterior of the
> TAPPINO home.*

MARIA

My house is on the television.

BRUNO/JOSEPH

Shhhh.

TELEVISION NEWS (V.O.)

The Ministry of Natural Resources transported the tranquilized moose to the
Wanabeeghin National Bush Sanctuary where he is being watched over by
Nature and Wildlife officials until he recovers and is back to running through
the bush.

TIMOTHY

He's alive. Alive. Our moose is alive.

GIUSEPPE

Teem, no believe everything you hear on the news. Those people probably shoot
him and eat him for supper tonight.

CARMELA

Dad. Not in front of the kids.

BRUNO

Carmela, would you stop saying *kids*. You only have *one* kid.

GINA

Bruno, don't be so rude.

TELEVISION NEWS (V.O.)

A Mr. Giuseppe Tappeen …

GIUSEPPE

Tappino!

TELEVISION NEWS (V.O.)

… of 172 Wawa Drive was fined and released for carrying a hunting rifle within city limits.

CARMELA

So that's what you did.

JOSEPH

That's what he did.

GINA

Yup. That's what dad did.

BRUNO

So, you made it on the local news.

TIMOTHY

Dad, Nonno was on TV.

DARRYL

That's right Tim. He was on TV.

MARIA

Now everybody know our business.

HONABIGI

Mr. Tappino, don't worry about it. That was pretty cool. I mean, not the jail part. But I know some people at work who would agree with what you were *trying* to do because, well, you know, you could have saved a lot of taxpayer money. Police. Moose Technicians. Firemen. All the commotion for a Moose. But don't tell anyone I said that.

GIUSEPPE

What? Really? Maria? You hear what she say? *(beat)* Bruno. Why you wait ten month to bring this nice girl home? *(beat)* Here. You take my chair.

HONABIGI sits down in GIUSEPPE'S chair.

MARIA

Ho, he no cool. He really stupido for what he do. Next time he no gonna go where he no suppose to go. Giuseppe, you better hurry up and paint-a the house before Michele come.

GIUSEPPE

No worry Maria. I got lots a free time. I'm gonna paint the house and make it look brand new just for you. And we gonna take care of Gina. *(beat)* Now let's toast.

EVERYONE

Yeah. Let's toast.

EVERYONE picks up a glass.

GIUSEPPE

To the baby. I hope *he's* healthy. But please, one thing I ask you when we are no more here, me, you mamma, you Nonni ... just remember, even if we come from far, far away from where we start our life, please remember to teach the children about us, our culture, our tradition. Even if you don't agree with everything we say and do, just try. For us. Ok? Salute!

EVERYONE

Salute.

GIUSEPPE

And to the moose. I hope those people bring him back to his home ... to his mamma ... with his famiglia. Salute.

EVERYONE

To the Moose. Salute.

THE YARD

MOOSE appears. EVERYONE freezes.

MOOSE

So, you met the Tappino's. Nice people, eh? They had some stuff to work out like all families do, but they're gonna be just fine. There's a lot of other locals I'd like to introduce you to, but I really have to be gettin' back to the Lodge. You know, if it hadn't been for Eva ... big blonde Polish Eva, walking out in her little slip to empty out the trash, well, it probably would have been just another day here in Way Up Bay. But it wasn't. So, you can blame all of this on Eva, or you can blame it on the place, Way Up Bay, or Nannabush, Nannabozho, Mishawooz, or you can blame it on the Great Spirit Manitou, if you want to. He's long overdue. Oh, and another thing ... I am *not* on the loose. Around here, a moose is never on the loose. You can call it whatever you want, but any place where there's more marsh and bush than city and the temperature drops to minus forty well, that's moose habitat. And that's why they call it *moose country*. Okay. I just had to get that off my chest. So, now you can all go. Go back to doing whatever it is you do in your neck of the woods and I'll just say ... arrivederci and ciao.

DAMN THOSE WEDDING BELLS!

1996
Tony Calabretta

"Chi si volta, e chi si gira, sempre a casa va finire.
No matter where you go or turn, you will always end up at home."
  —**Italian saying**

*The play is set in a brownstone apartment in an ethnic area of Brooklyn,
New York. The apartment is very well maintained. There are pictures of
the family displayed everywhere. Most prominently, that of the deceased
patriarch. There is a mirror by the entrance, and there is a hutch which
displays crystal glasses amongst other family artifacts.
The action takes place in the living room / kitchen area. The time is
the present.*

The cast

ANTHONY ROBERTINI, He is in his late-thirties; slightly overweight and balding. He wears glasses. He does not take pride in his appearance. Anthony comes across as a boy trapped in a man's body. He still lives at home, which puts him at the mercy of his very over-bearing mother, Nunziata. Since Anthony is, in fact, a grown man, he finds it nearly impossible to put up with the constant bombardment from his mother in her effort to control his life.

NUNZIATA ROBERTINI, *Anthony's mother*. A widow in her early sixties. A very over protective mother, and somewhat of a busy body. She's very inquisitive and always wants to know what everyone is up to even if she knows that it is none of her business. Nunziata also sees herself as very wise which often prompts her to speak in an opinionated manner. She believes that her family and friends would be much better off if they just listened to her and did what she told them to.

FRANK ROBERTINI, *Anthony's younger brother*. He is in his mid-thirties; lives on his own in Manhattan. His failed acting career has led him to be the local weatherman. Frank is a very suave and handsome guy, he is what we call a player or a ladies man. Frank knows how to turn on the charm and when to use it.

ANGELA RINALDO, *Anthony's love interest*. She's a chef at an up and coming trendy bistro in New York. Angela is a modern day woman who is getting her life together. She is very attractive which is one of the reasons Anthony falls for her so fast. One of the characteristics that sets her apart from the rest of the characters is the fact that she has no noticeable accents. She is in her mid-thirties as well.

LILLY, *Anthony's grandmother*. A spunky old broad in her eighties. Lilly never passes up an opportunity to slip in a sarcastic remark whenever the tension in the household needs breaking. Even in her sarcastic humor, everything she says is with love.

DAVID GREENBERG, *Anthony's best friend.* David is a divorced accountant who moonlights as a talent agent. A typical adult nerd who's been in therapy far too long. He comes across as a complete joke to those around him, but he is as serious as a heart attack. David is also in the same age group as Anthony.

CONNIE ROBERTINI, *Anthony's younger sister* and bride to be. Connie is a real drama queen. She's quick to judge and even quicker to jump to conclusions or react. She is somewhat absent minded which is one of the reasons she's not always taken very seriously by her family. She works as a hair dresser. Connie is a beautiful, outgoing woman in her early thirties.

ROSA VALDEZ, *Anthony's blind date.* A very sexy, thirty-something feminist. To say that she is emotionally unstable is an understatement. Speaks with a heavy Latino accent.

ACT 1
Scene I: A Friday morning in June, about 11:00 a.m.
Scene II: That Friday evening, about 8:30 p.m.
ACT 2
Scene I: That same Friday, about 10:30 p.m.
Scene II: The next day, Saturday afternoon, about 2:00 p.m.
ACT 3
One week later. Saturday, about 11 a.m.

ACT 1 SCENE I

(It is a Friday morning in June, about 11:00 a.m. The scene opens with LILLY and NUNZIATA in the kitchen. LILLY is sitting at the kitchen table, NUNZIATA is milling around the kitchen. CONNIE is off- stage.)

LILLY

> *(singing)*
> *"Lauretta mia, bimba dorata, la serenata te la canta papa ..."*
> *(to Nunziata)*

Te la ricordi Sonia? Sonia! Anyway, her husband's getting his prostate removed next week. Women, we have our problems as we get older, that's for sure. But men ... look at what they have to look forward to. I say it's God's way of paying them back for all those years they drove us crazy, when it did work!

NUNZIATA

Poor Sonia ... first her son had that terrible car accident, then her daughter gets divorced ... now this.

LILLY

She's cursed! Someone definitely put the evil eye on that family. I don't wanna say who but ... let's just say the woman I'm thinking of is a certified witch! I tell you, Nunz', if push came to shove, I'd show her a thing or two about cursing people.

NUNZIATA

Ok, Ma ... last time you thought about putting the evil eye on someone, that sweet Mrs. Collins broke her hip. And you felt so guilty, you spent the next month in church.

LILLY

She's not so sweet.

>   (resumes singing)
>
> "… la voce trema da l'emozione…"
>
>   (NUNZIATA hums along with LILLY.)

CONNIE (O.S.)

Ma, where's my black sweater?

NUNZIATA

Just where you left it, Connie.

CONNIE (O.S.)

Nevermind, I see it … thanks.

>   (NUNZIATA and LILLY resume singing. CONNIE comes out
>   of the bathroom putting on her sweater. Running through the
>   apartment, as if she's looking for something.)

CONNIE (Continued)

I'm glad to see you two have time to sing.

LILLY

At my age, this is considered a day at the opera.

>   (points to Nunziata)

Look, I have *pagliacci* right here.

>   (CONNIE goes over to kiss her grandmother.)

NUNZIATA

You look like a mad woman, slow down!

CONNIE

Can't. I gotta million things to do. Flowers … caterer. Then I gotta meet Joe for lunch to finalize the prenuptial agreement.

NUNZIATA

A prenuptial agreement? Ok. Connie, when you get married, it's for life. Never once did your father and I, God rest his soul, talk about leaving each other. Now you're talking about separation of property before there's even any property to separate.

CONNIE

A prenup doesn't mean that we're gonna leave each other. It's just a way to protect ourselves in business. After we get married, I plan on opening up my own hair salon and Joe wants to open up a garage.

NUNZIATA

Your own hair salon?

CONNIE

I tried talking to you about this, but—

NUNZIATA

Well you shouldn't go into business with the intention of failing—

CONNIE

I'm not—look, I gotta swing by the dress maker's. Why don't you come with me and I'll explain—

NUNZIATA

Which reminds me. I wonder if Anthony called for his tuxedo.

>   (beat)

No, you go ahead ... I've got plenty to do at home.
>   *(CONNIE and LILLY share a look;*
>   *CONNIE shakes her head and exits.)*

NUNZIATA (Continued)

Huh ... so Connie wants to open up her own hair salon?

LILLY

And this came as a surprise to you?

NUNZIATA

I'm a little surprised that she didn't tell me about it, that's all.

LILLY

That's all she's been talking about.

NUNZIATA

Whatever. She's making her life with Joe now. She doesn't need me to advise her anymore. Aaaall grown up and getting married next week. Wow how time flies.
>   *(beat)*

What's the thing you remember most about your wedding day, Ma?

LILLY

Are you kidding me, Nunz'? I have a hard time remembering what I had for dinner last night!

NUNZIATA

Moonlight Serenade ... that was our song. Domenic looked so handsome that day. Remember, ma?

LILLY

That was a long time ago.

NUNZIATA

It sure was.
>   *(beat)*

I just love weddings. Everybody's so happy. Laughing, dancing ... all that good food!

LILLY

I can't wait! Noise, sore feet ... indigestion.

NUNZIATA

I just want Connie to be happy, that's all.

LILLY

She will if she would stop acting like a fruit cake!

NUNZIATA

I know ...

LILLY

Don't worry about Connie. She'll be just fine.

NUNZIATA

I guess. I wish I could say the same for Anthony.

LILLY

Still living that swinging bachelor's life, is he?

NUNZIATA

You don't know the half of it. He hasn't left the house in weeks ... except to go to work. He just mopes all the time and "writes". I really hope he hits it off with that Rosa girl I told you about.
>   *(LILLY checks her watch; she doesn't wanna have this conversation.)*

LILLY
I have a hairdresser's appointment. I need to use the bathroom.

NUNZIATA
You're going to fix your hair, right?

LILLY
I don't want the girls criticizing me for the way I look.
(LILLY exits to the bathroom. Telephone rings.)

NUNZIATA
Hello? Hi Carla. How are you? Fine ... sure ... I've got two different sizes. One for eight eggs and one for twelve.
(ANTHONY comes out of his bedroom scratching his crotch, carrying his laptop. He is wearing loose sweat pants and a large T-shirt.)

NUNZIATA (Continued)
O.K., send her over ... bye.
(NUNZIATA hangs up the phone.)

NUNZIATA (Continued)
You are truly disgusting!

ANTHONY
(under his breath)
Someone had to inherit your traits.

NUNZIATA
What?

ANTHONY
I said I'm ... getting a treat!
(ANTHONY goes to the cupboard and gets himself a couple of twinkies and makes his way to the couch.)

NUNZIATA
You're gonna spoil your lunch. At least eat something a little healthier. I made some fresh blueberry muffins. I'll get you one.

ANTHONY
Don't.
(beat)
Connie leave already?

NUNZIATA
Yeah.

ANTHONY
Did you tell her the other band called for her last night?

NUNZIATA
Oh, I knew I forgot something.

ANTHONY
How could you forget? I reminded you twice last night!

NUNZIATA
I'll tell her when she gets back.
(ANTHONY's on the couch. He unwraps his twinkies.)

NUNZIATA (Continued)
Careful. Don't get anything on the couch.

ANTHONY
What's the big deal? It's vinyl.
NUNZIATA
No it's not! It's "pleather".
ANTHONY
"Pleather"? Wha—
                    (nevermind)
So how come Gentile's band canceled, anyway?
NUNZIATA
He had a hernia operation.
ANTHONY
Wow! He doesn't strike me as the type of guy who could lift anything, let alone something heavy enough to give him a hernia.
NUNZIATA
He got the hernia while trying to help his wife out of the bathtub after she slipped and threw out her back. It must've been hilarious! Can you imagine?
ANTHONY
I do everything in my power not to imagine the Gentiles in the nude.
                    (beat)
This time write it down and make sure she gets it.
NUNZIATA
I don't understand why you're making a big deal out of this.
ANTHONY
I'm making a big deal? I'm making a big deal? It's easier to stage a Broadway production than it is to prepare for this wedding.
NUNZIATA
Most of the fun is in the planning and preparation.
ANTHONY
I don't see you participating in any of the fun and games. You can't even give the kid a simple message.
NUNZIATA
Oh Dio mio ... with this message. Don't you have anything to do today ... like go for your tux?
ANTHONY
I got things to do, alright.
NUNZIATA
I meant things to do besides "writing". Something that'll get you outta the house for a while ...
ANTHONY
Don't even go there.
NUNZIATA
What?
ANTHONY
Just drop it!
NUNZIATA
Alright ... geez ...
                    (pause)

I just thought … it's a beautiful day … it would be nice for you to go out and get some fresh air …

ANTHONY

Fresh air brings on my allergies! And I know what you're getting at. People don't go for walks and magically end up coming home with some beautiful woman … not me, anyway. Unless I club her over the head and drag her home.

(LILLY walks in on his line.)

LILLY

I tried that once. I don't recommend it.

NUNZIATA

Fine …

(pause)

Can I ask you a question?

ANTHONY

There's more?

NUNZIATA

… without upsetting you?

ANTHONY

You can try!

NUNZIATA

Are you happy with … your looks?

ANTHONY

What?

NUNZIATA

Well, it's just that sometimes people don't feel good about themselves if they're not happy with the way they look. In your case, all you have to do is lose a little weight and maybe get yourself one of those hair units, even. Try something fun!

(ANTHONY is shocked.)

LILLY

A what?

NUNZIATA

A hair … unit … thing. You know …

(touches the top of her head)

Yeah, William Shatner has one and he looks terrific! You can't even tell it's a fake.

LILLY

Captain Kirk? Really?

NUNZIATA

… yeah … and they're not even that expensive. The butcher at Aldo's just got one and it only cost him $238.00.

LILLY

No wonder. It looks like the skin of some animal he just sold!

NUNZIATA

Go ahead, make fun. But he has no trouble finding dates.

ANTHONY

I wouldn't either if I didn't mind dating out of my own species.

NUNZIATA

Ok, forget the hair. What I'm trying to say is ... well, there's gotta be someone out there that interests you ... even a little.
(*ANTHONY doesn't reply.*)

NUNZIATA (Continued)

What about Maria Bettini? Have you spoken to her lately?

ANTHONY

Ma, please. I'm eating.

NUNZIATA

Give her a call. I know for a fact she's not seeing anyone.

ANTHONY

I'm shocked!

LILLY

Nunz', you think maybe he has the evil eye?

NUNZIATA

Of course! Whenever I feel a little off, and I don't know why, that's usually what it is.

LILLY

Get me a spoonful of olive oil and a glass of water.

ANTHONY

Get serious, will you? Ma, sit down.
(*CONNIE enters in a panic and starts sifting through papers in the living room.*)

NUNZIATA

Connie, what are you doing here? I thought—

CONNIE

Oh, please—I forgot where Joe told me to meet him. I left the address at home.

NUNZIATA

Why didn't you just call him ... or text him or something ...
(*This rings true to CONNIE.*)

LILLY

Thank God Joe's no brain surgeon either.

ANTHONY

Thank God? These people are gonna reproduce!

CONNIE

Well at least I have somebody to reproduce with!

ANTHONY

Okay, don't you start with me too, Connie! My love life is my business, understood? Nobody else's!

CONNIE

Love life? Anthony, the only way you'll ever get laid is if you crawl up a chicken's ass and wait!

ANTHONY

What men's toilet did you get that from?
(*CONNIE smacks him on the arm.*)

ANTHONY (Continued)

Owe!

CONNIE

Are you calling me a whore?

NUNZIATA

Connie, your language!

CONNIE

Jerk off!

NUNZIATA

Connie!

CONNIE

Love life! You wish!

> *(CONNIE storms out of the apartment.)*

LILLY

She forgot the address again.

ANTHONY

> *(to NUNZIATA)*

You see? You see what you just did, Ma?

NUNZIATA

How is this my fault?

ANTHONY

Because no matter what we talk about in this house you always twist it so that we end up discussing my personal life. So I don't bring a date to the wedding. Big whoop!

NUNZIATA

Anthony, please! Don't go getting all bent out of shape. People can't talk to you anymore without you taking their heads off.

ANTHONY

So why are people still talking to me?

NUNZIATA

Because we're fed up of seeing you so miserable all the time.

ANTHONY

I am not miserable!

NUNZIATA

Really? It's no wonder you're all alone. Look at your attitude.

LILLY

So why don't you leave him alone and stop wasting your time trying to set him up with every one of your friends' daughters!

> *(NUNZIATA is shocked that LILLY would just blurt this out.*
> *LILLY realizes what she said.)*

LILLY (Continued)

I mean ... leave him alone ...

> *(ANTHONY catches on.)*

ANTHONY

Set me up—what?

> *(NUNZIATA doesn't answer.)*

LILLY

I have to get my hair done.

ANTHONY
Not again, Ma ... PLEASE! I can't do this anymore. Did you lose your frickin' mind?
LILLY
On second thought, maybe I'll watch this first.
(NUNZIATA shoots her a look of death.)
ANTHONY
Just tell me that you didn't set me up on any blind dates ...
(NUNZIATA doesn't answer.)
ANTHONY (Continued)
Ma?
NUNZIATA
(pause)
It's not really a date ...
ANTHONY
Oh, Jesus ...
NUNZIATA
... it's more ... more like a ... meeting.
ANTHONY
Why is this so important to you? That you would go to these lengths! You truly believe that one woman can make that much of a difference in my life?
NUNZIATA
Yes!
ANTHONY
Well I can't wait to meet this person!
NUNZIATA
Good. Hang on to that sentiment.
ANTHONY
Unbelievable ...
NUNZIATA
It's good to meet women ... it'll help you get rid of some of those insecurities you have.
ANTHONY
I am not insecure!
NUNZIATA
Oh, no? You never went out with one girl I introduced you to. Not one.
ANTHONY
Take a hint! What I am is fed up with you constantly trying to manipulate my life. Who I see, or don't see, is my business.
NUNZIATA
Do you think that I enjoy doing this? Well I don't! I'm doin' it for you.
ANTHONY
Don't do me any favors!
NUNZIATA
Fine! It'll be a cold day in hell before you hear another word from these lips!
ANTHONY
Hallelujah!
(Silence. LILLY gets up.)

LILLY

Now, I can go get my hair done. Give *Nonna* a kiss, Antonio.

> *(ANTHONY goes over to kiss his grandmother.)*

LILLY (Continued)

Call me later Nunz'. Once you've regained your speech.

> *(NUNZIATA is about to say something but ANTHONY shushes her up. FRANK walks in dressed in lederhosen, carrying a nap sack. He meets LILLY as she's exiting.)*

LILLY (Continued)

Holy Jesus …

FRANK

Hey, Ma! Anthony!

> *(NUNZIATA and ANTHONY look him over.)*

FRANK (Continued)

What?

ANTHONY

Where'd you leave Hansel and Gretel?

FRANK

This …

> *(points to his clothes)*

… is because your best friend, my so called "agent", is a colossal idiot!

ANTHONY

David's an accountant.

FRANK

No kidding! He sends me to some audition for a commercial telling me it's a polka theme. Great. I walk in there ready to do my best rendition of 'Roll out the Barrel', only to see the other actors dressed in pin striped suits, smoking cigars—the works! After the director stopped staring at me, he asked me if I've ever played poker before!

ANTHONY

For a minute there, I thought maybe you picked up yodeling.

FRANK

Ha, ha.

> *(goes over to kiss his mother)*

How you feelin', Ma?

NUNZIATA

As well as can be expected under these circumstances.

> *(ANTHONY gives her a look as if to say I knew you couldn't stay quiet.)*

NUNZIATA (Continued)

And the only reason I spoke is because my youngest son acknowledged my existence. I respect my family members, so therefore I replied.

ANTHONY

Yeah, 'cause you're really capable of keeping quiet. You're a regular cappuccine monk.

FRANK

I'm … I'm just gonna go into the next room and change.

> *(FRANK exits to one of the bedrooms. Pause.)*

NUNZIATA
>   (explodes)
> Sure, it's fine if I have to talk to you to tell you where your clean socks are or to
> call you for supper. But as soon as I try to give a little advice—

ANTHONY
> Advice? Advice?

NUNZIATA
> That's right, advice! As soon as I try to give a little advice, I'm not allowed to speak.

ANTHONY
> That's the whole problem! All you do is talk.

NUNZIATA
> If you'd listen to me the first time, I wouldn't have to repeat myself twenty times.

ANTHONY
> Oh yeah? Okay! I'm gonna listen to you, but then you'll have to be quiet. I'm going
> out, like you suggested.

NUNZIATA
> Where?

ANTHONY
> You see the way you are? I thought you were gonna keep QUIET!

NUNZIATA
>   (talking to "heaven")
> You see, Domenic ... you see how your son talks to me?

ANTHONY
> Stop nagging him. That's what killed him in the first place.
>   (pause)
> I gotta get the hell outta here.

NUNZIATA
> Where you going?

ANTHONY
> For a walk.

NUNZIATA
> If you're going for a walk, you must know what direction you'll be walking in.
> People don't just wander!
>   (FRANK walks back into the room.)

ANTHONY
>   (singing 'The Wanderer')
> "They call me the wanderer, yeah the wanderer ... "

NUNZIATA
> Lovely, just lovely. My grown son acting like a grade school kid.

ANTHONY
> That's right, a baby! You have become unbearable lately. Do you at least realize that?

NUNZIATA
> Really? Well thank you very much for those kind words.

ANTHONY
> Any time.

NUNZIATA
> Can you at least tell me when you'll you be back?

ANTHONY

    With any luck, NEVER!
          (to Frank)
    Aufweidersein!
          (ANTHONY exits.)

FRANK

    Poor bastard.

NUNZIATA

    Oh, is that what you think?

FRANK

    Ma, please. Don't start with me now. I just came by to change.

NUNZIATA

    Well, thank you very much for stopping by. For a minute there, I thought it was me you came to see. God knows I hardly ever see you since you moved out.

FRANK

    Ma, I still have clothes here and I visit you five times a week!

NUNZIATA

    Your brother—ooh! He stays home so that I can watch him torture himself.

FRANK

    Look, I know living with Anthony lately hasn't exactly been a picnic, but you ... you have a way of bringing out the best in people.

NUNZIATA

    Real funny, Frank. We're getting to be a house full of Jerry Seinfelds in here.
          (beat)
    Speaking of ... how's your girlfriend?

FRANK

    Susan and I broke up last week.

NUNZIATA

    It's just as well. I never liked her anyway.

FRANK

    You only met her once for a total of five minutes.

NUNZIATA

    Exactly! You think she'd make an effort to try and get to know me.

FRANK

    We only dated a few times. Nothing serious. It's not as if we were getting married.

NUNZIATA

    Who knows if I'll live to see you get married, Frank.

FRANK

    Where do you get the energy?
          (There's a knock at the door.)

NUNZIATA

    Hello ...
          (NUNZIATA opens the door.)

ANGELA

    Hi, Mrs. Robertini?

NUNZIATA

    ... yes ...

ANGELA
I'm Angela ... Carla's daughter ...

NUNZIATA
Oh, hi! Come in, come in. I'm so happy to finally meet you! I'll get those cake pans for you.
                    (ANGELA enters.)

FRANK
Angela?

ANGELA
Frank! Oh my, God. I don't believe this ... Frankie ...
                    (FRANK goes over to ANGELA and hugs her.)

NUNZIATA
You two know each other? How nice.

FRANK
What ... what are you doin' here?

ANGELA
Having a flashback.

NUNZIATA
(looking for pans) Where did Anthony put those pans?

FRANK
So, how are you?

ANGELA
I'm shocked, to say the least.

NUNZIATA
                    (still looking for pans)
He's always baking something. Usually he's very organized when he puts things away.

ANGELA
Of all the places we could've bumped into each other—

FRANK
Stranger things have happened in this apartment, believe me.

NUNZIATA
Silly me. I just remembered. I left them at my mother's. Frank, be a sweetheart. Run upstairs and pick them up for me.

FRANK
No.
                    (beat)
I mean ... I don't even know what a cake pan looks like.

NUNZIATA
I'll be right back.
                    (NUNZIATA picks up a set of keys and exits.)

FRANK
                    (to Nunziata)
Take your time.
                    (to Angela)
So ... Angie Rinaldo. Holy crap. How long has it been?

ANGELA
It's ... been a while. When my mom told me to go to Mrs. Robertini's ... it didn't click that ... you know, that it was Mrs. Robertini, your mother.

FRANK
Or maybe it did click and you showed up here hoping to see me again.

ANGELA
Ahhh ... you've unraveled my plan.

FRANK
I can't get over this. So, tell me, what are you doing with yourself? You married? Kids?

ANGELA
I'm a chef. I just started working at Villa Carducci. And ... no I'm not married, but who knows how many kids I've got out there, right Frank?

FRANK
Villa Carducci. I'm gonna have to check it out some time.

ANGELA
You look like you're doing pretty good. I catch you on Channel 4 ... doing the weather from time to time.

FRANK
Just until my acting career takes off. (*beat*). You're not married, but you're definitely seeing someone, right?
> (*ANGELA looks at him; doesn't say a word.*)

FRANK (Continued)
... you're not?
> (*She shakes her head; same old Frank*)

FRANK (Continued)
What?

ANGELA
Nothing.

FRANK
No, tell me ... what is it?

ANGELA
You really haven't changed at all, have you?

FRANK
Why do you say that?

ANGELA
'Cause I know how you operate.

FRANK
How?

ANGELA
Forget it. You still live at home?

FRANK
No! God, no. I moved out. Now I spend far too much for a water front apartment.
> (*beat*)
What do you mean you know how I operate?

ANGELA

I haven't seen you in God knows how long and the first thing you do is put the moves on me. Wow.

FRANK

You keep saying things like that and you're gonna end up hurting my feelings.

ANGELA

Thanks to you, I know a little something about that too.

FRANK

You know ... there are two things I could never forgive myself for. One is for boiling my brother's turtle, man did Anthony love that thing ... and the other is for ... you know ... the way things ended between us ...

ANGELA

Frank. Things ended the way they did 'cause you stopped returning my calls.

FRANK

Will you at least do me a favor? Have dinner with me sometime.

ANGELA

What?

(FRANK lays it on thick now.)

FRANK

Please. I've been seeing this girl, Susan, for a very, <u>very</u> long time ... it was getting pretty serious. We even talked about marriage ... and, well ... we just broke up. I'd love to have someone to talk to. You were always a great listener.

ANGELA

You're gonna try to make me believe that someone actually got to you?

FRANK

Yeah ...

(long pause)

Look, I got another audition to go to. I'll pick you up tomorrow about eight, alright?

(She doesn't answer. Pause.)

FRANK (Continued)

Excellent. I'll see you then.

(NUNZIATA walks in carrying two cake pans. She bumps into FRANK as he's exiting.)

FRANK (Continued)

Later, Ma. I got run.

NUNZIATA

That's Frank for you. Always on the go. Come ... sit down.

(NUNZIATA places the pans on the table; she starts pouring two cups of coffee.)

NUNZIATA (Continued)

So, how do you know Frank?

ANGELA

We met at a resort in Vermont. We were both working there one summer.

NUNZIATA

I remember that, but I don't recall him ever mentioning you. Did you two have a <u>relationship</u> relationship?

ANGELA

I thought we did. I guess it wasn't that important to him if he never mentioned it.

NUNZIATA

He doesn't tell me anything unless I pry it out of him.

ANGELA

Can I ask you a silly question?

NUNZIATA

Go ahead. Try and out do anyone in my family.

ANGELA

Why would Frank boil his brother's turtle?

NUNZIATA

He actually told you about that? It was an accident. He wanted to surprise Anthony by giving the turtle a bath. The water was a little too hot, so ... Frank felt terrible. He hasn't spoken about it in ages. Why would he bring that up?

        (ANGELA just shrugs her shoulders.) ANGELA

I don't know.

        (beat)

Well, I ... I should get these pans to my mom. It was a pleasure meeting you.

NUNZIATA

Same here. Take both. She can use whichever one she needs.

ANGELA

Thanks again.

        (ANGELA exits. NUNZIATA goes to the phone. She finds a
        number in her book and dials.)

NUNZIATA

Hello, Mrs. Valdez ... it's Nunziata ... how are you? I'm calling about your daughter, Rosa ...

        (FRANK walks in. NUNZIATA notices him.)

NUNZIATA (Continued)

I'll have to call you back.

        (hangs up)

Frank. I thought you had an audition.

FRANK

        (indicates his cell phone)

David just called. They canceled.

NUNZIATA

I'm sorry, sweetheart.

FRANK

I don't know anymore, Ma. Maybe it's me. I must've gone to a dozen auditions in the past three weeks and nothing. Not even a call back. That alone is bad enough, but then to have to humiliate myself like I did this morning ... what's the use?

NUNZIATA

Awww. I got your favorite cookies.

FRANK

Those "S" shaped ones?

NUNZIATA

    If Anthony didn't get a hold of them.

             (NUNZIATA comes back with cookies.)

FRANK

    Where'd he go?

NUNZIATA

    I don't know and I don't care. He's a big boy now.

FRANK

    And growing by the minute! What were you guys arguing about before, anyway?

NUNZIATA

    You can't talk to him anymore without getting into an argument. All I did was tell him about this girl I wanted him to meet tomorrow, and he stormed out of here like a crazy man.

FRANK

    So what … now you're his pimp?

NUNZIATA

    Very funny. All I know is that if he'd find someone to keep him occupied, he'd be fine. Honestly, if he'd approach finding women with the same passion he has for writing, he'd have a harem.

FRANK

    Ma, leave the guy alone. All he needs is to get out of this apartment, have some fun and meet some people—on his own.

NUNZIATA

    I know that, but he doesn't go out "on his own"—unless it's to eat. Where do you suggest I take him?

FRANK

    A massage parlor.

NUNZIATA

    Boy, you're on a roll today. It wouldn't kill you to spend some time with your brother.

FRANK

    Why don't you ask David? Isn't he Anthony's best friend?

NUNZIATA

    Right. Where did he send you today?

FRANK

    Maybe Anthony would enjoy dressing up like Heidi.

NUNZIATA

    Come on, Frank? It'll be fun. Two brothers—

FRANK

    Fun? Like that time I took him to that pool party and he almost drowned. "My sinuses, my sinuses. I can't breathe!"

NUNZIATA

    You know he's afraid of water. Come on, sweetheart. You guys'll have a great time. Get David to come.

FRANK

    David? Oh, come on!

NUNZIATA

Do this for your brother ... please ...

FRANK

Fine. One night and that's it. And you, Ma, for the love of God, just leave him alone ...

NUNZIATA

I know what you're thinking, but I'm not doing anything wrong. I'd do the same for you.

FRANK

Don't threaten me like that!

> *(FRANK exits. NUNZIATA picks up the telephone and starts looking for a phone number.)*

NUNZIATA

> *(to herself)*

Okay. Rosa, Rosa ... Rosa.

> *(She continues looking for the phone number but is interrupted. LILLY walks in. NUNZIATA puts the phone down.)*

NUNZIATA (Continued)

Oh, hi Ma. Did you go to the beauty parlor?

LILLY

I just spent thirty five dollars to have my hair done, and she asks me if I went to the beauty parlor?

NUNZIATA

I don't understand why you throw away your money like that. Why don't you let Connie do your hair?

LILLY

Because Connie is not up to date with the latest gossip. Where's Anthony?

NUNZIATA

He went for a walk.

LILLY

A walk will do him good. He could stand to burn a few calories.

NUNZIATA

Did you have lunch?

LILLY

Not yet ...

NUNZIATA

Well sit down, I'll fix you a *panino*.

LILLY

Nah, I just came by to find out what time the fund raiser is.

NUNZIATA

We have to leave at four. Don't worry, I'll call you when it's time to go.

LILLY

O.K. And Nunz', don't be too hard on Anthony.

> *(LILLY exits. NUNZIATA picks up the phone again.)*

NUNZIATA

Finally. It's like Grand Central Station in here!

> *(finds her number and dials)*

Hello? Oh, Rosa? Hi. This is Mrs. Robertini ... good, how are you? ... so, your mother told me she spoke to you about my son, Anthony ... that's right ...

(ANTHONY opens the door; NUNZIATA doesn't notice him.
He stands at the doorway. She still doesn't notice him.)

NUNZIATA (Continued)

I just wanted to confirm for tomorrow afternoon ... listen, Rosa, just meet him, then take it from there ... trust me, he'll be here ... great ... two o'clock ... bye, Rosa ...

(NUNZIATA hangs up. ANTHONY totally startles her.)

ANTHONY

Who's Rosa?

(NUNZIATA jumps. She starts fidgeting.)

NUNZIATA

Jesus! You scared the life outta me.

ANTHONY

So ... who is she?

NUNZIATA

Who? Rosa? Oh, Rosa Valdez! You know ... no one, really.

ANTHONY

No one. So then why are you acting like Jerry Lewis? If you were talking to "no one" ... that means "no one" will be showing up here tomorrow afternoon ... at two, right?

NUNZIATA

I ... I mentioned it to you this morning ... sort of ...

ANTHONY

You don't give up, do you? Just ... leave me alone!

NUNZIATA

Again ... you're going into this with the wrong attitude.

ANTHONY

What kind of attitude would you like me to have?

NUNZIATA

For starters, you could be a little more enthusiastic.

ANTHONY

Enthusiastic about what? About spending my Saturday afternoons with rejects?

NUNZIATA

That's not fair! You haven't even met her. And you my son, are no Don Juan!

ANTHONY

I'll give you that. But she can't exactly be Marilyn Monroe either if she needs her mother to set her up on blind dates! This ... this is scarier than that petting zoo incident. Where you forced me to go and I was attacked by that goat!

NUNZIATA

All I ask is for a few minutes of your time, that's all.

ANTHONY

You ask for a few minutes of my time ... and any dignity that I have left.

NUNZIATA

Is that what you think? That I wanna take away your dignity. If you like her, great! If not, that's okay too. What's it gonna hurt? You know what always made everything better when you were just a little boy?

ANTHONY
    I'm afraid to ask.
NUNZIATA
    Pane e Nutella.
ANTHONY .
    I should've guessed it had something to do with food.
            (There's a knock at the door.)
NUNZIATA
    Come in. It's open.
            (ANGELA walks in.)
ANGELA
    Hi Mrs. Robertini.
            (ANTHONY notices ANGELA. He likes what he sees. He stands
            abruptly.)
NUNZIATA
    Angela! Come in, come in.
ANGELA
            (to Anthony)
    Hello.
            (ANTHONY goes to shake her hand.)
ANTHONY
    Hi ... I ... I'm Anthony.
ANGELA
    Angela. Nice to meet you.
ANTHONY
    Nice to meet you, too.
            (ANGELA returns one of the pans to NUNZIATA.)
ANGELA
    She insisted I bring one back to you ... in case you have to bake something
    yourself.
            (ANGELA has her back turned to ANTHONY. He starts to tuck
            in his shirt, straighten his glasses etc. Gets very fidgety.)
NUNZIATA
    I wanted to bake something, but ... who has the time?
ANTHONY
    Yeah. Making me miserable is a full time job.
NUNZIATA
    So, what kind of cake did your mother prepare for tonight?
ANGELA
    Chocolate cheese cake. My favorite.
ANTHONY
    That's my favorite too.
            (ANTHONY uses this to move in a little closer to ANGELA.)
NUNZIATA
    Do you do any baking yourself, Angela?

ANGELA

No, not really. I leave that to my mother. But all she bakes is cheesecakes. I tell her I like something, that's all I eat for months.

ANTHONY

You know, Angela. You're lucky she doesn't use a microwave or you'd be glowing in the dark.

> *(ANTHONY finds this a lot funnier than it actually is; laughs out loud. He turns his back to ANGELA; his facial expression tells it all: "I can't believe that came out of my mouth.")*

NUNZIATA

What she needs is some new recipes.

> *(beat)*

Anthony, why don't you lend Angela your cookbook?

> *(ANTHONY gets embarrassed by this.)*

ANTHONY

I ... I don't have a cookbook.

NUNZIATA

Sure. The one Connie gave you for your birthday.

ANTHONY

I don't even know where it is.

NUNZIATA

You were using it a couple of days ago. It can't be that far.

ANTHONY

I'll ... I'll have to look for it.

> *(pause)*

Oh yeah, yeah ... <u>that</u> cookbook. I'll find it and you can give me a call if you wanna pick it up ... or I can bring it over or something.

ANGELA

Great ... thanks.

NUNZIATA

Do you think your mother would exchange recipes with him?

ANGELA

I don't see why not ...

NUNZIATA

So ... are you going to the fund raiser tonight?

ANTHONY

Enough with the Spanish inquisition, already!

NUNZIATA

I'm just making conversation.

ANTHONY

Then converse, don't interrogate.

ANGELA

That's alright, Anthony. No, I don't think I'll be going.

ANTHONY

Given the way my mother is talking to you, I'd have to say that she met you ... once ... maybe twice before.

ANGELA
Very good.
ANTHONY
Sure, 'cause usually after the fifth or sixth meeting her file on a subject is complete.
She's very efficient. Very thorough.
NUNZIATA
Angela, can you tell him there's nothing wrong with getting to know a person?
ANTHONY
Where does it say that you have to do it under a certain time limit? This isn't a
game show.
NUNZIATA
There's nothing wrong with being curious. You're giving Angela the wrong
impression. You're making me sound like a busy body.
ANTHONY
I'm not even gonna touch that one.
          (beat)
Can I get you something to drink, Angela?
ANGELA
It's okay, Anthony. I'm fine, thank you.
NUNZIATA
I have this wonderful *Amaro* that my sister-in-law brought back from Italy ...
          (ANTHONY gets up, goes over to the hutch and is about to pull
          out the crystal glasses.)
NUNZIATA (Continued)
Get the glasses next to the sink. They're cleaner.
ANTHONY
Thirty years—you never used this crystal. She's waiting for the Pope to come visit.
ANGELA
It's okay, Anthony ...
          (ANTHONY goes over to the fridge to get himself a beer.)
NUNZIATA
Would you want to join us for lunch?
ANGELA
No thanks. I sampled the cheesecake before coming here.
ANTHONY
Did you sample the batter, or when it was in ... cake form?
ANGELA
... in cake form. Why?
ANTHONY
So ... your mother will be going to the fund raiser with a piece missing from
her cake.
ANGELA
She'll be selling it by the piece.
ANTHONY
Well, then ... that's okay.
          (takes a swig of beer)

NUNZIATA

Isn't it a little early in the day for a beer?

ANTHONY

We were ready to have hard liquor.

NUNZIATA

It's not the same thing. That liqueur is made from herbs. It helps your digestive system. It's practically medicinal.

ANTHONY

I had lunch, Ma.

NUNZIATA

That's no reason to drink.

ANTHONY

I'm thirsty. Can't a guy be thirsty?

NUNZIATA

Drink water! That's not like you—

ANTHONY

After this one, I think I'll hit the whiskey! So, how are you enjoying the spectacle so far, Angela?

ANGELA

Don't worry about it, the same thing goes on in my house.

ANTHONY

Good, 'cause it gets better. You see, every once in a while Mother and I lure some poor, unsuspecting person into our home and force them to watch us make total fools of ourselves.

NUNZIATA

I know why he's behaving like this, Angela—

ANTHONY

Don't! Just ... don't.

NUNZIATA

He always gets a little nervous the day before he meets a new girl.

    (pause)

ANTHONY

I just don't think Angela would be interested in our personal affairs.

ANGELA

Look, I should be leaving, I have a few errands to run.

ANTHONY

Well, we did it, partner!

NUNZIATA

I'm sure we didn't frighten her away. Right honey?

ANGELA

Exactly ...

ANTHONY

Please, give us a few more minutes.

NUNZIATA

Tell your mother to call me.

ANGELA

I will. Bye, Anthony.

ANTHONY

Angela. It was nice meeting you.

ANGELA

Same here.

> *(ANGELA exits.)*

NUNZIATA

Maybe you should eat a little something with that beer. Are you hungry?

ANTHONY

No, I picked up a hot dog when I went out.

NUNZIATA

You really should stop eating all that junk food, Anthony. There's a tuna sandwich in the fridge that I fixed for your lunch.

ANTHONY

I already ate. Besides, I told you never to fix me tuna for my lunches. I get all the cats in the neighborhood following me to work in the morning.

NUNZIATA

That Angela is a nice girl, isn't she?

ANTHONY

How can you tell? You didn't give her a chance to speak.

NUNZIATA

You wanna hear the best? She used to date Frank.

> *(ANTHONY takes in this bit of information then explodes.)*

ANTHONY

You just keep finding new ways to embarrass me, don't you?

NUNZIATA

How did I embarrass you?

ANTHONY

That little scene that just occurred, played out perfectly for you, right?

NUNZIATA

I don't know what you're talking about.

ANTHONY

Surprise, surprise!

> *(ANTHONY looks at her; guzzles his beer.)*

NUNZIATA

Stop being so dramatic and just relax, will you?

ANTHONY

Any more relaxed and I'll slip into a coma! That would solve a lot of problems, wouldn't it?

NUNZIATA

Anthony ...

ANTHONY

Forget it, Ma ... just forget it. You ... you'll never change!

NUNZIATA

You're the one who needs to change, Anthony. Not me.

> *(ANTHONY storms out. NUNZIATA stands there a second.)*
> BLACK OUT

ACT 1 SCENE II

(It is the same Friday about 8:30 p.m. The scene opens with what appears to be an empty apartment. ANTHONY comes limping into the apartment, carrying a newspaper. He is wearing jeans and a sport shirt. He sits on the couch, starts removing his shoe and checks his watch.)

ANTHONY
Holed up in a subway for three and a half hours.
(shoe's off; rubs his foot)
Ahhh ...
(CONNIE bursts into the living room.)
CONNIE
Anthony, did I get any calls?
ANTHONY
I just walked in.
CONNIE
Not now, this afternoon.
ANTHONY
I haven't been home all day. Who's supposed to call?
CONNIE
No one ...
ANTHONY
... you're not expecting a phone call ...
CONNIE
No ...
ANTHONY
Uh huh. If you're not expecting a phone call, then why—never mind.
(pause)
Connie, is everything alright?
CONNIE
No ...
ANTHONY
Do you want to talk about it?
CONNIE
Yeah ...
ANTHONY
You'll have to form some kind of sentence if you want this conversation thing to work. What's bothering you?
CONNIE
(crying)
It's Joe ... he stood me up for lunch today.
ANTHONY
Do you know why?
CONNIE
No ...

ANTHONY
Did you try calling him?

CONNIE
Yeah …

ANTHONY
Work with me here. Explain to me what happened.

CONNIE
Well, this morning I left to go to the dress maker's … then I was supposed to meet Joe for lunch … but I forgot where I had to meet him … that's when I came back home. Then I remembered where I was supposed to meet him, which is good, because when I came back home, I forgot to take the address of where I had to meet him. When I finished at the dress maker's, I went to the restaurant— that's where we were supposed to meet. When he wasn't there, I called his cell … no answer. Then I called him at work and they told me that he had left an hour ago … I waited and waited; I called him at home but he wasn't there either.
            (starts crying louder)
He doesn't wanna marry me!

ANTHONY
Connie, get a grip, will you? He probably forgot, it's that simple.

CONNIE
How could he forget to meet his fiancée a week before our wedding?

ANTHONY
This is Joe we're talking about. Look, there's probably a logical explanation for him not showing up.

CONNIE
You think so?

ANTHONY
Yes.
            (puts his arm around her; tries to cheer her up)
Don't go jumping to conclusions just because "Mr. Unforgettable", forgot about a lunch date …
            (motions to pick up a newspaper)
Owe!

CONNIE
What's wrong with your foot?

ANTHONY
Don't ask.
            (Telephone rings; ANTHONY answers.)

ANTHONY (Continued)
Hello …

CONNIE
Is it Joe?

ANTHONY
Hold on a sec …
            (CONNIE grabs the phone from ANTHONY; he gets up to check for any written phone messages.)

CONNIE

Hello? Joe, where the hell were you? I was running around until five o'clock this afternoon worried sick. Not knowing if you were dead or alive or if there was even gonna be a wedding. When I got home I had to take two ativans for my nerves and you don't even have the decency to call?

(pause; starts crying)

A car accident?

(cries louder)

Did you get hurt? ... thank God ... you did?

(checks her cell phone; cries even louder)

The battery died! Okay ... I'll meet you there in five minutes ... bye.

(CONNIE hangs up and rushes to get her purse.)

CONNIE (Continued)

Tell Ma I went out with Joe. That is if she bothers asking.

ANTHONY

Whoa ... what if I wanna go out?

CONNIE

Then ... go!

ANTHONY

Ma's not home yet.

CONNIE

So what? If you're so worried call her if you go out. You're the one she's gonna miss, Anthony. Not me.

(As CONNIE exits, she meets DAVID at the door. He seems very concerned about ANTHONY'S state. DAVID enters.)

DAVID

Hi, Anthony.

ANTHONY

Hey, David.

DAVID

How are you?

ANTHONY

I'm okay.

DAVID

Sure, anything you say, pal. You weren't at work today ... any particular reason you stayed home?

ANTHONY

David, please. I just got rid of my mother. But if you must know, the plant was closed today for an inspection.

DAVID

I just want you to know that you can talk to me.

ANTHONY

I'm glad to hear that. Can I get you a beer?

(ANTHONY gets up and heads for the kitchen.)

DAVID

If it's not too much trouble.

(notices Anthony limping)

Oh my God! What happened to your foot? Sit down. I'll get it myself.

ANTHONY

David, get a hold of yourself! You're starting to scare me.

DAVID

I didn't mean to scare you. I'm sorry, really ...

ANTHONY

Enough!

DAVID

Sorry.

ANTHONY

Did you stop taking your medication, again?

DAVID

No.

ANTHONY

Maybe you should adjust the dosage.

DAVID

So, what's wrong?

ANTHONY

It's a blister.

DAVID

Wow! How did you do that?

ANTHONY

I don't know. How do you get blisters?

> *(FRANK bursts into the room.)*

FRANK

Anthony! Good, you're here—where else would you be? And Greenberg is also here. Just for the record, David, when I said I'd swing by to pick you up ... I meant at your house.

> *(notices Anthony limping)*

What did you do to your foot?

ANTHONY

Since everyone is so interested ... I did a shit load of walking this afternoon. Now I got this huge blister on my heel ... my foot is killing me.

FRANK

You're the only guy I know who can go for a walk and injure himself. Get dressed. We're going to Spacco's.

ANTHONY

Spacco's ...

DAVID

Yeah, it's their fifth anniversary. They're making a big deal over the whole thing—

FRANK

Yeah ... yeah, Thanks for the info-mercial, David. Do you know who I bumped into today? Remember the Kowalski "twins"? I told them about Spacco's. And yes! They will be there tonight! Ooh ... those TITS! Four of them. That's right, Anthony, FOUR OF THEM!

ANTHONY

I'm not in the mood.

FRANK

Don't start this crap, alright.

ANTHONY

I'm not up to it, this blister—

FRANK

You're gonna stay home, God knows how long, because of a blister?

DAVID

Anthony, if you like, I can burst that blister for you in no time. All I need is some rubbing alcohol and a razor blade.

(DAVID starts off towards the bathroom.)

ANTHONY

David. Stop! What are you, nuts? I'm not going anywhere tonight in this condition.

FRANK

Condition? What are you, pregnant? If you wanna stay home, just say so. Believe me, you wouldn't be shocking me. But, please, don't use a blister as an excuse to vegetate.

ANTHONY

It's not an excuse.

FRANK

So then let Dr. Oz, over here, burst it, and let's get the hell outta here. Anthony, it's a tiny cut on the skin to let the water out. You put a bandage over it and it's done.

ANTHONY

I said no.

FRANK

You know what, I think you love staying in this house fighting with Ma. You say you hate it, but deep down inside, you get off on this shit. Ok, so wait for her to get home tonight so you two can have another huge scrap.

(ANTHONY thinks about this for a moment.)

ANTHONY

So, it's like a tiny cut, right?

DAVID

Anthony, trust me. I have had some medical training.

FRANK

You've been to enough psychiatrists, that's for sure.

DAVID

Hey! I happen to be an expert in handling crisis situations.

FRANK

Oh, Jesus …

DAVID

Remember my aunt Gertrude?

FRANK

(waves his hand in front of his face as if to indicate bad breath)

That aunt Gertrude?

DAVID

Remember her? It was a Saturday night, April 28, 1984. We had just finished supper. Roasted chicken, potatoes … string beans. I didn't eat the string beans. I was afraid of choking on that little thread. Aunt Gertrude got up from the table and went into the living room. I was helping my mother clean up when I started to hear this moaning sound.

> *(imitates a moaning sound)*

At first, I thought my dog got his paw stuck somewhere. Lucky. That was my dog's name, Lucky. The moaning got louder and louder and I realized it was coming from the living room. We all stopped what we were doing and rushed in to see what was wrong. We found aunt Gertrude sprawled out on the couch, clenching her jaw. Thank God she didn't pass out 'cause I don't think anybody would've given her mouth to mouth. Through the moaning and groaning she told us that there was a piece of a chicken bone stuck way in the back of her throat. There was no way my father would get near her. My mother couldn't. Given her heart condition and all. I was the only one left. So, I was elected to go in there and remove this piece of chicken bone. I took my mother's tweezers—we didn't have time to sterilize them—and a flashlight and I went in ... ever so slowly. I was just a kid, but I remember it as if it was yesterday. All that sighing and panting ...

FRANK
The scary thing is that he believes this really happened.

ANTHONY
I still don't know what this has to do with my foot!

FRANK
The point he's trying to make—at least I hope—is that things like blisters or something getting stuck in your throat are things that are fixed with simple home remedies. Now, don't turn this into a tragedy. Go get the razor and the rubbing alcohol.

> *(ANTHONY's reluctant; doesn't move.)*

FRANK (Continued)
Well, come on! We don't have all night.

ANTHONY
Alright!

> *(ANTHONY exits to the bathroom.)*

FRANK
You're a regular Shakespeare, David. That was one clever story.

> *(DAVID starts having a panic attack.)*

DAVID
I ... I can't breathe ...

FRANK
David, why are you freaking out? What's the matter with you?

DAVID
I can't touch him ... that story ... that story about my aunt ... I ... I exaggerated it. I can't go through with this ... Frank, I can't. What are we gonna do? What are we gonna do?

FRANK
David ... David ... get a grip! Don't screw this up! Just take the razor from him, and then I'll take over from there. Can you do that?

> *(DAVID nods.)*

FRANK (Continued)
Good. Now, take it easy ... just ... just think about something else.

DAVID

Good idea ... alright. Oh yeah, how did that polka audition go today?

FRANK

Audition? You sure you wanna go there?

>*(ANTHONY walks back into the living room, carrying a razor, some cotton balls and a bottle of rubbing alcohol.)*

ANTHONY

Here you go.

>*(reluctantly hands David the things)*

And be careful.

DAVID

>*(stares at the blade)*

All right, Anthony. You just sit down and relax. That's good ... real good. Just sit down and relax.

>*(he's about to have another panic attack)*

ANTHONY

David, why are you so nervous?

>*(to Frank)*

He's making me nervous!

>*(to David)*

You relax, O.K.?

FRANK

Thank you, David, but I'll take over from here.

>*(DAVID is still staring at the blade.)*

FRANK (Continued)

David!

DAVID

Huh? Are you sure?

FRANK

Gimme that!

>*(takes blade from David)*

DAVID

Alright then. Don't worry, Anthony. In a few minutes, we'll be heading for Spacco's, and if you play your cards right, we may just find you that girl you've been looking for.

ANTHONY

What do you mean, we—Oh ... so that's what this is all about. Get poor, pathetic Anthony a date for his sister's wedding. Jesus, you're the last person I'd expect this from. At least my mother has an excuse—she's my mother!

DAVID

It's no secret that you don't have a date ...

ANTHONY

I don't see any women breaking down the door to go out with you!

DAVID

I'm goin' through a divorce, here!

ANTHONY

That was three years ago!

DAVID

Yeah, well, at least I had a date to my sister's wedding.

ANTHONY

You're an only child! Thanks a lot, David.

FRANK

Yes, thank you, Einstein.

DAVID

Hey, what is it with you? Every time I say something, you associate me with another person.

FRANK

David, shut up! Let's get started.

DAVID

He has his sock on. He'll have to take it off.

FRANK

Thank you Larry King, for that enlightening bit of information.

DAVID

There you go again! Now I'm Larry King. I make a comment—I become someone else!

FRANK

Well ... take your sock off.

ANTHONY

I'll take it off. I know I have to take it off.

DAVID

I think I better rest. I may get a little queasy.

ANTHONY

You're gonna get queasy? I'm the one having his foot slashed!

DAVID

I always get queasy when I see a lot of blood.

ANTHONY/FRANK

Blood?

FRANK

Who the hell said anything about a lot of blood?

ANTHONY

Marvelous! They're gonna walk in here tonight to find three queasy guys passed out on the living room floor, with mangled feet and blood all over the place!

DAVID

He's a bundle of nerves. Maybe we should get him a drink to calm him down.

FRANK

I can use a drink myself.

DAVID

Now we're starting to make sense!

(heads for the bar; starts singing)

I say tomato, you say-

(DAVID stops singing; waits for FRANK to join in.)

FRANK

I'm not singing with you, David.

DAVID

> I say potato, you say-

FRANK

> Just get the bottle!

DAVID

> *(resumes singing by himself)*
> Tomato, tomato, potato, potato let's call the whole thing off.
>> *(DAVID pours a drink for ANTHONY and for FRANK.)*

ANTHONY

> That's the best damn thing you said all night.

FRANK

> Here. Drink this. It'll loosen you up. *Salute!*

DAVID

> *L'Chaim!*
>> *(They all drink. ANTHONY pulls his sock off and shows his huge blister to the audience.)*

ANTHONY

> I hope you don't mind, but I didn't have time to get a pedicure.

FRANK

> Alright, let's get this over with.
>> *(FRANK picks up ANTHONY'S foot.)*

ANTHONY

> Jesus Christ, your hands are like a block of ice!

FRANK

> I am a little nervous. It's not everyday I perform elective surgery in my mother's living room.

DAVID

> I better sit down. I'm getting queasy.
>> *(DAVID goes over and picks up a deck of cards. FRANK moves towards DAVID, all the time he's holding ANTHONY by the foot; drags him along the couch.)*

FRANK

> Again with the queasy. I swear on my mother's head, David. If you pass out, I'll see to it that you never regain consciousness again!
>> *(FRANK drops ANTHONY's foot.)*

ANTHONY

> Owe! Maybe we should just forget it.

FRANK

> You're dead! You're dead, Greenberg!
>> *(FRANK heads for DAVID.)*

DAVID

> Now you're gonna tell me this is my fault?

FRANK

> Shut up! I don't wanna hear you anymore! If you faint, or die … do it quietly. I need another drink.

ANTHONY

> I'm getting myself a double.

> *(ANTHONY goes over to the bar to get himself another bottle of booze. He takes a swig.)*

DAVID

> *(sits at the table and deals cards as if he's playing poker)*

Yeah, I'll have one too, Frank.

> *(FRANK pours a drink, puts down the bottle, and walks over to DAVID. DAVID throws down a card. ANTHONY continues to drink from the bottle.)*

FRANK

Why'd you throw out the jack? You had a two-way straight going.

DAVID

I'm trying this new strategy I read about.

FRANK

Put the cards down and pay attention. You're driving me to drink here, David.

DAVID

I'll get the car.

ANTHONY

> *(stalling)*

I would like to propose a toast!

DAVID

Excellent idea!

FRANK

To Connie's wedding.

DAVID

To your sister's wedding.

ANTHONY

Cheers!

> *(They all drink.)*

FRANK

Now ... you ready Anthony?

> *(picks up the razor blade)*

ANTHONY

What ... what's the hurry? Let's have another drink.

FRANK

One more and that's it!

ANTHONY

Salute!

> *(They all drink; ANTHONY continues to pound it back. DAVID goes back to his card game.)*

ANTHONY (Continued)

> *(lifts his bottle)*

I would like to propose a toast.

FRANK

Quit stalling!

ANTHONY

No ... no ... no ... no! I mean ... it's only right. You proposed a toast to my sister, it's only fitting that I propose a toast to yours ... ha, ha, ha ...

FRANK

> Very cute, Anthony!

DAVID

> At least you're not an only child. I think that's the root of my problems. Maybe that's why I have so much trouble making friends. I was always alone when I was growing up. No one to play with ...

FRANK

> Here he goes with the childhood stories. I thought I told you to shut up! I swear. I don't know how you get through the day without having to wear a helmet.

DAVID

> My therapist says ...

FRANK

> If I have to listen to another one of your therapist stories, I swear to God, I will take this blade and cut my jugular!

ANTHONY

> Hey, hey, hey. Let him talk. Go on, David.

FRANK

>> *(to Anthony)*
>
> I think you're getting delirious.
>
>> *(beat)*
>
> Anthony, your stall tactics were impressive ...
>
>> *(FRANK motions towards ANTHONY.)*

ANTHONY

> This is a true friend, Frank. You are, David, you are. I mean ... you see the sorry state I'm in ... and no matter how much of an asshole I am, you're there for me!
>
>> *(drinks)*
>
> I just want you to know that I appreciate that.

DAVID

> Thanks, Anthony.
>
>> *(ANTHONY goes to kiss DAVID on the cheek. DAVID turns as he delivers his line "Thanks, Anthony.". Their lips meet.)*

DAVID (Continued)

> That's the nicest thing anyone ever said to me.

FRANK

> Where did you grow up, in a cave? Alright, I had enough of this shit. Are we gonna do this or not?

ANTHONY

> Why should I?

FRANK

> You're just gonna have to trust me on this, alright?

ANTHONY

> Trust you? Trust you? You killed my turtle!

FRANK

> The turtle was an accident. An accident! Thirty years ago. You still haven't forgiven me!
>
>> *(goes for Anthony)*

ANTHONY

    Stay away from me!

FRANK

    David, grab him!

ANTHONY

    Help me, David, please!

FRANK

    Stand still so I can do this, you big baby.

ANTHONY

    Oh, you'd love that, wouldn't you?

FRANK

    Hey! You think I'm enjoying this? Well I'm not! I'm doing this for you.

        (gasps)

ANTHONY

    You're just like Ma! You're just like Ma!

FRANK

    How dare you ...

        (FRANK chases ANTHONY even harder. As ANTHONY tries
        to get away, he bangs his foot and falls onto the couch.)

ANTHONY

    Ah ... shit ... that hurts. Okay, okay, okay. You win. Just don't hurt me ...
    please dear God! Don't hurt me!

FRANK

    Show time!

ANTHONY

    AHHH! (Passes out).

        (Unbeknownst to FRANK, DAVID passes out.)

FRANK

    Anthony ... Anthony! David ... you believe it, he passed out! (notices that David
    passed out)

    Beautiful. Greenberg, you're a rock. Thank you for you support.

        (Drops Anthony's foot again. Starts removing David's shoe and sock)

    By the way, I never did get to thank you for that audition you sent me to.

        BLACK OUT

ACT 2 SCENE I

    (It is the same Friday night, about 10:30 p.m. The scene opens with
    DAVID at the kitchen table playing solitaire. ANTHONY and FRANK
    are curled up together, asleep on the couch. ANTHONY is in a tank
    top, and his legs are wrapped in a throw blanket. He's only wearing his
    boxer shorts under the blanket. A different pair of pants and a shirt
    are neatly laid out over the couch. The heel of ANTHONY'S foot is
    bandaged. ANTHONY wakes up. He pulls himself up and looks down
    at FRANK. FRANK looks at ANTHONY. In unison, they both turn
    to look at DAVID.)

DAVID

    Rise and shine!

ANTHONY

    Do you mind explaining this, David?

          (ANTHONY stands. The throw blanket falls to the floor, we discover that he's in his boxers.)

DAVID

    You spilled some brandy on your clothes before you dozed off, So I got you some clean ones.

          (ANTHONY starts getting dressed.)

ANTHONY

    Well … thank you.

DAVID

    Nice fruit of the looms.

          (FRANK and DAVID find this funny.)

FRANK

    They're pink!

DAVID

    With turtles on them.

FRANK

    Who the hell wears pink underwear?

ANTHONY

    Nonna gave them to me.

DAVID

    You weren't kidding when you said your family's got it in for you!

FRANK

    Or that you're not concerned with what women think. So, how's your foot?

ANTHONY

    It feels pretty good. Mind you, I'll probably develop gangrene and have to have it amputated.

DAVID

    You guys might think this is a little weird, but my foot is actually a little sore.

FRANK

    Really? Guys, please, I'm starving. Let's get the hell outta here. It's getting late.

ANTHONY

    It is getting late. I wonder why Ma's not home yet?

FRANK

    Minghia! Do you and her take turns staying home worrying about each other? You know the way these events go. Come on …

ANTHONY

    She usually calls if she's gonna be late. It's almost 11:00.

FRANK

    It's 10:35. She's gonna walk right through that door any second now. Get your jacket and let's get the hell outta here. Anthony, listen to me. You think women are just gonna show up in your living room and ask you out?

ANTHONY

    Don't worry. Ma's got that angle covered.

FRANK
I'm serious.
ANTHONY
Me too. You guys go ahead. I'm gonna stick around here and work on my screenplay.
FRANK
Snap out of it, will you? ... screenplay ... I haven't even read a decent Christmas card that you've written. Don't you wanna meet someone?
ANTHONY
Of course.
FRANK
Then?
ANTHONY
Yeah, but who am I gonna meet at a place like that?
DAVID
Anthony. The Kowalski twins!
ANTHONY
Stop calling them twins. They're not even related. Besides, I don't need to go there to get lucky.
FRANK
You're right. Stay home and get "lucky" with your right hand! It's gonna be swarming with hot, beautiful, available women—my mouth is watering just thinking about it.
ANTHONY
If I tell you why I don't wanna go out, are you gonna stop busting my balls? I already met someone, okay?
FRANK
You're shittin' me?

(ANTHONY shoots FRANK a dirty look.)

FRANK (Continued)
Sorry ... so who is she?
ANTHONY
I thought you were gonna stop bugging me.
DAVID
What's her name?
ANTHONY
Maria ... Deborah ... Gloria ... what's the difference?
FRANK
Easy ... so sensitive.
ANTHONY
Just forget I said anything.
FRANK
You are un-believable, you know that? You finally meet someone you like and you're even more miserable than before.
ANTHONY
You know ... it's easy for you good looking actor types to approach women, but me? It's like you said, Frank, these women are "gorgeous". Me, I'm plain at best.

FRANK

Anthony. If you want my opinion, I think you're beautiful. Whatta you think, David?

DAVID

Anthony, you're gorgeous. On my mother ... if you had tits, I wouldn't be able to keep my hands off of you.

FRANK

Listen, you're my brother and I love you. And I understand that maybe chasing women is not your thing ... or maybe you're afraid that they won't find you interesting or attractive ... whatever. But if you wanna at least hook up with someone, you're gonna have to start playing the "part". Jesus, Anthony. You ... you offer a woman a mutual fund when what she really wants is a night out at the casino!

ANTHONY

Play the p̲a̲r̲t̲?

FRANK

The "part". Make her believe that you're a womanizer—

DAVID

Who?

FRANK

Her ... any woman.

DAVID

... huh?

FRANK

Jesus. Shut up, David. (to Anthony) You play the bad boy or the "part" and she'll wanna find out what makes you tick. You know what I'm sayin'?

ANTHONY

Not really. But it has something to do with me lying.

FRANK

No. Not exactly. You don't have to lie ... just ...

DAVID

... create an illusion.

ANTHONY

I thought the foundation for a good relationship was honesty.

FRANK

Who the hell has been feeding you that crap? There's no such thing as a truly open and honest relationship where you can tell your partner anything—I mean anything.

ANTHONY

What?

FRANK

No such animal. Okay ... your wife one day notices you gawking at some gorgeous piece of ass and she asks you that question that every woman inevitably will ask at one time, "Honey, what are you thinking?" What are you gonna tell her?

ANTHONY

I don't know ...

FRANK

Are you gonna say, "Actually, I'm wondering what color her nipples are, and if she can do position 107 on a wing back chair."? No. You'll reply what any other normal man would and say: "Nothing, dear."

DAVID

And that would be a lie! Making you and your relationship dishonest.

ANTHONY

Somehow, I think you got the wrong idea about this relationship thing.

FRANK

Hey, you can stay home and contemplate honesty in relationships. Tonight, I'm going to hook up with some beautiful, unsuspecting woman, and feed her so much bullshit, that when she nods her head, she'll hear cowbells. And I will find out what color her nipples are and if she can do position 107 on a wing back chair! And just to make it interesting, I'll find myself a woman that's in her mid fourties; I hear that's when they're in their prime!

DAVID

I've been in my prime for eighteen years.

FRANK

Listen. I'm truly happy that you met someone. But you don't have to stay home and be faithful to a girl you barely said "hello" to! Anthony, reconsider. 'The illusion'. Be friendly ... charming. Go ... have fun for Christ's sake!

ANTHONY

I wouldn't know how.

FRANK

You're a writer. Pretend you're one of those charming characters in that movie you haven't written yet.

ANTHONY

No ... I don't know ... no, I'm really not up to it.

FRANK

I give up! Tell you what. You just worship this girl from afar. Keep a shrine of her in your room—pictures, candles. Stalk her so that you can get yourself arrested one day.

I'll be at Spacco's if you change your mind.

> *(FRANK exits.)*

DAVID

Come on, we'll go grab a beer and you can tell me all about her.

ANTHONY

No really, David. She said she might call ... she wanted to borrow a cookbook.

DAVID

Wouldn't it be funny if ... here you are waiting for a phone call, and she was at Spacco's?

ANTHONY

Hilarious. Plus, if I meet her there, I'll probably start acting weird and then I'll really blow it.

DAVID

Whatever you say. I'll see you later, buddy.

(DAVID exits. ANTHONY starts cleaning up. He begins humming to himself. He stops when he hears NUNZIATA at the door. NUNZIATA walks in cautiously.)

ANTHONY

How did the fund raiser go?

NUNZIATA

We had a pretty good turn out this year. How come you didn't go out with David?

ANTHONY

I wanted to get some rest. You know ... so that I'll be ready for that big "meeting" tomorrow afternoon.

NUNZIATA

How long are you gonna dwell on this for?

ANTHONY

I'm not dwelling on anything. I said I would meet her, didn't I?

NUNZIATA

Try to make the best of it. It's still not to late to catch up. You'll probably have a good time.

ANTHONY

Don't worry, I won't embarrass you by going to Connie's wedding alone.

NUNZIATA

That's not what this is about.

ANTHONY

Maybe not for you.

NUNZIATA

Did you get your tux?

ANTHONY

I'll go Monday after work.

NUNZIATA

If you'd like, you could try on the suit your father wore for our wedding? I'd have to shorten the pants a little, but it should fit okay.

ANTHONY

No ... don't touch his suit. I'll get the tux.
(pause)
You ... you and Pop started dating in high school, right?
(NUNZIATA is surprised at this question.)

NUNZIATA

Yeah ... our senior year. What ... what made you think of that?

ANTHONY

I don't know. So ... is ... is that when you realized he was the one for you? The man you were gonna marry?

NUNZIATA

It's hard to say ... I mean ... I didn't really think of marriage then, well at least not consciously.
(beat)
Why are you asking about your father?

ANTHONY

I've been thinking of him a lot lately.

NUNZIATA

What's bothering you, Anthony? Why are you bringing this up?

ANTHONY

Maybe I'm just getting old and sentimental. I remember taking a girl out for supper and then being able to sit and talk to her for hours. Now, after I'm finished eating, I look for a drafty place so I can pass gas.

NUNZIATA

Not sentimental, that's for sure.

ANTHONY

How come I never hear you talk about him anymore?

NUNZIATA

I actually find it gets more difficult as time passes. Now, I'm happy just thinking about him. Thinking about all the beautiful memories he left me. To this day I can't listen to Moonlight Serenade without getting emotional.

ANTHONY

I wonder if he realized how lucky he was to have left someone behind to remember him.

NUNZIATA

I'm sure he knew, Anthony. I'm sure he knows.

> *(ANTHONY leans over and kisses her on the cheek.)*

ANTHONY

Ah, what the hell. I think I will catch up with the guys.

NUNZIATA

Good.

> *(pause)*

You okay?

ANTHONY

Yeah.

NUNZIATA

You can talk to me, you know.

ANTHONY

I know. Are you gonna be alright?

NUNZIATA

Yeah.

ANTHONY

Connie should be home soon. She's with Joe.

NUNZIATA

Go. Have a good time.

> *(ANTHONY checks his wallet.)*

ANTHONY

Oh, Ma ... you wouldn't have fifty bucks to lend me, would you?

> *(NUNZIATA goes into her purse and takes out fifty dollars. As she's giving him the money, she holds his hand.)*

ANTHONY (Continued)

Thanks, Ma.

> *(ANTHONY kisses his mother and exits. NUNZIATA finds herself alone in the apartment. She notices the picture of her*

husband, curls up on the couch as the lights fade.)
BLACK OUT

ACT 2 SCENE II

(It is Saturday afternoon about 2:00 p.m. The scene opens with CONNIE in the living room putting on lipstick in front of the mirror. She's getting ready to go out. ANTHONY walks in on her, checks the time.)

ANTHONY

Connie ... it's almost two o'clock—

CONNIE

Don't worry, I'm leaving. I would've been outta here a long time ago, but I've been sick all morning. Maybe I'm bulimic.

ANTHONY

Connie, you have many problems, but bulimia, really?

CONNIE

Okay, so then how do you explain this? Last night Joe fixed me a nice supper ... and halfway through the baked zitti, I got up, went to the can and puked my guts out! I was lucky to make it to Spacco's afterwards.

ANTHONY

The way Joe cooks, you got off light!

CONNIE

Yeah, you're probably right. Dinner was pretty nasty. So, did you have fun last night?

ANTHONY

It was interesting to say the least. Man, these places ain't cheap, that's for sure.

CONNIE

You're telling me ...

ANTHONY

But ... watching David screw up every one of Frank's pick up attempts. Can't put a price tag on that.

CONNIE

So who was that hottie <u>you</u> were chatting up last night?

ANTHONY

Who?

CONNIE

That blond with the fake boobs ... green skirt ...

ANTHONY

She thought I was Miguel. The bus boy. She kept asking me for more ice.

CONNIE

Okay, Miguel. I'm outta here. Have fun!

(CONNIE kisses him on the cheek and exits.)

Miguel ...

ANTHONY

(A tango plays in the background. ANTHONY checks himself out in the mirror and practices how he's going to greet Rosa.)

ANTHONY (Continued)
>(in a Latin accent)

Hello, Rosa. Welcome to Antonio's hideaway. Please. Come in, come in. No.
>(typical Jersey guy. Grabs his crotch.)

Yo, Rosa . . . how you doin', uh? Definitely not.
>(There's a knock at the door. He snaps out of it. Music stops.)

ANTHONY (Continued)

How the hell did I let myself get talked into this?
>(ANTHONY opens the door. ROSA walks in as if she owns the place.)

ROSA

Hola!

>(ANTHONY stands at the door liking what he sees. Looks up to
>the heavens and mouths "Thank you.".)

ANTHONY

Well, olay to you too.

ROSA

It's *hola*, not olay. *Hola* is Spanish for—.

ANTHONY

Yeah, I know. I was trying to be—*Buongiorno*. That's Italian for hello. I'm
Anthony. That's English for Antonio. Pleased to meet you.

ROSA

My name is Rosa.
>(ROSA goes to the couch and sits with her legs curled up. She lifts
>her skirt to mid-thigh. Pats the couch, indicating for ANTHONY
>to go sit with her.)

ROSA (Continued)

Come and sit with me, Antonio.

ANTHONY

I . . . would you like some coffee, or a drink?

ROSA

No, thank you. I don't believe in poisoning my body with chemicals such as
caffeine or alcohol. I prefer to find ecstasy the natural way; satisfy the needs of
my body with a clear mind.

ANTHONY

O—kay!
>(ROSA walks over to ANTHONY and passionately kisses him.)

ROSA

Mm . . . oh . . . yes . . .

ANTHONY
>(pulling away)

Easy . . . you're slobbering all over me.

ROSA

What's wrong? Is it my breath?
>(ROSA goes for her purse; takes out her breath freshener spray.)

ANTHONY

It's not your breath. Your bodily odors are in tact. It's just that I . . . well we
barely said "hello". I'd like to get to know you first.

ROSA

We've introduced each other, what's left for us to say. Your mother set us up because you're desperate. Any conversation at this point would be meaningless small talk. But if you'd feel better talking first ... let's talk!

(ROSA walks back and sits on the couch.)

(Indicates for him to go sit with her. ANTHONY goes.)

ROSA (Continued)

Talk!

ANTHONY

Yeah, I'd feel better if we'd talk first. So ...

(pause)

I can't just talk ... I mean ... I have to have something to talk about ...

ROSA

What do you do for a living?

ANTHONY

I'm a writer. Actually, I work in a meat packing factory, but I'm really a writer ... movies, TV shows ...

ROSA

Fine. I work for Green Peace.

(ROSA kisses ANTHONY all over and starts unbuttoning his shirt.)

ANTHONY

Gotta save those whales!

(ROSA continues kissing him and unbuttoning his shirt.)

ANTHONY (Continued)

There you go again ... will you please control yourself? You must've been real popular in high school!

ROSA

Not really, my father never let me out of his sight. (ROSA kisses him more and more.)

ANTHONY

... you're steaming up my glasses ...

ROSA

Do you know what it's like spending your teenage years in confinement?

ANTHONY

Today you choose to rebel against your father?

ROSA

(violently releases him)

Don't you dare psycho analyze me. I've seen enough therapists in my life to last us both a lifetime.

ANTHONY

Oh, boy ...

ROSA

Let me ask you a question. Do you think you're better than me because you want to talk to me before you screw me? What difference does it make if we have a conversation first? Well?

(ANTHONY'S at a loss for words.)

ROSA (Continued)

Oh, sure. It would satisfy your macho male ego, thinking you're in control of the situation. But you know as well as I do that from the second you saw me, all you could think about is how fast you could get me undressed and make hot, passionate love to me.

> *(getting hysterical)*

Sex! SEX! That's what's on your mind, no? And how good I'd be in bed?

ANTHONY

I am starting to wonder about the color of your nipples ...

ROSA

> *(unbuttons her dress)*

Then, let me end the suspense ...

> *(ROSA slips her dress off from the shoulder straps. ANTHONY watches in amazed confusion as it falls to the floor.)*

ANTHONY

You—are very, <u>very</u> hot—

ROSA

Oh, so you do find me attractive?

> *(ANTHONY nods his head rapidly. ROSA grabs him and tries to kiss him. He reluctantly moves away from her.)*

ANTHONY

... do I have a say in any of this?

> *(ROSA pushes him violently.)*

ROSA

You male chauvinist pig!

ANTHONY

So now I'm a pig? Two seconds ago you were ready to jump in the sack with me.

ROSA

It's fine for a man to make a move on a woman, but when a woman shows her affection to a man, she's considered a bitch, a slut, a *puta*!

ANTHONY

What affection? You—

> *(At this point, she is totally out of control.)*

ROSA

You will not have my body. I am a woman in control of my body and my destiny!

ANTHONY

Now would be a good time for you to call one of those therapists.

ROSA

The only therapy I need is the therapy of a <u>real</u> man!

ANTHONY

Get a hold of yourself, woman!

ROSA

Woman! That's what I am. A woman, not a whore. I want you to stand there naked and humiliate yourself in my presence the way men have humiliated women for centuries. Undress!

> *(ANTHONY'S frozen. He doesn't know what to do.)*

ROSA (Continued)
> UNDRESS!

>> *(ROSA makes a move towards ANTHONY and ends up chasing him around the room. He removes his own shirt and throws it at her. She catches it.)*

ANTHONY
> There! My shirt's off! Happy?

ROSA
> The only time I'll be happy is when men stop killing each other like the pigs that they are. When famine ceases to exist. When oppression in third world countries is CRUSHED!

>> *(ROSA wrings his shirt and throws it on the floor.)*

ANTHONY
> I'm calling *nueve uno uno.*

>> *(goes for the phone)*

ROSA
> Don't bother ... I must be leaving.

>> *(ROSA regains her composure and slips her dress back on.)*

ROSA (Continued)
> I'll call you sometime.

>> *(ROSA exits.)*

> Thanks for the warning.

ANTHONY
>> *(ANTHONY stands there, unbelieving. Telephone rings.)*

ANTHONY (Continued)
> Hello? Hey David, *che passa?* ... yeah, she just left ... nah, not my type. Pretty sure Frank would love her. Listen, I'm not gonna make it tonight ... remember that girl I told you I met? Yeah, well, I think I'm gonna ask her out tonight. O.K., see you later ... *ciao.*

>> *(NUNZIATA walks in quietly. ANTHONY doesn't notice her, but she notices that he has his shirt off. NUNZIATA starts to panic thinking he had sex with the girl.)*

NUNZIATA
> Anthony?

ANTHONY
> Hello, Mother.

NUNZIATA
> Where's Rosa?

ANTHONY
> She left.

NUNZIATA
> I hope there was no sex going on in my house. You know how I feel about that. I don't care how desperate you are.

ANTHONY
> Nothing happened, Ma.

NUNZIATA
> So then why are you half naked?

ANTHONY
Because—
NUNZIATA
Why are you half naked!?
ANTHONY
Because the girl is a nut case, that's why. She should be tied up. Although she'd probably enjoy it.
NUNZIATA
Oh my God. I guess saying things didn't go very well is an understatement.
ANTHONY
What gave it away, Ma? This is the last time you humiliate me like this!
> (NUNZIATA abruptly moves towards the phone. Starts looking through her phone book.)
ANTHONY (Continued)
What are you doin'? Who are you calling?
NUNZIATA
Mrs. Levine.
ANTHONY
What for—who?
NUNZIATA
Mrs. Levine. To tell her and her daughter not to bother coming over tomorrow.
ANTHONY
This is insane. No. This is worse than insane. Rosa … now that's insane. This. This is worse!
NUNZIATA
I spoke to her a couple of weeks ago … they were just planning to come over like that …
ANTHONY
People don't just come over "like that"! You had this whole god damned thing planned and you weren't even gonna tell me about it.
NUNZIATA
Are you insinuating that I'm sneaky?
ANTHONY
> ("if the shoe fits")

Hey …
NUNZIATA
I told you a million times, all I ever wanted to do is be helpful.
ANTHONY
You wanna be helpful? Help me call Mrs … whatever her name is … and tell her and her daughter not to bother coming over. Not tomorrow, never! I'm over this!
NUNZIATA
What does it look like I'm doin'?
> (dials)

I'm sorry about this, okay?
> (ANTHONY doesn't reply.)
NUNZIATA (Continued)
Okay?

ANTHONY
>Alright.

NUNZIATA
>No need to get into an argument.
>>*(on the phone)*
>Mrs. Levine ... hi. It's Nunziata. Listen, we'll have to do this another time ...
>Anthony's not feeling well ... diarrhea ... I'm sorry ... I'll talk to you later.
>>*(hangs up)*

ANTHONY
>Diarrhea?

NUNZIATA
>I had to think fast ...

ANTHONY
>Yeah, but diarrhea?

NUNZIATA
>That was all I could think of.

ANTHONY
>You'll be leaving those people with a great mental picture of me. Then you
>wonder why I don't have any girlfriends.

NUNZIATA
>Just call your brother and find out if he's coming for supper tonight. I gotta go
>to the bathroom.
>>*(NUNZIATA exits to the bathroom. ANTHONY's about to dial.*
>>*He mumbles to himself. After a few seconds, FRANK walks in.*
>>*ANTHONY puts down the phone.)*

ANTHONY
>I was just about to call you.

FRANK
>Check these out.
>>*(hands him a business card)*
>My very own channel four business cards.

ANTHONY
>>*(reading the card)*
>"Franklin Roberts?"

FRANK
>I'm changing my image.

ANTHONY
>You got a real problem, kid.

FRANK
>So what's up?

ANTHONY
>Nothin'. You coming for supper tonight?

FRANK
>Can't. I got a date. I hope Ma did the ironing.

ANTHONY
>There's a couple of your shirts in my closet. How <u>is</u> Susan?

FRANK

Don't know. I'm not seeing her anymore. But breaking up with her did open the door for me to hook up with an old girlfriend.

ANTHONY

You mean there's a woman out there who would actually come back for seconds?

FRANK

All it takes is a little of that Robertini charm. You missed out on that trait. A little begging never hurt. And when all else fails, I give them the old broken heart routine.

(FRANK exits to one of the rooms.)

FRANK (O.S.) (Continued)

"Please help me ... I'm on the re-bound ... I need someone to talk to, Angela ... "

(Hearing FRANK say "Angela" makes ANTHONY feel like he just got kicked in the stomach. FRANK enters carrying a shirt.)

FRANK (Continued)

I haven't seen her in ages, then bam, outta nowhere, here she is standing in our living room—I don't remember, did you ever meet Angela?

ANTHONY

I met her briefly yesterday ...

FRANK

That's when I saw her again, too. Not bad, huh? I think I'll probably take her to dinner—give us a chance to catch up—then ... we'll see.

ANTHONY

Sounds like fun.

FRANK

You alright?

ANTHONY

Yeah ... it's just my stomach.

FRANK

Tell Ma to make you some chicken *brodo. Ciao.*

(FRANK exits. NUNZIATA enters.)

NUNZIATA

Was that Frank I heard?

ANTHONY

Yeah. He can't make it tonight. He's got a date with Angela.

NUNZIATA

Oh wow! I thought he and Angela were over and done with.

ANTHONY

Obviously not.

NUNZIATA

They spent the summer together in Vermont a few years ago. Did you know that?

ANTHONY

No. No, I didn't.

NUNZIATA

It's funny the way things turn out, isn't it? Huh.

ANTHONY

You sure you cleared it with Mrs. Levine?

NUNZIATA

You heard me talk to her on the phone. *Nonna* forgot to take her cannoli. I'll be back in a minute.

> *(NUNZIATA exits. ANTHONY sits for a minute, then breaks down. There's a knock at the door. He regains his composure and answers the door.)*

ANGELA

Hi, Anthony.

ANTHONY

Angela . . . come in.

ANGELA

Thanks. And thanks for lending me your cookbook.

ANTHONY

Oh! I . . . didn't even realize you borrowed it.

ANGELA

I'm sorry. I came by, you weren't around—

ANTHONY

No problem. Did you forget something?

ANGELA

No. No . . . my mom got her hands on your book and she's experimenting. You think I borrow that cake pan again?

ANTHONY

Sure. If I can find it.

> *(ANTHONY starts looking for the pan.)*

ANGELA

You're probably wondering why someone my age runs errands for her mother like a little messenger.

ANTHONY

Not really. I was wondering if your mother owned any of her own kitchen utensils.

> *(ANTHONY finds the pan and gives it to ANGELA.)*

ANTHONY (Continued)

Here you go!

ANGELA

Thanks.

> *(There's an awkward moment, finally ANGELA motions to leave. ANTHONY decides to go for broke. He starts playing the "part".)*

ANTHONY

I'm . . . glad I could find that pan for you. I barely know where anything is around here. Well, with hardly ever being home and all . . . you know . . . I use this apartment as sleeping quarters—sometimes.

ANGELA

Really?

ANTHONY

Are you kidding me, I'm a party animal. Yeah, just last night I was over at Spacco's.

ANGELA

Really? You have a good time?

ANTHONY

Oh, yeah … really tied one on. All that dancing, I got this huge blister. My foot's killing me.

ANGELA

All you have to do is cut—

ANTHONY

I'm familiar with the process. How come everyone in my family seems to know you, yet we've never met?

ANGELA

I guess you weren't looking hard enough. No. I just got out of a really crappy relationship and I moved in with my folks until I could get my act together.

ANTHONY

That's good. I mean it's good that you moved in with your parents, not that you broke up. Unless of course, you wanted to break up, then that's good too. So, what happened?

(realizes that he may be getting personal)

I'm sorry, that's really none of my business.

ANGELA

No, that's okay. I guess we had different interests, that's all. I'm more like you. I enjoy going out and meeting people, whereas his idea of a fun evening is staying home to watch TV.

ANTHONY

Imagine that.

ANGELA

It was for the best. Too bad it took eighteen months to realize it. So, what's your story? Besides being a dancing machine.

ANTHONY

I work in a slaughter house. Yup, that's me … a meat packer by day, a screenwriter by night, and panic stricken when I'm left alone with my mother.

ANGELA

You're a writer, huh? Have you written anything I may have seen?

ANTHONY

I doubt it. I don't have anything produced yet.

(pause)

I don't have anything written yet either.

ANGELA

How did you get into writing?

ANTHONY

Writing's my passion. Believe it or not, but I get a great deal of satisfaction out of sitting and staring at a blank sheet of paper for hours on end.

ANGELA

So you write movies … wow.

ANTHONY

Yeah. Although with the influence I get from my family, I should be writing my will.

ANGELA

Oh, come on, it can't be that bad. Your mother seems like a wonderful lady.

ANTHONY

> Mother Theresa herself. What about you? What do you do?

ANGELA

> Let's see. I'm a chef. I—

ANTHONY

> You cook. Do you enjoy it?

ANGELA

> I love it . . .
>> *(beat)*
> I hope I'm not out of line, here . . . I mean . . . I don't know you very well, but somehow, you don't strike me as your typical slaughter house worker.

ANTHONY

> Why, what does your typical slaughter house worker look like?

ANGELA

> . . . I'm not sure . . . a more muscular physique . . .

ANTHONY

>> *(jokingly)*
> Angela, if I wanted to be insulted, I would've gone out with my mother.

ANGELA

> No . . . no. It's not about your physical appearance—I can see why you write. You're very funny—

ANTHONY

> You mean "ha, ha" funny, right?

ANGELA

> I meant "ha, ha" funny, yes. You got the whole package. The sense of humor, the charm, that adorable way of talking . . .

ANTHONY

> You think the way I talk is adorable? Angela, that word hasn't been used to describe me since I was three.
>> *(pause)*
> You know . . . I gotta confess something. I was kinda hoping you were gonna be at Spacco's last night.

ANGELA

> I'm sure there'll be plenty of opportunities for us to hang out.

ANTHONY

> Yeah . . . I'm sure . . . actually I was wondering—
>> *(ANGELA's cell phone rings.)*

ANGELA

> Sorry, Anthony. Let me get this.
>> *(on the phone)*
> Oh, hey Frank . . . just pick me up at work, it's easier that way . . . ok, see you then . . . ciao.
>> *(hangs up; to Anthony)*
> Sorry. You were saying?

ANTHONY

> Actually I was just gonna say that . . . I'm sure we'll bump into each other. You know how that jet-set life is, right?

ANGELA

Right. It was real nice time talking with you.

ANTHONY

It was real nice talking with you too.

> *(Pause. ANGELA walks away)*

ANTHONY (Continued)

Angela ... you take care of yourself.

ANGELA

And ... you write something soon.

ANTHONY

I hope I do.

> *(ANGELA exits. ANTHONY closes the door and takes a long hard look in the mirror, totally dejected.)*

ANTHONY (Continued)

Jet-set ... yeah, right. Who am I kidding?

> *(ANTHONY is about to sit on the couch but before doing so, he looks at it as if it's his mortal enemy. He finally sits and picks up his writing pad. Ponders for a moment and puts it back down again. NUNZIATA walks in.)*

NUNZIATA

I thought I heard someone in the apartment.

ANTHONY

From upstairs?

NUNZIATA

I heard the door open and close a couple of times. I thought maybe Rosa came back.

ANTHONY

That's not the worst thing that could've happened to me today. But thanks for trying.

NUNZIATA

You alright?

ANTHONY

Drop it, Ma. I don't wanna get into it.

NUNZIATA

What happened all of a sudden?

ANTHONY

Nothin' happened, alright.

NUNZIATA

Obviously something did happen. I leave for five minutes to come back and find you moping.

ANTHONY

Can you just forget it?

NUNZIATA

If it's about this afternoon. I apologized.

ANTHONY

Okay, Ma. Apology accepted.

NUNZIATA
So tell me what's wrong.
ANTHONY
Jesus Christ! You're gonna keep on busting my balls until you drag me into this,
right? LEAVE ME ALONE! Fuckin' shit, man.
NUNZIATA
Hey! I don't deserve to be talked to like this. After all I do—
ANTHONY
And we're off! Every time we have a discussion, you start with the drama.
"What I did for my kids", by Nunziata Robertini. What have you done for me,
Ma? Explain it to me.
NUNZIATA
Go to hell!
ANTHONY
No … you wanna do this? Ok, let's do it. Answer the damn question. What are
you doing for Connie now? What?
NUNZIATA
I haven't had the time lately—
ANTHONY
Of course not! It's her wedding and you haven't spent two minutes with her since
this whole circus started. You're too busy finding your pathetic son a girlfriend—
and you're not doing it for me, you're doing it for yourself because that's what
you want.
NUNZIATA
Bullshit! You couldn't be further from the truth.
ANTHONY
Did you ever stop and think that maybe I'm in this situation because of you?
NUNZIATA
Because of me? Stop feeling sorry for yourself. If you're not happy with the way
your life turned out, it's your own fault. Not mine.
ANTHONY
Oh, really? You think I'm happy being stuck in a crappy job, with no future?
NUNZIATA
Thank God for that job. I'd hate to think what your life would be like if you
were unemployed!
ANTHONY
You just don't think that I'm capable of doing anything else with my life! And
it's exactly because of that … that I have no life!
NUNZIATA
You don't have a life because you're too afraid to get out from under my skirt!
ANTHONY
Are you joking me? Are you fucking joking me?
NUNZIATA
You blame me, but it's you. You think it's easy living with you, Anthony? Always
moping, moody, pissed at the world … watching you blame everyone else for
your problems but yourself. You don't like who you are … CHANGE!

ANTHONY

So what are you saying? That if I'm living like this it's because I like it? You think I want this? You think I'm happy with the way my life turned out?

NUNZIATA

You think I am? Being widowed with three kids at thirty five years old?

ANTHONY

So why didn't you do something about it? No wait. You did. You chose to make me pay for what happened to you. When my father died—

NUNZIATA

Don't you dare drag your father into this!

ANTHONY

When my father died, all I ever heard from you was how I had to be strong . . . for Connie, for Frankie . . . for YOU! And I was strong. I was goddamn it! But you weren't. You just gave up. I spent my life looking out for this family. And all I get is guilt from you and bullshit advice from Frank . . . and Connie burdening me with all her crap because you just don't give a shit! I've always denied myself for everyone else and now I'm paying for it. You should all be ashamed of yourselves.!

NUNZIATA

Ashamed? You . . . you miserable little bastard! How dare you? What did you sacrifice for this family, what?

ANTHONY

Holy Christ . . . you have to be fuckin' kidding me.

NUNZIATA

Don't call how you chose to live your life a sacrifice. You made your choices. It's your own fault that you're stuck in a job you hate . . . and that you're not the writer you wanted to be . . . or that you're living at home . . . that you're overweight and that you dress like a slob! You just don't have it in you to change and I'm sorry for that. And it hurts me that you turned out to be such a bitter person and that you don't even like yourself. But don't you dare blame me. 'Cause that's too easy, Anthony. To blame your own mother for your miserable life.

ANTHONY

It's not easy, ma. But it is true.

NUNZIATA

Just get the hell out of my life!

> (ANTHONY storms out. NUNZIATA breaks down realizing
> what has just been said as the lights fade.)
> BLACK OUT

ACT 3

> (It is the following Saturday morning about 11:00 a.m., the day of the
> wedding. The living room is decorated with flowers etc. It is evident
> that there is a wedding about to take place. NUNZIATA is on the
> telephone as the scene opens. She is wearing a bath robe, holding a
> make-up brush. DAVID is pacing, looking for things to straighten out.)

NUNZIATA

I hope you got those orchids for the table of honor. When I called yesterday to confirm the order, one of your employees told me they weren't on the list ... I don't remember his name ... Juan ... yeah, that's him ... they are? ... very good. Thank-you.

> *(hangs up)*

Like I really need this today.

> *(NUNZIATA exits to her bedroom. The telephone rings.)*

DAVID

I'll get it!

> *(answers phone)*

Hello? ... just a second ...

> *(calls out)*

Mrs. Robertini, it's the caterer, he wants to talk to you.

NUNZIATA (O.S.)

What does he want ... I'm busy.

DAVID

> *(on the phone)*

Can I take a message? Uh huh ... uh huh ... hold on a sec. (calls out)

He said they're out of cannelloni, do you want the manicotti?

NUNZIATA (O.S.)

Tell him, you know where he can put the manicotti!

CONNIE (O.S.)

> *(yells out)*

Oh my God ... I forgot to get something borrowed!

DAVID

Mrs. Robertini, what do I tell him?

CONNIE (O.S.)

Tell him there's not gonna be a wedding if I don't find something borrowed to wear!

> *(continues whining to herself)*

NUNZIATA (O.S.)

Tell him there's no way I'm paying for cannelloni if he gives me manicotti!

CONNIE (O.S.)

Is anybody listening to me?

DAVID

QUIET! Please.

> *(about to have a panic attack)*

Mrs. Robertini, we take the manicotti, right?

NUNZIATA (O.S.)

Tell him I want a better price!

DAVID

> *(on the phone)*

I really think you should discuss this with—

CONNIE (O.S.)

I knew something like this would happen! Does anybody care?

DAVID
> *(on the phone)*

Just a minute.
> *(calls out)*

Connie, what is your problem?

CONNIE (O.S.)

I need something borrowed!

DAVID

There's a pair of pink fruit of the looms in your brother's drawer—knock yourself out!
> *(on the phone)*

No, not you. Okay, listen, the manicotti will be fine. All right, thanks.
> *(DAVID hangs up the telephone, NUNZIATA walks in.)*

DAVID (Continued)

Mrs. Robertini, I'm going home ... see if Anthony showed up or something. You better lock up. Someone could just walk in and help themselves.

NUNZIATA

I will. Call me if you hear something.

DAVID

I promise.

> *(DAVID exits. NUNZIATA puts the chain on the door and exits to her bedroom. Seconds later, LILLY tries to enter the apartment but the chain on the door prevents her from fully opening it. She sticks her head through the opening.)*

LILLY

Oh my God! I hope they didn't leave without me. Nunziata, open up. Nunziata!
> *(LILLY is frantic and continuously knocking.)*

NUNZIATA (O.S.)

I'm coming, already!

> *(NUNZIATA opens the door to find LILLY there, holding a large bouquet of flowers. She is wearing a very loud dress and flowers in her hair.)*

LILLY

Why the barricade on the door?

NUNZIATA

I'm practicing for when I live alone.
> *(CONNIE comes running out in her bath robe.)*

CONNIE

Anthony? Oh, hi *Nonna*.

LILLY

Have you heard from him?

NUNZIATA

No.

LILLY

Nunz', remind me to take some pepto bismol before we leave.

NUNZIATA

I haven't spoken to him in a week.

LILLY

And he will be forever grateful.

NUNZIATA

This is no joking matter. I didn't think it would go this far. This has got to be one of the worst weeks of my life.

CONNIE

Well, I really enjoyed spending this past week with you.

NUNZIATA

That's not what I meant, sweetheart.

> *(breaks down)*

I'm worried ...

CONNIE

I'm worried too, Ma.

LILLY

At the very least, we should be grateful that he's staying with a good friend like David.

NUNZIATA

David was just here ...

CONNIE

And?

NUNZIATA

Anthony didn't show up for Joe's stag party the other night, and when David got home, Anthony wasn't there.

LILLY

> *Oh, Dio mio ...*

NUNZIATA

If Anthony doesn't show up today, I'll never forgive myself.

CONNIE

I'm sure that if you just talked to him ...

NUNZIATA

If I'd see him I would.

LILLY

Nunziata. I've watched you do what you thought was right these past few weeks and I didn't get involved. But now you're gonna listen to me. You have to <u>talk</u> to him. And when you do, just remember that Anthony loves you more than anything. Don't let that go to waste. He needs to know that he can have his own life, and that you can still be a part of it. Take it from someone who knows.

> *(pause)*

We have a wedding to go to. Go finish getting ready. Come on, Concettina, I'll help you get dressed. *Santa Maria Goretti* this girl is gonna be late for her own wedding.

> (CONNIE gives LILLY the evil eye as they're exiting to
> CONNIE'S bedroom.)

LILLY (Continued)

Oh, don't you evil eye me, you. I practically invented that.

> (CONNIE and LILLY both exit.)

NUNZIATA

She's right.

(NUNZIATA exits to the bedroom. After a couple of seconds ANTHONY walks into the apartment. He looks a little different. He is not wearing his glasses; he is wearing a tuxedo and his hair is neatly groomed. Notices that there's no one around. He goes into the hutch and defiantly pulls out a crystal glass. He walks into the kitchen. He opens the freezer, but there is no ice. The phone rings. NUNZIATA runs out to answer. NUNZIATA stops and notices ANTHONY. She stares at him; answers the phone.)

NUNZIATA (Continued)
Hello ... yeah, David. He's already here. Bye.
> *(pause)*

Anthony ...

ANTHONY
You're out of ice.

NUNZIATA
Oh ... thanks ... I'll pick some up. I'm glad you came.

ANTHONY
I'm here for Connie.

NUNZIATA
She really missed you. She's gonna be thrilled. And *Nonna* is worried sick. I don't give her enough credit sometimes. She's right, though. We should talk ...

ANTHONY
Maybe this was a mistake, after all.

NUNZIATA
Why do you say that?

ANTHONY
Because it's true.

NUNZIATA
Why do you wanna hurt me like this, Anthony?

ANTHONY
Who's hurting who? Connie missed me ... *Nonna* was worried about me. What about you?

NUNZIATA
I missed you ... I worried about you ... and I wouldn't want anything more than to talk to you again. What more do you want me to say?

ANTHONY
Nothing. You said enough last week.

NUNZIATA
We both did. But I'm willing to move on.

ANTHONY
You have nothing to lose.

NUNZIATA
You actually believe one of us can win something out of this?

ANTHONY
At least you have a home to live in.

NUNZIATA
Anthony—

ANTHONY

Look, I didn't come here today to fight with you.

NUNZIATA

To make peace?

ANTHONY

I'm here for Connie ... and my father.

NUNZIATA

Oh, Anthony. When your father died, I made it my mission in life to make sure that my children didn't miss out on anything. I didn't want you growing up having any regrets, or even worse, hating your father for not being there for you. You gotta believe me that I did my best. And I truly thought that to look out for you, I needed to have you near me all the time. And you know what, Anthony. I really liked that. I love the fact that you're always there for me and that you think that my well-being and happiness are your responsibilities. It makes me feel wanted ... needed ... loved. I guess I'm afraid to lose some of that. But I don't want you to stop living your life. I never wanted that for you. I thought about what happened last week how you blamed me for the mess your life was in. It was a long time coming. I guess in some way we both realized then that you had to move on. I know you hate me for saying those things and for driving you out. But I'd rather you hate me for that, than for ruining your life. You're a good person and you have so much to offer. I wanna make sure you get your chance.

ANTHONY

You know, Ma ... sometimes it's ... it's just hard for me to look inside myself, admit who I am and change ... you know ...

NUNZIATA

I know it's hard but I also know what it's like to look back at a life time and ask yourself "what if"? I don't want you to have to live with that feeling.

> *(LILLY enters.)*

LILLY

I made it. Not a scratch. She's your daughter, you deal with her.

> *(she glances over to Anthony, then turns back; she doesn't recognize him)*

You got a butler?

ANTHONY

Hi, *Nonna*.

LILLY

> *(puts her glasses on; looks him over)*

Antonio!

> *(she hugs and kisses him then taps him on the cheek)*

If you wanna worry your mother, that's one thing. You do this to me again, I'll hunt you down and kill you.

CONNIE (O.S.)

Ma ... where's the blush?

NUNZIATA

I borrowed it. One small favor. Don't let your sister know you're here yet. She'll never finish getting ready.

CONNIE (O.S.)
I'm breaking out!

NUNZIATA
Calm down! You're gonna get an anxiety rash.

LILLY
I don't believe I'm related to that girl ... or to this one.

NUNZIATA
She's been a total basket case all week. It's good that you're here. It's the best gift you could've given her. Come on, Ma. Come and help me make myself beautiful!

LILLY
I'm your mother, not David Copperfield!
    (NUNZIATA and LILLY exit to her bedroom. ANTHONY
    looks around, realizes he should make the best of this day.)

CONNIE (O.S.)
Oh, no! Ma ... Ma ... I got a run in my nylons! Stupid garter.
    (no answer; yells)
Ma ... where are you?

NUNZIATA (O.S.)
Connie, please! I gotta get dressed!

ANTHONY
    (in a woman's voice; Italian accent)
You mamma busy. Grandma ... can-a she help?
    (CONNIE comes running out of her bedroom.)
Anthony, is that you?

CONNIE
    (lets out a joyous yell)
I knew you'd show, you big jerk! Does Ma know you're here?

ANTHONY
No, Connie. You're doing such a great job of keeping it quiet.

CONNIE
Oh my God! It's bad luck to see the bride before the wedding.
    (CONNIE runs back to her room.)

ANTHONY
Connie ... that superstition applies only to the groom. I'm not the one marrying you. And every morning when I wake up, I thank God. By the way Connie, I love what you did with your hair.

CONNIE (O.S.)
Yeah, well at least I have hair.
    (ANTHONY finds himself alone in the living room. He walks
    over to the mirror and admires himself.)

ANTHONY
You look good, Anthony. Pretty good.
    (ANTHONY looks around to make sure he's alone. He turns on
    the stereo and France Joli's 'Come To Me'—the slow intro part of
    the song—comes on. To an imaginary girl:)

ANTHONY (Continued)

    Excuse me, Angela . . . may I have this dance?

        (starts to slow dance)

        *(FRANK and ANGELA walk in. ANTHONY doesn't notice
        them. They watch him for a couple of seconds.)*

FRANK

    Whatta ya do for an encore?

        (ANTHONY notices them. FRANK turns off the music.)

FRANK (Continued)

    Where the hell have you been? Ma was so upset last night, I had to sleep over.

ANTHONY

    You see. You can take on some responsibility.

FRANK

    Where were you?

ANTHONY

    I don't have to answer to you. And lose the attitude, alright?

FRANK

    Sorry . . .

ANTHONY

    Now's not the time.

        (a little uncomfortable) .

    Hi, Angela, good to see you again.

ANGELA

    Nice to see you too, Anthony.

ANTHONY

    So, how's our little sister. Did she drive you nuts last night?

FRANK

    Are you kidding? She was up every hour on the hour trying on her dress to make
    sure it still fit. That's apart from when she'd have mom diagnose a new sickness
    for her. I tell you, there was enough material here last night for you to write a
    mini-series. I gotta hand it to you. I don't know how you did it all these years.

ANTHONY

    Neither do I.

FRANK

    And I must congratulate you on your new appearance.

ANGELA

    You look great.

FRANK

    Yeah, you look good without your glasses. Can you see?

ANTHONY

    Not a thing, no.

FRANK

    So, is there something you wanna tell me?

ANTHONY

    No. What?

FRANK
> *(pulls Anthony away from Angela's view)*

Did you ...
> *(indicates the act of fornication with his hands)*

... get a little *minghia* ... last night?

ANTHONY

Why, 'cause I—
> *(indicates his own clothes)*

I think you've been playing with your barometer a little too long.

NUNZIATA (O.S.)

Frank?

FRANK

How does she know I'm here?
> *(yells out)*

WHAT?

NUNZIATA (O.S.)

Go get some ice.

FRANK

I don't get it. What, she waits for me to show up so I can run her errands? Get me a cake pan, get me some ice ...

ANTHONY

It's ok. I'll run out and pick some up.

FRANK

Take it easy. You stay here and entertain our guest, I'll go. Oh, yeah, if Susan calls, tell her I'll meet her at the church.

ANTHONY

I thought you two split up.

FRANK

Ah. Since she already bought her dress and I did invite her in the first place ... we decided to have another go at it. Besides, it'll give Ma something else to talk about.
> *(pause)*

Hey. I'm glad you made it.
> *(FRANK kisses his brother on the cheek and exits. ANTHONY finds himself alone with ANGELA. He starts to get nervous.)*

ANTHONY

Can I ... get you something? A drink ... with no ice? A cake pan?
> *(ANTHONY laughs to cover up his nervousness.)*

ANGELA

The house is decorated very nicely.

ANTHONY

Yeah, all these flowers ... when I walked in here this morning I thought I had died.

ANGELA

How's your foot?

ANTHONY

Good ... good. My foot's good. Yeah ... it's a good foot!
> *(pause)*

It's warm in here.

ANGELA

Yeah . . .

(Pause; ANGELA sits on the couch.)

ANTHONY

Don't get too comfortable, you may get stuck to the "pleather". You'd be surprised at the noises you could make with this thing on a hot day!

ANGELA

So, Anthony, when's your date getting here?

ANTHONY

No date . . . nobody . . . no . . . no one at all.

(pause)

And you? . . . my brother, he said something about Susan . . . does that mean . . .

ANGELA

I asked him for a lift. There's only so much walking I can do in high heels.

ANTHONY

So . . . Frank and Susan . . . wow . . . he's always full of surprises.

ANGELA

They make a nice couple.

ANTHONY

Great couple . . . <u>great</u> couple . . . good for him . . .

(Another pause; ANTHONY needs to find his courage.)

ANTHONY (Continued)

Listen, Angela . . .

(ANGELA waits for him to speak, but ANTHONY doesn't say anything.)

ANGELA

Anthony—

ANTHONY

Angela, please . . . I gotta get through this. I've been rehearsing this speech in my head ever since I first laid eyes on you. Trying to figure out the best way to, you know . . . ask you—My whole life . . . I never had the courage to go after something I really wanted . . . especially if that something would make me happy. Maybe I was afraid of the disappointment or rejection . . . you know . . . if I don't get disappointed, I can't get hurt. Or . . . or maybe I just believed that good things could never happen to a guy like me. So why bother? But if I'm gonna salvage whatever's left of my life, I can't live like that anymore. So, I apologize in advance if I'm gonna make you feel uncomfortable, but I'm gonna have to just come out and ask you . . . what do you . . . how do you feel about someone like me?

(She looks at him intently, definitely moved by his out-pouring. Then—she leans in to gently kiss him.)

ANGELA

I was expecting you to ask me out a week ago. But I do understand that you had to work things out first. You don't give yourself enough credit. You're a warm, genuine person . . . who just lacks a little confidence, that's all.

ANTHONY

Wow . . . I can't help but feel that I almost blew it.

ANGELA

Anthony, believe me. I wasn't gonna let you blow it.

(ANGELA smiles at him and kisses him again. ANTHONY
starts laughing.)

ANTHONY

Sorry ... I'm just not used to this. Angela ... you probably figured this out already
... but do you remember how I told you that I was a party animal? Nah. I'm to
homebodies what the Maharishi is to yoga!

ANGELA

Beautiful. I could use someone around the kitchen to taste test my recipes.

ANTHONY

I guess I should break out the cholesterol pills.

(They kiss again, this time more passionately. DAVID walks in
on them. He breaks up their kiss. He pushes ANGELA away and
hugs ANTHONY.)

DAVID

Anthony! Oh, Anthony ... I was worried sick.

(continues hugging Anthony)

ANTHONY

You could let go now.

(DAVID lets go of ANTHONY.)

ANTHONY (Continued)

I want you to meet Angela. Angela, this is my very, very best friend ... David
Greenberg.

DAVID

So this is the girl. Mazeltov!

(ANTHONY nods. DAVID hugs ANTHONY and kisses him
again.)

ANTHONY

He's very affectionate.

(NUNZIATA enters.)

NUNZIATA

Oh good! Everybody's starting to arrive.

(she goes to Angela and takes both her hands)

... Angela ...

ANTHONY

Ma ... don't cause a scene ...

NUNZIATA

We'll set another place at the table of honor for you dear.

(FRANK enters carrying a bag of ice.)

FRANK

OK, let's get this show on the road.

DAVID

Angela ... you look familiar. Were you ever in therapy with a Doctor Libman?

(FRANK pops open the champagne and starts filling the glasses.)

FRANK

Is that all you ever talk about? No, David, she was never in therapy. You're the only mental case here today.

     (ROSA enters in the doorway. She looks over to ANTHONY.)
     (Stands there for a second then makes a bee-line for DAVID.)

ROSA

Baby ...

DAVID

Rosa. I thought you were gonna wait in the car.

ROSA

I was getting lonely.

ANTHONY

I guess you should've tied her up a little tighter.

DAVID

Oh, man, thanks for introducing me to her.

ANTHONY

I'm glad things are working out.

DAVID

Working out? We've already talked about the possibility of moving in together.

FRANK

Maybe you and Rosa can even get married and raise a whole bunch of little whackjobs.

     (LILLY walks in.)

FRANK (Continued)

Connie, come out here ... we wanna propose a little toast!

LILLY

Excellent idea, Frank. All this joy is killing me!

     (CONNIE walks into the living room dressed in a gorgeous wedding
     gown. Everyone admires her—the oohs and aahs from everyone
     in the room.)

CONNIE

     (very peaceful)

I'm ready.

NUNZIATA

Oh ... my ... baby ...

FRANK

You look beautiful.

LILLY

God bless you.

CONNIE

Anthony?

ANTHONY

     (admires his sister)

I wish I had something inspiring to tell you, Connie ... but I don't. Quite honestly, up until a few days ago, I couldn't even hear church bells without experiencing an anxiety attack. So, I'm just glad I'm able to be here. No. I'm happy to be here. A toast. I can only wish upon you, Connie, that your home is filled with as many good memories as this one.

CONNIE
I'm gonna cry.
>   *(hugs Anthony)*

ANTHONY
And so you should.
>   *(Everyone toasts.)*

DAVID
Congratulations, Connie.

FRANK
Usually you congratulate the bride after she's married.
>   *(Honking of horns is heard off stage. FRANK looks out the
>   window.)*

FRANK (Continued)
Let's go, Connie. Your limo's here. *Nonna*, come on, you'll ride in my car.

LILLY
No way. I'm taking the limousine. Anthony, let's go. I'm not letting you out of my sight.

ANTHONY
I'll catch up with you in a minute, *Nonna*.
>   *(LILLY exits. ANTHONY whispers something in ANGELA's
>   ear then exits to his bedroom.)*

NUNZIATA
Angela, help me with my corsage please.

CONNIE
Hurry, Ma.

DAVID
Let's go Rosa. Frank, wait up. I'll follow you.

FRANK
It's four blocks away. Even you couldn't get lost going there.

DAVID
I don't see how me following you can change your life.

FRANK
I don't even like you, David. Don't follow me!

DAVID
Rosa, did you bring your prozac?
>   *(DAVID, ROSA, FRANK, & CONNIE exit.)*

ANGELA
>   *(finishes helping Nunziata with her corsage)*
There. We're all set. You look wonderful.

NUNZIATA
I'm really glad you came.

ANGELA
I'm glad you asked me to. Thank you.
>   *(she hugs Nunziata)*
Come, they're all waiting.

NUNZIATA

You go ahead, dear.

> (ANGELA exits. NUNZIATA appears to be waiting for ANTHONY to come out of his room. She picks up the picture of her late husband. ANTHONY walks back into the living room holding a CD. He goes to her.)

ANTHONY

I've been meaning to give you this for a week now.

> (NUNZIATA takes the CD from him and reads the title aloud.)

NUNZIATA

"Moonlight Serenade". Oh, Anthony.

> (ANTHONY opens his arms to her and they hug. Moonlight Serenade starts to play in the background. They walk off together. The music grows louder; lights fade; a single light shines on the Father's picture. To black.)

THE END

HISTORICAL PLAYS

JOHNNY BANANAS

1983
Michael Macina

"He mentioned a play he had been writing based on the life of his great grandfather, Giovanni Macina, known around the financial district of Toronto as Johnny Bananas. Johnny was an Italian immigrant who made a living selling bananas on the corner of Bay and King streets. An old school immigrant with a pugilistic approach to solving personal issues, be it with the authorities or friends and family, Johnny was legendary figure on this corner pretty much until the day he died."
—**Damiano Pietropaolo**

ACT ONE

1902–1917

PAPERS

Union Station, March, 1902

MICHE stands on a train platform, dressed in a sober North American business suit, mandolin in hand.

MICHE
Napoli New York (CHORUS)
All aboard Buffalo
Salute Canada
Allô Toronto (bis)

Two bucks in your pocket
riding that train
Jew Greek or Wop
it's always the same

You buy em for two cents
you sell em for four
arbeit laboro
a cart then a store

(CHORUS) (bis)

You dock here in March
you work cause you're poor
it's ten cents a day
there just ain't no more

Your wife should stay home
she's double the fare
you can't live alone
it's better she's here

(CHORUS) (bis)

Two bucks in your pocket
riding that train
Jew Greek or Wop
it's always the same

You buy em for two cents
you sell em for four
arbeit lavoro
sole mare amore

(CHORUS) (bis)
> *A crowd of immigrants steps off the train.*
> *Among them is GIOVANNI MORA, a redhaired twenty-two-*
> *year-old, carrying three battered bags.*

GIOVANNI
Suona signore, suona.
MICHE
Si paga, la musica. Hai dei soldi?
GIOVANNI
Due dollari.
MICHE
E tutto quell che hai?
GIOVANNI
Si, guarda.
> *GIOVANNI turns his pockets inside out. Behind them, there is*
> *much joyous kissing.*
MICHE
Allora, ti serve una giobba.
GIOVANNI
Una giobba?
MICHE
Si, una giobba, lavoro, Parli inglese?

GIOVANNI
Sure.
MICHE
You got papers?
GIOVANNI
Hé?
MICHE
AHHH … A WOP.
GIOVANNI
Non capisco.
MICHE
With Out Papers. W.O.P. Senza documenti. Tu.
GIOVANNI
No no, ho documenti, io.
MICHE
Mostra. Ah ah ah, guarda. W.O.P. Without papers. This paper says you got no papers.
GIOVANNI
Scusa?
MICHE
No papers, no giobba. No stay in Canada. No work.
GIOVANNI
Slow please.
MICHE
You need papers to work, I got. You need place to stay—allogio, per dormire—I got. Sai firmare?
GIOVANNI
Non scrivo.
MICHE
Doesn't matter. What's your name? Tuo nome?
> MICHE is writing something on a piece of paper.
> At the end of the platform, a hurried JIMMY shouts at his brother.

JIMMY
Giovannino, Giovannino.
MICHE
Giovannino, grazie.
GIOVANNI
Giacomo.
JIMMY
E la moglie, dov'è la moglie?
GIOVANNI
Aiaiai, Anna, Anna.
> ANNA, a diminutive woman of twenty-four, has descended cautiously from the train, an infant in her arms.
> JIMMY throws his arms around her.

GIOVANNI
Anna, mio Fratello. Guarda la bambina, Giacomo.

JIMMY
Piacere Signora. Anna, scusami.

MICHE
Anna. E la bambina?

GIOVANNI
Si chiama Teresa. Guarda com'è bella.

MICHE
Ah yes, very nice. Giorno Teresa, giorno.

JIMMY
Chi è?

GIOVANNI
He give to me giobbo.

JIMMY
Come?

MICHE
I give him papers to stay.

JIMMY
He no stay. Torna in Italia.

GIOVANNI
No no, rimango.

ANNA
No, torniamo in Italia.

GIOVANNI
Basta Anna.

JIMMY
Giobba you need, I find. You, we don't need. Vai.

GIOVANNI
Mi serve lavoro, Giacomo.

JIMMY
Ti troverò lavoro, io.

> JIMMY rips the paper from MICHE's hand.
> ANNA returns to the train.

MICHE
Per favore, he needs this paper.

GIOVANNI
Anna, rimani qua.

ANNA
Torno in Italia.

JIMMY
He's no work for the padrone.

GIOVANNIA
Il padrone? Anna!

JIMMY
Si, il padrone. Ten centa day, you bring you own shovel. Nice padrone, he look after you. You change you giobba, he fix you leg. Vai, lasciaci.

JIMMY pushes MICHE away rudely.
GIOVANNI has gone to fetch ANNA.

MICHE

Too bad for you, paesano. No papers, no giobba, you see. Ciao Giovannino. Ci vediamo un'altra volta.

MICHE wanders off with the crowd.
ANNA returns with GIOVANNI.

GIOVANNI

Ma, che è successo?

JIMMY

Where you learn English?

GIOVANNI

I learn on a, on the big, bigga …

ANNA

Sheep, sheep, sheep.

JIMMY

Ah, you learn on a bigga boat.

GIOVANNI

Sure.

JIMMY

That's good. Andiamo a casa.

ANNA

No.

GIOVANNI

Aiaiai.

JIMMY

Cos'è Anna?

GIOVANNI

Te l'ho detto, non abbiamo soldi per tornare. Devo lavorare, qua, in Canada.

ANNA

Dimmi che torneremo quando avrèmo il denaro.

GIOVANNI

Non posso.

ANNA

Come, non puoi?

GIOVANNI

Perche è finite. Hanno venduto la fattoria.

ANNA

O Dio, O Dio. Ti odio Giovanni, ti odio.

ANNA slumps and almost hits the ground,
saved by JIMMY.

JIMMY

What? They sold the farm? L'hanno venduta?

ANNA

Mascalzone di bugiardo.

GIOVANNI

Basta, Anna, si. L'hanno venduta.

JIMMY
> They sold the farm.

GIOVANNI
> Si, finisce.

JIMMY
> Perchè?

GIOVANNI
> Non so.

ANNA
> Sapesci tutto. Non mi hai detto niente.

GIOVANNI
> Non abbiamo più niente.

JIMMY
> What are they gonna do, Mamma e Papà? Che fanno?

ANNA
> E io, che farò io in questo paese?

GIOVANNI
> Ho bisogno di uno giobbo, Giacomo.

JIMMY
> Giobba, Giovanni, giobba.

ANNA
> Ho freddo, io.

JIMMY
> Non mi chiamo più Giacomo. They call me Jimmy here. I know. I know where
> to get you a giobba. Andiamo.
>> *JIMMY picks up their bags and leads them off the train platform.*
>> *ANNA is reluctant to push off.*

CARTA

A street in St. John's Ward, the next day.

*MICHE stands in a white apron next to a chair covered in a
white cloth.*

MICHE
> This is the land of milk and honey. Frozen milk and frozen honey. Sixteen
> monthsa yeara snow. They call it the Ward, St. John's Ward. Jews, Wops and
> Chinese who never smelled each other's smells before. Six monthsa yeara mud
> and horse manure in the streets. And carts. Thousandsa carts, all loaded with
> bananas. Who ever saw a banana before he walked into this ice box? Three
> monthsa yeara sun in a good year. Ah sole, sole, ti ricordi?
>> *GIOVANNI pulls a run-down cart laden with GREEN
>> bananas toward MICHE, giddy with satisfaction.*

GIOVANNI
> Si si, splende il sole. Ma nevica.

MICHE
> Sun and snow. Should you laugh or cry?

GIOVANNI

Come manna, dal Cielo.

MICHE

From heaven, manna falling right into your hands. Metti il carro davanti ai buoi, sai?

GIOVANNI

Come?

MICHE

You put the cart before the horse.

GIOVANNI

I am horse.

MICHE

You're an ass. Push it, idiot.

> *MICHE pushes GIOVANNI aside and turns the cart around.*

MICHE

Guarda, spingila, spingi.

GIOVANNI

Ma chef ai, tu?

MICHE

Even a mule's not so stubborn.

> *GIOVANNI turns the card around.*
> *He and MICHE engage in a tug of war.*

GIOVANNI

Parla Italiano, non capsico.

MICHE

Più testardo di un mulo. Mille fruttivendoli nella strada e non ce ne sta uno che tira la carta. Sei pazzo, guarda. Si spinge, la carta.

> *MICHE wins out with a graceful spin of the cart and rests his case.*

GIOVANNI

Ma allora.

MICHE

Ma allora, si. Per favore, il cappello, bravo. Damello. Very nice, the peasant look. May I see?

> *MICHE snatches GIOVANNI's hat and pretends to be interested*
> *in it.*

MICHE

Just what I thought. Chi ha tagliato questi capelli? La tua moglie? She cut this, your wife? You look like you just got off the boat.

GIOVANNI

Il treno. Ciao.

> *GIOVANNI grabs his hat and is about to move on.*
> *MICHE whips the white sheet from the chair and offers*
> *JOHNNY a seat.*

MICHE

Come here Johnn, prendi posto.

GIOVANNI

Come mi hai chiamato?

MICHE

Sit in the chair Johnny, I cut your hair. How you like like?

> *JOHHNY hesitates, fascinated with the transformation of his*
> *name and with MICHE, then sits.*

JOHNNY

Sempre così.

MICHE

The same, shorter, okay. You know this expression, okay? No you don't, you don't know nothin yet. Where you from? Da quale regione vieni?

JOHNNY

Un villagio contadino.

MICHE

So you're campagnolo, so what? Sew buttons, be a tailor. Could be fuller on top.

JOHNNY

Non si tocca.

MICHE

Sono barbiere. That's my job, touchin people's hair. Taglio, si o non?

JOHNNY

Si.

MICHE

Okay. So whaddaya want with bananas? There's five hundred bananamen in the streets. You're never gonna sell no bananas. Work on the railroad, in the North. La ferrovia, sai? Huge country, Canada, needs a railroad. How much you sell these bananas? Capisci?

JOHNNY

Yeah.

MICHE

Okay. How much you sell the bananas?

JOHNNY

Four centa pound.

MICHE

Average. How much you pay? (PAUSE) How much you pay? Quanto costano le banane?

JOHNNY

Two centa pound.

MICHE

So you make two cents. You get them from the Siciliani? You should find out how much he pays. Two years ago, I got off the boat, didn't know what I was gonna do.

JOHNNY

Che fai?

MICHE

Trust me. You need to change the style. There's a certain look you ain't got. You need that look that says you know a peach from a plum, ripe from rotten. You look like you just got off the boat.

JOHNNY

Il train.

MICHE

Same thing. When I got here, there was no Italian barber. Put all my money into this place. Five bucks for a chair and scissors. I never cut no hair before. I'm a shoe maker, for the love of God. Calzolaio, capisci?

JOHNNY

No he fin sopra i capelli. Finish.

> *JOHNNY has pulled off the white apron and stands opposite*
> *MICHE.*

MICHE

I only did one ear.

JOHNNY

How much?

MICHE

Shave an a haircut, due bit.

JOHNNY

Come?

MICHE

Due bit. That's a Canadian expression. Shave and a haircut, due bit. Twenty-five cents. Barba e capelli, due bit.

JOHNNY

No barba.

MICHE

You'd be surprised the difference the shave makes. Specially on a good-lookin boy like you. Aspetta. Don't move. (MICHE snips a hair over JOHNNY's ear.) Keep your hat on, nobody's gonna know the difference. Try to develop some personality. You ain't always gonna have that hair. You got ten cents? No? Sixabanan ten cent. Gimme sixabanan. The name is Michè.

> *JOHNNY rips some bananas off the cart.*

JOHNNY

Ciao Michè, grazie.

MICHE

Prego. Remember what I told ya, the railroad. Sudbury, I heard it's beautiful, sun shines all the time. Take them bananas home and put em next to the furnace. In three days they're ripe. Don't eat em green. Ciao Giovannino.

> *JOHNNY has pushed his cart off.*
> *MICHE has removed his barber's shirt.*

MICHE

Been here one day and already he learned one new expression, two bits. In a year, if he's lucky, he might have six bits under his mattress. In a year—who knows, in a year? In a year, he could be back home.

ROOMABOARDA

JIMMY's pensione, April, 1903.

ANNA sits on a bed nursing her child.
JIMMY sits at the window, fidgeting.

JOHNNY

(OFF) Sixanana ten cent, who wantsa buy?

JIMMY

There he is.

ANNA

Non mi importa niente.

JIMMY goes out to intercept JOHNNY.

JIMMY

She don't want the cart around here.

JOHNNY

We put behind the house.

JIMMY

She don't want it behind the house.

JOHNNY

Who?

JIMMY

Mrs. Green.

JOHNNY

Don't eat em green.

JIMMY

And no more bananas in the basement.

JOHNNY

What are we gonna do with em?

JIMMY

That's your problem. Anna non è contenta.

JOHNNY

Non è mai contenta. What now?

JIMMY

You was out all night, John.

JOHNNY leaves the cart outside and goes into the pensione.
He heads for an armoire.

JOHNNY

Ho bisogno di una camicia pulita.

ANNA

Ho bisogno di soldi.

JIMMY

Them's my shirts, don't touch.

JOHNNY

For what do you need money?

ANNA

Torno in Italia.

JOHNNY

Quest'è buona, eh Jimmy? She's goin back.

ANNA

Sono stufa di te, di lui, di questo schifo di paese. Freddo come una ghicciaia.

JOHNNY

All night I was pushin that cart through the mud and the shit. You got no idea. You sit here all day. You don't even go to the market. Torno a casa and there's no clean shirt.

ANNA

You smell like cigar.

JOHNNY

Lavoravo. I work when I smoke. Jimmy, this is private.

ANNA

Bugiardo.

JIMMY

That's my bed she's sittin on.

ANNA

Where's the money?

JOHNNY

I gotta buy more bananas.

ANNA

Ladro.

> There is a knock on the door.
> A hush falls over the trio.

JOHNNY

Did you pay the pigione?

JIMMY

I wasn't here last night.

ANNA

I was here, alone, all alone. Sola soletta.

JOHNNY

Where were you, she was here all alone?

JIMMY

I'm in love. With a Scotchwoman. She's beautiful. She's got red hair.

GREEN

(OFF) Mister Mora.

> *JOHNNY re-buttons his dirty shirt, opens the door a fraction.*

JOHNNY

Yeah.

GREEN

Not you, the other one.

JOHNNY

I got the money for the roomaboarda.

GREEN

I rent the room to him. As far as I'm concerned, you don't live here.

JIMMY

It's okay Mrs. Green, he's movin out from here. They're goin back. Aiaiai, non è possibile.

> *MOMMA and POPPA stand in the doorway, bags in hand.*
> *Mrs. GREEN pushes in ahead of them as the family embraces wildly.*

GREEN

Alright Mister Mora, this is the last straw.

ANNA

E il colmo Giovanni, è il colmo.

MOMMA

Giacomo, mio figlio. Anna.

JIMMY

Mamma, Papà.

JOHNNY

They're not stayin Mrs. Green. They're touristi.

POPPA

No, rimaniamo. E finita, la fattoria.

GREEN

They're not stayin.

JIMMY

Come finite, Papà?

POPPA

Non esiste più. L'hanno presa, la fattoria.

ANNA

Lo seppi, io.

JIMMY

Never rains but it pours.

POPPA

Come?

JIMMY

Canadian expression.

MOMMA

Ci sta un'altra stanza?

ANNA

No, è tutto.

JOHNNY

This is my Mamma, Mrs. Green. E la donna della casa.

MOMMA

Piacere Signora.

GREEN

They're not stayin eh? That's what he said about you. But your wife was pregnant.

JIMMY

I didn't know she already had the baby.

GREEN

And now she's gonna have another one. One is already too many.

JIMMY

Another what?

ANNA

Si, ne aspetto un altro.

> All stare at ANNA, then MOMMA showers her in kisses;
> POPPA whacks JOHNNY on the back.

POPPA
Buona a qualcosa, tu.

MOMMA
Che belle notizie Anna, brava, brava.

GREEN
Yes, very nice. But not here, and not with a man like him. Out, all night. I had inspectors here.

JOHNNY
Che dice, Jimmy?

ANNA
La polizia.

MOMMA
Polizia, perchè?

GREEN
No polizei. But I expect they'll be here next. First the city inspectors, then the police. I don't need that. I don't need that cart in my backyard. Or the bananas in the basement with all the spiders. Mister Mora, I'm telling you . . .

JOHNNY
Just one night, here's the rent. They go in morning.

POPPA
Cos'è Giovanni? Non possiamo rimanere qua?

GREEN
No.

JIMMY
Just for one day, Miss Green.

GREEN
No.

MOMMA
Ci sta qualche problema, Signora?

GREEN
No. Mrs. Mora can stay because of her condition. But I don't want bananas or anybody else.

MOMMA
Ah grazie Signora, mille grazie.

POPPA
Noi siamo riconoscenti. Molto gentile, Signora.

JIMMY
They be gone by morning.

JOHNNY
I move the cart. Papà, vieni con me?

POPPA
Si si, vengo. Che faciamo?

> Mrs. GREEN has been ushered out the door.
> JOHNNY swipes one of JIMMY's shirts.
> POPPA is on standby.

JOHNNY
Andiamo lavorare Papà.

MOMMA

Vuoi mangiare qualcosa Anna, hai il viso pallido.

JOHNNY

That's right Anna, you look sick. Greens you need. Ricordati Papà, dell'insalata per Anna.

POPPA

C'io una fame, io.

MOMMA

Dov'è la cucina, Giacomo?

JIMMY

Ain't no kitchen, Mamma.

MOMMA

Come?

JIMMY

Quest'è la cucina.

MOMMA

Ah?

> JOHNNY kisses MOMMA when ANNA turns her cheek to his peck.

JOHNNY

You comin Jimmy?

JIMMY

I better stay, in case of inspectors. That's my shirt.

JOHNNY

Ciao.

> JOHNNY and POPPA go.
> MOMMA spots some fruit in a bowl.

MOMMA

Cos'è questo?

ANNA

Sono banane.

MOMMA

Banane?

ANNA

Si, si mangiano.

> MOMMA takes a bite of unpeeled banana.

JIMMY

No no no no Mamma. Così, guarda. (Peeling one for her.) Takes time to get used to the taste. Ti abiturai. Why didn't you tell me there were inspectors here last night? They coulda sent us back. Vuoi tornare in Italia, tu, is that what you want?

ANNA

Vuoi tenere la bambina, Signora?

MOMMA

Vergogna Anna, sono Mamma, capisci, Mamma.

FUOCO E FIAMME

A back alley, April, 1904.

*The cart stands half-laden with bananas. MICHE sits on it
with a hand organetto.*

MICHE
Oh roses like a rich compost
Toronto is aswarm with wasps
a little crap makes roses grow
there's pricks and stinks in every plot

Yes, Johnny's salad patch needs rain
and Anna's roses need a fence
Toronto's going up in flames
to pray for rain is common sense

Well, years of April rain yield trees
but minutes make of them mere stumps
the salad patch must have a fence
and trees make wood, that's plain enough

But what's the reason, what's the cause
why some have wood and some have none
the mangiacake he makes the laws
the Wop has got to play along

Oh roses like a rich compost
Toronto is aswarm with wasps
a little crap makes roses grow
there's pricks and stinks in every plot

> *Voices drift in from the alley as MICHE moves off.*
> *JOHNNY and JIMMY enter with some wood as a young man*
> *of JOHNNY's age, Bill PRICE, looks on, unnoticed.*

JOHNNY
Acqua, Papà, acqua.
JIMMY
We ain't gonna find no water. There's no time.
POPPA
Facio pipi.
JIMMY
Non è necessario, Papà. No pipi.
POPPA
Brucerà, la carta.
> *POPPA is about to pee on the wood as JOHNNY and JIMMY*
> *return for more.*
PRICE
Stay right where you are.

POPPA

Giovanni.

JOHNNY returns and stares down PRICE.

JOHNNY

Non gli dare retta. Vai.

PRICE

Just hold it.

JOHNNY

Big fire, eh.

PRICE

Hey, you kapish the English?

JOHNNY

You capisci Italiano?

PRICE

No kapish. I don't wanna kapish.

POPPA

O. O. Capisc-o.

PRICE

This is private property. You're stealing. That's against the law.

JOHNNY

You a cop?

PRICE

I'm a lawyer. Fire or no fire, I'll make a citizen's arrest and have you thrown in the slammer.

JIMMY throws a new load on the cart.

JIMMY

We're helpin fight the fire.

PRICE

That doesn't mean you can steal.

JIMMY

Building's fallin down all over the place. We gotta stop it. They need this wood.

PRICE

You're stealing this wood.

JOHNNY

Just looks like it. Legname, andate subito. You like oyster?

PRICE

What?

JOHNNY breaks open a crate of oysters and shucks a slimy-shelled mollusc.

JOHNNY

Look at that, beautiful. Legname, Papà?

POPPA

Assagiala, è buona, l'ostrica. In tutti i mesi con la letter r, come Aprrrrile.

PRICE

What's he saying?

JIMMY and POPPA have gone for more wood.
JOHNNY grabs PRICE by the arm.

JOHNNY

Don't do that.

PRICE

You threatening me?

JOHNNY

Where you live?

PRICE

Why? So you and your friends can come over and beat me up. I'm not afraid of you, Wop.

JOHNNY

I never talk to no English person before.

PRICE

That's not my problem.

JOHNNY

Where you live?

PRICE

You want to come and talk to me?

JOHNNY

Maybe. I bring to you some bananas.

PRICE

I don't eat bananas.

JOHNNY

You give to you friend. Where you live?

PRICE

Jarvis Street.

JOHNNY

What number?

PRICE

Two eleven.

JOHNNY

Te lo ricorderai, Jimmy? That's my brother.

> *JIMMY and POPPA have returned with wood.*

JIMMY

Two eleven, va bene.

JOHNNY

I'm Johnny. That's Papà. Tonight we deliver to you some bananas. You a lawyer, eh?

PRICE

That's my profession, that's what I do.

JOHNNY

Good, maybe you help us.

JIMMY

E avvocato, Papà.

POPPA

Ah si, abbiamo bisogno di un avvocato. Piacere Signore.

JIMMY

Papà needs a lawyer for some things in the old country. They took our farm away over there.

PRICE

Who did?

JOHNNY

The government, they say they build a railroad.

PRICE

That's terrible.

POPPA

Si, è una cosa terribile. Non c'io più niente.

JIMMY

We got nothin left. We were kings. They took everything—farm, animals, olive trees, vines, everything. They gave him a ticket to America.

POPPA

It's no right.

PRICE

I don't know if I can do anything.

JOHNNY

Tonight, we deliver. We talk about this.

PRICE

Second floor in the back.

JIMMY

We'll be back, sure.

PRICE

Where are you taking the wood?

POPPA

Ci vediamo, avvocato.

JOHNNY

Sta sera, Papà. No kidding Price.

> JOHNNY and JIMMY push the cart as POPPA waves from the back of it, where he is seated.

BAMBINI

The rear of the Mora home, April, 1905.

MOMMA pokes the earth with a stick. Mrs. GREEN appears with a brown bag in hand.

MOMMA

Terra ingrata, perchè ti rifiuti di fruttare?

GREEN

Buon giorno, Signora.

MOMMA

Hallo Miss Green, vado a cercarla.

GREEN

No no, let her be. I brought something for the family. Time to turn the soil again I see. For you.

> *Mrs. GREEN offers the bag to MOMMA.*
> *She toys with a plaid scarf at her neck.*

MOMMA

Ahhh, un pollo, grazie. E un po magro, ma è bello. Lo spennerò.

GREEN

I knew you were having money problems. And I wondered if you could do me a favour. Since it's Friday ...

MOMMA

Aspetta, non capsico. Anna!

GREEN

No please ...

> *ANNA is standing in the shade of the door.*
> *MOMMA goes into the house.*

MOMMA

Guarda che bell pollo, l'ha apportato Signora Verdi.

ANNA

You like to come in?

GREEN

I just wanted to know how you were feeling.

ANNA

A little better, thank you.

GREEN

I'm glad. Time heals all wounds. I know how difficult it can be. I lost my first two, both boys. I just can't carry them. Now of course I have two beautiful daughters. God calls some of us back at an early age. God has his reasons. (PAUSE) I hope you can use the chicken.

ANNA

You shouldn't worry about us.

GREEN

Well, I do. It's kosher, I hope you don't mind. My neighbour, Mrs. Bertelli, she moved away. I wonder if you could do something for me.

> *MOMMA has returned with a metal basinette.*
> *ANNA cries out at the sight of it.*

GREEN

No. Use something else. A sugar bag.

MOMMA

Conservo le penne. Sono buoni per cuscini.

GREEN

Not here Signora, inside.

MOMMA

Non ti preoccupare. Guardate come escono.

ANNA

Va bene Mamma. It's okay Miss Green, she wants the feathers. You want me to do something.

GREEN

Don't worry about it. Another time.

ANNA

You bring us the chicken. What do you want?

GREEN

I made a cholent, it's in the oven. I wondered if you could start the fire for me tonight. Like before.

ANNA

You leave open the door, I do for you.

GREEN

Perhaps your mother could do it.

ANNA

She doesn't know how. I fix for you.

GREEN

Thank you, Mrs. Mora. I want you to have this.

ANNA

No, already we have the chicken.

GREEN

At the factory, we have hundreds.

ANNA

We don't wear this colour.

GREEN

Take it, please. It's a gift.

MOMMA

Prendila, per le bambine.

ANNA burst into tears again and goes.

ANNA

I cannot take this. Excuse please

GREEN

I shouldn't have come here. Please give her this.

MOMMA

No worry for Anna. Very strong. Soon another one. Grazie Signora. Aiaiaiai.

GREEN

What is it?

MOMMA

Venerdì. Friday. No meat.

GREEN

That's right—no meat on Friday.

MOMMA

Ma, si mangiarà dopo mezzanotte.

GREEN

You can't eat meat. I can't light my stove. Just because it's Friday. It's a funny way we have, isn't it? No no, pull the feathers the other way.

MOMMA

Non ti preoccupare Signora. Ah America, America, anche i polli sono, contro natura.

GREEN

I see you've got a few violets coming up over here. Blue ones, see? And this vine is taking. Who would have thought? You're going to have a lovely garden. And in a few years, you'll have grapes for wine. Watch the scarf in the chicken innards.

MOMMA
   Grazie per la sciarpa, thank you. Ciao Signora.
GREEN
   Yes, ciao.
MOMMA
   Bye-bye Miss Green.

Mrs. GREEN goes as MOMMA plucks the chicken, the plaid
scarf around her neck.
When Mrs. GREEN is gone, MOMMA wipes her eye.

BOCCHSACARRU

A siding, Union Station, April, 1907.

MICHE appears, looking much more affluent, next to an open
boxcar.

MICHE
   Hurry hurry hurry hurry (CHORUS)
   hurry where the money's made
   busy busy busy busy
   busy people never wait

   I could be makin real money
   workin on the railroad
   I'd have an English puscemeni
   fillin in my time card

   But I'm still here, I love the South
   even when it's grey
   and Johnny Mora's rich enough
   to be my boss, and so I stay

   (CHORUS)

   You got a head, it's yours to use
   you got a nose, and two good eyes
   you smell a deal, you look obtuse
   you sniff the spots that catch the flies

   you hear the talk, it gets around
   it takes some cash and if you're quick
   you steal the keys to open doors
   the key don't work? So use your fist

   (CHORUS)

Sudbury, it's sunny and cold
I never been there, I hate the railroad
MICHE stops suddenly, spotting JOHNNY.

MICHE

Oh oh, arriva il bossu.

JOHNNY

Hé, fruittvendolo, non abbiamo tempo di suonare. Il bocchsacarru aspetta,
Andiamo. These bananas belong to me. The bocchsacarru's gonna be leavin any
minute. Goin back for more. Scarica.

MICHE

Sciurissimo bossu. Mister Loblaw wants his banane, he's gonna get a thousand.
Scarico.

JOHNNY

Where's the other carta?

MICHE

Just me today, bossu.

JOHNNY

Tell your brother for me he don't exist no more. Scarica, precipitevolissimevolmente.
PRICE enters precipitevolissimevolmente.

PRICE

Don't load the cart.

MICHE

Mannacia l'America.

JOHNNY

These bananas got a customer. Train's goin back for more.

PRICE

This train ain't goin nowhere. Basta.

JOHNNY

I need the money, you need the money. Scarica.

PRICE

The money can wait. Don't load the bananas.

JOHNNY

I can't wait. Scarica.

MICHE

Decidi. Scarico o carico? This way or that way? Whaddayou want? Just tell me.

PRICE

Into the boxcar.

JOHNNY

Fuori dello bocchsacarru.
> *JOHNNY and PRICE move the bananas in opposite*
> *directions.*
> *MICHE stands back.*

PRICE

Johnny, we just wait three or four days.

JOHNNY

They all be rotten.

PRICE

Put em on ice.

JOHNNY

That's gonna cost more than it's worth.

PRICE

Believe me.

> *JOHNNY throws down his (new) hat.*

JOHNNY

Santa Madonna, non capisco più niente. What's goin on? Am I talkin Arabico or what? These bananas are sold. In fifteen minutes I can get cash. Two and a half centa pound.

PRICE

In four days they're gonna be worth four centa pound.

JOHNNY

What are you, crazy?

PRICE

Jesus, Jesus, Jesus. You never listen to nothin I tell you. La testa dura.

JOHNNY

Hey Mister Mangiacake, I don't need your pearl of wisdom.

PRICE

Why should I cast them to swine anyway?

MICHE

Ah, finalmente, ho capito qualcosa.

JOHNNY

Tu, scarica. Okay Bill, I deliver the bananas, you get you money back, that's it. You buy your own bananas from now on.

PRICE

There ain't gonna be no more bananas.

JOHNNY

Why? Somebody eat em all?

PRICE

Cause there's gonna be a strike.

MICHE

Striku?

PRICE

That's right. A train strike. No more frutti frutti, kapish. Hé paesan? Price is going up.

> *POPPA rushes in, flailing his arms.*

POPPA

Giovanni, apsetta, aspetta.

JOHNNY

Not now, Papà. Lasciaci.

POPPA

Conserva le banane.

PRICE

You're givin em away for nothin. You're throwin away our money. My money.

JOHNNY

I know what I'm doin.

PRICE

You think you do.

POPPA

Non hai capito niente.

JOHNNY

Si Papà, ho capito. Price, you a lawyer, you tell me about papers. You tell me how to get back my farm. Didn't work, don't matter. I don't tell you how to run your business.

PRICE

You don't understand business.

JOHNNY

So how come I'm makin deals with Loblaw? Why? Because I can't go home, because you didn't do nothin about the place in Italy with all the nice cows and horses and pigs. So I gotta work here. And what's my business here? Bananas. Cause I understand bananas. You're an Orangeman, I'm a bananaman. Siciliani think they got the banana business by the balls. But we're gonna show them something. Cause I don't care about the railroad. Papà, Michè, scarica.

POPPA

No Giovanni, non si vende.

PRICE

Not even the Sicilians are gonna get bananas. In four days, these bananas are gonna be worth twice as much.

JOHNNY

In four days they be rotten. What about next week?

PRICE

Next week there ain't gonna be no bananas. No apples, no oranges, no nothin.

JOHNNY

Wrong.

PRICE

You gonna end this strike all by yourself?

JOHNNY

Next week I'm gonna be in Buffalo.

POPPA

Buffalo? Che ferai a Buffalo?

MICHE

I got a brother in Buffalo.

JOHNNY

I know who's got bananas in Buffalo.

PRICE

How you gonna get them across the border?

JOHNNY

That's your giobba. We're gonna buy a trocku.

PRICE

A what?

MICHE

Ahh, a trocku, very smart.

PRICE

With what are we gonna buy a trocku?

JOHNNY

That's why we gotta sell these bananas.

PRICE

What about gas?

JOHNNY

Cheaper in Buffalo.

PRICE

Who's gonna drive?

JOHNNY

Papà.

PRICE

He can't drive.

JOHNNY

He learned to push a cart.

PRICE

He hasn't got papers.

JOHNNY

That's your giobba. We leave on Monday.

PRICE

I can't get papers in four days, on the weekend.

JOHNNY

You can't get no papers? I thought you were my partner. I been waiting five years for these papers. I don't think I need no papers.

POPPA

Giovanni, che succede?

JOHNNY

Domanda lui.

POPPA

Signor Bill, che succede?

PRICE

Who's got bananas in Buffalo?

JOHNNY

That's my business. Loblaw is waitin. You gonna get us papers? Next week we gonna be the only ones in the city with bananas.

PRICE

Okay, okay. I'll call my father. But there are no guarantees. He's a judge now, he's got to be careful. Alright, Mike, let's get Mister Loblaw his bananas.

JOHNNY

Just one thing. Here. Tell your wife thank you very much but he don't wear pink. Gonna call him Pete.

PRICE

It was a boy? Congratulations. I had some blue ones in the other pocket. Here they are.

The men exchange pairs of knitted booties.

JOHNNY
Va bene. Papà, Michè, andiamo.
MICHE
I ain't seen my brother for two years.

SARDINE

The Mora bedroom, May, 1909.

JOHNNY lies in bed next to TERESA, ANGEL and, at the other end, ANNA.
He steals from bed in his trousers, searching for his boots. The second boot drops from his hand.

ANNA
Giovanni.
JOHNNY
Si?
ANNA
Ho fatto un sogno.
JOHNNY
What did you dream?
ANNA
Rats under the bed.
JOHNNY
We're the only rats here, eatin cheddar cheese night and day.
ANNA
They came to bite the baby.
JOHNNY
Dormi.
ANNA
La pigione.
JOHNNY
Braunstino don't need our rent money. He's just gonna buy another building like he did last week.
ANNA
Dammi i soldi.
             ANNA leans out of bed and searches JOHNNY's pockets.
JOHNNY
Non toccare le Tasche. What's this? Cos'è, Anna? Orrecchini? Where you get this?
ANNA
He gave it to me.
JOHNNY
Who? Braunstino? For what?
ANNA
Ai, mi fa male. Ah no, sanguine dal naso.
JOHNNY
Give them to me. You don't take nothin from him.

ANNA is holding her nose with one hand; with the other she boxes JOHNNY on the ear.

ANNA

Guarda che hai fatto, brutto.

JOHNNY

Ai, why you hit me?

TERESA

Momma, she kicked me.

JOHNNY

(IN A LOUD WHISPER) Sta zitti, tutti. That's it, Anna, no more Braunstino strozzino. You give those back to him. That's ten weeks' rent. We move from here. Sporco Bastardo, I'm gonna kill him. Scarpa, scarpa, dov'è la mia scarpa?

POPPA appears in the half-light, shoe in hand; TERESA screams.

TERESA

Aiii, Poppanonno.

JOHNNY

Papà, what are you doin, are you crazy?

ANNA

Teresa, tappa la bocca.

POPPA

Montanaro contadino scarpe grosse cervello fino.

JOHNNY

Si si si. Go to your room.

POPPA

Mi chiamo Raffaelle.

JOHNNY

That's your name, so what?

POPPA

Si chiama Pietro, lui.

JOHNNY

Papà, this is Canada. How can he be Raffaelle? Then everybody's gonna call him Ralph. That's no good, I told you a thousand times. Let him sleep. Cos'è?

POPPA

Il dente di lupo.

JOHNNY

The wolf's tooth. He's gonna put that in his mouth and choke to death. He's only got three teeth of his own, why you givin him this?

POPPA

Contr'il malocchio.

JOHNNY

Malocchio? There's no evil eye in this country.

MOMMA has stolen from her closet to see what is going on.

MOMMA

Come? Malocchio si trova dovunque.

JOHNNY

There is no malocchio in Canada. There are no rats. There's just us, livin like sardines in the can.

MOMMA
Raffaelle, che fai qui?

POPPA
Me dicono che si chiamerà Pietro.

JOHNNY
But that's his name, for two years now.

MOMMA
Very nice. Come San Pietro. Raffaelle, a letto. Giovanni.
POPPA pads back into the closet.

MOMMA
Dov'è Anna?

JOHNNY
I don't know, she's gone.

MOMMA
La giacca—dove vai?

JOHNNY
I'm gonna buy a new trocku.

MOMMA
Trocku we don't need. Already you have one, doesn't work.

JOHNNY
A new trocku, Mamma, a red trocku with yellow lettere, says Johnny Mora,
fruit vendor.

MOMMA
Giovanni, è domenica. On Sunday we go to church. Ti vesti, Teresa.

TERESA
It's too early to go to church.

MOMMA
Hai sentito?

TERESA
How come Angel never has to go to church?
*TERESA parades past her father and grandmother toward the
bathroom.*

MOMMA
Aspetta? Giovanni, ti aspetta Anna nel gabinetto?
JOHNNY shakes his head no; TERESA continues.

MOMMA
Va bene, Teresa, al gabinetto. Allora, che ti prendi?

JOHNNY
I'm sick and tired Mamma, of livin like sardines in the can, eatin lentiche night
and day. You and Papà sleepin in the closet. Teresa and Angelina sleepin in the
same bed with us. Pietro sleepin in a basket.

MOMMA
Ho capito. Raffaelle.
POPPA returns from the closet.

POPPA
Si?

MOMMA

Ti vesti, andiamo a chiesa.

POPPA

Ma noi siamo soltanto alle sei.

MOMMA

Vai. Vengo con te.

> *JOHNNY is left alone for a moment when ANNA returns*
> *with a rag over her nose.*
> *She gets into bed.*

JOHNNY

I'm gonna buy a trocku. La pigione can wait. (PAUSE) It's Sunday, I can still buy a trocku. Tomorrow I sell the other one. (PAUSE) Vai a chiesa? No. Quando ritorno, ti voglio nel letto, capisci? I want the bed flat and perfect and you in it. We're not doin it in Braunstino's bathroom no more. It's six in the morning, how can they go to church now?

> *TERESA returns and lays her nightclothes on the bed.*

TERESA

Ciao Momma.

ANNA

Where you go?

TERESA

To church. Sun's not even up.

> *MOMMA and POPPA come out of the closet, dressed for church.*

POPPA

Perchè non si chiama Pietro Raffaelle?

JOHNNY

Papà, you want to call him Pietro Raffaelle, that's your business. His name's Petie, punto.

MOMMA

Andiamo tutti. Teresa.

TERESA

Angel's pretending to be asleep.

JOHNNY

So's your mother.

MOMMA

Anna, nel armadio. Angelina, dormi. Giovanni, spogliati.

> *MOMMA motions ANNA into the closet;*
> *ANNA stands waiting for JOHNNY to undress.*
> *JOHNNY starts to undress but stops at removing his pants; the*
> *others leave.*

ANNA

E la pigione?

JOHNNY

We need the truck more than he needs the rent. I give him back his earrings for the rent. Pietro, the wolf's tooth, just give it to me for luck for now. When you're grown up, I give it back, I promise.

ANNA
Giovanni, adesso.

· **GUERRA**

City Hall, May, 1915.

MICHE stands beside a display of bananas. POPPA prepares a show of halved watermelons atop an open-back truck that reads "Johnny Mora, fruit vendor" on the side.

MICHE
There's a war on, don't you know there's a war on? Somewhere, there's always a war on. And you never know whose side you're on, because they can change the law or they can change their mind, and all of a sudden you're on the other side.

POPPA
Quest'è il mio cornu.

MICHE
It's a free country.

POPPA
I am here first.

MICHE
Sixabanan ten cent who wantsabuy?

POPPA
Watermela nicea fresh. Who wantsa buy?
                JOHNNY enters, machete in hand, ready to kill.

JOHNNY
Dov'è la carta? Papà?

MICHE
I got bananas today. No more bananas.

JOHNNY
Ritorn'al tuo posto. Go where you supposed to be.

POPPA
Il sangue non è acqua.

MICHE
You can't get blood from a stone. I'm ready.

POPPA
Non voglio più ti parlare.
                POPPA waves JOHNNY off with a flourish of his own machete.
                JOHNNY returns the gesture defiantly.

JOHNNY
We cover both sides. Go back where I told you. People gonna be here any minute, just dyin for a piecea watermelon. Where's the cart?

POPPA
Ho bisogno di meloni.

JOHNNY
I gave you melons.

POPPA

Rotten. Sono molli, guarda, come te, nella testa.

> *POPPA has sliced a watermelon with his machete and hits*
> *JOHNNY over the head with one of the pieces.*

MICHE

Attenzione, arriva il Carnevale. Banaaane.

JOHNNY

We're in business together, not against one another.

POPPA

You think I'm stupido? Lousey meloni, who's gonna but this? Ottantacinque anni, io. Mi credi scarso? I no work for you.

JOHNNY

Good, go sell you meloni someplace else.

> *The conscription parade has arrived.*
> *Mayor CHURCH carries a sign reading:*
> *ANDIAMO FAR LA GUARRA;*
> *Miss HUMBLE, an enthusiast of voluntary enlistment, a sign*
> *reading: WE GO TO FREE TRENT AND TRIESTE;*
> *The SIGNORA, a ravioli vendor, the sign:*
> *BRITTANI ECCOCI QUA.*

MICHE

Sixabananaten cent.

SIGNORA

Ravioli deliziosissimi. Free, free.

POPPA

Watermela nicea fresh. Fivecent.

JOHNNY

These are my meloni Papà. Ten cent. Go away.

> *CHURCH positions himself to address the crowd, Miss*
> *HUMBLE at his side.*

CHURCH

Aitalo-Canadians, andiamo far la Guerra. On this, your national feast day, we raise the red, white and GREEN in front of City Hall. My name is Tommy Church and I'm the Mayor of this city. I want you to know my ancestors were Irish.

MICHE

Attenzione a lui, Signora, è pazzo.

SIGNORA

No no no no, è bravo, è il sindaco.

CHURCH

The Aitalian has been called the New Irish, come here to escape the grinding poverty of the homeland, the bestie paesani.

JOHNNY

Last year it was Wops out of the country.

CHURCH

And this year the Aitalian has turned a deaf ear on the Kaiser. Hundreds of young Aitalian boys from Winnipeg, Vancouver, the Prairies, are come here on the Traino deli Aitaliani to prove themselves men of the land, Canadians strong and true.

SIGNORA

Ravioli per tutti quelli chi si arrualano voluntari.

MICHE

Qualsiasi cosa per il denaro, hé Signora?

HUMBLE

It is your duty to enlist.

CHURCH

That's right Miss Humble. Will you lead us in the anthem you have composed for the overseas campaign, "We're from Canada"? Rocco d'Angelo and his band will join Miss Humble in her composition.

HUMBLE

Thank you, Mayor Church. Thank you, you fine Aitalo-Canadian boys who have joined up, and thank you Canada, our glorious country, strong and free. Let us keep it ever so.

King and our country
We're from Canada (bis)
A land beyond compare
where the sun shines bright
and the stars at night
look down on our fields so fair

POPPA

Signora, se permette?

SIGNORA

Si, gusta I miei ravioli. Gustateli tutti.

PRICE

Johnny.

JOHNNY

Jesus Chris, I don't believe it. Papà, guarda.

POPPA

Signor Bill.

JOHNNY

You look like a post officer.

PRICE

I'm an officer, Royal Artillery.

HUMBLE

On to victory (bis) we will help to fight the foe and the maple leaf is our emblem dear as marching on we go

POPPA

Come stai?

PRICE

Bene, bene.

POPPA

Good, good.

> Miss HUMBLE finishes her song to the applause of MICHE, CHURCH and the SIGNORA.

MICHE

Brava, brava bis, bis.

SIGNORA

Si, è bravissima. Mangia.

CHURCH

Aitalo-Canadians, after me. To Union Station, to the Traino deli Aitaliani. Andiamo to Trent and Trieste. On to victory.

CHURCH leads his little band away.

MICHE

Hé, where's my ravioli. Dove andate?

SIGNORA

Vieni con noi, vieni.

PRICE

Gonna join up, Johnny?

JOHNNY

Somebody shoot me.

PRICE

Not if you shoot first. I'll teach you how. It's easy, like driving a car. You just point and pull the trigger. Use your quick Canadian wits to know when to pull the trigger. That's what you have to learn.

MICHE

He's no Canadian.

PRICE

This is his chance to become a real Canadian. You too, Mike. No questions asked. Join up now before they bring in conscription.

MICHE

Who's that?

PRICE

Conscription means they can force you to join whether you want to or not.

MICHE

I'm not no Canadian.

PRICE

That's not gonna matter. You join now, you get better treatment. The government will look after you when the war's over. It's a job. You can pay me back the money you owe me, Johnny, that you used to buy this here truck.

JOHNNY

Nobody's buyin my melons these days.

POPPA

Because they rotten.

MICHE

Hé Price, they leave without you.

PRICE

They don't need me. I find my men my way. Where you livin, Johnny?

JOHNNY

Same like before.

PRICE

Let's go see your kids. I haven't seen them for years. I got three kids now.

JOHNNY

Same like me. Papà, prendi I miei meloni.

POPPA

Nobody wants.

JOHNNY

Give em away.

POPPA

Never give away.

JOHNNY

Then let em rot.

MICHE

Hé, sei pazzo, tu. E una cosa seria, la guerra. You wanna get yourself killed?

POPPA

Giovanni, non dirmi che vai con loro.

PRICE

Lemme tell you somethin, men. If you join up with me, you'll probably never be issued a gun. They'll give you a shovel. We're reserve. But with all the benefits.

JOHNNY

Take the meloni Papà. You sell em, you keep the money. Find the cart and bring it home.

POPPA

Perchè non mi ascolti?

JOHNNY

Eighty-five years old, Bill. Leaves the cart all over the place. Forgets where he put it.

PRICE

Still go the fighting spirit. That must be where you get it from. Chip off the old block.

POPPA

Dove vai?

JOHNNY

A casa Papà, calma calma.

POPPA

Mascalzone.

MICHE

Vieni con me, Poppanononno. We go to the station and sell the bananas and meloni. Then we have a drink.

> POPPA walks away from MICHE and his son.
> PRICE is somewhat embarrassed by the bad feeling he has aroused
> between father and son; JOHNNY takes him by the shoulder
> and they go.

SCOPA

The Mora kitchen, June, 1917.

JIMMY and JOHNNY pitch cards in a game of scopa on the kitchen table. MICHE stands apart, playing a guitar.

MICHE
>Patria famiglia
>shovels, guns and bombs
>fifteen years in Canada
>marching up and down
>
>In the drill hall here's a starling
>flying up and down
>and the starling's always stealing
>when nobody's around
>
>Patria famiglia
>shovels, guns and bombs
>fifteen years in Canada
>marching up and down
>
>Colonel bought his own horse
>soldiers, they have none
>Captain bought his own boots
>one day they were gone
>
>Patria famiglia
>shovels, guns and bombs
>fifteen years in Canada
>marching up and down

>   *MICHE watches as JOHNNY and JIMMY count.*

JIMMY
>Figura for twelve, two for thirteen.

JOHNNY
>Twenty-one for one, five gold for one. I win.

JIMMY
>Lucky at cards, unlucky in love.

JOHNNY
>Come?

JIMMY
>Canadian expression. My deal.

>   *TERESA enters, takes dishes from armoire.*

TERESA
>I can't set the table with this going on.

JIMMY
>We can't play cards with you settin the table.

ANNA
>(OFF) Apparecchia la tavola.

TERESA
>I can't they're playin cards.

ANNA
>(OFF) Basta con le carte.

TERESA
    This is Angel's job.
JOHNNY
    Vuoi una sberla? Do what your mother says.
            JOHNNY picks up the cards as TERESA sets the table.
            ANNA appears, a suitcase in her hand, MOMMA beside her.
ANNA
    Jesu Maria Giuseppe, Giovanni Mora, per l'amore di Dio. Cos'è questo? Cos'hai
    fatto?
JOHNNY
    What does it look like?
            ANNA drops the case, goes to JOHNNY and boxes him on the ears.
ANNA
    You wanna die and get killed and leave me and your children to die?
JOHNNY
    It's what has to be. Basta o ti schiaffeggio.
            JOHNNY defends himself, hitting ANNA back.
            MOMMA and JIMMY pull them apart.
MOMMA
    Zitti tutti. Basta Giovanni. Raffaelle.
JIMMY
    Giovanni, fermi.
ANNA
    Mi fai schifa, tu, questo paese. Non has senso.
JOHNNY
    We're gonna build a railroad. Shovels, not guns.
ANNA
    No ha senso.
JOHNNY
    It makes perfect sense. They're gonna look after ya.
ANNA
    Who, who? Price? He leads you there.
JOHNNY
    The government. They give you money, more money than we ever had.
ANNA
    You got no brain, you got no heart either? Idiota. (HITS HIM AGAIN) What
    about your children? What about me? E io, Giovanni, e io? Ne aspeto un altro.
            She slips to the floor, silencing all.
POPPA
    (ENTERING) Che è successo qua?
JIMMY
    Jesus, she's havin a nosebleed.
JOHNNY
    Vado in Inghilterra Papà.
POPPA
    Come?

JOHNNY

I'm goin to war. I'm goin over there.

TERESA

No Poppa, no.

JIMMY

Jesus Joh, Jesus. Can't you tell them she's pregnant?

POPPA

Ma perchè vai in Inghilterra?

MOMMA

La guerra, idiota, la guerra.

POPPA

Sei pazzo, Giovanni? E lo businessu, e la tua famiglia? La tua moglie? La tua
Mamma? Io?

JOHNNY

I signed, I gotta go. If I don't go, they're gonna throw me in the can.

POPPA

Parla italiano.

JOHNNY

Se non vado, mi mandano in prigione.

ANNA

If you go, I never speak to you again. Capisci? Io non ti parlo più.

> ANNA rises and exits, TERESA following, then MOMMA.

MOMMA

Vigliacco. Te l'ho detto.

> JOHNNY upsets the kitchen table with the dishes on it, sits in
> a chair.
> POPPA immediately begins picking up.

POPPA

Bene, bene, e adesso spezza I mobili.

JIMMY

That ain't your table

JOHNNY

Whose is it if it's not mine?

JIMMY

I helped you pinch it from the Army, remember?

JOHNNY

Jesus Jimmy, Jesus, Jesus, Jesus. I never thought they were gonna send us.

JIMMY

Did you think you were just gonna march up and down the drill hall all day?

JOHNNY

I can't get out of it Jimmy, I tried.

JIMMY

You shoulda never joined up in the first place.

JOHNNY

I just couldn't no more.

JIMMY

Couldn't what?

JOHNNY

    Bananas and apples and meloni. Fifteen years and nothin to show. Why? Because he sold la farma. Papà sold it, he sold us, everything that ever belonged to us in Italy.

POPPA

    Insolente, vergogna. Non saic he dici. La farma is to me. La mia fattoria, la mia terra. They steal from me, not from you. Why? To build the railroad. But they don't build. They steal my farma, they keep.

JOHNNY

    We were kings Jimmy, do you understand?

JIMMY

    It don't matter, it's gone now.

JOHNNY

    Mamma, muoio di fame. Mamma. See Jimmy?

JIMMY

    What's to see?

JOHNNY

    There's nothin to eat.

JIMMY

    You got soup.

JOHNNY

    Same as yesterday.

JIMMY

    Better the second day.

POPPA

    Quando parti?

JOHNNY

    Domani Papà.

JIMMY

    You gonna say goodbye to Julia?

JOHNNY

    I don't know, why?

POPPA

    Ho fame anch'io.

JIMMY

    We probably gonna get married when you're gone.

JOHNNY

    That's nice. She's beautiful for a Scotchwoman.

        ANNA has returned with JOHNNY's uniform.
        She throws it on the ground.

ANNA

    Decidi. Price o me. Now. You make up your mind.

        JOHNNY is unmoving.
        ANNA attacks him; POPPA leads her away.

POPPA

    Calma Anna, calma. Non partirà.

JIMMY

    He's gonna be dead when you get back.

JOHNNY
He's gonna live to a hundred. And you gonna marry the Scotchwoman. How can you do that?

**END
ACT ONE**

ACT TWO

1919—1974

BORDANTI

The Mora home, June, 1919

TERESA sits at GAE's feet as he taps out a rhythm on a snare drum. MICHE, sitting opposite, strums a guitar.

GAE
Più rapidamente, sai? Prestissimo. Bam ba ba ba ba ba ba, bam ba bam ba, bam ba ba ba ba ba, bam ...
MICHE
No no, qualcosa di romantico, una storia di amore. Everybody loves a love story. Ascolta. E una calzone agrodolce. Sweet and sad. Una ragazza chi aspetta il suo fidanzato. Torna da soldato ma ...
TERESA
In inglese per favore.
MICHE
In Italian and English. Devi imparare a parlare italiano, sai?
TERESA
Some day I'll learn. Play the song and be quiet.
MICHE
How can I play and be quiet? Okay. Comincia così.
            GAE plays a slow introduction on the drum.
            MICHE bids him to speed it up; GAE plays a jazz rhythm.
            MICHE silences GAE and begins on his own; during the reprise
            of the song, GAE will re-introduce the jazz rhythm and they
            will sing the song together in an up-tempo version.
            JOHNNY appears half-way through the song.
MICHE
    E tornato da soldato
    he come back from the war
    è sempre innamorato in love like before

Ma la sua prediletta
but the darling of his eye
s'è stancata, non l'aspetta
she has said her last goodbye

Nell'amore splende il sole
in alto mare com'in città
se le nuvole arribano
la donna fugirà

The light of love shines forever
on every corner of the world
but if love is clouded over
you will not find the girl
                    In the reprise of the song, TERESA nestles up to GAE.
JOHNNY
Teresa, who are these guys?
TERESA
Poppa. E lui. Momma.
JOHNNY
Quiet. Who are they?
TERESA
Bordanti.
JOHNNY
Ancora?
TERESA
Boarders Poppa. They help us with the rent.
JOHNNY
I want them out of here.
TERESA
No Poppa, this is Gae.
JOHNNY
I don't care, I want him out.
TERESA
He's my friend. Gaetano, quest'è il mio Poppa.
GAE
Piacere Signore.
TERESA
He plays drums in the Rocco D'Angelo band. He's learnin the violin too.
JOHNNY
La porta, la porta, vai.
                    *JOHNNY takes GAE by the seat of the pants and shoves him
                    out the door.
                    He returns for MICHE, who is on his feet.*
MICHE
Calma Signore, calma. I get my bag. (EXIT)

TERESA

No.

JOHNNY

Bordanti we don't need.

TERESA

You wrecked it, you wrecked everything. You been away eight months after the war was over. You coulda been dead for all anybody knew. You come home and in ten minutes you wrecked everything.

JOHNNY

Anna.

TERESA

She's not talkin to you. Gaetano. Gaetano.

JOHNNY

Teresa, rimani qua.

> *TERESA runs out after GAETANO, followed by MICHE with his bag and guitar.*
> *PETIE comes running in and rushes into his father's arms.*

PETIE

Poppa, Poppa.

JOHNNY

Who's this. You grew two feet. Anna.

PETIE

You kill any Germans Poppa?

JOHNNY

Only at cards. Look, German money, and French money and here's some English money, it's for you. Where's your Mamma?

> *ANGEL comes running to her father also, preceding ANNA, who stands in a doorway with a child in her arms.*

ANGEL

You came back.

JOHNNY

Of course I came back, to see my little Angel. Anna.

ANNA

Si chiama Ettore.

JOHNNY

Ettore, Ettore. Dammelo. You sure that's gonna be his name?

ANNA

E finita tra noi.

> *JOHNNY has taken ETTORE and has tried to kiss the iron ANNA; PETIE and ANGEL are clinging to him.*

JOHNNY

Angel, take my bag to your room and open it. I brought you something. Petie, I wanna talk to your Mamma, go to your room.

PETIE

This is my room.

JOHNNY

Go help your sister.

PETIE

I wanna be with you.

JOHNNY

I'm here, Pietro. Anna, it's not finished. I love you, you're my wife. Two years I been thinking about this moment. Per l'amore di Dio, Anna.

ANNA

Non c'è niente nel mio cuore per te.

JOHNNY

No Anna, guardami. E bello, Ettore. I brought you something, look, from Parigi, Paris, the city of Gods. Dell'ambra—amber, the tooth of a goddess, from Paris, the city of light. Anna.

> ANNA throws the amber to the floor and crushes it with her foot.

ANNA

Dammi il bambino.

JOHNNY

We got four kids we gotta bring up. It's gonna get better. I changed, you changed. Look at our faces. Don't cry. Anna, you get wrinkles from the salt like the sailors in the sea. Sara meglio, credimi. Rimango. Mi sei mancava, Anna, I missed you.

PETIE

You never wrote no letters.

JOHNNY

Your Poppa can't write.

ANNA

Ti credio morto.

> ANNA takes ETTORE away. ANGEL returns with a present, tearing the wrapping from it.

JOHNNY

Pietro, how has she been, your Mamma?

PETIE

We didn't know what happened to ya.

JOHNNY

Didn't nobody tell ya where I was?

PETIE

I don't know.

JOHNNY

Where's Poppanonno and Mommarella?

PETIE

Mommarella died, then Poppanonno.

ANGEL

A doll.

JOHNNY

It's from Paris.

ANGEL

I'm too old for dolls.

JOHNNY

I thought you might like it. It's French.

PETIE
That's when we got boarders. Three of em.
JOHNNY
Where's the truck?
PETIE
We had to sell it.
JOHNNY
What about the cart?
PETIE
It's out back.
JOHNNY
So we start again from nothin. Nuovo da capo.
ANGEL
There's a boy at school walks me home every day.
JOHNNY
You're too young to walk with boys.

INDISCREZIONE

JIMMY's pensione, July, 1920.

*JOHNNY sits on a chair, putting on his shoes and socks, whistling.
MICHE and GAE stand to one side, singing and playing an
allegro accompaniment to:*

MICHE/GAE
Indiscretion's been the fashion
worn by men in every age and
women shared their secret passion
out of sight and off the stage so

Nothing's new about two lovers
hot as coals when lights are low cause
your wife's home, the husband's gone
what to heck, we're all alone

Indiscretion's out of season
when the lady's not quite sure her
husband's brother should be seen in
circumstances quite so lurid

Passion is an odd compulsion
making men forget their wives and
kids and family, all that matters
passion rules a lonely life

Indiscretion is the fashion
what to heck, we're all alone but
if the lady's not quite sure her
passion rules her—tell her jokes

> GAE runs off with TERESA at the end of the song, MICHE
> following.

JIMMY

What to hell is goin on here?

JOHNNY

I took a bath. I was all smelly.

JIMMY

That's right, you stink. You don't just come over here and take a bath when I'm not here.

JOHNNY

I thought we were goin to the races.

JIMMY

Looks like you already been to the races.

JOHNNY

I heard a funny joke.

JIMMY

Keep it to yourself. I just saw Julia on the street. I wanna know what you said upset her.

> JOHNNY is nervous; JIMMY is poking at him and JOHNNY
> fears he will retaliate.

JOHNNY

Lay off. Guy is talkin to his friend Alberto.

JIMMY

You got some fuckin nerve.

JOHNNY

Alberto, he says. Listen to my joke.

JIMMY

He says, Alberto listen to my joke?

JOHNNY

No, you listen idiot. If she was cryin, it's got nothin to do with me. I told her a joke.

JIMMY

Some joke, makes a pregnant woman cry.

JOHNNY

You wanna hear the joke?

JIMMY

You lie through your teeth.

JOHNNY

Alberto, he says, you likea woman with smelly armpits and long stringy hair hangin down? Alberto says, "No, why you ask me that?" Alberto, he says, you likea woman with big long neck and droopy tits and bad breath? Alberto says, "No, why you ask me that?"

JIMMY

What are you talkin about?

JOHNNY

Ascoltami. Alberto, he says, you likea woman with big flat feet and fat legs who fart at the table when you eat you supper? Alberto says, "No, why you ask me that?" Guy says, "Alberto, why you screw my wife?"

JIMMY

That's a lousey fuckin joke.

JOHNNY

You and your wife got a lousey sense of humour.

JIMMY

Doesn't sound like your sense of humour is appreciated around here, so maybe you shouldn't come around here no more.

JOHNNY

You tellin me you don't want me around here no more?

JIMMY

That's what I'm tellin ya.

JOHNNY

Ho capito. Bye-bye. Never talk to you again. Never.

JIMMY

She told you she was pregnant, right?

JOHNNY

What does she have to tell me for. You can see it.

JIMMY

So you thought it's safe, you can screw her now. You been wantin to do it all these years.

JOHNNY

Sei pazzo, Jimmy, sai?

JIMMY

You ain't getting it at home and it's drivin you bananas. Well, you ain't gonna get it here, capisci?

JOHNNY

Sporco bastardo, vai fa'n culo.

JIMMY

Well, it's true ain't it.

JOHNNY

You're never gonna know the truth.

JIMMY

It's alright, she already told me everything.

JOHNNY

You believe what she tells you?

JIMMY

Yeah, I believe her. She's my wife.

JOHNNY

That's good. So believe me, I'm your brother. I never touched your wife, even though I mighta thought about it.

JIMMY

Fuck off, just fuck off, get out.

JOHNNY

I think it's nice, after all these years, she's gonna have a baby. What is she, thirty-eight years old now? Better late than ever, hé? Ciao. Ci vediamo. You phone me when you're ready to say you're sorry.

STORU

Mora Groceteria, July, 1923.

A telephone rings interminably inside a run-down storefront groceteria.
JOHNNY rushes to the wall phone, stepping around disarrayed bushels of peanuts and potatoes.

JOHNNY

More Groceteria, we deliver. Pronto. Si Signora. Bellissime barbietole, two pounds red beets. Pepi verdi? Rossi, certe. Just one red pepper. Five poundsa tomato, va bene Signora. This afternoon, prego. (HANGS UP) She's gonna turn her husbands insides red and his face white with tht order. Pietro.
PETIE enters, a hang-dog look on his face.

JOHNNY

You got your wheels? How you gonna do deliveries with no wheels?

PETIE

Take the truck.

JOHNNY

Truck's got other business. It's Friday.

PETIE

We didn't get paid.

JOHNNY

It's Friday, you didn't get paid?

PETIE

Trainer wasn't there. He's the one who pays.
JOHNNY pulls PETIE by the ear in a quick move; PETIE squeals and squirms.

JOHNNY

Why do you lie to me? Trainer said you didn't show up this morning. He phoned lookin for ya.

PETIE

I quit.

JOHNNY

What to hell did you do that for?

PETIE

I don't like it there.

JOHNNY

Why?

PETIE

The jockeys are queer.

JOHNNY

I need you there. I wanted you to find out if they were usin the foo-foo on that horse.

PETIE

They been usin it on him all week. He ran through the rail on Tuesday.

JOHNNY

I need to know if they used it on him today.

PETIE

They put it on his tongue before the race.

JOHNNY

What do you think, I'm stupid?

> TERESA, *eight months pregnant, enters with ANNA and*
> *ANGEL.*
> *JOHNNY is still twisting PETIE's ear.*

JOHNNY

We got deliveries to make. Five pounds beet.

TERESA

Giorno, Poppa.

JOHNNY

Giorno, Teresa. You make me feel old. When's this one due? Angel, help your brother. Brought the Mommarella too.

ANNA

Pietro, il tuo lonccio.

TERESA

I ain't seen ya for four months. Do I get a kiss?

> *ANNA gives PETIE his lunch as JOHNNY pecks TERESA on*
> *the cheek.*

JOHNNY

Save some of that for me.

TERESA

You're runnin this store like it was a fruit cart.

JOHNNY

You wanna talk about how to run a store? Two poundsa GREEN pepper Angel.

PETIE

She said red.

JOHNNY

So give her red.

TERESA

We're givin up the store on Havelock.

JOHNNY

I told you, but you don't listen to your Poppa. Location is everything.

TERESA

Yeah, you told us. Well, we got a new store on Queen Street. The baby is gonn be here any day.

JOHNNY

You two startin a marchin band?

TERESA

We're gonna rent the kitchen and when we get more money we're gonna rent the whole house.

JOHNNY

For the trumpets and drums.

TERESA

I'm gonna need a place to stay.

ANGEL

What else Poppa.

JOHNNY

Ten poundsa tomato. What about him?

TERESA

Gae is gonna live in the store part with one of the babies, little Johnny I guess.

JOHNNY

Married four years, pregnant three times and here you are again.

The doorbell rings; PRICE enters hesitantly.

PRICE

Hiya Johnny, I was just passing by. I noticed the name the window and I figured it had to be you.

JOHNNY

Hé Bill, Bill, come in, come here. Look at you. Place is a mess. Remember my daughter?

PRICE

Angel.

ANGEL

I'm Angel.

TERESA

Teresa.

PRICE

Theresa, I'm sorry, how are you?

TERESA

Fine, thank you.

JOHNNY

Sure, this is Teresa, the one who went out the door one day to pay the phone bill and never came back. Her husband steals her away to Italy like a nogoodbum and runs away with the money.

TERESA

I paid the phone bill. And we eloped, we did not run away.

ANGEL

Right out the back window.

TERESA

I did not.

ANGEL

That's how he got your suitcase.

JOHNNY

And now she's back. Now I got eight kids.

TERESA

Poppa, I need a place for the babies and me for a few months.

JOHNNY

A few months? A few months. You share the bedroom with Angel like before.
One baby sleeps with you and little Johnny can sleep in a basket like everyone else
done. Mommarella's not sayin nothin, so I guess it's fine by her. You remember
my wife, Bill?

PRICE

Yes, piacere Signora. I was just on my way to the office and I thought I'd drop in.

JOHNNY

Don't go. My boy Petie and me, we're just gonna make one delivery and then we're
goin over to the track. Why don't you come with us?

PRICE

I've got some things that will have to be . . .

JOHNNY

My boy Petie show you around the place. I tell you what horse to bet.

PRICE

I didn't know you could bet. Of course, I guess you can do that. You know, I never
been.

JOHNNY

You never been? Thrill of a lifetime. Just one race. Two, we can bet the double.

PRICE

Why don't you let me make a phone call.

JOHNNY

Telephone is right there. What a thing, eh, phone.

TERESA

Poppa, Gae and me are gonna need the truck to move.

JOHNNY

Sure. When?

TERESA

This afternoon.

JOHNNY

No.

TERESA

Poppa, we paid for half that truck.

JOHNNY

The half that works or the half that don't? You tell Gaetano to phone me.

TERESA

Poppa, it's ours too,

JOHNNY

Tonight, Teresa. I'll help you move. Not now. Okay? Petie, andiamo. Where is he?

ANGEL

He went home to get his bike.

JOHNNY

I need him now. Angel, go home and tell him to get back here.

ANGEL

Aw, no.

JOHNNY

Never mind, I'll go get him myself. Okay Bill, you ready?

PRICE

Sure, let's go.

JOHNNY

Okay, truck is loaded, got my keys, andiamo, Anna, stai attenta allo storu.

PRICE

Nice to have met you again, Signora.

> *JOHNNY and PRICE go out, leaving the women.*

TERESA

Allora, che fai Momma?

ANNA

Rimango.

ANGEL

Go home Momma. I'll look after the store. How you gonna answer the phone anyway? You don't talk English no more.

TERESA

I have to go and help Gaetono. Ciao Momma. Angel, make sure everything's okay, please, tonight, the truck.

> *TERESA goes, pausing as the phone rings.*
> *When it is obviously not GAE, she leaves.*

ANGEL

Mora Groceteria, we deliver. Pronto. Si? Say it again. Momento. (COVERS THE RECEIVER) They don't speak English.

ANNA

Pronto. Si, si. No delivery today.

> *ANNA hangs up, sits on a crate, looks around, gets up and goes; ANGEL runs after her.*
> *MICHE enters the empty store.*

MICHE

So who's minding the store? Nobody seems to mind if nobody's minding the store. Is this any way to run a business? But what business is this anyway? Sometimes you wonder why you're workin and what it is you're doin. Why should you get up at six in the morning and go the market when Loblaw'was there an hour before and bought everything at half of what you pay. Loblaw—had a kid, called him Bob. Bob Loblaw. What's he know that Johnny Mora never learned. What business is he in, really?

TRAFFICANTE

The Mora home, September, 1927

> *ANGEL sits on the back steps, wedding veil and needle and thread in hand.*
> *ETTORE comes home from school with some books under his arm.*

ETTORE

You gonna do my homework with me?

ANGEL

I gotta make dinner Hector.

ETTORE

Don't call me that.

ANGEL

Then I won't call you at all.

ETTORE

You're gonna stick yourself with that needle.

> ANGEL's hand is shaking as she sews. JOHNNY's call is more
> aggravation.

JOHNNY

(OFF) Anna, è l'ora di cena.

ANGEL

She's not here. It's Thursday. (QUIET) Why do you have to yell like that?

ETTORE

Here comes Teresa and Gae.

> TERESA enters carrying a newborn and goes inside with
> TERESA [GAE?] after brief hellos.
> GAE is button-holed by ETTORE outside.

ETTORE

You gonna help me with my spelling, Uncle Gae?

GAE

Cos'è? Ahh, un abbecedario. English.

TERESA

Where is everybody?

ANGEL

It's Momma's day to go out.

TERESA

Since when does she go out? Where does she go?

ANGEL

Out, she goes out, we don't know where.

TERESA

What does he think about that?

ANGEL

He don't like it. That's why I'm makin dinner.

GAE

Okay, I say and you ... va bene. Cog. Coog. Cos'è?

ETTORE

Lemme see. Cough, cough, like (COUGHS) when you cough.

GAE

Tossa, tossa. Cough.

ETTORE

C-O-U-G-H. Cough. Next one.

TERESA

    Is everything ready?

ANGEL

    Nothin's ready, nobody's ready. The dress ain't finished. Hector hasn't got no suit.

TERESA

    Are you sewing this veil? Why are you sewing your own veil?

ANGEL

    We couldn't afford no dressmaker.

TERESA

    Ah no, let me finish it.

GAE

    Altoff.

ETTORE

    Altoff? That can't be right. Lemme see. Although.

GAE

    Al-tho.

ETTORE

    A-L-L-T-H-O-U-G-H. Although. Next one.

GAE

    Al-tho.

JOHNNY

    (OFF) Who's makin supper?

TERESA

    I'll set the table.

ANGEL

    Nevermind, you got the baby.

ETTORE

    I wanna eat too.

GAE

    Thro.

ETTORE

    T-H-R-O-W. Throw. Next one.

GAE

    Throwf. Troff. Trufe.

ETTORE

    What? Lemme see.

TERESA

    Is everything ready in Chicago? Have you talked to him?

ANGEL

    I'm afraid to call him.

TERESA

    Afraid? Why?

ANGEL

    I'm afraid he'll get angry.

ETTORE

    Through, through, like through the door. T-H-R-O-U-G-H. Through the door.

GAE

True. That's crazy. Looks just the same. Why you learn this? Why don't you just learn numbers, English is too crazy. Troff, trufe, non ha senso.

JOHNNH enters the kitchen.

JOHNNY

I'm hungry, where is it? Ah la piccola Dorothea. Ciao Teresa.

ANGEL

There you go Poppa, insalata e polpettone.

TERESA

Ciao Poppa.

JOHNNY

It's cold. Your husband gonna eat everything cold?

JOHNNY stares at ANGEL's cold salad and meat-loaf.
A MAN has approached GAE and ETTORE.

MAN

I'm looking for Johnny Moro.

GAE

Mora. He's in there.

ETTORE

Poppa, there's a man outside.

JOHNNY

What does he want?

GAE and ETTORE go in; the MAN follows.

GAE

I want to talk to you.

JOHNNY

So talk. Who's your friend?

ETTORE

Start now.

ETTORE has pulled a stopwatch from a pocket.

MAN

They said at the poolhall I might want to talk to you.

JOHNNY

About what?

MAN

Income taxes.

JOHNNY

Ncommitecchsi. That's a good one, eh Gaetano?

GAE

Si si. We take the train to the wedding.

JOHNNY

Good, more room for us in the car, right Ettore? What are you doin?

MAN

That your Model T out back?

JOHNNY

Nice car, eh? Ettore, che fai? Portami una birra.

GAE
We need the money you owe us for the train.

JOHNNY
You want your money? Here's your hundred bucks. Now I don't owe you nothin.
>   *JOHNNY has pulled a wad from his pocket and peeled off*
>   *some bills.*
>   *ETTORE has pulled up a trap door, lighting the MAN's eyes.*

ETTORE
Anybody else want a beer?

MAN
You make that yourself?

JOHNNY
Is that what you want? Why don't you say so?

GAE
Chiudi la porta.

JOHNNY
Come?

>   *The room stops; something is wrong.*

MAN
Johnny Bananas, they call you.

ETTORE
You don't want this beer?

MAN
I'll take one, thank you. I'd like to talk to you outside, Mister Mora.

JOHNNY
Sure, I just finish this. Angelina, brava, brava. Chiama Price.

MAN
Now, Bananas.

JOHNNY
Sure.

ETTORE
Takes you ____ minutes and ____ seconds to eat.

TERESA
Cos'è Poppa?

>   *JOHNNY and the MAN step outside.*

GAE
Cops.

ANGEL
That's all I need. They're gonna put him in jail. You stupid little.

ETTORE
Hey.

GAE
It's not his fault. He don't make the beer.

>   *ETTORE winces at the blow he received from ANGEL.*
>   *JOHNNY returns, agitated, violent.*

JOHNNY
Who let him in?

GAE

I did.

JOHNNY

You idiot. Money, money, give me the money.

GAE

We need it for the train.

JOHNNY

Gimme the money or there ain't gonna be no train and no wedding. Soldi, soldi.

GAE

So they catch you, eh, you happy now?

JOHNNY

You shut your face or I punch you in the nose.

>   *JOHNNY goes outside with the money, returns and sits at the*
>   *table; he opens a beer.*

JOHNNY

Ettore, Angel, sta zitti.

ETTORE

She hit me.

JOHNNY

You deserved it. You been told, strangers outside.

ANGEL

Now they're never gonna make it to Chicago. The wedding is ruined.

JOHNNY

Nothing is ruined Angelina. We leave tonight. As soon as your Momma gets back. And I get somethin to eat.

TERESA

The dress ain't finished.

JOHNNY

Your Momma will fix it.

TERESA

She can't do everything.

JOHNNY

She shoulda been here. (SILENCE) Here, take your hundred dollars. Go home. See you in Chicago. Go.

>   *TERESA and GAE sneak off, leaving the veil.*

ETTORE

I ain't got no suit.

JOHNNY

We buy you one there. Tomorrow.

ETTORE

That mean I don't have to go to school tomorrow?

JOHNNY

No school.

ETTORE

I got a spellin test.

JOHNNY

Wedding's more important.

ETTORE
Was that guy a cop Poppa?
JOHNNY
Yeah, that was a cop.
ETTORE
You goin to jail?
JOHNNY
Be quiet, Ettore, you upset your sister. Nobody's goin' to jail. We're gonna go to Chicago and your sister is gonna have a beautiful wedding in her beautiful dress. What's this?
ETTORE
Stopwatch.
JOHNNY
____ minutes. That's fast, eh? That's about how long it takes to get married. Over before you know it. Angelina, you're gonna be beautiful and Ettore's gonna carry the ring.
ANGEL
Oh my God, the ring.
JOHNNY
Calma, calma. I got it. And Ettore's gonna look after it, right? Where to hell is your Momma?

RUSSIA

Teresa's bedroom, September, 1928.

ANGEL lies in bed, TERESA at her side.
TERESA
Doctor said there's gonna be a bed Friday. They wanna operate Monday.
ANGEL
Oh God. (SILENCE) Who's gonna pay for it.
TERESA
You shouldn't worry about that right now.
ANGEL
I should let Carlo sell the store so he can come here and pay for the operation? I don't even want him here.
TERESA
He said he's comin. He's gonna take you back after the operation.
ANGEL
Back to what?
TERESA
He said he's sorry and he wants you back. His brother's gonna take him into the canning. He wants me to phone back right now.
ANGEL
I gotta talk to him.
TERESA
You stay where you are.

ANGEL

I'm not dead yet.

> *ANGEL gets out of bed despite TERESA's attempts to keep her there.*
> *ANNA blocks her exit.*

ANNA

Angelina, dove vai?

ANGEL

I gotta talk to him Ma, lemme go.

> *ANGEL begins to cough; a baby cries.*

ANNA

Guarda che hai fatto.

ANGEL

Jesus, Jesus, Jesus, where is he?

ANNA

Where you leave him, in Chicago.

TERESA

That's enough Momma, basta.

ANNA

La tua bambina grida.

ANGEL

I can't stand babies cryin.

TERESA

Better get used to it. Babies cry all the time. What do I tell Carlo?

ANGEL

Tell him I want him here to talk to him. No, wait.

TERESA

What about the hospital?

> *ANGEL starts to cry; she coughs.*
> *ANNA puts the covers over here; TERESA goes.*

TERESA

There's no question; you're goin to the hospital.

ANGEL

I just wanna sit up, Momma. Leave me, go.

ANNA

Ingrata.

ANGEL

I'm sorry, you make me miserable. You make everybody's life miserable. Like you make Poppa's life miserable.

ANNA

You don't know how he makes me suffer. You don't know.

ANGEL

I don't know what it is to suffer? Are you blind? I'm pregnant, I got pleursy. They're gonna take my lung out. I might not live, the baby might not live. Do you understand that? You don't. You're too stupid.

ANNA

Sono stupida, io?

ANGEL

I used to think you were just plain stubborn, like him. But you're not. You're stupid. Not cause you never been to school. There's nothin in your noodle. I'm talkin to ya, but the words ain't getting through. It's like you're in another world. (COUGHS)

ANNA

Basta. You make it

ANGEL

How can it be worse? What could be worse? Carlo's in Chicago tryna sell the store so he can come here and be with me and I don't want him. Do you understand, Momma, I don't love him?

> ANGEL cries in her mother's arms.
> The baby has stopped crying offstage.

ANGEL

He hit me Momma, when I was pregnant.

ANNA

Shh shh.

ANGEL

How can you live with Poppa and not sleep with him? It's been ten years since the war. What keeps you together? Tell me, I wanna know if I'm gonna be like you.

ANNA

You are no like me. Carlo is no like him.

ANGEL

(PAUSE) Where do you go Thursdays?

ANNA

Che ti prendi?

ANGEL

Petie seen you comin out of Mr. Green's. Mrs. Green's been dead five years. Does he touch you and kiss you? Are you in love with him?

ANNA

E gentile. E tutto. I love only one man.

ANGEL

Is that what you call love? It's a mess. Una russia, una vera russia. Your life, my life, it's all a big mess. It's not love keepin you together, it's hate. You know what Momma? Poppa never told nobody except me. He almost died in the trenches, from the gas. They kept him in the hospital five months after the war. His lungs are as bad as mine. And he never told nobody, cause he's stupid. Stubborn like you.

ANNA

You don't know what you say. How could I not know? He is my baby, he cries to me. You don't know yet what is between a man and his wife. I know what he does. But I stay with him.

ANGEL

Why?

ANNA

Because once I loved him. C'hai bisogno di dormire.

> TERESA returns with her newborn.

TERESA

Carlo will be here Sunday. Poppa's downstairs Momma. He wants you to go home to make supper for the boys. He wants to see you Angel.

> *ANNA kisses ANGEL and goes; ANGEL turns away from her sister.*

TERESA

I'll tell him you're sleeping. It really wouldn't hurt to see him, you know?

ANGEL

None of it makes sense, why people love and hate.

TERESA

It all makes sense, but in a different way than you thought before.

MALEDIZIONE

The Mora kitchen, September, 1928.

ANNA and JOHNNY aruge offstage.
PETIE and PRICE study their cards at table as MICHE strums a jazz guitar.

MICHE

A brisc', a lisci', a marked-up deck
Johnny's sure he knows his cards
from back or front those one-eyed jacks
eying him wherever they are

Please keep an eye fixed on the goat
she-goats eat most anything
and nannies favour paper most
bills are best which picture kings
Some guys make it on the market
some have made their mark in love
Johnny has a secret target
up his sleeve he has a trump

A brisc' a lisci' a marked-up deck
Johnny's sure he knows his cards
from back or front those one-eyed jacks
eying him wherever they are
> *MICHE picks up his cards as JOHNNY enters.*

PETIE

Hé Captain, che fai?

PRICE

I'm thinkin, I'm thinkin.

MICHE

Thought he was a Colonel.

JOHNNY

They made him a General. Attorney-General. Numero uno in the whole place. Who's in?

MICHE

I'm out.

PRICE

I fold. Everything okay Johnny?

JOHNNY

She don't like parties. I win.

PETIE

Hold it. That don't beat two pair. Clean sweep.

MICHE

Ain't it past your bedtime, kid?

> PETIE takes all the money on the table.
> JOHNNY takes two dollars and shuffles.

JOHNNY

Deuce for the kitty. Gimme a beer Petie. We're goin down the river. Five-ten, no limit.

MICHE

Hé Price, how come booze ain't illegal no more and you still can't buy it?

JOHNNY

Bill gonna change the law, right Bill.

PRICE

It's not up to me. I'll have another one Petie.

MICHE

Petie's gonna have to invest in the stock market if he keeps on winnin like this.

PRICE

Stick to an honest livin, at the track.

PETIE

I hearda guys makin a thou a week on Bay Street.

PRICE

Sellin stocks that don't exist. Six weeks, shit's gonna hit the fan. There's gonna be a change in the weather.

MICHE

You gonna stop em?

PRICE

You bet. For five.

PETIE

Call.

JOHNNY

Raise ten.

MICHE

Sweepstake match. I'm in for fifteen.

JOHNNY

Stockmarket, you're all dreamers. Price again, two aces.

PRICE

The name is Bill, for five.

PETIE
> Bump you ten.

MICHE
> Fold.

JOHNNY
> Michè, che succede? Nothin left in your sock? Keeps his money in a sock. He's into the sock market.

MICHE
> Johnny got his money buried in the backyard. Last week, goat ate a hundred ones.

JOHNNY
> Pietro, che fai?

PETIE
> Your play.

JOHNNY
> Check.

PRICE
> Call, for fifteen.

> *MICHE goes to get the beer which never appeared.*
> *ANNA stands in the doorway with a bowl of water and a cruet*
> *of oil.*

PETIE
> Check.

JOHNNY
> Check. One card down times three.

PETIE
> Attenzione Poppa.

> *JOHNNY watches ANNA pour three drops of oil three times*
> *into the bowl of water.*

ANNA
> Chi vi ha fascinato
> occhio, pensiero, desio cattivo
> chi toglierà il fascino
> Padre, Fliglio, Spirito Santo
>
> Vergogna truffatori. Non è una casa da gioco. Mi esce degli occhi. Malefico, nelle griffe del diavolo. Tutti all'inferno con lui. Pietro a letto. Finita la partita. Ho parlato Giovanni. E l'ultima volta. Never again in my house or you are out, all of you, father, son and friends. I will not have the devil in my house.

> *ANNA goes, leaving MICHE with the bowl.*

JOHNNY
> Non ci sta neache due dollari sull tavola.

PRICE
> What is it Johnny?

JOHNNY
> There's not even two dollars on the table and she's sending us all to hell.

PETIE
> I'm in.

JOHNNY

You didn't look at your card.

PETIE

I don't have to. Gotta gettused to that in Italian families, Bill.

PRICE

Sky's the limit?

JOHNNY

Sky's the limit.

PRICE

For fifteen. That's very frightening.

PETIE

I'm out. Yeah, it's meant to make other players nervous.

JOHNNY

Raise ten. Why don't you look at your cards?

PETIE

I don't have to. Three spades up, could have the King wired. Could be a full house or a flush.

PRICE

I don't like sharks at my table. See you.

JOHNNY

Show me. Full house. That's nice. But it don't beat two pair both the same and the Black Lady.

MICHE

Not if you deal standin up.

JOHNNY

I don't cheat at cards, capisci?

MICHE

Yeah, and the Pope's not Italian. Here's your beer.

PRICE

How could I lose with a full house? No thanks.

MICHE

You asked for it.

JOHNNY

Never had so much fun, eh General. Complete with side show. Who wants to play a little forty-four? I know where there's a good game. Play all night.

PRICE

I gotta get some fresh air.

PETIE

This way General.

> PETIE guides PRICE out the back door.
> JOHNNY picks up a phone.

JOHNNY

I'll call find out how they're doin. (ON PHONE) Pronto. Sono Johnny. Ciao. Arrivo in dieci minuti con un sempliciotto. Yeah, the General. He's loaded. He's a mark. Price. No kiddin. Who else?

> PRICE has returned.

PRICE

    I forgot my beer.

MICHE

    Maybe you shouldn't drink no more.

PRICE

    This game on the up and up Johnny?

JOHNNY

    Where we're goin? Sure.

PRICE

    No, this game here.

JOHNNY

    You want your money back?

PRICE

    I always played straight with you.

JOHNNY

    That's a laugh. You got me to join the army. Said we were goin to dig ditches and we wound up on the front line, mustard bombs exploding in my face.

PRICE

    Believe me, Johnny, that's not what I was told. I didn't know. Sometimes you just gotta take what comes and do the best you can.

JOHNNY

    I never cheat my friends, okay? Never.

PRICE

    Are you my friend?

JOHNNY

    Yeah, I'm your friend.

PRICE

    Okay.

JOHNNY

    Okay, so are we gonna play a little forty-four?

PRICE

    I can't. I can't see straight. Wife's gonna kill me.

JOHNNY

    Michè? They got coffee there, you know?

MICHE

    Why don't you just call it a night?

JOHNNY

    You're all afraid of women, that's what it is.

PRICE

    Only one thing you forget Johnny. When we were in the trenches, you showed me how to mark cards. That's a one-eyed jack.

    PRICE turns over a card on the table.

PRICE

    I had it in my hand so many times I felt the corner. I always played it straight with you John, always.

    PRICE leaves.

MICHE

You still got somebody on the phone there?

JOHNNY hangs up.

JOHNNY

You got a C note you can lend me, Michè? No? Guess I gotta go win it back from the Sicilian who took it off me a week ago. You wanna play Michè?

MICHE

No, you go play. Take it easy, John, hé?

JOHNNY leaves, putting on a felt hat.

APPLE JOHNNY

Woodbine Race Track, October, 1934.

A group of men descend from a streetcar.
JOHNNY tries to sell them apples from a little basket over is arm.

JOHNNY

Apple here, lovely apple, fit for the king. Ontario spy, rose red, nothing like this on the inside. Proszipana, djunkwya. Five cent, rose red, let's go, first race is gonna start.

ETTORE appears, sixteen and unshaven.

ETTORE

You look like a goddam orphan just got off the boat with his basket of apples.

JOHNNY

Go bet your money Ettore.

ETTORE

I changed my name.

JOHNNY

To what?

ETTORE

George.

JOHNNY

(LAUGHS) Like the King. Your Momma know that?

GEORGE

She wants to see ya.

JOHNNY

Then why did she kick me out? Ariappa, first race is gonna start.

GEORGE

Cause you weren't contributin nothin. We been eatin stewed tomatoes for five months. Can't afford no eggs for pasta.

JOHNNY

Well I can't afford no eggs, so go away.

GEORGE

Where to hell is the money goin Poppa?

JOHNNY

What money kid? There's a Depression goin on, or maybe you didn't notice.

GEORGE
    Don't call me kid, Poppa.

JOHNNY
    I don't know if you're my kid anyway.

GEORGE
    What about the relief money?

JOHNNY
    They cut it off.

GEORGE
    They cut it off?

JOHNNY
    Don't say what I say, you sound like a bird.

GEORGE
    Why did they cut it off?

JOHNNY
    Said I'm not a Canadian. I fought in their fuckin war, but I'm not a Canadian.
    Up their backass.

GEORGE
    Aw shit Poppa.

JOHNNY
    Why aren't you in school?

GEORGE
    I quit.

JOHNNY
    You quit? Why did you quit?

GEORGE
    I gotta get a job. It's just me'n Momma.

JOHNNY
    How you gonna get a job you can't read and write?

GEORGE
    Who reads you the Racing Form?

JOHNNY
    Be a garbage collector. Hector Hector garbage collector.

GEORGE
    Don't say that, Poppa, don't say it.

JOHNNY
    But it's true. Like a little bird with black eyes. You see things and you steal,
    stealin radios that don't work. You think I don't know? You think the cops don't
    know who's got all the radios that don't work? They don't care. Not worth nothin.

GEORGE
    Yeah, well I know you got your army pension. You gonna blow it all in there?

JOHNNY
    I only bet the double. Six and nine. Who told you I got a pension?

GEORGE
    Price. He wanted to know if you were okay. He said he got some papers you gotta
    sign. I didn't tell him you ain't been home for a month.

JOHNNY

Tell your Momma I'm home after the second race.

GEORGE

We ain't got no home. We're stayin with Petie.

JOHNNY

So I go to Petie's.

GEORGE

His wife's gonna have a baby.

JOHNNY

Good.

GEORGE

Then we're gonna have to move.

JOHNNY

Since when do you smoke?

GEORGE

That girl I been seein.

JOHNNY

Bad for you, make you cough.

GEORGE

We're gonna get married.

JOHNNY

You're not old enough to shave.

GEORGE

She's gonna have a baby.

JOHNNY

Why didn't you wear rubbers.

GEORGE

Wasn't old enough to buy em.

JOHNNY

How much money you got?

GEORGE

Two, three bucks.

JOHNNY

Six and two in the double.

GEORGE

You just said six and nine.

JOHNNY

Six and two is gonna win.

GEORGE

Then why did you say six and nine?

JOHNNY

Maybe six and nine is gonna win. Don't talk to me no more. People think I'm not open for business. Here comes the streetcar.

GEORGE

You are the craziest, stupidest, stubbornest son of a bee ever walked the face of the earth and I love ya Poppa. When are you comin home?

JOHNNY
>After the second race.

GEORGE
>I'll wait.

JOHNNY
>Go get a Racing Form. Find out who's up in the third race.

GEORGE
>Why?

JOHNNY
>What if we win the double? Apple here, rose red. Fit for a King. Ontario spy, we got em red. Go on.

INCOGNITO

Robertson Confectionery, November, 1944.

The sound of breaking glass brings JOHNNY and PETIE running into the storefront.

PETIE
>Awww nooo. We're all fightin the Germans now.

JOHNNY
>They don't know Italy changed sides?

PETIE
>I better get a broom. Katie's gonna be furious. They can't read? It says Robertson's Confectionery for the love of Mike, not Luigi's Groceteria. Where are you goin?

JOHNNY
>To get a broom.

PETIE
>One of us has to watch the store. Never mind. Jesus, how can people be so stupid?
>>*JOHNNY and PETIE rush out.*
>>*MICHE appears from nowhere, GAE beside him.*

MICHE
>Rocks are coming through store windows rockets flare all over London true Canucks are killing Germans who is throwing rocks you wonder?

GAE
>Mussolini's big on black shirts Canadian boys are dressed in khaki shoot the Wop and drag him in dirt Canadian boys will send him packing.

MICHE
>Them little Nips they want a war more beef less rice will give them muscle the B.C. Japs all live in fear cause now the Yanks are in the tussle.

GAE
>Ship Britain wheat and ship em nickel another day, another dollar drink their wine and eat their treacle give em credit, there's no bother.

MICHE
>Economics win a war Depression meant you'd not a cent Hitler wants to fight some more we'll blitz him full of full employment.

GAE withdraws and MICHE follows.
GEORGE enters and ducks behind a counter.
PETIE and JOHNNY return with two brooms.
The phone rings.

PETIE

Robertson Confectionery. Alberto, I'm busy.

JOHNNY

What's this? It's a cash registra.

PETIE

They put a rock through the window. I don't know who. I don't take nothin on hockey. Who's playin?

JOHNNY

The Leafs, it's Saturday. There's a silver dollar in here.

PETIE

Leave it, it's for Pete Junior. I can't talk now Alberto. I don't make odds on hockey. Ciao. What to hell are you doin here?

GEORGE emerges from behind the counter.

GEORGE

I gotta talk to youse.

JOHNNY

You look like a wet rat. What's this for?

PETIE

Business is boomin all over the place except here. Katie said we needed a cash register to make the place look serious. Whadda you want Georgie? I ain't got no money to give ya.

GEORGE

I got no place to stay.

PETIE

Whose fault is that? Move, I gotta sweep up.

A solemn-faced TERESA and GAE come in.
There is a silence.

JOHNNY

I'm gonna listen to the Leaf game on the radio.

TERESA

Don't run away Poppa. He ain't stayin with us no more. I can't stand it.

JOHNNY

Whaddaya want me to do, end the war?

GEORGE

I want you to do somethin for Chrissake.

PETIE

I told you to go see that guy. You didn't do it.

GEORGE

I can't work at no job Petie, how many times do I gotta tell ya?

PETIE

Why? You're in my road.

GEORGE

Cause they got my number.

JOHNNY

Number, what number?

GAE

Insurance numbers. Now everybody's gotta have a number to get a job. Even me they want to give a number.

GEORGE

That's how they find ya.

PETIE

Yeah well, I don't want em to find ya here. I got enough problems as it is. You shouldn'a run away.

GEORGE

It ain't my fault you're drawin heat for makin book.

PETIE

Why are you kickin him out all of a sudden?

TERESA

I just can't take it no more. Every time I think about young Johnny lying dead on a beach someplace over there and Georgie hidin in the basement.

GEORGE

You all think it's my fault, don't you, young Johnny went and got hisself killed?

PETIE

Young Johnny knew what he was doin. He volunteered. Just like his grampa.

GEORGE

I never told him to run out on the beach and get himself exploded into a thousand pieces.

TERESA

Stop.

> *TERESA runs out of the store; GAE will follow.*

GAE

You see. We can't do this anymore. She cries night and day. And then he comes out of the basement like some animal and he smells and the children take him his food like he was a dog. Me too, I can't think of him, my son. He just can't stay with us no more.

PETIE

Well, he ain't stayin here.

> *PETIE goes out with the broom and dustpan.*

GEORGE

Jesus Poppa Jesus. I went through the whole fuckin camp lookin for him. I knew we were gonna go over and I knew they were gonna send us right into the middle of it.

> *GEORGE cries on his father's shoulder.*

JOHNNY

Okay boy, okay. You ran away and they're lookin for ya. Just don't let it turn ya into a slob. Cause that's what you're actin like. It's too bad about Teresa's boy, but he knew what he was doin. Just keep your nose clean until the war's over. There's gonna be thousandsa guys like you. A hundred times I coulda went AWOL. Night before they sent us into the trenches . . .

GEORGE

Five years the war's been goin on. How long can I wait?

JOHNNY

Could go five more. Shoulda thoughta that at the time.

GEORGE

At the time I wasn't thinkin.

PETIE returns.

PETIE

So what are you gonna do?

GEORGE

What am I gonna do? What am I gonna do? I don't know what I'm gonna do. They're gonna find me through the numbers. I thought Poppa with with all his big shot friends was gonna help me. But he's just a big talker.

JOHNNY

You wanna know what to do? I'll tell ya. Turn yourself in.

GEORGE ·

What? I don't believe my ears.

JOHNNY

You heard me. Go to jail and turn yourself in.

GEORGE

I must be losin my mind.

JOHNNY

Nobody can do nothin. You gott turn yourself in, then we can get you out. You broke the law.

PETIE

That's right Georgie.

GEORGE

Who are youse to lecture me about breakin the law?

PETIE

That's what Price said. You tell em who you are and what you done and then maybe he can get you off.

GEORGE

Is he coverin up your little bookie operation too?

PETIE

You wanna keep livin like a rat?

JOHNNY

Go inside and shave. I take you to the station.

PETIE

Katie's asleep. Can't he shave somewheres else?

ANNA enters with a plumed chicken.

ANNA

Santo Dio, è lui. Ettore, Ettore, poverino.

GEORGE

Si Momma, sono io.

ANNA

Pietro, il pollo. Preparo la cena per lui.

PETIE

We're takin him in, to jail, like Price said.

ANNA

No, rimanerà con noi.

GEORGE

It's what has to be Momma. I can't take it no more.

ANNA

Mangiarà con noi sta sera.

PETIE

Yes Momma, he can have dinner. Poppa, the chicken. Georgie, I wanna talk to you.

JOHNNY

I wanna listen to the hockey on the radio.

PETIE

You can pluck the chicken while you're listenin.

> *JOHNNY and ANNA leave with broom and chicken.*

PETIE

Your wife been callin here.

GEORGE

I got nothin to do with her no more.

PETIE

She was gonna turn you in.

GEORGE

Figures, doesn't it? Bitch.

PETIE

What are you doin Georgie? Aren't you in enough trouble already?

GEORGE

Get off my back, will ya?

PETIE

You gonna spend your whole life knockin women up and leavin em? She knows about this other broad. Everybody knows. What are you usin for brains? That's why nobody wants ya. Think about it. You're a weasel. See this rock? It was meant for you. Katie and me are gonna have to pay for a new window.

GEORGE

Don't give me no Protestant holier than thou bullshit brother, or I'll knock your teeth back a foot.

ANNA

(RETURNING) Basta le due. Ettore, vieni. Pietro, vergogna. Vergogna Pietro, vergogna.

SANTA

TERESA's bedroom, Christmas, 1947.

> *JOHNNY is removing his trousers, a Santa costume beside him on a bed. He pulls his trousers up as TERESA and GAE burst in.*

GAE

There are two dozen people down there.

TERESA

I'm going to the toilet. I can't go to the toilet?

GAE

Go, go. Just don't be half an hour. They're all waitin for the dessert so we can have the Santa.

TERESA

Why can't you put out the dessert? Or are you too drunk?

GAE

The table, it's full of dishes.

TERESA

You got five daughters, on of them can clear the table. I gotta go.

JOHNNY

Teresa, you're gonna give yourself a nosebleed.

GAE

What are you doin in here?

JOHNNY

You want a Santa? He's gotta put on his red dress.

TERESA

I'm havin a nosebleed.

> *She runs out, hand to nose. GAE suspects JOHNNY has caused the hemorrhage.*

JOHNNY

Goat needs milkin, Gaetano.

GAE

She's dry.

JOHNNY

She gets looked after better than your wife.

GAE

Better than when you had her.

> *GAE leaves in a huff as ANGEL enters.*

ANGEL

It's okay Poppa, I seen boxer shorts before.

JOHNNY

Why don't you knock? It ain't a barn.

ANGEL

Merry Christmas.

JOHNNY

With a fur coat like that, it musta been a Merry Chrissmas.

ANGEL

Momma's not havin such a nice Chrissmas.

JOHNNY

She coulda come here. Your sister made ravioli.

ANGEL

I made a lovely turkey. For a change Momma didn't have to cook.

JOHNNY

She made Chrissmas dinner for fifty years.

ANGEL

She might not be makin too many more.

JOHNNY

Somebody else's turn.

ANGEL

Momma is gonna move in with me.

JOHNNY says nothing, puts on the jacket.

ANGEL

What could it cost ya to spend Chrissmas with her Pa?

JOHNNY

More of the tradition here. Your sister's havin' a nosebleed just like your mother used to do.

ANGEL

She can't spend Chrissmas at home for Chrissake.

JOHNNY

I told her, I don't spend Chrissmas alone.

ANGEL

You might be spendin a lotta time alone from now on. I came to invite you for cake and coffee. The kids wanna see ya.

JOHNNY

I gotta play the Santa over here.

ANGEL

But you ain't got no gifts to give.

JOHNNY

Your mother goes to your place, I'm moving in here.

GAE sticks his head back through the door.

GAE

No you're not. Thought you were makin dinner at your place.

ANGEL

Just dropped over to wish everybody a Happy Chrissmas. Merry Chrissmas Gae, Poppa. Anybody wants to drop by our place, they're welcome. We're just around the corner. Ciao.

ANGEL goes; JOHNNY is still half-dressed.

GAE

Kids are waitin Santa Claus.

JOHNNY

Gaetano.

GAE

Si.

JOHNNY

You come from Bari, vero?

GAE

Si. Perchè?

JOHNNY

Santa Claus comes from Bari. Why don't you be Santa.

JOHNNY removes his Santa outfit.

GAE

You're the old man around here.

JOHNNY

Ah sì, è vero. But I'm too skinny. You need a fatter Santa. Whose wife cooks for him.

GAE

The kids are waitin.

JOHNNY

Santa's gotta go see Mrs.Santa. She got sick from what she ate. If Santa Claus is Italian, how can he live at the North Pole?

CINQUANTA ANNI

ANGEL's home, February, 1952.

*ANNA sits motionless, staring out a window. ANGEL enters
with a bag of peanuts, turns on the television.*

ANGEL

That hairdo girlie, it drives me nuts. You look like a Red Cross donut lady and the war's been over for seven years. How come broads like you get on television? Don't you ever go to the movies.

*ANNA turns to stare at ANGEL; ANGEL notices a presence
in the room.*

ANGEL

Ma, don't do that. Sweet Lord, you took my breath away. I wish you'd stop lurkin around the house like a sneakthief. My heart is pounding like I saw a ghost. Don't do that to me. Come sit and watch the television.

ANNA

Non mi piace la televisione.

ANGEL

You don't like nothin no more. Come and look at this dame, she bugs me. Talks like a bee stung her in the lip. Like a real Canadian, ya know? You probably can't see the picture. That's it, isn't it. Why don't you go see the doctor? You need glasses.

ANNA

Cinquanta anni fa.

ANGEL

What's that? (SILENCE) Fifty years. Fifty years ago what? That's when you came here. Yeah, well that's a long time.

ANNA

Avevamo fiori tutto l'anno.

ANGEL

Yeah, well this is Canada and you're gonna have to wait for your flowers till the snow melts. Was it snowin when you got here?

ANNA

E grigio il Canada. In Italia la luce è chiara, bianca, pura, il cielo azzuro.

ANGEL

I can't understand ya when ya talk so much Italian. Geez, I can remember when you used to swear like a trooper. Soon as you left Poppa, you went right back to bein the immigrant. Cause you never wanted to be here. But you're here. You coulda gone back to your aunt. Carlo said he's pay. But you didn't wanna go and now she's dead. Can't say as I blame ya, though. War didn't leave e'm nothin they say.

ANNA

Tentacinque anni fa.

ANGEL

No, the second war I'm talkin. Right. Thirty-five years you ain't talked to him. You musta talked to him at least once. You still love him, don't ya. Why don't you call him?

ANNA

Sei pazza, Angelina?

ANGEL

You're the one who's crazy about him, not me. You gonna tell me about the red hair he used to have again?

ANNA

Capelli castani. Sono bianchi adesso.

ANGEL

He just lives down the street for cryin out loud. You think he's happy with that big long facea his? He remembers too. How can he forget? Phone him. I didn't tell ya. Carlo got himself a new job. Yep, una bella giobbicella, managerri. Teresa wants you to call. The kids all want Mommarella's ravioli. Ain't nobody can make em like you. You should be stayin with Teresa, not here. She's got ten kids and they all love ya. I love ya too, but you're so stubborn it drives me nuts. Ma, Ma. Ma!

ANNA

Perchè urli?

ANGEL

You didn't say nothin. You stopped movin.

ANNA

Vado al gabinetto.

ANGEL

Somethin wrong with your kidneys Ma?

ANNA has left.

ANGEL

I used to know the Italian word for that. Rene. Cause every time it was raining you used to make a kidney stew. Now when it rains, you piddle on my Persian rug. I hope I'm never like you.

JOHNNY BANANAS

A downtown corner, spring, 1974.

JOHNNY MORA is ninety-four years old. He wears a straw hat, white shirt, black pants, white socks and army boots. He sits erect, blinking like a pigeon, atop an upended orange crate in a sea of basketsful of cherries, apples, oranges, pomegranates, peaches, pears, plums, bananas. Little signs with reverse N's and S's stick up from the baskets and crates. He squawks like

an excited bluejay. JIMMY, ninety-two, approaches in an
overcoat and felt hat.

JOHNNY

Apples peach pearplumpomenagran orangebanan, ariappa, let's go. First race is gonna start. There goes the bell. I got all this to sell.

JIMMY

Gonna sell me an apple?

JOHNNY

Lovely apple, twenty-five cent.

JIMMY

Greenwood today, eh John? Make your fortune.

JOHNNY

I'm a millionaire, nineta four years old millionaire. Had a thousand bucks a thousand times.

JIMMY

How much money you make today paesano?

JOHNNY

More than you Jimmy. Lookit this. Hundred apple, hundred orange. That's fifty bucks.

JIMMY

You gotta pay the taxi to get this stuff here.

JOHNNY

I got a guerhausa.

JIMMY

You got a what?

JOHNNY

Guerhausa.

JIMMY

Warehouse. Warehouse. You got a warehouse. Seventy years you been here, you still ain't learned to speak proper. You got two G's you gonna lend me?

JOHNNY

(LAUGHING) Two G's? You wanna pay for your funeral before you're dead?

JIMMY

I got a business proposition. Don't laugh, it's gonna make money.

JOHNNY

You gonna build a skyscrapper with two G's?

JIMMY

I'm gonna open a boxing club.

JOHNNY

You couldn't win a fight with a dead chicken.

JIMMY

Hey look, I got a meatball sandwich. Veal cheese and oregano. It's a nice one.

JOHNNY

You got a bowl of spaghettini in the other pocket? What are you doin with this big coat?

JIMMY

I get the chills in my legs. Have some.

JOHNNY

So where's your boxing club?

JIMMY

There's a place in the west end. We get a boxing license, we can open a club. With a room in the back for cards and stuff.

JOHNNY

You should sell popcorn.

JIMMY

We can do that too.

JOHNNY

No, on the street, like Dino.

JIMMY

Easier to get a boxing license.

JOHNNY

I don't need no license. I'm one of a kind. I got the system beat. Goinna Florida. Beautiful oranges kissed by the sun.

JIMMY

Hialeah, goin to the dogs.

JOHNNY

Better your money on the ponies, better odds.

JIMMY

Mutual fund creams ten per cent right off the top. Might as well take it off the top yourself. Ettore is gonna run the club for us. Georgie.

JOHNNY

Jimmy, you're ninety-two years old. Ettore is just a boy. He's only fifty. Money burns a hole in his pocket. Partners, worst way to do business. He already asked me for money. Two days ago he was here. I used to give him money when he was a boy. You know what he used to do with it? Used to buy the girls ice creams. He's still doin the same thing. Kids all over the place don't know who the father is. He's got five girlfriends all at the same time. Three of em got kids called George. What makes you think I got money?

JIMMY

You just told me you're gonna make fifty bucks. You don't pay no rent. They feed you at the hospital. You got a pension.

JOHNNY

I told you you should join the army.

JIMMY

Look what it done to your lungs, emphysemas.

JOHNNY

I'm gonna live to be a hundred. I'm a winner. Got two tickets for the Queen's Plate. Best seat, you bet.

JIMMY

What kinda seats you got?

JOHNNY

Best one, right on the horse.

JIMMY

You gonna watch the Leaf game tonight? Playoffs.

JOHNNY

Nineteen fifty-two, best hockey ever played.

JIMMY

Same year Anna died.

JOHNNY

Never been hockey like that. Beat the Russians in over-time.

JIMMY

I'm gonna watch the game at the old men's home. They got colour now. I'm takin an apple.

JIMMY is about to go; JOHNNY panics.

JOHNNY

Dove vai?

JIMMY

I gotta find two G's.

JOHNNY

You think it's gonna rain?

JIMMY

April showers bring May flowers.

JOHNNY

Come?

JIMMY

Canadian expression. So you're not gonna lend me no scratch?

JOHNNY

You make me laugh.

JIMMY

Why?

JOHNNY

You hat.

JIMMY

What about my hat?

JOHNNY

You look like you just got off the boat.

JIMMY

Least I don't wear white socks with my army boots.

JOHNNY

Keeps my feet warm.

JIMMY

I gotta go. See you John.

JOHNNY

Ciao Giacomo.

JIMMY shuffles off.

JOHNNY

Ciao Ciao Canada. Sixteen monthsa yeara snow. Just like Russia. Canada, che russia. Appleorangebanan, we got em fresh. Ariappa, let's go, first race is gonna start. Sixabanan ten cent, who wantsa buy?

FINE

IN SEARCH OF MRS. PIRANDELLO

2015
Michaela Di Cesare

"In 1894 he married and in the late mid- and late nineties his wife bore him three children. But the comfort and equanimity of his domestic and literary life were shattered when the family Sulphur mines in Sicily were destroyed by floods, leaving his father and father-in-law bankrupt. Hitherto financially dependent on them, now to support himself and his family, Pirandello was dependent upon a university lecturing post. His wife's mental health gradually deteriorated, and she became prey to suspicions and rages, which led eventually to her being confined to an asylum. Pirandello gave up teaching only in 1922. By that time, he had begun to acquire international status as a dramatist."
— **Cambridge Guide to World Theatre**

ACT ONE

A note on characterization. The Searcher and The Librarian are human. Antonietta wears the mask of madness. All other characters have an element of traditional Sicilian marionette. The Searcher is always The Searcher—she steps into moments in Antonietta's life, in her place, as part of the search. Only when The Searcher wears "the mask" near the end has she crossed the line into full embodiment.

The Searcher and Antonietta are in separate folds of time. When Antonietta's fold is pierced, she can see & hear The Searcher. The Searcher is being unconsciously influenced by Antonietta until they meet in the same fold of time.

Prologue

Lights up on Antonietta in her shadowy cell. She is catatonic. The Searcher is following a map, weaving in and out of light and shadow. She comes upon the tomb of Luigi Pirandello.

THE SEARCHER
    She's not here. She's not here? Where is her body? Where the fuck is her body? You have to be kidding me. This place is a lie.

The Searcher paces in frustration. She fixes her eyes on the tomb with pure rage. She looks around. She pulls down her pants, squats and pees.

Confinement

Antonietta stirs from her catatonic state. She watches The Searcher.

ANTONIETTA

I know you. I recognized your voice the minute you called out. It pierced my fold of time the tiniest bit. Enough to wake me. They want you to think lines are everywhere. Lines make up the universe, they say.

Dominant lines. Strings. Phallices. Straight. Hard. Direct. But the folds are everywhere. The folds are microcosmic representations of life. Soft petals. The vulva. The fat backsides of babies. The universe is folding in on itself. Each time you make a choice, you create a fold, an alternate life that runs overtop.

THE SEARCHER

Can you believe they're acting like she never existed? She's a footnote. How does a woman become a footnote? Superscript 1: The great burden Nobel-prize winning Sicilian playwright Luigi Pirandello carried was his wife, Maria Antonietta Portolano—hah, Map!—She went insane. She persecuted him with an unprovoked and crazy jealousy. In 1919, she was finally institutionalized and she remained there for forty years, until her death. End of footnote.

The Searcher addresses her husband, who is unseen.

THE SEARCHER

Hey babe, I know I said this was the last stop. I'm so sorry.

ANTONIETTA

She's not sorry, but she doesn't know that.

THE SEARCHER

I need to look in one last place.

ANTONIETTA

To be sure I did everything I could.

THE SEARCHER

To be sure I did everything I could.

Access to Knowledge

The Searcher enters the light, she's standing at a door.

THE SEARCHER

Let me in! Please. I am begging you to let me in.

The Librarian is on the other side of the door.

THE LIBRARIAN

Siesta. No open.

THE SEARCHER

Please. I heard you have an extensive private collection and I go back tonight. To Canada. I just need to verify something about Pirandello—

The door opens.

THE SEARCHER

I should have known that's the magic word around here. About Pirandello's wife.

THE LIBRARIAN

You mean Pirandello.

THE SEARCHER

I mean his wife.

THE LIBRARIAN

You want to know about Pirandello.

THE SEARCHER

I need to know where Antonietta was buried.

THE LIBRARIAN

Have you seen the tomb? Official Pirandello museum house?

THE SEARCHER

I saw the tomb. She's not there.

THE LIBRARIAN

She?

THE SEARCHER

His wife.

THE LIBRARIAN

You look like Antonietta.

The Searcher and The Librarian stare at one another for a beat.

THE LIBRARIAN

Go ask. Very nice museum house. They tell you.

THE SEARCHER

I can't go back there.

THE LIBRARIAN

Very easy. 10 minutes by car. Drive Sicilian style.

THE SEARCHER

I can't go back there because I pissed on his tomb. Me. Pipi on Pirandello.

Beat. The Librarian doesn't know what to think.

THE SEARCHER

I had high expectations for the museum house. I knew he was buried there and I assumed she would be too. It was so hot when I arrived, sweltering. From the moment I walked through the front door it was all busts. Busts of Luigi and some darling little poems about Sicily.

One bust was donated by Marta Abba, that bitch, right in the foyer of the family home. Che vergogna. Did you know he left all of his literary rights to Abba when he died? He gave HER his plays.

THE LIBRARIAN

Si, because his wife

The Librarian makes "cuckoo" gesture with his hand.

THE SEARCHER

Pirandello's work showed me I had a place in the theatrical canon. Before him all we studied was Shakespeare and Miller. Then I played The Stepdaughter from Six Characters in Search of an Author. And I knew her. He was writing people I recognized. He made me believe I could do that too. Give legitimate voice to the people and places I love. But Antonietta's story was not in the museum house. They told me the tomb was out back. A 2K hike on a rocky road, 40 degrees out and all these tourists. This one girl was kissing the tomb, she didn't look like she'd ever even read a play. Like she'd think 6 Characters was about Twitter, you know? There was a group of shirtless guys. They were taking selfies, shirtless selfies at the tomb. Hashtag dead author. Hashtag proud to be Italian.

THE LIBRARIAN

Hashtag Sicilian Stallion

THE SEARCHER

I waited patiently for them to be done. I thought this couldn't possibly be what Pirandello wanted when he asked for cremation, to leave no trace of his existence, to disappear into the Sicilian soil. He couldn't have imagined all the busts and the plaques and the streets and the squares and the parks and the gelateria. Pirandello gelateria.

THE LIBRARIAN

They make excellent straciatella flavor.

THE SEARCHER

The tourists were called back to their bus for lunch. I was finally able to get close to the tomb. And she wasn't there. I was hot, tired, thirsty—e d'improvviso avevo bisogno di fare pipi.

> Beat. The Librarian starts laughing and The Searcher joins him.

THE SEARCHER

My husband- my husband, wow, I'm on my honeymoon. So not used to saying that. He found me with my pants down and he didn't even ask. That's a good man.

THE LIBRARIAN

What you are looking for, Signora?

THE SEARCHER

Maybe you have some letters that Antonietta wrote?

THE LIBRARIAN

We have Pirandello letters.

THE SEARCHER

I have those too. But she must have replied.

THE LIBRARIAN

We don't have index card for Antonietta. No one ask about her before.

THE SEARCHER

I can create the card. Please just give me an hour.

THE LIBRARIAN

You need to cover your shoulders. And the bathroom is over there.

THE SEARCHER

My husband is watching the rental car, with all our bags. Do you have a parking lot?

THE LIBRARIAN

No. But we have a Sicilian marionette museum.

The Searcher looks at the marionettes. The other actors take on the form of sinister marionettes, watching.

LUIGI (V.O.)
We're like so many puppets hung on the wall, waiting for someone to come and move us or make us talk.

Flooded

THE SEARCHER
I'll start with what I know to be true. The sulfur mine disaster of 1903. Antonietta's first breakdown that manifested as catatonic shock.
Luigi descends from the marionette museum.

LUIGI
Brava, Antonietta.
The Searcher sees him, recognizes him, is in shock.

LUIGI
You've dragged your husband home from work once again. What is the emergency? This better not be another letter from a foolish schoolgirl.
Luigi picks up a letter to read.

LUIGI
My dearest daughter, my heart aches to tell you this, but our fortune is lost. The mines in Aragona have flooded. What renders this catastrophe worse is that just a few short weeks ago, your father-in-law invested your dowry and all the Pirandello family savings into those mines. We are all destitute. I blame myself for marrying you to Luigi. You used to be a wealthy miner's daughter, my dear, and now you are a failing writer's wife. My only daughter, all the treasure I used to have, has been washed away with the flood. With love and regret, Your dying father. Oh my sweet Antonietta—
Luigi turns toward The Searcher. She is still unmoving, freaking out a little. Like a little girl whose celebrity crush has just appeared out of thin air. Luigi hugs and kisses her.

LUIGI
I am sorry. Do you hear me?
Luigi exits. The Searcher touches her face where he kissed her.

THE SEARCHER
What the f—

Searching

ANTONIETTA
Fill in the blanks. The places where I'm missing. Hear the notes I am not playing. Footnotes.

THE SEARCHER
This is the land Google forgot. Who uses a card catalog any more?

ANTONIETTA
Sicily 1893.

THE SEARCHER
The marriage agreement.

ANTONIETTA
Who benefits from a young virgin?

Sicilian Carriages

Signor Portulano approaches The Searcher. She takes his arm. They are riding in a carriage.

SIGNOR PORTULANO
You don't need to think. I will tell you what to think. I am not certain what the nuns have taught you, but marriage is a woman's principal duty through which she can bring honour to her family. Honestly, a simple girl like yourself cannot hope for much better than this.
The Searcher opens her mouth to speak.

ANTONIETTA
Quiet or he'll hurt you.
The other carriage pulls up.

SIGNOR PORTULANO
Ah, here is the Pirandello family carriage. I warn you: behave yourself.
Signor Portulano pinches her hard on the side of her arm.

SIGNORA PIRANDELLO
You must consider this match, after everything your father has done to preserve our mining business. Why, he shot a man!

LUIGI
Yes. We both know how impulsive Father can be.

SIGNORA PIRANDELLO
Your broken engagements prove you're just like him.

LUIGI
There was only the one! You couldn't expect me to go through with marrying cousin Caterina after her illness rendered her quite … unrecognizable.

SIGNORA PIRANDELLO
Thankfully Antonietta is revered as the most beautiful girl in this town. That's why her father sent her to the nuns.

LUIGI
In this town? That isn't saying much.

SIGNORA PIRANDELLO
She has the exotic beauty of a gypsy girl with all the refinement of good breeding.

LUIGI
Mother, I simply cannot believe that I am meant for marital happiness.

SIGNORA PIRANDELLO
Yes, yes. I know. You are melancholic. You suffer. Your sister told me all about your bizarre letters. She thought you were going to be a suicide.

LUIGI

Those were private!

SIGNORA PIRANDELLO

Oh look! Some other townsfolk have happened upon our path, entirely by chance. Signor Portulano.

SIGNOR PORTULANO

Signora Pirandello.

SIGNORA PIRANDELLO

The heat wave hasn't let up.

SIGNOR PORTULANO

No. It hasn't.

SIGNORA PIRANDELLO

Who's there with you? Is that Antonietta?

SIGNOR PORTULANO

Yes. Here she is.

SIGNORA PIRANDELLO

Oh, what a coincidence! My son is here with me. Luigi, say hello.

LUIGI

I detest when you bid me to say hello. As though my own common sense would not dictate that I greet fellow human beings with whom I cross paths. Hello.

SIGNOR PORTULANO

Say hello.

There is a drawn-out pause.

ANTONIETTA

Buongiorno.

THE SEARCHER

Hello

LUIGI

Well that's out of the way then.

SIGNORA PIRANDELLO

You probably need to return to work, Signor Portulano.

SIGNOR PORTULANO

You know what they say. A sulfur empire can easily go up in smoke. Good day.

The pairs part ways. In Portulano's carriage

SIGNOR PORTULANO

Well?

The Searcher doesn't know what to say.

SIGNOR PORTULANO

I don't care. You will marry him. The merger between our two families will allow me to retire and live well, something a man without sons must be concerned about.

The carriage departs. The scene dissolves.

THE SEARCHER

By all accounts her life starts here and ends right over there. From a carriage to a cell. From trot to rot. From silence to incest.

Madness

Rome. 1919. Antonietta leans out of her cell and yells.

ANTONIETTA
   Incest! My husband and my daughter. Incest! I will not stop hollering until all of
   Rome knows the truth. Your beloved author, UN MANIACO SESSUALE!
   The lights go out on the cell.
THE SEARCHER
   And then he himself writes in Henry IV
LUIGI (V.O.)
   "It's convenient for everybody to insist that certain people are mad, so they can
   be shut up. Do you know why? Because it's impossible to hear them speak!"

My Wife

THE SEARCHER
   What did you mean by that?
ANTONIETTA
   An admission. Rome 1924.
LUIGI
   My home is haunted by her absence.
THE SEARCHER
   Yes!
LUIGI
   The long, empty corridors mock my solitude.
THE SEARCHER
   You begged to have her back. Five years into her confinement, you changed your
   mind. Why?
ANTONIETTA
   Writer's block.
LUIGI
   I wonder if she would have been happier, healthier, had she married a miner and
   not a writer. Had she continued to live in her small village. Had her mind not
   been so forced as it was to attempt to understand … things. I put everything
   aside to care for her. My colleagues marveled at my sacrifice. I stood patiently
   by as they won awards, were produced in foreign countries, had tawdry affairs …
   I waited patiently for my wife to get well and come back to me. I searched for
   Antonietta in every lucid moment, every familiar smile, every hint of lime. I write
   to you in hopes that you will see fit to release my wife into my care.
   Luigi exits, Searcher runs after him.
THE SEARCHER
   Wait! Did she reply to this letter?
ANTONIETTA
   He never liked my letters.

The Courtship Letters

ANTONIETTA
　Sicily 1893.
LUIGI
　My lovely Antonietta, as I write this letter I am fantasizing about your reaction.
　I imagine you've received this unworthy scrap of paper and held it to your bosom
　all day long, waiting for the perfect moment to unfold my words and to spend
　some time alone thinking only of me. Is the paper warm, love? Was it strapped
　tightly underneath your silk corset, serenaded by the fluttering of your delicate
　heart? I can hardly contain my joy when I think that heart will soon belong to
　me. Oh, Antonietta, you cannot know, you could never imagine, the darkness
　that lurked over me before the day I saw your angelic face. I thought there was
　nothing for me to live for. I was jaded; I had no hope that any member of your
　sex could truly make me happy, so unimpressed was I by the rough and crude
　girls at the university and even less impressed by the simple village girls from
　Agrigento. You will be the wife I dreamed of but never dared believe existed.
　A type of resurrection is what I feel, Antonietta. You saved me from myself.
　Before you, I was merely a corpse. I showed no signs of life. I had no appetite,
　no eagerness, I was in a kind of daze. Thoughts of love only made me feel more
　like a dead man. I hope I have not shocked you, Antonietta mia. I only wish for
　you to understand how complete you've made me. My heartbeat is counting
　down to our wedding day. I love you, tesoro mio. Please write back soon. Luigi.
　　　The Searcher scrambles to find Antonietta's response. She does.

ANTONIETTA
　Dear Luigi, my Zia Linda took me to the furniture shop today. She says every
　new bride must pick out a kitchen table. What do you think of mahogany?
　Yours, Antonietta.
　　　During the following monologue, The Searcher is discovering
　　　more of Antonietta's letters.

LUIGI
　Do you really not know what to say to me? Do you expect me to believe that you
　are that unschooled? That innocent? How do you think I feel when after I have
　poured out my soul for you to read you return with the most banal, most unpoetical
　reply. Oh to think that I expected more from you than from other women. To
　think I raised you above your sex. Do you wish to remind me that my family
　needs your dowry? I hate to remind you, but there is as much sulfur in your
　blood as in mine.
　Your flesh reeks, as all other flesh, as any other woman. Why do you torment
　me? Why with all this distance between us do you punish me with this frigid,
　unfeeling behaviour? Now those old feelings are stirring up in me again. Perhaps
　happiness is not a state of being that I am meant for. With disappointment, Luigi.

Voice

> *The Searcher starts waving a stack of letters and screaming. The Librarian rushes in.*

LIBRARIAN
Cosa è successo? Lizards? I come spray. Bye bye.
ANTONIETTA
I wrote letters. Nice letters.
> *The Searcher runs to the librarian, papers in hand.*

THE SEARCHER
These are letters Antonietta wrote! Her voice, it was here all along. In this creepy, possibly haunted, lizard-infested—
> *The Librarian clears his throat.*

THE SEARCHER
I need to photocopy all of these.
LIBRARIAN
No copy machine. Read here.

She Speaks

ANTONIETTA
Sicily 1894. Lina Carissima, It was so kind of you to pay us a visit on our honeymoon. Your family's beach house was lovely. We are very happy. Right now, your brother Luigi is jumping from room to room singing, "Muglieri Bedda!" I received a lovely card from Sister Nella. Would you please thank her on my behalf? I have placed her photo on my desk, here. I like to think she is watching over me through that photo, making sure I am a good wife. Please send your little Linuccia to visit us any time. What can I say? I normally can't abide children—
THE SEARCHER
You and me both.
ANTONIETTA
But that girl has stirred an affection in me. I don't think I could be a good mother, but as an aunt I am full of patience. Your loving sister-in-law, Antonietta.
THE SEARCHER
Sister Nella . . . where can I find her?
ANTONIETTA
Sicily 1893. My special place beneath the lime tree. My mother was buried under a citrus tree like this one.
The only mother I'd ever known was the Sicilian soil.

Sicilian Limes

> *Sister Nella and Sister Pia come running in. They need a moment to recuperate. Sister Pia is carrying a corset.*

SISTER PIA

Antonietta! Antonietta!

SISTER NELLA

Antonietta, your father will be cross. We aren't supposed to let you run wild.

THE SEARCHER

Oh God.

SISTER PIA

Excuse me?

ANTONIETTA

I won't tell him.

SISTER PIA

I won't tell him, *Sister Pia*. Can you believe her impudence, Sister Nella?

THE SEARCHER

You're Sister Nella!

SISTER NELLA

Calm yourself, child. Come, let me dress you. You can't be jumping about like this. Didn't we explain that certain parts of your body . . .

SISTER PIA

Are more/developed.

SISTER NELLA

/Bouncy.

SISTER PIA

Bouncy? Really?

SISTER NELLA

Plump.

SISTER PIA

Tight is best. To contain all the . . .

SISTER NELLA

Bounce.

SISTER PIA

If men saw women unrestrained, no work would get done in this town!

SISTER NELLA

And besides, today is a special day.

> *The two nuns start to dress her and do up her hair. They tie a corset on her.*

ANTONIETTA

My father came to visit every Saturday. He would take me down into the mines all heat and sulfuric gas, and tell me how grateful I should be for my inheritance since it was for love of me alone that he never re-married and produced a male heir. Then he would take the dirt and hold it to my nose. To remind me where I come from.

SISTER PIA

You seem flushed. Are you sick? The Good Lord will have to see you through it.

SISTER NELLA

You must meet your husband-to-be!

> *Sister Pia hits her.*

SISTER PIA
    Shh!
SISTER NELLA
    Was it a secret?
SISTER PIA
    Yes.
SISTER NELLA
    Oops.
SISTER PIA
    Now that's enough.
SISTER NELLA
    It's Luigi Pirandello!
                Sister Pia hits her again.
SISTER NELLA
    I don't know what's the matter with me.
SISTER PIA
    After the whole mess with that invalid Caterina, poor dear, he needs to marry a
    good Sicilian girl.
THE SEARCHER
    I don't know if I'm good.
SISTER PIA
    What you are is beautiful, rich and an only child. The holy trinity of
    marriageability.
SISTER NELLA
    You poor motherless dear. You need initiation into womanhood and all you have
    are two vestal virgins to guide you.
SISTER PIA
    Don't say virgin like that!
SISTER NELLA
    We must perform the sacred mother-daughter pre-marriage ritual.
SISTER PIA
    There is no sacred mother-daughter pre-marriage ritual.
                Sister Nella looks at The Searcher expectantly.
THE SEARCHER
    C'e la luna mezz'o mare ...
ANTONIETTA
    No. That's anachronistic.
SISTER NELLA
    (Repeating the song) C'e la luna mezz'o mare
THE SEARCHER
    Mama mia me maritari
ANTONIETTA
    This did not happen.
SISTER NELLA
    Figghia mia, a cu te dari
THE SEARCHER
    Mamma mia pensaci tu.

SISTER NELLA

If I give you to the farmer He will come and he will go But he'll always have his plow If he agrees to marry He will plow you, oh my daughter.

SISTER PIA

Oh santo Gesu!

> *Antonietta puts a lime in The Searcher's hand. There is a moment of channeling. The Searcher is taken aback by it.*

ANTONIETTA

Sister Nella, what about the writer?

THE SEARCHER

Sister Nella, what about the writer?

SISTER NELLA

If I give you to the writer He will come and he will go But he'll always have his pen If he agrees to marry He will pen you, oh my daughter.

SISTER PIA

Enough! Signor Portulano is coming and he will not accept this nonsense! Get that lime out of your mouth. Why do you insist on such a vulgar habit?

ANTONIETTA

It makes me feel something. Sweetness then bitterness.

THE SEARCHER

It makes me feel something. Sweetness then bitterness.

SISTER NELLA

Well then I'd say you're ready for marriage.

SISTER PIA

Sister!

SISTER NELLA

Why do you think I became a nun? Marriage is always sweetness followed by bitterness.

SISTER PIA

Please don't tell your father that Nella let the secret slip. His temper will flare and none of us wants that.

SISTER NELLA

(whispering in Searcher's ear)

If you marry Luigi, he will take you to Rome. Far away from your father.

ANTONIETTA

Far away from my father.

THE SEARCHER

She wanted to get married.

ANTONIETTA

You must make him happy. Sicily 1894.

White Linens

THE SEARCHER

The wedding night.

> *The villagers/wedding party can be heard outside. They are demanding the bedsheet, calling for blood. Luigi enters.*

LUIGI
> I've finally understood. Wedding day festivities are actually meant to torment the bride and groom in a sadistic fashion. They have employed medieval torture devices on us. That dress must be cutting into your vital organs—look at that bodice! And I don't believe we've eaten a thing all day. Are you hungry?

THE SEARCHER
> No.

LUIGI
> Thirsty?

THE SEARCHER
> No.

LUIGI
> What are they hollering about out there?

ANTONIETTA
> The bed sheet. They wouldn't leave until they'd seen it.

LUIGI
> The bed sheet! I refuse to submit to that archaic practice. Why, the insult!

THE SEARCHER
> It is pretty asinine.

ANTONIETTA
> I didn't mind.

LUIGI
> Nonsense, we hardly know one another. I wouldn't want your first experience to be—

ANTONIETTA
> My first experience.

LUIGI
> We should spend the night talking, getting acquainted privately.

THE SEARCHER
> Okay. Let's talk. Luigi, I need you to tell me—

ANTONIETTA
> They wanted to see the sheet!

THE SEARCHER
> Wow. That's distracting.

LUIGI
> Don't fret, my love. I'll go out onto that balcony right now and tell them—

ANTONIETTA
> He was going to embarrass me.

THE SEARCHER
> You broke off your engagement with your cousin Caterina.

LUIGI
> She was a nut.

THE SEARCHER
> Did you want to get married?
>
>> *During the following speech, Antonietta unlaces the The Searcher's corset so that it falls off.*

LUIGI

I wanted you. My father asked very specifically, through my mother because we don't really talk, for my approval. I should think if anyone was forced, it was you. And the tepid manner with which you replied to my letters only proves it. Do you always do as you're told? Is that what you're doing now? You want to give yourself to me only because they are demanding the bed sheet. Because it's the next logical step?

THE SEARCHER

Wait a minute. You don't want to consummate the marriage?

ANTONIETTA

He wanted them all to go home saying that I could not make him happy. Or worse. That I had some fault to hide. My father would have been livid.

THE SEARCHER

Portulano will be livid.

LUIGI

Your father? The man who tried to stop the wedding in a fit of jealousy yesterday?

THE SEARCHER

I know you had sex while in University.

LUIGI

That was different. I had no respect for her.

THE SEARCHER

Her. There's a her. A specific her.

ANTONIETTA

Jenny Shulz.

LUIGI

Would you have preferred a them?

THE SEARCHER

Your cousin—

ANTONIETTA

Who was extremely fat by the way

THE SEARCHER

You respected her. Did you sleep with her?

LUIGI

Antonietta, per favore, you are bringing up such indecent topics on our wedding night.

ANTONIETTA

I couldn't go back.

> *Antonietta pushes The Searcher onto Luigi.*

ANTONIETTA

The entire village was waiting.

THE SEARCHER

What's happening here?

LUIGI

Why are you behaving this way? So forward. It's disgusting.

ANTONIETTA

I didn't go back.

> *Antonietta unpins her hairpiece and stabs herself in the thigh.*
> *The Searcher feels this pain and cries out. Antonietta grabs the*

*bedsheet and rubs it between her legs, then drops it into The
Searcher's hands. The Searcher, terrified, shoves it at Luigi.*

ANTONIETTA
I would not be fodder for their gossip.
*Luigi walks to the balcony and drops the sheet. The crowd cheers.
One man says, "Il melone era rosso" which means "The melon
was red."*

Morbid Jealousy

The Librarian enters

LIBRARIAN
La cercatrice, did you find more letters?
THE SEARCHER
No. Sorry. I'm fine.
LIBRARIAN
I go tell your husband more waiting. He fell asleep con la testa honking the horn.
The Librarian exits.
THE SEARCHER
Tell him—
ANTONIETTA
Tell *me* why I am here. What is my diagnosis? Being a woman? Being a wife?
THE SEARCHER
Morbid jealousy. Otherwise known as Othello syndrome.
ANTONIETTA
Oh jealousy. Is that all?
THE SEARCHER
To me a diagnosis of Morbid Jealousy sounds like you're envious of dead people.
Which, you know, on a bad day who isn't? A wife's jealousy? That's not morbid.
That's normal. You tell a woman all her eggs, literally, have to sit in this one
basket, and you expect her not to be afraid of dropping the basket and cracking
all her eggs? Do you know how terrifying it is to see everything you've ever wanted
oozing into the abyss?
ANTONIETTA
Yes. I followed him. I searched for him. I lived for him.

Lessons

ANTONIETTA
Rome 1899.
THE SEARCHER
Antonietta was pregnant for the third time.
ANTONIETTA
I was also barefoot.

DEAN

I'm truly sorry about the handcuffs, Mrs. Pirandello. Marco, our head of security, he scares easily. He's from Florence, you know.

THE SEARCHER

That's fine uh ...

ANTONIETTA

Dean Garibaldi.

DEAN

Your husband should be here very soon. The campus is quite big.

> *The Searcher does not reply.*

DEAN

Not like the schools in Il Caos, I imagine.

THE SEARCHER

Porto Empedocle. Luigi is from Caos.

DEAN

Oh. Charming. I bet you could walk from one village to the next. Can I offer you a coffee?

> *Luigi enters. The Dean stands.*

DEAN

Professor Pirandello, there seems to have been some confusion. Your wife—

LUIGI

I am truly sorry, Dottor Garibaldi.

DEAN

She was searching for you.

> *The Dean takes Pirandello aside and whispers in his ear. Then the Dean exits.*

LUIGI

Antonietta, is everything okay?

THE SEARCHER

Yes.

LUIGI

The children?

ANTONIETTA

The woman next door was watching them.

LUIGI

Antonietta! Is it true you were you hiding in the bushes outside my classroom?

THE SEARCHER

That's what they say.

LUIGI

Why?

> *The Searcher breaks away, thinking to herself.*

THE SEARCHER

Why would you do this?

ANTONIETTA

I said I didn't want children and there I was, pregnant with a third!

LUIGI

What are you going on about? You embarrassed me at work! You have no shoes on!

THE SEARCHER

Why do you think I would come here? To embarrass myself like this. In front of your boss. In front of your students—

ANTONIETTA

His students.

THE SEARCHER

(remembering Luigi's own words)

This better not be another letter from a foolish schoolgirl.

ANTONIETTA

They began to adore him.

LUIGI

You found Mariella's letter. It was nothing. She's stupid. She's . . .

THE SEARCHER

Why did she write you a love letter?

LUIGI

You'd be surprised at what students say to augment their grades.

THE SEARCHER

I don't believe you.

LUIGI

Antonietta, please. You are the one who forced me to take this horrendous job. You are forcing me to live this tedious life. Do you mean to tell me you didn't realize I'd have to interact with young girls on a daily basis?

THE SEARCHER

You kept the letter. If you felt nothing for her, you wouldn't have kept it.

ANTONIETTA

We've been through this before!

LUIGI

What do you—

THE SEARCHER

Jenny Shulz.

LUIGI

Not that again.

THE SEARCHER

Yes. That again.

ANTONIETTA

That always!

LUIGI

I knew her in university. I won't be held accountable for something I did over a decade ago. That isn't fair.

THE SEARCHER

You kept all her letters.

ANTONIETTA

And her indecent photo.

LUIGI

I will not do penance for that any more.

THE SEARCHER

And now you've kept this girl's love letter.

LUIGI

I kept it in case her flattery eventually developed into folly—I could prove that the advances were one-sided.

THE SEARCHER

You're always here. After classes, late at night sometimes.

LUIGI

Yes, wife! I am always here. Do you know how difficult it is to put my pen to paper with two young children screeching at home?

THE SEARCHER

I know that even the smallest distraction can take hours to recuperate from. You're trying to access a world that exists somewhere between reality and dream.

LUIGI

(overlapping)

Between reality and dream. I was just now trying to express something like that in my preface.

THE SEARCHER

I've studied you well.

LUIGI

Why did you come here today?

ANTONIETTA

I wanted to see her. I wanted to see if you loved her.

Quiet

THE SEARCHER

Rome 1934. The nurse's log. This is the day Pirandello won the Nobel prize! Antonietta didn't speak when given the news. She hadn't spoken in 10 years.

ANTONIETTA

Nuns and nurses. Nurses and nuns. They wrote reports about me. Folded them up. Filed them away. He wrote plays about me. Fattened them up with my juices. Poor nurses. I don't do. I don't act. I don't want. That is also what the critics write of his plays. Sometimes. Sometimes they are a revelation. How does he know madness so well? He is being awarded today. A high honor.

LUIGI

Thank you. By sounding the depths of madness I have made important discoveries. I have penetrated deeply into the obscure borderland between reality and dream. For the success of my literary endeavours, I had to go to the school of life. I would gladly believe that this prize is not given so much to the virtuosity of a writer, which is always negligible, but to the human sincerity of my work.

ANTONIETTA

I don't speak because I have nothing to say that will make a difference. I will outlive him. I will outdie him. Here in this odorless place. I don't speak and I don't do because there is nothing worth doing. But I do want. I want Sicily. I want to be home. I want to be an island.

THE SEARCHER

She never spoke again. She spent another 25 years, sitting motionless, staring. And then she died. "Expired spontaneously"

ANTONIETTA

I was dreaming.

The One Who Got Away

THE SEARCHER

I wonder if she was thinking of him then. He was long dead. And when he died he was in love with Marta Abba. This might sound stupid, but you really want to be the one your husband is thinking of on his death bed.

ANTONIETTA

That is stupid.

THE SEARCHER

When it's time to reflect on life decisions and what it would have been like to have married someone else. It's not romantic being the one who stayed. Every artist has a secret love. Ted Hughes. Rodin. All of Fellini's muses, his city of women.

ANTONIETTA

I envy your version of love. You expect it to be unconditional, the way women of my time were taught to love men. We were told to repair and forgive. Forgive and repair. Keep folding. You, the new woman, the equal woman, you want to be special, individual, unforgettable. How terrifying to want to break the mold rather than fit in, tucked away.

LUIGI (V.O.)

Here is a piece of earth. If you stand staring at it and doing nothing, what does the earth yield? Nothing. Just like a woman.

As You Desire Me Sicily

ANTONIETTA

Sicily 1894. The morning after the wedding night.

LUIGI

Sister Nella said I might find you here. I'm sorry about what happened last night. I imagined a happier wedding night.

THE SEARCHER

I shouldn't have been so insistent. Testa dura.

LUIGI

I was stubborn too.

THE SEARCHER

Do you think I could be a good wife?

LUIGI

You will be. But last night you changed so suddenly.

The Searcher retorts with a direct Pirandello quote.

THE SEARCHER
Has it ever happened to you, to find a different self in yourself? Have you always been the same?

LUIGI
What a poetic question! Your mind. It's fascinating.

THE SEARCHER
It's yours, actually.

ANTONIETTA
I believe we've been here before. And we'll be here again. I believe in cycles.

ANTONIETTA
I believe in time folding onto itself.

THE SEARCHER
I believe in time folding onto itself.

LUIGI
Folds of time. How interesting.

THE SEARCHER
Don't you believe in anything?

LUIGI
I believe in you. I believe that you've saved me.
                    Beat.

LUIGI
My past troubles you a lot.

ANTONIETTA
Yes. Because it's folding right over us. Crushing us.

LUIGI
You are different from every woman I've ever known.

ANTONIETTA
It's only a matter of time.

THE SEARCHER
It's only a matter of time.

LUIGI
I would never betray you.
                    Beat.

LUIGI
My father carried on an affair behind my mother's back and I was the one who discovered it. I have hardly been able to tolerate looking at him since. It was with a young niece of his. He was asked to be her guardian when her parents passed … He turned out to be a very dedicated guardian. I've never forgiven him for the hurt he caused my mother.

THE SEARCHER
The first time I read your work—

ANTONIETTA
This is different!

LUIGI
You've read something of mine?

THE SEARCHER

I've read it all. I fell into obsession. My whole life my obsessions have been what my love life could never be. I built up this idea of who I wanted you to be. I wanted to be good—

LUIGI

Good enough for me?

THE SEARCHER

As good as you. You made me want to be better. Then I found out about her and now I don't know what to think.

LUIGI

You don't need to worry about the past any more.

THE SEARCHER

Do you think artists can marry—happily?

LUIGI

Of course I do.

THE SEARCHER

What if the artist is always taking, without giving back? Do you ever worry about destroying the person you love with your obsessions?

> *Luigi kisses her passionately. An overhanging lime falls down/ Antonietta drops it on them.*

LUIGI

What's this?

ANTONIETTA

I wanted to show you what I love most about Sicily.

> *The Searcher turns away, feeling guilty. Luigi exits.*

MAP

THE SEARCHER

But then we—they—she—She went to Rome.

ANTONIETTA

Do all roads really lead to Rome? What if you are an island? No man is an island, but a woman can be. I am an island. I am Sicily. Rome is landlocked. Rome is eternal.

> *The Searcher finds the following information.*

THE SEARCHER

Some mental illnesses are sparked by a move from a rural to an urban setting!

ANTONIETTA

So many cocktail parties. Rome 1894.

When in Rome

> *Luigi is at a cocktail party chatting with a writer, Gabriele D'Annunzio.*

LUIGI

You must be joking, Gabriele. A woman writing? From Sardinia?

GABRIELE

Deledda is her name

LUIGI

Why, that's practically Africa.

GABRIELE

Said the Sicilian.

LUIGI

Ah, yes, but I can pass for a Northerner, can't I? Anyway, the trick to all that is write about one's roots like an anthropologist would. Be from the South, but not of it—

GABRIELE

They like her style. I daresay she might be successful.

LUIGI

I don't think much of the woman of letters. Of course, she cannot be regarded as a woman. The woman, by nature, is passive and art is active. This does not mean that an active female mind cannot exist. It simply means that it cannot truly belong to a woman.

GABRIELE

I like her prose. I see the charm in it.

LUIGI

Preposterous. We write for posterity—how many streets or schools are there named after women writers? There just aren't. She might have some low-born fans today, but in a few years, no one will know her name. Us, there will be parks and schools and town squares named for us. Parco Pirandello. Strada D'Annunzio. We're the godfathers of the Italian theatre.

THE SEARCHER

The Godfathers. Who says that?

GABRIELE

Can you repeat that, Signora Pirandello?

ANTONIETTA

I would never have contradicted him in public.

The Searcher takes the lemon and sucks on it.

GABRIELE

She only speaks your dialect. How charming.

LUIGI

Yes, my wife, she would never pass for a Northerner. She is pure—

GABRIELE

Exoticism.

He twists a lock of her hair.

LUIGI

Now, now. You'll make Luisa mad with jealousy.

GABRIELE

Luisa! I've moved on from her. Heiresses are all dazzle and no passion. I'm seeing an actress now.

LUIGI
> An actress?

GABRIELE
> Eleonora Duse.

LUIGI
> You bastard!

GABRIELE
> Let me tell you, she is not as quiet and demure as your little Sicilian Lime. With her, everything is rhetoric. Life is poetry. You should write plays, my boy. Write plays and the actresses will come.

LUIGI
> I'm a married man, Gabriele. My time for frolicking with actresses is past.

GABRIELE
> Signora Pirandello, you are a lucky woman. If I happen to have a fatal heart attack while romancing actresses, you will be married to the greatest author in this country.

> *Gabriele clinks her glass and walks off. Luigi and The Searcher stay.*

LUIGI
> I married a good girl for the very reason that she would not let strange men fondle her at parties!

THE SEARCHER
> You're blaming me?

ANTONIETTA
> Who else?

THE SEARCHER
> He reached for my hair. What should I have done?

LUIGI
> Not say a word of course. Just keep sucking your citrus fruit.

THE SEARCHER
> Oh, I get it. You're not making any money publishing poetry. You're living off your wife's dowry and you resent that.

LUIGI
> You have no clue how difficult it is to create art. I don't need your materialism, a God-given feminine attribute, weighing down on me.

ANTONIETTA
> There are jobs at the University.

THE SEARCHER
> There are jobs at the University.

LUIGI
> At the university? You know what I think of teachers. They are the eradicators of creativity in young minds everywhere. Their worshiping of administrative laziness makes it such that true ART could sit on their faces AND THEY STILL WOULD NOT SEE IT!

THE SEARCHER
> And what did you mean your time for frolicking with actresses is past?

ANTONIETTA
> What actresses

THE SEARCHER

What actresses

THE SEARCHER

did you frolic with?

LUIGI

None! Where would I find an actress?

THE SEARCHER

But you wish to frolic?

LUIGI

No. I wish to write. Gabriele can frolic all he wants. When his brain goes syphilitic, I'll have one less competitor.

THE SEARCHER

She will be young and fair.

LUIGI

Who?

THE SEARCHER

The actress.

LUIGI

There is no actress!

THE SEARCHER

One day you'll realize what a liar you are.

LUIGI

Calm yourself. We are in public.

THE SEARCHER

Oh yes. I should be calm, shouldn't I? An active female mind does not exist after all.

LUIGI

You were offended by that?

THE SEARCHER

Tell me again what you think of the woman of letters.

LUIGI

You're having another episode. We're leaving.

ANTONIETTA

Didn't you think I could smell the sulfur on my skin when you took me out? **Why did you take me here, away from home?**

LUIGI

Simple. No actress would ever fix my dinner.

> *The Searcher squirts the lemon from her drink into his eye.*

LUIGI

Ah! What has gotten into you?

ANTONIETTA

I was pregnant.

LUIGI

I'll take the job at the university.

Heavy

ANTONIETTA

Rome 1895. Dearest Lina, my head is aching and my body is deformed. I am too big for 6 months! I am afraid that this will be a creature full of nerves, like its mother. I can't go out any more. The other night I dreamed it was a boy. Luigi says he dreamed it was a girl. But dreams are dreams and I don't believe.

THE SEARCHER

I had that dream again last night. I never married you. I was married to this impostor and deep down I knew he wasn't my husband. Something was wrong. So I went to look for you. When I found you, you were married to her and you didn't recognize me at all. You looked right at me and you didn't know me. And you were happy with her. You seemed to enjoy the life you would have had without me. Without me being so . . . so sad all the time . . . I know it's hard to love me. I know because you say I'm still searching, I'll never be happy and it makes you tired. You just want me to stop. Stop looking. So in my dream I went home to the impostor. He knew and I knew. But it was better that way. You were happy. I wanted you to be happy. When I woke up, I watched you sleep, I leaned in very close. I thought if I was quiet enough, I could hear if you were dreaming about me too.

ANTONIETTA

My Lina, I have not left my bed for 10 days. The child does not let me sleep. I am unrecognizable. Completely wasted away. It seems my son is bigger than me and when I look at him I hardly believe he is mine. I can't recognize myself in motherhood. That image of a smiling woman cradling a babe is not my reflection. He won't drink my milk and all I can do is cry and cry. You asked about the baptism. I will let Luigi write on that subject as I am in no mood to celebrate.

LUIGI

My dear sister, it is true that my wife has not left our bedroom for quite some time. I understand her preference. In bed, my real love has always been the sleep that rescued me by allowing me to dream.

THE SEARCHER

Those moments when I'm not dreaming, when my mind is awake, but my body is heavy, the in-between, those are the moments that belong to worry: Maybe I should be a teacher. My work won't survive. I won't survive my work. I should want to be a mother. Maybe that's the only permanence. I ask myself if I actually believe in marriage. I can't decide, but I confirm that I love you. We're different. We're not the institution, the tradition, the patriarchy. I decide I want to die first. I start to think that if you die first it would make a great play. I hate myself for thinking that.

ANTONIETTA

Dear Lina, my son is growing so fast! He's become quite brown which I suppose is my fault and I regret it.

Though it means he must be my son.

THE SEARCHER

She was obviously suffering from postpartum depression. And Luigi—

ANTONIETTA

He was writing. He didn't notice me. He wouldn't have noticed if I had strangled our son to death and flung myself off the roof.

THE SEARCHER

He was distracted. I get distracted too sometimes. Gets me into big trouble. I disappear in the middle of conversations to eavesdrop on another one, or because something is coming together in my mind and I just need to retreat for a moment, **or an hour**. But is it possible to be that oblivious to what your spouse is going through?

ANTONIETTA

Of course. There is always a sacrificial lamb. Some of us choose to be sacrificed. Rome 1896.

Arguments

Luigi and The Character are arguing in his study. The Searcher watches them for a moment.

LUIGI

That's the most preposterous thing I've ever heard! Come back to me when you have a better story.

THE CHARACTER

But it's the truth.

LUIGI

The truth. You cast your wife away like that? With no sense of responsibility?

THE CHARACTER

You are not supposed to judge my actions. Only write.

LUIGI

Only write? I cannot only write. I must interpret, discover, be inspired.

ANTONIETTA

Luigi?

THE SEARCHER

Who's that?

LUIGI

Antonietta. My love, I am so sorry. Why did you get out of bed?

THE SEARCHER

I heard shouting.

LUIGI

I apologize. I was just trying to get some writing done.

THE SEARCHER

You were talking to a character again.

LUIGI

Yes.

THE SEARCHER

Which one? Was that The StepFather?

ANTONIETTA

I was terrified.

LUIGI

How did you know?

THE SEARCHER

He cast his wife away. Like you.

LUIGI

I can't talk to you when you're like this. Do you know how exhausting it is to follow the invisible threads of your logic?

THE SEARCHER

You seemed to be conversing just fine before I got here.

LUIGI

I am very busy. What do you want?

THE SEARCHER

Is it worth it? Are you ever really here, physically and mentally?

LUIGI

I really wish you would sleep.

ANTONIETTA

Sleeping was *your* real love, remember?

Who's the Schizo?

THE SEARCHER

It's not that he talks to his characters that bothers me. It's that they talk back. That sounds schizo to me.

ANTONIETTA

Go back. Repeat. Fold.

THE SEARCHER

Schizophrenia. Catatonic Schizophrenia!

ANTONIETTA

The mines were flooded. My birthright. My home.

Catatonia

THE SEARCHER

Rome 1903. The flood. The catatonia.

> *The Searcher freezes again. She knows Luigi is coming. Every time Luigi interacts with her body, it changes in shape and remains frozen.*

LUIGI

I must take our jewelry to the pawn broker. It will feed the children for a week.

> *Luigi is packing around The Searcher.*

LUIGI

I have come to the only possible solution. Your father hates me and my family; that much is clear. But surely he would take in his daughter and his grandchildren if I was out of the picture. Do you understand, Antonietta? I must die. Without a husband, you can return home. In time, it will feel as though I never existed. As though we were never married. Do you hear me, Antonietta? I must DIE!

ANTONIETTA

Don't move!

> *Luigi gets a shotgun from his desk and holds it to his head. He looks at Searcher and she does not flinch. He points the gun at her: nothing. Luigi suddenly becomes fascinated.*

LUIGI

You really are absent, aren't you, my wife? How interesting.

> *Luigi sits down and begins writing.*

THE SEARCHER

He was fascinated

ANTONIETTA

By my complete inability to cope with reality

THE SEARCHER

He was inspired

ANTONIETTA

By my desire to retreat into the catacombs of my mind. While I transported myself down into the lost mines, he wrote.

THE SEARCHER

He was manipulating my body.

ANTONIETTA

While I mastered the art of disappearing at will, he mastered his art publicly.

THE SEARCHER

Schizophrenia, presenting with catatonia, that's not a diagnosis in the early 1900's ... It's dementia praecox ... First diagnosed by Dr. Emil Kraeplin ... who was lecturing in Bonn ... at the same time Luigi was a student there!

ANTONIETTA

Freeze. Stop time fold.

THE SEARCHER

Bonn. 1891.

ANTONIETTA

No. 1891 is wrong. Not my timeline. Our marriage was not arranged yet. This is my story!

The German Doctor

> *Luigi approaches Dr. K, who is busy packing up his papers.*

LUIGI

I enjoyed your lecture very much.

> *Dr. K does not notice him.*

LUIGI

Excuse me. Dr. Kraepelin?

DR. K

Oh. Hello.

LUIGI

I was intrigued by what you had to say.

DR. K

Thank you.

LUIGI

The study of the human mind. It's a passion of mine.

DR. K

Are you a neurology student?

LUIGI

No. I'm a man of letters. I'm obtaining a degree in Philosophy and Philology—

DR. K

Why did you come to my seminar?

LUIGI

I am interested in constructs of reality. In the power of the mind to reconstruct one's surroundings. I also believe that human psychology helps me to write characters. I'm an author.

DR. K

How nice. I really do need to catch my train back to Heidelberg.

LUIGI

Caterina—

THE SEARCHER

The cousin.

LUIGI

The woman I was engaged to—she suffered from those same episodes you were describing.

ANTONIETTA

Why are we discussing her?

DR. K

The woman you were engaged to? You are no longer engaged?

LUIGI

She's locked away now. I witnessed one of her episodes and I wrote a novella, in the shortest time it has ever taken me to write one. As if something superhuman was guiding my hand, I wrote a story about a man obsessed with a troubled young lady.

DR. K

Ah yes, every writer needs a mad muse.

LUIGI

You said in your talk that the conditions favorable to producing this disease could create latent symptoms that are then exacerbated—

DR. K

You want to know if you caused her breakdown.

DR. K

She was not pleased when I chose to come to Bonn for my studies.

LUIGI

Patients suffering from dementia praecox often fear unwantedness—deriving from maternal deprivation. Had the girl been raised without a mother?

ANTONIETTA
Like me.

LUIGI
No. Her parents. My aunt and uncle, they are very doting parents.

DR. K
You didn't mention she was your cousin. Do you know of any biological factors, then? Family history of madness? Complications at birth?

LUIGI
The family line is very healthy.

DR. K
Social deprivation in youth?

LUIGI
Her parents are protective, but not overly so.

DR. K
I'm afraid the girl you mention has no verifiable factors.

LUIGI
I didn't mean to waste your time.

DR. K
You don't look Sicilian. That is good. I'll be publishing a paper soon proving a predisposition to this mental affliction in certain races. Those who are small, frail and darkly complexioned are at higher risk. Southern blood, for example, makes a resort to the knife, to violent mania, an instinctive act on the slightest provocation. I will be suggesting that these afflictions may eventually be bred out of the general population.

LUIGI
Bred out?

THE SEARCHER
Bred out?

DR. K
I believe psychiatric illness should be observed through experimentation like with the other natural sciences.

LUIGI
You mean working upon the mind to produce the symptoms of the disease?

ANTONIETTA
Fold. Fold.

DR. K
I believe that a man has the right to do anything to a weaker mind.

LUIGI
Even experiment for the sake of art?

ANTOIETTA
This is piercing. All this talk.

DR. K
I am talking about the future of the human race. You are talking about stories.

LUIGI
Forgive me if I believe there is no difference between those two things.

Carriages Part 2

ANTONIETTA

Are you suggesting that he knew before he married me what I could become?

THE SEARCHER

I need to see the arrangement again. Sicily 1893.

> *The Portulano carriage trots away. Signora Pirandello smacks*
> *Luigi behind the ears.*

SIGNORA PIRANDELLO

Maleducato! You embarrassed the girl on your first encounter.

LUIGI

She seems dim.

SIGNORA PIRANDELLO

She's shy! She grew up motherless in a convent.

LUIGI

Maternal and social deprivation. Interesting. How did her mother die?

SIGNORA PIRANDELLO

Giving birth to the girl. It was a difficult pregnancy and—

LUIGI

Complications at birth!

SIGNORA PIRANDELLO

Yes, but not to worry. The nuns assure me she is healthy as a mare. And anyway her saint of a mother died because Portulano went mad temporarily. He would not let the doctor see his wife undressed. A real fit of jealousy.

LUIGI

The father is mad?

SIGNORA PIRANDELLO

Once, he was mad once. That one time. But not to worry. It's mostly gossip. The girl is so calm, she hardly seems—

LUIGI

She'll make a good wife.

SIGNORA PIRANDELLO

Repeat that please.

LUIGI

I will turn her into a real woman. A woman with character.

ANTONIETTA

His characters, the people he built and transformed, it was they he truly loved.

SIGNORA PIRANDELLO

You will go through with the marriage?

LUIGI

She will be my salvation.

SIGNORA PIRANDELLO

Your salvation!

LUIGI

Ah Antonietta. She smells of limes.

ANTONIETTA

His characters had access to him in ways I never did. He knew them intimately. Anyone who was not a character, who could not contribute to the work was dead to him. I *was* jealous. Morbidly jealous.

The Searcher begins to overlap in English after Antonietta begins the following speech.

ANTONIETTA

Hai mai pensato di andar via e non tornare mai piu? Scapare e far perdere ogni tua traccia, per andare in un posto lontano e ricominciare a vivere, vivere una vita nuova, vivere davvero?

THE SEARCHER

Have you ever thought of going away and never coming back? Running away and leaving no trace, to go a faraway place and start living all over again, to live a new life, to truly live?

One Character in Search of a Wife

Mattia Pascal has been summoned by the previous speech.

MATTIA

What's this? The quiet little wife is auditioning for my part. Those are my words.

THE SEARCHER

Mattia Pascal.

MATTIA

The one and only.

THE SEARCHER

Luigi speaks to his characters in private. Why would you appear to his wife?

MATTIA

What makes him so special?

THE SEARCHER

He's the author.

MATTIA

My story is already told. And it's earned your family quite some money.

THE SEARCHER

Yes. Luigi wrote it after the mines flooded. He was suddenly inspired.

MATTIA

You're welcome.

THE SEARCHER

I'm busy. What do you want?

MATTIA

This play will take him away from us. He will start a new life and never look back.

THE SEARCHER

This coming from a man who faked his death to escape his loyal wife.

MATTIA

All husbands fantasize about death.

THE SEARCHER

That's not true.

MATTIA

Of course, if I had a wife like you I wouldn't fake my death.

Mattia grabs her forcefully.

THE SEARCHER

What are you doing?

MATTIA

He will erase us. But we're not dead. We are the ones who live, who feel, who breathe.

THE SEARCHER

You're mistaken. You don't know who I really am.

MATTIA

Or maybe it is only I who knows you. You said it yourself, characters must appear to the author. That play is yours. Destroy it.

THE SEARCHER

I could never do that.

ANTONIETTA

I could. When a character is born, she acquires at once such an independence, even of her own author. She acquires for herself a meaning which the author never thought of giving her.

The Searcher gives in to Mattia's embrace.

THE SEARCHER

Characters are immortal.

MATTIA

Wives are not.

THE SEARCHER

Do you know what happened when I died? What did they do with my body?

Mattia breaks away from her.

MATTIA

I forgot I was conversing with a nut. YOU MUST STOP HIM from staging this play.

THE SEARCHER

Why does it bother you so much?

MATTIA

You said it. In a novel, I am immortal, unchangeable. My story will live through the ages. Theatre is ephemeral. It is lowly. It will put me in many bodies and change my story depending on the whims of such lunatics as actors and such egomaniacs as directors.

THE SEARCHER

He will be lauded for bringing Italian theatre out of the dark ages. Sicily will forget clowns and marionettes and buffoonery. Generations to come will know Luigi Pirandello had talent.

MATTIA

Does he?

ANTONIETTA

Does he?

THE SEARCHER
>That part is undeniable.

MATTIA
>Or is he merely observing?

THE SEARCHER
>Observing me?

ANTONIETTA
>Observing me.

MATTIA
>It's all you. Every word is you. Since the change.

THE SEARCHER
>The change?

MATTIA
>You wear the mask of madness now.
>
>>*Mattia places an identical mask to Antonietta's on The Searcher.*

Wrecked

ANTONIETTA
>Rome 1918. The night I realized I was transformed. Fold.
>
>>*Antonietta removes her mask. Now The Searcher is the only masked one. They have switched places, in a way.*
>>
>>*The Searcher throws the play on the ground and squats to pee. A mirror of the moment at the top of the play.*

LUIGI
>You ruined it. You ... why would you?

THE SEARCHER
>That wife. That terrible wife. She's not me.

LUIGI
>The play is not about you. How many times do I need to tell you to distinguish my work from reality.

THE SEARCHER
>She doesn't do anything. I'm searching. She's not searching.

LUIGI
>What are you searching for?

THE SEARCHER
>You.

LUIGI
>Here I am, Antonietta!

THE SEARCHER
>No, you go away. You talk to your characters. You disappear inside your mind.
>
>>*The Searcher moves into the shadows. Luigi follows. The argument continues behind the screen.*

LUIGI
>I am here. You won't let me near you. You won't let me touch you.

THE SEARCHER
You once spoke to me as though I gave you joy, your muglieri bedda.
LUIGI
You did once.
THE SEARCHER
And now?
LUIGI
You've changed.

> *The Searcher freezes in place, catatonic. In the following scene, Antonietta can manipulate her body.*

Jenny

ANTONIETTA
Change. My husband did not favor change. Jenny, his lover from his days in Bonn, wrote him a letter when they were both old and near death and I had been locked away for over a decade. She wrote, let's see one another one last time. Luigi wrote back. He was very touched. But he preferred to remember Jenny as a young student and to die with only good memories of the way she was. "Good" meaning "not old" and "not saggy" and "not mad." Or not *too mad*. Just enough madness to be a muse, to be controlled. The truth is he had recently fallen out with our daughter because she chose to marry and move far away. This news did not surprise me. He wallowed in the throes of depression until he met the young actress, Marta Abba. Then all was right again.
The worst thing a girl could do in Luigi's eyes was change. Grow up. Become a woman.

Reality

> *The Librarian enters. The Searcher is frozen in a position he takes to be normal. Or at least normal for her. He notices the increased disarray of the library.*

THE LIBRARIAN
La signora, Miss Honeymoon, your husband—You forget all about him. He eat 3 arancini, 6 canoli and a lot of espresso. La vedova Saracino is feeding him. You should go before she eat him. He looks like a tasty man.

My Wife's Madness

ANTONIETTA
Rome. 1919.

> *The Searcher unfreezes. In her new masked form, she watches Luigi almost like a predatory animal would.*

LUIGI

My dear colleague and friend, Gabriele, perhaps it's already been a while since the news of my irremediably tragic familial conditions have reached your ears. Is that true? My wife, dear Gabriele, has been mad for years. Since the collapse of our family mines. And I am my wife's madness—which certainly proves that hers is a true madness—I, I who have always lived for my family, exclusively, and for my work, exiled from all human contact, so as not to give her, so as not to give her madness, the slightest reason to suspect me.

This has changed nothing, unfortunately, because nothing can help. La pazzia di mia moglie sono io.

ANTONIETTA

We're like so many puppets hung on the wall, waiting for someone to come and move us or make us talk.

THE SEARCHER

You're an impostor. You think I don't know. When you go into your study and shut the door. All the voices.

Always watching me. Always laughing at me. At your mad wife. You are making me this way! I can't move, I can't breathe, without you and your minions watching, watching me. And the children look right through me, as though I were a ghost in this house, they wish I was dead, all children should have dead mothers, maybe I am dead, maybe you are my punishment for being such a bad girl, such a wretched little girl who killed her mother. I want my daddy. Papa! Papa, come get me! I want my father. At least he knew I was bad and he told me I was bad and he treated me like I was bad. No lies, no pretense. I'm bad not mad. Bad and sad.

LUIGI

It is convenient to insist that certain people are mad.

THE SEARCHER

Incest! Incest! My husband and my daughter! He is in love with his own daughter.
There is more commotion in shadow. We see a figure with a gun. A gunshot is heard.

LUIGI

You are sick. Oh, this is catching! This is catching, this madness! Our daughter tried to kill herself! Is that what you wanted?

THE SEARCHER

Is that what you wanted?

LUIGI

I have been patient. I have tried to live my life at the mercy of your illness but I can not do that any longer if it means our child's life is in danger.

THE SEARCHER

Give me a divorce and I will go.

LUIGI

You can get a divorce. I won't stop you.

THE SEARCHER

Good.

LUIGI

But first you need to be deemed mentally sound.

ANTONIETTA
    How?
THE SEARCHER
    How?

Redemption

ANTONIETTA
    Rome. 1924.
THE SEARCHER
    A letter.
ANTONIETTA
    A fold.
THE SEARCHER
    A folded letter.
ANTONIETTA
    Hand delivered by a wrinkled nun.
THE SEARCHER
    Sister Nella?
ANTONIETTA
    Nella died. This was a different nun.
Luigi
    My love, when I think of you in that place I wonder how we've arrived here. You
    and I. I don't have a home without you. Please return to me and we can go on as
    before. I have written a letter to the hospital regarding your release. You need
    only consent and you will be discharged. The head doctor says you've shown
    improvement and may be suited to home care at this stage.
ANTONIETTA
    Dear husband, it is true I have changed a great deal. For one thing, I have improved
    at writing letters. I have spent the last five years waiting for you to send word and
    release me. I hoped that eventually you would feel guilt over the lies and pretense
    you used to get me to come here. If I recall correctly, I was promised a divorce.
    And yet, here I am, still your wife. I will not be reprising my role. I would rather
    play the insane patient than the obedient wife. I have found a sort of happiness
    here. They have told you I am fit to release? I don't believe I'm well enough at
    all. I'm mad, don't you remember? I am not myself. I wear a different face now, a
    terrible mask, which is no longer a mask, but madness, madness personified. You
    should use that line in a play. Consider it my last gift to you. Goodbye.
        Antonietta stabs herself in the thigh.

You're Not Me

    *The Searcher feels the pain once again. Is shocked into awareness, removes
    the mask. Now the folds have been completely pierced. The Searcher can
    see Antonietta for the first time.*

THE SEARCHER

Why would you do that?

ANTONIETTA

One of us is in the wrong fold. Or is this a new fold?

THE SEARCHER

Why would you throw your freedom away like that?

ANTONIETTA

I did no such thing. I made a choice. The first choice I ever made.

THE SEARCHER

And the last. You stayed in confinement voluntarily? You chose 35 more years of solitude.

ANTONIETTA

Meglio sola che male accompagnata.

THE SEARCHER

I'm an idiot. I believed you didn't deserve to be locked up. Apparently you did.

ANTONIETTA

What right do you have to judge me?

THE SEARCHER

This is not what I wanted to find.

ANTONIETTA

Well boo hoo. I am not your cause. I am a person. You wanted me to be a victim so that you could save me. Now you find I don't need saving and you're disappointed?

THE SEARCHER

Did you lie about the incest?

ANTONIETTA

Is it a lie if I am mad? Or is it a lie because I'm mad. Can it be the truth even though I'm mad?

THE SEARCHER

The truth is important.

ANTONIETTA

Life is full of infinite absurdities—

THE SEARCHER

Which do not need to appear plausible because they are true. Don't quote your husband at me! This is important. I wanted to expose the truth for every woman who has ever been called a lying crazy bitch. Do you understand? It's a responsibility we have.

ANTONIETTA

Not we. You are not me. I am not every woman. Every woman is not you.

THE SEARCHER

No one knows your name.

ANTONIETTA

Yes. Probably the other Marie Antoinette is better known.

THE SEARCHER

You're a footnote.

ANTONIETTA

What's so bad about that?

THE SEARCHER

    I would never want—

ANTONIETTA

    Ah. YOU would never want to be a footnote. Why are you so afraid of disappearing, Mrs—what's your name?

THE SEARCHER

    His plays were garbage before he shattered your mind and spilled it onto the page, and you know it! You are his body of work.

ANTONIETTA

    Speaking of bodies.

THE SEARCHER

    Where is it?

ANTONIETTA

    I chose confinement. What do you do with the corpse of a madwoman who must be erased?

THE SEARCHER

    No. No. No.

ANTONIETTA

    Rome is eternal.

THE SEARCHER

    They never sent your body home.

ANTONIETTA

    Are you mad?

THE SEARCHER

    No!

ANTONIETTA

    Barren.

THE SEARCHER

    What?

ANTONIETTA

    Are you more afraid of being unloved or unknown?

THE SEARCHER

    You aren't supposed to know me.

ANTONIETTA

    I know that you cannot, no matter how hard you try, escape the dreadful silence that follows you. The silence that keeps you awake at night so that you must fill it with thoughts. Grinding your teeth, sweating, pulling his body closer but feeling no comfort, because you're searching

THE SEARCHER

    What am I searching for?

ANTONIETTA

    I couldn't speak for you, though I have my theories.

THE SEARCHER

    You! I was searching for you.

ANTONIETTA

You found me. Life is long. Death is longer. My choices were not your choices. Confinement in society or confinement locked away. For me, it was better to be folded over.

> *Antonietta kisses her on the forehead.*

ANTONIETTA

The burial ground is behind the asylum in the outskirts of Rome. You should be satisfied. I am.

THE SEARCHER

And if I'm not satisfied?

ANTONIETTA

I recognized you from the start. I know your type. I was married to your type.

> *Antonietta exits.*

A High Honour

THE LIBRARIAN

Basta. One hour is over. I give tour now. And your husband said he is leaving for Palermo international airport in 5 minutes, wife or no wife. Did you keep promise?

THE SEARCHER

Sorry?

THE LIBRARIAN

You make index card for Antonietta?

THE SEARCHER

She would prefer not to be unfolded.

LIBRARIAN

So all this mess is for what?

> *The Searcher looks at him, he exits. She looks around at the mess.*
> *Then she looks out at the audience, still searching.*

FRESCO

2102
Lucia Frangione

"During the Second World War, 31,000 Italian Canadians were labelled enemy aliens, and then fingerprinted, scrutinized and forced to report to local registrars once a month. Just over 600 men were detained and sent to war. They were business owners, workers and doctors, they were fathers, daughters and friends. When the authorities came to their door, when they were detained, there were no formal charges, no ability to defend themselves in an open and fair trial, no chance to present or rebut evidence. Yet, still, they were taken away to Petawawa or to Fredericton, to Kananaskis or to Kingston. Once they arrived at the camp, there was no length of sentence. Sometimes the internment lasted a few months; sometimes it lasted years, but the impact lasted a lifetime. These are stories that have gone untold for far too long, stories that have been silenced by shame and fear. This is injustice that has laid heavy on far too many generations."
  —**Prime Minister Justin Trudeau**, May 27, 2021,
  Apology for the Internment of Italian Canadians During WW II

The original production was developed with the Bellaluna Ensemble
Susan Bertoia, Aaron Freschi, Stefano Giulianetti and Marco Soriano
Italian translation by Stefano Giulianetti and Marco Soriano
Furlan translation by Marisa De Franceschi
Special thanks to Ray Culos and Lynne Bowen
and dramaturg DD Kugler

This story is dedicated to Nonna and Nonno.

Fresco was originally produced by Bellaluna Productions in association with The Vancouver Italian Cultural Centre as part of the A Question Of Loyalty exhibit, funded by the Government of Canada. It premiered at the Shadbolt Centre March 21–24 2012 and the VECC March 27–31 2012. It was directed by James Fagan Tait and starred Susan Bertoia (Rosina, Young Rosi, Nunzio) Stefano Giulianetti (Gaetano, Rosi) Michael Rinaldi (Michael, Ninetta) and Marco Soriano (Alessandro, Cecilia). Set and props were designed by Catherine Hahn, sound by Paul Tedeschini, costumes by Carmen Alatorre, multimedia by Flick Harrison and stage managed by Ben Cheung.

CAST LIST

Rosina Marino—42, pregnant. She's a Canadian of Italian and English heritage (Michael's daughter). She is performance artist. She speaks English with a Canadian accent.

Michael Marino—89, [17 when WWII begins] a retired lawyer, Rosi and Gaetano's son. Born in Canada. He speaks English with a Canadian accent.

Alessandro Bertin—late 30s. A barber. Born in Veneto, Italy. He speaks Italian and English with an Italian accent.

Gaetano Marino—mid 40s. Gaetano runs a boarding house and coffee shop. Michael's father. Born in Calabria. Speaks Italian and English with an Italian accent.

Young Rosi Marino—mid 40s. Gaetano's wife, Michael's mother, laundress and boarding house manager. Born in Friuli. Speaks Carnic Furlan, a bit of Italian and broken English with a heavy Furlan accent.

Nonna Chorus:

Rosi—mid 80s [can be doubled with Gaetano]. This is Young Rosi as an old Nonna. Speaks Italian around the other Nonnas, and her English is much better though it still is spoken with a Furlan accent.

Cecilia—mid 80s [can be doubled with Alessandro] a Nonna in black. Rosi's sister, speaks with a Furlan accent.

Ninetta—mid 80s [can be doubled with Michael] a Nonna in black. A friend of the family. Speaks with an Italian accent.

Charles (Carlos) Marega—68 [can be doubled with Rosina] a sculptor. A friend of the family. Speaks English with a slight Italian accent.

Nunzio—60s. [can be doubled with Rosina] a shoemaker.

Judge H—50s [can be doubled with Michael] a judge.

SETTING

Strathcona, Vancouver, BC 1938–2013

Scene One

> A two-storey house, circa 1914, Union street, Vancouver.
> The front door is the gateway into the history this house holds
> its primary point of tension being 1938–43. Outside is the
> present day. Around the house and its neglected articles, waits
> and rumbles a ghost world of Italian-ness. The Strathcona
> garden gate may have crumbling lions, reminiscent of the Lion's
> Gate bridge. A crow perches. Caws. Pecks. Shakes off the rain.
> A snatch of distant music ..."Cassetta In Canada"

... Quando Martin vedete solo per la città forse voi penserete Dove girando va. Solo, senza una meta. Solo ... ma c'è un perché: Aveva una casetta piccolina in

Canada con vasche, pesciolini e tanti fiori di lillà, e tutte le ragazze che passavano di là dicevano "Che bella la casetta in Canada"!

> *[When you see Martin alone in the city perhaps you'll wonder where he's wandering to. Alone, without a goal. Alone ... but there's a reason: He had a little house in Canada with tanks, fish, and many lilacs, and all the girls who passed that way said "What a beautiful little house in Canada ...!"]*
>
> *Curiously, a big white embroidered tablecloth hangs, and who knows for how long, on the clothesline.*
> *It is a crisp bright day. The crow caws, caws ...*
> *Rosina enters. She carries a folded black umbrella in one hand and tucked under her other arm is a sign on a stake, obscured by her black jacket. The crow continues to caw ... did it just say ...?*

CROW

Caw caw . Fresco! Si ... Fresco. Brrrr ...

> *Nah. She stands in front of the old house for a moment and stares at it. Sighs, sadly remembering.*

ROSINA

Hello, old house ...

> *She looks over at the laundry, how odd. She touches the tablecloth, curious.*

ROSINA

Whose laundry is this?

> *She heads up the stairs and knocks with authority, scattering crows. She knocks again and yells through the window to any possible squatters.*

ROSINA

Is anybody still home? The lease expired a month ago, all tenants should be cleared out ... Michael Marino was your landlord ... I'm his daughter. I'm putting the house up for sale.

> *She decides they're gone. She heads back down the stairs and stabs the "For Sale By Owner" sign into the front lawn.*
> *Suddenly, the whole house gasps as though the front yard itself has been punctured painfully. The wind whips into a frenzy, rain begins to pelt, a murder of crows swoop down on Rosina as she is blown in circles trying to hoist her umbrella. The tablecloth billows and out rolls like a bocce ball a little red kerchiefed black clad old Nonna Rosi. She sits up, startled.*

ROSI

Che?! [what?!] I justa roll over in my grave. Why?

ROSINA

incredulous Nonna?!

ROSI

tender when she notices Rosina ... *but sees the "for sale by owner" sign, gasps* Oddio! [dear God!] Not the house!

ROSINA
Dad told me to sell it …!
Rosi yells to the sky in full Medusa rage.

ROSI
Where is my son?! Michael!
The elements rage with her and this yell of Rosi's evokes Michael
who is dropped out of the sky by crows. He falls with a scream
behind the house. He enters, an old man, dusting himself off,
pissed.

MICHAEL
Ma! What do you want?!

ROSINA
Dad!

ROSI
I give you my key to the house with the lucky golden horn, why?! You promise
me you never sell the house!
Rosi snatches the house key out of Rosina's hand.

MICHAEL
Yeah, I promised. But my daughter did not! The house is dilapidated now, Ma …

ROSI
That's because you rent it out for twenty years instead of move there with your
wife …!

MICHAEL
Strathcona is a slum!

ROSINA
It's starting to gentrify …

MICHAEL
Maybe if you had moved to Commercial Drive in the sixties with the other
Italians—

ROSI
The other Italians make the nest like the crow.

CECILIA
Caw caw!

ROSI
They fly from Strathcona to the Commercial Drive, to the Burnaby, and then
that's it. They sleep. But not us. Why move? Gaetano built this house with his
own hand. We stay!
Crows flutter at a safe distance, Michael eyes them suspiciously.

MICHAEL
to Rosina You should get eight fifty for the land at least, the house is a tear down.
Another gasp from the Nonnas, unseen.

ROSINA
What?! It's a beautiful old home. Whoever buys it can apply for Heritage status—

ROSI
The foundation is good!

MICHAEL
The roof is shot, it needs to be rewired, re-plumbed … there's nothing worth keeping.

A crack of thunder or the like. Whispered collective voices of
Nonnas make Michael and Rosina freeze in their tracks.

VOICE OF NONNAS

You think there is nothing left. But the house is full of us.

They cackle quietly, amidst broody crows. Rosina is startled and
spins around as a newspaper blows by and smacks Michael in the
face, carrying him off. Mandolin music as the Nonnas dominate.
Cecilia, a Nonna, emerges from the shadows.

ROSINA

Dad!

CECILIA

What about Zia Cecilia's bomboniere you love? The Capodimonte shepherd girl?
Her sheep all covered with dust, still back of the cupboard ...

The Nonna chorus "baas" like sheep, unseen. Ninetta emerges
from the shadows then fades away again.

NINETTA

What about the bottle of Nonno Gaetano's grappa he hide in the basement? He
too proud to use the cane, fall down the stairs and die ...?

Rosina relives the falling, as she walks down the front door
stairs. Rosi unfolds a picture of St Anthony in her palm.

ROSI

And what the about the sticker of St. Anthony they paint over in the bedroom?
The saint I pray to before I kiss my rosary goodnight and pass away in my sleep?

Cecilia brings out the mandolin in her arms, as though it were
a hurt child.

CECILIA

What about your father's mandolin up in the attic? The spiders they spin the new
string?

Rosi and Cecilia and crows dance around Rosina playing the
broken mandolin badly and cornering Rosina so she's got her
back up against the "For Sale by owner" sign.

ROSI and CECILIA

Don't sell the house, non vendere la casa, non vendere la casa ... *[don't sell the house]*

Michael enters again, grabs the mandolin and tosses it aside
with disdain.

MICHAEL

How is she going to keep it, Ma?

ROSI

Make this your home, Rosina!

ROSINA

Nonna, Dad's right. Even if I get a couple of renters downstairs and buy out my
brother's half, I'm going to have a four hundred thousand dollar mortgage—

MICHAEL

And she'll have no money for renovations. She'll be house poor. Rose, let it go.

ROSINA

You always Anglicize my name. Call me Rosina!

NONNAS
Si!
MICHAEL
You don't even speak Italian.
NONNAS
Si!
ROSINA
Whose fault is that?
NONNAS
Papà!
ROSINA
You were never around enough to teach me.
NONNAS
Si!
ROSINA
You were always in court.
MICHAEL
You want to preserve your heritage? Then take Italian lessons at the Italian Cultural Centre. Don't get sentimental about a building. Life here was not so Beautiful, Principessa. [*Princess*]
NONNAS
The girl has respect for her family, unlike you!
MICHAEL
to Rosi Don't talk to me about respect, I named her after you, didn't I?
> *Rosi snaps the sky and it suddenly turns all warm and sunny.*
> *She and Cecilia lead Rosina into an Italian heritage moment.*
ROSI
And I was named after my Nonna Rosina and she was named after her Nonna Rosina ...
MICHAEL
And each one of those roses was a real thorn in the side.
ROSI
We were all born in Friuli. On the farm. In the house made of the white stone—
CECILIA
And it crumble like a block of the goat cheese. And it hang off a cliff in the middle of the Carnic Alps.
ROSI AND CECILIA AND ROSINA SIGH WITH NOSTALGIA, CECILIA STRUMS THE MANDOLIN.
ROSINA
Then why did you leave?
MICHAEL
They were uneducated, superstitious, dirt poor. If they had a cavity, they'd pull the tooth right out of their own mouth. One of the reasons why Nonna Rosi never smiles.
ROSI
ignores Michael In Friuli, Mamma run the farm with me and Cecilia. We have the garden, the chicken ... the sheep.

MICHAEL

But they didn't drink fancy cappuccino, they drank crap chicory. And they didn't eat osso bucco. They ate whatever they could find the hooves, the brains, the pig snout. *pushes his nose up like a pig*

ROSI

The muso! *[snout]* Hey, my muset *[cotechino]* taste better than your business lunch rib eye steak for the snob! *She pushes her nose up like a stuck up pig*

MICHAEL

I'm saying being Italian isn't so romantic!

CECILIA

butts in to keep the story going for Rosina Anyway! In Friuli ... we'd we cut the wool, the sheep all skinny, so cute all shy. And we do with the weave to make the blanket.

ROSI

And we sell in the market. Our Father send the money when he work in Canada. We had a good life.

> *Another sigh of nostalgia.*

CECILIA

But then Mamma got the tumor in the stomach and she die.

ROSI

So we come to Halifax. On a boat. Nineteen days.

MICHAEL

Then six days on a CPR to Trail, BC.

ROSI

Our father, he work at the smelter. I never know him since I was the baby.

CECILIA

He ashame because we dress Italian with three dress on top the other not warm for the weather.

ROSI

He was the big man with the big fat hand—

CECILIA

With a new wife already I hate. I marry Vittorio, Rosi marry Gaetano—

MICHAEL

And they all got the hell out of Trail.

ROSI

Your Nonno Gaetano built this house 1914. Then I have Rossano, Matteo, Orisia, Marino, Giuseppe and then this one. *smacks Michael's head* The black sheep.

MICHAEL

Why am I the black sheep? I'm the only one with a university degree!

ROSI

And you're the only one who don't speak Furlan or Italian! I'm a very proud to have a lawyer of a son. But you all the book smart, not the heart smart.

MICHAEL

If this is about Papà, he can come out here and *yells to the house* fight like a man!

ROSI

All these years, you still don't forgive?

ROSINA

Forgive what?

MICHAEL

You wouldn't understand, Rosina.

ROSINA

Understand what?

> *NONNAs converge and expand with a murder of crows that*
> *swoop down and shoo MICHAEL away with defiance.*

NONNAS

Let the girl judge for herself! Vattene! *[go away]*

> *Michael is shooed off.*

ROSI

So. Why can't you handle the mortgage, Rosina? You got the good job? You went
to university.

ROSINA

I studied performance art, Nonna.

ROSI

Cosa?! *[what]*

CECILIA

Non lo so. *[I don't know] forced polite* I would like to see you perform—you get
the free tick for the family?

ROSINA

It isn't theatre, it's the anti-thesis of theatre. Never mind.

ROSI

But you get paid?

ROSINA

Well, all I had this month was an Abramović inspired sitting with the disenfranchised
on Main and Hastings. It was only twenty four hours and we didn't get a grant.

CECILIA

How you gonna make money you only do one show and you don' sell tick and
it's not on the stage?! Ma che strane queste cose! Non ci capisco niente *[I don't
understand, this is so stupidly strange]*

> *Rosina smiles tightly. Tricky.*

ROSI

Ma smettila, Cecilia! *[back off Cecilia] turns* Rosina, relax. We gon' help you with
your life. But first, you want Juice, Coke, Fresca, Orangina, Chinotto, espresso,
anisette? What you want?

ROSINA

I want you to teach me your language sitting here on the front porch, I want to
dip pizzelle in honey in the kitchen, I want to plant peppers and tomatoes in the
garden Nonna … I want to live up to your name, but I think it's too late. There's
nothing Italian left in me, and yet people hear "Rosina Marino" they assume I
can cook, sing opera and my Nonno is a Mafia hit man.

ROSI

Your Nonno had nothing to do with the Camorra. And the fifth column no exist
ghost! They say la mano nera?! *[the black hand]*

CECILIA

Your Dad tell you Nonno was "al fresco?"

ROSINA
    Al fresco?!
ROSI
    Shh!
NINETTA
    A fascist?
ALL NONNAS
    SHH!
ROSINA
    No, no, it's a joke, Nonna.
ROSI
    Who joke?
ROSINA
    Me, Nonna, nobody. Me …
ROSI
    squints Not funny. You are Italian with your blood! And some, they think Italian
    we break the strike, we all got the knife in the back. People jealous because we
    not afraid of nothing. We cheat the system? Yeah. So what. The system it cheats
    us first. And then the war, Madonna mia. We make the best, even if we only got
    the scrap. And so will you!
NONNAS
    Arrangiarsi!
ROSINA
    What is arrangiarsi?
NINETTA
    How you say in English?
CECILIA
    Making do.
ROSI
    Even if everybody take the grape and we only get the skin … we gon' make brovada
    with the turnip!
NONNAS
    Arrangiarsi!
ROSI
    Even if everybody take the pure silk and we only got the old bed sheet we gon'
    crochet the edge with the ricamo linen on the table. Ha!
NONNAS
    Arrangiarsi!
ROSI
    People don't pay for the performance art? Then find something they do! Work with
    your hands. Don't let anyone call you the small head.
ROSINA
    The small head, Nonna?
ROSI
    Si.

CECILIA

Italians, Spanish, Greek, all the small head. You see the English, head like melone. That's why the English the woman they die when they got the baby.

NINETTA

Melone on the stick for the head.

ROSI

The government with the doctor say big head make more smart. Only big heads for to come to Canada. Only the small heads when they need the hard work done.

CECILIA

But Italians—we work with our hands and we build this city!

NINETTA

With the Chinese. The Cinese.

ROSI

Chinese work hard.

CECILIA

Same the Filipino.

NINETTA

Nice small head like a chestnut.

ROSI

Your Nonno, he was the first once on the street he build the toilet in the house. The first to have the lion on the gate. The first to grow the grape! We keep this house until we die. And you better keep this house until you die!

ROSINA

But Nonna, I'm an artist—

ROSI

So you're poor. Ma. So what.

NONNAS

Arrangiarsi.

ROSI

That is the English side, it get all the panic when you have no money. Boo hoo.

CECILIA

Not all the English are bad. Especial your Mom.

ROSI

Her family, I like.

CECILIA

And the Irish. They're clean.

ROSINA

They're clean?

CECILIA

The soap with the man in the wood. I like. The Irish spring.

NINETTA

Ahh ... *remembers now* Irish Spring *signature whistles* "and I like it too"!

ROSI

Vancouver, 1940s, for sure you know we are in *British* Columbia.

NINETTA

It is the Italians who are the poor ...

ROSINA
>Really?

CECILIA
>Now, the poor is the Vietnamese. Same thing.

ROSI
>But we made it through the depression, you can make it through 2012, Ma—.

NINETTA
>The Italians, we bring the sun.

ROSINA
>How?

ROSI
>Ros*ina*, you cannot get out of bed without the poor. You want clean sheet?

CECILIA
>Clean shave.

NINETTA
>Shoe shine.

ROSI
>Caffe.

CECILIA
>Newspaper deliver when the sun come up …

NINETTA
>Right there in the bottom of our apron.

ROSI
>in our cup.

CECILIA
>in our hand—

NONNAS
>We bring the sun.

Scene Two

> *Italian sunrise. It should be industrious, bright, social, hopeful,*
> *cheerful.*
> *Some images to play with, up for interpretation, but should be*
> *a pattern that gets repeated later:*
> *black kerchiefs fly up, birds flying at dawn, Vancouver wakes*
> *up with Italians knocking on the boarding house doors to wake*
> *people up,"Buon giorno!". Laundry being snapped and folded,*
> *steam from the espresso maker, SHHHCH SHHHCH*
> *SHHHHHCH, train chug, streetcar ding, shoveling coal,*
> *furnace door slamming shut, shoe shine, newspaper called out,*
> *"L'Eco", barber clips, mandolin and singing as café tables are*
> *put outside and chairs set right side up. The sequence should*
> *end with: they all snap back an espresso.*

ALL
    Ahhh!
                    Crow caws. They all watch it fly over their heads.

ALL
    pleased Fresco.

Scene Three

                    An idea builds . . .

ROSINA
    You used to have a coffee shop in the front. Didn't you? In the forties.
                    Nonnas whisper unseen
NONNAS
    Si . . .
ROSINA
    I wonder if that means the house still has commercial zoning?
NONNAS
    Si . . .
ROSINA
    Then I could do the same thing!
NONNAS
    Si!
ROSINA
    I could turn it back to its former glory, put some tables outside, call it "Fresco!"
                    Michael storms up and grabs the cup out of Rosina's hand.
MICHAEL
    Are you crazy? It wasn't just a coffee shop, it was a boarding house in the back and
    a barbershop in the front. They all lived upstairs.
ROSINA
    What barbershop?
MICHAEL
    Rosina, you know nothing about business. You're an artist. *Michael goes over and
    covers Rosi's ears about Rosina's indiscreet lifestyle* You do your little prancing around
    in Milan with the transvestites—
ROSINA
    covers Cecilia's ears We don't say that word anymore, Dad. It was a fluid-sexual
    Fluid-cultural exploration of identity, yes—
MICHAEL
    You dip yourself in polenta and fly around naked—if your Nonna Rosi knew
    about that one she would roll over in her grave again.
ROSI
    not hearing I would what? What?
ROSINA
    I only did that once. And it was semolina.

MICHAEL
Once! Who in their right mind does that and then asks people to pay for it?
Do something normal!

CECILIA
not hearing anything I cannot hear, something wrong with my ear ...
Michael and Rosina release the Nonnas

ROSINA
I won't cater to the bourgeoisie!

MICHAEL
The only people who complain about the bourgeoisie are the ones who owe them
money.

CECILIA
With the university you could also be a teacher—

ROSI
Or a lawyer like your Papà—

CECILIA
Or the pharmacy. So I always get the right pill for the heart and the *indicates bowel
obstruction* per la stitichezza. *[for the constipation]*

MICHAEL
She's an artist, Mamma. I want her to do something she loves, but something great!
We didn't leave Italy and work this hard for you to make coffee.

ROSINA
I know but I can't live hand to mouth anymore. Maybe I could put a little stage in
the corner, have performances on the weekend. A coffee shop could be fun and it
would bring the family business back to life.

MICHAEL
It's dead for a reason.

ROSINA
What are you ashamed of?

MICHAEL
Nothing! I fought in WW 2 and liberated Italy. Not like Bertin with his bust of
Mussolini.

ROSINA
Who?

    *Alessandro Bertin pokes his head out the window, finally
    someone calls his name.*

ALESSANDRO
Alessandro Bertin barber. And business partner with your Nonno Gaetano. Alla
sua disposizione signorina. *[at your service]*

MICHAEL
Here's another one who complains about the bourgeoisie!

    *He crawls out the window and approaches Rosina charmingly,
    drawing her into a dance, Michael argues for her attention.*

ALESSANDRO
Ah ... Rosina, you're as beautiful as your Nonna Rosi, like a key cut for the same
door. Oopah! *Dips her*

MICHAEL

He's a fascist!

ALESSANDRO

All the men in my family are good looking. But unfortunately all the Bertin
women look just like me with a bun. And that is the luck of my sister.

MICHAEL

Parasite!

ALESSANDRO

Interesting to be called a parasite by you, Michael, who lived off my family's
money for ten years. *To Rosina* To understand why your Nonno and I spent
World War two Al Fresco ...

ROSINA

You spent it what?

ALESSANDRO

Al Fresco.

MICHAEL

There's no need for her to know!

ALESSANDRO

You have to understand Mussolini and why Italy loved him. To understand that
you have to know what it is like to be so poor you split an egg eight ways on
Sunday. Right, Gaetano?

> *Gaetano pops his head out of the same window Alessandro*
> *came from.*

GAETANO

So, show the girl. Forza, racconta! *[tell her the story]*

ROSINA

Nonno! My God, I've almost forgotten what you look like.

GAETANO

I'm an innocent man, Rosina.

MICHAEL

No. No, you weren't.

> *Gaetano slams the window shut, angrily.*

ALESSANDRO

Rosina, do you really want to come in through this door and enter the house of
your family?

MICHAEL

Don't do it!

> *Offers the door, she reaches towards the knob.*

ROSINA

Yes.

ALESSANDRO

I will give you a day in July, nineteen thirty eight. To understand, you will have
to become like your Nonna Rosi. You will have to contend with your Nonno,
Gaetano. And your father, Michael, when he was a boy. And, you will have to
contend with me.

MICHAEL

Rosina, please ... be careful what you open ...

ROSINA
    I agree.

Scene Four

> *Rosina reaches for the door and opens it. The door spins and
> the whole world transforms into Union Street July, 1938. The
> mood should be jovial, inter-cultural, harmonious but gritty
> around the edges, poor. Some suggested historic images to play
> with: a game of Mungo Sungo on Powell, Chinese merchants
> on Pender, Jewish junk cart "any bottles and rags?" Italian
> vendors "anybody want coallllll?" Theatre going women with
> long yellow bird of paradise feathers hanging down their back.
> Bootleggers, prostitutes. Sacred Heart's church bell ringing for
> vespers. Laundry sheets, folding them, snapping them, it turns
> into the barber bib over the customer. The sequence should end
> with: Michael enters, a sixteen year old boy playing the mandolin.
> He is singing a lighter happy rendition of Russ Columbo's
> Prisoner Of Love, Gaetano may join him in snatches as he sets
> up the coffee shop, but they're soon over-ridden by the Nonnas.*

MICHAEL
    Alone from night to night, you'll find me
    too weak to break the chains that bind me
    I need no shackles to remind me
    I'm just a prisoner of love
MICHAEL/GAETANO:
    for one command, I stand and wait now
    from one who's master of my fate now
    I can't escape, for it's too late now
    I'm just a prisoner of love ...
> *Nonna chorus parade overtakes Michael. They are full of
> newspapers, patriotism, pride, Italian flags, picnic baskets, they
> do a little fascist song, Giovenezza. They surreptitiously place a
> bust of Mussolini in Alessandro's barbershop while they sing.*

NONNAS
    Giovinezza, Giovinezza,
    Primavera di bellezza
    Per la vita, nell'asprezza
    Il tuo canto squilla e va!
    E per Benito Mussolini,
    Eja eja alalà
    E per la nostra Patria bella,
    Eja eja alalà ...
    [Youth, Youth, the beautiful springtime of life, in times of hardship your song rings
    out! And for Benito Mussolini, hooray hooray hooray, and for our beautiful
    Homeland, hooray hooray hooray ...]

Scene Five

Young Rosi shushes and shoos the marching Nonnas off the street.
She grabs her broom, notices the brush end is screwed off the
pole. Alessandro enters with flourish, snaps his fingers and tosses
Michael a pair of black shoes.

ALESSANDRO

Michael, I want to see my face shining back at me.
Michael grabs the shoes and heads out to the porch with his
brushes, calling back a challenge:

MICHAEL

Minichiello has offered me five cents more an hour at the Dodson hotel ...

ALESSANDRO

O, then go. And pay for your own room and board.

GAETANO

You hear how good my boy is getting on the mandolin? Soon he can join the band.

YOUNG ROSI

Michael, what you do my broom? And why you wet?

MICHAEL

We went rafting up False Creek ...

ALESSANDRO

making fun, poling with the stick Aren't you a little old to be playing Tom Sawyer?
Gaetano corrects Young Rosi's English, gives her a newspaper.

GAETANO

"what ARE you doing WITH my broom" Rosi. Here. Read. Learn English.

YOUNG ROSI

No sta dimi cemûd fevela, tu che tu crôds di save dût. No sai parce che ti ai sposât!
[Don't tell me what to say. Why I ever married you, I don't know.]
Alessandro screws the head of the broom back on, gives his shop
a quick sweep.

MICHAEL

What did she say?

GAETANO

I have no idea. Friulano is the language of wrath. She only knows twenty words
in English, I only know twenty words in Friulan, you don't speak Calabrese, so
together we talk like children.

YOUNG ROSI

Get to work. Capisci? *[understand?]*
She playfully tousles Michael's hair while he continues to
shine shoes.

MICHAEL

calls out Get your shoe shine!
Young Rosi turns on the radio. A popular song is playing. She
likes it. Sways to it, Gaetano sees her, pulls her into a dance,
she laughs and does a turn with him then a bit shy, shrugs out
and heads for her laundry basket.

MICHAEL

quotes, aside to Gaetano Dad, next time you gotta play it cool. Say, "Frankly my dear, I don't give a damn."

GAETANO

What's that from?

MICHAEL

Gone With The Wind.

GAETANO

You got time for The Orpheum?

ALESSANDRO

You got the extra dime?

YOUNG ROSI

He sneak out with the English girl, Margarita.

MICHAEL

Margaret.

YOUNG ROSI

English girl all slut.

MICHAEL

Ma, she's Anglican.

YOUNG ROSI

her point Si! Anglican! All divorce! Putane! *[slut]*
Alessandro chuckles, Young Rosi begins to take the wash off the line.

GAETANO

Michael, that's exactly what your mother was doing when I first saw her. I came with Alessandro to her Papà's house—

ALESSANDRO

He was foreman of the smelter and we wanted our last week of pay.

GAETANO

I see this beautiful young girl in the backyard with her step mother ... *Gaetano re-enacts with Young Rosi, she protests but really she is amused* Excuse me, Signorina Lazzara ...

YOUNG ROSI

Ah, never mind.

GAETANO

Lei parla Italiano?

YOUNG ROSI

Furlan. Little English.

GAETANO

I happened to see you work hard and have a strong back. You are also very pretty even though you are short.

YOUNG ROSI

You have suitcase. You go back to Italy?

GAETANO

No. My dream is to open a boarding house in Vancouver. And I make my own roast for the coffee, Calabria style. Maybe you would consider marrying me and making a better life? I am not handsome but I am kind.

YOUNG ROSI
You won't beat me or give me syphilis?

GAETANO
No!

YOUNG ROSI
I say goodbye to sister, I finish wash. Come back two hours. We go to church.

GAETANO
Okay. You have made me very happy!

YOUNG ROSI
Don't be late.

MICHAEL
laughing incredulously That's it?!

YOUNG ROSI
Si.

GAETANO
That's it.

> *Alessandro turns over his "open" sign, presents the barber chair to Gaetano. Young Rosi takes the time to pull out a paper to read with her espresso.*

ALESSANDRO
Gaetan, you grow a beard so fast, your chin looks like the ass end of a badger.
> *Gaetano rubs his beard, why not? Agrees to a shave. Gets lathered up. Alessandro is king here. Gaetano notices the new sculpture. They speak in English often for Young Rosi and Michael's benefit and they speak Italian to keep things from them.*

GAETANO
Ma che cos'e' questo? Don't you think it's a bad idea to have Il Duce in the barbershop? *[What's this?]*

ALESSANDRO
Why?

GAETANO
Ma e' il profilo di Mussolini. *[It's the profile of Mussolini.]*

YOUNG ROSI
notices Che? *[what?]*

ALESSANDRO
What do the RCMP know about art? Nothing. I'll tell them it's a bust of my Zio Francesco.

GAETANO
And they'll tell you it's a bust of your cazzone. *[penis]*

ALESSANDRO
My cazzone would be too large for the mantle.

YOUNG ROSI
People gonna think we be like you, they see in the window.

GAETANO
Rosi, let me talk. Alessandro, we don't like this on our property.
> *Young Rosi starts to exit with the newspaper. Alessandro yells after her.*

ALESSANDRO

If you're Italian you're fascist. Whether you like it or not. Like the Canadian, you're liberal, whether you like it or not.

GAETANO

indicates the sculpture again You're being a big son for Italy impressing the vice consul. *whispers, in Italian* Why'd you ask me to join the Circolo Giulio Giordani ...?

> *But no good, Young Rosi has heard this and comes scooting back, horrified.*

YOUNG ROSI

Che?! You what?!

GAETANO

Per la Madonna ... *[Mother of God]*

YOUNG ROSI

Gaetano! I tell you no join!

ALESSANDRO

You joined the Colombo lodge in Trail.

YOUNG ROSI

Italy not with the German back then.

> *Michael overhears this, it's loud enough. He stops shining the shoes and listens.*

GAETANO

macho offended O, Rosi, you tell me nothing, you understand?!

YOUNG ROSI

What you think gonna happen, if Hitler he make the war on the English, eh?

ALESSANDRO

Non lo fara. *[won't happen]*

GAETANO

Relax.

YOUNG ROSI

How good to be fascist in Canada then?

GAETANO

Come on—

YOUNG ROSI

They gonna shoot us like dogs!

ALESSANDRO

Non lo fara. *[won't happen]*

GAETANO

I don't go for the speeches, I go for the prosciutto and buns!

MICHAEL

Yeah Ma, its not like he's a member. Right, Dad?

YOUNG ROSI

Gaetano, did you sign?

GAETANO

Guardati nel tuo piatto. *[Never mind]*.

ALESSANDRO

Sono I fatti suoi! *[A man's business is his own.]*

GAETANO

I will decide what I will decide. Lascia mi stare! *[Now leave me alone].*

ALESSANDRO

stops the shave Hey, relax, you're gonna end up with your throat cut and not over politics!

GAETANO

Rosi, let me have the paper. I want to read L'Eco.

ALESSANDRO

You have to read at least five papers to even get a slice of the truth these days.

GAETANO

I want to know what Boccini has to say to depress me.

> *Young Rosi hands him the paper, disgusted with him.*

YOUNG ROSI

Take. I depress already.

ALESSANDRO

Why is nobody talking about what Hitler is doing to the Jews?

GAETANO

corrects her English Take it. I'm depressed already. My handsome husband that I love and trust to do what's best.

YOUNG ROSI

Ti crôdarai ogni muart di vescul. *[Furlan expression When a Bishop dies/when pigs fly]*

> *Young Rosi grabs her espresso cup and heads into the house.*

ALESSANDRO

Mussolini says the Aryan race is a joke. The Germans were "illiterate when Rome had Caesar, Virgil and Augustus."

GAETANO

Look at him quoting Il Duce. *Turns the page* Okay, who did the Nazis eat for breakfast?

ALESSANDRO

It wasn't a wienerschnitzel.

MICHAEL

They just attacked Austria.

ALESSANDRO

Maybe today they're going to relax, have a coffee with whip cream, and take a piss.

GAETANO

Wienerschnitzel is almost exactly the same as the Cotoletta alla Milanese. But which one would you rather eat? Wienerschnitzel or Cotoletta alla Milanese.

ALESSANDRO

Cotoletta di pollo. I don't like pork.

GAETANO

Unless it's Mussolini's pork.

> *Michael and Gaetano laugh, good one.*

ALESSANDRO

Zitto! *[quiet]* Here comes "Charles" Marega.

> *Alessandro gets ready to cut Carlos' hair. They address the dignified moustached fellow with respect, Michael hangs around to listen.*

MICHAEL/GAETANO

Buongiorno Signor Marega.

CARLOS

Per favore. Carlos.

ALESSANDRO

Carlos, come sta?

CARLOS

Do I look like the millionaire, Andrew Carnegie? Am I Sam Plastino with the Heatley Hotel? Or Battistoni and can give you bread from Venice bakery? No. So why does my family keep sending me their children's children to live with me?!

ALESSANDRO

Out of every egg springs a Veneziano.

CARLOS

Two more cugini from Toronto. *[cousins]* They are laying off Italians like they have the plague.

ALESSANDRO

Are they skilled?

CARLOS

Diggers and muckers. The family thinks I'm still a world-famous sculptor. They don't know—nobody wants the old style anymore. And nobody wants a "fascist". I have ten dollars to my name.

ALESSANDRO

You are all over the city, Carlos. They just put your leoni on the Lions Gate bridge.

CARLOS

Out of cement, Alessandro. Cement! And that will be my last commission. Mark my words. To be honest, now that Bertha is gone—

GAETANO

God rest her soul.

CARLOS

I don't care anymore.

ALESSANDRO

But you still teach at Vancouver Art School?

CARLOS

Yes. The young. The young. Everybody wants the young. Speaking of which, I have a good Italian girl for you, Michael.

MICHAEL

That's okay, Senor Marega—

GAETANO

He's only sixteen.

CARLOS

My niece, Filomena. *shows a picture* Fourteen, small chest but nice big hips.

MICHAEL

I'm fine.

GAETANO

Listen, Michael, the Canadian girls are good for the movies but they can't cook.

CARLOS

Better Filomena comes here because if you go to Italy right now Mussolini is gonna grab you and put you in the army …

ALESSANDRO

Three years in the army so what? Then I had a job building the autostrade while the rest of the world was in the middle of the Depression.

Carlos makes like a puppet

CARLOS

O! I don't have to be Mussolini's Arlecchino to be a son of Italy. *[puppet/fool]* On Monday

I help with the ballila. *[children's club]* Tuesday

I got the Figli d' Italia. *[brothers of Italy]* Wed

practica de musica. *[music practice]* Saturday

somebody always got a Prima Comunione, a wedding. *[first communion]* Then Sunday Sacro Cuore. *[Sacred Heart church]* Brancucci wants me to sign the paper for the Circolo Giulio Giordani. I say "No disrespect Vice Consul, but I'm already Italian enough!" I talk to Marino Culos and he says not on his life. You know it says on your membership I pledge to fight for Mussolini with my blood. No way Il Duce. Not anymore. You have turned into a mad man.

GAETANO

What?! To fight for Mussolini with my blood?!

CARLOS

Yes. If you are a member of the Circolo Giulio Giordani, it has it in the small print.

GAETANO

I didn't read that part.

Michael listens very closely, anxious about his Dad signing.

ALESSANDRO

Stupido it's nothing! The Circolo is for socializing. Do you have Mackenzie King over for dinner, talk about foreign policy? No. I don't like everything Mussolini does either—

CARLOS

Like attacking Ethiopia with tanks and mustard gas!

GAETANO

Better than the communists take it.

ALESSANDRO

If Canada was fascist maybe we wouldn't have so much unemployment and poverty.

MICHAEL

astonished What?! How?

CARLOS

Bah!

GAETANO

Mussolini built five thousand new farms.

ALESSANDRO

He reduced imports.

GAETANO

He got the trains running on time.

CARLOS
Si, he did a lot of good before he became power crazy—I even made a sculpture of him! But—

ALESSANDRO
He solved the Roman Question between Italy and the Holy See.

MICHAEL
The Mediterranean Sea?

ALESSANDRO
good Lord The Vatican See. He fixed the Lira at ninety to a pound.

GAETANO
He helps the Italians hold their head up in a world that doesn't take them seriously.

CARLOS
Listen to the Mezzogiorno talk, keep up the fascist propaganda and we'll all end up in jail. Mussolini is Hitler's whore. He's possessed with the devil. Never mind the shave, I have changed my mind.
>   *Carlos stomps out.*

ALESSANDRO
yells after him Carlos, I believe in equality. Your "democracy" is all about greed. And since the great war the entire world is being infected with socialism a nice theory that doesn't work.

MICHAEL
You really believe that?
>   *Alessandro grabs a newspaper and hucks it at Michael.*

ALESSANDRO
Michael, Michael, Michael, you tell me what has Mackenzie King done? Eh?

MICHAEL
He gave us unemployment insurance, old age pension, social services ...

ALESSANDRO
Okay, fine. But the man has no sense of style.

GAETANO
Democracy might work if everyone was civilized—

ALESSANDRO
But the masses are stupid.

GAETANO
We need a firm hand or the crooks take over. Mussolini put the mafia behind bars.

ALESSANDRO
He drained the Pontine marshes, not even Augustus Caesar could do that!

MICHAEL
The Pontine Marshes?

ALESSANDRO
An entire province, south east of Rome, full of water—

GAETANO
Italy had malaria like a plague, all the time.

ALESSANDRO
Mussolini got the job done. Made five new cities.
>   *Suddenly the radio is turned up. Young Rosi rushes in with the*
>   *news announcement, shushing the men, aghast. It's about*
>   *Mussolini's anti-Jewish legislation being put into practice.*

YOUNG ROSI
Sh!
NEWSCASTER v/o
in the background Italian citizens both nationally and abroad were shocked today when Benito Mussolini enacted the Manifesto della Razza, a set of anti-Semitic laws that strip all Jews and some African races of their Italian citizenship and with it any position in the government, educational, financial or medical professions in particular. / The manifesto of race allows authorities to confiscate Jewish property. All marriages between Italian and Jews are now abolished. This is a huge about face for Mussolini and has created quite the upset in Fascist Italy, with citizens already concerned about the influence Germany has over Italian policy. Pope Pius XII is publicly protesting the new laws.
During this announcement, they speak.
YOUNG ROSI
Alessandro, listen what Mussolini do to the Jews.
ALESSANDRO
Impossible, he would never do that!
They listen to the radio a bit ...
YOUNG ROSI
Never say never.
Young Rosi heads into the house, Gaetano looks at Alessandro, the news has hit him hard. Gaetano begrudgingly follows his wife. Alessandro picks up his sculpture. Michael watches.
ALESSANDRO
Ah, Mussolini. You had such a perfectly shaped head. Vaffanculo. *[fuck you]*
He drops the sculpture and it smashes.

Scene Six

This Italian sunrise should echo the sequence of the first Italian sunrise except the light is greyer than before: rainy, suspicious, nervous, parsimonious. Suggested images to play with: black kerchiefs fly up, birds flying at dawn, workers eying each other suspiciously, whispering about each other as they pass, as the city wakes up with Italians knock on the boarding house doors "Good morning". Steam from espresso maker, steam train, shoveling coal, furnace door, slam shut. Newspaper called out, everyone grabs one anxiously and opens it up immediately, fearfully. The sequence should end with: a round of espresso shots, they all go to snap one back, then stop, think better of it, sniff the coffee suspiciously, leave it on the table untouched and scorned.

ALL
No Uh uh.
They sit down in their café chairs. Crow caws. They all watch it fly over their heads. They are all chilled with the cold, pull their jackets up.

ALL
>Fresco.

> *They all part ways, suspicious of each other, leaving full dirty cups. Voices accuse in whispers throughout: fascists, WOPs, dirty dago, greasy Italians, Canadian nigger, traitor, strike breaker, Fifth Column. These voices start to be embodied by bullies who surround Michael as he's walking down the street, the name calling escalates and they attack him. They beat him up. He manages to scramble himself away, grabbing his mandolin, bleeding and torn. He escapes through the front door and turns once again into the old man, gasping for breath. Rosina burst through the door behind him into the reality of the present.*

Scene Seven

> *Rosina slams the door shut. She walks down the stairs, looks at Michael in a new light, touches him gently as he recovers, still shaken from the memory of the beating.*

ROSINA
>Dad ...

MICHAEL
>Give me a minute. Don't fuss.

ROSINA
>I had no idea ...

MICHAEL
>Bah! What do you expect? We were immigrants, that's all. It takes a while to get established. You want to talk to a First Nations about racism, okay, there you've got a story. The Japanese.

ROSINA
>And from this you became a lawyer, you were on the school board ... the odds you faced. I'm proud of you.

MICHAEL
>Now she says this.

ROSINA
>Why didn't I ask more questions? The stories I could have passed onto my child.

MICHAEL
>What child?!

ROSINA
>I'm pregnant.
>> *The Nonnas suddenly straighten with the shocking news.*

ROSI/CECILIA
>COSA?!

MICHAEL
>What?! How?

ROSINA

A shadow came over me and I said "my Lord, my Lord".

ROSI

Rosina, you no marry!

CECILIA

The baby gone be bastardo!

MICHAEL

Not by that guy from Montreal.

ROSINA

His name is Jorgen. Yes.

ROSI

The man is a Danish.

CECILIA

I know the Danish, I like with the strawberry in the middle.

MICHAEL

Does he know?

ROSINA

I haven't told him yet.

ROSI

Oh my God …

ROSINA

I wasn't sure if I was going to keep it.

> The Nonnas exit, pulling out rosaries, praying madly

MICHAEL

You're forty-two years old. That things gonna have three heads.

ROSINA

The ultrasound looks great, I'm four months.

MICHAEL

Why didn't you tell me and your mother?

ROSINA

Mom knows. She's happy.

MICHAEL

To have you pregnant with no husband and no work with no maternity leave? She's happy. She's gonna be doing a lot of freakin' babysitting.

ROSINA

Opening a café could help me support a child.

MICHAEL

And Danish isn't going to help you?

ROSINA

He's an artist, Dad, he makes no money. And his company is in Montreal.

MICHAEL

Don't give up, Rosina. You're a beautiful dancer. You could make a better living—

ROSINA

I'm not a dancer, I'm a performance artist.

MICHAEL

Whatever you call it … when you move. But then you open your mouth and wreck everything.

ROSINA
So you don't like it when I get political.

MICHAEL
I don't like it when you're trying to be someone else.

ROSINA
Then let me find out who I am!
Rosina charges through the door again, returning to

Scene Eight

March 23, 1939. Alessandro's barber chair is empty. He looks outside his shop. Sighs. Young Rosi enters with panini, Gaetano follows with coffee. It is tense between all of them. Definitely we feel Young Rosi is not impressed with Gaetano and Alessandro who are sticking with each other.

ALESSANDRO
shouts We're open! Even the Italians are boycotting the Italians.

GAETANO
Where is Michael with the paper?

YOUNG ROSI
offers Cotoletta? Polo. *[cutlet? Chicken]*

ALESSANDRO
Speaking of Cotoletta, has Gandhi had a sandwich yet?

YOUNG ROSI
Week. Before.

GAETANO
Last week, Rosi. You say "last week".

YOUNG ROSI
weary Lassaimi a pâs. *[leave me alone]*

GAETANO
Week before is fine ... you're right.

ALESSANDRO
Your English is getting better, Rosi.

YOUNG ROSI
Si. And my Furlan is getting worser. Soon I forget everything and speak nothing good.

GAETANO
Why do the English call our Indians Indian? They don't look Indian to me.

ALESSANDRO
Everything is Indian if it isn't blonde.

YOUNG ROSI
To Gaetano You. You could be an Indian.

GAETANO
Don't even joke, those people take a lot of shit oppressione. *[oppressed]*
Michael runs in with his mandolin around his back.

MICHAEL

You won't believe who died!

GAETANO

Who?

MICHAEL

Charles Marega.

ALESSANDRO

Carlos?!

YOUNG ROSI

Signôr Benedêt! *[Dear God.]*

MICHAEL

He was teaching a class, reached for his hat, fell down. Dead.

GAETANO

You're kidding.

MICHAEL

I was downtown for band practice.

Silence and still.

GAETANO

No more backyard fountains for the rich in Shaughnessy.

YOUNG ROSI

He was so happy for the lions.

MICHAEL

It's gonna hit the papers big.

YOUNG ROSI

No, it won't.

MICHAEL

He's one of the greatest sculptors in North America.

ALESSANDRO

Yeah. But he's one of us.

GAETANO

He's gonna be lucky if he gets a grave.

Alessandro pours a round of drinks. They all do a toast.

GAETANO

Carlos Marega.

YOUNG ROSI

I like the girls he do on the Sun building.

MICHAEL

The maidens.

ALESSANDRO

The Caryatids.

GAETANO

Except they only got one leg.

ALESSANDRO

They're Greek.

GAETANO

Greek women only have one leg? Why?

YOUNG ROSI
So they don't run away. We should be happy we alive and we got the two legs.
ALL
Arrangiarsi.

> *Another toast. Then Young Rosi cleans up lunch and Bertin gets*
> *back to work at the barbershop. Crows are in the background,*
> *mischievous.*

MICHAEL
You coming to swear allegiance at the hall with Branca?
GAETANO
Mr. Big Shot Angelo Branca.
ALESSANDRO
If Italy joins the war ... it doesn't matter what petition we sign or how much
money the Italian community raises for the Red Cross—
MICHAEL
They bought an ambulance with those donations. People remember that.
ALESSANDRO
No they don't.
MICHAEL
You better do something, Alessandro. Carlos was right. Everyone knows what a
fascist supporter you've been. My family is going to be implicated by association.
GAETANO
Big words from the young lawyer.
MICHAEL
Branca is going all around British Columbia speaking to the Italians ... Field,
Trail, Kamloops, Kelowna ...
GAETANO
Branca tries to look like a saint but look at the murderers getting out of jail! And
you want to go to law school. He must love you.
MICHAEL
He's keeping an eye out for me.
GAETANO
An eye and a tooth.
MICHAEL
You're jealous because he's in City Hall—
GAETANO
He let Joe Celona walk. Joe owns all the brothels—
MICHAEL
He's the youngest prosecutor in the province. He fought the same odds you did,
Dad, and who are you? Nobody!

> *Gaetano and Michael start to wrestle in the barbershop, Alessandro*
> *ad lib protest for them to stop, Young Rosi bursts in, breaks up*
> *her men.*

YOUNG ROSI
Don't talk to your father like that. He is not the nobody. He makes excellent coffee!

> *Michael exits, angrily.*

GAETANO

to Young Rosi That's the best you can do?!

YOUNG ROSI

The boy is right, Gaetano!

GAETANO

Remember whose house you're in!

YOUNG ROSI

I'm in the house of a man who makes friends with the enemy! *to Alessandro* Your Mussolini is power hungry. Look deda deda dee ... Corfu, Albania ...!

ALESSANDRO

I'm trying to work here. You want to talk politics, woman, then go outside. Gaetano what's wrong with you, you don't teach your wife her place?

GAETANO

Rosi, leave the men alone! You want to go back to your Dad in Trail so he can beat you? You want to go back to Italy so you can starve? Fine.

YOUNG ROSI

A nûs train tal čhâv colpe la to braure stupide. *[we're all going to get shot in the head over your stupidity]*

ALESSANDRO

Ti piace avere le palle schiacciate da una morsa. *[you enjoy having your balls in a vice]*

GAETANO

You know where the war is, right here. Over the kitchen table.

> Gaetano turns on the radio, tries a few dials, can't find any
> news, lets a song play.

ALESSANDRO

notices Here comes Nunzio. Really. *calls out to him* After a year? Come inside my shop. I dare you. Giuda! *[wimp/traitor]*

> Nunzio does not enter, but stands at the door to goad
> Alessandro through addressing Gaetano loudly. Gaetano tries to
> be cordial to both men. Nunzio has a paper in his hand.

GAETANO

Buon giorno, Signor' Nunzio. *[Good morning]*

NUNZIO

Gaetano, I make the best shoes in the city. Best cobbler in town. And who is coming to my shop? Nobody!

GAETANO

I know. Hey, give me a look at your paper, eh?

NUNZIO

Listen, I fought against Germany WW I with the Canadians.

ALESSANDRO

Where's Rossini, your life would make such an opera!

NUNZIO

Gaetano, my brother died of influenza and his body was stacked up under a tarp with all the others in the alley behind the undertakers at Pender ...

GAETANO

Yes, Nunzio ...

NUNZIO

I shared my bread with the hobos in the 30s, when the city was giving them seeds to plant food on public land . . .

GAETANO

Si.

NUNZIO

Don't tell me I'm not loyal to this country!

GAETANO

This will all blow over very soon.

NUNZIO

has come here to yell this You better hope so, my friend. Because today *opens up newspaper to flaunt* Slovak and Hungary are officially at war—and you're a business partner with a fascist in a country that is about to declare you the enemy.

ALESSANDRO

Get out of my shop!

Scene Nine

This sequence is the building menace of war over the next fifteen months pass: soldiers being deployed, Mussolini shaking hands with Hitler. It ends on the day that war is declared between Italy and Britain, June 11, 1940.
Some ideas: Branca and crowd in the Silver Slipper Hall [the Hastings Auditorium] pledging allegiance to Canada with hundreds of Italian Canadian citizens. Speeches by Mussolini, Chamberlain, Mackenzie King overlapping. Unmarked train pulling into the immigration building. RCMP mobilizing. The burning of the documents in the Vice Consul's office in the basement furnace of the marine building as he yells out in Italian "we're at war". Knocking on the doors as Italian men are being grabbed in the middle of the night out of bed, at work. This sequence ends with: Alessandro is taken away by two guards. He shouts out:

ALESSANDRO

No trial?! No lawyer?! And this is the glory of democracy?! You know what this really is?! Fascist!

Two guards grab Gaetano at the café while he's making coffee. Black grains fly up.
Michael walks in on Gaetano apprehended. They say nothing to each other. In that moment Michael turns his back on his father and walks away.
A crowd of NONNAs bundle past and in the middle of the chaos, Young Rosi climbs up and out, trying to get heard, trying to see- trying to reason, desperate, but is smothered and taken off with the crowd.

YOUNG ROSI
Where are you taking my husband?! What did he do?! What did he do?! Gaetan!

More image ideas to play with: Immigration building top floor, barred holding bin. Men
were all shoved together, being taken away by guards and put on unmarked guarded trains.
This sequence ends with: Rosi is thrust forward
in the chaos of the crowd, she waves a white hanky, yells—

YOUNG ROSI
Gaetan!

NONNAs look at her, whisper. She immediately pulls her hand down, but watches, tracks the movement, watches, but ashamed to cry out again.

YOUNG ROSI
Quiet devastation, to herself Ca ch'o soi. *[I am here]*

Ominous huge black crows tower over Michael. He smashes the mandolin. He's terrified. He runs, the shadows screech and peck at his heels. He open the door, slams and locks it trying to shut out the shadows and crows but they seep through the layers of wallpaper and around the corners. Knocking, knocking. He hobbles down the stairs, now an agitated, haunted old man.

MICHAEL
Rosina, Rosina, don't make me remember ...

Rosina is left on the other side of the door, locked out, she is the one knocking.

ROSINA
Dad! Dad!

END OF ACT ONE

ACT TWO

~

Scene One

Back to the same position, Rosina yelling through the door to her father on the other side. Underneath this, the Nonna chorus whispers "Giovinezza".

NONNAS
Giovinezza, Giovinezza,
Primavera di bellezza
Per la vita, nell'asprezza
Il tuo canto squilla e va!
E per Benito Mussolini,

618

Eja eja alalà
E per la nostra Patria bella,
Eja eja alalà ...

> *Rosina yells through the door at her aged Dad.*

ROSINA

Why didn't you tell me they took Nonno?! Please let me in. Please.

> *Michael hobbles up, agrees to open to the door. They sit on the step.*

MICHAEL

No warrant, just a knock on the door and he was grabbed by the RCMP and led away in handcuffs. Because he joined that club? Because he did something we didn't know? Or was it simply because he was Italian? He was put on a guarded CPR train to a secret internment camp. We didn't know if he'd be shot, if he'd be put on trial, there was no communication. They took Alessandro too. Forty-one men from Vancouver, eight from Trail ... over six hundred across Canada. After several months we finally got a letter in the mail with a big red POW stamp on it. He was at a camp in Kananaskis.

ROSINA

I've gone camping there.

MICHAEL

He cleared roads, worked in the kitchen.

ROSINA

The only vivid memory of Nonno is when I was six—

> *Gaetano walks out the front door.*

GAETANO

You want Coke, bambina? Sip a the Coke?

ROSINA

No, Nonno, I said "skipping rope".

GAETANO

Ahhh! The rope! *skips with Rosina.* Skip the rope, like Italian Stallion, like Rocky Balboa, good for the heart! Wait, I get.

> *He dashes into the house, quickly returns with a rope and a
> cross necklace.*

ROSINA

He pulled a little wooden cross around my neck.

GAETANO

Important to Nonno. Special. Don't lose. I make when I go camping.

ROSINA

Now I understand what he meant by camping, because God knows Nonno did not own a tent.

MICHAEL

I'm surprised he gave you that. It was Mamma's but she refused to wear it. Okay, so. You have your keepsake. You can put it in a jewelry box in your nice two-bedroom apartment after you sell this house.

> *Rosina looks at the sign, is somewhat convinced. Michael takes
> her arm and attempts to lead her away from the house but they
> are intercepted by Rosi who lays in a major guilt trip that starts
> soft and boils into a somewhat incoherent rant.*

ROSI

You gon' wear the pain in the neck from Nonno but not the pich of your father, not the pich of me in the locket? Okay. You live your life, Rosina. Never mind I scream in my grave when they rip down my house and build the Loonie Toonie store with the candle of the Madonna, Mari di Jesù Crist [mother of Jesus] for smoking the druggies with the crack of cocaine and they open up the Starbuck who always burn the bean NEVER MIND! Oh Canada! They like espresso now! If we alive today and make the caffe, we have a million stella buck too!

Cecilia joins her, carrying grocery bags from Bosa Foods, concerned she's getting upset.

CECILIA

Oh yes, everyone love Italy now. Look at this Bosa. Millionaire. Start out with one truck and the crate of grape. And he keep the store open all these years and Canadians they learn Italy got the best. Now all the store have the pasta, even the Orecchiette.

ROSI

The prosciutto slice thin …

CECILIA

For the English to wrap around their melone. Hahaha! *Wraps it around her head*

ROSI

But back in the old time—no tomato in the store!

CECILIA

No garlic. The English they like just a the salt and just a the pepper.

ROSI

And the big piece of meat in the oven.

CECILIA

Dry.

ROSI

Dry!

CECILIA

Like a rock they cook so long it turn grey.

ROSI

You have to cut with the big knife at the table, you have to be like the butcher in front of your family.

CECILIA

Like a hunter, kill the roast beef! *attacks food with knife*

ROSI

Maybe some potatoes they eat. White and they smash like food for the baby.

CECILIA

Dry!

ROSI

Dry! No wonder they got bad teeth. And the bread, like cake.

CECILIA

You put the knife with the cheese on the top and it break the hole. How you make sangwhich?

ROSI

Now everybody smart. They like the Italian because we stay long enough for them to figure it out! And our house still stand because the strong foundation. And Michael, you had a good life here.

CECILIA

All the poor they play together. We help each other out. The Japanese, good people, they got Powell. The Chinese they got Pender.

ROSI

And we share Strathcona with the Jews.

CECILIA

I like the Jews. They're clean with the chicken.

ROSI

Michael, you remember you have the birthday and everybody come? Even the black boy from Hogan's alley.

MICHAEL

His name was Tom. Ma. Not "the black boy".

ROSI

Same thing. And he afraid, he stay in the yard. He never been invite inside the house of the white. And Gaetano say "don't be stupid, get in the house, you the same as everybody else, Black Boy!"

MICHAEL/ROSINA

immediately correct Tom.

ROSI

Shame is not on your father's shoulder. This is a house of honor.

CECILIA

Shame is for all the people who hate the poor.

ROSI

If you gonna tell the history, tell it right. I dare you, my son. Go back. See your father. Rewrite your history where maybe you are not the hero.

> *Michael has a little stare off with his mother. He takes the challenge and boldly goes through the door, Rosina scurries to follow.*

Scene Two

> *This scene is once again an echo of the Italian sunrise pattern, except it is in the Kananaskis internment camp. Barbed wire, armed guards. Palimpsest on door frame reveals Kananaskis Hut 33. The mood: rigid, terrifying, full of isolation. We enter the internal internment. So much of the conflict is now in their heads. Visual ideas to play with: Knocking on prisoner's doors "get up". Prisoners enter in a line, blue jackets with red circle targets revealed on their backs. Futurist disjointed, mechanical, isolated. Black kerchiefs fly up and out like birds flying at dawn. Steam donkey for logging gangs. Trains, shoveling coal, furnace door, slam shut. Wood carving, painting, soccer, singing. Barber*

*clips for the prisoners, the snap of the laundry being pulled out
and folded. The sequence ends with: Whistle blows, lunch
break for road clearing work gang. Thermos cups opened up,
they all take a swig.*

ALL
Ahhh!

*Work whistle blows. They all put away their cups and get back to work like a human
machine. Stop. Crows caw. They all watch it fly over their heads. A whistle is blown
they all suddenly stand and turn their backs in an obedient prison line up. They yell
out, almost like a "yes, sir!" to a captain:*

ALL
Al Fresco!

*The prisoners grab their jackets over their heads, ready to sleep.
One, paces in a circle around and around and around, the
other sings a fascist song, Alessandro and Gaetano lie in bunks
beside each other. A moon rises, as red as the one on their backs.
Gaetano sings very softly ...*

GAETANO
Alone from night to night, you'll find me
too weak to break the chains that bind me
I need no shackles to remind me
I'm just a prisoner of love
For one command, I stand and wait now
from one who's master of my fate now
I can't escape, for it's too late now
I'm just a prisoner of love ...

Alessandro can't stand the pacing or the singing.

ALESSANDRO
Basta! *[stop]*

Silence. Stillness. After a moment, someone weeps in the black.

ALESSANDRO
softer Stop.

*The weeping stops. Only the forest makes sounds now, in the
deep black night.*

Scene Three

*A laundry sheet is dropped, Young Rosi is in her yard, doing
the wash. She notices the broken mandolin, picks it up gently,
sadly. Michael enters with a bag of books on his back, stops in
his tracks when he sees his mother.*

YOUNG ROSI
What happened to this?

MICHAEL

It broke.

YOUNG ROSI

Hm.

MICHAEL

Leave it.

YOUNG ROSI

Michael, walk with me to 33rd and Heather. You have time before Italian lessons.

MICHAEL

Ma. They shut down the school.

YOUNG ROSI

Si. I forgot. Then walk with me now.

MICHAEL

You are not an enemy. I am not an alien.

YOUNG ROSI

I don't want to go alone. And if you don't register with the RCMP ... we got enough trouble.

MICHAEL

I was born here. We all crammed into the Silver Slipper hall and pledged allegiance to Canada. We agreed to turn in traitors ...!

YOUNG ROSI

Today I talk with Genoveffa in Benny foods ... and the RCMP come in the store, "speak English; no more than five of you." We talk about the sugar ration! You think Ninetta she gonna be spy for the German?! She don't barely know how to read.

MICHAEL

I refuse to be humiliated over something my father did!

YOUNG ROSI

He's not a fascist, Michael, he's a push over.

MICHAEL

He was a member!

YOUNG ROSI

He sign a paper. Because Luigi sign a paper and Vito sign a paper and Biaggio and Alessandro sign a paper ...

MICHAEL

Why?!

YOUNG ROSI

They all want to be big shot businessmen for Italy. Scratch the pen on the paper like he scratch his ass. Where's my basket with the fruit?

MICHAEL

The cornucopia?

YOUNG ROSI

No corn, fruit. With the zucchini, the bread, the grape ...

MICHAEL

Cornucopia. The harvest. Trust me.

YOUNG ROSI

In Italy we trick, we see the picture ... Canada the corn-cope. They say there is snow but the snow is dry. Like sand. You don't feel the cold.

MICHAEL

Ha.

YOUNG ROSI

Your Dad probably better off than us. At least they feed you at the prison camp.
We have no customer for six month. No social assistance, they freeze all the
saving account ... I sell the car, I sell my wedding ring, I sell my silver spoon ...
I got nothing left. Bertin can't pay his rent ... I can't pay the mortgage.

MICHAEL

We have to sell the house.

She shakes her head.

YOUNG ROSI

Chel a mi fâs fûr. *[That would kill me.]*

MICHAEL

I don't think we have a choice, Ma.

*A woman who doesn't show emotion, does for a split second
here. She nods.*

YOUNG ROSI

Everything you work so hard for, eh? Delicât. *[delicate]*. Like the bird who hit the
window. Bam! So fast. *deep breath of resolve* Your Zia Cecilia take us in.

MICHAEL

They have seven kids, there's no room!

YOUNG ROSI

The basement, we share by the furnace, she put a little cot.

Michael puts his head down, distraught.

MICHAEL

I'd rather sleep in the park. At least I wouldn't owe anybody. *starts to walk away,
turns* You know, the last thing I said to Papà? ... I called him a "nobody".

YOUNG ROSI

He knows you don't mean.

MICHAEL

No, Mamma. I do. I do mean it.

He leaves her alone.

Scene Four

*Internment camp, Kananaskis. Alessandro pulls out a deck of
cards while Gaetano is whittling the wooden cross.*

ALESSANDRO

Scopa?

GAETANO

Okay, bene. *[okay, good]*

ALESSANDRO

Hai Sentito? *[have you heard?]*

Unseen guard's voice warns:

V/O GUARD NONNA

In English!

ALESSANDRO

You know that boy who would stick his head through the barbed wire fence and stare out at the woods?

GAETANO

The blonde kid?

ALESSANDRO

Yeah. Eight doctors in this camp and the man dies.

GAETANO

What did he die of?

ALESSANDRO

shrugs, shame likely Nothing wrong with his body.

> *Alessandro shrugs. They play cards.*

GAETANO

You want me to say I miss my wife. I do not.

ALESSANDRO

Liar.

GAETANO

E che ne sai te? *[What? Why do you say that?]*

ALESSANDRO

Oh big man. Nothing bothers you. Bugiardo. *[liar]* Every night you cry like a baby. "Not even a picture of my wife do I have. My grandchild won't know me. I'll be shot and buried like a dog and dug up by a bear and eaten and shit out again among the pine needles."

GAETANO

That was the first week. It's better now. I never said I'd be shit out again. And sure I worry about Rosi, all the time. I am glad she has Michael who speaks English but I don't know how she is surviving. And yet, it's been six months, I don't want to go back. When I am with her I can never get enough of her. I beg for her legs at night and she pushes me off. I hope for a meal and I get rice and brodo. I keep telling jokes hoping someday she will laugh. I am a little bird looking for crumbs. And now that I'm away ... I am forgetting about her legs and I am finding my own.

ALESSANDRO

You miss your son the most, you know how I know? You never talk about him.

GAETANO

Michael is seventeen. I miss him when he was a small boy. I do not miss the big man he's trying to be. Taller than me. Quicker than me. Always wants to wrestle so he can pin my shoulders to the floor. I know this is necessary for a boy. To beat his father down. But do I miss it? No. How about he can beat down the memory of me and how about my wife can serve soup to an empty chair?

ALESSANDRO

What you miss is your business. You dignity. Your power.

GAETANO

You want me to say I am angry? What if I told you ... I think they did the right thing. What do they know of my loyalty? If I was Canada, I would do the same.

ALESSANDRO

Why make you a prisoner of war?! They have nothing on you!

GAETANO

If I am a prisoner, why have I never felt so free? I can't be a father, I can't be a husband, I can't be in business. I can only be a man. In the woods. I can only be the one who listens to the owl and carries the water and counts the stars. Finally, there is no war for Gaetano. Everything stops except the brook. The wind. The circle of the sun. The change of the water from fog to rain to snow to mud to dew to sky. I think this is the first time in my life I have had silence. The first time I have felt ... like my own man.

ALESSANDRO

Your own man. What are we charged with? We don't know. All our civil liberties —gone. And you're a disgrace of a man to be taking it so lightly!

> *They break into a fight, they are pulled apart. Eventually,*
> *Gaetano sits down beside a pensive Alessandro. Starts shuffling*
> *the cards again. Deals Alessandro in. Picks his own hand up,*
> *sorts it. Alessandro decides to pick his hand up and play.*
> *A letter comes for Gaetano and a package. Young Rosi dictates,*
> *Michael writes, as Gaetano reads what they sent him.*

YOUNG ROSI

My dear and loving husband, I am sending you the biscotti you like and some of this season's sopressata. I know you don't like the one with the fennel, but that is the only one we have left. It has been nine months.

MICHAEL

adds We have had to liquidate all our assets and I put the house up for sale.

YOUNG ROSI

Some men have come home from the camp, but not you. I believe it may have something to do with joining a club I asked you not to join. Your dearest most devoted and faithful wife, Rosi.

> *Gaetano dictates to Alessandro. Meanwhile Gaetano carves out*
> *the wooden cross necklace.*

GAETANO

My dearest most devoted and faithful wife, Rosi ... I joined nothing that would lead me to think it might cause my family to suffer. Thank you for the biscotti and the sopressata. I shall need a hammer to chew them both. Bertin has arranged for his brother-in-law to buy the house from you. And then we can buy it back from him when we get on our feet, he promises. This war will be over in a couple of weeks. Your husband who loves you like Christ loved the church, Gaetano.

> *The letter is stamped with a big red POW stamp and given to*
> *Young Rosi.*

Scene Five

> *Michael as an old man and Rosina have been peering in at*
> *this. They turn.*

MICHAEL

We lost everything within twelve months, like a lot of businesses ...

NONNA ROSI

Okay, we don't need to tell her all that, Michael ... Nonno and I are fine with the money ...

MICHAEL

Pasqualini's bakery, his wife ended up in the hospital for her nerves ...

NONNA ROSI

That none of our business ... okay ...

MICHAEL

Mamma started drinking at night—

NONNA ROSI

Enough! Very good very good ...

MICHAEL

laughs Oh, now we don't want to talk about the history, eh Mamma? Where maybe we're not the hero?

ROSI

Never mind!

> *Michael is scooted off again.*

ROSI

Biele figure! *[put on the good face]* Rosina! Let's talk about you. You gone have baby! Everybody happy!

> *The other Nonnas come out and coo.*

ROSINA

How can it be happy, Nonna? I need to stay in Vancouver where I'm close to friends and family but Jorgen can't leave Montreal ...

ROSI

Perfetto! He can visit.

ROSINA

What kind of life is that for a child? It's not like the old days.

NINETTA

It's exactly like the old days!

ROSI

The men in my village, all the time, Americans. *[Italian pronunciation, Americani, those who leave]*

CECILIA

They go for the work all summer
America, Canada, Australia, Europe ...

NINETTA

Si. They all go.

ROSI

Since the days of Cristoforo Colombo!

CECILIA

Emigration because there's not enough work, leave the women and children, send the money back home.

NINETTA

Bye-bye.

ROSI

Come back for enough time to make the baby—

CECILIA

Oopah!

NINETTA

Then bye-bye again. Never have to change the diaper.

ROSI

Italian in Canada, mostly all the men. The women still in Italy. Only a few of us, eh Cecilia?

CECILIA

The rest of the women they come after the second world war, 1956, 1966, lots, with the children. Make a good life.

NINETTA

Very good.

ROSI

But even here, the woman at the house and the men—off the logging

CECILIA

Off the fishing

NINETTA

Si, they all go.

ROSI

Off the mining

CECILIA

Off the railroad

NINETTA

Bye bye.

ROSINA

That's lonely.

ROSI

No!

CECILIA

No!

NINETTA

No! What hard is now all retire, all the time, Pasquale in the kitchen, in the garden, in the living room watch the soccer too loud, drive me crazy boss me round I wish to God he go fishing again.

ROSI

It's true.

CECILIA

It's true.

ROSI

The man they got to be gone for some time or they like lion. No good the cage.

CECILIA

They like the bear, no good the teeth.

NINETTA

They like the crocodile. No good the bath tub.

ROSI

Cosa?

CECILIA
Che?
NINETTA
With the bubble … Never mind. That private business.
ROSI
So, tell Jorgen about the baby, Rosina. It could be the best kind of life.
CECILIA
He come, he stay for a little while, he bounce a the baby, he help pay the rent and then—
NINETTA
Bye bye!
ROSI
It's good!
CECILIA
Trust me.
NINETTA
It's the old way. It's good.
ROSINA
But what about the men? Nonna. How did they feel? Separated from their families, only good for a pay-cheque. What's behind the "bella figura"?
She heads back through the door.
ROSI/MICHAEL
Wait!
ROSINA
No.
Rosina walks through the door and enters the Kananaskis internment camp.

Scene Six

Gaetano is handed another letter that Young Rosi reads out.

YOUNG ROSI
My husband who loves me like Christ loved the church, we are living with my sister and it is a joy to accept her charity. *[not]* I am doing laundry and washing floors for food. Michael is driving taxi and it is hard for him to finish high school. Despite your beautiful and holy, if not naïve optimism, the war continues and we are now thirteen and a half months apart. I am sending you a jar of brodo. With fennel. Your favorite. Bertin's brother-in-law has bought the house. I don't trust him. Your ever devoted white dove of truth, Rosi.
Gaetano reads out a letter back.
GAETANO
Between you and my son my soul sleeps easy knowing my family appreciates all that I have done for them over the years. Your stag that leaps over the cedars of Babylon to pant by your stream. Gaetano.
Rosi starts to write, she doesn't know how …

Gaetano starts to write, no, lets go of the paper.
He doesn't have to. What's the use?
Gaetano and Alessandro are clearing lumber.

GAETANO

I'm surprised you volunteered—

ALESSANDRO

Twenty cents a day, better than nothing.

GAETANO

I've never cleared lumber before. At least we keep busy.

ALESSANDRO

The city without women.

GAETANO

What do you think the red moon is for? Looks like Japanese.

ALESSANDRO

It's a target, Gaetan. So if you try to run away, you're easy to shoot.

Silence, the men keep on working. After a while, Gaetano
watches Alessandro and finally asks:

GAETANO

What are you thinking?

The inside of Alessandro's head explodes. It should be full of
contrasting images and ideologies that build into a frenzy as he
is now becoming disillusioned with everything he once believed
in. Alessandro has been steeped in Fascist ideology and Futurism,
an artistic movement that came out of world war one and greatly
influenced fascist ideology and its propaganda. But now he is
faced with fascism's ugly side notably anti-Semitic activity and
colonization. But that said, democracy and communism have
also revealed their dark sides to him. Suggested images: Works
by artists such as Severini, Marinetti's Futurist manifesto "We
will glorify war, the world's only hygiene". Futurism trademark
theatre elements: humans as machines, speed, blur, scorn for
women, destruction of the old, glorification of the new and of
youth, how this can relate to a deck of cards. Nazi propaganda,
Allies speeches and images . . .
Rosina watches this . . . aghast . . .
What ends this sequence: This overwhelms and crushes
Alessandro, this contrast and conflict in his head. He doesn't
know what to believe. Bombarded, he shouts out:

ALESSANDRO

What is the truth?!

ROSINA

How can you believe in this shit? I hate what you have done to my family. To
my people.

It all fades away, leaving him broken. He goes back to the same
motion of logging as before.

GAETANO

Hey. I'm talking to you. What are you thinking?

ALESSANDRO
　　Nothing.

*Rosina grabs Alessandro by the arm and pulls him through the
door and into her reality.*

Scene Seven

ROSINA
　　I'm asking you something!
ALESSANDRO
　　You are more like me than anyone else!
ROSINA
　　What?! Fascists are violent—
ALESSANDRO
　　Says the performance artist who worships Artaud and the theatre of cruelty.
ROSINA
　　It isn't actually cruel. We try to shatter society's false reality—
ALESSANDRO
　　—with a violent physical determination.
　　　　*Nonnas come out to rescue the audience and themselves, sensing
　　　　an intellectual debate.*
NINETTA
　　I don' understand, you understand?
ROSI
　　Maybe I just don't want my head to hurt.
NINETTA
　　Let's do a little tarantella. More better.
ROSI
　　Si.
　　　　*Ninetta and Rosi do a little goofy dance on the side for the
　　　　people in the audience who don't want to engage in this next
　　　　scene. It should be extremely silly. They happen at the same
　　　　time and continues until noted.*
ALESSANDRO
　　Your work is a watered down spin off from the Surrealists and the Dadaists who
　　all copied Italian Futurists. Marinetti's manifesto was Mussolini's bedtime story.
ROSINA
　　The point of my work is to break down old constructs in order to explore the new—
ALESSANDRO
　　Exactly! For you this is just a "style", for me it's life and death. When I realized
　　the heart was full of contradictions, technology was all I could count on. When
　　"tradition" meant starvation, when religion meant suffocation, when "culture"
　　became a luxury for the rich, I toppled it!
ROSINA
　　Big fat words—

ALESSANDRO

My childhood was spent in the mud of the great war, listening to the baby scream and scream and then not make a sound ... because my mother was too starved to make milk—

ROSINA

I'm sorry that happened to you, but—

ALESSANDRO

That's when I started to crave the abstract. When my tears and snot were smeared with my own father's blood, my cult became youth.

ROSINA

But Alessandro, you didn't seek out the new, you sought to rule the world with the fantasy of resurrecting the dominion of the ancient Roman empire. And it's all men! Men and their glory, men and their pride, men and their violence!

ALESSANDRO

You know what's a fantasy? Peace. Men and women have always been at war. I chose fascism to fight communism and to rebel against my country's class system. You chose performance art to fight your family's patriarchy. You fly around naked in polenta to rebel against Daddy. Hypocrite. Look to your own arrogance. An artist should bleed every time they create. Do you? Maybe I was wrong but I bled. So don't preach to me, "fascio femminile". Because when a man has done everything he can to be a man ... and he fails, you women say "I told you so". What do you think you're going to get for that? Love? *He spits in her general direction.* You get scorned. You women. Like a mare with a bad back who is too tough to eat.

> *Alessandro and Rosina split apart. She storms through the door.*
> *Too hard for her to take.*

ROSI

Okay, they're done. Signôr Benedêt ... *[dear God]*

NINETTA

Si.

Scene Eight

> *Gaetano receives another letter, this one excites him, he's overjoyed.*

GAETANO

I got a letter from my son! From Michael!

> *He heads to a private corner to savor it. Michael dictates the letter out loud, coldly.*

MICHAEL

Papà, I have enlisted in the Canadian Armed Forces to give our family some dignity back. When I return I'm going to finish high school and apply for law school. When I am a lawyer working for a law firm, I am going to buy the house on Union Street back for Mamma. The house you lost. Your wife's son, Michael Marino.

> *This letter kills Gaetano.*

Scene Nine

Camp "review process", Gaetano is lead in to see the officials.

JUDGE H
Gaetano Marino?

GAETANO
Yes, your honor.

JUDGE H
Please be seated. We are moving prisoners of war out of Kananaskis-

GAETANO
Do I get to go home?

JUDGE H
Most men are being released. Some are being interned at Petawawa in Ontario. You will now have the opportunity to plead your case. What is your view of fascism?

GAETANO
I have lived in Canada for over twenty years. All six of my children are Canadian citizens. We're all good Catholics.

JUDGE H
Please answer the question, what is your view of fascism?

GAETANO
I am not a fascist. During the Depression when everybody was starving over here and Italy had bread on the table people were saying—

JUDGE H
What people?

GAETANO
Newspapers were saying, the vice consul was saying, the fascists maybe had a better way to organize the people, share the resources.

JUDGE H
Did you sign a pledge to fight for Mussolini as a member of the Circolo Giulio Giordani?

GAETANO
The clubs were having speeches; I went for the picnics. We were starving and they had nice buns. What offense have I done?

JUDGE H
We have received letters petitioning your release. One from the local priest and one from a prominent lawyer. We have a way you can prove your loyalty to Canada.

GAETANO
I'll do anything.

JUDGE H
Join the Canadian armed forces.
          Pause.

GAETANO
And you'll release me?

JUDGE H
Yes.

GAETANO

Alright. But … on one condition. Don't send me to the Italian front.

JUDGE H

Why not?

GAETANO

I don't want to be pointing my gun in the face of my brother. I am sure you understand. Send me anywhere else.

JUDGE H

I can't guarantee that.

GAETANO

Then I accept internment.

JUDGE H

Understood Mr. Marino. You may return to your barracks.

Gaetano leaves. Alessandro enters.

JUDGE H

Alessandro Bertin.

ALESSANDRO

Yes. Gaetano's son has joined the Canadian army, did he tell you that? The man is innocent, don't send him to Petawawa. The bust of Mussolini was mine, convincing him to join the clubs, it was all me—blame me.

JUDGE H

So, you are a fascist.

ALESSANDRO

Please let him go.

JUDGE H

Answer the question. Are you a fascist?

ALESSANDRO

Yes, I was. Not anymore. But it isn't you who convinced me otherwise. It is Mussolini and I hope he gets strung up like a dog. I pray for the liberation of Italy.

JUDGE H

So, if you are not a fascist, what are you?

ALESSANDRO

Am I an Italian? Am I a Canadian? Am I a Jew? What does any of that mean. All I can know for sure, at this point is … I am a man. When we have things good we want a little bit more and we take. We get greedy and bold and take more. Until it is taken from us. You know, back home in Strathcona, all the children, blacks, Italians, Japanese, whatever they all play together. And here. The Italians, the Germans, we all play soccer on Sundays, baseball, choir, we have a band. We paint. We carve. All this camaraderie. We have nothing. So we have everything. That is all I know. Politics are meaningless.

Alessandro leaves.

JUDGE H

Almost seven hundred men. And I have yet to come across a criminal.

He throws his papers.

Scene Ten

This sequence is mainly to show a passage of time: the men are shipped to Petawawa, the continuation of the war. The mood should be weary, uncertain, beaten down, shame, survival. Suggest images: the internment of the Japanese, the bombing of Pearl Harbor. War images. Soldiers returning wounded or dead. Liberation efforts in Italy as Italy joins the allies. Young Rosi scrubs floors for a living. Alessandro and Gaetano continue to work in the camp and Petawawa has some high rollers in the camp from back East the mayor of Montreal, some prominent criminals, doctors, a real mix with all the laborers. Nonnas sing something like "God Save The Queen". Woman making packages to send to soldiers, rationing of groceries. This sequence should end with Michael in uniform saying good-bye to his mother.

Scene Eleven

This sequence is the end of the war. The mood is shortly jubilant and then sobering as families are reunited or not and rebuilding has to happen. Suggested images to play with: Nonnas shout out in a short parade announcing the war is over. Men are given clean shirts in the camp and paid for their labor and sent home on the train. The sequence ends with: Young Rosi and Gaetano just look at each other, his return.

GAETANO
Powell Street is so empty, they take all the Japanese.

YOUNG ROSI
Yes. My God.

GAETANO
Gaetano pulls a wad of bills out of his pocket I made a hundred and twenty dollars for my work at the camp. It's something.

YOUNG ROSI
Not enough to buy back our house.

GAETANO
They need someone at the floating log camp at Tahsis Inlet. To cook for the men. I've been offered.

YOUNG ROSI
Where is that?

GAETANO
Up North. Does it matter?

YOUNG ROSI
You gonna make me a white widow.

GAETANO

Sit down please.

He's never really taken charge before. She sits.

GAETANO

When I first saw you I said to myself, "This girl is too beautiful for me. But she has had a hard life and I can make her happy." Now ... I don't know. Have you ever been happy, Rosi?

YOUNG ROSI

Don't be stupid.

GAETANO

No, think back. I want you to think about when you were happy. Because as long as I've known you, I've never seen this.

ROSI

You want me to do a little dance for you, Gaetano, make a smiley face like a come une matucele? *[half wit?]* Put some flowers in my hair "welcome home my brave camper!" I was happy when my children were born.

GAETANO

No. I would say you were relieved. Do you want to go back to Italy? The house is still there, Rosi, hanging off that cliff. All our children are grown. I can take work on the island and send you enough to live.

YOUNG ROSI

You're tired of me?

GAETANO

No. Rosi. I want you to be happy for once in your God damn life.

YOUNG ROSI

A decent woman doesn't leave her family. We need to put Michael through law school. He's still over there, they have him in Germany, doing war relief.

GAETANO

He's alive at least?

YOUNG ROSI

Si. I will stay with my sister in the basement, you go to the lake up North, come home when you can.

It's like a business deal, they nod. No affection.

Scene Twelve

ROSINA

So that's the deal they made.

MICHAEL

Yes. For the sake of the children. So. Work out a deal with Jorgen for the sake of your child.

ROSINA

He said he loves me and will help if I choose to keep the baby but he doesn't want to live in two cities. Too difficult. He says it's better that I move on.

MICHAEL

Rosina, he doesn't love you. He's lying to make himself feel better. Love means courage. It means sacrifice.

ROSINA

Does it? We are so proud of being able to make due. "Arrangiarsi". We sacrifice too much and then we are left unsatisfied. Our country is built on people who leave their homes because they are not satisfied. Unhappiness is in my blood. That's what it is to be Italian. We're always splitting our eggs eight ways on Sundays. And I am the last of the Rosinas and I am full of all of your thorns—we are like the crows ...

All the Nonnas come out in their blacks.

ROSINA

Flying over the city, moving from home to home—

NONNAS

Caw caw

ROSINA

Never satisfied calling it all crap—

NONNAS

Cacca Cacca Cacca!

They all line up, and as she snatches their kerchiefs it is like she is snatching their life—she approaches Gaetano.

ROSINA

Gaetano Marino my Nonno, you rebuilt your life and your business but there is no statue for you either. Not even your family saves your memory. You are gone.

She snatches his kerchief from him.

ROSINA

Zia Cecilia, Zia Ninetta, outliving your husbands by thirty years and raising your children and their children. Who visits your marble square at the mausoleum? You are gone.

She snatches two more kerchiefs.

ROSINA

Nonna Rosi ... the hardiest of all the climbing roses, I loved you. Your house is going to be torn down to the ankles, to the nubs. And you are gone.

She snatches another kerchief.

ROSINA

Dad ... Dad ... all your war medals in a box, all your papers in the file cabinet, your property liquidated and your firm taken over by partners. For what? I could really use your advice. I want to stroll in the park with you in your three hundred dollar shoes, pointing to the lions on the bridge, feeding your Panini to the birds. I always complain the white flour will kill them ... I want to hold your big wide hand ... but you are gone.

She snatches his kerchief. We realize he is dead too, a ghost. All the kerchiefs fly out of her chest like black doves. She collapses in a heap of grief and ideally Michael floats back up into the sky with a murder of crows.

Scene Thirteen

> *A crow hobbles over to the huddled Rosina and pecks at her*
> *shoulder. Rosina looks up. Her Nonna Rosi is standing above her.*

ROSI

Rosina. What you talking about? You are not the last Rosina. *She touches her belly*
And you are not alone.

> *Michael appears again, maybe in the sky.*

MICHAEL

You have history wrong. Like I did.

ROSI

Let me tell you about my Gaetano. But I tell you in Friuli. For once let me speak
with my full tongue! I will put you in my heart. Now speak! Speak!

ALESSANDRO

Let the lions roar!

GAETANO

Let the maidens stand on their one good leg!

MICHAEL

Let the crows fly!

> *Young Rosi speaks her monologue freely and passionately, finally,*
> *in Friulan and there are subtitles [and for the audience]*

YOUNG ROSI

Il gno omp al e un omp brâv cun un sol vestît. Al a i čhavêj neris tanche Il čharvon.
e i voi celest come il mâr. Ma no lu viodevi. I čhalâvi simprit viers čhase, pensant
di torna in Italie, torna cun me mari. Torna a sinti las sôs ninenanes, sinti la sôs
mans cha mi čharecavin. Torna in daûr quant cha l'ere cualchidun chal viodeve
di me. E i eri a chi tai braĉs cun un chal voleve fâ dût chest. Quant che a me l'an
puartât vie, par nuje—par avet firmât une čhiarte, a ere la miôr robe ch'al
podeve sucedi. I vin pierdût il nestri negozi, I ai sčhugnûut la a vivi cun me sûr.
But then the miracle happened. I started to see him fresh.

[My husband is a humble man with one good suit. His hair is as black as coal and
his eyes are as blue as the ocean. But I could not see him. I always had my face
turned homeward, thinking if I could get back to Italy I could get back to my
Mother. To her lullabies and her fingers running softly through my hair. Back to a
time when someone could take care of me. And here I was in the arms of a man who
wanted to do that and I would not let him. When he was taken away, for doing
nothing but being perhaps a little reckless with his signature, it was the best thing
that could ever happen to us. We lost the business, I had to live with my sister, yes.]

GAETANO

Fresco.

YOUNG ROSI

I started to miss him. I started to want him. Sometimes I iron his shirt all over
again because the steam would lift the smell of his skin.

> *Back to the same position as they were in the last scene together . . .*

Scene Fourteen

YOUNG ROSI
    Si. I will stay with my sister in the basement, you go to the lake up North, come home when you can.

GAETANO
    Okay. I'm going to sleep. Is it through here? I don't want to wake your sister. Or am I on the sofa?

YOUNG ROSI
    You want fresh towel for the shower?

GAETANO
    I want to go to bed.

YOUNG ROSI
    But you work, and maybe you travel, I don't know where you been. Gonna be more comfortable you take a shower.

GAETANO
    Okay.
            As she darts out to get a towel, he takes off his boots.

YOUNG ROSI
    You got the gray in the hair more.

GAETANO
    You look the same.

YOUNG ROSI
    You're the only man I know who goes to an internment camp and comes home a little bit fat.

GAETANO
    I was doing the cooking. One week the Italians, one week the Germans. Even the guards came to eat with us.
            Pats his belly apologetically, she hands him the towel.

YOUNG ROSI
    No. I like it.
            He takes the towel carefully.

GAETANO
    Thank you.
            He goes to walk away but she grabs the end of the towel and then hugs him to her fiercely, not letting go for dear life.

YOUNG ROSI
    I am happy to see you, Gaetano. I am happy. Happy.
            He is surprised and moved by this affection. They stay embracing.

Scene Fifteen

            Bertin walks into his barbershop, alone, defeated. He sits in his barber chair, numb.
            Young Rosi saunters in, almost casual, turns on the radio.

YOUNG ROSI

Gonna take me three years to get this house clean again. You know, I never like your brother-in-law. But for him to let us move in and do our business, until we can pay … I guess you good for something, Alessandro.

ALESSANDRO

Your English is much better, Rosi.

YOUNG ROSI

Now. Make him sell it back for a good price.

> *Gaetano comes in, carrying Bertin's shoes. He turns over the "open" sign. He bends down, takes off Alessandro's dirty boots from the camp and replaces then with the nice shoes and buffs them up with a cloth. This makes Alessandro weep in the silence of his friend's kindness. When Gaetano is done, he stands, walks over to the cabinet, gets out the razor, hands it to Alessandro.*

GAETANO

I haven't had a decent shave since I went camping.

> *They embrace, good friends, and trade places.*

Scene Sixteen

> *As Alessandro shaves Gaetano, there is a post war sequence. The mood should be optimistic, confidence and pride growing, economy starting to turn around. Ideas to play with: a brief visual history of Strathcona, Vancouver, post war. Nonnas chatter in Italian and come out with picnic baskets. Alessandro works with increasing confidence. Young Rosi turns the radio to a pleasing song and dances a bit. Maybe a few customers come streaming in, one by one under the barber's bib. This sequence ends with: Gaetano's shave is done, he gets out of his chair, everything quiets down and Alessandro admits:*

ALESSANDRO

My mother always hoped I'd become a rabbino [rabbi]. But instead, on Saturday morning, I am here. Men come into my shop … the working men. Covered in grime from the deeps or full of dust from the smelter or stink like fish from the docks … they come here. Wash all off that sludge. All that nothing-more-than-an-animal … immigrant labor. I clip their hair, I shave their face, and slowly, as the man underneath emerges … he remembers his name. He remembers his dignity. He remembers his family and why he is working so hard. He remembers that in some language he knows poetry. In some country he can sing songs that others know the words to. In some other world that is not this, he is a king. I am like a rabbi with a straight blade. I wash them clean as snow, and they are momentarily reminded they are a child of God.

Scene Seventeen

> *Young Michael walks up the stairs of the house and knocks on the door. He has a suitcase and he's wearing his armed forces uniform. He's back from the war. He stands, waits, takes his hat off. Knocks on the door. No answer, starts to walk down the steps a bit, Young Rosi opens the door, gasps with joy.*

YOUNG ROSI
Michael!

> *She rushes to her son, hugs him. He hugs her back. Gaetano is seen in the frame of the door. Michael looks at him, stony. A while. Stand off.*

MICHAEL
You have nothing to say to me?

GAETANO
What do you want. A medal?

> *Gaetano closes the door. Michael turns and walks away. Young Rosi is caught between the two. One by one they all turn to Rosina and ask:*

MICHAEL
Can you live in this house?

GAETANO
Can you live in this house?

ALESSANDRO
Can you live in this house?

> *Rosina is left with this question as they all fade away.*

Scene Eighteen

> *Rosina is alone. Just her and the house. She approaches the "for sale" sign.*

ROSINA
Yes.

> *Rosina nods, pulls out the "for sale" sign and throws it. The Nonnas cheer and then immediately bombard her with intrusive familial smothering.*

NONNAS
Arrangiarsi!

MICHAEL
Alright. But don't just sell coffee. You're an artist, Rosina. We didn't come this far for you to cheap out on your dreams.

ROSI
You can still make the performance and the coffee!

CECILIA

Have the room for the rest upstairs, the student maybe. The Chinese I like. They're clean.

MICHAEL

Maybe a little stage in the corner ...

ROSI

You could run the daycare like your Zia Sue!

CECILIA

Make a little classroom, teach the acting?

MICHAEL

The coffee shop could also be an art gallery and you could bring in musicians in the evenings.

ROSI

Seat about fifty around the tables—eh?

CECILIA

Oh si! Get the license for the liquor—!

MICHAEL

Do a little baking—

ROSI

Crochet ricamo, have for sale in the window—

CECILIA

Maybe a few Italian imported olive oil, the pasta, put up the shelves—

ALL

We help you with your life!

ROSINA

Basta!

> *With Rosina's shout for silence, all the Nonnas and Michael shush up immediately and we hear a baby cry. ROSINA enters the house as the sun sets.*

Scene Nineteen

> *Rosina turns on a light that says FRESCO Studio And Café. She comes out again with a baby in a blanket, bouncing her. She looks down the street, a bit frustrated, no business. Calls out like Alessandro did:*

ROSINA

We're open!

> *Rosina continues to rock the baby as the NONNAs enter and coo around the child.*

ROSI

Everybody goes to bed with the Italians. If they're lucky.

ROSINA

What do you mean, Nonna?

ROSI

The latest café serving grappa under the table—

CECILIA

Will be an Italian.

NINETTA

The late picture show—

ROSI

The last dance at the wedding with the band.

CECILIA

An Italian will be the last one at the poker table stealing away your mortgage.

NINETTA

The Italian will be the one you pay to rock your child to sleep while you are out walking under the moonlight with your husband, a yellow bird of paradise feather in your hat.

ROSI

And in the middle of the night, it will be an Italian whispering in your ear to make love.

> *Italian sunset. The mood should be sensual, a bit dangerous, sexy, delicious as Italians do all this above.*

ROSI

This is why in the middle of the day—

ROSINA

Yes Nonna?

ROSI

We take a god damn nap.

> *All ghosts return through the walls of the house, back into the fabric. Back into Italian-ness. Rosina rocks her baby and enters the house. The business sign left on, glowing in the dark. A snatch of distant music … "Cassetta In Canada" drifts through the door, as does the sound of an espresso maker.*

The End.

MODERN-DAY
SOCIAL DRAMAS

GOD IS A GANGSTER

(Inspired by conversations with Freddie Kohl,
60's rock star in Malibu, California)

2012
Nick Mancuso

"The text, inspired as it was by the very 'real' plight of the homeless alcoholic tramps of Toronto and Los Angeles, is the original material performed by me at the European Theatre Festival at the National Theatre in Timisoara Romania. It has so far received only one performance in English. It was subsequently translated into Romanian and has been performed at various times at the National Theatre in Timisoara. There are intentional spelling and grammatical errors in this English version of the text. These errors serve a purpose. Since this is not a literary work but an actor's 'performance piece' the misspellings and grammatical shifts are extensions of the character in vivo. In the Romanian version of the play a 'double' a kind of mimetic clown was added who tails the tramp throughout the play echoing his inner sentiments and commenting on his condition. In stark silence. It was a brilliant conceit. The theatre translated the title into *Domneu es un Mafiot* (*God is a Mafioso*) and a huge banner was hung in front of the building announcing that title. Needless to say the intent caused a scandal and made the National News when death threats were issued against the actors.

God is a Gangster is not a play but what I term a 'psychologue,' an inner monologue. It is part of 5 other psychologues which I wrote, including *Hotel Praha* which I staged and performed at Theatre Passe Muraille in Toronto and *Glances for A Window* which was recorded at the University of Toronto. This psychologue is meant to be actor friendly. It can be performed and played by any actor as he so wishes. Or totally ignored which I suspect it will be. Since the actor may if he wishes improvise or change the material to suit his style and liking many versions are possible. What's important is that the actor play out the homeless tramp and give him life. Spelling errors and all. *God is a Gangster* is a tragedy wrapped in the leafy papyrus of comedy."

—**Author Notes**

Lights up to reveal in center stage an alleyway. It's Christmas eve. A homeless tramp (God) is rummaging through the garbage. He looks up towards the audience.

MUSIC UP. CHRISTMAS MUSIC. JINGLE BELLS TO I'LL BE HOME FOR CHRISTMAS. TRAFFIC NOISE.

GOD

> *(Coughing, smokers cough)*

Hey you gotta smoke. Can I buy a smoke off ya? Yeah yeah I know I'm not supposed to smoke but what the fuck I'm God. I can do whatever I want … Cancer?? I am cancer!! Who gives a shit … I'm freezing.

> *(He walks haltingly towards us, limping.*
> *A cat howls.)*

Shut the fuck up. I said shut the fuck up. Can't stand cats.
Always trying to steal the show. To think those nasty Egyptians insisted on worshiping cats. Stupid dirty cats with fleas and lices and god knows what else. I mean, I know what else … I gotta lie down. I'm exhausted … People have no idea how much energy it takes to run the Universe. You have any idea? … Talk about calories. I don't have ta worry about my weight. It never stops. Galaxies. Universes. Time-space continuum, quarks, black holes, to say nothing of the billions and I mean billions of creatures wandering around needing food, shelter … love. Family. Children. House. Money. Food. To say nothing of keeping the clock ticking … U try it? Here!

HOLDS OUT OLD BROKEN CLOCK

Go ahead make it tick.

THE CLOCK STARTS TICKING.

A CAT MEOWS, COMES TO HIM

Come here pussy cat. Do not fear what they fear … say to those with fearful hearts, "Be strong, do not fear; your God will come, he will come with vengeance; with divine retribution he will come to save you." Well won't he?? You hungry? Here I happen to have an open tin of salmon, from the upper streams of the Fraser where the giant sturgeon once upon a time floated by. Yup. Saved it just for you. Go ahead eat it. It's Canadian. Salmon is going, the cod already gone, so thick Giovanni Caboto, or John Cabot to you anglos, couldn't steer his ship through the shallows. I made so many. An abundance. And what did you guys do? Ate em all up.
Yum! Yum!

SINGS

The TRAMP improvises an aimless tune.

Everything gone. I'm standing on stone. Christmas eve and it's raining. Nobody gives a shit. Why should I? Global warming? Gimme a break. I'll show you warming. Look into the centre of the sun. You want hot? I'll show you hot.

(PAUSES)

A SIREN, THEN A HUMAN SHOUT—A DRUNK RAILING OBSCENITIES

Nice. real nice … sir? Sir? And the son of man hath not a rock to lay down his head … all around me men are freezing here in the land of abundance. And the son of man hath not a place to lay down his head …

HE PLACES IT ON THE GROUND. HE STROKES THE IMAGINARY CAT.

So do not fear, for I am with you; may ye not be dismayed, for I am your God. I will strengthen you and help you; I will uphold you with my righteous right hand. For the riches of the wicked are stored for the righteous …

TO PASSERSBY

Sir. Sir. It's Christmas Eve. Could ya help out an old altar boy, father. Will work for food.

TO CAT

You still hungry? Tough shit I aint got no more food food far ya!! Join the club cat but hey I could make it come out of the sky if I wanted to just like that swami bupkuskananda in India only he ain't God, he is a swami, swami, bologni … how's about a salami sandwich with pickles and mustard?

THE CAT SCRAMS

(He makes a face.)

Love … hate … love … would love a bologny sandwich meself with wonder bread and mustard of love. And a good cold Budweiser. To make thee fart. Anaconda lord of farts and disappointments. How'd I end up on the street me a former altar boy with so much promise. But promises aren't enuff …

You see that's your problem. Always love me. Love me. You don't get it it's not love me … Take care of me. Please me. It's love you. Take care of you. Please you. Please me. Love you.

Love me why don't you love please don't leave me I love you I love coffee I love the smell of napalm in the morning I love to. Ah bullshit … I could use some real food. And a good hot cuppa java … Dunkin' Donuts. Only they won't let me in on accounta I stink. I need me some teeth. And the son of man hath not a place to …

HE HUMS

THEN SINGS BURSTING INTO SONG

Hmmm hmmm hmmm hmmm hmmm
Hmmm hmmmm hmmm let the sun shine in Let the sun shine
Let the sun shine
The suuuun shine in ...[1]

MORE VERSES UNTIL HE IS DOING IT BROADWAY STYLE

Silent night. Holy fucking night. The rain comes down. As the rain comes down.
Began to realize that every single drop had a particular meaning. It was a message.
Ever notice that? What's it doing raining in the middle of winter? Each drop had
a particular meaning. What happened??

> *(He halts. Stares at someone in the audience, slobbers)*

What are you looking at buddy? Or buddy asses. You looking at me. I don't see
anybody else around here?? What are you looking at?? What do you think you
see? A bum, a homeless wreck of a human being? A churk gangster is that what
yu think? That. God is (wait for it) a ... gangster is that so. God is a gangster???
Yeah, yeah, I go to the movies too ... love the gangster movies if I wasn't God
the only other thing I wanted to be was a gangster ... god as a gangster ...
funnneee ... not.

> *(pauses)*

I get so pissed off these days. Maybe I got a blood sugar disorder. Maybe
hyperinsulinism. thyroid problems. Who knows ...

HE GRABS HIS THROAT

I mean I'm billions of years old. I mean old. I mean really old, I got a right to be
sick, medical insurance. Wheee, forget it stop payments and you got bupkus. And
I don't get the girls anymore ... they don't give me a second look—no one does.
I'm a bum in a world of abundance. Yeah. Abundance millions of millionaires
and while I starve in misery in this rat-infested alley there are people hooting
and hollerin and have great old time having parties and throwing away more
food in one night that I get to eat in a week but hey who gives a fuck I'm God,
no, when I was young, when I was young. Forget about it. Then I had that son
of mine and bango it's all over. He gets all the action. And I get bupkus. What
night is this? Oh, holy night?? Silent night??

CAR HORN SCREECHES AND LIGHTS PASS HIM BY.

Hey hey asshole. What's the rush?? Ahhhhh!!! Ahhhh!!! Ahhhhhh!!!!
"There was an ancient mariner/ and he stoppeth one of three/ by thy long beard
and glittering eye/ why stoppest thou me??" My feet are killing me. My toenails
are going black and falling off. Does he write? Does he call? I know he thinks of
me. He's thinking about me all the time but does he call, does he write?? Eh,
invisible dreams eh. What's a postage stamp cost?? And then. That younger
brother of his. Holy ghost ... holy mackerel. Invisible dreams. Doen't even

---

1. From *Aquarius/Let the Sunshine In*. Song by The 5th Dimension 1967.

breathe like he never existed. What a family. Now when I was. King. Of the hill king of Sparta. And top of the world. It was different. Communication is the key to everything. Communicate guys! I need a drink of aqua velva. No wonder I drink, you would too with kids like that.

HE TAKES BOTTLE OF AQUA VELVA FROM HIS POCKET AND GULPS IT DOWN,

AH HA!!! WHOOO! A little dab'll do ya!!! It did me!!!
(He leans against a garbage and rubs his feet. To an imaginary passerby —a shadow)
Hey how ya doin? Have a blessed night. Got thee some spare change for a meal?
I could use a meal once in a while with a clean tablecloth. Got thee any? Have a blessed night and oh Merry Christmas to youse and go fuck yourself!
"Fish heads, fish heads—eat them up yum.

HE CONTINUES TO HUM. IT SNOWS.

"Snow. Snow. Make up your mind." Or should I say: Make up mine ...

SHADOWS WALK BY HIM, CRISSCROSSING, SHADOWS ON SHADOWS.

No no no. Ain't gonna go to rehab. No no no. I'm God I don't need rehab, I found Jesus. hell, I made him ... I ain't complaining. Everything is perfect. My hands are perfectly freezing ... That's all. My hands and my feet are as cold as ice and at 10 below the cold moves right up to my knees, into the bones. It's great. And I'm havin trouble breathin it's great and at 20 below it gets real interesting And at 40 ... fogget about it cause ya can't. Fogget ... about. It I'll start a fire

HE PACKS SOME OF THE CRAP TOGETHER.
AND TRIES TO LIGHT. GOES OUT. TRIES AGAIN. TAKES
OUOUT SMALL CAN OF KEROSENE.
IT LIGHTS. SQUIRTS SOME OF INTO HIS MOUTH ...

Mmm mmmm delisccccccccc

HE FALLS OVER AND LIES THERE FOR ABOUT A MINUTE.
THEN HE STIRS ...

Fuck me on a small stick ... head ... ache ... oh ... HE RETCHES. STOPS.
STARTS.

HE STARTS A COUGHING FIT

... Other than that, I'm ok. Gotta lot to be grateful for. Thank you, God, for aftershave lotion ... thank you, Jesus ... wanna lay down on a bed or roses but lay me down on a bed of nails. Am born from the wind and my name is no-one.

HE GULPS THE REST OF IT

Hey you!!!

TO PASSERBY

Come back here!!
I'm God, asshole ... have a blessed night . . . I hope you get all yr Christmas shopping done. Have a blessed night.

HE RETCHES. HE IS SICK, VERY SICK.

"Blessed is he that considereth the poor: the Lord will deliver him in time of troubles. The Lord will preserve him and keep him alive; (well he's keeping me alive.) And he shall be blessed upon the earth: and thou wilt not deliver him unto the will of his enemies. The Lord will strengthen him upon the bed of languishing: thou wilt make all his bed in his sickness." Assholer!!! I'm standing on stone!!!

HE PANTS FOR A FULL MINUTE. THEN.

HE THROWS THE BOTTLE OF AQUA VELVA

Assholers ...

BLACKOUT

THUNDER

LIGHTS UP TO REVEAL HIM IN THE SAME POSITION.

Go ahead call the fuckin cops ...
Ah fuck you! Fuck all of ya fuck yaz all and the horse ya rode in on, yer jags and yes Mercedes and yes private jets, livin behind walls and gates in your olivine suits and yr goose and duck soirees and yr yr fuckin orgies and . . . wandering around in yer fancy olivine suits, Dolce e Gabbana, yr suit screwing everyone with your important business appointments, fer time is money yer broads, yer houses, yer tribes, yer bribes yer countries, yes important lives vanity vanity for all is vanity saith the preacher. fuck you all—I got a mind to. ah forget about it ... cause ya can't. Forget about it cause ... ya. Can't. What about me?? Where are my gifts?? Where's my Christmas Eve gifts?? Fogge about it cause ya can't!! It's Christmas Eve where is my fucking Lear jet?? Where?? Where's my fuckin lear jet?? I'm God don't I deserve it all?? Where's my cute little bundles of joy??

BLACKOUT

THEN IN DARKNESS WE HEAR

(sings)
"Fish heads. Fish heads. Tiny . . . little.
"No aint gonna go to rehab. No no no." Fogget about it . . .

LIGHTS UP. HE'S ON THE GROUND, HOLDING HIS HEAD. THE AQUA VELVA NEW RESTORED. HE LOOKS IN SHOCK.

How the fuck I do that?
"Give ear oh heavens that I may speak!!"
Hear oh earth the words of my mouth!!
No I went in for that controlled drinkin' thing the govt has got for us alkies and guess what it worked. I control every drink I want. Now I'm gonna control some more."
Works every time. Controlled drink number one.

HE SHOOTS IT BACK.

Controlled drink number 2

HE SHOOTS IT BACK

Controlled drink number 3

HE SHOOTS IT BACK

Controlled drink number 4

HE SHOOTS IT BACK

Controlled drinking 223345
Now you might be wanderin what God is doin drinkin and smoking!! So what??
I'm a marborough man but I can't get em up here in the Northlands. Just injun tabbakki. And it makes me cough. Fogget about it . . .
Ya see that's my problem. I don't forget nothing. 4235 B.C., July 4th 4:02 pm—right here. (Points to his head.)
In this noggin. I mean everything. Everywhere that ever was that ever will be in every planet . . . Every universe. Every godddam things down to the molecular level is right in here. And if I forget about it . . . poof gone . . . vanished. You think I won't remember this? This is. Like a crystal. A cosmic computer. You can't even begin to imagine pr understand how could ya?? . . . locked forever in my memory, forever. And none youse rich fucks will get away with anything cause I am Toth and Siva, Horus and Zoroaster, Ahura Mazda, and Mithras, the Buddha and if I forget abut poof—gone—like it never existed!! Like youse never existed!!
That's a big responsibility right? You try it on for size.
Go ahead . . . I dare ya . . . remember everything. Forever and ever. Now. Can't do it can ya. can. That's why im God and yur not. All inside of this here noggin.

HE SLURPS A LONG WALLOP OF SWEET CHEAP WINE, COUGHS. AND HOOTS ... HE RUMAGES THRU HIS KNACKSACK.

Heah it is.

IT'S A PHOTOGRAPH OF THIS MAN WITH A WIFE AND DAUGHTER IN FRONT OF A HOME—SUMMER

This was me. 10 years ago ... HE POINTS, that's my lovely wife Sarah and that's my little girl. She died. and Sarah ran away ... and this man here. Why. That used to be me. Before I was God ...

HE RUBS THE PHOTO AND THEN PUTS IT AWAY IN THE SACK

Theres a couple a things I wann get clear about. And don't get me wrong. I appreciate the smoke. But Life ain't fair. Get it through yr heads once and for all. Get that piece of relevant information at the beginning of the journey and you won't have any trouble at the end.
   (He coughs)
What is this? Natural tobacco. What the fuck is natural?
It's all natural. I made it . . . it's natural. Plastic?? It's natural. Comes from trees don't it? Anythin I make is natural atomic bombs, natural, garbage natural. Recycling or not. Natural. What's with the recycling?? Save the planet?? ... Get it straight, can't ya ... it's saves yourselves natural. Organic. Living. Alive. Tunas cans? Save yourselves. Natural. Cardboard boxes? Natural. Sodium hydrochloride. Natural. Formaldehyde? Natural. Everything is natural. I made it so its natural. Prove to me it's not. Save yourselves.
Go ahead ... I dare ya ...

HE SIPS.

There's a couple a things I wann get clear about. And don't get me wrong. By the way. I appreciate the smoke.
   (He coughs)
What is this? Natural tobacco. What the fuck is natural?
It's all natural. I made it ... it's natural. Plastic?? It's natural. Comes from trees. Anything. Get it straight ... it's natural. Didn't I just say that?? What the fuck is wrong with me. Didn't I just say it. Organic. Living. Alive. You know why? Cause I made. Use a little of that God given logic ... Did I just repeat myself? I think I'm getting alzheimers. I'm turning into a senile old fart, a toxic whore of an ole fuck. Well that would make sense. Old, I am the Ancient of Days ... what happened?? What happened to me??
   (pauses)
"I am the eternal circle, whose circumference is everywhere and who centre is nowhere. I am. That I am." Tell them.
Be honest. About it. To me it's all the same, to yu it's different. If I say unto you the sun shineth on the good and wicked alike, you tell me theres a special room

in hell reserved for people like me, kind of an anthroposphcal point of you, anthrogenic know what I mean. Only I ain't people. I'm God. But you think I'm a bum and human being and I am. A bum and human. But I'm God.

(CHANGES VOICE AND ACCENT, HISPANIC)

"Let me splain sumin do you. Sarah was jewish but I married her anyway. She was my childhood sweetheart and we were sweet on each other from the beginning. She had. (HE STUTTERS.) She hadda hadda. Abi. Abigale. Oh dear God in heaven. My darling little girl. Where did yu go. To Heaven. Don't you worry, baby. Pappa's going to be there soon. Sh sh sh don't cry. Oh dear god in heaven. And the Sarah her heart broke into a million pieces and they gave her the meds and she lost her mind and she ran away, just ran ran away. I'm God. G. O. D. God god god god help me god god am god. Sarah … Sarah. Sarah.

AS HE WEEPS AND PRAYS

BLACK OUT

LIGHTS UP

STARING HARD INTO AUDIENCE

YOU don't believe do you?? You want a magic trick, a miracle of some kind, don't you? Like bending a spoon. Then you say it was a trick anyway. Or making a beautiful broad appear out of the thin air.

HE TAKES A FORK FROM HIS KNAPSACK AND BENDS IT WITH HIS HANDS.

See it's bent. You figure it out how I did that …

A BEAUTIFUL BROAD APPEARS OUT OF THE THIN AIR.

Then you say it's done with mirrors.

SHE DISAPPEARS.

There now do you believe me?? … no no not at all. I created this entire fucking universe and everything and everyone on it and I keep on creating it nanosecond by nano, in it, within it, without it and you act like its nothing out of the ordinary like its an everyday occurrence as a matter of fact. You create a universe why don't you one with 11 sides??
It's like the word creation. Which is it? Creation is what? This? This ain't creation? Anyone know what this is I mean this. Let me spain it to you. Creation is what is. Is … What … is—get it now? It's this. This is this. Om tat sam. I am that I am get it. But ya don't. A don't get it. Do yas??

A SIREN CALLS AND LIGHTS FLASH

Hey you know what tonight is don't ya? That's right it's Christmas eve—my son's birthday. Let me ask you something. Don't you get a little confused sometimes? I mean the crucifiction. Concentration camps. Terrorist bombings. All in my name. Kinda weird ain't it. My son shows up spreads the good news. Love thy neighbor. Love thine enemy. Be nice to each other . . . love one another and then bango a few years later you're killing each other in his name. My name. What's with that?

Deus vult Will of god

Zing off wid yer head

You looking? To Fuck with me? Fuck with me? You wanna fuck with me??

I may be a homeless old tramp but what the fuck are you?? I got a degree I went to the University of Fuck. I went and dwelt by the brook Cherith, that is before Jordan.

And the ravens brought me bread and flesh in the morning, and bread and flesh in the evening; and I drank of the brook. I . . . I.

CONFUSED AND DAZED, STARING AS THOUGH LISTENING TO SOMETHING DISTANT.

A TRAIN HOOTS

I love trains. When I was a kid. I grew up near the tracks and I heard em hoot in the deep heart of the night warm in my fathers house . . . warm. what happened. Lord? Lord?

Why am I talking to myself.

HE STARTS TO WHEEZE AND COUGH.

Unbeleivable. She throws me out. On the street. For the lips of a strange woman whose lips drop as a honeycomb, and her mouth is smoother than oil: ·
But her end is bitter as wormwood, sharp as a two-edged sword.

Her feet go down to death; her steps take hold on hell. (He rises and dusts himself . . . looks around)

This place is a rat hole—You guys make more garbage than anyone else in the universe . . . What's with the garbage?

YOU ALL STINK UP THE PLACE!!

The problem. With youse. Is that you like to sit around all day . . . sit around and make trouble for everybody—let's start with Adam and Eve, your mommi and your poppi. Not so nice. Not nice people. And look at their kids. You think it was a coincidence one of them killed the other one. A random happening?? Like Columbine??

I give them gardens, I put in pear trees, cherry trees flowers, rhodendrons, hippos, pussy cats, fluffly coulds—Let's face it was beautiful—nice and warm so you

don't need to wear no clothers. No insects what can I tellya?—These I made later, no scorpions, later, no rattlesnakes, later, no man eating tigers later, spiders, coachraches, later—one snake, one lousy snake—a small one and one apple tree for effect—and I think to myself—leave the apple tree—what do you think— apples grow on trees?? Well they do but you know what I mean?? Leave the apple tree, the tree of the knowledge of good and evil—god and evil—leave it.
Eve.
Eve. Whoso findeth a wife findeth a good thing. Yeah right. Like that wife of mine running off with my kid and my boss. The two of them. Not a word you coulda have knocked me over.
Eve, Eve, Eve—nice ass, perfect tits—let me tell you ... like bunnies ... lots of bunnies, the first playboy bunny that ever was. Beautiful, naked. Eve. OK so I made her from some ribs, so what, look at the results. For Even in laughter the heart is sorrowful.

CHANGES VOICE

Eat ye not of the tree of the knowledge of good and evil.
In other words stay the fuck away. Stay. The fuck. What's the big deal? Away. From the fucking tree and the fucking apples. Think of it as a window display. For effect.
What's so difficult about that. Eat watermelon. Eat bananas, eat pineapples, eat kiwi, eat figs.—no apples. Is it. That. So hard? No tell me true. Was I asking too much? I wanna know. What was so hard about that?—Eat ye not of the tree of knowledge of good and evil. Leave it alone. Mind your own business. Go about your day. But leave it alone. But noooooo that wasn't good—you needed an extra admonition—leave it alone or I'll knock er lights out.
And that's what I did what I was forced to do ... you never listen ...
You know the rest of it. Decay death working in the steel mills, starvation, old age, a total fuckup. Over one stinking apple. But it was the principle of the thing. I give you free rent, free food, free fucks, even free booze and one simple request —eat ye not of the tree of knowledge of good and evil. Notice I don't say good vs evil, good and evil, one word good and evil, notice? Good an devil. Get it? And you got steel mill towns and ethnic cleaning.
After a while, even I lose my patience and I start with the thunderbolts and the quakes and the floods. Are you starting to get it. Let me tell something. I'm a nice guy. But don't piss me off—what is it with you people?? I mean all of you.

HI NOISE OF A JET PLACE TAKING OFF

Now take Noah. There was a good guy. Gets drunk fucks one of his daughter. Take David, handsome intelligent ... bright ... smart. Falls for this broad ... gets her husband killed off so he can fuck her. Nice guy. Solomon ... a million wives. Brilliant. What's with the wives. Harems. Bordellos. You just can't get enough. And he's not the only one. The whole book is full of oldmen screwing young broads, fucking their maids, their daughter, screwin around on their wives and then getting pissed off when god ie ME decides to send a few opillars of fire and sturm unt drung to burn em up and stop them from knocking in the doors of honest people in order to fuck their wives daughters, sons—so I send these H bomb and wipe em out like the scumbag vermin they are and they figure hey I'm an angry wrathful guy and then want to send me to anger management and rehab. What's wid dat. I give them the rules plain and simple ten commandments and they act like it's all news to them. Like they were born yesterday in a manner of spacing. Maybe I made a mistake giving you that thing between your legs. It was an experiment. A joke and you took all so seriously. Like chocolate. Why did I ever invent chocolate. I had no idea. Who knew?? I could use a drink. Ya see you drove me to digits all your fault cause you don't want the truth. You just wanna party have lots of broads and all the money in the world and lo and behold you think you're happy and then you go and blow yer head off one way or another. I'm starting to think we have here is what you call a co-dependent relationship especially you guys in the mideast. I'm not prejudiced. You all the same to me. I don't care what you call me, honest—I don't give a rat's ass. A rose by another other name . . .

What's with the there is no god but god. Think about it. There is no God? But God. You just said there is no god and then you tell me there is. Which is it. God or no God. Come on the clocks ticking. I have precious to waste. I mean I don't. I'm busy . . . guy

(There is the sound of a garbage truck in the distance)

I hate those fucking things. So polluting fillup the air with garbage dust. What. Cat ya figure out another way?? Of doing it. So come on . . . there is no god . . . But there is. I'm confused and what's with the million and one gods —one's not good enuff for ya? You gotta have the god of the door, the god of the underwear, the god of the retail, the . . . it's Christmas eve, him you remember me you don't. What am I chopped liver. What about my birthday? What about God's Birthday? You know god the father?

I know I know you think I'm some homeless old bum, out of mind on aftershave and mouthwash and shoeshine polish and cheap, cheap wine . . . I don't give a fuck what you think . . . I am God. Go ahead call the cops. Arrest me, throw me in jail, throw me in the looney bin . . .

Why do I waste my time with you people??

TAKES OUT A WORN BIBLE

(takes a swig)

Here it all is—verbum deo. You didn't know I could speak Latin, did you. I invented latin . . . think about it . . . by the way you know what night this is . . . ? Ok. Here it is . . . "It is God who arms me with strength and makes my way perfect. He makes my feet like the feet of a deer; he enables me to stand on the heights. He trains my hands for battle; my arms can bend a bow of bronze. You give me your shield of victory, and your right hand sustains me; you stoop down to make me great. You broaden the path beneath me, so that my ankles do not turn." God. Where is my son mentioned??

HE HOLDS OUT THE BIBLE

No Where that's where. Ok Isiah. But then he was I was Isiah. Hard to explain. Not so hard. Before I was I was. Isiah. In the bible in black in white . . . go ahead and look.

"Praise be to the name of God for ever and ever; wisdom and power are his. He changes times and seasons; he sets up kings and deposes them. He gives wisdom to the wise and knowledge to the discerning. He reveals deep and hidden things; he knows what lies in darkness, and light dwells with him."

Where is he mentioned?? Where??

"The LORD is my rock, my fortress and my deliverer; my God is my rock, in whom I take refuge. He is my shield and the horn of my salvation, my stronghold. I call to the LORD, who is worthy of praise, and I am saved from my enemies. The cords of death entangled me; the torrents of destruction overwhelmed me. The cords of the grave coiled around me; the snares of death confronted me. In my distress I called to the LORD; I cried to my God for help. From his temple he heard my voice; my cry came before him, into his ears."

So where he is mentioned??

So where is my son in all this mishigash??

It's Christmas eve, the night you celebrate my only begotten sons birthday. Did you get that my son. Only begotten. He's my son . . . he's not me . . . get it?? I'm me and he's my son and he goes and he sits on the right hand, not the left hand. What's so complicate about that?

So what's all the hoopla?

Is the son the father? Does he get to steal my thunder?

Where is it written you should be praying to him and not me? Didn't he tell you? He told you. Over and over but no you wanna make a rock star out of him.

"Don't you know that you yourselves are God's temple and that God's Spirit lives in you?" Here it is. One of the scribes came near and heard them disputing with one another, and seeing that he answered them well, he asked him "Which commandment is the first of all?" Jesus answered: "The first is, 'Hear O Israel: The Lord our God, the Lord is one; you shall love the Lord your God with all your heart, and with all your soul, and with all your mind, and with all your strength.' The second is this: 'You shall love your neighbor as yourself.' There is no other commandment greater than these."

It's in the bible in black and white.

"Are you the son of god?"

"You say so."

You say so. Get it. You not me. Later he tells the thief. "Verily verily," —that's how they used to talk only Arameic, not American—"I say unto you. Today you will be with me in heaven." And who do you think he was talking to near the end there when he rolls his eyes . . . father, father eloim eloim. Why have you abandoned me and then he says. it is finished. are you all half deaf?? Who's he talking to . . . himself?? Only by me will ye enter the kingdom. Only by me means only by my teachings. by the word I bring you. Why is that so hard to figure out?? Fucking brilliant. You people. Rock stars . . . university profesors, theologians, rabbi, ministers, priests, popes and kings. You disgust me.

Ok I blame myself, I blame myself ... I should never let him do all that crucifiction strum unf drang, but he talked me into.

How else are we gonna get their attention, he says to me.

Ok says I ... you want drama ... you got drama 2011 years of drama and tsouris ...

   (he scratches his leg)

I think I got fleas ... why? Does that disgust you. Nothing human disgusts me. So why should it disgust you. I stink? That's your opinion. To my self I smell like a bed of roses.

   (he sniffs)

THE STAGE FILLS WITH THE SMELL OF ROSES

What a night. Look at those stars ... through those clouds. Of garbage and smoke ... look at those stars. You know I wanted to be an astronomer when I was a kid no really ...

   (He points to heaven)

See those stars. Made those stars. all 45 700 56780934 trillion zillion of them. All of them with meticulous detail and guess what kids?

I made you! Every molecule. And I made the angels. The seraphim, and I made HIM, Lucifer, the angel of light, and called him up to me and put him on the right side of my throne and gave him the kind of smarts only god could dream up and what does he do?

He tries to muscle in on my territory. Like a bum. You know the principal difference between a dog and a creation of mine is don't ya. Between an angel of pure light and a mutt is that a mutt won't bite you for feeding him ... for taking care of him. Ok I didn't say that ... Mark Twain said it but then I created Mark Twain ...

What a character! What balls! To muscle in on my territory after I raised him up. All kind and nice like, ready to give him territories and what does he do BAM!! He tries to snatch it out my hands like a low life. I treated him like a son and what. Ah. There's a reason for everything but I not getting into besides it's Christmas Eve.

I said to my real son I said. Son, I called him son. Don't bother, they'll crucify you. If you try to help them ... they will fucking kill you.

They call you a bum, a gangster, a troublemaker—go ahead heal the sick, make the blind see, give legs to the lame and balm to the lepers —food to the hungry and free the prisoners and then you watch—what happens. walk on water why don't you ...

The first cosmic law is this—no good deed goes unpunished, got it? But he wouldn't listen not to me not to pappi. Not to his mother. And then he rolls his eyes heavenward: "Eloim eloim. Why have you abandoned me??"

What did he expect me to do, rend the heavens and reach down and take him off that cross and blow up the fucking place???

What did he expect would happen?

There's no figuring out people ... even I can't figure em out and I made em. Like Job, remember him? He's in the first part of the book in fact he's in the oldest part of the book, I mean the oldest, there's a reason for that I'll splain it to you all later. I'll be holding private sessions for those that want em in my dressing room especially the blonde in the front row, for 500 bucks. just kidding no. I'm not, just kidding. No I'm not. Just kidding. No I'm not.

Job's a good guy a little boring but a good guy, the only thing wrong with him is nothing, nothing's wrong, nice family good sexy wife lots of children she bears him, big healthy happy farm family, rosy cheeks and all, lots of food, even the barnyard animals are happy, the sheep the goats, the swine the pigs are laughing. Everything is going along swimmingly as those British pricks might say, I'll get to the British pricks later, I got a bone to pick so one day Lucifer angel of light, better known as Satan, the liar the deceiver, the actor, remember the ACTOR sidles up to me really sweat like, big red blue eyes flaring and says to me, "Boy that Job, he's a real good guy, says his prayers by night, gives you the burnt offerings, honors the Sabbath, all 10 commandments, ALL TEN!!! Everything in order, loves the lord god with all his heart and soul and his mind and might." BANG!! "100 silver drachmas he turns against you once the going get rough."

Bang. "You're on," says I. I can't resist a good bet. We'll talk later.

Don't ask, it just spilled out the me, ok maybe I got a bit of a gambling problem, I love a good bet, expect the unexpected and because as I have often said time and time again I amno. Not RE-SPECTER of persons.

BANG—YOUR ON!

And so it begins—I throw the book at him locusts, plagues, famines, earthquakes floods he loses it all wife children house the full catastrophe THIS is before came up with concentration camps cover the poor bastard in sores I mean bleeding pus and fart sores loses his hair his teeth his friends no one I mean no one will give him a helping hand, all his fair-weather friends. We love you Job as long as you got money, and land and property and prestige; they bolt like demented jackrabbits, a few even snicker in his face. Hey Job, you're getting what you deserve. Why would God do this if you hadn't done some thing wrong, good point. Good point. You musta done something, no helping hand here just. Must be you.

It's beautiful. They avoid him like the plague, there in his hour of sorest need, tell you something and he keeps praying and praying and loving and loving and a fasting and a praying finally last straw he breaks down weeps and weeps and wails and on his broken blistering knees looks up to the heavens in my general direction. "Why oh god ... why??" Why why why??

Why? Cause I'm God and yer not!!!

All the rivers run into the sea, yet the sea is not full.

The eye is not satisfied with seeing, get it. Geerout!! And that's when I let him have it full blasters

Why? Says I: "Cause I'm god and your not." Cause I feel like it ok? And then I hit him with the old Elizabethan rag, the great shakeasperan shit shot. Love that guy what a playwright but then he stole it all from me and my writings but we'll get into that later and says I to a crumbled mess of a human being, King James style. WHERE WERT THOU WHEN I CREATED THE UNIVERSE ... were wert thou when I created the UNIVERSE??

(Pause)

And that shut him up tight a nun's cunt ... and not another peep out of him, not even a tiny squeak of a fart, you could hear the boards creek and the wind in the

distant hills blow like desert songs. Of emptied broken-hearted. Shards. I like that word. Empty …
Where. Wert. Thou.
When I.
Created
The universe …
And then bingo I gave it all back 10 fold—I restored the harvest the locusts had eaten …
And I made a hundred silver drachmas in the bargain.
You could heard a pin drop …

THE BEETHOVEN MOONLIGHT SONATA PLAYS THROUGHOUT THIS …

In the beginning God created the heaven and the earth.
And the earth was without form, and void; and darkness was upon the face of the deep. And the Spirit of God moved upon the face of the waters.
And God said, Let there be light: and there was light.
And God saw the light, that it was good: and God divided the light from the darkness.
And God called the light Day, and the darkness he called Night. And the evening and the morning were the first day.
I love Beethoven. Stole it from me. I dictated. He wrote. Then I made him deaf, just to prove a point!!!
And then I made youse guys!!!
So God created man in his own image, in the image of God created he him; male and female created he them.
And I saw everything that I had made, and, behold, it was very good. Perfect. Should have been all over then no??
But ye can not well accompany the devil. Can ye??

SOUND OF WIND AND THUNDER. TAKES OUT SMALL RADIO FROM HIS POCKET AND FIDDLES. TAKES OUT AIR HARMONICA—"DAISY. DAISY."

Love short wave. Gives me this mystical feeling.
Looks like snow. It's warming. Or snow? Let me check the scores. Yup Yankees won. As I predicted. Stockmarket down. 112 points. Missed one. I just made 22 trillion.

HE PUTS OUT TO FEEL THE FIRST FLAKES.

Love snow. Just love it. It's a fine invention of mine. Soft and gentle on Christmas Eve, is there anything more beautiful??

SILENT NIGHT HOLY NIGHT PLAYS IN THE DISTANCE

THE TRAMP IS PACING, TRYING TO KEEP WARM. STAMPING HIS FEET.

It's great, hate the winters, sleeping on a grate freezing my fucking ass off, so it's fine with me. But I find it all so humiliating sometimes. So embarassing. All those feet in front of my face and sometimes I fall asleep and when I wake up I think I'm back home in my bed, my mother's house with the cute little ducks on the wall. And the peanut butter and jam sandwiches for lunch at school.

HE STARTS TO TEAR UP

I miss my mamma, especially since I never had one and am self created. It's tough being self created I tell ya. It's lonely at the top. Believe me. "Innumerable devils have compassed me about … Be pleased, O Lord, to deliver me: O Lord, make haste to help me." Help me, Lord. Ok I will.

BLACKOUT

LIGHTS SLOW UP THEN A VOICE. MUSIC

Waiter. Water. For my daughter. For my daughter. Waiter. Water … water … water. Water. Water. Water. Water. Water. She drowned.[1]

BLACKOUT—END OF ACT ONE

ACT TWO

~

LIGHTS SNAP OPEN. GOD IS RUMMAGING. HE FINDS AN OLD RIPPED UP UNDERWEAR. A CHILDS DOLL. A TIN CAN. A LIGHT BULB.

GOD

What?? So I'm rummaging. So what? What's it to ya? I'm hungry. Whose do you suppose this was?? What little girl?? My little girl? My little girl? I'm supposed to be some kind of a fucking joke, is that what I'm supposed to be?? You drive by in your limos, on your way to your strip clubs and your swingers parties with tinted windows and you stare at me like yu are looking at a martian or something. I'm a human being folks, just like you. Every morning come to and grab my crotch and inch by inch I go down the hill to this corner right inch by inch rags blowing in the freezing wind on the freeway where the cars can't stop or sometimes stops and I put up a sign—WILL WORK FOR FOOD. SIGNED GOD.

---

1. Riff on *I Want the Waiter (With the Water)*. Song by Ella Fitzgerald 1995.

You know what youse are?? You're a bunch of arseholes!! You think you rich fucks are gonna get away with anything?? Your seriously misguided—go ahead with your banks and yur credit cards and you insurance companies—here insure this!!

IT THUNDERS AND LIGHTNING FLASHES

Yeah yeah I know a coincidence. As you get into your Porches and your Mercedes and your Lear Jets and while you have your high and mighty end meetings o figure out how to screw your fellow man ponder if there is enough money in the world to insure that your assholes won't fall off!! End run that!!
Behold, a virgin shall conceive, and bear a son, and shall call his name Immanuel. Butter and honey shall he eat, that he may know to refuse the evil, and choose the good.

HE STARTS TO BUILD A CHRISTMAS TREE OUT OF GARBAGE

For unto us a child is born, unto us a son is given: and the government shall be upon his shoulder: and his name shall be called Wonderful, Counselor, The mighty God, The everlasting Father, The Prince of Peace.

HE IS RIPPING UP THE CARDBOARD AND THE WOODEN CRATE TRYING TO BUILD A FIRE.

I'm freezing. I need a match NOW. I really need shelter NOW. It's 20 below, this is gonna kill me. Me feet and legs are numb, I may not make it thru another night. I need help I need companionship. I need warmth. Please God don't let me die this way.
You have no idea, who I am. Was. And you don't care. Why should you. You're all so busy running around like scared rats. Keep running. Just keep running and whatever yu do don't look back cause something might gaining on you. You're just rats ... scared ugly rats. Living in feces and garbage. Me I live in paradise. This is heaven. You've got it all backwards and I laugh at you and feel sorry for you.

HE CHUCKLES AND COUGHS ...

Emphysema.
I had an important job on Wall Street, over 200 grand a year, perks bonuses expense account, a Seville 5 bathroom 5 bedroom house, cause you know I was so important and of such service to the company my boss loved me. True love. One day ... my boss he takes me aside and tells me I'm one of his best and for this reason they were gonna let me off easy no pension, no green parachute, no nothing the com. No really. I got a law degree from Queens, and then. I don't know what happened. The bottle, I guess. I pissed myself off?? ... I kept working longer and longer hours like they said, like they told me. trying to make a living for me for my wife and my child, not knowing and I work harder and harder and

longer and longer hours and I come home and then that day came and everything is goner, where my kids, where is she?? Then I hear this animal moaning coming from my old basements gone, they're gone, i can't find them and then. The moaning gets louder and louder. I call out to them and I go downstairs and she's hiding and she tells me Sarah. Sarah.

WHERE IS SARAH?? WHERE IS SARAH?? DEAR GOD IN HEAVEN WHERE IS SARAH??

After the funeral she change, such a little coffin, like a dolls and she had this look in her eyes like something inside of her had been broken. This look. In the hospital they gave her these meds and then she came back home and just sat staring into the walls, just staring and then she was gone. Every thing gone. The furniture, the bank accounts. everything. Gone in an instant and I just ... fell apart. Just fell apart ... Is it too much to ask dear lord?

9: (For we are but of yesterday, and know nothing, because our days upon earth are a shadow:)

Is it nothing to you, all ye that pass by? Behold, and see if there be any sorrow like unto my sorrow ... I hit the bottle and the bottle hit me right back.

Nothing made sense anymore. Not life. Not death. Career. Home. Country. Day and night. The stars, the moon, the sea. Nothing.

They put me in a mental ward. I ended up in Bellevue. They put me on meds said I was clinically depressed. I couldn't get out of bed in the morning ... they fed me intravenously. After a year of drugs and therapy they threw me out. I was healed. I went home. But. There was no home left there was nothing for me. The street, the alleyways. jails. Night and cold and then. I realized that I was God. God. God ... and when I got it I left everything and I flushed the meds down the toilet, those cocksuckers.

HE PAUSES AND STARES INTO SPACE.

I think I pissed myself ...

THUNDER

Hear that? That's me talking. Clearing my throat as it were. Going ahem ahem. May I be so bold. May I be so bold as to try to get it into your thick heads that the hour of judgement is nigh and I cain't seem to get no satisfaction. By the way the Stones. They work for me, not the other Guy. Dylan ... me, the Beatles. Me boy was it ever me. Celine Dion, the other Guy. Sinatra let's just say. It's a toss up. Beethoven me. Listz me, Chopin me, Vivaldi me, big time. Mozart 100 percent me, Bach.

Now you may find it funny, or tragic or sad. But the world I made and the world as it is now. It's two very different things. There's this world here.

HE GESTURES

And then there the world you guys made ... but soldiers are dying everyday in this world, soldiers, civilians, men women children, old sick grandmothers, rich businessmen or sooo ... men and women are strapping on bombs and blowing themselves to smithereens!! We have made a covenant with death, and with hell are we at agreement.

War. What part of thou shalt not kill don't you get??

HE SNAPS HIS FINGERS

Come on, come on think about it.

Think about it. In the beginning there was the void, I mean the word and the word was made flesh, meaning what ... meaning youse. You're the flesh I'm talking about and if you are the incarnation of the word, then youse all are incarnations of me. My word. Which is law.

So go figure it out. First there was nothing, zero squilch, nada, empty space and then I speak and fill it up. And there you are and there I am and there you are ... and there I am. I am that. I am. I'm popeye the sailor man. SHUT UP, SHUT THE FUCKUP! Your wars!!! Then said I, Woe is me! for I am undone; because I am a man of unclean lips, and I dwell in the midst of a people of unclean lips. You are all of you unclean, not I!!

HE RUMMAGES THRU THE GARBAGE, TAKES OUT A BOTTLE OF SCREECH AND A SOGGY CIGARETTE ...

Now I know some of youse out there, is thinking what's God doing smoking and drinkin—to these individuals I say: SO WHAT!so the fuck what. What business is it of yours what God does or doesn't do or if he dies on a cross in some godforsaken hole in a corner of the infinite galaxy, or sits under a tree gazing at his navel.

I am Alpha and Omega, the beginning and the ending, saith the Lord.

HE SINGS AND DRINKS

If your travellin in the north country fair
Where the winds blow heavy on the borderlines
Remind me to one, to one who lives there
For she once was a true love of mine ...[1]

HE DRINKS.

Fuck ... after shave ... I'm drinking after shave lotion. Oh the shame the shame. The humiliation ...

---

1. *Girl from the North Country.* Song by Bob Dylan 1963.

SHADOW OF A POLICEMAN CUTS ACROSS THE ALLEYWAY

Oh oh. Cheese it. The cops. Why good evening officer. Taking a break from the evening's festivities at the goose and duck soire? Am I drunk?? Sure I'm drunk. Sir I can assure you occifer than nothing the purest of spring waters has passed thru these lips. Move on? Oh Lucifer how thou art fallen. Why certainly I would love to move on but where to? To earth? To heaven? Where is my home? For the son of man hath not a place to lay his head. And I need a shave honest. Occifer.

VOICE

Move on.

GOD

And where should I move to? And once I get there I'll still be god and still be everywhere at once so why push it down the street? I'll still be there. All the same to me here or down the street ... don't you get it? Ok ok forgive my importance occifer ... forgive my self importance but let me explain something to you sometimes I can be the biggest shithead yo have ever know and in you worst nightmares—I can be a gangster like yu have never known so would be very careful to tread in my presence, capisce? And you can arrest me and put me in a prison and give me the opportunity to hang myself.

Cancer, disease, taxes, war, concentration camps are a picnic compared to what I am capable of doing. I created stars billons of them, for kicks and the cockroach just for laughs. So who are you? Set thine house in order: for thou shalt die, and not live.

If I speak in the tongues of mortals and of angels, but do not have love, I am a noisy gong or a clanging cymbal. And if I have prophetic powers, and understand all mysteries and all knowledge, and if I have all faith, so as to move mountains, but do not have love, I am nothing. Occifer.

VOICE

Move on!!!

MAN

Yes. yes. move on.

GOD

Tremble and fear me if you have any sense left in that noggin of your because I can blow you back into the dark ages if I feel like it so don't get me feeling that way—play nice—stay cool—all I ask is a little respect—a little bonhomie, a little admiration—be nice to me and I will be nice to you—cosmic law—don't sweat the small stuff and it's all small stuff—give us this day our daily bread and all that stuff—daily not yearly, not monthly—are yu getting it? And no outer darkness and gnashing of teeth for you—no trembling in awe and perdition—Are. You. Getting it??

A GIANT SHADOW CROSSES OVER HIM

HE IS STARING INTO THE NIGHT SKY

What is that a UFO? Why am I scared all the time, if I'm made of love why do I shake and tremble and make the universe shake and tremble? What's with that?

I need a smoke but I've run out and a drink. I got the shakes bad this time. (HE HOLDS HANDS OUT) Look. Look. Look upon my works. Ye mighty and ... despair. For I am a wrathful god, a jealous god, a vengeful god and. Grind your bones to make my daily bread. For where wert thou when I did created the world? I didn't ask for much ...

SINGS

god said to Abraham, "kill me a son"
abe said, "man you must be putting me on"
god said, "nooo"
abe said, "what??"

god said, "you can do what you want, but the next time you see me coming, you better run"
abe said, "where you want this killing done?"
"Take it on down to
Highway 61"[1]
Zoom

THE OLD TRAMP TAKES OUT HARMONICA. HE PLAYS, FRANTIC ...

I used to play one of these in the 60s I was part of a famous rock and roll band. Groupies, millions, adoring fans, wrecked hotels, swimming pools full of blondes. The whole 9 yards. I died a wreck a drug addict and alcoholic. Died my heart stopped and when I came to in the hospital. I was me. This guy. And then I discovered who I really was—God. I was god. Dog. D.O.G.
God! What? That spells dog? God is backwards?
I got a little ADHD?
I wasn't happy.
I had fame , I had money. I wasn't happy. I had babes. I had baubles. I had fancy cars. The money was stolen. The babes betrayed me. The cars were repossessed, the baubles disappeared like soap scum in wind. Everyone betrayed me. The houses, the travel, the vacations in Tahiti, the whores in Thailand, the adulation, the awards—all bullshit. My wife throws me out, my business manager rips me off, everyone throws their backs to me and here I am an old bum in an alley way bumming smokes and regaling you assholes with my tales. For I am Job.

TO WALKING SHADOW

"Spare a nickel spare a dime spare a nickel spare a dime" (superfast, and then over the speakers located on different parts of the stage, the garbage bin, the walls, the sidewalk, voices—spare a nickel spare a dime).

---

1. *Highway 61 Revisited.* Song by Bob Dylan 1965.

And then SHE broke my heart—who Mary Magdalene? Yeah Mary Magdalene, that fucking whore … The people that walked in darkness have seen a great light: they that dwell in the land of the shadow of death, upon them hath the light shined. Thou hast multiplied the nation, and not increased the joy: they joy before thee according to the joy in harvest, and as men rejoice when they divide the spoil. I lose everything, the very universe I created … weird ain't it? I create it and then I destroy it, weird ain't it, destroy it create it, destroy it create it ho hum … For unto us a child is born, unto us a son is given: and the government shall be upon his shoulder: and his name shall be called Wonderful, Counselor, The mighty God, The everlasting Father, The Prince of Peace.
Of the increase of his government and peace there shall be no end. It's Christmas Eve.

IT'S RAINING. THE HOMELESS WRECK IS COVERED IN GARBAGE A BOTTLE OF AQUA VELVA IN HIS FILTHY HANDS—BOTTLES STREWN EVERYWHERE. HE GROGGILY COMES TO. THUNDER.

I'm I'm in my mouth which doth cleave and my tongue. My tongue. I have been shipwrecked before … 3 times and scorned beated with the lash and the rod. 39 times. starved and laughed at … beaten tortured and imprisoned. For. What the fuck where am I? The voice said, Cry. And I said, What shall I cry? All flesh is grass, and all the goodliness thereof is as the flower of the field:
The grass withereth, the flower fadeth: because the spirit of the Lord bloweth upon it: surely the people is grass.

HE SHIVERS. SOUND OF RAIN HE SINGS

"Waiter, water. For my daughter
for my daughter bring some water.

IT'S A WESTERN JAZZ TUNE CIRCA 1934

"Water for my daughter. Waiter.
oh king of satyrs.
Whyever dost thou refuse
to grasp boldly the sword. And use
only fierce words for thy weapons of war.
Of war! War! War! War! If a man takes
his knife for sharpening. Thou grandest
thy teeth
And upon her forehead was a name written, MYSTERY, BABYLON THE GREAT, THE MOTHER OF HARLOTS AND ABOMINATIONS OF THE EARTH.
And a mighty angel took up a stone like a great millstone, and cast it into the sea, saying, Thus with violence shall that great city Babylon be thrown down, and shall be found no more at all.
I SHOULD HAVE KILLED THE MOTHER FUCKER!

Taken a knife and sliced him open from stern to stem and her that rounded bitch from hell!!!! Walkin by me like that. Ignoring my very existence! Like I don't exist, like I am so homeless wretch you all can ignore. I am on the street. You should all be ashamed!

"Waiter. Water. For my daughter."

The voice of him that crieth in the wilderness, Prepare ye the way of the Lord, make straight in the desert a highway for our God.

Every valley shall be exalted, and every mountain and hill shall be made low: and the crooked shall be made straight, and the rough places plain:

And the glory of the Lord shall be revealed, and all flesh shall see it together: for the mouth of the Lord hath spoken it.

And when I cam into the office that morning Joe Edwards my boss, looks at me and says—"Looks like we're gonna have to let you go Mike."It's a roundup. But Joe says I. Ah joe I been working here for 30 years. I expected a gold watch not kick in the teeth for my hard years of labor. And he steals everything from me. That cocksucker. Everything.

HE RISES

I get home. She's gone, taken my daughter, my son, cleaned out my back bank account. The taxes. How could I pay the taxes. The taxes. And a certain man from Galilee did come to him to Jesus saying "If you are the Messiah. then tell me why I am such a rich asshole."And he could not answer him. He hath no form nor comeliness; and when we shall see him there is no beauty that we should desire him.

He is despised and rejected of men; a man of sorrows, and acquainted with grief: and we hid as it were our faces from him; he was despised, and we esteemed him not. Surely he hath borne our griefs, and carried our sorrows.

Go thou ... today. I see to you verily I will see you in heaven.

SHOUTS

"Show me a token for good!!! That they which hate me may see it, and be ashamed: because thou, Lord, hast helped me, and comforted me."

SOUND OF A SIREN. THEN THE WIND. A DOG BARKS.

How many beatings can a man take?

As many as he can. And they hung him on a tree that his ribs might break and his lungs fill up and he suffocated and rolling his eyes before his death he said to the great green hoc age heaven—forgive them father for they know not what they ... doo doo. Dooo waiter, water for my daughter. For my daughter and me and while you're at it a good long draft of Calvados. Briocon unitas.

Lets eat ...

"Waiter, water. for my daughter
for my daughter bring some water.
Oh daughters of Zion!!

OUT OF THE GARBAGE HE MAKES A TABLE AND CHAIR.

Ah better, much better let's see what's on the menu today. What no chateaubriand? No surf and turf?

HE RETCHES

ONE OF HIS TEETH FALLS OUT. HE STARES AT IT A LONG TIME THEN PUTS IT IN HIS POCKET.

I can't feel my feet. My legs are numb. Maybe I should see a doctor. Or something.

SHADOWS AND HONKING OF HORNS

HE CLOSES HIS EYES. AND CONCENTRATES.

I once had a home and a son and a wife. But no longer do. I once had a job and a place and a car and a life and a mother and a father. And I had brothers and sisters and uncles and aunts and cousins and friends and went to school and I went to university and I was successful in my career. And it was all taken away. Because everything must be taken away before you will listen to my still quiet voice. Because your brain has too much noise and traffic and roaring. Because the nations of the earth are at war and brother fights brother. Because some take everything and other nothing.
I once had a home and a wife and a son. And my son was crucified on he cross as a deliverance of your sins. And you were forgiven and washed in the blood of the lamb. Because I am the Lord thy God, creator of heaven and earth!!
What mean ye that ye beat my people to pieces, and grind the faces of the poor? Woe unto them that call evil good, and good evil. Behold, a virgin shall conceive, and bear a son, and shall call his name Immanuel.
Butter and honey shall he eat, that he may know to refuse the evil, and choose the good.
May I know to refuse the evil and choose the good!
Behold. A child is born. A great light in the world and his name shall be . . .

A CLOCK CHIMES MIDNIGHT

Happy Birthday.

MUSIC UP. IT GETS LOUDER AND LOUDER, SHATTERING AS DOES THE LIGHT THEN;

BLACKOUT. SIRENS. SOUND OF SNOWFALL.

LIGHTS UP TO REVEAL EERIE EARLY MORNING LIGHT. THE BUM IS DEAD WRAPPED UP IN RAGS AND CARDBOARD A NEWSPAPER BLOWS. CHRISTMAS MUSIC PLAYS. THE LIGHTS DIE OFF TO BLACKNESS.

THE SUMMONED

2016
Fabrizio Filippo

"The set resembles that of a keynote address or product launch—a bare stage and a large screen backdrop. Aldous acts as narrator and addresses the audience directly. As well as participating in scenes with other characters. He does this interchangeably, sometimes with lighting speed. These shifts in address are not delineated in the text, nor are various leaps in time that flash back to various moments in the characters' past. What is intended with this devise is the drifting sense that memory and the telling of it has, moving in and out of realities without clear lines, disorienting us if just momentarily in time and place."
—**Playwright's Production Notes**

The Summoned received its premiere at Tarragon Theatre in the Mainspace from April 19 to May 29, 2016 with the following cast:

John Bourgeois:	**Gary**
Rachel Cairns:	**Isla**
Fabrizio Filippo:	**Aldous**
Kelli Fox:	**Laura**
Maggie Huculak:	**Annie**
Tony Nappo:	**Quentin**
Alon Nashman:	**Walky-Talky (voice)**

Director:	**Richard Rose**
Costume Design:	**Charlotte Dean**
Video Design:	**Kurt Firla**
Sound Design:	**Dylan Green**
Lighting & Set Design:	**Jason Hand**
Props Design:	**Michelle Tracey**
Fight Director:	**John Stead**
Stage Manager:	**Kate Sandeson**
Assistant Director:	**Joel Bernbaum**
Apprentice Stage Manager:	**Jacki Brabazon**
Script Coordinator:	**Ali Joy Richardson**

CHARACTERS

ALDOUS	Annie's Son	30's	Male
ANNIE	Hotel Manager	60's	Female
QUENTIN	Security Consultant	40's	Male
GARY	Company President	60's	Male
LAURA	Lawyer	60's	Female
ISLA	Aldous' Girlfriend-ish	20's	Female
KAHN (VOICE ONLY)	Tech Mogul	60's	Male
WALKY-TALKY (VOICE ONLY)		40's	Male

SETTING

The set resembles that of a keynote address or product launch—a bare stage and a large screen backdrop. As scenes change so do images and text projected onto the backdrop. What's on the screen corresponds sometimes literally to the scenes and sometimes abstractly. There are suggestions in the stage directions for certain passages, but otherwise the director should take license with this device.

A NOTE ABOUT TIME AND DIRECT ADDRESS

Aldous acts as narrator and addresses the audience directly, as well as participating in scenes with other characters. He does this interchangeably, sometimes with lightning speed. These shifts in address are not delineated in the text, nor are various leaps in time that flash back to various moments in the characters' past. What is intended with this device is the drifting sense that memory and the telling of it has, moving in and out of realities without clear lines, disorienting us if just momentarily in time and place.

Aldous plays a young Kahn when necessary, as well as Isla playing a young Annie.

> *Pre-show text on the screen reads: "IF IT CAN BE DONE IT WILL BE DONE."*
> *ALDOUS enters without warning. No light shift. Nothing. He wears a headset and carries a small remote control with which he can manipulate what's projected on the screen. He watches the audience, waits for them to settle.*

ALDOUS

Isn't it great to be alive? I'm excited. I'm excited for myself and I'm excited for all of you.

> *ALDOUS clicks the remote: HOUSE LIGHTS DROP.*
> *He clicks again—on the screen it reads in large letters: "ANNIE MANN".*

ALDOUS
As of this very moment typing 'Annie Mann' into a search engine gets you about 9,920,000 results. The first two are regarding a dating site for women looking for "any man".
Then there's an organic bakery and then somebody named Annie Manning and her blogs and then 'Annie 'Da Man', a transgender Icelandic DJ who spins the hottest clubs in Reykjavik. And her blog. (Beat.) And Aimee Mann. (Beat.) And amiable manatee. (Beat.) But not Annie Mann.
ALDOUS clicks the remote. ANNIE enters, hand on her belly.

ALDOUS
Not this Annie Mann.

ANNIE
Aldous.

ALDOUS
Yes, Mother?

ANNIE
Staff gone as per request. The procedures of Kahn's will are ... detailed.
She goes to adjust the collar on his shirt. ALDOUS leans away.

ALDOUS
How many guests?

ANNIE
Uh, two. Plus the executor of the will.

ALDOUS
Security?

ANNIE
Notified.

ALDOUS
Three guests total?

ANNIE
The last time I remember it this empty was ...
ANNIE puts her hand on her belly, ALDOUS notices.

ANNIE
Nerves nerves.

ALDOUS
She had a dream that all this was an elaborate hoax, an attention grabber Kahn could parlay into a presentation of some kind, a launch during which he unveiled in the most shocking way possible ...
ALDOUS clicks the remote. On the screen it reads:
"PRODUCT". Strange silence from ANNIE.

ALDOUS
She wants to tell him something.

ANNIE
I wanna tell you something.

ALDOUS
But obfuscates.

ANNIE
I had this dream ...

ALDOUS

Tells him about the dream instead.

ANNIE

... in an auditorium ...

ALDOUS

... Kahn facing hundreds or thousands of slavish followers whose minds are being smashed to bits.

ANNIE

At some point, I don't remember exactly when, he started concluding presentations with a quote he, uh, made up.

ALDOUS

A quote he claimed was William Shakespeare so often and for so long if you Google it now it actually says Shakespeare wrote it. Do it. Google it. Quote: "It is not in the stars to hold our destiny but in ourselves" ...

ANNIE

... end quote.

> *Strange silence.*

ALDOUS

She wants to really talk to him. But can't seem to. Has never been able to.

ANNIE

Aldous—

> *Her Blackberry goes off. She pulls it out, checks it ...*

ALDOUS

This morning, first thing, she read a post bemoaning current dramatic shifts in technology. Everything's-changing-so-fast sort of thing. She doesn't agree, thinks humans are currently in the middle of nothing more than tweaking stages of things that have already been invented. "You want to see things changing fast?" she thinks. "Look at the years between 1910 and 1918 ..." Electric power electric light telephone telegraph automobile airplane ocean liner subway helicopter radio phonograph typewriter sewing machine air conditioner elevator mustard gas the moving picture ...

> *Words appear in a jumble all over the screen: "ELECTRIC POWER ELECTRIC LIGHT TELEPHONE TELEGRAPH AUTOMOBILE AIRPLANE OCEAN LINER SUBWAY HELICOPTER RADIO PHONOGRAPH TYPEWRITER SEWING MACHINE AIR CONDITIONER ELEVATOR MUSTARD GAS THE MOVING PICTURE".*
> *All the while, ANNIE's phone dings over and over.*

ANNIE

(Re: Phone.) It's a text wave. Text-quake. Text-nado.

> *ANNIE circles the stage, texting back as fast as she can.*

ALDOUS

She considers how the turn of the twentieth century changed what we are. We lost our grip on nature or rather nature lost its grip on us. She thinks about the trauma that comes from re-conceptualizing one's place in the universe over and over like that. How did we ground ourselves amidst such an onslaught? Love? Love, she thinks, but not with certainty.

Because deep down she feels there is nothing technology can't get its hands on. There is no fundamental reality it can not mutate beyond recognition. Even love. It isn't man vs. machine, she thinks. Machine won. Over a hundred years ago. The question now is—

ANNIE

(To phone.) Stop now!

> ALDOUS, slightly startled, steps away. ANNIE's phone dings
> and dings.

ALDOUS

The question now is, how far from our nature will tech take us?

ANNIE

(Sings softly.) *Heeeere am I . . .*

ALDOUS

She thinks about how everything began for her. She remembers events occurring in an instant, in a . . .

> ALDOUS clicks the remote. Screen: "SPARK".

ALDOUS

She sees Kahn as if by a magician's trick, a soul pulled out of a hat, a hat pulled out of the

universe. She remembers turning to him, taking him in as he took her in, nothing between them but bell bottoms and punch cards and inklings that become matter as fast as thought, popping into realized bits at the moment of conception. "Greetings," he says the first time he sees her, the image of her a revelation. As if having known him a lifetime she asks, "Have you ever heard of something called the Homebrew Computer Club?" He responds, "And you *aaaaaare?*"

ANNIE

Now. They're coming now.

> ALDOUS clicks the remote. On screen: "BOY".

ALDOUS

A child materializes out of floppy disks and random memories. She considers hours spent staring into those little eyes, how beyond any kind of . . . anything it was, beyond any of her imaginings, beyond the inscrutability of even the most elegantly written code. Who is he? Whose is he? How can this creature occupy her thoughts so unceasingly, so all-encompassingly? He's an equation she can never hope to solve, stomping around in her thoughts like a little mental dictator, dragging her kicking and screaming out of this distant, abstract, theoretical mindlock in which she prefers to curl up into her every waking moment. It was around this time a rival company managed to get an offer to Annie to head up their R&D. How is that possible? She thinks. My brain is drowning. Everything else, everything thought process she had before becoming a mother falls away like fairy dust, and never comes back. (Beat.) Can't sleep. Takes pills.

ANNIE

I can't get security detail today.

ALDOUS

His first day of school, she asks how his teacher is and how the kids are and he shrugs. His emotional distance is heartbreaking for her. As he grows, the boy turns further inward, if that's possible, and further from his feelings. She's certain he possesses a great intelligence. And yet ...

On screen: A jumble of report card grades—mostly C's.

ANNIE

Push back the cleaners and pull up food service.

ALDOUS

She didn't like what school seemed to be doing to him, turning him into a rube for the military industrial complex, making an isolated soul out of him. She tried for a while to home school him. Stupid idea. All that time together. Drove them further apart. An urgency in her tone.

ANNIE

Aldous ...

ALDOUS

She reeeeally wants to tell him something, but every time she tries to form the words she can't bring herself to. She's terrified to crack open this door she knows will never close.

ANNIE reads her phone, large letters across the screen:
"PLANE HAS LANDED!!!!!!!!!!!"

ANNIE

The internet is the best thing to have ever happened to the exclamation mark. (Singing nervously, unconsciously ...) "*Heeeeere am I sitting in a tin caaaan ...*"

ALDOUS

Why are you singing?

ANNIE

Was I?

ALDOUS

Never heard you sing. (Then ...) She unconsciously throws her phone across the room.

ANNIE unconsciously throws her phone across the room. She gets on her hands and knees, begins searching for the phone.

ANNIE

The plane's already landed. How does a plane land eight hours early? The man is messing with us from the grave.

ALDOUS

Can I ask?

ANNIE

Uh huh?

ALDOUS

How long've you worked for him?

ANNIE

Can you find my phone?

ALDOUS

(Beat.) Yup. I'll call it.

ANNIE's phone rings.

ALDOUS

Someone's calling you.

ANNIE goes to where the ringing is coming from. She grabs her phone, looks at the screen. ALDOUS' NAME AND NUMBER appear on the screen.

ANNIE
Says you're calling me.
ALDOUS checks the screen of his phone.

ALDOUS
Nope.

ANNIE
The only other time I remember the place this quiet was when we closed down for two days because we had those rolling blackouts. Remember it? You were junior high-ish.

ALDOUS
I sort of remember.

ANNIE
(Re: Phone.) I've been looking at air traffic and weather and I don't see a reason for this flight to come in early. After we're done re-prepping, stay overnight at Isla's. 'kay?

ALDOUS
At Isla's?

ANNIE
Could you? I was thinking.

ALDOUS
Could I stay at Isla's?

ANNIE
You've slept over at Isla's before.

ALDOUS
Have not.

ANNIE
Right. Fine. But the will apparently states there are to be no other guests.

ALDOUS
I'm not a guest.

ANNIE
Trust me. Call Isla.

ALDOUS
She's not . . . in town.
ALDOUS receives a text. He checks his phone.

ALDOUS
Huh. It's Isla. For some reason she says she's coming here now. I guess she's in town.

ANNIE
That's weird. Now? Why?

ALDOUS
I don't know. Weird, huh?

ANNIE
She just texted you that right this second?

ALDOUS
Weird, right? I thought she was out of town.

ANNIE

> She can't come ... be here. She—
>> *A MAN dressed in black suit, stylish glasses, dishevelled, enters.*
>> *He looks around. He has an older, large walky- talky on his*
>> *belt and is talking on a burner phone.*

MAN

> (On phone.) Incorrect. (Beat.) Incorrect. (Beat.) Incorrect. (Beat.) Incorrect.

ANNIE

> I'm sorry, the hotel's closed for a private function.

MAN

> (On phone.) I gotta go.
>> *MAN hangs up the phone, snaps it in half and discards it in*
>> *his side bag. He grabs the walky-talky.*

MAN

> (To walky-talky.) I'm in. Over.

WALKY-TALKY

> Copy that.

ANNIE

> You have a walky-talky from an eighties cop show.

MAN

> Never underestimate the stealthiness of *true analog*.

ANNIE

> They called they're own security. That's you, right?

MAN

> I'm on the security side, yes. I oversee elements, both real time and digital.

ANNIE

> What about the guys I usually use?

MAN

> The guys you use are more security "guard" types. They don't hover in this sort of stratum. They've been notified, B-T-dubs.

ANNIE

> What's your name?

MAN

> (Pause.) Quentin.

ANNIE

> Who hired you?

QUENTIN

> People handling Kahn's estate. They did a lot of stuff without telling you. You should know the guests have landed.

ANNIE

> I'm aware. Last name? Yours?

QUENTIN

> (Ignoring her.) What I'm allowed to tell you is that Kahn's President was in Hong Kong meeting with Chinese-multinationals. Tech billionaire dies, President gets called outta there earlier than scheduled, and apparently there's also a pretty big deal Silicon Valley lady lawyer coming. So, count them, two flights—one commercial, one private and a third, totally empty Boeing from an undisclosed location.

After they landed at Kennedy the passengers were taken to Newark and Laguardia, then—check this out—four helicopters land in the outlying area, one at Buttonville, one at Hamilton International, one at Billy Bishop. Then two minivans. One hotel.

ANNIE

Where'd the fourth helicopter go?

QUENTIN

Riiiiight …?

ANNIE

Complicated travel itinerary.

QUENTIN

A certain amount of paranoia comes with Kahn I'd say. In life and in death.

ANNIE

Last name?

QUENTIN

Mine?

ANNIE

Uh ya.

QUENTIN

Jones. (Beat.) Tyler Moore. (Beat.) Fonzerelli. (Beat.) Look, just enjoy the ride. Without a million questions if at all possible.

ANNIE

What firm do you work for? .

QUENTIN

That would be a question.

ANNIE

In terms of security detail—

QUENTIN

There's vans at the northwest and southwest ends of the block on the residential side and units off the highway ramp exit and entrance and of course on either end of the property in the parking lot.

ANNIE

We'll have to feed them.

QUENTIN

Already taken care of. Meals provided by a restaurant called "The Department of Taste". Japanese fusion, I believe. One of the hottest places in town and they usually don't do take out. So everything's taken care of, we just need you to—
        ALDOUS clicks. The screen: "FACILITATE." ALDOUS

She's made the better part of a life ensuring people have a place to do important things in secret.

ANNIE

Why was the Boeing passenger-less?

QUENTIN

I'll inform you of developments the moment they tell me I can inform you of said developments.

ALDOUS

That's actually the name of a restaurant?

QUENTIN

Who is that guy?

ANNIE

This is my son. He lives here. Helps me run the place.

QUENTIN

Oh yes.

ANNIE

But he's leaving. As per, uh, stipulations.

QUENTIN

His absence wasn't requested. In fact, quite the opposite. He *can't* leave. (To ALDOUS.) You can't leave, so you know.

ANNIE

Why can't he leave?

QUENTIN

Because he's a beneficiary.

ALDOUS

I'm a ... (To ANNIE.) That's not what you were trying to tell me.

ANNIE

No.

ALDOUS

I'm in *Kahn's* will? That's insane. I'm going to buy Facebook.

> QUENTIN *pulls a smartphone out of his side bag, starts capturing photos of the surrounding area. As he snaps each pic a word appears on the screen:* "SHITTY", "RUNDOWN", "AIRPORT", "HOTEL" ...

QUENTIN

You don't have wifi?

> *He types and swipes at lightning speed on the tablet.*

ANNIE

Wifi's dangerous if you're trying to make people feel not vulnerable. We aim to provide the least vulnerable accommodations.

QUENTIN

We in 1982? All communications will be jammed once the last guest arrives.

ANNIE

We have plug-in in the rooms.

QUENTIN

Which we shall unplug. You say your son lives here with you? In the hotel?

ANNIE

Yes. And he works with me.

QUENTIN

How 'Psycho'. The movie, not the mental illness. You mind if I look around?

ANNIE

For what?

QUENTIN

Ssssstuff.

> QUENTIN *walks around, scanning.* ALDOUS *clicks the remote. The name* "QUENTIN" *appears.*

ALDOUS

First two pages of Quentins is all "Tarantino". He looks out the window at the vast airport parking, considers what he's here to do, considers the people on their way. VIPs. An abbreviation that to him has become synonymous with the word "criminal". His mind links back to an online entity he follows on various media: RoyBatty-underscore-1-8-2016. He thinks about how badly a person like that would want to find themselves in the middle of what's about to go down here today.

> QUENTIN *pulls out another burner phone. Dials a number.*
> *Through the following, he listens then presses buttons on the*
> *dial pad.*

ALDOUS

RoyBatty-underscore-1-8-2016 is a web handle that first appeared as a BBS Sysop for an early hacktivist organization named 'Cult Of The Dead Cow'. You all completely understood that, right? The man or woman behind this handle is now considered in some circles to be the Bansky of information leakers. No one knows his/her real name, or how he/she gets the access he/she does. It has been suggested he/she was the real person behind Cablegate, the Sarah Palin e-mail hack, Bilderberg . . . He/she is named for Rutger Hauer's character in the movie Blade Runner, the one who delivers the 'Tears in Rain' speech. I'm just geeking out right now. One of Quentin's main objectives here today is to make sure all doors remain closed to someone like Batty.

> QUENTIN *snaps the phone in half, discards the remnants in*
> *his side bag. He draws a can of air freshener out of his bag, sprays*
> *it into the air.*

ANNIE

What is that? What are you doing?

QUENTIN

There were some specific directions concerning the reading of the will. Air freshener was one of them.

ANNIE

Are you kidding? You need to check with me when—

QUENTIN

No, I don't.

> QUENTIN's *WALKY crackles.*

WALKY-TALKY

Gary Alameda approaching in red minivan. Over.

QUENTIN

Copy that.

ANNIE

(Re: Walky.) Who's on the other end of that?

QUENTIN

I'm not at liberty to, you know.

> QUENTIN *exits.* ALDOUS *crosses, clicks the remote. Search*
> *engine RESULTS are projected in a jumble.*

ALDOUS

Gary Alameda. About 476, 000 results. Oh look, he's the 15th result on the third page? Looks like someone's been search engine *de*-optimized. (He is shocked when the audience doesn't laugh.) Really? I thought that was so much funnier when I wrote it. Gary has been with Kahn since the beginning, since the company that started it all: LogSecure. He is President of Kahn's current technology systems corp 'SysRefresh'. 'Sysrefresh'. Sounds vaguely like toilet bowl cleaner. Kahn wasn't the best at naming things. Kahn knew Gary when he was at Texas Instruments. He liked what he saw, he said, "Let there be Gary" and then there was Gary. Gary is the worst thing that ever happened to disorder. He takes chaos and pummels it into certainty. He may not ever be liked but he will always be indispensable. They will always need him because no matter what happens, no matter how big and bad the monsters get, Gary makes sure they pay out on time.

GARY enters pulling a small suitcase. QUENTIN follows.

GARY

(On the phone.) No, you tell them if they don't stop their little blackhat armies from buzzing like shit-flies around our systems we're going after your government for human rights violations. (Pause.) Yeah, well that's the thing about information, you can delete it, overwrite it, burn it, take a crap on it. It never really goes away. You tell them I don't personally care what they do to their 12-year-old sweatshop hackers, but the world might. And if not, some diabolical darknet cult will.

GARY hangs up. When he sees ANNIE—

GARY

My God.

ALDOUS

Here, now, standing before him. The person who in some ways looms larger to him than even the god they are gathered for.

ANNIE

Hi Gary.

ALDOUS

This man who runs multinationals looking back at her like he's her lap dog.

GARY

You look—You in a relationship?

ALDOUS

He wants to touch her but is afraid she might disintegrate. Or he might. Or the world around them might.

GARY

Who the hell are you?

ANNIE

He's my son.

GARY

Right right right.

GARY approaches, gives her a big bear hug.

ALDOUS

The woman Kahn loved.

ANNIE

(Being squeezed.) Hiya.

GARY

What's that smell?

QUENTIN
    Air freshener.
GARY
    Who the hell are you?

ANNIE
    Security.
QUENTIN
    In that zone.
GARY
    Air freshener?
ANNIE
    Apparently in the will's directions.
GARY
    Jesus. He wants to control what we smell?
ANNIE
    He controlled everything. *Is* controlling everything.
GARY
    Good to hear nothing's changed.
                GARY looks around, annoyed.
GARY
    This is really one of his places?
ANNIE
    Uh huh. Can I take your bag?
GARY
    Looks like a government building ate a crack house and shat this place out.
                GARY hands her his suitcase.
GARY
    Stupid day. What the hell are we going to do without him, Annie? What are any
    of us going to do? You should see Hong Kong right now. The air is about to
    become sentient.
    QUENTIN pulls a translucent plastic folder out of his side bag and draws a
    document out of it. He hands it to GARY, who takes the document absently.
QUENTIN
    This is an agreement you'll need to sign before we proceed with any of the ...
    proceedings. (Re: document.) You can take some time to look it over if you want.
GARY
    Security is in charge of this stuff now?
QUENTIN
    Different kind of situation I think you'll agree. I'm also different kind of secur—
GARY
    Whatever. Who has a pen?
                QUENTIN searches himself, no pen.
QUENTIN
    Who ... has ... a ...?
                ALDOUS clicks. The word "PEN" projected in huge letters.
                ANNIE searches herself, no pen. Laughs to herself.

ALDOUS

This is the kind of thing Annie finds humorous, the irony of not being able to find a pen, here, now, where they are congregating because of a tech giant, in this time when every person has in their pocket the technology to publish a book or make a movie, but not to scratch a mark on a piece of paper.

ISLA enters, not expecting to see all these people.

ISLA

(To QUENTIN.) Oh hey. Who are you? (To GARY.) And who are you? It's a party. Hey

Annie. (To Aldous.) Hi, kid.

ALDOUS

Sup, girl.

GARY

Who the hell are you?

ALDOUS

She's Isla.

ISLA

I'm very Isla.

ALDOUS

I thought you were out of town.

ISLA

Flight was cancelled. Not even rescheduled. Just cancelled. No more flight. Like it disappeared.

> *She moves to ALDOUS as if drawn to him, gives him a sort of distant awkward kiss. ALDOUS receives it awkwardly and distantly, though he is equally drawn to her.*

ANNIE

What are you doing here?

ISLA

I was totally asked to be here.

ANNIE

You were asked to be here? By whom?

ISLA

Dunno. Lawyers. They sent me a van. I was about to head to the airport and then I found out about my flight and then I got a call from these guys who said they were lawyers—

GARY

Strange men you don't know who claimed to be lawyers sent you a van and you got into it?

ISLA

Yup.

ANNIE

(To QUENTIN.) What does she have to do with any of this?

QUENTIN

(Referencing phone.) All I know is she's supposed to be here.

ALDOUS
I'm in the will.

ISLA
Whose will?

ANNIE
(To ISLA.) You have a pen?
>	*ISLA happens to have a pen in her pocket.*

ISLA
Hey, yeah, I do!
>	*She pulls it out and gives it to ANNIE, who gives it to GARY who quickly goes to sign the agreement.*

GARY
Pen doesn't work.
>	*ANNIE laughs.*

GARY
What's so funny?

ANNIE
Inside pen joke. With myself. There'll be a pen in the room.
>	*GARY gives the pen back to ANNIE who gives it back to ISLA, who draws on the back of her hand with it.*

ANNIE
Aldous, can you show Gary to his room?

ISLA
(Re: Pen.) It's working for *me*.

ALDOUS
Which room?

ANNIE
Four-eleven.

ALDOUS
(To Gary.) Come with me.
>	*GARY exits. ISLA follows.*

ANNIE
Seriously, why does Isla have to be here?

QUENTIN
Your son's girlfriend?

ANNIE
(Annoyed.) Not technically.
>	*Pause.*

QUENTIN
How'd you know the man with the Star Trek villain name?

ANNIE
What?

QUENTIN
How did you know—

ANNIE
Kahn? None of your business?

QUENTIN

You were in an early unauthorized biography. You can't find it on shelves anymore. I think I saw a picture of you and him next to an early computer console, an 'Altair' or a 'KENBAK' or something, in the mid-seventies.

ANNIE

Then why'd you ask how I know him?

> *Pause.*

QUENTIN

I don't know.

ALDOUS

Kahn and Annie met the year the term "personal computer" was coined.

> *ANNIE and QUENTIN exit. ALDOUS clicks. The screen reads: 'ALTAIR 8800'. ISLA enters.*

ISLA

You ever heard of something called the Homebrew Computer Club?

ALDOUS

And you *aaaaare* ...?

ISLA

People trade info and hardware for a kit called the Altair 8800. It's a build-it-yourself personal computer.

ALDOUS

My name's Kahn.

ISLA

This guy Wozniak invented a machine called an "Apple" and gave away the schematics at one of the meetings. I mean "personal computing" ... (She makes an explosion sound.) You seem sort of rich. Are you rich?

ALDOUS

(He laughs at her boldness.)

ISLA

(She laughs at his appreciation of her boldness. Then ...) Buy me an Altair.

ALDOUS

It's a stupid hobbyist machine.

ISLA

Don't kid yourself. They're so backlogged no interfaces or peripherals are available until they catch up with the orders. It's a movement.

ALDOUS

How much is it?

ISLA

Five.

ALDOUS

Fine. Do I get your name now?

ISLA

Really? You'll just buy one for me like that?

ALDOUS

Yup.

ISLA

    The vaults are going to be blown open, you know. The access to data alone. The possibilities. I see so much … (Can't find the words.)

ALDOUS

    What? What do *you* see?

ISLA

    Need for security.

ALDOUS

    (Beat.) Huh. That's what you see?

ISLA

    With easy access to data that's the first thing I see.

ALDOUS

    That's so—

                ALDOUS makes an explosion sound.

ISLA

    I know who you are. You're the guy who was kicked out of MIT for hacking into their systems. I want to make stuff with you.

ALDOUS

    What kind of stuff?

ISLA

    Everything but babies.

ALDOUS

    What's wrong with babies?

ISLA

    Babies are stupid. I want to shatter paradigms.

ALDOUS

    Well, it's important to have realistic goals. What's your name?

ISLA

    Annie Mann.

ALDOUS

    (Pause.) I love you, Annie Mann.

ISLA

    Good. That's so good.

                MUSIC: Opening chords to "Space Oddity".
                ISLA and ALDOUS kiss deeply. GARY enters. ALDOUS and
                ISLA part.

GARY

    (Finishing a story.)—and then the whole thing fell on me.

ISLA

    That's totally "oh no".

ALDOUS

    Yeah, oh no. Totally.

GARY

    All the folding chairs and the sound system and the digital projector. I'm lucky to be alive.

                ALDOUS clicks the remote. ISLA stops in front of a part of the
                screen that has the word "GARY'S ROOM" projected onto it.

GARY

And all my employees standing around me, and not one had the urge to jump in there. To help me. Not for the sake of common decency or job advancement or even instinct. There's apparently no good reason to save my life.

ISLA

(She laughs.) That's sad.

GARY

You're a funny little thing aren't you? Are you guys an item?

> Both ISLA and ALDOUS start to talk, realize they're interrupting the other, stop to let the other speak and, when the other is silent, start to speak again. Then they stop again. Then start again.

GARY

Jesus, shut up. (To ISLA.) Do you work here, too?

ISLA

I'm a flight attendant. (To ALDOUS.) We should probably go and see if Annie needs anything.

GARY

I was talking.

ISLA

Actually I think *I* was talking. And then he was talking.

GARY

Well, I'm fucking talking now.

ISLA

Well, I'm fucking listening.

> GARY laughs.

GARY

Okay, okay. Where was I?

ISLA

You were saying that there's no good reason to save your life.

GARY

You're a smart ass. It's been a stupid day. Both of you go away.

ISLA

'kay.

> ISLA exits. SOUNDS OF: 'Speak and Spell' intro music.

ALDOUS

The year Texas Instruments manufactured a break-through in speech synthesis …

> ALDOUS clicks the remote and 'SPEAK & SPELL" is written on the screen as well as the computerized voice accompanying the toy: "Speak and spell." Gary opens his suitcase and pulls out circuit board after circuit board. He's not happy with them.

GARY

Perfboards? Seriously? I said etched PCBs.

ALDOUS

Perfboards are cheaper.

GARY
Sure. To manufacture. But then we lose speed during assembly. And the overall quality loss isn't worth it. See that's the thing about saving money. If you make a shit product that doesn't *make* money, there's no money to save.

ALDOUS
Do you know who I am?

GARY
You're the dweebus they brought in to predict the future.

ALDOUS
If you know who I am then you know how much influence I have. Why would you speak to me that way?

GARY
I'm infrastructure. I can talk to almost everyone like that. Especially the tech kiddies.

ALDOUS
Seems to me you need something to give a shit about, Gary.

GARY
Does it?

ALDOUS
Can I give you some advice? Get out of hardware.

GARY
Why?

ALDOUS
You wanna spend your life making toys that don't last long? Or building fortresses that last forever?

GARY
You have something in mind apparently.

ALDOUS
Online security.

GARY
(Laughs.) Like ARPANET kinda stuff?

ALDOUS
ARPANET is military, I'm talking beyond military.

GARY
There is nothing beyond military.
            GARY exits. ANNIE enters.

ALDOUS
She really wants to tell him something.
            LAURA enters.

ANNIE
(Struck.) Laura.

LAURA
(Struck.) Annie. (Beat.) Wowwy.

ALDOUS
When they see each other, they see the only other woman across a playground of boys with toys.
            They hug.

LAURA

> My God. How's your son?

ANNIE

> We're gonna do that? We're gonna be the kind of women who talk about our kids right off?

LAURA

> Okay fine, let's talk about our husbands. (She laughs at her own joke.) Please tell me you're working on something incredible.

ANNIE

> I run this place.

> > *LAURA looks around. Then back down to her phone.*

LAURA

> You? That's what *you* do?

ANNIE

> Yes.

LAURA

> What is that smell?

ANNIE

> Air freshener.

LAURA

> (Off what she's reading on phone.) Oh God.

ANNIE

> Something wrong?

LAURA

> Putting out fires. Kahn was big into digital rights and, I mean, the shear amount of money he gave … the moment he's dead, everyone goes ape shit. Did he set up a trust? Who's going to manage it? Etcetera. (Re: phone.) Ha. I just typed "etcetera".

ALDOUS

> Laura Kessler—3,880,000 results. This particular Laura Kessler is the first result on the first page. Round of applause. Come on give it up. (Hopefully the audience applauds.) She's a legal pioneer, was literally there at the creation of Internet law, figuring out the rules of cyberspace on the fly as Kahn's general counsel. He credits her for having once taught him that the role of the corporation is to create a problem, and then to provide the product that fixes it. In the case of online security that problem is freedom. Laura is also, incidentally, a hugely influential advocate for a free internet.

LAURA

> (To ANNIE.) I haven't seen you since. (Beat.) When was the last time you saw him? He tried to see you so many times.

ANNIE

> There was a year he left a message on my service every single day. An entire year.

LAURA

> Wow. To be loved like that.

ALDOUS

> Leave a message at the …

> > *ALDOUS clicks. Screen reads: "TONE".*

ALDOUS
Hi Annie we have Kahn on the line for you please give us a call when you get a chance hi Annie he's been trying to get in touch with you for some time you are not responding to any of his messages hey Annie you got a note letter wire cable package—Mother?

ANNIE
I don't want to see him.

ALDOUS
Why not?

ANNIE
Because I don't.

ALDOUS
He's … Kahn. And your boss. (Then …) If a man like that really wants to see you … I mean, a man like that doesn't give up. Ever. No matter what.

ANNIE
I'm going to go listen to the radio.

ALDOUS
Why not just fire up the ole gramophone?

ANNIE
There's no shame in the radio.

ALDOUS
This next song is dedicated—

> ALDOUS clicks: "ANNIE, TALK TO ME!" "ANNIE, CALL ME!" "CALL ME BACK, ANNIE!" in various fonts and sizes all over the screen. MUSIC: The opening guitar chords for "SPACE ODDITY".

ALDOUS
Then it finally stopped.

ANNIE
Then it stopped.

> Screen goes blank.

LAURA
Let's talk about our kids. How's your boy?

ANNIE
He's fine. I don't really feel like talking about he barely leaves the house. Hotel. I don't know. He helps me out here. I still think he's special somehow, but it's, I don't know, who knows? Your kids. Your kids.

LAURA
Insufferable successes. Achievers. They've exceeded their potentials in every way possible. My daughter is a fabulously successful journalist. *Journalism!* A dying industry and she thrives in it.

ANNIE
So great.

LAURA
I've always instilled in them the importance of certain principles, you know … uh … (She thinks too long.) … punctuality.

ANNIE
   (Beat.) Punctuality's good.

LAURA
   This is one of Kahn's places.

ANNIE
   Yes.

LAURA
   And you run it.

ANNIE
   Kahn flies in … *used* to … fly in … (ANNIE can't continue.)

ALDOUS
   … he used to fly in controversial figures from all over the world, get them out of danger's way, put them up in a secret locale. Who would suspect a budget airport hotel in Toronto?

ANNIE
   He asked me to run it. Make sure these people are well taken care of.

LAURA
   Amazing.

ANNIE
   Salmon Rushdie stayed in 319. Snowden in 420. We gave Ai Weiwei the whole 5th floor.

LAURA
   Oh, okay, wow.

ANNIE
   I managed to impress you.

LAURA
   Everyone's got an inner starfucker.

ANNIE
   Can I show you to your room?

LAURA
   Yes, please. I need a shower. How's the water pressure in this place?

ANNIE
   Um. Yes. Good.

LAURA
   (She stares at ANNIE again.) You. Toronto.

      ANNIE and LAURA exit leaving ALDOUS alone on stage.
      He turns out to the audience, takes it all for a moment.

ALDOUS
   Looks like everyone has arrived.

      ANNIE enters on her phone just as QUENTIN enters on
      his phone.

QUENTIN
   (On phone.) It's Quentin.

ANNIE
   (On phone.) Uh huh. Everything all right?

QUENTIN
   (On phone.) Why?

ANNIE

    (On phone.) Because you're on the phone talking to me and you just walked right
    past me.

    QUENTIN hangs up, snaps his burner phone, discards it.

QUENTIN

    I saw something on Reddit that made me think someone was sniffing us. I've
    radioed the posted guards, no one has seen anything. If I see so much as a curious
    hashtag, we shut the show down.

ANNIE

    Of course.

QUENTIN

    We're blocking communications now that everyone's arrived. No texts, no emails,
    no Tinder. And no one is allowed to leave. Did I give a waiver to Laura? You have
    to sign a waiver.

ANNIE

    Confidentiality?

QUENTIN

    And everyone waves their right to privacy and consent and what not.

ANNIE

    Consent? To what?

QUENTIN

    Look, I'm guessing you people are all about to get a lot of money. A lot. Like
    jabillions. That doesn't ever come for nothing. You have to be here, do what
    you're told and don't ask questions. (Beat.) I'll take the waiver to …

    ALDOUS clicks—on the screen the words: "LAURA'S ROOM".
    ANNIE exits. LAURA enters reading the agreement.

LAURA

    For the reading of a will? Does he want the rights to our first born as well?

QUENTIN

    I'm not here to negotiate the thing.

LAURA

    And if we don't sign …?

QUENTIN

    You may as well just get back into one of those vans and head back to wherever.

    LAURA signs the paper, hands it to QUENTIN, who exits.

ALDOUS

    The year a little computer called the 'Commodore 64' broke retail records …

    ALDOUS clicks and on the screen an image of the
    COMMODORE 64 LOGO.

LAURA

    (To ALDOUS.) This is the worst licensing agreement I've ever seen.

ALDOUS

    Annie signed it. She knew what she was signing. I just need you to put it into motion.

LAURA

    The market's on fire right now. Does she understand what she's giving away?

ALDOUS

    She does. Yes. She understands exactly what's happening.

LAURA
>She gives you full ownership of all IP. Why would she sign this? How can you make her sign this?

ALDOUS
>I'm not making her sign anything. Whose lawyer are you?
>>*LAURA and ALDOUS kiss suddenly. Passionately.*
>>*ANNIE enters, in her own world. An aspirin bottle in her hand, she pops it open and takes two.*
>>*LAURA notices ANNIE, pulls out of the kiss.*

LAURA
>Annie. Uh …
>>*QUENTIN enters, followed by GARY and ISLA.*

ISLA
>He was like a … a computer guy, right?

GARY
>A computer guy? A *COMPUTER* guy??? Who the hell is this person?

QUENTIN
>Ask her if she knows who the Beatles were?

ISLA
>Shyeah. Like a band right?

GARY
>Like a band?! Like a *BAND*?!!!!

QUENTIN
>Cool your duals, Gareth.

GARY
>This "computer guy", as you so retardedly put it, built the first online security company. Ever.
>>*ISLA doesn't react.*

GARY
>That does nothing for you? (No reaction.) National Scrabble champ by the time he was …?

QUENTIN
>Six.

ISLA
>Scrabble?

GARY
>Classical piano prodigy—

QUENTIN
>Eight.

GARY
>—*at eight*?

ANNIE
>Piano wasn't real. He just thought it sounded genius-y.

QUENTIN
>Really? Interesting. What else wasn't real?

ANNIE
>Brazilian Jujitsu master.

GARY

The fact that he claimed he was adopted.

ANNIE

No, that's true. He and Jobs had that in common. Not wanted as babies. Rabid ambition. Blah blah.

LAURA

I was adopted, I didn't turn into a ... He was in foster homes. That's when he gave himself the name Kahn. Wanted to give himself a name that sounded like a bad guy.

GARY

(To ISLA.) Was one of the guys that shrank the electrical transistor down to the size of a quarter. Do you realize what that did to computing as we know it?

ISLA

Nope.

GARY

Jesus.

QUENTIN

Tell her he invented gravity.

GARY

(Losing it.) The guy was instrumental in the anti-apartheid movement, the Velvet Revolution, Tiananmen Square ... If you don't shoot me an impressed look I will gouge your pretty eyes out.

LAURA

Eventually he had to move to Panama. No extradition treaty. Since then no one claims to have seen him in person. Except for Bono.

ISLA

(Impressed.) Like from U2? Damn.

GARY

That's it? That's what gets you? He was friends with Bono?

QUENTIN

That *is* pretty awesome.

ALDOUS's cell phone rings. He checks it.

ALDOUS

(To ISLA.) Says you're calling me.

ISLA

Ha! Weird.

ISLA checks her phone.

ISLA

Nope.

QUENTIN rushes to them, takes both their phones, looks at them.

QUENTIN

Interesting.

QUENTIN gives them their phones back and bounds off.
GARY, LAURA and ANNIE exit.

QUENTIN

(Into walky as he goes.) We've got a cell phone comm breech on the lower level. Over.

ALDOUS clicks. On the screen: "ISLA STACHANSKI."

ALDOUS

Googling "Isla Stachanski" gets you . . .

Screen: "ZERO".

ALDOUS

. . . zero results. That's impossible. Someone somewhere is making certain she doesn't "exist".

ISLA

I'd have sex with Bono. Even though he's old. Actually, there's a ton of old guys I'd have sex with.

ALDOUS

Nothing attaches to Isla. She is attached to nothing. She's a flight attendant. She literally spends most of her time not attached to the ground. She has an apartment she sleeps in a couple times a week, a technically "not-boyfriend" who she randomly met staying at this hotel during a stop over, a guy who couldn't possibly put any demands on her since he barely leaves his house. Hotel.

ISLA

Does that bug you? That I'd have sex with a ton of old guys?

ALDOUS

She claims to be fearless to the point of it being a psychological condition, routinely finds herself in the middle of, let's just say, compromising situations. She blames her intrepidness on a mysterious visit to the hospital when she was eleven and it looked like she was going to die. No one knew what was wrong with her. At the behest of an anonymous donor doctors were flown in from . . . *somewhere* and they saved her life. After that Isla was pretty sure the universe would take care of her. Turns out it would be to a ridiculous degree.

ISLA

Why do you think I was, like, requested?

ALDOUS

When she couldn't pay her rent a few years ago, a check from a matured savings bond or something else that might happen in 'Monopoly' showed up in her mailbox. When, after stumbling drunkenly out of a bar and into an alley with some guy who had a face tattoo, she was very nearly raped. Lo and behold, an unseen shooter put a bullet in that tattoo. The shooter was never identified. When, in her late teens, she visited a live volcano—

ISLA

You remember when you were a kid and you thought you could control traffic lights with your mind?

ALDOUS

Despite very different upbringings, Isla and Aldous share some parallel childhood experiences.

ISLA

You think I'm in the will?

ALDOUS

Why would you be? You don't even know who the guy was.

ISLA

Of course I know who he was, I'm not an idiot. I was just fucking with those guys. I actually met him once.

ALDOUS
You did?
ISLA
A few years ago, when I was taking tix at the airport. Would you like a window
seat, Mr. Kahn?

ALDOUS
It's just Kahn. One name. Like Cher.
ISLA
Oh my God. Sorry. Window seat?
ALDOUS
I don't know, what do you think?
ISLA
Personally, I'm like, you're going on a plane. And I know you've done it a million
times, but still you are about to freaking fly through the air and I'm like how
could you not want to see that through a freaking window?
ALDOUS
When God or whoever it was made you, they threw away the design specs.
ISLA
Soooo window seat?
ALDOUS
Two years after the movie War Games exploded personal computing ...
            ALDOUS clicks and we see the 'War Games' LOGO on
            the screen.
ISLA
OH GOD!
            ISLA and ALDOUS drop to the floor, make love.
ALDOUS
Oh Annie!
ISLA
Don't come inside me.
ISLA
Don't. Don't.
ALDOUS
I know. I know.
ISLA
(Beat.) What's that smell?
ALDOUS
What do you mean?
ISLA
Why does it smell like a bakery?
ALDOUS
Air freshener. Tahitian Vanilla. I like it.
            They laugh together, flip over. He stops fucking her.
ISLA
Don't stop fucking me.
ALDOUS
You know I have a stupidly low sperm count.

ISLA

Is that supposed to be hot?

ALDOUS

Can I come inside you? Just this once.

ISLA

(Pause.) Sure.

> *He fucks her. They come with exhilaration.*

ISLA

Get off! I said *don't* come inside me!

ALDOUS

You said "sure".

> *ISLA throws ALDOUS off her, who leaps to his feet. ISLA*
> *holds her belly and slowly exits. GARY enters and crosses.*

ALDOUS

So what I want you to do is locate every abortion clinic within, I don't know, say in the greater Bay area and make some donations. Tell them to look out for a possible walk-in.

GARY

Why?

ALDOUS

Also, I'd like to have Annie monitored very closely. Track everything. Her movements, her conversations, what she's reading, everything ...

> *GARY exits. LAURA enters.*

ALDOUS

Why won't she see me?

LAURA

She won't discuss it.

ALDOUS

She stopped coming to development meetings.

LAURA

She says she wants out. Of everything. She says she knows you have her under surveillance and she wants you to stop. She's filing a restraining order.

ALDOUS

That's a tad severe. Should I ask her to marry me?

LAURA

Excuse me?

ALDOUS

Is that what this is all about? I mean, she knows I'll take care of her.

LAURA

I think restraining orders are generally not cries to get married. You would marry her?

ALDOUS

Sure. Why not?

LAURA

I don't know. You're kinda/sorta fucking *me* like a lot ...

ALDOUS

    I fuck you like I'm taking down a gazelle in the Serengeti. What we have isn't a love thing.

LAURA

    Yeah, okay. That.

ALDOUS

    (Pause.) I'll find a way to get her back.

        LAURA exits. ALDOUS's eyes roll back into his head and he
        faints. ANNIE rushes in.

ANNIE

    Where is he where's my son the school called and they said he had a seizure of some kind and they rushed him here where is he I want to see my son what do you mean I can't see him this is against the law I'm going to call someone the police ...

        ALDOUS rises, ANNIE gets quiet. He steps up to face her.
        LAURA and GARY enter.

ALDOUS

    Been a long time.

ANNIE

    (To LAURA and GARY.) He's not supposed to be standing this close. That was in our agreement.

LAURA

    I know.

ANNIE

    He's breaking the law right now.

LAURA

    I know.

ANNIE

    How's my son? What's happening in there?

LAURA

    I don't know.

        ANNIE rushes to ALDOUS and knees him in the groin.
        ALDOUS goes down.

LAURA

    Annie!

GARY

    Holy shit!

ALDOUS

    (Scrambling to his feet.) Ha ha. That was. I thought she was going to kiss me.

ANNIE

    Where's my son?

ALDOUS

    I'm taking care of it.

ANNIE

    What are you taking care of?

ALDOUS

    (Turns to GARY and LAURA.) Give us a sec.

GARY

    Are you sure?

ALDOUS

    Yeah.

          GARY and LAURA exit reluctantly.

ALDOUS

    It's wonderful to see you.

          No response.

ALDOUS

    How's your money situation?

ANNIE

    What?

ALDOUS

    You need money?

ANNIE

    What's happening in there?

ALDOUS

    Hey, what grade is he in now?

ANNIE

    Don't ask me that kind of question.

ALDOUS

    He's older, though. You must be bored. I have a job for you. I need someone I can trust. I'm not going to force you to do anything you don't want to do, but I'd be appreciative.

ANNIE

    What sort of job?

ALDOUS

    It involves strategizing, scenario building, maybe not the most intellectually challenging but sort of thrilling. You'll be helping protect incredible people. Good people. At least by my standards.

ANNIE

    My mind's not what it used to be.

ALDOUS

    Trust me, you can handle this. Let's go check on your boy.

          ALDOUS turns to go.

ANNIE

    I've thought about it over and over. (Beat.) I was on the pill.

ALDOUS

    The pill isn't a hundred percent.

ANNIE

    You have a stupidly low sperm count.

          He doesn't know what to say.

ANNIE

    The smell.

          Silence.

ANNIE
> It did something to me, Kahn. Changed me. Irrevocably.

ALDOUS
> I'm going to make things right. But you have to trust me. Blindly.
>> *She looks at him for a long beat.*

ANNIE
> When do I start? The job.

ALDOUS
> You guys will have to relocate.
>> *ANNIE turns to go.*

ALDOUS
> Mother, what happened to me when I was twelve and I was rushed to the hospital?
>> *She stops.*

ANNIE
> We talked about that.

ALDOUS
> No, we didn't.

ANNIE
> You had a seizure.

ALDOUS
> Caused by what?
>> *GARY, QUENTIN and LAURA wheel conference room chairs
>> onto the stage.*

QUENTIN
> (Mid-conversation.) ... irrefutable proof that the whole honeybee thing is a vast conspiracy of The Megacorp. They want to control the planet's food supply. That's just fact.

GARY
> Where the hell did you read that?

QUENTIN
> (Into WALKY.) We've moved to ...

>> *Screen reads: "CONFERENCE ROOM."*

WALKY-TALKY
> (Crackle.) Sit tight. Over.

QUENTIN
> Roger that.
>> *GARY, LAURA, ANNIE and ALDOUS sit.
>> QUENTIN pulls out an aerosol can and sprays a long stream
>> around them.
>> Everyone checks their phones. Everyone realizes they have
>> no reception.
>> ISLA enters.*

ISLA
> Oh. Everybody's here. Aw, you guys look super sad. Why you sad?

GARY

It's the reading of a will, nimrod

ISLA

Right. I'm hungry. Quentin, are they gonna give us food?
                    MENU appears on the SCREEN.

ISLA

Yummy.
                    Pause.

GARY

Hey, Quinlan.

QUENTIN

Quentin.

GARY

What's the set list?

QUENTIN

Set list?

GARY

Ya. Like what's happening next. I knew him. Really well. And I know that every
second of these proceedings has been written down in painstaking detail some-
fucking-where.

QUENTIN

I get told things minute-to-minute.

GARY

Ya. I'm the President of the company. I was once his boss. I've worked more closely
with the guy than—

QUENTIN

Good for you. Everything you know, I know.

GARY

Ya. At least tell me how long we're going to be here.

QUENTIN

Dunno.

GARY

Ya. Ballpark.

QUENTIN

Dunno.

GARY

I'm handling a corporation in shock, here. I can't just, I can't just *BE* here and not
tell people when I'm going to *BE* there, wherever they need me to be.

QUENTIN

Well, he wanted you to *BE* here.
                    Pause.

GARY

Can I at least get a cell signal?

QUENTIN

No.

WALKY-TALKY

Is everyone seated? Over.

ISLA
	(Eyes light up.) Who's that?
QUENTIN
	Not at liberty. (Into WALKY.) Everyone seated. Over.
ISLA
	(To QUENTIN.) Who was that? Who was that? Who was that? Who was—
		She gives up.
GARY
	That air freshener is ... God this is fucked.
		MUSIC: Opening chords to "Space Oddity".
		ANNIE hears the music and leans forward. QUENTIN, still
		standing, falls sleep.
GARY
	What was I talking about? My employees? The urge to save me ...? Where are we?
	Conference room.
		GARY and LAURA stare out with vulnerability. ANNIE
		listens to the music, nods her head to the beat. ALDOUS and
		ISLA register this with one another.
ISLA
	Ummmm ...
		They suddenly pull out their phones and check. They realize
		they have no reception.
		LAURA giggles, first softly. She tries to suppress it but can't. It
		grows louder and more intense. She pulls it back, shocked.
ISLA
	You okay?
LAURA
	I don't know. Stop it, Gary.
GARY
	(Without looking up from his phone.) Stop what? I'm not doing anything.
LAURA
	Stop shooting me your horrible vibes. That's all you've been doing since I got here.
GARY
	In terms of vibes, that's all I got. Horrible ones. Take 'em or leave 'em. (Re: phone.)
	I've got no bars! NO BARS!
LAURA
	Put away your phone right this second.
ISLA
	Yeah, it's rude. Let's talk about food. Yum. Quentin, did I see a menu?
		LAURA laughs involuntarily. Stops herself.
ISLA
	I definitely saw a menu.
		LAURA laughs.
ISLA
	I'm killin' it.
GARY
	(To LAURA.) Stop it, for Christ's sake.

LAURA
> (Laughing, terrified) Can't for some reason.

GARY
> Jesus. Quincy! Can we get things moving?

QUENTIN
> My name isn't Quincy.

GARY
> I know, I did that on purpose, it's a tactic. Why did I say that? Is the executor of the will here?

QUENTIN
> *I'm* the executor.

GARY
> (Pause.) What?

QUENTIN
> I'm the executor.

GARY
> You're a security guard.

QUENTIN
> I'm executor by proxy. (Holding up walky-talky.) These guys represent the estate and I'm the only one who has access to them. So looks like I'm judge, jury and executor.
>> *Silence.*

GARY
> So, what? Are we supposed to sit here indefinitely?

QUENTIN
> All you need to be aware of at the moment is that you can't leave. None of you. Contractually. According to the agreement you all signed. There's a clause that stipulates you must abide by all conditions and if not they reserve the right to withhold whatever portion of the estate is bequeathed to you. They request you do not leave. Did you think this wasn't going to be weird?
>> *QUENTIN falls asleep again. LAURA giggles.*

GARY
> Will you stop crazy laughing!

LAURA
> Okay. I just … I feel so …

LAURA
> What's going on?
>> *Pause. LAURA stands and looks around as if taking her surroundings in for the first time. She tried to recall where she is and what is happening.*

LAURA
> Etc. Punctuality. Menu. (Giggles.)
>> *ALDOUS clicks, MENU text appears on the screen. LAURA sits back down, laughs. Throughout the following, she giggles sexually.*

ISLA
I'll read it. Totally. (Reading.) "Miso soup with mussels, tofu with crab sauce, chirashi sushi, miso glazed black cod with sautéed broccoli, yuzu crème brûlée."
LAURA realizes she has been getting more and more sexually aroused. Stops. Looks at everyone around her.

LAURA
I'm not eating Japanese takeout. From a place I've never heard of. Especially if I slept with him. With Kahn.
Beat.

ISLA
Did you just say you slept with Kahn?

LAURA
I said I refuse to eat Japanese fusion takeout.

ISLA
(Loving this.) Yeah, it's super below us.

LAURA
I'm not being a snob it's a health issue we had a thing for about a year. (Realizing what she just said.) I'm sorry, Annie. While you were together. Before you were pregnant. (Unable to stop herself.) Well, during. Once. Twice. The first time I didn't know. I knew. What is happening? I feel compelled to tell you. I honestly feel possessed. (Laughing.) I'm sorry, Annie. I don't find any of this funny. You should know it was just sex. Not ... you know ... anything more than ... But like such great sex, oh God, like nothing I'd ever experienced before, like *up against the wall and tearing open your stomach and your intestines pouring out*, you know.

ISLA
Oooh. Intestine sex.

ANNIE
I knew.
Pause.

LAURA
You ... knew?

ANNIE
I've always known.

LAURA
Back then? You knew?

ANNIE
Yes.

ISLA
A woman knows.

LAURA
My God. If I'd known you knew ...

ANNIE
Then what?

LAURA
I don't know, I could've ... it's just something that would have changed ... everything.

ANNIE
Would it have?

LAURA

A piece of information like that is a ... well, it's a game changer. You find out one thing like that ... it's like finding out you, I don't know, like finding out you have an extraordinary singing voice or ... there is no God.

ISLA

Not like exactly comparable.

LAURA

(To ISLA.) Can you please shut your stupid face?

ISLA

Sorry. I heart confrontation.

LAURA

The point is it's one piece of information and a whole other reality. In an instant. What if it was more than sex? I did not allow myself to so much as entertain the notion because I didn't want to hurt you.

ISLA

If you didn't want to hurt her maybe not *slammin'* him would've been a way to go.

ALDOUS

(To ANNIE.) You and Kahn were together?

> *Stunned silence.*

LAURA

He doesn't know? (Silence.) You don't know?

ALDOUS

Nope.

LAURA

How is that possible?

ALDOUS

She never talked about it. How would I know?

LAURA

Because it's like really obvious.

ALDOUS

She never told me anything. About anything. Like ever.

> *LAURA bursts out laughing. LAURA*

Not sure where this is coming from. I feel like such a terrible person.

GARY

Because you fucking are. Can we please get to hearing this thing and hopefully all become disgustingly wealthy and get out of here?

ISLA

Wait. Aren't you already disgustingly wealthy?

GARY

Who?

ISLA

You.

GARY

Me?

ISLA

Yeah.

GARY

    Am I disgustingly wealthy?

ISLA

    Yeah.

GARY

    No. You want a game changing piece of information? I live off a line of credit I established when the motherfucker went crazy and disappeared. For the third time. I went down with him so many times. He built me up financially and then ruined me—

        GARY suddenly bursts into tears. LAURA keeps giggling.
        MUSIC: Opening chords of 'Space Oddity'.

ISLA

    I'm having the. Weirdest. Best. Time.

        Music stops. GARY stops crying. LAURA stops laughing.

GARY

    That was nuts.

ISLA

    Aw, little guy.

GARY

    I didn't see that coming. That just completely just ... fucking ... happened.

LAURA

    A guy we loved died, Gary. It's fine to cry.

GARY

    (Crying.) I can't stop. Why can't I stop? Stop crying! Stop it! I've had just about enough of you, Laura.

LAURA

    I didn't say anything!

GARY

    Why he ever wanted you around I'll never fucking know.

LAURA

    Because I'm brilliant.

GARY

    I suppose having a massively available vagina didn't hurt.

LAURA

    Don't you dare cling to some misogynist re-framing of—

GARY

    I can't stand you.

LAURA

    I was every bit as valuable, if not more valuable than you ever—

GARY

    I couldn't stand you the moment I met you.

ISLA

    (Applauding ferociously.) Ya!

        GARY turns to her.

GARY

    What is your damage?

        ISLA stops clapping.

LAURA

(Realizing/remembering.) Wait a second. You know what, Gary? I don't remember when we met. That's funny.

GARY

What do you mean? How could you not? On the trip. The big trip. Remember? All of us, the four of us. The four of us together driving to Stanford to go to ... the meeting ... the club ...

LAURA

Homebrew? You weren't on that trip I don't think.

GARY

Of course I was. The trip to Stanford.

LAURA

The trip to Stanford he always talked about. The Homebrew Computer Club meeting. When we, quote: "Realized the potential of the personal computer".

GARY

Yeah. That trip.

LAURA

You weren't there, Gary. It was Annie and Kahn, myself and that guy who wouldn't wear shoes.

ANNIE

That guy who figured out *SWITCH! MODE! POWER SUPPLY!*
                    On the screen: "SWITCH! MODE! POWER SUPPLY!

ANNIE

Sorry, it's just that, uh, he never gets talked about and without him every computer in the world would be overheating.

QUENTIN

Guy's name was Rod Holt.

ANNIE

You know your tech history.

QUENTIN

I'm not good with compliments so heart-shaped emoticon and winky-face.
                    *On screen: A HEART-SHAPED EMOTICON and WINKY-
                    FACE EMOTICON.*

GARY

Rod Holt wore shoes. And he wasn't on that trip.

ANNIE

Who was it then?

LAURA

(To Gary.) How would you know? You weren't even there. Kahn met you at Texas Instruments. That was years after that trip.

GARY

(She's right.) Holy shit. (Beat. Cries softly.) Why do I remember being there?
                    ALDOUS clicks the remote. Projection: "MYTH".

LAURA

Because it was part of his dumb creation story, the way he wanted people to see the catalyst of his empire. He told it at the beginning of presentations. Every interview. All four of us driving to Stanford.

GARY

But I really remember being there.

LAURA

You go around thinking "this is reality" and then you find out one piece of information.

GARY

Yeah, but I was ... (Beat.) I met Wozniak there. That was ...

LAURA

You weren't on that trip.

GARY

(Beat.) ... the trip to Stanford.

LAURA

You weren't. Gary, you weren't there. It was Annie and Kahn, myself and ...

ANNIE

Not Rod Holt.

Silence.

GARY

Who?

EVERYONE but ALDOUS and ISLA stand. The screen reads: "GLITCH". They pull out their phones, sit and check. They realize there's no reception. QUENTIN is standing with his finger unconsciously on the aerosol nozzle, spraying.

ISLA

Something's in the air freshener.

WALKY-TALKY

Quentin. Move quickly to Isla with your walky-talky.

QUENTIN stops spraying. He moves quickly to ISLA. An ELECTRONIC SOUND emanates form the walky and ISLA faints instantly.

ALDOUS

What did you just do?

QUENTIN

Dunno.

WALKY-TALKY

(Crackle.) Aldous?

ALDOUS

(Pause.) Yes?

WALKY-TALKY

Isla's fine, we wanted to talk to you alone. Do you wanna know what's happening to everyone? Over.

ALDOUS

Sure.

WALKY-TALKY

They're buffering. Over.

ALDOUS

Who're you?

QUENTIN

Lawyers.

WALKY-TALKY

Not quite buffering. Something like it. A molecular hardware glitch. You wanna know what's in the spray?

ALDOUS

Okay.

WALKY-TALKY

GNR. Genetic nanobio-robotics. Microscopic robots you breathe into your bloodstream. Apparently affects something in the frontal lobe. Breaks down inhibitions. Heightens overall emotionality. Breaks down anticipatory and reflective thought patterns.

ALDOUS

Soooo alcohol?

WALKY-TALKY

Different. "MomentSoft" was Kahn's name for it.

ALDOUS

"MomentSoft"?

QUENTIN

Man can not name a thing to save his life.

WALKY-TALKY

This what is affecting everyone. He said he wanted them all to be open. To be unguarded with, quote, "full imagination and emotionality." He said he wanted everyone to, quote, "let go of the wheel". So that they might believe. Over.

ALDOUS

Believe in what?

WALKY-TALKY

Quote, "The possibility of all things." End quote. MomentSoft doesn't affect you.

ALDOUS

It doesn't?

WALKY-TALKY

You're different. So's Isla.

ALDOUS

How are we different?

WALKY-TALKY

One sec. Let me check if we … (Pause.) Yeah, we have no idea.

A tone plays through the WALKT-TALKY. ALDOUS crosses to help ISLA stand. She doesn't seem aware of what just happened.

ISLA

(Seeing ALDOUS.) Oh hey, baby. (Looking around.) Oh right. (Beat. Laughing.) Oh riiight. What was I talking—

WALKY-TALKY

La la la la la la la la. Wasn't important.

ISLA

Oh, good.

GARY cries softly.

ISLA
 Aw, Gary.
GARY
 Fuck you.

> *ANNIE crosses to ALDOUS, smacks him.*

ALDOUS
 Ow!
ANNIE
 Be more.
ALDOUS
 I'll try.
ANNIE
 Sorry.

> *LAURA laughs low.*

GARY
 How sad is this? When was the last time we even saw the fucker? He used to message me a thousand times a day. So fucked up because I realized one day that I was thinking of him as if he were, you know, a part of my life, that he felt so much a part of my life. But I realized that I hadn't seen him in nine years. In person. Nine years. Is that a real relationship? Doesn't seem right, doesn't seem, I don't know, the natural way to have a friendship. Why is everything exploding in my brain? I'm so fucking sad. I'm so mad. I'm sad and mad.

LAURA
 You have a complex understanding of your emotions.

GARY
 And I guess the thing that hurts the most, you know, is that ... Jesus, I feel like such a little bitch saying this ... it's just that ... I don't think he ... I wish he ... aw ... I wish he loved me. (Through sobbing gasps.) I don't think he loved me. He didn't love me.

ANNIE
 Don't be stupid.

GARY
 Am I stupid, too?

ANNIE
 Why do you say he didn't love you?

GARY
 First of all, I'm the least lovable guy maybe ever. And he was happy before I came onto the scene. All those guys were happy before guys like me jumped in. Selling hardware out of their garages. Never imagining how big they could get. Everything was being shared, it was all open source. You wanna know the truth? I think it was fucking beautiful. Guys like me turned the movement into a business. Made people rich beyond belief, but the money took all the fun away. I hate money. What am I saying?

ANNIE
 You're being a suck, Gary. The companies started getting too big to be run by smelly bearded anarchists. And if they wanted them to thrive they had to have people who knew how to handle infrastructure. And, make no mistake, he

wanted his company to thrive. So we could do the things we started to do. The big things.

QUENTIN

Which things?

ANNIE

The big ... ones.

QUENTIN

Which?

ANNIE

I don't. Recall.

>*QUENTIN goes to speak. They all turn to him. He stops himself.*

GARY

Yes? (Beat.) Quentin?

QUENTIN

What?

GARY

(Pause.) Did you want to talk?

QUENTIN

Did I—(He stops, confused.)

LAURA

(Beat.) It looked like you wanted to say something.

QUENTIN

I do.

GARY

(Pause.) Well fucking go.

QUENTIN

First of all my name is Quentin. Oh yeah, you said Quentin that time. Nevermind. Oh wow, okay. Just ... I wanted to ask about some stuff I may have read previously or heard here today. Okay. How, considering the size the mainframe would have had to have been over thirty years ago, did you build—no, wait, that's a stupid nerd question. I'm going to ask something else. How did you ... (Beat.) ... this is a question for Annie ... how did you end up living in a crappy airport hotel catering to the illuminati of fugitives?

ANNIE

I don't understand. The question.

QUENTIN

Yeah, you do. It might be a hard question to answer, but for sure you understood it. I'll ask a different one? They're just flooding my brain. It's delightful in a sort of horrifying way. What happened when Aldous went to the hospital? When he was rushed to the hospital when he was twelve?

ANNIE

I don't, uh ... know.

QUENTIN

How could you not know?

ANNIE

I don't, uh, want to, uh—

QUENTIN
    What's your auto-fill?
ANNIE
    My—
QUENTIN
    When you type your name into a search engine, what are the automatic words in
    the drop down?

> *ALDOUS clicks. Across the screen: "ANNIE MANN" typed.*
> *Then a drop box with various options: "ANY MAN", "ANNIE*
> *DA MAN", "AIMEE MANN", "AMIABLE MANATEE" ...*

ANNIE
    I'm not in the habit of typing my name into-
QUENTIN
    I can just type it in myself I guess. Dumb question. I think it's wrong that your
    son doesn't know how much you had to do with Kahn's empire? Just saying. My
    opinion. (To ALDOUS.) Your mom is super cool, dude. She was the Woz to Kahn's
    Steve. She was the Woz, man. She was one of those people who conceptualized so
    many things at the beginning. And the algorithm, that made the software possible.
    That the company was built on. The first basic non-military data encryption
    algorithm. Your mom developed the algorithm for LogSecure.
ANNIE
    How do you know this?
QUENTIN
    I read things. That are on paper.
ALDOUS
    But ...? (Beat. To ANNIE.) If that's true, then why wouldn't you want to tell me
    that? Why wouldn't you want to tell me that you were like ... what were you?
    Were you a programmer?
ANNIE
    Little bit.

> *ALDOUS raises the remote. SOUND OF a computer*
> *rebooting. Screen reads: "CONCEPTION".*

ALDOUS
    Say that again, Annie.
ISLA
    It uses enzymes to control the flow of specific protein as it moves down a strand
    of DNA.
ALDOUS
    This is kind of a fundamental building block when it comes to molecular electronics,
    so I'm going to ask her to say it again.
ISLA
    My design uses enzymes to control—
ALDOUS
    Again.
ISLA
    It uses—

ALDOUS

My God. (Silence.) My God. (Pause.) You know what you've come up with?

ISLA

Uh, yeah.

ALDOUS

A molecular transistor. A *molecular* transistor.

ISLA

Theoretically.

ALDOUS

I can barely keep it in my brain. I might cry.

QUENTIN

Aldous, your mother is every woman you've never heard of in the history of technology.

ANNIE

Quentin.

QUENTIN

She's Ada Lovelace. She's the Los Alamos wives. She's Hedy Lamarr, actress and did you know also developer of an early form of spread-spectrum broadcasting?

ANNIE

Quentin!

QUENTIN

And then Kahn erased your contribution. He deleted you from everywhere. From databases. Wikipedia. He erased you the way powerful men erase everything they don't like, through prolonged and forceful misinformation.

> *QUENTIN's walky crackles.*

WALKY-TALKY

Quentin. Next phase. Over.

> *QUENTIN immediately leaps into action, heads down the line holding his bag open.*

QUENTIN

It's time to get your riches, bitches. Phones and anything else that can capture an image, please.

> *Everyone drops their phone into the bag as he goes.*

LAURA

Are we gonna get these—

QUENTIN

Shut your face, Hilary Clinton.

GARY

HA!

QUENTIN

You too, bald Gordon Geko. All of you. Just shut up.

> *QUENTIN takes a stack of computer tablets out of his bag and distributes them to everyone.*

QUENTIN

Digital copy of the last will and testament. Touch the screen to begin.

> *A bunch of scrolling and tapping. As they read, what starts as excitement dissolves into a devastated silence.*

GARY

He didn't leave us ... anything? None of us?

LAURA

None of us?

GARY

(Trying to contain his rage.) I ... I ... need to ... to go murder a squirrel.

GARY gets up to go.

QUENTIN

You can't leave.

GARY

Try me.

QUENTIN

The doors are locked from the outside.

GARY

That's illegal.

QUENTIN

Sue whoever.

LAURA

(Re: Tablet.) Gary, keep reading.

GARY reads.

GARY

(To ISLA.) You better look at this, moron.

ISLA

Me?

ISLA taps on her tablet, scrolls.

ISLA

(Reading off her tablet.) It says, "thanks for the window seat." Says he left me ... (She reads.) Holy cow. Holy cow.

GARY

Everything. He left her the entire thing. All his shares in the company. The entire estate.

LAURA

Doesn't become active, for some reason, for a period of ... minimum six months. Conditionally. There's a clause. A conditional bequest. She has to, "after the allotted time period upon receipt of said bequest" ... (She reads silently to herself.) ... decide fair terms for the rest of us?

GARY

This is stupid. Who the fuck is this girl? Let's fucking kill her! I'm being emotional and hyperbolic obviously!

LAURA

She gets everything. Then gets to decide what we get.

GARY

(To ISLA.) I think you're terrific, by the way. Have since I met you earlier today.

ISLA

(Stunned.) Thanks a lot, buddy.

WALKY-TALKY
> (Crackling.) 'kay, that's done. Quentin, inform the beneficiaries that there's a verbal request. Over.

ANNIE
> Verbal ... request?

WALKY-TALKY
> That the young man go upstairs into one of the rooms we've prepared. Over.

QUENTIN
> That the—

ANNIE
> That you've prepared? What have you prepared it for?

QUENTIN
> We've—

WALKY-TALKY
> We've sterilized it, loaded in some equipment.

QUENTIN
> (Into Walky.) You guys want me to talk or—

WALKY-TALKY
> Electronic devices are prohibited.

QUENTIN
> I'm gonna let you take this.

ANNIE
> Don't go.

ALDOUS
> What do you want me to do up there?

WALKY-TALKY
> Watch a video. That's all. Watch a video he left for you.

ALDOUS
> For me?

ANNIE
> Don't go up there.

WALKY-TALKY
> If you don't go, it means the will's instructions were not followed properly, which means everything becomes null and void and no one gets anything. FYI. Over.

LAURA
> (Beat. To ALDOUS.) You should go.

WALKY-TALKY
> Give Quentin your watch ...

ANNIE
> Don't.

> ALDOUS rises, turns to QUENTIN, hands him his calculator
> watch.

ANNIE
> He's your father.

> ALDOUS turns to ANNIE.

ANNIE
> You knew that, right?

ALDOUS

Nope.

ANNIE

How could you not know?

GARY

Pretty much couldn't get more obvious.

ANNIE

I guess it's good that you know before going up there. It would be wrong if you found out that way.

ALDOUS

Because it's not wrong for me to find out this way?

> ANNIE doubles over as she gets an extreme wave of pain in
> her belly.
> Lights go black.
> On the screen: A blue dot of light. It morphs and warbles into
> various abstract digital patterns when prompted by a distant,
> tinny, digitally distorted voice.

KAHN

Aldous? (Pause.) Aldous? Hi. (Pause.) Hello. Are you there? Can you hear me? It's Kahn. It's me. It's not a video like they told you it would be. You're going to think it's nuts but I'm just gonna say it and see how it lands. You are hearing a voice module that translates my ... well ... my electromagnetic field. It was extracted from my body and then uploaded into the biodrive. In essence, we're talking about consciousness. My body started dying a little over twenty-four hours ago and my team was set and ready to initiate the scanning process in time. They uploaded my field and ... (Distortion.) Are you getting this? Can you hear me?

> ALDOUS steps in front of the screen.

ALDOUS

I can hear you.

KAHN

This tech, you understand, it's why I disappeared, every single time I disappeared. Either to work on it in utmost secrecy, or hide from people who wanted to kill me to get it. We're talking about a major leap in life extension science. If you can upload your programming then hopefully you can download it. Right? Body dies, the part that makes you you goes into a storage unit, you find another carrier, let's call it a "device". (Distortion.) But that get's tricky because this device has to be robust. You can't just upload into some average, stupid, dirty person. So we realized we needed to go ahead and build our own if it were possible. A healthy and beautiful one. One that would last long enough for me to be done with my "housing", as it were. You know what I'm saying? I'm saying ... (Distortion.) Super sorry about the voice quality. You wouldn't believe how hard it was to make me sound this good. Are you there?

ALDOUS

I'm here.

KAHN

You are here, aren't you? Your presence feels nice. I wish I could see you. It's a cliché, but in the end I found myself wishing I had none of it. Or rather I would have readily traded it all in … the money, the power, the influence. I would have given it all away if I could just be hanging with all you guys. To be by your mom's side watching viral vids or playing 'Stratego'. You know what I want right now? More than anything? God, I want to … (Distortion.) Sorry, was that inappropriate?

ALDOUS

You dropped out there.

KAHN

Can you hear me now?

ALDOUS

Yes.

KAHN

I wish I could … (Distortion.)

ALDOUS

No, I lost you.

KAHN

Now?

ALDOUS

Yes.

KAHN

(Distortion.) … your mom. I wish I could be doin' it with your mom. (Pause.) You hear me?

ALDOUS

(Wishing he hadn't.) Yes.

KAHN

I'm entirely aware of how inappropriate that was but I felt the need to say it. And I have another thing to say that you might not like so much. Something you really should know.

ALDOUS

I know. You're my father.

KAHN

No. That's what we told Annie. I *did* have intercourse with her to make it appear that that's how you were conceived, but truth be told, you don't really have a father. Or mother. Early nanobio. That's what you owe your life to. You're the first one ever made.

ALDOUS

(Pause.) Made?

KAHN

She carried you to term. She took care of you your whole life. But she was just a womb, biologically speaking. And a caregiver. We needed someone we knew we could have significant influence over. I had to devise a way to keep her close but not entrap her, you understand. So she wouldn't feel the need for you guys to run. Thus, the job. At the hotel. Look, this is … put simply … a team built you. Inside Annie. A team of nanobots. You're a bio-molecular self-sustaining device. When you were twelve we almost lost you. You remember when you were rushed to the hospital? It was a glitch in your operating system. Something happens at puberty. It was the last time I saw Annie in the flesh. So, yup, I'm not your dad.

And she's not genetically your mom. It's also important to note that Annie doesn't know any of this. She thinks you're her kid. And she feels deeply unsettled about the fact that she never seemed able to ... well ... love you? Love you. Like a mother loves her son.

> *Pause.*

KAHN

> You there?

ALDOUS

The tech isn't there. It can't be.

> KAHN

> Would I tell people if the tech was there? Seriously. This has been my life's work and you think I'd, what, Instagram it? Aldous, I hacked a woman's womb to grow you. *Without a sperm and without an egg.* The tech is there. You're the most amazing thing ever built.

ALDOUS

> Are you telling me I'm a robot?

KAHN'S VOICE

> No! Not a robot! Don't ever say that! You are a living, breathing, thinking biological device. You are superintelligence. You are the technological singularity.

> *The lights start flickering. ALDOUS looks up.*

KAHN

> See what you're doing there?

ALDOUS

> Wow. I *am* doing that, aren't I?

KAHN

> Remember when you were a kid and you thought you could control traffic lights with your mind?

ALDOUS

> That was real.

KAHN

> A sort of by-product of your functionality. This tendency to link to other devices. But with no consistency. We're still figuring it out.

ALDOUS

> So you're also saying that the way I am ...

KAHN

> What way?

ALDOUS

> This way of being ... this failure to launch, how I feel ... unable to connect to people and go out there and thrive in the world.

> *Lights stop flickering.*

KAHN

> Oh yeah, fully programmed. Like I said, the way we decided to go is to have you stay put so you wouldn't damage yourself.

ALDOUS

> Oh. (Beat.) What did you build me for?

KAHN

Because it's insanely cool, for one thing.

ALDOUS

That's the reason I'm alive. Because it's cool?

KAHN

At least there *is* a reason. Most people there's none. And, actually, yeah, there is another reason and I'm really kind of surprised you're still not catching on. But then again you didn't even put together that I was your father. Which I'm not. But you should have, given the overwhelming evidence, at least considered it. So, I'm going to say something to you but I need you to listen close and stay open minded.

ALDOUS

Stop.

KAHN

What?

ALDOUS

I get it.

KAHN

Eureka.

ALDOUS

You want me to be your ... device.

KAHN

Yes.

ALDOUS

You want to, like, body snatch me.

KAHN

If you want to put it in 1950's B-movie terminology ...

ALDOUS

But that's what you're talking about.

KAHN

Yes.

ALDOUS

Why don't you just abduct me and do whatever you want? Why are you selling me?

KAHN

You have to agree to it. I programmed free will into you. This has to be by choice.

ALDOUS

Why?

KAHN

It's a question of quality. Turns out that within the difference between robot and superintelligence, there lies free will. And when I'm in you, I want ... well ... superintelligence. Aldous, we're almost there. We know we can upload, and now we need to find out if we can download. I'm risking my life, however you want to define that. So would you be. But if we get this right then what's next is ... we've prepped it for Annie.

We're going to save Annie. She's very sick right now, Aldous.

Pause.

KAHN

Don't believe me? Want to see her stats? We've been monitoring her for a while. You should see how we're able to do that now. Everything from blood pressure to an EKG without ever needing to be in the room.

ALDOUS

I'm not sure I can keep having this conversation.

KAHN

We're going to save her though. With Isla. (Pause.) Isla's the same tech as you. Well, she's a slightly more advanced version. She's had a lot of bug fixes. We gave her a likability factor that frankly eclipses yours, and the inability to retain memories of trauma. Talk about free will. She leaps before she looks. It's a crapload of work keeping someone who lives in the eternal present like that from destroying themselves. Practically had to give her her own secret service. But when the time comes we won't have to sell her on any of it.

ALDOUS

She's a flight attendant, weren't you concerned about losing her in a plane crash?

KAHN

It's statistically the safest job we could have arranged for her.

>   *Pause.*

ALDOUS

What happens to me? What happens to my "field"?

KAHN

You go into the biodrive, eventually we hack another womb and build you a device.

ALDOUS

And until then?

KAHN

Oh my God. Such good stuff.

ALDOUS

Like …

KAHN

So much good stuff.

ALDOUS

Like …

KAHN

You become pure electronic consciousness. Pure electronic thinking. I'm right here right now in that place and I'm here to tell you it's really freaking good.

ALDOUS

Doesn't sound that good.

KAHN

It's amazing. You move like thought. You can fully interact with machines. Just machines.

ALDOUS

Not … humans?

KAHN

Not directly. I think you, especially, would like it.

>   *Silence.*

ALDOUS

    If I did it, I'd be doing it for her?

KAHN

    And for all of humankind. Think about what you have the opportunity to be a part of. NOTHING SHORT OF THE POTENTIAL FOR HUMAN IMMORTALITY.

ALDOUS

    If I did it, I'd be doing it for her.

KAHN

    For Annie. Yes.

ALDOUS

    You think she didn't love me?

KAHN

    I didn't exactly say—

ALDOUS

    Yeah, you did.

KAHN

    Yes, I did. Look, the way I see it, she was this genius, this visionary and then ... you were ... (Pause.) ... born. You ruined her. What would it feel like right now to save her?

        Extremely long silence as ALDOUS deliberates.

ALDOUS

    (Softly.) Okay.

ANNIE

    WHERE IS HE?! WHERE'S MY SON?!

        Lights go very bright.
        QUENTIN, LAURA, GARY and ISLA hold ANNIE back
        from going up to the room.

ANNIE

    HE'S BEEN UP THERE FOR HOURS! I WANT TO SEE MY SON! IS HE STILL UP THERE?! WHERE IS MY SON?!

        ALDOUS turns to them.

QUENTIN

    He's right there! Look! Just look at him! He's right in front of you.

ANNIE

    Oh. I didn't ... see you ... somehow.

        Their eyes connect. She calms. EVERYONE lets go of her.

ANNIE

    Are you ...? Are you all right?

ALDOUS

    Boy, am I.

    ANNIE goes to him, stops.

ALDOUS

    Yes. Come.

        She doesn't.

ALDOUS
    What's wrong?
            ALDOUS takes a step toward ANNIE and she backs away.

ALDOUS
    What's the matter?
ANNIE
    Nothing. You're okay?
ALDOUS
    Oh yeah.
ANNIE
    You look ...
            ISLA rushes to ALDOUS, hugs him.
ALDOUS
    (Ecstatic.) Aw, wow.
            ALDOUS hugs her tight.
ISLA
    You feel weird.
ALDOUS
    This feels good. Being hugged. Talking through vocal chords.
ISLA
    That's a weird thing to say.
            She lets go of him.
ALDOUS
    So how is everyone? You guys well?
GARY
    What happened up there?
LAURA
    Did you watch the video?
ALDOUS
    (Remembering.) Oh yeah. It was long.
GARY
    Yeah?
ALDOUS
    Mmhm. He wanted me to relay some information to all of you. Each of you.
            Pause. He takes them all in.
GARY
    What is it?
ALDOUS
    Seeing you guys. In the flesh. This is so unbelievably exciting. You guys look ...
    (He makes a strange, overwhelmingly excited noise.)
GARY
    Annie, what is going on with your son?
ALDOUS
    I feel deeply deeply connected to you ... Quentin.
QUENTIN
    That's ... what?

ALDOUS
Are you just so honored to be here?

QUENTIN
Ssssure.

ALDOUS
You're a good person. You take big risks for what you believe in.

QUENTIN
I do?

ALDOUS
Can I, can I, can I make physical contact with you?

QUENTIN
Nope.

ALDOUS
Completely fine. Now I'm about to draw the curtain on some pretty heavy stuff, Quentin, and as a witness, you're integral to this process. (He discovers his belly, lifts his shirt, tickles it pleasurably under the following.) But if the vibe right now is too much for you you let me know. Okay? What I'm saying is, if you want to leave you're free to leave but you have to do it now. And, of course, we'll erase your memory.

QUENTIN
I'll stay.

ALDOUS
I'm so glad. I intended for you to be here, you know. I chose you specifically.

QUENTIN
Why?

ALDOUS
I know who you are. Who you really are. I've known since you were just a brat posting on GeoCities and message boards about our unreleased upgrades.

QUENTIN
What're you talking about?

ALDOUS
It's an age old origin story. You were a programmer plebe at LogSecure who wanted to be on the management team for one of our initiatives in the early nineties, I don't even remember what it was. You didn't get the job, you developed a burning hatred for the company and then you became our primary leak source. Yeah, we knew about you. But it didn't bother us. Not until you started cracking encryption algorithms. I want you to recognize, however, that that disappointment we caused, you not getting your promotion, made you the legend you are today.

QUENTIN
I'm not sure what you're—

ALDOUS
You're not?

QUENTIN
No. I'm—

ALDOUS
You're not sure.

QUENTIN
(Beat.) I'm—
ALDOUS
What I'm talking about.
QUENTIN
(Beat.) I—
ALDOUS
RoyBatty-underscore-1-8-2016? (Pause.) Really? Not sure?
        QUENTIN is speechless.
ALDOUS
I'm gonna let you chew on that. Who's next? Gary.
        ALDOUS moves to GARY, grabs him by the shoulders.
GARY
Why are you touching me?
ALDOUS
I can't tell you how much he loved you. And that you would ever doubt it says more about his failings than anything. Who else was there? Who else was ever there for me but Gary?
GARY
You're freaking me out.
ALDOUS
That's what he said. In the video. He said he loved you.
GARY
He said that?
ALDOUS
Yes.
GARY
How did he say it? In the video. Exact words.
ALDOUS
Exactly like I just said it.
        GARY weeps.
ALDOUS
Aw, look at you. Oh, beautiful man. Beautiful beautiful man with so much in his heart. This is it, isn't it? This is everything. All this ... fffffeeling. I have to sit down. No I just have to breathe.
        He takes a big breath.
ALDOUS
Laura.
LAURA
What?
ALDOUS
Your turn. You remember when you were having the affair with him? That raw unexplainable connection, that frankly, admit it, you haven't had since.
LAURA
He said that in the video?

ALDOUS

And poor girl you never really had the chance to define what that was for yourself, that thing you had. You know, because of the reality of the situation. Well, let me clear it up once and for all. You're his biological sister. (Silence.) It was only when he went looking for his birth parents that he found out about the daughter they also gave up, which is you. (Pause.) You're my family. We're our only family.

LAURA

Where's my phone I need to call my kids.

ALDOUS

You mean my niece and nephew?

LAURA tries not to throw up.

ALDOUS

You should also know at some point I knew you were my sister and continued having sex with you.

LAURA

Why ...?

ALDOUS

Because it's liberating. I mean think about it, if you can have sex with your sibling over and over again and not have a problem with it then there's almost no social construct you can't demolish.

LAURA laughs maniacally.

ALDOUS

I know, right? There is no God and you have an extraordinary singing voice.

LAURA sits where she stands. Cries. QUENTIN

It's not you. You're not him. You're not Aldous.

ALDOUS touches his nose then points at QUENTIN.

ALDOUS

Good boy, Quentin. Now ...

ALDOUS turns to ANNIE.

ALDOUS

Hi, Annie. Are you ready to get messed up?

He approaches slowly. ALDOUS

You wouldn't answer my calls. You wouldn't answer my e-mails. Every time I came near you, police. I've been wanting to see you for so many years. Other than on closed circuit screens.

ANNIE

Stay away.

ALDOUS

Don't be afraid. Your ideas built me. And you'll get credit for it. You'll get everything, actually.

ANNIE

This isn't happening.

ALDOUS

It is. And it's happening fast. We're gonna need to talk about your health super soon. I hope now's a good time. Vaginal bleeding. Need to urinate with frequency. Feeling of general pressure in the pelvic or abdominal area. You should've seen a doctor a long time ago.

ANNIE

    Stop.

ALDOUS

    (Grave.) It's in the ovaries, Annie. Could be related to the nanobio. To Aldous's conception. You've got about six months. But we have the capability to radically extend that. Are you paying attention, Quentin?

QUENTIN

    Can I write stuff down?

ALDOUS

    You don't have a pen. We'll give you an info sheet later. Everyone here is marked to be the first. I'm looking at a bunch of Neil Armstrongs right here in front of us. Here's the plan: We all keep this info in the vault while RoyBatty leaks the hell out of it. Next thing you know it'll be all over robotics conferences, Solve for X, Sci Foo Camp ... (Glances out at the audience.) ... auditorium stages and convention centres everywhere, the story being told about the day you were summoned in secrecy to a cheap airport hotel and shown how we are going to kick ... death's ... ass.

        ALDOUS clicks the remote. 'MYTH' appears on the screen.

ALDOUS

    And this you'll have actually been there for, Gary.

GARY

    (Through tears.) What if I'm not sure I want to live that long?

ALDOUS

    Oh baby, you don't have to decide right this second. We don't even have your device ready. We're growing it. Yours too, Laura.

GARY

    Am I going to get ... money?

ALDOUS

    Well, that's gonna be up to Annie, isn't it? I love you, Annie Mann. Never stopped, always will.

        ALDOUS rises, moves to ISLA.

ALDOUS

    Your device is ready. (Moves to ISLA.) Isla's robust.

ISLA

    Whaaa ...?

ALDOUS

    She's all system go. And I know you. You weren't gonna go along just to get along so I embedded it all with a little incentive. Once you transfer into the girl, everything's yours.

ISLA

    Awesome.

ALDOUS

    You decide who gets what. Even me. You control it all. The company and the tech. You get to be who you should've been this whole time.

ANNIE

    No.

ALDOUS

Okay, but if you refuse then the board of directors decides.

GARY

Annie don't let that happen. We're assholes.

ANNIE turns to ISLA, who is moved by this.

ISLA

(To ANNIE, through tears.) I would love to be you.

ANNIE

This can't be real.

ALDOUS

You of all people know how real it can be. You were the first to conceptualize everything, down to the delivery platform. Aerosol exposure. Microscopic robots in the air. You thought that up.

ANNIE

Where's my son?

ALDOUS

He was never your son.

ANNIE

I want to see my son.

ALDOUS

He's in the grid.

ANNIE

Pardon?

ALDOUS

He's electricity. He's inside your phone and mine. Aldous, do something to show us you're here!

The lights flicker.

ALDOUS

He likes the lights thing.

ANNIE

What did you do to him? How did he agree to this?

ALDOUS

It was complete free will. He completely gave himself to us. Once I told him the truth.

ANNIE

What truth?

ALDOUS

That you couldn't love him.

ANNIE

Oh God. Oh my God.

The lights flicker.

ANNIE

My little boy … You *made* my life … (To ALDOUS.) You told him I didn't love him? What could you possibly know about love?

ALDOUS approaches her.

ALDOUS

I'm here, aren't I? Against incredible odds. I'm giving you everything I spent my life building. And I'm giving you the greatest gift that can be given. *Life.*

ANNIE

My god. Is this real?

Lights go dark momentarily then come back up.

ANNIE

My boy. My boy.

She turns to ALDOUS, touches him to see if he's real.

ALDOUS

You want to bring him back? You can bring him back. It's up to you now.

ANNIE

Can you prove it? Prove it's you.

ALDOUS

Ask me something that only I would know the answer to.

ANNIE thinks.

ANNIE

The night we first made love ... what was playing on the radio?

Pause.

ALDOUS

(Singing.) *"Check ignition and may God's love be with you ..."*

MUSIC kicks in: "Space Oddity".

ALDOUS leans in toward ANNIE in for a kiss. Just as their lips are about to touch MUSIC drops out and ALDOUS takes a step away. He turns out to the audience. Let's the moment hang.

ALDOUS

The question now is how far from our nature will tech take us. (Pause.) Buckle up, friends.

ALDOUS swoops back in and kisses ANNIE passionately as MUSIC kicks back in loud. ANNIE can't help but be drawn to him. It really feels like Kahn. She kisses back with full force, losing herself in him.

ALDOUS opens his arms out wide to demonstrate to the audience that ANNIE is, in fact, kissing him. Mission accomplished! Suddenly ANNIE becomes horrified, pulls away. She drops to her knees.

ISLA stands, the remote now in her hands—she clicks it. The screen reads: "PRODUCT".

ISLA comes downstage to where ALDOUS started the play, takes the audience in with an exhilarated smile. She clicks the remote. MUSIC ends abruptly.

ISLA

I'd like to close with a quote by, uh, William Shakespeare: "It is not in the stars to hold our destiny but in ourselves." (Silence.) Thanks everyone. Thanks for coming. Have a magnificent life.

The lights flicker. ISLA clicks the remote. The screen shrinks down to a blue dot and then goes BLACK.

END OF PLAY.

Biographical Musings

PROFESSIONALLY ETHNIC

2006
Bobby Del Rio

"I wrote this play a decade ago. So when I hear over and over again how relevant the play's themes are, it actually makes me sad. This play is the theatricalization of many years I spent working as an anti-racism political activist. It is my hope that one day this play will be viewed as redundant—as society will have adopted my point of view years before."
— **Playwright's Note**, *Professionally Ethnic*
2017 SummerWorks Program

CHARACTERS:

WILLIAM—20s, ambiguously 'ethnic', moralistic, angry
KYLE—20s, white, funny, good heart
TRACY—20s, black, smart, grounded
GERRARD—50s, white, takes himself VERY seriously

SYNOPSIS:

An ambiguously ethnic actor is offered a chance at stardom—if he is willing to play up an ethnic identity he doesn't agree with …

> *2 guys are arguing. They are WILLIAM, (20s, ethnic) and KYLE (20s, white). They are shooting hoops with WILLIAM's mini basketball hoop above his garbage can.*

WILLIAM
That play was shit.
KYLE
I found it fascinating.
WILLIAM
How could it get nominated for a fucking best play award?
KYLE
It was an interesting story. (*hits a basket*) White boys shoot 3s. I think it's in our genes.
WILLIAM
It's just cause it was Chinese. (*misses shot*) How do you do that?
KYLE
You wouldn't understand. It's the golf gene.

WILLIAM

> 2 words: Tiger Woods.

KYLE

> 2 more words: Everybody else.

WILLIAM

> Go to hell. And as for the play shit, every other play was a white play. They wanted 'diversity', so they took a shitty Asian play and hyped it up. They do it with every race every year. It's the guilt award.

KYLE

> That's racist.

WILLIAM

> I can't be racist.

KYLE

> Cuz you're not white?

WILLIAM

> Yep.

KYLE

> That's bullshit.

WILLIAM

> Hey man, I don't have to pussyfoot around the issues. My skin gives me the carte blanche to say whatever I want.

KYLE

> Ethnicity is not a license to be an asshole.

WILLIAM

> I'm not trying to be an asshole. But if a play isn't good enough to compete with the best, it shouldn't be honoured as such.

KYLE

> Yeah, but when every single category is completely dominated by us white people, there has to be a way to create a level playing field. Plus, I totally dug that play. I think the identity stuff is interesting. It's like different.

WILLIAM

> It's not fucking different! It's an excuse for every playwright of colour to start asking their grandparents stories of the 'old country' so they can get grant money! It's ghettoization. It's a step backwards.

KYLE

> What the fuck do you know, man? Have you ever written a play?

WILLIAM

> I don't have to be a playwright to have an opinion.

KYLE

> What are you: a theatre critic? Maybe they just found those stories compelling. The muse, or whatever, can take many

WILLIAM

> It's fucking bullshit, man. To succeed as an ethnic artist, you have to grasp on to your exotic appeal and milk it for everything it's worth. That's fucking bullshit. I'm an artist. Straight up. I don't wanna have to bust out a dashiki or play the sitar or learn the language my parents speak so I can get attention.

KYLE

You're so fucking angry, dude.

WILLIAM

Yep.

KYLE

Just work on your audition technique. That's something to do. (*Hits a three.*) Korver pops another 3!

WILLIAM

Why don't I work on banging your mother?

KYLE

Mother jokes? That's so 1995.

WILLIAM

I'll 1995 your mother.

KYLE

If you touch my mother, I'll get you lynched. (*Hits yet another three.*) Korver's on fire!

WILLIAM

Lynch away, whitey. (*WILLIAM dunks on the tiny hoop, ripping it down.*) LeBron!

KYLE

Okay Gandhi's angry brother, I'm sick of this 'sports for midgets' thing anyway.

WILLIAM

Okay, well prepare for the real deal. Don't forget: basketball at 2 tomorrow.

KYLE

Your shit is mine.

WILLIAM

You got lucky last game. Tomorrow, I bust out the crossover.

KYLE

Bust out whatever you want. It's not gonna help. (*looks at watch*) I gotta make some calls, check my email, but I'll meet you at the court tomorrow at 2 ...

WILLIAM

Cool.

> The artistic director, GERRARD, (56, white) of a powerful
> theatre company is speaking on a panel.

GERRARD

And this initiative will ensure that opportunities abound for ALL of our artists from all different backgrounds ...

> TRACY (20s, black) comes up to the microphone to make a
> comment.

TRACY

Mr. Smith?

GERRARD

Call me Gerrard. (*He smiles at her.*)

TRACY

Well Gerrard, I am grateful for your commitment to diversity.

GERRARD

Thank you.

TRACY

I also appreciate you taking time out of your busy schedule to speak on this panel.

GERRARD (*smiling*)

This kind of panel is essential if we are to have an inclusive Theatre.

TRACY

But I would be remiss if I did not state my disappointment at the glaring imbalance of visible minorities on your board of directors. (*There is a big stir created on stage because of this comment.*) As much as these incentive programs are appreciated, unless the entire brand identity of your organization is changed, the issues remain the same. My question is: why can't people of colour penetrate your power structure?

GERRARD

That's an important question, and it's exactly what I'm trying to do. Our theatre company is big. It is influential. And I believe we have a responsibility to find solutions to these pressing issues by placing inclusion at the center of our artistic vision.

TRACY

But

GERRARD

Okay, everyone. That's all the time we have for today, but please feel free to track us down on your own time to let us know what's on your mind. It is our hope that important panel discussions like these will lead to fair and equitable solutions to all involved. Thank you and good night.

>*WILLIAM and GERRARD meet at a Chinese restaurant.*
>*GERRARD enters.*

GERRARD

I'm glad you could make it.

WILLIAM

Of course.

GERRARD

This is one of my favourite places.

WILLIAM

I've never heard of it.

GERRARD

Yeah, it's quite good. Great ma po dou fu. [or some other fancy dish]. (*pause*) Anyway.

WILLIAM

Right.

GERRARD

So I wanted to thank you for taking the time to meet me.

WILLIAM

Certainly.

GERRARD

I want you to take a look at something. (*He pulls out a laptop computer. He turns it on, and opens a file.*) Read this.

WILLIAM (*reads*)

"… only one visible minority performer was good enough to be considered for the company …"

GERRARD

That's you.

WILLIAM

That's me?

GERRARD

You were the one. I was specifically looking for actors of colour at the showcase. You were the one I found.

WILLIAM

Hmm.

GERRARD

I just thought you should know.

WILLIAM

Well, that's quite a compliment.

GERRARD

You earned it. Of the 9 non westerneurocentric performers, you were clearly the best.

WILLIAM

But you never hired me?

GERRARD

Well, the writer insisted on someone else for that role; and anyway we were still trying to figure out how to integrate multiculturalism into the fabric of our longterm vision. And now we have a plan.

WILLIAM

That's encouraging.

GERRARD

You haven't heard the plan.

WILLIAM

The plan is the encouraging part.

GERRARD

Okay. Here it is: Setting the new international standard for multicultural artists.

WILLIAM

Wow.

GERRARD

"Everybody gets a chance to be represented."

WILLIAM

Hmm.

GERRARD

Not bad for a whitey, eh?

WILLIAM

Not bad.

GERRARD

You haven't heard the best part.

WILLIAM

What's the best part?

GERRARD

I want you to join us.

WILLIAM

Me? I've auditioned for you twice and never been hired.

GERRARD

I want you to play the lead.

WILLIAM

Me?

GERRARD

This community needs to see that you don't have to be white to be a star. And you will be our new star.

WILLIAM is revealed with his girlfriend: TRACY.

TRACY

How'd it go?

WILLIAM

It's the lead!

TRACY

Holy shit!

WILLIAM

I know.

TRACY

He's

WILLIAM

I know.

TRACY

You're totally a token.

WILLIAM (*taken aback*)

But ... it's like here I am sitting at a table with one of the most powerful men in theatre, and he offers me a job. The job. Straight up. "Take this job."

TRACY

But—And?

WILLIAM

It felt right.

TRACY says nothing.

WILLIAM

You think it's totally for show?

TRACY

Well ...

WILLIAM

Like "Ethnics On Parade" or something? "See them act! See them dance!"

TRACY

This is when it's shitty to have a conscience.

WILLIAM

I still believe in talent.

TRACY

You must be very lonely. WILLIAM says nothing.

TRACY

You should have heard him speak. Gerrard Smith is a complete fucking hypocrite. He's going on and on about his great plans for multiculturalism in the arts, when

his company hasn't appointed one fucking ethnic board member in the last
10 years!

WILLIAM

Well, this initiative sounds like it will change the balance.

TRACY

Yeah, but what's really going to change? He uses you for your exotic cache, gets
more grant money for doing it, and still all the people running the show are white!

WILLIAM

Well, at least I get a job.

TRACY

I know you do, honey. And that's great. But until we get more people of colour
running shit, we're picking up table scraps.

WILLIAM

Looks like your law school friends are rubbing off on you.

TRACY

Hey man, it's a good thing. This Equity Studies course is like the coolest course
ever! I'm totally going into Labour Law.

WILLIAM

I'm glad that you finally have some focus, but I worry.

TRACY

About?

WILLIAM

Well, it's like you see all these people who are all about 'the cause' or whatever.
But as soon as they get a piece of the pie, they're gone. It's like political activism
is just another way to make contacts.

TRACY

Give me some credit.

WILLIAM

It's not that I don't think you're awesome. I do. I think you're totally doing the
right thing, and trying to make a legitimate change. But I wonder how long you
can really sustain the fight.

TRACY

As long as it takes.

WILLIAM

I mean, it's like if you didn't have to starve, why would you? Once you get a big
job offer, why wouldn't you take it? You can just justify it by saying you're 'helping
the cause from the inside' or

TRACY

I totally get your point. But this is me. I'm for real, William. My mother raised
me and my 2 sisters by herself. It may sound like another cliché of the single
black mother who worked her ass off to feed her kids. But that's what this is.
That's who I am, and I will not forget that!

WILLIAM

I know.

TRACY

And when you see your mother take a shitty job because the white people won't
hire her for anything better, it makes you angry. It makes you angry when the

little white princesses get fancy computers and cars for their birthday and down payments on their condos as presents from daddy for graduating from university … You know what I got for graduating from university?

WILLIAM

A hug.

TRACY

A hug. A big, long hug. And you know what? That was the greatest present I could ever hope to receive. When my mother stared at me with that pride as the first woman in the family to graduate from university, and one of the few AfricanCanadian women to graduate from the University of Toronto, I knew that I would spend the rest of my life fighting for people like my mother.

WILLIAM

I know.

TRACY

And that's not going to change because some rich white dude thinks I can make him richer by giving me a job. No fucken way.

WILLIAM

You're gonna do it, Tracy. You're gonna make her so proud.

TRACY

Alright, no more of this weak woman shit. You're like oppressing me or something. I got class.

WILLIAM

Oh, shit! I gotta run to the court! Kyle's probably there already. (*He kisses her.*) I love you. And I support you.

TRACY

I know you do.

WILLIAM

I'll be back around 10.

> *Basketball court.*

KYLE

Take the job!

WILLIAM

I don't know, man.

KYLE

TAKE THE JOB!

WILLIAM

But

KYLE

If I was an actor, I would totally take the job!

WILLIAM

It's a different situation, man.

KYLE

I mean, I totally hear you. You don't wanna be the monkey at the zoo or whatever. But it's like a big deal, man. Every play you drag me to—all the dudes are white. Like almost always. You're like pissed off all the time because you can't get the same opportunities. Well, here it is. Finally, it's working FOR you. You're gonna be like the man! You're gonna be like a role model for kids and shit.

WILLIAM

It's just the circumstances

KYLE

Man, I hear you, but get over it. I got my job because of my dad. There you go. Did I get a degree in Engineering from Waterloo? Yes. Did I work my fucken ass off? Yes. Did I get my job because of it? Nope. My dad hooked me up. That's the way it works, man.

You gotta have the shit when you get the gig, but anything you do to get the gig is just the rat race ...

WILLIAM

It just feels shitty, dude.

KYLE

Oh man, you're totally a whore. But do you think for a second that some white dude would hesitate to take the job because it was set in Ireland?

WILLIAM

You're hilarious.

KYLE

Take the job. Now shut the fuck up and break the ice. (*KYLE gives WILLIAM the basketball.*) I have 45 minutes to embarrass you, then I have to Chat with 'Roxanne' on MSN!

TRACY

Today I'd like to talk about solutions. In this class, we are all painfully aware of the systemic barriers facing the visible minority movement today. I'd like to discuss the notion of art as a tool for social change. I guess because my boyfriend is an artist, I've learned quite a bit about the role of the ethnic artist, and the responsibility of their art. I am a firm advocate of the power of art to educate. I am under no delusions that artists contain the ability to instantly ignite social change, but I believe their unique role in society is that of 'the informant'. They provide a forum for stories that are shut out of the mainstream, and create a space where important debate can occur about taboo issues like racism. Obviously, for the purposes of this class, finding equitable solutions through art is the ideal conclusion.

GERRARD

A new world is upon us, gentlemen. No longer can we sit atop this mighty perch without adapting to the everchanging world around us. Multiculturalism is not a buzzword. It is not a trend. It is the new reality. As the premier theatre company in this country, we are best positioned to capitalize on these shifting demographics. While some of you may see fear, I see opportunity. I see a niche market waiting to be conquered. We must not fear change, we must embrace it! An understanding of the multicultural market will translate into wealth 20 years from now. This selfpreservation is essential. I present to you now a longterm vision for a way to incorporate multiculturalism into the fabric of our organization: William. (*Enter WILLIAM.*)

WILLIAM

What's up?

GERRARD

Our intention is to brand this young man and the community he represents as vital to the true fulfillment of our mission statement. When people see William, they will see us. We will translate our slogans in all of the diverse community papers. William will be the personification of a new type of Canadian: An edgy, sexy, exotic Canadian.

WILLIAM (*impressed*)

Thanx.

GERRARD

A Canadian just like us, but so much more. A hybrid of cultural values that will lead us in the pursuit of long and lasting change. I present you with William: our star for the 21st century!

Thunderous applause.

TRACY

How'd it go?

WILLIAM

It was fucken weird.

TRACY

Whatdya mean?

WILLIAM

It was like me and 15 old white dudes just chilling out.

TRACY

Weird.

WILLIAM

Supposedly they have a black guy. But "he's not here today".

TRACY

Marcus Banks. That guy's whiter than Carlton from Fresh Prince.

WILLIAM

They were asking me all these questions about my 'culture'. What was it like being 'different'? How can we 'bridge our differences'? There was this big gala with like egg rolls and fajitas and mango salad and samosas. I was all like, "Where's the wine and cheese?". And everybody laughed. And I was like, "No, seriously." They laughed again. In fact, they laughed at almost everything I did. So I just started making fun of white people with (uses 'white' voice) this voice. They loved it! They couldn't get enough of it! (normal voice) It was some weird ass shit.

TRACY

Well, at least you're in.

WILLIAM

Yeah, I guess I'm in. But it was really fucken weird. I felt like this imposter. I was like James Bond dressed up in a Turban—and everyone was buying it. I even made some shit up about my parents getting an arranged marriage.

TRACY

How did they meet again?

WILLIAM

Leafs game.

TRACY

Right.

WILLIAM

So, yeah. I guess I'm like this professional ethnic now.

TRACY

Interesting.

WILLIAM

Yeah.

TRACY

So, should I like bow or something?

WILLIAM

I don't know.

Enter KYLE.

KYLE

Dude, I got your message. Does this mean we can't be friends anymore?

WILLIAM

Well, I didn't tell them my best friend was white. It might lose me the gig. I think we have to have like a public fallingout.

KYLE

Dude, you're so gonna get laid for this!

TRACY

Excuse me?

KYLE

I mean ... metaphorically. He's gonna get metaphorically laid ... by the man.

TRACY

Right.

WILLIAM

I don't know, man.

KYLE

Shit. You're like the least ethnic person I know. My cousins from Saskatchewan are more ethnic than you.

WILLIAM

Hey man, I know how to use chopsticks.

KYLE

Yeah, but you use them during sex.

TRACY

You told him that???

Beat.

KYLE

I was joking.

There is an awkward silence in the room.

WILLIAM

Anyway, man. Yeah. Shit's fucked up, I'm professional coloured folk, but I got a gig and we're gonna celebrate!

KYLE

Pizza?

WILLIAM

Always.

TRACY

Remember we get 2 dollars off because.

WILLIAM
They fucked up the

KYLE
Order last time. One big happy family.

WILLIAM (*playfully*)
Shut up, whitey!

KYLE (*same*)
Darkie!

TRACY (*same*)
Honky!

KYLE
Nubian princess!

TRACY
Okay fuckers, turn on the hockey game. My Habs are taking out your Leafs tonight.

GERRARD
And in the midst of this chaos, there will be one constant: our brand. A place where ideas and multiculturalism intermingle, intermix, interact. We will become a type of race of our own: a race of artists! A place of creativity AND community! Multiculturalism AND multilateralism! Diversity and divinity! Immigrant artists will look to our company as a type of 'sacred ground'. Funding bodies will see the inevitable evolution—with our company leading the way! We will not simply become part of the multicultural community, we will LEAD the multicultural community!! We will BECOME the multicultural community!! Gentlemen, I welcome you to a new era in our evolution ...
The apartment.

WILLIAM (*in a thick Spanish accent*)
Give me the fucking money, gringo! You want to talk about pride? Let's talk about money, chico! Your fucking money! I'm gonna pull out my blade, vato!

TRACY
Did you get it?

WILLIAM
I don't know. I did the "LA Gangstaspeak" that they wanted, but who knows?

TRACY
I don't know how you do it.

WILLIAM
I don't know either. I just try to act like Cheech and Chong.

TRACY
No, I mean I don't know how you allow yourself to be oppressed on a continual basis.

WILLIAM
Oh, right. That. Nobody watches TV anymore anyway. Everybody's on MySpace.

TRACY
Why can't you just march in there and tell them, "I'm not an ethnicforhire, asshole! I'm a real actor!"

WILLIAM
The casting directors would love that.

TRACY

Why can't you be a casting director?

WILLIAM

I'm an actor.

TRACY

Can't you be both?

WILLIAM

You really don't understand my world, do you?

TRACY

Not really.

WILLIAM

Yes, it totally sucks that I have to wait for them to be casting some generic ethnic gangster for me to get an audition, but I'd rather

TRACY

"Audition for those parts than not audition at all." That's your problem, my brother. You're taking handouts from the white man because you're too afraid to confront him.

WILLIAM

I'm not too afraid to confront him. I'm too smart to get blacklisted.

TRACY

Somebody's gotta take a stand against this bullshit!

WILLIAM

Well, when he does, I'll take his audition spot.

TRACY

Pathetic. How's your ethnic Marlon Brando thing going?

WILLIAM

Oh, Gerrard? I don't know. Last time we talked, he mentioned something about changing my name to make it sound more ethnic. I think he's losing his mind a bit.

TRACY

Did I tell you I'm writing a paper about you?

WILLIAM

Is this like a sexual prowess thing?

TRACY

No pervert, I'm writing about your experiences as an ethnic artist.

WILLIAM

Now that sounds really fucking boring.

TRACY

I'm writing a paper about using ethnic art as a tool for social change.

WILLIAM

I don't want to be your 'tool'.

TRACY

Ethnic artists have the unique ability to communicate racespecific struggles to mainstream audiences by using their uncensored artistic arenas to educate.

WILLIAM

Oh, fuck.

TRACY

I'm not talking about tokenism. I'm talking about media that's not controlled by a Caucasiandominated corporate board with an economic agenda.

WILLIAM

Right. Whatever. Where's the remote?

TRACY

William. I want to interview you.

WILLIAM

I'm not really an artist. I don't make anything. I just audition for shitty tv shows and complain a lot.

TRACY

Yeah, but your perspective as an ethnic artist trying to persevere in a whitedominated society is totally relevant. Plus, it'll mean we can spend more time together.

WILLIAM

Any chance we can do this during intercourse? I'm an avid multitasker.

TRACY

Nope. Plus the interview has to last more than 4 minutes. (*She smiles.*)

WILLIAM

Low blow. And not true at all. (*TRACY looks at him.*) I was drunk.

TRACY

Let the games begin.

GERRARD

Gentlemen, there are 3 core areas we must target in order to successfully support William (possibly soon to be known as Vikram) as the symbolic realignment of our brand.

TRACY

Hello, everyone. My extensive research with my subject, let's call him 'Subject 4 minutes', has revealed he is impacted by the following information . . .
The two scenes go back and forth. A "/" indicates where an overlap should begin. Through this, William is seen brushing his teeth (or some mundane activity). This slowly stops as he focuses on these voices—as if they are in his head.

GERRARD and TRACY

Number 1. Education slash outreach.

GERRARD

Extensive data must be collated in order to identify / consumer trends.

TRACY

There is considerable work needed in order to educate the general public about the current state of ethnic / artists and the challenges they face

GERRARD

Marketing must be developed to strengthen our brand based on ethnic cues.

GERRARD and TRACY

Number 2. Mentoring slash partnerships.

TRACY

In order to penetrate the mainstream, we must create an influx of influential / ethnic decisionmakers.

GERRARD
  The ethnic community presents numerous opportunities to partner up with
  established ethnicbased / businesses slash media.
TRACY
  As ethnic clout increases, we will be well positioned to make organizational change.
GERRARD and TRACY
  Without preestablishing allies, we will find it considerably more difficult to make
  significant gains.
GERRARD
  Number 3.
TRACY
  Infrastructure.
GERRARD
  Once we have established a market presence, there is a great need to maintain
  the community idiosyncrasies and simultaneously maintain our position.
TRACY
  Once we are able to infiltrate the majority, we must implement a mechanism that
  perpetuates our newfound political power.
GERRARD
  We must tread the line between partner and owner.
TRACY
  We must not rely on donated gains.
GERRARD
  We must not jeopardize our capital.
TRACY
  We must create a system of power redistribution.
GERRARD
  But we need to find an infrastructure that utilizes multicultural influence
TRACY
  It is here that we must focus our attention most desperately
GERRARD and TRACY
  In line with our—
GERRARD
  Revenue.
TRACY
  Beliefs.
GERRARD
  But of course, this is just the beginning of our market research.
TRACY
  But of course, these are just the initial findings of my thesis.
GERRARD and TRACY
  Thank you.
              Basketball court.
KYLE
  You look tired, man.
WILLIAM
  Dude, they're killing me.

KYLE

You're like always so busy these days.

WILLIAM

Between Tracy and Gerrard, I'm starting to feel like the guy from A Clockwork Orange. They're always asking me questions, and testing me out in these fucken weird psychological ways.

KYLE

You actors are into some weird shit.

WILLIAM

No man, it's this ethnic shit. I swear to God, it's like the new terrorism. Everybody's dissecting it, and analyzing it, and synthesizing it, and

KYLE

Buddy, I'm an engineer. I go through this shit every day. We hire people solely to filter information and look for distinct patterns. It's like totally segmented analysis.

WILLIAM

Well, I don't know what the fuck it is, but it's stressing me out. My life was fine until I found out I was ethnic.

KYLE

When did you find out?

WILLIAM

Like 2 months ago.

KYLE

Just get out of it.

WILLIAM

Which one?

KYLE

I guess I sorta mean both.

WILLIAM

No, man. Tracy is cool. She's just been really militant since she started her Equity Studies course. And Gerrard is totally hooking me up with some peeps. He's totally pimping me to all these corporate types. All I gotta do is 'act different from everybody else', and I'm totally a star.

KYLE

Yeah, well try not to lose your soul. Professional ethnic or not, you're still my best friend.

WILLIAM

Thanx, man. I'll be alright. I just need to think about something that doesn't have the word 'race' or some politically correct synonym in it.

KYLE

How 'bout 'pussy'?

WILLIAM

You're a fucken lowlife. But I love you, man.

KYLE

Rippers at 11. Meet me in perverts row.

WILLIAM

You're intense

KYLE

    I like to participate, man. Call me an investor in the stock of life.

WILLIAM

    Sure, whatever. As long as I don't have to think.

KYLE

    That I can guarantee. Now leave me. I can't deal with you ethnics anymore.

WILLIAM

    Yeah. Me either.

          Boardroom. Epic music swells.

GERRARD

    Since the dawn of time, there have always been heroes. Moses parted the Red Sea. Martin Luther King Jr. led a revolution of idealism. And now I present to you the next great legend of the modern day: Vikram Bagadu! (*Reveal WILLIAM dressed in a strange eclectic combination of ethnic attire.*) A product of our new corporate culture, Vikram exemplifies the very essence of our new and strange world! He has been displaced from his homeland (*WILLIAM looks quizzical.*) but he has learned to assimilate in this Darwinian tragedy of epic proportions. His very existence is the aggregate existence of ALL of us. He is beautiful. He is now. He is ... ETHNIC!

          Thunderous applause. WILLIAM looks uncomfortable.

          Later.

WILLIAM

    Can we talk about something?

GERRARD

    Yes, my star. What would you like to discuss?

WILLIAM

    Well, I feel like we're REALLY playing up my heritage.

GERRARD

    It is essential.

WILLIAM

    I mean, don't get me wrong. I'm totally happy to be here. I just feel a little strange.

GERRARD

    Vikram

WILLIAM

    William.

GERRARD

    Sorry. Vikram, as a star, you no longer belong to just yourself. You become a public commodity. There is an expectation now. You represent so many things to so many people. When little boys and girls go to sleep at night, they will be dreaming of growing up to be exactly like you.

WILLIAM

    Even the girls?

GERRARD

    Vikram, I know it may sound strange to say. But ... I love you.

          The apartment.

WILLIAM

    All I know is that he loves me.

TRACY

This is some fuckedup shit right here.

WILLIAM

Baby, do I have a right to complain?

TRACY

I don't know if 'complain' is the word …

WILLIAM

Well, what's the word? Surely, there's some term for this that you guys use in your class?

TRACY

The word is 'fuckery'. This is some freaky shit right here.

WILLIAM

Do you think he really loves me?

TRACY

Willy, that's not the point. We need a …

Enter KYLE.

KYLE

I've got a plan!

TRACY

… plan.

KYLE

Okay Will, I've been thinking about your freaky white dude, and I think I know what to do …

WILLIAM

Anything.

KYLE

It's gonna take a bit of planning, but it just might work … And Tracy, I'm gonna need your help too.

TRACY

Anything.

KYLE

Can you make us some sandwiches?

TRACY

Fucker.

KYLE and WILLIAM start laughing.
Press Conference.

GERRARD

Thank you everyone for coming. I am pleased to have such an overwhelming turnout to our official launch. PROJECT: COLOUR YOUR WORLD has been the jewel in our crown of achievements. In what we surmise will set an international precedent, we have taken the liberty of inviting the world press for this monumental occasion. No longer will our countries be divided by differences in language, ideology and tradition. Today we have created a new bridge, a new universal standard, a new collective understanding! I present to you now the fruits of our labour: the new representation of all the world's people—Mr. Multiculturalism himself—Vikram Bagadu! (*Reveal KYLE, dressed as the quintessential Harvard preppie.*)

KYLE (*with affected preppie voice*)
    Hi, everyone. I'm Vikram Bagadu. I represent all of you. And I'm happy to be here. Hey, is that a cocktail wienie? (*GERRARD is speechless.*) What's the problem? Never seen an ethnic dude before?

                    Apartment.

TRACY (*reading*)
    In the most embarrassing display this reporter has ever seen, Gerrard Smith was observed screaming, "Where is my Ethnic? Where is my Ethnic?" as Vikram Bagadu displayed 'ethnic pushup' after 'ethnic pushup'. Considering Mr. Smith's poor record of visible minority board members—revealed to us by a secret source (*TRACY smiles*)—it's safe to say that Gerrard's 'pioneering' days for multicultural people have come to an abrupt end."

KYLE
    But did it say I'm hot?

TRACY
    Honey, you're adorable.

WILLIAM
    Dude, when you started doing that rain dance, I thought I was gonna lose my shit.

KYLE
    Hey man, that was the one and only time I'm ever going to represent every culture in the world in front of the world's most powerful media outlets. I had to milk it for everything it was worth.

WILLIAM
    And you did. That was awesome. (*WILLIAM gives him props.*)

TRACY
    So that's that.

                    Classroom.

TRACY
    In conclusion, I believe that the responsibility of the ethnic artist is a collective responsibility. His/her journey can only be completed by incorporating the wants and needs of the audience as well. The inherent power lies in the art's ability to bring attention to universal truths. The artist may imply, state or suggest, but the political outcome remains beyond the artist's sphere of influence.

                    Back to previous scene.

TRACY
    Gentlemen, now it's time for the most important cultural tradition of all. (She grabs the remote and turns on the tv. They turn their attention to the television.)

KYLE
    Your Habs are gonna get bitchslapped tonight.

TRACY
    Not if I have anything to say about it, white boy.

WILLIAM
    We'll see.

KYLE
    Go Leafs go!

WILLIAM
    Go Leafs go!

KYLE and WILLIAM
    Go Leafs go! Go Leafs go! Go Leafs go!
TRACY (*simultaneously*)
    Leafs suck! Leafs suck! Leafs suck!

        The lights fade during the repeated chants.

        The End.

PAOLOZZAPEDIA

2019
Adam Paolozza

"When Anna asked me to include *Paolozzapedia* in this anthology I was flattered but also a little hesitant: so much of the work I do is gestural, visual. Its expressive power comes from its 'liveness'. The text is just a small component of a larger set of theatrical elements. If presented alone, in all its fragility, bereft of its relationship to the image, how well would my little script read off the page? You, dear reader, will be the judge of that. I trust your imagination more than up to the task. Lastly, it might be helpful to mention that *Paolozzapedia* is a memory play. Memories are presented as experiences whose meaning remains open, changing the more we return to reflect and meditate upon them, the more we grow. To evoke this, the storytelling in the piece follows a poetic logic more akin to collage than to traditional dramaturgy."
—**Playwright's Note**

Credits from the Original *Paolozzapedia* Production
Originally produced by Bad New Days, in partnership with Theatre Passe Muraille. Presented in Toronto from February 16th to March 3rd, 2019.
Stage Play Devised & Created by The Company
Original Concept & Script Written by Adam Paolozza
Directed by Adam Paolozza and Kari Pederson
Dramaturgy by Kari Pederson
Creative Producer Victor Pokinko
Featuring: Adam Paolozza, Christina Serra, Eduardo Di Martino, Maddie Bautista and Matt Smith.
Voice Overs recorded by Adam Paolozza
Set and Costume Design by Allie Marshall
Lighting Design by Andre Du Toit
Puppet Design by Adam Paolozza (hand puppets), Jessie Byers (hand puppets) and Graeme Black Robinson (large puppets)
Pulcinella Masks by Amleto & Sara Sartori, and Adam Paolozza
Original Music and Sound Design by Matt Smith
Stage Management by Dylan Tate-Howarth

The set consists of two large, white fabric screens on wheels that move positions throughout the show. When moved and reconfigured they can function as a curtain, a screen, a wall, etc. The floor is also painted white. The background of the entire two storey playing space at Theatre

*Passe Muraille is covered in laundry lines with white clothing hanging
making the space appear like the ghost of an old Italian village.
Situated to the left of the audience's view just offstage, there is a small
kitchen area with a coffee maker, hot plate, microwave and other
electronic instruments, such as a synthesizer.
As the audience light lowers, chef MATTEO (played by composer and
sound designer Matt Smith) walks to the kitchen area. MATTEO
begins to cut vegetables in preparation for a tomato sauce that he will
make throughout the show.
Eventually MATTEO whistles for ADAM to enter.
ADAM enters to address the audience.*

SCENE 1: PROLOGUE

ADAM

Grazie Matteo.

Good evening my name's Adam Paolozza and as you probably guessed from the
title this play is about my family.

As this show is about origins we would like to take a moment to acknowledge the
origins of the land we're standing on and its traditional caretakers: the Mississaugas
of the Credit, the Chippewa, the Anishnabeg, the Haudenosaunee and the many
other First Nations, Inuit and Métis peoples who have shared this land.

I would also like to acknowledge my own origins. I come from two small villages.
On my father's side I come from a small village in Italy, in the province of
Campania. It's a little medieval town on top of a foot hill. It's called Baselice.

The other small village is about forty five minutes east of here, it's called Oshawa.

A lovely place, there's a GM plant and Sting once played a free concert there in solidarity with the striking workers—grazie Sting!

Before we start I want to tell you a little bit about some of the things that came together during the making of this show. To give you some context.

One thing that happened was that I decided very consciously to start studying my Italian cultural heritage. Specifically two phenomena: carnival and mask. And specifically this mask: which is a character called Pulcinella.

(ADAM holds up a Pulcinella mask)

Pulcinella traditionally comes from Naples. They're the Italian version of a trickster character. They're sort of the spirit of the people of Naples. But I became really interested in another, less known aspect of Pulcinella: their role as a spirit guide. Pulcinella exists between the world of the dead and that of the living. During the time of the year when the Carnival celebrations take place, like on All Hallow's Eve here in Toronto, during times like these the door between the world of the dead and the living opens. Pulcinella straddles both worlds and connects us to the ancestors.

The other thing that happened was that right during the creation of the piece my father had a stroke. He was recovering while we were making the show and all of these questions about life, death, time and childhood were hanging in the air. I think this created the fertile soil from whence *Paolozzapedia* sprang.

*(ADAM pauses, taking in the audience, ADAM also takes a
long look at the Pulcinella mask in his hand)*

So: Family, Carnival, Pulcinella, Life and Death ... have you got all that?

Ok. I think we're ready now. Sit back, relax and we'll see you on the other side.

ADAM exits

SCENE 2 The Burden of Consciousness

*As ADAM exits the music from the 80's Italian pop song
Gloria, by Umberto Tozzi, plays very loud.
ADAM and the other actors enter and perform a 'bow' as if
they have just finished the show. All performers are holding
their masks, not having put them on yet.
Note: all of the performers in the show play a different Pulcinella,
each wearing a unique Pulcinella mask. As Pulcinella is a
character 'type' and not a specific person, each Pulcinella in the
play also has their own unique name, which is based off of the
name of the actors who play them. Eduardo Di Martino's
Pulcinella is called EDUARDO; Maddie Bautista's is called
MADDALENA; Christina Serra's is called PADRONA, a
nickname which means 'boss'. ADAM is now called
PULCINELLA.
All of the performers bow three times and exit after the third
bow leaving EDUARDO onstage.
The lights shift.*

*EDUARDO performs a slow movement as he gets up from
bowing, standing up in a way that evokes the feeling of a child
growing up. EDUARDO slowly begins putting on the Pulcinella
mask and continues to stand upright, gazing around the space
while the following prerecorded VOICE OVER is heard,
underscored by a recording of a string quartet playing
Schubert's Serenade.*

VOICE OVER

"Since your father's brush with death you start to ... obsess? Obsess over certain older memories, revisiting them again and again, holding them up to the light to find some new meaning in them, to help you through this dark time.

There are only fragments, images, moments.

But if you could somehow get them in the right order, the right constellation, they would start to tell a certain kind of story.

The problem is that sometimes you're not sure if the memories are yours or if you absorbed them after hearing family stories told by others. Memory is funny like that.

Your earliest memory, however, is certain: as a child of two or three you said to your mother, "Mom I wish I was still a baby. Because babies have no worries, they just exist."

Ah, the burden of consciousness!

Even then!

Your sense of yourself rests on this deep sadness, a maternal melancholy. You were already nostalgic even then for that undifferentiated connection, for your time before language.

The human is the sad animal who stood up on their hind legs and—perhaps it was only an accident at first, but the kind of accident life rushes to, takes advantage of—the first human stood on their hind legs and for the first time saw themselves as separate from the world, a figure against a ground, in context, self conscious."

The VOICE OVER and the Schubert music end together.

Silence.

Slowly, EDUARDO begins breathing heavily and pushing, as if giving birth or taking a massive shit. The lights shift.

MATTEO cracks an egg and starts cooking it. The sounds of MATTEO's kitchen are amplified and played on the speakers in the auditorium, creating an ASMR effect.

We hear screaming and crying coming from behind the white screens. These cries join EDUARDO's.

The flats open to reveal MADDALENA and PADRONA inside a large piece of white fabric that is gathered in the shape of a large bird's nest. They scream and cry, as if they were new born babies, the image of little chicks in a nest.

MATTEO adds the amplified sound of a coffee grinder to the sound of the egg cooking in butter. These sounds meld with the cries of the performers into an anarchic crescendo until ...

PADRONA yawns and claps her hands forcefully to stop them all crying.

SCENE 3: Morning Coffee

PADRONA
> Buon giorno.

MADDALENA
> Buon Giorno.

EDUARDO
> Buon Giorno.

> > *Led by MADDALENA they all sing a working song as they*
> > *unravel the nest, unfold the fabric and set it down on the stage.*
> > *The song is a traditional Pugliese 'call and response' verse form,*
> > *with MADDALENA calling out the strophe and the whole*
> > *group singing the antistrophe in harmony.*

MADDALENA
> Amore, amore, c'e m'ha fattu fare?
> ('Love, love, what have you made me do?')

EVERYONE
> La strada di Toronto tira tira ...
> ('The road to Toronto pulls me, pulls me ...')

> > *When they have finished with the fabric PADRONA calls to*
> > *them all "Caffè!" and they all walk over to MATTEO's kitchen*
> > *area to get a coffee.*

EVERYONE
> *(One after the other rhythmically)*

EDUARDO
> Grazie Matteo—

MADDALENA
  Grazie Matteo—
PADRONA
  Grazie Matteo!

> *The sound of grunting is heard off stage.*
> *The white screens open to reveal ADAM/PULCINELLA's legs,*
> *as if he were sitting on a toilet just invisible off stage.*

PULCINELLA
  (Looking between his legs)
  Nothing!
  Da quaranta giorni ho provato a cagare e ancora niente!
  For forty days I try to make a poop and still nothing.
  Mamma mia.
  Sono tropp' tropp' bloccato.
  In my hometown, Baselice, there is an espressione and it goes like this: 'Si Nicola cacava non muoreva'—'if Nicholas had shit he would not be dead.'
  I don't know who is this Nicholas and why he cannot shit but if I don't go soon I'm afraid I'm a' gunna die! Mamma mia!
  Ah, life! (*Exiting the bathroom.*)
  Oh! (*Pausing himself before entering the stage. He thinks ... idea!*)
  Courtesy flush! (*He mimes flushing the toilet and the sound of flushing is heard*).
  To work! A lavoro!
PADRONA
  (*To PULCINELLA, indicating her watch*) Pulcinella!
PULCINELLA
  Arrivo Padrona! ('Coming, Boss')

Normalmente I love the mattina! In the morning, everything is possibile. But today, oggi … (*taking a coffee from* MATTEO) … Grazie Matteo! Come spiegare? È difficile comminciare oggi quando non posso lasciare ieri. It's difficult to start today when I cannot let go of yesterday, if you catch my drift (*indicating his constipation*).

PADRONA

A lavoro!

MADDALENA

A lavoro!

EDUARDO

A lavoro!

> *They all leave to start setting the stage for the next scene, except*
> PULCINELLA. *PADRONA indicates to PULCINELLA to*
> *come as well.*

PADRONA

Pulcinella! Get to work!

PULCINELLA

Arrivo!

Normally I'm like my Papa: one smell of the caffè and—BOOM—Cacá! But today … molto difficile! And what a day! It's moving day, my mother keeps calling me non-stop from Italy to 'check in', and worst of all I cannot *GO!* (*indicating constipation again*)

> PULCINELLA *starts to sing Yesterday by The Beatles. Everyone*
> *is setting up a clothing line across the stage. There are three*
> *white shirts hanging off the line.* PULCINELLA *isn't tall*
> *enough to attach the line to the side of the stage and* MATTEO
> *comes to help.*

PULCINELLA

Ah! Grazie Matteo.

(*indicating how much taller* MATTEO *is than he*) Canadese alta; Italiano piccolo!

> *To get out of helping finish the set change* PULCINELLA
> *imitates the sound of a cell phone ringing in his pocket and*
> *then takes out his cell phone.*

Ah, cellulare. (*to audience*) It's my mother. (*to phone*) Ciao, mamma, come stai? Scusa one second. Si mamma ma ascoltami, mamma ascolt … ascolt … (*yelling into the phone*) … ASCOLTAMI MAMMA! One second, (*to audience*) my mother started a new business and she needs some advice. (*back to phone*) Si mamma ma … no, WIX is no good, wix no good, è meglio Squarespace. Devi 'click click drag' … si 'click click drag'.

> PULCINELLA *keeps talking to his mother as he exits the stage.*
> *The lights shift.*
> EDUARDO, MADDALENA *and PADRONA take up a*
> *position behind the clothing line, animating the empty shirts as*
> *if they were blowing in the breeze. Suddenly a hand puppet,*
> *PUNCH, appears as if it were attached to the sleeve of one of*
> *the shirts, played by PADRONA.*

SCENE 4: In which hand puppets PUNCH and TINA discuss the nature time

PUNCH (*Speaking in an over-the-top Italian accent. To audience*)

Surprise! You didn't know I was there, did you!

Ok, shh! Shh!

I'm going to tell you something, ok? I'm going to help you with this show. Because I am from Naples, (*bows quickly*) thank you, and I understand culture. But first off, congratulations, you made it to the theatre! You changed your pants, you left the radio on for the dog and you put on your nice coat, not the one you wear to Tim Hortons, and you made it here. So, congratulations, big night of culture for you!

Now, I am from Naples, (*bows quickly*) thank you, so I know a lot about art. We invented theatre, we invented classical music, basically we invented culture. So, listen to me. Canadese theatre is … is … not bad … it's *okay* … (*mockingly*)

You like a lot of the 'farming' and that's ok. You know that famous Canadese show I'm talking about? It was made right in this theatre, in the 70's. What's it called? Oh, yes! *The Farming Show*? That's it! (*he laughs*).

Anyway.

This show is not like that, ok? This show is about big ideas, life and death.

Now, it's no big surprise that we're all going to die one day. And if *that* is a surprise, well, again, big night for you! (*he laughs sarcastically*)

Now where was I? Oh, yes. So: we are all going to die. This show is about that. But it's also about time. Now I know what you're thinking: I have no time, where did the time go, time, time, time! I tell you something: you have the time! Time is everywhere! Time is up, time is down …

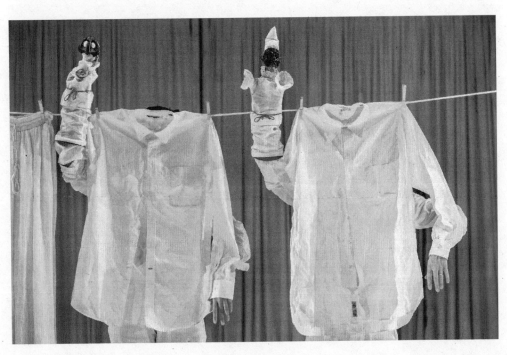

> *TINA, another hand puppet operated by MADDALENA,*
> *appears and talks to PUNCH*

TINA

(*interrupting*) Punch! Punch! I have to tell you something!

PUNCH

Not now!

TINA

Precisely! There is no now! Time as we know it does not exist. I was reading this book by Italian physicist Carlo Rovelli ... and it said ...

PUNCH

Rovelli? He is my cousin, (*bows quickly*) thank you.

TINA

... and Signore Rovelli was saying the entire universe is made of events rather than things! And the things that are most 'thing-like' in the universe, like rocks, are actually just events that take place over long periods of time, like millions of years, and are only able to take place because of the unique quantum effects that make it so, until they finally turn into dust!

EDUARDO

(*with only his head sticking out of the shirt*) Will I turn to dust?

PUNCH

(*to EDUARDO*) Oh, nobody's talking to you!

TINA

(*to PUNCH*) Precisely! Think about it this way: pasta that was made today did not exist yesterday, and if it's good, it will not exist tomorrow ...

PUNCH

... because I will eat it.

TINA

Precisely! *Things* don't just hang around forever. They come and go. Everything is an event passing in and out of being. This place is an event, this clothesline is an event ...

EDUARDO

... Am I an event?

PUNCH

Oh, this guy!

TINA

Precisely! We are all events within a bigger event that is the earth, within a bigger event that is the solar system, within an even bigger event that is the univer ...

> *PULCINELLA interrupts with his loud phone conversation*
> *offstage. This startles the puppets and they disappear.*

PULCINELLA

... no mamma! The CRA is never going to call you! It's a scam. Mamma, you don't even live in Canada! (*he makes an Italian hand gesture of desperation to the audience*)

> *PULCINELLA unties the clothesline and the other workers*
> *reappear.*

PADRONA

Pulcinella! Put this away and when you're finished, get the chair!

PULCINELLA
    The chair, si!
            The workers move the screens to change the scene.

SCENE 5: Father and Fishing.

> *The lights shift.*
> *PADRONA sits alone in a chair centre stage lit by a soft blue*
> *light from offstage, creating the image of an 'old man' Pulcinella*
> *watching television late at night.*

VOICE OVER
    After your dad's stroke, but not necessarily because of it, you start to think about
    how you've always had a problem with the present.
    For you life was always *to come*.
    Yet now you're more afraid of the future than ever.
    You remember when you were a kid your dad coming home from work every night,
    heating up his dinner and then watching the news until he fell asleep. You really
    remember the sigh he let out as he sank into the couch.
            (Sighs)
    An insufficient gesture.
    Despondent and beautiful.
    Unlike you, your dad thought that everything would get better and better. Getting
    better all the time.
    Giuliano Paolozza.

It became 'Jules' in Canada in grade one after the other kids teased him: "Giuliano plays the piano!" He didn't speak English so he just lay his head down on his desk and cried.

He loves fishing. He never catches any fish but you both know that isn't the point. He loves the fishing as much as the catching. You usually never go, preferring to read at home, took after your mother that way.

But now you go because you sense that there are only so many invitations left. At some point during the last time you went dad says: "You know, in the end all you really have are the good days."

Somehow you knew he was going to say that. When he was teaching you about fishing he was really teaching you about time. Not passing it but occupying it. In the end, you just have these moments.

You haven't been fishing again since the stroke ..."

> *Lights shift.*
> *Everyone changes the space, moving screens, etc. MATTEO calls "Lunch Time!"*
> *They all sit on the steps at the back of the stage, that connect the main level to the balcony. They eat sandwiches, each one sitting one step above the other, in a row, like three chickens.*
> *Lights up on PULCINELLA on the balcony level above, on the toilet again.*

SCENE 6: Lunch

PULCINELLA

Oh, dio mio, santa Maria, san gesú! Per favore lasciatemi cacare!
> *(Looking between his legs)*

Still nothing!

(Rising from the toilet.) Sono sempre constipato.
> *(Pulcinella sits with the others. PADRONA offers him a sandwich)*

PULCINELLA

(To PADRONA) No, grazie. *(To audience)* Eh! Sapete una cosa!? When I was a child I had a piccolo problem with the uh ... how do you say it ... the sphincter! And every night my mother, with this little finger, would go like this *(mimes putting pinky finger in baby's bum)* to massage the muscle and make it all work again. My mother!

Why are you laughing? It's a normal thing!

Ah, my mother. *(feigning nostalgia)* Where is she now? *(as if suddenly annoyed)* She's in Italy, she calls me five times a day! Mamma mia!

> *PADRONA and the others finish eating and join PULCINELLA on the balcony. They start preparing puppets that they will use in the next scene. To stall for time while they get ready, MADDALENA comes to the balcony railing, to address the audience.*

MADDALENA

(*Still munching on her sandwich*) Wow, what a *beautiful* view from here, eh! (*Looking into the audience*). Hey! It's my cousin Margareta! Hey Margareta! Thank you for coming all the way from Woodbridge! Hey, Eduardo, come here. Margareta, you're looking for someone to date, yes? Well, here's Eduardo: he takes care of his skin, he plays the banjo and he's the next Baryshnykoff! Eduardo, you have something to say to make the sparks fly?

EDUARDO

(*Visibly nervous*) Ahem ... ciao ...

PADRONA (*to* EDUARDO)

Hey, Romeo, let's go!

> *Everyone turns sharply to face the audience on the upper balcony. Lights shift and old fashion Italian music starts. The actors all operate puppets now—some on their hands, some life-size— forming a large family procession. They walk ceremoniously in step, making their way down the stairs towards centre stage for a family portrait.*

SCENE 7: "The Italian Side"

> *Throughout this scene the performers and puppets continually rearrange themselves into different family photo poses. With each formal pose they temporarily 'freeze' as the lights flash like a camera, capturing their image before they melt again into chaotic movement, laughter and argument. The music fades and a VOICE OVER is heard.*

VOICE OVER

The Italian side. Furniture covered in plastic, white plaster walls and gory crucifixes, the smell of coffee, must and marble.

Your dad was the youngest of eight children and three have passed on.

It's funny which stories you tend to remember them by. Like Uncle Mike and Uncle Tony. They went to the grave feuding with each other over a banana stolen in the 1960's.

Uncle Tony wore daisy dukes with lifts and black dress socks. His backyard was full of marble statues and when you were a kid you whispered to your mom, "Uncle Tony's backyard is sexy!"

Uncle Mike smuggled sausages and cheese out of Italy in a hollowed out Cadillac. Mike died in '94 in a snorkeling accident and now he appears to your mother in dreams whenever someone in her family passes away.

When you were young you liked saying you were Italian at school but it didn't really come natural to you, you didn't really feel authentically anything.

Except once on a family vacation in your Dad's village. The whole village was in the piazza and you and your sisters looked around and noticed that everyone looked exactly like you. They even stood like you. 5000 kms away from home in a place that you've only been to once and you disappear completely into the crowd. For a split second you felt ... what was that feeling?

> *(Everyone moves out of the family portrait formation.*
> *PULCINELLA and PADRONA move down stage. Each of*
> *them holds a grandparent puppet: NONNO and NONNA.)*
> *(During the next section of narration NONNO and NONNA*
> *interact with each other and with their puppeteers.)*

Then there were your grandparents. Rosalia and Vincenzo Paolozza. Neither spoke English or Italian that much. You didn't call them Nonna or Nonno because you didn't really speak Italian.

Rosalia used to smile a lot for you. You got your underbite from her. She had dark eyes and a perm.

Vincenzo was handsome and always wore a three piece suit. He smoked a lot and once when you were five and nobody was looking he offered you a little hit off his cigarette.

> *(NONNO lights a cigarette. MADDALENA, hidden behind*
> *PULCINELLA, blows powder to simulate the smoke that*
> *NONNO exhales. NONNA hits NONNO on the shoulder.)*

You coughed and he laughed. You don't remember the sound of their voices but often wonder now that they're gone and you speak Italian, what would you actually ask them? And what would the dead have to say anyway? So much dust."

SCENE 8: A joyful interlude.

> *The following scene is silent. PULCINELLA and PADRONA gently take off NONNO and NONNA puppets. They carry them offstage, holding the limp puppet bodies like children.*

MADDALENA and EDUARDO each take a corner of the large fabric that covers the floor. PULCINELLA and PADRONA re-enter and each take a corner, as well. They signal to each other to all pull it up and it floats in the air above their heads while soft, bubbly music plays.
The image evokes the tenderness of childhood, afternoons spent folding laundry with mothers, blankets taken and shaken out for family picnics, the parachute game, etc.
They float it up one last time, extra high, as they deftly slide a small bed onstage. PULCINELLA and PADRONA quickly lie on the narrow bed, and the fabric settles on them like a sheet, transforming the stage into the image of an old couple lying in bed.

SCENE 9: Your Parent's Bedroom

The lights shift. EDUARDO enters on tip toe and stops at the foot of the bed, watching the two sleeping bodies. He stands transfixed.

VOICE OVER

Last year on Christmas eve you walked into your parents room and caught them asleep. You needed the wrapping paper your mom still keeps in the bedroom closet and you didn't know they were in there.

It was as if you saw them as old for the first time.

And it was strange because they also seemed young.

For a moment the bed became monumental, outside of time.

You saw yourself watching them. You remember them when they first had you in their 20's, babies themselves. You remember when they turned 40, all the cheesy t-shirts, hats and mugs they got. You thought 40 was so old and they had all the answers.

You felt safe then.

Now you're 40 and more afraid of the future than you were when you were a boy and begged them to sleep in their bed.

But tonight, seeing them asleep like that, so frail and innocent, you want to take care of them.

You want them to be happy.

You think of all the time they've spent arguing and you ask: Why?

It's so easy from the outside to have the answer; as if you could just say to them: Do this, don't do that, and choose to be happy.

You think that everyone has a choice to be happy and work things out.

But then you wonder why that same advice doesn't work for you.

Lately, when you think of your parents you can't help weeping and maybe this is all towards a reason why.

> EDUARDO exits as the VOICE OVER finishes. The old couple
> in bed pull the blanket away from each other in a slapstick
> style. Then the woman sits up, facing away from the man, and
> lets out a deep 'SIGH'. An image of intimate loneliness.

SCENE 10: Moving Day

> *The bed is struck offstage and the screens move again.*
> PULCINELLA *comes forward holding a stained mattress.*

PULCINELLA

Moving day!

Oè! Eduardo, Maddalena, Padrona, mettet' tutto sta roba qua, lì!

('move all this junk over there')

(*to audience*) Moving day. Not exactly my favourite day. It's the 50th time I've moved in two years. Look at my new apartment: two metres by two metres only $3500/month—grazie Toronto! (*As he says this he gives the "up yours" gesture*). Ah, rental crisis.

But, guarda questo qua: look at this: my mattress! I raised it from a pillow. Questa è la storia de la mia vita. This is the story of my life. (*He indicates all the stains on the mattress*). Guarda questo qua: this one here: was my brother Franco. My mother and father when they one time try to make'a 'boom boom' una volta my father pull out and he "splooge" all over the mattress, he missed and so Franco doesn't exist. Rest in peace Franco.

This stain here is the water that broke when I was born from my mother.

Oh, and questo qua, qua, qua, qua, qua, qua ... (*he points to several stains and grins at the audience, pausing for effect*) ... adolescenza. Do you know adolescenza?

> (*PULCINELLA performs his lazzo of 'puberty' miming all of its effects from growing hair, to masturbating, to getting caught masturbating. This lazzo was improvised slightly differently each night in response to the audience and usually culminated in some kind of a grotesque, comedic orgasm*)

Sapete una cosa? The French call an orgasm a little death: piccolo morte. And this always seems strange to me because it's like the life and the death all mixed together. Oh, maybe it's this: because when you make the life (*mimes orgasm with emphasis on crotch*) your face makes a look of death (*mimes orgasm again with emphasis on the face*). Ah, the French, very paradoxical!

Anyway, I gotta go, the moving truck is a' double parked.

Ah, my mattress! The only thing I have left with me from Italy.

Maddalena, vai, let's go! After you help me move I'll get you a pizza!

MADDALENA

Pizza Pizza?

PULCINELLA

(*confused*) Well, ok, if you want *two* pizzas I'll get you two pizzas!

> (*PULCINELLA tries to sing the Pizza Pizza theme song from the 80's: "Call 967-11-11, call Pizza Pizza, hey, hey, hey!" but gets the numbers and the words all wrong.*
> *He exits singing.*)

SCENE 11: Memory Montage

MATTEO from the kitchen/sound booth, starts to play a surreal, remixed version of the Pizza Pizza theme song, picking up from where PULCINELLA left off.

During this scene all of the performers move the white screens into different formations, creating different angles and openings between screens to reveal a montage of images that relate to key moments in the show. For example: MADDALENA is revealed wearing snorkeling gear to recall an uncle who drowned; an arm pushes through a hole in the screen holding a banana, which it slowly peels, recalling the family feud between two uncles. The images flow one into the other but gradually we become aware of the presence of a figure in a black cloak holding an hourglass. The figure of DEATH crosses the stage as the music changes from a dreamy synthesizer soundscape to the sound of many percussive bells and shakers, as in a carnival procession.

After DEATH exits, the music changes again, it is now something like the electronic sound an MRI machine makes, only less piercing. All the screens are moved offstage to reveal MADDALENA and PULCINELLA, each on one half of the stage in a spotlight, as if in a split screen.

MADDALENA on the left is like a newborn child, trying to learn how to crawl, stand and eventually walk.

PULCINELLA on the right is in a chair, trembling, performing some kind of neuro physio-rehab gesture with his arm, which recalls the kind of physiotherapy ADAM's father underwent following his stroke.

As MADDALENA takes her first tentative steps, the music shifts, the lights shift and the two screens each pass from one side of the stage to the other, disappearing PULCINELLA and MADDALENA and leaving the stage completely empty.

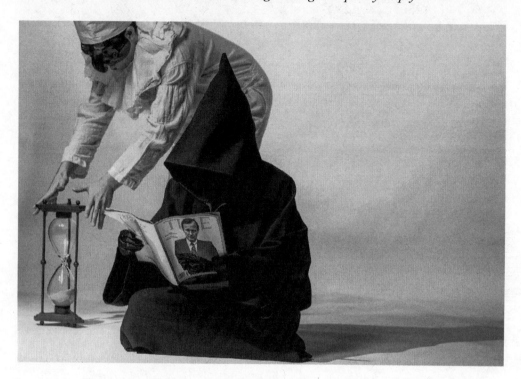

SCENE 13: The Puff of Smoke

After a very long silence the fog machine releases a single puff that hangs in the air above the stage, like a cloud or like a puff of smoke from a cigarette.

Slowly, everyone wanders on stage to watch the puff of smoke as it disappears in real time.

Silence.

PADRONA claps her hands and gets them to get the next scene ready.

SCENE 14: Old Pulcinella and TV reprise

The scene is the same as the earlier scene with PADRONA sitting centre stage lit by an offstage tv set. PADRONA sits silently like a tired old man for some time. The sound of the microwave beeps three times and stops. The VOICE OVER begins.

VOICE OVER
If it's true that there are no things in the universe, only events, then the meaning of our lives is not "out there" like some absolute truth to be discovered. And if the past is not truly fixed, then it, too, is a site of potentiality.

SCENE 15: The END

The tv light goes out and PADRONA disappears behind a screen.
The lights shift.

EDUARDO comes in front of the screen into a spotlight and starts breathing heavily and pushing as if pregnant or taking a massive shit, just as he did at the beginning of the show.
When he reaches a climax of noise a spotlight light comes up to reveal PULCINELLA on the upper balcony, sitting as if on the toilet again.
Both EDUARDO and PULCINELLA scream and mime pushing, as if trying desperately to shit.

Eventually we hear the tiny, comic sound effect of a single turd
dropping into a toilet.
PULCINELLA rejoices.

PULCINELLA

Oh, finalmente! Excuse me dear public, I know it's a little anticlimactic, but a
little something is better than a little nothing, if you catch my drift! Padrona!

PADRONA

Si?

PULCINELLA

Sono finito jamma magnà ('I'm finished, let's eat!').

Festive music plays and everyone carries on a small table with a
pot of pasta in the centre. They set it for each other and then sit.
MATTEO brings over the wine and PADRONA makes a toast.

PADRONA

Brindisi! ('a toast') A la vita! ('to life') La morte! ('to death') e, a la legerezza!
('and to levity!').

ALL

Salute!

They drink to the audience's health.
In a very quick movement they down their wine and change
positions to look like they've been drinking for hours and they've
suddenly passed out.
The lights snap to a new state to accentuate this. Then we hear
the final VOICE OVER.

VOICE OVER
The end.
It's just a moment like any other. But once you sense it, nothing is ever really the same. You realize that there is only so much time left and even if you had forever you could never hold onto all those moments, squeezing every last little bit of meaning and beauty from them.
Everything is so much more manageable in hindsight.
It's the present that's so damn hard to swallow. And it keeps coming at you, now, and now, and now. Still now. And if you hoped the end would provide some epiphany, you have to let that go. The real epiphanies came when you least expected them: at inopportune moments, perfect and useless.

Slow fade to black.

The End.

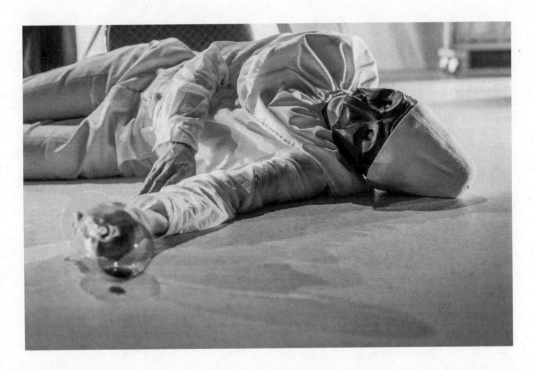

BOYFRIEND

2017
Liana Cusmano

"The natural voice is transparent, it reveals, not describes, inner
impulses of emotion and thought, directly and spontaneously. The
person is heard, not the person's voice. To free the voice is to free
the person, and each person is indivisibly mind and body."
—**Kristin Linklater** *Freeing the Natural Voice*

My grandmother is tiny
and old
and Italian
and she knows just enough English to ask me:
"So, you have boyfriend?"
The Italian word for *boyfriend*
is the same as the Italian word for *fiancé*.
And so the best way for my grandmother to strike out in the dark
to sidestep linguistic landmines
is to use English words that are as unfamiliar to her
as the concept of being with someone
even when you have no intention of marrying them.
Every time my grandmother and I
have a conversation about a *boyfriend*
I know that each of us will be reminded
of just how many things we don't understand.
We are as close as two people can be
when they are part of one family
that is split between two completely different worlds
like two different recipes for pasta sauce
like the *arrabbiata* of two different generations.
My grandmother doesn't understand
why I can't just do things the way she did and
the way her mother did and
the way my mother did
as if we were all objects on an assembly line
instead of items crafted by hand.
When I tell my grandmother
that I have something important to say to her
she asks me if I'm pregnant.
When I tell her that I'm bisexual,
when I tell her about men and women and people

and about how much love I have to give
she says that she would have preferred it
if I'd been pregnant.
Over the years
no small improvement stamped on a report card
has ever gone unseen
no schoolyard grievance
or petty workplace dispute
has ever been left unheard.
But the pillow-forts and the vegetable garden
the home-cooked meals and the morning espressos
and the countless episodes of *Jeopardy!*
now feel like they were building blocks
in a house of Italian playing cards.
When I tell my grandmother that I am dating someone
small, gorgeous, vegan, feminine and Jewish
she groans like she can see the faraway spectre of her
healthy, bilingual great-grandchildren
rapidly disappearing into nothingness,
she mourns them as if they were the only thing that ever mattered.
She doesn't see the simple elegance of my own devastation
when she serves me her scandalised and bewildered disappointment:
"Wouldn't it be better for each of you if you had a man,
instead of one another? Wouldn't it be better for this girl
if she had a man, instead of you?"
When we broach the topic of the *boyfriend*
I start to believe that maybe there are exceptions
that the rules of my childhood no longer apply
that maybe not every small joy or great disappointment
is understandable or valid.
It's only when we discuss the concept of the *boyfriend*
that I understand that I will have to pick and choose
which of my grandmother's words and thoughts and actions
I will allow to affect me, because the alternative is to be fractured
and splintered
by her opinion on something she can't
and doesn't
and will never understand.
The words in my mouth are like stones in my pockets
when I say "Neither one of us wants a man right now,
if we have chosen one another
over every other man, woman, person
haven't we already proved that each of us is enough?
Doesn't that prove that I am
enough just as I am?"
My grandmother has told me that she loves me always,
forever, without exception,

with or without a *boyfriend*.
I choose to believe her.
That deadly distinction
between *you are not enough*
and *I love you anyway*
is a twisted and double-edged reassurance
that I would not accept from anybody else
but my grandmother is tiny
and old
and Italian
and she loves me and she is mine.
And this is all that matters,
that love is what I pick and choose to remember
when there is so much that still hurts
and so much that I still don't understand.
That love is all that matters,
that love is a bridge that can be crossed
even in translation.

CONTRIBUTORS

TONY CALABRETTA. Born and raised in the heart of Montreal's Plateau borough, Tony Calabretta has been an active member of the film, television, and theatre scene for over three decades. As a playwright, Tony's plays, *Damn Those Wedding Bells!*, *Don't Blame it on the Stork* and *The Glam Mothers* have garnered rave reviews from critics and audiences alike wherever they were staged. *Damn Those Wedding Bells!*, and *The Glam Mothers* have both been adapted for the screen, with filming of *The Glam Mothers* having been completed. His plays capture the raw grittiness of family struggles, while being able to maintain a comedic balance that has audiences laughing and crying. Tony's unique writing style caught the attention of legendary Canadian playwright, Michel Tremblay, who insisted on translating *Damn Those Wedding Bells!* into French, and toured the play across Quebec. Again, it was met with sold-out performances and excellent reviews, proving that Tony's storytelling transcends languages.

Tony is also a very accomplished actor having appeared in over eighty films and television programs, not to mention countless plays. His body of work has solidified his place within the Montreal acting community earning him the respect of his peers and the industry at large. Amongst his many accolades, his interpretation of one of the lead characters on the CBC-Radio Canada co-production of *"Ciao Bella"* landed him an Outstanding Performance—Male nomination. Tony continues to be an active member of the film, television, and theatre community in Montreal.

LIANA CUSMANO. Writer, poet, filmmaker, and arts educator, Liana (Luca/BiCurious George) is the 2018 and 2019 Montreal Slam Champion and runner up in the 2019 Canadian Individual Poetry Slam Championship. A participant in the 2019 Spoken Word Residency Program at the Banff Centre for Arts and Creativity, their poems and short stories have been published in anthologies and literary magazines. Liana has performed their work in English, French and Italian, and given readings in Montreal, Lisbon and Shanghai.

They wrote the short film *La Femme Finale*, screened at the 2015 Cannes Film Festival, and wrote and directed the award-winning *Matters of Great Unimportance*, screened at the 2019 Blue Metropolis Festival. Their work explores heritage, queerness, and mental health. Their first novel, *Catch & Release* (2022), was published by Guernica Editions. They are a 2022 finalist for the QWF Spoken Word Prize.

BOBBY DEL RIO [ROBERTO ADRIANO DEL RIO] graduated from the University of Toronto at Mississauga (UTM)/Sheridan College Theatre and Drama Studies program in 2001 (Minor in English). He began his playwriting career with a splash, winning the Robertson Davies Playwriting Award in 2000 for *When Children Fall*. The play was remounted at SummerWorks 2000, becoming one of the hits of the festival. His next play, *Christian Values (2001)*, was the Number Three selling hit of the Toronto Fringe Festival—landing Bobby on the cover of *NOW Magazine*. He was also the subject of a 22-minute documentary on *Bravo*, that aired nationally across

Canada. Bobby was only 23 years old. His play, *The Market (2010),* was adapted into a feature film (directed by Bobby). The film received a distribution deal during the pandemic. Bobby also wrote (and starred in) *Professionally Ethnic* at SummerWorks 2017. The play was named on *NOW Magazine* lists for: Outstanding Play, Outstanding Production & Outstanding Ensemble. The play was first published by *Canadian Theatre Review* in 2009. Favorite titles include: *Child Hood (2005), Porn Life (2007), Power Struggle (2017), The Trial of Ken Gass (2013),* and *Half-Chinx Taking Over the World (2004).*

MICHAELA DI CESARE is a playwright and performer with a Master's Degree in Drama from the University of Toronto. Michaela's solo show *8 Ways my Mother was Conceived* was presented in Toronto, Montreal, New York City, Ottawa, Hudson, Winnipeg and Stratford. Michaela wrote and performed in *In Search of Mrs. Pirandello* (2016 WildSide Festival Centaur Theatre) followed by the world premiere of *Successions* in the 2017/2018 Centaur Theatre season (Outstanding New Text, METAs 2018). Her play FOMO *(Fear of Missing Out)* premiered with Geordie Productions in September 2019 (Outstanding New Text Nomination, METAs 2020). Her play *Ex-tra/Beautiful/U* won first place in the 2017 Write on Q competition presented by Infinithéâtre and received its world premiere in their 2023/2024 season. Michaela was playwright-in-residence at Centaur Theatre for the 2019/2020 season writing *Mickey & Joe (Good. Bad. Dirty. Ugly).* Her play *Hot Blooded Foreigner* was commissioned by Tableau D'Hôte Theatre. Screenwriting credits include the web series *Sex & Ethnicity* and the short film *The Carcass.* She is developing a feature length holiday romance *Mistletoe & Mari-nara* and a comedy series *The Simulators.* As an actor, her theatre credits include *Winter's Daughter* (Tableau D'Hôte Theatre / Segal Studio), *A Bear Awake in Winter* (Next Stage Theatre Festival/Factory Theatre), *Gratitude* (Oren Safdie/MainLine Theatre), *Birds of a Feather* (Roseneath Theatre), *Urban Tales* (Centaur Theatre/Urbi et Orbi), *A Midsummer Night's Dream* (Humber River Shakespeare) and *State of Denial* (Teesri Duniya Theatre). Film & TV credits include NBC'S *Transplant, Mob Hits, No Good Deed, Mafia INC, The Engagement, The Bold Type, Mike, Fatal Vows, A Stranger in My Home, Sex & Ethnicity.*

TONI ELLWAND is a graduate of York University's Theatre program in Performance. She has been a professional actress since 1984. She began her professional career at the Stratford Festival in 1983 under the direction of John Hirsch. Toni has worked in Theatres across Canada, and she had the privilege of playing at the Festival of Madness in The Arts in Muenster Germany for Workman Arts. As well as working in Theatre, Toni has also been busy in the film and television scene. You can find her on IMDB or just google her! Toni is also a playwright, producer, and director. As well as *Cause Unknown,* Toni wrote the Toronto Fringe hit *La Donna Immobile,* and *The Mummy Files.* She also helped with the workshopping of the play *Ciao Baby,* based on the poetry of Gianna Patriarca. She directed her husband, Greg Ellwand's play *GREG ELLWAND'S BREAD!* She and her husband have also produced several plays over the years. She is also a published author. One of her short stories can be found in: *CURAGGIA: Writing By Women of Italian Descent.* Toni is married to actor, Greg Ellwand and they have three daughters and three grandsons! She would like to dedicate her portion of this anthology to her grandsons: Giacomo, Marco, and Tasman.

FABRIZIO FILIPPO is an award-winning creator, writer, and director. Most recently he wrote, directed and was co-showrunner of *SORT OF*, a half-hour for CBC and HBOMax (Sphere Media Prodco)—which has gone on to win a Peabody Award, Canadian Screen Awards and is nominated for the prestigious Rose d'Or. Before that, he wrote and directed the critically acclaimed and award-winning short-form series *Save Me* (iThentic Prodco, CBCGem) which was nominated for a number of international festival awards and a Webby. He has over 20 episodes of true crime under his belt as a director and has developed television for 20th Century Fox, Amazon, CBC, Showcase, and Global Television. As a playwright, he was nominated for a Dora Award for his play *The Summoned*. He also co-created and directed half-hour hit comedy *Billable Hours* (Temple Street Prodco) in which he starred. As an actor you might also know him from projects like *Lives Of The Saints* opposite Sophia Loren, indie hit *way-downtown*, or the first Showtime *Queer As Folk* reboot. People are sometimes impressed when they find out he had an arc on the hit *Buffy The Vampire Slayer*.

LUCIA FRANGIONE is the author of over thirty plays including *Espresso*, *Leave of Absence*, *Kindred*, *The Thin Man*, *Cariboo Magi* and *In a Blue Moon*. She has been produced across Canada and in cities like Chicago, NY, Boston, London and Warsaw. Her first novel, *Grazie*, was published by Talon books in 2023. Frangione is an award-winning actor and is launching a podcast called Cuppa Stories. She is honoured to be included in this anthology with such gifted writers and she is proud to call herself an Italian Canadian.

DIANA IUELE-COLILLI was born in Toronto. She obtained her BA at the University of Western Ontario, and her MA in Italian Studies and PhD in Italian Linguistics at the University of Toronto. She is a Professor of Italian Studies at Laurentian University in Sudbury, Ontario where she teaches and conducts research in the areas of Italian language, linguistics, culture and Italian-Canadian studies. Her academic publications include *Lettura e conversazione* (co-author, 1986), *I friulani di Sudbury* (1994), *Italian Faces: Images of the Italian Community of Sudbury* (2000), *The Harvest of a New Life* (editor, 2002) and *After the Age of Immigration: The Lives of Italian-Canadians* (editor, 2007). Her published plays include *I panni sporchi si lavano in famiglia* (with Christine Sansalone, 2008), *Ma che brava gente!* (with Christine Sansalone, 2009), *Vita di tutti i giorni* (with Christine Sansalone, 2010), *Nozze all'arrabbiata* (with Christine Sansalone, 2011), *Il tempo vola* (with Paul Colilli, 2016), *Le bocce della morte* (with Christine Sansalone, 2019), *Una vita per ogni stagione* (with Christine Sansalone, 2019), *La sala verde* (with Paul Colilli & Christine Sansalone, 2017), *Divorzio alla canadese* (with Paul Colilli & Christine Sansalone, 2017), *La luna di fiele* (with Christine Sansalone, 2020) and *Una sorpresa foriú* (with Christine Sansalone, 2020).

MICHAEL MACINA (1951–2006). "I first met Michael Macina in the lobby of Hart House Theatre on the University of Toronto campus. It was the fall of 1973.We were both enrolled in the MA Programme in The Graduate Centre for the Study of Drama and were waiting our turn to audition for Martin Hunter's upcoming production of Shakespeare's *Troilus and Cressida*. Landing a role in a Hart House Drama Centre production often brought students and seasoned professionals together on the historic stage. It was a time when academic research and theatrical production were attempting to form a long-lasting marriage of true minds. It was an ideal playground for an actor like Michael Macina, who was at home in academic circles as well as the bohemian circuit of the vibrant theatre scene in Toronto. In our tedious wait we exchanged pleasantries. He mentioned a play he had been writing based on the life of his great grandfather, Giovanni Macina, known around the financial district of Toronto as *Johnny Bananas.*

"Johnny was an Italian immigrant who made a living selling bananas on the corner of Bay and King streets. An old school immigrant with a pugilistic approach to solving personal issues, be it with the authorities or friends and family, Johnny was legendary figure on this corner pretty much until the day he died. I had just returned from a year in Florence doing agit-prop street theatre with Teatro Lo Scaleo, and Michael was just back from a stint in Strasbourg training with Roger Blin, the iconic embodiment of the bohemian French theatre that goes back to Antonin Artaud and Samuel Beckett. Michael had native proficiency in French and felt very much at home in the *poet-maudit* tradition of the streetwise intellectual, the *flaneur* with a strong satiric outlook on art and life. Neither of us felt quite at home in the Anglo dominated emerging theatre scene in the 1970s.Yet here we were auditioning for Shakespearian roles in the hope of getting into the nascent Anglo centered theatre community. Michael landed the role of Thersites and Martin offered me a production role as apprentice director. Thus began a collaborative friendship among the three of us that was to last a lifetime. Mostly it was centred on how to bring *Johnny Bananas* to life on the professional circuit in Toronto. After an unnecessarily long gestation *Johnny Bananas* finally made it into the mainstream with a production co-directed by Martin Hunter and me.

"Following an initial run at the Adelaide Court Theatre and The Columbus Centre, Michael adapted the play into a radio serial, *The Bananaman*, which was heard nationally on the CBC radio program *Morningside.* In my view this was the first cultural event of any significance in Toronto to bring together, so to speak, two solitudes: an emerging culture of ethnic theatre and the established hegemony of Anglo theatre culture.

"While waiting our turn to audition, Michael broke into the verse of a blues song he was composing:

> *I've been reading Dostoevsky.*
> *He says life is pretty risky ...*

"For me it was friendship at first listen. Nimble of mind, multitalented on stage and on the page, fun to be with, Michael was an intellectual artist equally at home in the Anglo, French-Canadian and Italian-Canadian cultural communities. Emotionally, however, he was deeply rooted in a world in which many *Johnny Bananas* survived in the concrete jungle by their persevering courage and determination to pull their families out of centuries old poverty.

"Michael remained a rebel to the end. He was an authentic bohemian who refused to be trapped into any academic or theatrical fakery. And if anyone tried, he was ready to puncture their bubble with a fiery outburst worthy of Johnny himself, or a sharpness of wit he might have picked up in his performance of Thersites. By the time of his untimely death in 2006, life had indeed proved to be risky business for Michael. Whether by choice or force of circumstances he could never find a firm existential footing. Even though he remained on the margins of Toronto's theatre scene he had a finger

in every pie and contributed to the founding of many theatre companies in Toronto such as Actors' Lab, Buddies in Bad Times, Theatre of the Autumn Leaf, and Necessary Angel Theatre. Johnny Bananas, however, remained a life-long creative adventure."
Damiano Pietropaolo, Former Head and Executive producer, CBC Radio Drama

NICK MANCUSO. Internationally known actor Nick Mancuso has been referred to a "one of Hollywood's best kept secrets." A stage, film and TV actor, he is a 40-year veteran of over 200 movies and TV shows, having worked in over 12 countries and in 3 languages. He was born Nicodemo Antonio Massimo Mancuso in 1948 in Mammola Reggio Calabria, in the Aspromonte region of southern Italy, and migrated with his family to Toronto in 1955.

He began his acting career in the mid 60's as a founding member of many of the so-called underground theatres of Toronto, including Toronto Free Theatre, Canadian Stage, Factory Lab Theatre and Theatre Pass Muraille. In 1970 he was artistic director of Pier One Theatre in Halifax Nova Scotia, and by 1976 was a member of the Stratford Company playing opposite stage giants Maggie Smith, Hume Cronyn, Jessica Tandy and Jeremy Brett. His work at Stratford brought him to the attention of theatre critic Walter Kerr in New York resulting in him being placed under contract to ABC and legendary TV producer/writer, Stephen J Cannell. He was brought out to Hollywood in 1977 and then starred in Columbia Pictures *Nightwing* directed by veteran director Arthur Hiller. In 1979 he worked with one of America's greatest playwrights Tennessee Williams on the original play *Tiger Tail* and *Night of the Iguana* in Atlanta Georgia. He has since then worked for every major network and Hollywood studio.

In the mid-80's he starred as the lone ranger mystery man *Stingray* for NBC. His other TV starring role series include *Matrix, Call of the Wild, Mysterious Forces Beyond, Total Recall*. He recently appeared in NBC's *The Firm*. (2012) In 1981 he won the Canadian Oscar "The Genie" for his breakthrough performance as a cult victim in the MGM/UA film *Ticket to Heaven*. Over the years he has played opposite every major Hollywood star of the 50's, 60's 70's and 90's, from Charlton Heston (with whom he starred in *Motherlode* with Kim Bassinger) to Sophia Loren (*Lives of the Saints*), Raquel Welch, and Catherine Deneuve. His extensive work in Hollywood, Canada, Italy, Spain, France, and Russia has garnered him the reputation of being one of the silver screens most versatile and experienced working actors. He has played every role imaginable in his extensive and unusual career from comedies to horror movies, from action adventure, suspense thriller to romantic leads and mob bosses. He is also well known for his Christian and faith-based movies, such as *Revelation, Messiah, Apocalypse*. As well as martial arts movies such as *Rapid Fire* with Brandon Lee and *Under Siege* with Stephen Segal. His early horror movies *Black Christmas* and *Deathship* are cult classics.

Nick is also a screenwriter/producer having produced several award-winning movies in the last few years including *The Last Gamble* (U.S.A) starring Steve Bauer directed by Joe Goodavage. His other credits include *Anna, Teresa e le Resistenti* (Italy) and *The Resurrection of Tony Gitone* (Canada). A published poet, essayist, playwright, he has performed his plays in Canada, New York, and Europe, recently performing his one man show at the "European Theatre Festival" in Timisoara Romania, to great acclaim. His electronic compositions *Wintertins, In Parenthesis, Die Moulds* have played in Zagreb and on Danish radio. His adaptation of Plato's *Apologia, The Death of Socrates*, which he wrote and performed, was aired by the CBC in Canada.

Mancuso is a painter and digital artist as well as a filmmaker, director and teacher of his original system for actors, based on his book *Acting (is) for Everyone*. He is a student of Yoga, Aikido, Tai Chi, Chi Kung and Tibetan meditation as well as a practicing Christian. He holds a degree in Psychology and Philosophy from the University of Toronto and Guelph. His many acting awards include The Genie (Canada, Best Actor), "Il Polifemo D'Argento" and "Il Ciak di Calabria" (Italy), Houston Film Festival (Best Actor, twice), Best Supporting Actor, New York International Independent Film Festival, and he has received Lifetime Achievement Awards from The Italian Film Festival (Canada) and the AOF Film Festival (U.S.A.) and has been the subject of several documentaries. Three of his films, *Ticket to Heaven* (1981), *Maria Chapdelaine* (1984) and *Heartbreakers* (1983) have been inducted into the National Film Review in Washington D.C. In 1984 he rejected an offer by the-president of the Academy of Motion Picture Arts and Science, Charlton Heston, for membership, on "philosophic grounds." In 1988 he was referred to by the *L.A. Times* as a "Renaissance Man" and Kevin Thomas called his work in *Ticket to Heaven* "the performance of the decade."

DINA MORRONE was born in Thunder Bay, Ontario, to Italian Immigrant parents from Calabria (Perito, near Cosenza) who passed on their love of storytelling, making people laugh, and the importance of being bilingual. From an early age, Dina's maternal Nonno, Rocco, encouraged her to write, perform and put on a show. At the age of four, along with her sister, Anna, she took the stage at the Italian Banquet Hall Annual Christmas Party and sang in English and Calabrese. The surreal moment of all eyes on her, the thunderous applause, and a box of Black Magic Chocolates for her efforts left her with a burning desire to be in front of an audience. Although paternal Nonno, Giuseppe, back in Calabria, was an incredible singer (tenor), Dina did not inherit his singing gene! And that was pretty much the end of her singing career. Numerous school plays (no musicals), talent shows, and figure skating shows followed. After joining a modeling school/agency, Dina discovered a love for fashion design. She attended Toronto Metropolitan University (Ryerson) Fashion Program, but upon graduation, decided she didn't want to sit behind a sewing machine and moved to Rome, Italy, where she worked as an actress/TV host/model/voiceover actor for ten years.

She left Rome for LA and joined Theatre West, where she is the current vice-chair of the artistic board and regularly attends the Playwrights workshop. She also attended UCLA Creative Writing. She produced several solo festivals including *Portraits of Humanity 2* (14 shows), *SOLOpalooza 2.022* (10 shows), *Who I Am*, for Black History Month, and the revival production of *Moose On The Loose*. The world premiere of *Moose On The Loose*, a comedy about an Italian family and a Canadian moose, took place at Theatre West in 2011. The show was a hit and was subsequently picked up and produced in Canada. Mel Brooks said, "I cannot tell a lie. *Moose On The Loose* is really funny and surprisingly moving." Based on her encounter with the Maestro, Federico Fellini, Dina's one-woman show, *The Italian in Me*, was awarded the Valley Theatre Award for Best One-Person Show.

Dina's voiceover work keeps her busy on features, TV shows, commercials, animation, video games, and announcer at awards shows: *Luca, The Bad Guys, Avatar, The Morning Show, Ferrari, The White Lotus 2, Fiat, Mafia 2 Video Game*, etc. In 2012, the LA Bureau of the FBI invited her to give the Keynote Address at their annual Memorial. Past Speakers included Sherri Lansing, Ernest Borgnine, Joe Mantegna, and Dr. Oz.

Since 2015, Dina has been Executive Contributing Editor and Contributing Feature Writer at *The Eden Magazine*, a lifestyle consciousness magazine. She has interviewed the likes of Gina Lollobrigida, Blair Underwood, Louis Gossett Jr., Bruce Dern, Paolo Sorrentino, and John Salley, to name a few. Dina is a member of The Academy of Canadian Cinema & Television, Playwrights Guild Of Canada, Dramatists Guild Of America, Producers League of LA, L'Accademia Italiana Di Cucina, Canadians Abroad, Italian Cultural Institute, and Le D.I.V.E.

TONY NARDI. A multi-award winner for his work in film, television and theatre, Tony is a Canadian actor, playwright, director and producer. A four-time Genie Awards Nominee, he has won twice for Best Actor for his roles in *La Sarrasine* (1992) and *My Father's Angel* (2001), for which he had also received a Best Actor award at the Sonoma Wine and Country Film Festival in 2000. He received the Guy L'Écuyer Award for his role in *La Déroute* in 1998. In 2010, the year marking the 30th Annual Genie Awards, he made the Academy's 30th Anniversary Top 10 list in the Lead Actor category in Canadian cinema—a ranking based on the number of wins and nominations over the 30-year period.

He collaborated on the screenplays for *La Sarrasine* and *La Déroute*. In television, he received a Gemini Award nomination in 2006 for his role in *Il Duce Canadese* and a Best Actor Award at the Geneva International Film Festival, Tous Écrans/All Screens, in 1999, for his role in *Foolish Heart*. He has performed in more than sixty (60) plays ranging from classics to more experimental and collective-driven works. He received a Montreal Gazette Critic's Award in 1979 for his role in *Nineteen Eighty-Four*, a Dora Mavor Moore Award for Artistic Excellence—Collective—in 1985 for *La Storia Calvino*, garnered a Dora Award nomination in 2001 for his role in *A Flea in Her Ear*, and a Dora Award in 2002 for Outstanding Performance for his role in *The Lesson*. In 2007 he received a Best Actor Thespis Award for *Two Letters*.

As a playwright, his first play, *La Storia dell'Emigrante*—written in Calabrian—in collaboration with Vincent Ierfino, played in Montreal in 1979 and 1980, and in Toronto in 1982, and won the 1st James Buller Award for Best Original Canadian play at the Ontario Multicultural Theatre Festival at Harbourfront. *A Modo Suo (A Fable)*, written and presented entirely in Calabrian, received a Dora Award nomination (Outstanding New Play) in 1990. An English translation in collaboration with poet/author Antonino Mazza was published in its entirety in the Fall 2000 issue of the *Canadian Theatre Review*. In 2007 *Two Letters* was nominated for a Dora Award (Outstanding New Play). In 2008 he was nominated for a Siminovitch Prize in Theatre (long list) for playwriting. In 1992 he received the 125th Anniversary of the Confederation of Canada Medal, awarded to Canadians for significant contribution to their fellow citizens, to their community, or to Canada.

ADAM PAOLOZZA is an award-winning performer, director, writer, producer, and arts educator. After completing the two-year program in theatre creation at École Jacques Lecoq in 2003, Adam formed the ensemble TheatreRUN in Paris, France with fellow graduates. Over the next two years TheatreRUN created two shows and toured in France, USA, and Edinburgh. This was a formative period where Adam developed a love of devising, touring, and producing independent theatre. Adam returned to Canada in 2005 and established himself as a physical performer, creator, and director, as well as a teacher of clown, mask and movement. In Toronto, he's worked with a variety of collaborators such as Why Not Theatre, Theatre Smith-Gilmour, Zou Theatre, Fixt Point Theatre, Ahuri Theatre, Guillermo Verdecchia, interdisciplinary artist Kari Pederson, JMar Electric, Tomson Highway, composer Arif Mirabdolbaghi, pianist Greg Oh, and many more.

In 2014 Adam created *Bad New Days* to produce his own projects and explore his vision of a contemporary poetic theatre of gesture. "I'm searching for an autonomous theatre that responds to, rather than reflects, contemporary existence. A theatre based in a practice dedicated to formal experimentation and collaborative, devised creation. I'm pursuing a theatre of affective interruption, cultivating an encounter between audience and performer that challenges the traditional ways through which we perceive meaning. My hope is to foster a more active, empathetically engaged spectatorship, encouraging the audience to experience the work as an aesthetic 'caesura' in their lives, an existential pause in which to reflect on the world. I believe theatre has the potential to open up new space for radical thinking precisely because it is an art where meaning is held 'in suspense', so to speak, as pure potential." Adam and Bad New Days have been collectively nominated for 27 Dora Mavor Moore awards, winning personally for Performance, Direction, Playwriting and Production. He is an RBC Emerging Artist Award nominee and a K.M. Hunter Award nominee. He is a former Urjo Kareda resident artist and a former member of the Playwrights' Unit at Tarragon Theatre. Bad New Days is a former RBC emerging company in residence at Canadian Stage.

Adam is a dedicated teacher. He's been a sessional instructor at the Soulpepper Academy, taught at Toronto Metropolitan University (formerly Ryerson), Brock University, the University of Toronto and Humber College. He has given independent workshops in Scotland, France, India and China as well as all over Canada, using his own unique interpretation of the Lecoq pedagogy. Adam's goal as instructor is to help students develop a spontaneous mind and body connection through a coupling of formal technique and improvisation. He is a graduate of École Internationale de Théâtre Jacques Lecoq, Ryerson Theatre School and has studied Corporeal Mime with the Decroux company Intrepido in Paris. Adam studied Commedia Dell'Arte with the late Marcello Magni of Théâtre de Complicité. Most recently he studied mask making with the Sartori family in Abano Terme, Italy, and he's taken Butoh classes with renowned dancer and choreographer Mariko Yoshioka.

CHRISTINE SANSALONE is an associate professor in the department of Modern Languages and Literatures at Laurentian University. Her areas of expertise are contemporary Italian theatre, cinema and literature as well as Italian-Canadian studies. She has written articles on Italian cinema, Italian bourgeois theatre, Italian Canadian literature and, most recently, on the internment of Italian Canadians during World War II. She is also the co-author of eight plays based on the Italian Canadian community in Sudbury. Together with her colleague Diana Iuele Colilli she co-directs *Le Maschere Laurenziane*, a student theater group housed in the Italian Studies Program at Laurentian University. She is the co-editor of three special issues of *Italian Canadiana* [31 (2017), 32 (2018), 33 (2019)].

ACKNOWLEDGEMENTS

THIS ANTHOLOGY OF plays was brought about by many hands and inspirations: Domenico Pietropaolo, notably, who encouraged and supported the project from its inception. Since first supervising my Doctoral studies at the University of Toronto's Drama Centre, as it was then called, Domenico always believed in me and encouraged my academic strivings as worthy and meaningful. I am forever grateful. Any lasting value of my historical work including the introduction to this volume is mostly by way of his incomparable example. Thanks to friend and colleague Tony Nardi for amongst other things our existential tirades on Canadian theatre out of which in May 2017 emerged the idea for this anthology. We were having coffee at the Tim Hortons at University and College, and as we discussed the state of Italian Canadian theatre to-day, it occurred to me how ironic it was that we were sitting at the historic border site of Toronto's post-1840s immigrant enclave known as The Ward. Newcomers of multi cultures, including Italian artists and artisans, lived, and worked there, striving, mostly faceless and nameless. It is their voices that I wish to honor with this book. Gratitude to Jessica Johnson not only for expert copyreading with me but the coercions only a cherished friend and ideal reader can reel off: "You must cut this! This is too dry. What?" But mostly for taking to my endless tales of Italian Canadian theatre history and its unsung pioneers with such respect. Lee Lewis for her insightful reading and compassionate listening (over marvelous dinners) to my awe and outrage while I was discovering some of this remarkable history. As a Canadian Theatre Pioneer herself, Lee's insights into theatre-making generally and Canadian theatre specifically including the grand tradition of Yiddish theatre and the overlapping traditions of music and puppetry will remain treasured memories. Salvatore Bancheri provided welcoming contexts at the University of Toronto's Italian Department and University of Toronto Mississauga to present my research to students. His love of theatre and commitment to the recording and teaching of Italian Canadian theatre history in all its manifestations from educational to community is deeply valued. Sincere thanks are also due to Damiano Pietropaolo, Frank Spezzano, Alberto Di Giovanni and Sarah Hunter for their shared knowledge, warmth, and generosity, and to Rocco Galati, Gianna Patriarca, Antoni Cimolino, Pal D'Iulio, Roberto Martella and Nick Mancuso for supporting the work always. Special thanks to Inna Viriasova for her translation of Myroslav Irchan's drama book, but mostly for her unassuming intelligence and poise at a difficult time for any Ukrainian who loves their homeland. Sincere thanks and respect to some of my favorite people in the world: librarians and archivists. They include Ann Smith, Erin Patterson, Agnieszka Hayes and Jean Kelly at Acadia University, the archivists at the Beaton Institute, Guelph, York and Manitoba University libraries, the New York Public Library and Archives Canada. Special thanks to R. Dennis Moore at the Multicultural History Society of Ontario. Terry Aulenbach deserves special thanks for his good-humored patience and technical savoir-faire. Christine Sattler deserves recognition for her meticulous transcription work on *Johnny*

Bananas. Thank you, Guernica, and editor Michael Mirolla, for your infinite patience and thoughtfulness, and David Moratto for your visual artistry. Apologies to anyone I may have inadvertently overlooked.

Finally, to Canadian playwrights of Italian heritage, past, present, and future: This is for you.

ABOUT THE EDITOR

BORN IN ITALY and raised in Toronto, Anna Migliarisi holds a BFA in Performance from the School of Dramatic Art, University of Windsor, and an MA and PhD from the Centre for Drama, Theatre and Performance Studies, University of Toronto. She has taught at Toronto Metropolitan as well as the universities of Waterloo, Guelph, and Toronto. Her scholarly publications include numerous articles on directorial history as well as four books: *Renaissance and Baroque Directors: Theory and Practice of Play Production in Italy* (2003); *Directing and Authorship in Western Drama* (2006); *Stanislavsky and Directing, Theory Practice and Influence* (2008); and *About Directing* (2014). The present work, *Canadian Plays of Italian Heritage,* was inspired by Anna's experience as an actor and co-producer of the groundbreaking critically acclaimed production of Tony Nardi's *A Modo Suo (A Fable)* in 1990. Not only has she worked professionally in theatre and film but for the past two decades has trained young actors and passed on her love of theatre and drama as a tenured Professor at Acadia University.

Printed by Imprimerie Gauvin
Gatineau, Québec